# FUNDAMENTALS OF MARKETING

## McGraw-Hill Series in Marketing

# FUNDAMENTALS OF

# MARKETING

## NINTH EDITION

**WILLIAM J. STANTON**
University of Colorado

**MICHAEL J. ETZEL**
University of Notre Dame

**BRUCE J. WALKER**
University of Missouri–Columbia

**McGRAW-HILL, INC.**
New York   St. Louis   San Francisco   Auckland   Bogotá   Caracas
Hamburg   Lisbon   London   Madrid   Mexico   Milan
Montreal   New Delhi   Paris   San Juan   São Paulo
Singapore   Sydney   Tokyo   Toronto

2 3 4 5 6 7 8 9 0 VNH VNH 9 5 4 3 2 1

ISBN 0-07-060952-7

*This book was set in Palatino by York Graphic Services, Inc.*
*The editors were Bonnie K. Binkert and Judith Kromm;*
*the designer was Joan Greenfield;*
*the production supervisor was Diane Renda.*
*Photo editing was done by Research Plus.*
*New drawings were done by Hadel Studio.*
*Von Hoffmann Press, Inc., was printer and binder.*

*Cover photo and p. iv: "Edetta" by Vasarely, 1984. Acrylic on canvas. Courtesy of Circle Gallery.*

See photo credits on pages vii–ix.
Copyrights included on this page by reference.

**Library of Congress Cataloging-in-Publication Data**

Stanton, William J.
   Fundamentals of marketing/William Stanton, Michael Etzel, Bruce Walker.—9th ed.
     p.    cm.—(McGraw-Hill series in marketing)
   Includes bibliographical references and index.
   ISBN 0-07-060952-7
   1. Marketing.    I. Etzel, Michael J.    II. Walker, Bruce J.    III. Title.    IV. Series.
HF5415.S745     1991
658.8—dc20                                          90-42292

# PHOTO CREDITS

**CHAPTER 17**

p. 428 Robert Phillips/The Image Bank.
p. 431 Jon Feingersh/Stock, Boston.
p. 437 Pete Saloutos/The Stock Market.
p. 440 Owen Franken/Stock, Boston.
p. 441 Century 21 Real Estate Corporation.
p. 443 Bob Kinmonth.

**CHAPTER 18**

p. 450 Bernard Asset/Photo Researchers.
p. 453 BASF Corporation.
p. 461 United Stations Radio Networks.
p. 462 Courtesy of Mike Etzel.
p. 464 This advertisement is reproduced with the permission of the Dial Corporation, owner of the registered trademark displayed therein and of the copyrights pertaining thereto. All rights reserved.
p. 466 Brian Smith.
p. 468 Reprinted by permission of Reebok International, Ltd.
p. 471 Los Angeles Dodgers.
p. 472 Bettye Lane/Photo Researchers.
p. 477 Margot Granitsas/The Image Works.
p. 479 Richard Pasley/Stock, Boston.
p. 480 Phil Moughmer/Third Coast Stock Source.

**CHAPTER 19**

p. 484 Bill Wassman/The Stock Market.
p. 487 Marco Wallroth.
p. 489 Credit Suiss.
p. 490 Lufthansa German Airlines.
p. 497 Courtesy of Carnival Cruise Lines.
p. 498 Alaska Airlines/Livingston & Company.
p. 499 AT&T.
p. 501 Marco Wallroth.

**CHAPTER 20**

p. 506 Mark Gibson/The Stock Market.
p. 509 Yellowhammer Advertising Agency, London.
p. 511 General Foods.
p. 514 San Francisco Ballet.
p. 518 Marin County Free Library.
p. 519 (top) The Salvation Army.
p. 519 (bottom) Spencer Grant/Stock, Boston.
p. 521 Reproduced with permission. © American Heart Association.

**CHAPTER 21**

p. 524 David Pollack/The Stock Market.
p. 526 Benetton Services, Corp.
p. 528 SAAB/Saab-Scania of America, Inc.
p. 530 Francie Manning/The Picture Cube.
p. 535 Tom McHugh/Photo Researchers.
p. 539 No credit.
p. 541 Robert Wallis/SIPA Press.
p. 544 George Hall/Woodfin Camp & Associates.
p. 550 Thomas Fletcher/Stock, Boston.
p. 552 Miro Vintoniv/The Picture Cube.
p. 554 Thaine Manske/The Stock Market.

**CHAPTER 22**

p. 558 David Stoecklein/The Stock Market.
p. 561 Courtesy of Ford Motor Company.
p. 564 Lennox Industries, Inc.
p. 567 Sony Corporation.
p. 569 Howard Johnson, Inc.
p. 572 Maytag Company.

**CHAPTER 23**

p. 580 Courtesy of Procter & Gamble.
p. 583 Courtesy of Hewlett Packard.
p. 587 Light Images.
p. 589 Rob Kinmonth.
p. 591 H. Wendler/The Image Bank.
p. 592 Courtesy of International Business Machines, Corp.
p. 599 Bob Daemmrich/The Image Works.

**CHAPTER 24**

p. 604 Dick Luria/FPG International.
p. 606 Randy Matusow.
p. 608 Fred McConnaughey/Photo Researchers.
p. 610 Beryl Goldberg.
p. 612 Bob Daemmrich/The Image Works.
p. 617 Herb Snitzer/Stock, Boston.
p. 620 No credit.
p. 622 McGraw-Hill Photo.
p. 627 Sailors/The Stock Market.
p. 629 Steve Hansen/Stock, Boston.
p. 631 Sears, Roebuck & Co.

# ABOUT THE AUTHORS

**William J. Stanton** is Professor Emeritus of Marketing at the University of Colorado—Boulder. He received his Ph.D. in marketing from Northwestern University, where he was elected to Beta Gamma Sigma. He has worked in business and has taught in several management development programs for marketing executives. He has served as a consultant for several business organizations and engaged in research projects for the federal government. He also has lectured at universities in Europe, Asia, Mexico, and New Zealand.

The coauthor of the leading text in sales management, Professor Stanton has also published several journal articles and monographs. *Fundamentals of Marketing* has been translated into Spanish, Portuguese, Italian, Indonesian, and Bangladesh, and separate editions have been adapted (with coauthors) for Canada, Italy, and Australia. In a survey of marketing educators, Professor Stanton was voted one of the leaders in marketing thought, and he is listed in *Who's Who in America* and *Who's Who in the World*.

**Michael J. Etzel** received his D.B.A. in marketing from the University of Colorado. Since 1980, he has been Professor of Marketing at the University of Notre Dame, where he served as chairman of the Department of Marketing from 1980 to 1987. He has also been on the faculties of the University of Kentucky and Utah State University, and he has had visiting appointments at the University of South Carolina, the University of Hawaii, and the University of Innsbruck.

In over twenty years of teaching, Professor Etzel has taught a wide variety of marketing courses, from fundamentals through the doctoral level. He was recently awarded a Fulbright teaching and research fellowship to lecture and conduct research in Austria.

Etzel      Stanton      Walker

His research in the areas of marketing management and buyer behavior has appeared in the *Journal of Marketing*, the *Journal of Marketing Research*, the *Journal of Consumer Research*, and other publications.

Under the auspices of the American Association of Advertising Agencies, Professor Etzel served as a faculty intern at Ted Bates Advertising in New York. He has directed the American Marketing Association's School of Marketing Research since 1981 and has also been active in the AMA's Education Division and Marketing Research Division.

**Bruce J. Walker** is Dean of the College of Business and Public Administration at the University of Missouri–Columbia. He received his doctorate in marketing from the University of Colorado.

Professor Walker has been on the faculties of the University of Kentucky and Arizona State University, where he served as chairman of the Department of Marketing from 1982 to 1989. During his teaching career, Professor Walker has taught a variety of courses, including principles of marketing, to undergraduate and graduate students.

Professor Walker's research, focusing primarily on franchising, marketing channels, and survey-research methods, has been published in the *Journal of Marketing*, *Business Horizons*, *Journal of Marketing Research*, and other periodicals. He has also coauthored and co-edited a number of books, including a college textbook, *Retailing Today*.

Besides speaking to business groups in the United States, Professor Walker has also made presentations and conducted seminars for executives, faculty, and students in Europe. Active in the Western Marketing Educators Association and the American Marketing Association, he has served as president of WMEA and as vice president of the AMA's Education Division.

To
Kelly and Little Joe
Chris, Gretchen, and Kate
Pam, Therese, Steve, and Scott

# CONTENTS IN BRIEF

# CONTENTS

## PART TWO: TARGET MARKETS

# PART THREE: THE PRODUCT

# PART FOUR: THE PRICE

# PART FIVE: DISTRIBUTION

# PART SIX: PROMOTION

# PART SEVEN: MARKETING IN SPECIAL FIELDS

# PART EIGHT: MANAGING THE MARKETING EFFORT

# PREFACE

## Building a Foundation for the 1990s and Beyond

As we prepared this edition of *Fundamentals of Marketing*, we had the remainder of the 1990s and the 21st century in mind. Most of today's undergrads will be about 30 years old at the start of the new century. Ahead will be the prime years of potentially rewarding professional careers and personal lives. Just how rewarding that time will be depends in large part on two factors—the knowledge foundation that is built in the 1990s, and the ability to adapt to the environmental changes and challenges that occur in the 1990s and beyond.

And changes there certainly will be. Technological advances are occurring in so many fields at such a pace that it is difficult to envision the scene in the year 2000. Applications of fiber optics and laser surgery, for example, seem boundless. Concern for the physical environment, especially in North America and Europe, is likely to be a controlling factor in many economic and political decisions. Advances in information-processing capabilities will make instantaneous communication commonplace within ten years. Breakthroughs in fuel technology and manufacturing processes should dramatically affect the nature of the products we buy. We will probably see the start of space colonization, three-dimensional interactive home entertainment systems, waterless machines for washing clothes, and perhaps a cure for cancer.

One development that we can count on as this century ends and the next one begins is the growing internationalization—even globalization—of business relationships. Virtually every career field is becoming increasingly international in scope. In autos, cameras, and consumer electronic products, we all have seen the effects of competition from Japanese products. Four other Asian countries on the Pacific rim—Korea, Taiwan, Singapore, and Hong Kong—are increasing competitive pressures in international trade. The economic unification of the 12 nations of the European Community in 1992 also poses major marketing challenges for the United States and Japan.

In response to, or perhaps even in anticipation of, these developments, marketers will have to change their ways and learn to make decisions quickly. For instance, they will have access to sales data from the prior week, maybe even the prior day. With these data, they will have to determine inventory or production levels for the next time period. Also, they will have to select from a growing variety of media in planning how best to communicate with consumers. And, to cite one more example, marketers will have to choose between domestic and foreign markets and determine how to compete effectively against firms from the United States and many other countries. Marketing during the remainder of this decade and into the next century will be more dynamic, challenging, and exciting than ever before!

**WHAT'S NEW IN THIS EDITION**

This book has been substantially revised to reflect the changing social and economic forces that will seriously challenge marketing management in the near future. Some of the many new and updated features are:

- International marketing is given significantly greater attention. Not only have we updated the separate chapter devoted to the topic, but we also have added numerous international examples in the text plus an *International Perspective* box in every chapter.

- Coverage of services marketing has been considerably expanded. Our long-standing separate chapter on the marketing of services has been completely rewritten to reflect the growing importance of and current activity in the field. Moreover, we have increased the use of services examples throughout the book and have added cases involving services organizations.
- Marketing ethics receives added emphasis. This is accomplished with an *Ethical Dilemma* box in every chapter and with expanded coverage of marketing ethics in Chapter 24.
- The text has been reorganized to some degree as suggested by reviewers and adopters. The related topics of market segmentation and demographics have been combined in one chapter, thus reducing the number of chapters in the book. The chapter on managing channels of distribution has been shifted to the beginning of Part 5 in order to provide an overview of the distribution function before discussing specific middlemen. The marketing planning chapter has been moved to the final part of the book, where it is coupled with a chapter on marketing implementation and evaluation for a unified treatment of managing the marketing effort.
- Several chapters have been substantially rewritten. These include Chapter 1 (The Field of Marketing), Chapter 2 (The Marketing Environment), Chapter 4 (Market Segmentation and Demographics), Chapter 5 (Consumer Buying Behavior), Chapter 12 (Managing Channels of Distribution), Chapter 14 (Retailing: Markets and Institutions), Chapter 19 (Marketing of Services), Chapter 22 (Marketing Planning and Forecasting), and Chapter 24 (Marketing: Appraisal and Prospects).
- Seventeen of the 24 cases are new, and 11 of the new ones focus on well-known companies such as McDonald's, Nike, and American Express.
- All chapter-opening vignettes are new.
- Examples and footnote references have been updated throughout the book.
- The package of teaching and learning supplements has been expanded and improved for more effective use by instructors and students.

## THIS BOOK'S BASIC STRUCTURE

Those who are familiar with earlier editions of this book will find that we have retained the features that have made it a widely used teaching and learning resource. At the same time, we have carefully revised, improved, and updated the book to carry students through the 1990s.

The writing style continues to make the material clear and interesting to read. Frequent, timely examples illustrate concepts and enliven the presentation. The organization allows topics to flow logically for easy reading, and the section headings simplify outlining.

Numerous end-of-chapter discussion questions are intended to be interesting and thought-provoking. Virtually all of the questions require the *application* of text material, rather than rote repetition. Each of the 24 short cases focuses on one or more topics covered in the text. The cases provide students with an opportunity for problem analysis and decision making.

The book's basic theme, approach, and organization have been retained from previous editions. The central theme is that marketing is a total system of business action rather than a fragmented assortment of functions and institutions. Although some attention is directed to the role of marketing in our socioeconomic system, the book is written largely from the viewpoint of a marketing executive *in an individual organization.* This firm may be a producer or a middleman, a business or a nonprofit organization, and a provider of goods and/or services to domestic and/or foreign markets.

The marketing concept is a philosophy that stresses the need for a customer orientation compatible with society's long-run interests. This philosophy is evident in the framework of the marketing-management process. A company sets marketing objectives, taking into consideration environmental forces that influence its marketing effort. Management next selects target markets. The company then has four strategic elements—its product, price structure, distribution system, and promotional activities—with which to build a marketing program that will reach its markets and achieve its objectives. In all stages of the marketing process, management should use marketing research as a tool for problem solving and decision making.

This framework for the marketing process is reflected in the book's organization. The text is divided into eight parts as follows:

- Part 1 introduces the field of marketing and also includes chapters on the marketing environment and marketing research and information systems. An appendix on careers in marketing follows the introductory chapter.
- Part 2 is devoted to the analysis and selection of target markets in both consumer and business areas.
- Parts 3 through 6 deal with the development of a marketing program. Each of these parts covers one of the four components of the marketing mix. In Part 3, we discuss various topics related to the product component.
- An organization's price structure is the subject of Part 4. A related appendix on financial accounting is included in this part.
- Part 5 focuses on the distribution system, including channels, wholesaling and retailing institutions, and physical distribution.
- Part 6 is devoted to the total promotional program, including advertising, personal selling, and sales promotion.
- In Part 7, we apply marketing fundamentals to three special areas—services (rather than goods), nonprofit (rather than business) organizations, and international (rather than U.S.) markets.
- Building on the foundation formed by the first seven parts of the book, Part 8 deals with the management of the total marketing effort in an individual organization. Using the framework of the management process, we discuss marketing planning as well as marketing implementation and evaluation. This concluding part of the text also includes an appraisal of the role of marketing in our socioeconomic system and a brief look at the future in marketing.

## TEACHING AND LEARNING SUPPLEMENTS

This textbook is the central element in a complete package of teaching and learning resources that have been completely revised and considerably expanded for this edition. The package includes the following supplements:

- A *study guide* for students provides chapter outlines, test questions, real-world cases for each chapter, and exercises that involve the students in practical marketing experiences.
- A *book of readings* contains a series of recent marketing articles from *Business Week* magazine keyed to the parts of the text.
- A *set of video cassettes* highlights well-known companies, including some

that are featured in the text cases, and provides insights into the firms' marketing strategies. These video segments, which range in length from 10 to 25 minutes, complement and extend the text discussion.

- A set of *Lotus spreadsheet exercises* consists of text-related problems adaptable for use on *IBM and IBM compatible* personal computers.
- A *simulation* is available for use on *IBM and IBM compatible* personal computers. This "computer game" is a straightforward one-product simulation calling for a series of marketing decisions.
- An *instructor's manual* provides lecture outlines for each chapter, including many real-world examples not found in the text. This manual also includes commentaries on the end-of-chapter questions, the 24 cases, the *Ethical Dilemmas*, and the exercises in the student study guide.
- A collection of more than 200 full-color *transparencies*, most of which are *not* in the text, is available to adopters.
- *Slides* of all transparencies are available to adopters who prefer this alternative to overhead transparencies.
- A *test bank* includes an extensive assortment of multiple-choice, true-false, and short-answer fill-in questions for each chapter. All questions are categorized by difficulty, and the page in the text where the rationale for the correct answer appears is presented for each question. This test bank also is available for Mac and IBM compatible computers.
- A *customized testing service* is available to instructors from McGraw-Hill by mail or toll-free telephone number.

## ACKNOWLEDGMENTS

Many people—our students, present and past colleagues, business executives, and other professors—have contributed greatly to this book over the years. Several cases in this edition were prepared by other people; in each instance, authorship is identified. Professor Stephen W. Brown of Arizona State University provided considerable insights and materials for our revision of Chapter 19 (Marketing of Services).

The revised *Study Guide* was prepared by Professor Thomas J. Adams of Sacramento City College. The excellent *Test Bank* was prepared by Professors Betty and Thomas Pritchett of Georgia College. For his fine efforts in developing the computer exercises, we are indebted to Professor C. Anthony di Benedetto of Temple University. Likewise, we acknowledge with appreciation the contribution made by Professors Michael L. Ursic, Willbann D. Terpening, and James G. Helgeson of Gonzaga University, who developed the simulation that is part of this text package. We also thank Tim Christiansen and Maria Muto of Arizona State University for helping us prepare a comprehensive instructor's manual.

Many changes in this edition were inspired by reviews prepared by the following professors:

| | |
|---|---|
| Gordon Barnewall | *University of Colorado at Denver* |
| Holland C. Blades | *Missouri Southern State College* |
| John J. Buckley | *Orange County Community College* |
| John Bunnell | *Broome Community College* |
| Kenneth E. Crocker | *Bowling Green State University* |
| James C. Douthit | *Middle Tennessee State University* |
| Chaim M. Ehrman | *Loyola University of Chicago* |

| | |
|---|---|
| Richard H. Goodwin | *Broward Community College* |
| William R. Lowry | *Central Connecticut State University* |
| James McAlexander | *Iowa State University* |
| Mary Ann McGrath | *Loyola University of Chicago* |
| Malcolm L. Morris | *University of Oklahoma* |
| Lester A. Neidell | *University of Tulsa* |
| Wayne Norvell | *Kansas State University* |
| W. Daniel Rountree | *Middle Tennessee State University* |
| Robert Ruekert | *University of Minnesota* |
| Gary M. Smith | *Westark Community College* |
| Lois J. Smith | *University of Wisconsin—Whitewater* |
| Richard J. Stanish | *Tulsa Junior College* |
| Clinton B. Tankersley | *Syracuse University* |
| Addie L. Weinstein | *Miami University (Ohio)* |
| Richard A. Wozniak | *Northeastern Illinois University* |

We appreciate the insightful and constructive comments provided by all of these reviewers.

Finally, we would like to recognize, with gratitude, the efforts of the people at McGraw-Hill who did so much to make this book an effective and attractive teaching and learning resource. We especially want to thank our sponsoring editor, Bonnie Binkert, for her patience and gracious manner. Our developmental editor, Judith Kromm, similarly helped us through the critical editing and pre-production stages. Judy Motto had the very large task of coordinating the preparation of all elements in the supplemental package, and she carried it out well. Safra Nimrod, our photo editor, added life and color to the book. Dan Loch developed and implemented the plans to inform instructors about the ninth edition. To all of you, we say, "Thank you so very much."

*William J. Stanton*
*Michael J. Etzel*
*Bruce J. Walker*

# FUNDAMENTALS OF MARKETING

# PART ONE

# MODERN MARKETING AND ITS ENVIRONMENT

An introduction to marketing, the marketing environment, marketing research, and the role of marketing in organizations today

Part 1 introduces the field of marketing. In Chapter 1 we explain what marketing is, how it has developed, and how it is continuing to develop. We also introduce the concept of the management process in marketing. In addition, the chapter considers the role of marketing both in our overall socioeconomic system and in the individual organization. The organization may be a business firm or a nonprofit organization; it may be marketing goods, services, ideas, people, or places; and it may be marketing them domestically or internationally.

In Chapter 2 we discuss the environmental forces that shape an organization's marketing program. Although the environment is largely uncontrollable, the management of an organization must strive to identify, anticipate, and respond to important environmental influences. Chapter 3 explains the role of marketing information systems and describes the procedure in a marketing research project. Marketing information systems and marketing research are major tools used in marketing planning and decision making.

# CHAPTER 1
# THE FIELD OF MARKETING

## CHAPTER 1 GOALS

"What is marketing?" Chapter 1 answers this question, and the answer may surprise you. After studying this chapter, you should be able to explain:

- The relationship between exchange and marketing.
- What marketing means in a business sense.
- Marketing's evolution in the United States.
- The marketing concept.
- The difference between selling and marketing.
- What is involved in the management process in marketing.
- The importance of marketing in the global economy, in the American socioeconomic system, in an individual organization, and to you personally.

Do the following diverse situations have anything in common?

- Two companies, Colorocs Corp. and Canon U.S.A., compete in David and Goliath fashion in the emerging market for color photocopiers. Consumers like the machines but are put off by their prices, which are several times those of black-and-white copiers.
- Civic leaders in Cincinnati, Ohio, promote the city's "quality of life" when they urge corporations to relocate to their city.
- Various churches conduct surveys of members and nonmembers to learn more about their spiritual and social needs.
- A supermarket on the Navajo reservation in northern Arizona stocks not only ordinary grocery items but also distinctive items, such as skinned sheep heads and 25-pound bags of flour, that are desired by residents of the area.
- Club Med, which operates resorts around the world, changed its advertising to emphasize vacation flexibility rather than sexy models. Increased competition in the travel industry and a slight

drop in the number of North Americans visiting Club Med resorts prompted the changes.
- Using closed-circuit television, a funeral parlor in Chicago has a drive-through lane in which relatives and friends can view their deceased loved one. The drive-through service meets the needs of people who cannot or do not want to go inside for a more traditional viewing.
- Several manufacturers are trying, with limited success, to achieve consumer acceptance of a toothpaste that fights plaque, a condition that causes gum disease. Apparently consumers do not yet consider plaque to be a serious dental problem.

These situations vary greatly with respect to products, types and sizes of organizations, geographic settings, and even the activities carried out. However, despite these great differences, all involve *marketing*—because they are attempts to understand consumers, seize an advantage over competitors, gain a foothold in a market, or create a program that will satisfy customers. Welcome to the dynamic, challenging, and potentially rewarding world of marketing. •

## NATURE AND SCOPE OF MARKETING

The situations just presented—and countless others in everyday life—involve marketing. Sometimes we carry out marketing, or at least participate in it, without even realizing it! Perhaps the best examples are our frequent experiences as purchasers of goods and services. But as you progress through this course, you probably will come to realize that you have experience as a marketer as well as a consumer.

### Broad Dimensions of Marketing

Ordinarily marketing is considered an activity or function performed by business firms. However, marketing also can be carried out by other organizations and even by individuals. Whenever you try to persuade somebody to do something, you are performing a marketing activity. You engage in marketing when you ask someone to donate to the Salvation Army, fasten a seat belt, vote for your candidate, or swap their tickets to a concert for your tickets to an athletic event.

Within this broad dimension, there is great variety with respect to (1) marketers, (2) what they are marketing, and (3) their potential market. The category of *marketers* might include, in addition to business firms, such diverse social units as a political party trying to market its candidate to the public, the director of an art museum providing new exhibits to generate greater attendance and financial support, a labor union marketing its ideas to members and to company management, and colleges trying to shift demand from overenrolled to underenrolled courses and majors.

In addition to the range of items normally considered as goods and services, *what is being marketed* may be ideas, such as reducing air pollution or contributing to the United Way; people, such as an entertainer or a political candidate; and places, such as industrial plant sites or a place to go for a vacation.

In this general context, *markets* encompass more than the direct consumers of products. For example, a state university's market is made up of legislators who provide funds, citizens living near the university who may be affected by university activities, and alumni. A firm's markets may include government regulatory agencies, environmentalists, and local tax assessors.

In this case who is the marketer and what is being marketed?

## THE CONCEPT OF EXCHANGE

Broadly viewed, *the essence of marketing is a transaction—an exchange.* Marketing occurs any time one social unit (person or organization) strives to exchange something of value with another social unit. Thus marketing consists of all activities designed to generate and facilitate any exchange intended to satisfy human needs or wants.[1]

**Exchange** is one of three ways in which a person can satisfy a need. Suppose you want some clothes. You can make them yourself. Or you can steal them or use some form of coercion to get the clothes. Or you can voluntarily offer something of value (perhaps your money, your services, or another good) to another person who will voluntarily exchange the clothes for what you offer. It is only the third alternative that we call an exchange in the sense that marketing is occurring.

Within the context of marketing, the following conditions must exist for an exchange to occur:

- Two or more social units—people or organizations—must be involved. If you are totally self-sufficient in some area, there is no exchange.
- The parties must be involved voluntarily, and each must have wants to be satisfied.
- Each party must have something of value to contribute in the exchange, and each party must believe it will benefit from the transaction.
- The parties must be able to communicate with each other. Assume that you want a new sweater and a clothing store has sweaters on sale. If you and the store are not aware of each other—you are not communicating—then there will be no exchange.

**Business Dimensions of Marketing**

While it can be interesting to consider marketing in its broadest context, this book concentrates on the business of marketing as carried out by organizations and individuals within our socioeconomic system. These organizations may be business firms in the usual sense of the word *business.* Or they may be what is called a nonprofit organization—a hospital, university, United Way, church, police department, or museum, for example. Both types of organizations face essentially the same basic marketing problems.

Now many executives in those organizations, as well as many household consumers, think they already know a good bit about the business of marketing. After all, churches run newspaper ads and museums sell copies of famous paintings. And people at home watch television commercials that persuade them to buy. These people purchase products on a self-service basis in supermarkets. Some have friends who "can get it for them wholesale." But in each of these examples we are talking about only one part of the totality of marketing activities. Consequently we need a business definition of marketing to guide executives in business and in nonprofit organizations in the management of their marketing efforts.

Our definition of marketing—applicable in a business or a nonprofit organization—is as follows:

**Marketing** is a total system of business activities designed to plan, price, promote,

Some nonprofit organizations, such as the United Way, market the concept of contributing to their cause.

---

[1] In this book the terms *needs* and *wants* are used interchangeably. In a limited physiological sense we might say that we "need" only food, clothing, and shelter. Beyond these requirements we get into the area of "wants." More realistically in our society today, however, many people would say that they "need" a telephone or they "need" some form of mechanized transportation.

and distribute want-satisfying products to target markets to achieve organizational objectives.[2]

This definition has two significant implications:

- The entire system of business activities should be customer-oriented. Customers' wants must be recognized and satisfied effectively.
- A marketing program should start with an idea about a new product (good, service, idea, person, or place) and should not end until the customers' wants are completely satisfied, which may be some time after the sale is made.

**Difference between Marketing and Selling**

Many people, including some executives, still do not understand the difference between selling and marketing. In fact, many think the terms are synonymous. However, as shown below, there are vast differences between the two activities.

| Selling | | Marketing |
|---|---|---|
| Emphasis is on the product. | **vs.** | Emphasis is on customers' wants. |
| Company first makes the product and then figures out how to sell it. | **vs.** | Company first determines customers' wants and then figures out how to make and deliver a product to satisfy those wants. |
| Management is sales-volume-oriented. | **vs.** | Management is profit-oriented. |
| Planning is short-run-oriented, in terms of today's products and markets. | **vs.** | Planning is long-run-oriented, in terms of new products, tomorrow's markets, and future growth. |
| Stresses needs of seller. | **vs.** | Stresses wants of buyers. |

When selling is emphasized, a company makes a product and then persuades customers to buy it. In effect, the firm attempts to alter consumer demand to fit the firm's potential supply of the product. When marketing is practiced, a much different approach is taken. The firm finds out what the customer wants and then develops a product that will satisfy that need and still yield a satisfactory profit. In this case the company adjusts its supply to the will of consumer demand.

**EVOLUTION OF MARKETING**

The foundations of marketing in America were laid in colonial times when the early settlers traded (exchanged) among themselves and also with the Indians. Some settlers even became retailers, wholesalers, and itinerant peddlers. However, the evolution of marketing in the United States is usually measured from the Industrial Revolution in the latter part of the 1800s. Since then, marketing in U.S. business has evolved through three stages of development. But understand that these stages depict the *general* evolution of marketing. Although many firms have progressed to the third stage, some are still in the first or second stage, as is shown in Figure 1-1.

---

[2]The American Marketing Association, the largest professional organization in the marketing field, recently developed a very similar definition: "Marketing is the process of planning and executing the conception, pricing, promotion, and distribution of ideas, goods, and services to create exchanges that satisfy individual and organizational objectives." See Peter D. Bennett, ed., *Dictionary of Marketing Terms*, American Marketing Association, Chicago, 1988, p. 115.

**FIGURE 1-1** Three stages of marketing evolution in the United States.

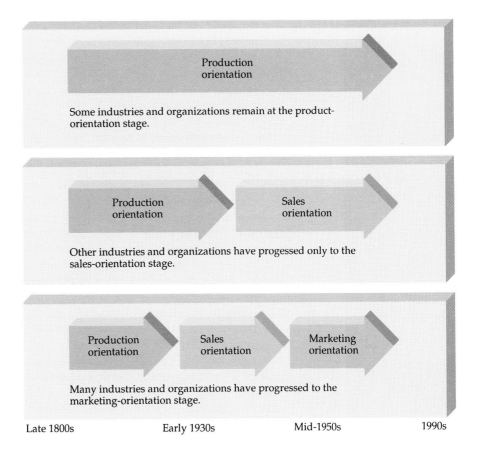

Some industries and organizations remain at the product-orientation stage.

Other industries and organizations have progessed only to the sales-orientation stage.

Many industries and organizations have progressed to the marketing-orientation stage.

Late 1800s          Early 1930s          Mid-1950s          1990s

## Production-Orientation Stage

In this first stage a company typically is production-oriented. Executives in production and engineering shape the firm's planning. The function of the sales department is simply to sell the company's output, at a price set by production and financial executives. This is the "build a better mousetrap" stage. The underlying assumption is that marketing effort is not needed to get people to buy a product that is well made and reasonably priced.

During this stage the term *marketing* is not yet used. Instead, producers have sales departments headed by executives whose job is to manage a sales force. This stage dominated in the United States until the Great Depression in the early 1930s.

## Sales-Orientation Stage

The Depression made it clear that the main problem in the economy no longer was to produce or grow enough but rather was to sell the output. Just making a better product brought no assurance of market success. Firms began to realize that the sale of products required substantial promotional effort. Thus the United States entered a period when selling activities and sales executives gained new respect and responsibility from company management.

It was also during this period that selling acquired much of its bad reputation. This was the age of the "hard sell" characterized by the unscrupulous used-car dealer or door-to-door sales person. Even now some organizations believe that they must operate with a hard-sell philosophy to prosper. In the United States the sales stage lasted from the early 1930s into the 1950s, when the marketing era emerged.

## Marketing-Orientation Stage

By the early 1950s the United States had completed the transition from an economy disrupted by World War II to a peacetime economy. Manufacturing plants were turning out tremendous quantities of consumer goods to satisfy the demand that had built up during the war. As the postwar surge in consumer spending slowed down, many firms found that demand fell short of their production capabilities. Aggressive promotional and sales activities did not resolve the problem. Thus the evolution of marketing continued. Many companies decided they needed to focus on the needs of their customers and carry out a broader range of marketing activities to be successful.

In this third stage, attention is focused on marketing rather than on selling. The top executive responsible for this activity is called a marketing manager or vice president of marketing. Several tasks that traditionally were managed by other executives become the responsibility of the top marketing executive in this stage. For instance, inventory control, warehousing, and some aspects of product planning are turned over to the head of marketing. To be most effective, this executive should be brought in at the beginning, rather than at the end, of a production cycle. Marketing should influence all short-term and long-term company planning.

A key to effective marketing is a favorable attitude toward marketing on the part of a firm's top executives. The following statement reflects an understanding of this point: "Marketing begins with top management. Only top management can provide the climate, the discipline, and the leadership required for a successful marketing program." We are *not* saying that marketing executives should hold the top positions in a company. Nor are we saying that the president of a firm must come up through the marketing department. But it is necessary that the president be *marketing-oriented*.

Many American business firms, as well as some nonprofit organizations, are presently in this third stage in the evolution of marketing. How well these companies have implemented a marketing orientation, however, is questionable. Some firms are using the appropriate titles and other external trappings, but they are finding it difficult to become truly marketing-oriented.[3]

## THE MARKETING CONCEPT

As business people recognized that marketing is vitally important to the success of any organization, a new philosophy of doing business developed. Called the **marketing concept,** it emphasizes customer orientation and coordination of marketing activities to achieve the organization's performance objectives.

## Nature and Rationale

The marketing concept is based on three fundamental beliefs:

- All planning and operations should be customer-oriented. That is, the organization and its employees should be focused on determining and satisfying customers' needs.
- All marketing activities in an organization should be coordinated. In reality this belief means that marketing efforts (such as advertising, product planning, and pricing) should be combined in a coherent and consistent way and that one executive should have overall authority and responsibility for the complete set of marketing activities.
- Customer-oriented, coordinated marketing is essential to achieve the organization's performance objectives.

[3] A practical game plan for achieving a marketing orientation is presented in Adrian F. Payne, "Developing a Marketing-Oriented Organization," *Business Horizons*, May–June 1988, pp. 46–53.

**FIGURE 1-2** Components and outcomes of the marketing concept.

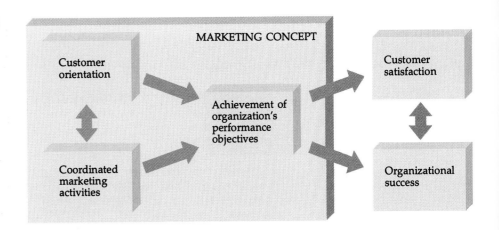

MARKETING CONCEPT

Customer orientation

Coordinated marketing activities

Achievement of organization's performance objectives

Customer satisfaction

Organizational success

The marketing concept is equally applicable to businesses and nonprofit organizations. Of course, objectives may be fundamentally different depending on whether the organization is in the business or nonprofit sector. A business firm's objectives, unlike those of a nonprofit organization, ordinarily revolve around profits.

Customer orientation and coordinated marketing activities are the means used to achieve the end that is sought, namely achievement of the organization's performance objectives. Figure 1-2 illustrates this relationship. Sometimes the marketing concept is simply stated as "The Customer Is King (or Queen)!" As helpful as it is to stress customer satisfaction, however, this motto must not be allowed to replace achievement of objectives as the fundamental rationale for the marketing concept.

## The Societal Marketing Concept

This firm may be satisfying some of its "customer" groups and not others.

Off and on for more than 20 years, the marketing concept has come under fire. There have also been calls to make the concept more socially responsible. Its critics charge that, although implementing it may lead to business success, it may encourage actions that in some way conflict with a firm's responsibility to society.

From one point of view, these charges are true. A firm may totally satisfy its customers (in line with the marketing concept), while also adversely affecting society. To illustrate, an Ohio steel producer might be supplying its customers in Texas with the right product at a reasonable price, but at the same time be polluting the air and water in Ohio.

Actually the marketing concept and a company's social responsibility can be quite compatible. The key to compatibility lies in extending the *breadth* and *time* dimensions of the marketing concept. With this revision we would have, in effect, a **societal marketing concept.**

When the concept's *breadth* is extended, a company recognizes that a market includes not only the buyers of a firm's products but also other people directly affected by the firm's operations. In our example, the Ohio steel mill has several "customer" groups to satisfy. Among these are (1) the Texas buyers of the steel, (2) the consumers of the air that contains impurities given off by the mill, and (3) the recreational users of the local river where the mill releases its waste matter.

An extended *time* dimension means that a firm should take a long-term view of customer satisfaction and performance objectives, rather than concen-

## AN ETHICAL DILEMMA?

### Ethical Dilemmas—What and Why

Because marketers try to influence behavior in intensely competitive environments, sometimes their work has ethical implications. However, issues of ethics are often ambiguous. Thus there are situations in which the behavior of a marketer might be judged inappropriate and unethical by some and totally acceptable by others. We think it is important to be aware of some typical ethical dilemmas in marketing and to take the opportunity to consider how you would respond to them. With that in mind, we have included boxes like this one in every chapter of this book. In most instances there are no absolutely right or wrong answers. That's why we call them Ethical Dilemmas. We hope you find them interesting and helpful in refining your own sense of ethics.

### The First Dilemma

Americans spend $2 billion a year on bottled water, but by law it need be only as pure as tap water. The International Bottled Water Association estimates that more than a third of all bottled water is simply filtered municipal water, but it can cost 700 times more. If you were a retailer, would you consider it ethical to stock a brand that you knew was filtered tap water?

trating only on tomorrow. For a company to prosper in the long run, it must do a good job of satisfying customers' social and economic demands.

Thus the marketing concept and a company's social responsibility are compatible if management strives over the long run to (1) satisfy the wants of its product-buying customers, (2) meet the societal needs of others affected by the firm's activities, and (3) achieve the company's performance objectives.

## THE MANAGEMENT PROCESS IN MARKETING

To successfully apply the marketing concept, whether the traditional or societal version, an organization has to effectively manage its marketing activities. It must engage in skillful marketing management. The *marketing* part of the term *marketing management* was defined earlier, but what about the *management* part? **Management** is the process of planning, implementing, and evaluating the efforts of a group of people working toward a common goal. (The terms *management* and *administration* are used synonymously here.)

At this point we need at least a brief discussion of the management process in marketing because we use management concepts and terms throughout the book. In-depth discussion is deferred until Part 8, which focuses on managing the marketing effort.

### What Is the Management Process?

The **management process,** as applied to marketing, consists basically of (1) planning a marketing program, (2) implementing it, and (3) evaluating its performance. As shown in Figure 1-3 the *planning* stage includes setting goals and selecting strategies and tactics to reach these goals. The *implementation* stage includes forming and staffing the marketing organization and directing the actual operation of the organization according to the plan. The *evaluation* stage is a good example of the interrelated, continuing nature of the management process. Evaluation is both a look back and a look ahead—a link between past performance and future planning and operations. Management

**FIGURE 1-3** The management process in marketing.

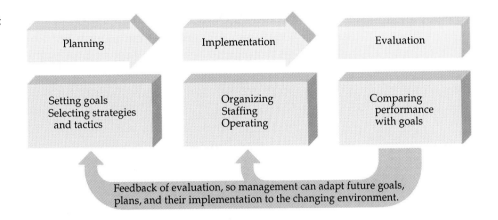

looks back to analyze performance in light of organizational goals. Findings from this analysis of past performance are then used to look ahead in setting the goals and plans for future periods.[4]

During the past 20 years businesses have devoted substantial attention to the planning phase of the management process. In their preoccupation with planning, however, business executives typically have given relatively little attention to the implementation stage. In the authors' opinion, this is unfortunate. After all, if you don't carry your plans through and put them into practice—implement them—then your plans really are of no value. You may have the best plan for an upcoming ball game, but if you can't execute that plan—make it work in the game—then that plan is not worth very much to you.

An encouraging prospect is that many companies have become disenchanted with the lopsided emphasis on planning. Executives are becoming increasingly vocal in their demand for more effective *implementation* of their companies' plans.

## Management Terminology

Several basic terms continually appear in discussions of business and nonprofit marketing. Let's look at how these terms will be used in this book.

### OBJECTIVES AND GOALS

We treat two terms—*objectives* and *goals*—as synonyms. An **objective,** very simply, is a desired outcome. Effective planning must begin with a series of objectives that are to be achieved by carrying out plans.

To be worthwhile and workable, objectives should be measurable, time-defined, and specific. Consider these examples:

| Weak (too general) | | Workable |
|---|---|---|
| Increase our market share. | $\longrightarrow$ | Increase our market share to 25 percent next year from its present 20 percent level. |
| Improve our profit position. | $\longrightarrow$ | Generate a return on investment of 15 percent next year. |

[4]Many writers and executives use the terms *control* and *evaluation* synonymously. We distinguish between them. To speak of control as only one part of the management process is too restrictive. Rather than being an isolated managerial function, control permeates virtually all other organizational activities. For example, management *controls* its operations through the objectives and strategies it selects. Also, the type of organizational structure used in the marketing department determines the degree of *control* over marketing operations.

## STRATEGIES AND TACTICS

A **strategy** is a broad plan of action by which an organization intends to reach its objective. The word *strategy* originally applied to the art of military generalship. In marketing, the relationship between objectives and strategies may be illustrated as follows:

| Objectives | | Possible strategies |
|---|---|---|
| Reduce marketing costs next year by 15 percent below this year's level. | $\longrightarrow$ | Cut back warehouse inventories and eliminate slow-moving products. Reduce number of sales calls on small accounts. |
| Increase sales next year by 10 percent over this year's figure. | $\longrightarrow$ | Intensify marketing efforts in domestic markets. Expand into foreign markets. |

Two companies might have the same objective but use different strategies to reach it. For example, two firms might each aim to increase their market share by 20 percent over the next 3 years. To do that, one firm's strategy might be to intensify its efforts in domestic markets. The other company might select the strategy of expanding into foreign markets. Conversely, two companies might have different objectives but select the same strategy to reach them.

A **tactic** is an operational means by which a strategy is to be implemented or activated. A tactic typically is a more specific, detailed course of action than is a strategy. Also, tactics generally cover shorter time periods than strategies. Let's look at an illustration:

| Strategy | | Tactics |
|---|---|---|
| Direct our promotion to males, ages 25–40. | $\longrightarrow$ | Advertise in magazines read by this market segment. Advertise on television programs watched by these people. |

To be effective, tactics must parallel or support the strategy.

## Strategic Planning

"If you don't know where you are going, then any road will take you there." The moral of this management axiom is that all business and nonprofit organizations need a well-conceived plan. Most fundamentally, planning is studying the past to decide in the present what to do in the future.

In a management context, **strategic planning** may be defined as the managerial process of matching a firm's resources with its market opportunities over the long run. Developing plans for the entire company provides the framework within which strategic planning is done in the firm's various divisions, including marketing.

**Strategic marketing planning** essentially consists of (1) selecting target markets and (2) designing a marketing mix. Strategic planning in marketing is applicable to nonprofit organizations as well as business firms.

## TARGET MARKETS

A **market,** discussed later in detail, consists of people or organizations with needs to satisfy, money to spend, and the willingness to spend it. A **target market** consists of a group of customers (people or organizations) at whom the seller directs a marketing program.

A firm may have a single target market—such as all small businesses in a metropolitan area that need moving services for purposes of office relocation.

More likely, a firm will have multiple target markets—such as the preceding target plus all large households that need moving services for purposes of residential relocation.

Target-market selection must be based on careful analysis of market opportunities. Usually the selection process involves some form of research and market segmentation, which will be described later in the book. When target markets have been selected, the firm can proceed to the second step in strategic marketing planning—designing an appealing marketing mix.

### THE MARKETING MIX

The combination of the four primary elements that comprise a company's marketing program is termed the **marketing mix.** The design, implementation, and evaluation of the marketing mix constitute the bulk of a firm's marketing effort.

The four elements of the marketing mix are:

- *Product*—Managing the product ingredient includes planning and developing the right goods and/or services to be marketed by the company. Strategies are needed for changing existing products, adding new ones, and taking other actions that affect the assortment of products carried. Strategic decisions are also needed regarding branding, packaging, and various other product features.
- *Price*—Management must determine the right base price for its products. It must then decide on strategies concerning discounts, freight payments, and many other price-related factors.
- *Distribution*—Even though marketing intermediaries—primarily wholesalers and retailers—are largely a noncontrollable environmental factor, an executive has considerable latitude when working with them. Management's responsibility is to (1) select and manage the trade channels through which the products will reach the right market at the right time and (2) develop a distribution system for physically handling and transporting the products through these channels.
- *Promotion*—Management needs to inform and persuade the market regarding a company's products. Advertising, personal selling, sales promotion, and publicity are the major promotional activities.

The four ingredients in the marketing mix are interrelated; decisions in one area usually affect actions in the others. Each of the four also contains countless variables. A company may market one item or several—related or unrelated. The item may be distributed through wholesalers or directly to retailers, and so on. Ultimately, from the multitude of variables, management must select the combination that will best adapt to the environment, satisfy target markets, and still meet marketing and organizational goals.

## IMPORTANCE OF MARKETING

Coca-Cola is sold in virtually every country in the world. Sales of Japanese autos continue to increase in the United States. We can choose from numerous brands of personal computers and airlines. Many students at your school obtained good jobs following graduation last term. Effective marketing is a common denominator in these diverse situations. As these examples suggest, marketing plays a major role in the global economy, in the American socioeconomic system, and in any individual organization. It also has significance for you personally, if not in business then at least in your role as a consumer.

## In the Global Economy

Most nations today—regardless of their degree of economic development or their political philosophies—recognize the importance of marketing. Indeed, economic growth in developing nations depends greatly on the ability to design effective marketing systems for their raw materials and industrial output.

Russia is even trying to introduce some semblance of an open-market system into its rigid, centrally controlled economy. In light of these economic reforms, some U.S. firms are planning to manufacture and market in Russia on a joint-venture basis with Soviet organizations. RJR Nabisco, for example, plans to produce and market cereals, crackers, and Camel and Winston cigarettes in the Soviet Union. Eastman Kodak, Chevron Oil Company, and Johnson & Johnson are also planning to enter the Russian market.[5] These examples suggest that a global marketplace is emerging. In many (perhaps most) national markets, companies from numerous countries compete aggressively.

Consider the U.S. market, for instance. Until the late 1970s, the United States provided a large domestic market for American firms, and there was no significant foreign competition in most industries in that market. But the picture changed dramatically through the 1980s as foreign firms improved their products and their marketing expertise, and then successfully entered the American market. Many imported products have achieved large sales—office equipment, autos, apparel, watches, semiconductors, and consumer electronics (TVs, stereos), for example. As a result the United States has been running large annual trade deficits, meaning that imports greatly exceed exports.

[5]See Louis Kraar, "Top U.S. Companies Move into Russia," *Fortune*, July 31, 1989, p. 165.

Alphagraphics, a print-shop organization, is among the many firms that see marketing opportunities in the Soviet Union.

**TABLE 1-1 Some major global players from the United States**

Ten companies with foreign sales accounting for a substantial share of total sales.

| Company | Foreign sales as % of total | Best-selling products abroad |
|---|---|---|
| Dow | 55 | Industrial chemicals |
| Hewlett-Packard | 52 | Computer workstations |
| Merck | 50 | High-blood-pressure medicine |
| Caterpillar | 50 | Earthmoving equipment |
| 3M | 46 | Pressure-sensitive tape |
| Boeing | 46 | Commercial airliners |
| Eastman Kodak | 45 | Film for amateur photographers |
| Sun Microsystems | 42 | Computer workstations |
| Scott Paper | 38 | Bathroom tissue |
| Ford Motor | 25 | Escort automobile |

Source: Alex Taylor III, "The U.S. Gets Back in Fighting Shape," *Fortune*, Apr. 24, 1989, p. 45.

In the early 1980s, the competition facing U.S. firms came primarily from Japanese companies. Later, companies in the four "Asian tigers" (Korea, Taiwan, Singapore, and Hong Kong) added to competitive pressures. In the 1990s, continuing competition from these Pacific Rim countries will be augmented by a new challenge from Western Europe. Starting in 1992, the 12-nation European Community will eliminate internal trade barriers and adopt uniform technical, financial, and marketing standards. A more integrated European Community will open major marketing opportunities for internationally minded U.S. firms, but at the same time, it is expected to stiffen competition.

More and more American firms—many large ones and even some rather small ones—are moving into foreign markets. Many companies are concluding that achieving profit and growth objectives is most likely through a combination of domestic *and* international marketing rather than sole reliance on domestic marketing. As shown in Table 1-1, some large American firms derive a substantial percentage of their total revenues from foreign sales.

The significance of global marketing is reflected in the large number of international examples you will find throughout this book. Also, because of its special characteristics, an entire chapter will be devoted to international marketing.

**In the American Socioeconomic System**

Americans have developed marketing to the greatest extent. Aggressive and effective marketing practices have been largely responsible for the high standard of living in the United States. Today, through relatively efficient mass marketing, we enjoy products that once were considered luxuries and still are so classified in many countries.

Since about 1920 (except during World War II and the immediate postwar period), a strong buyers' market has existed in the United States. That is, the available supply of products has far surpassed total demand. Making most products has been relatively easy; the real challenge has been marketing them.

## AN INTERNATIONAL PERSPECTIVE: How do companies achieve success in foreign markets?

Not every company or industry should view the world as a mass market. In some industries—luxury cars, for instance—a company can do quite well by marketing to one limited niche. Mercedes, Ferrari, and Porsche, for example, are not threatened by the global mass marketing of Ford, Toyota, or Volkswagen. But for most industries in the 1990s, many different countries comprise their market.

A professor at the University of Pennsylvania identified 136 industries where the name of the game is international operations. These industries ranged from A to Z (accounting services to zippers) and included autos, banking, consumer electronics, entertainment, pharmaceuticals, travel services, and washing machines.

For a company that wants to go global, there is no handy formula for success. However, management should heed all or most of the following guidelines:

- Develop new products suitable for the world market.

- Make yourself at home in the three most important markets—North America, Europe, and Asia.
- Base your profit centers on product lines, not on countries or regions.
- "Glocalize" your operations—that is, make *global* decisions on strategic questions about product research and financial capital. But let *local* organizational units make tactical decisions about such matters as packaging and advertising.
- Overcome narrow-minded attitudes and train people to think internationally.
- Open senior positions to foreign employees.
- In markets that you cannot penetrate on your own, seek joint ventures or other alliances with local firms.

Source: Jeremy Main, "How to Go Global—and Why," *Fortune*, Aug. 28, 1989, p. 70.

### EMPLOYMENT AND COSTS

The significance of marketing in the U.S. economy might be more easily understood in quantitative terms. *Between one-fourth and one-third of the civilian labor force is engaged in marketing activities.* This figure includes employees in retailing, wholesaling, transportation, warehousing, and communications industries, as well as people who work in marketing departments of manufacturers and those engaged in marketing in agricultural, mining, and service industries. Furthermore, over the past century, jobs in marketing have increased at a much more rapid rate than jobs in production. The great increase in the number of workers in marketing reflects its expanded role in the economy.

The cost of marketing is another measure of its significance. On the average, *about 50 cents of each dollar we spend at the retail level goes to cover marketing costs.* These costs should not be confused with profits, however. Nor should it be assumed that goods and services would cost less if there were no marketing activities.

### CREATION OF UTILITIES

The range of utilities created by marketing is another indication of its importance in our socioeconomic system. **Utility** may be defined as the attribute in an item that makes it capable of satisfying human wants. Marketing gives rise to four types of utility—place, time, possession, and image—and plays a supporting role in creating a fifth type—form utility.

**Place utility** exists when a product is readily accessible to potential customers. Making a product available to consumers when they want it adds **time utility. Possession utility** is created when a customer buys the product—that is, ownership is transferred to the buyer.

Furniture produced in Grand Rapids, Michigan, in April is of little value to a man in Los Angeles who wants to buy the furniture for a Christmas present. However, by performing marketing activities—in this case, transporting the furniture to Los Angeles and locating it in a store near where that man lives—we have added value to the furniture. Thus, marketing has created *place utility*. Then by storing the furniture—another marketing activity—from April until December, marketing has created *time utility*. Finally, *possession utility* is created when the man buys—acquires ownership of the furniture from a retail store.

**Image utility** is a more subjective, difficult-to-measure concept. It is the emotional or psychological value that a person attaches to a product or brand because of the reputation or social standing of that product or brand. Marketing, especially advertising and other forms of promotion, often contributes greatly to the creation of image utility.

Image utility ordinarily is associated with prestige or high-status products such as designer clothes, expensive foreign automobiles, or certain residential neighborhoods. However, the image-utility value of a given product may vary considerably depending on different consumers' perceptions.

**Form utility** is what we ordinarily refer to in business as production—the physical or chemical changes that make a product more valuable. When lumber is made into furniture, form utility is created. This is production, not marketing. However, marketing research may aid in decision making regarding product design, color, quantities produced, or some other aspect of production.

Businesses, like some final consumers, may be interested in image utility.

Business Gifts
That Are Remembered,
Forever.

TIFFANY & CO.

**In the Individual Firm**
Marketing considerations should be an integral part of all short-range and long-range planning in any company. Here's why:

- The core of business success is customer want satisfaction, the basic social and economic justification for the existence of virtually all organizations.
- Although many departments are essential to a company's growth, marketing is the sole revenue-producing activity. This fact sometimes is overlooked by production managers who use these revenues and financial executives who manage them.

American business has long been oriented toward production: products are designed by engineers, manufactured by production people, priced by accountants, and then given to sales managers to sell. This approach generally won't work in today's environment of intense competition and constant change. Just *building* a good product will not result in its success, nor will it have much bearing on consumer welfare. The product must be *marketed* to consumers before its full value can be realized.

During the past two decades, marketing has become much more prominent in a growing sector of our economy that includes service firms and nonprofit organizations. Recognizing the importance of marketing in such organizations, we will use services and nonprofit examples throughout this book to illustrate marketing fundamentals. In addition, since services marketing and marketing in nonprofit organizations have special characteristics, we devote separate chapters to each type later in the book. For practical purposes, however, we briefly describe the development and role of marketing in service firms and nonprofit organizations here.

**IN SERVICE FIRMS**

The United States has moved beyond the manufacturing stage of economic development to become the world's first service economy. Services account for over two-thirds of the nation's gross national product. Almost three-fourths of the country's nonfarm labor force is employed in service industries, and about one-half of all consumer expenditures are for the purchase of services. Furthermore, projections for the year 2000 indicate that services' share of all these categories (gross national product, employment, expenditures) will increase.

Despite the fact that our economy has been *services*-dominant for some time, most of our marketing until recent years was *goods*-dominant. Writing and discussion about marketing focused on concepts and strategies related to tangible goods (such as groceries, clothing, machine tools, and automobiles) rather than on intangible services. Now some of the most marketing-oriented firms are in the services sector—for example, Federal Express, Disney, American Airlines, and Marriott Corp.

**IN NONPROFIT ORGANIZATIONS**

During the 1980s many nonprofit organizations realized they needed effective marketing programs to make up for shrinking government subsidies, a decrease in charitable contributions, and other unfavorable economic conditions. Colleges faced with declining enrollments, hospitals confronted with empty beds, and symphonies playing to vacant seats all began to understand that marketing was essential to help them turn their situations around.

Today charities, museums, and even churches—organizations that formerly rejected any thought of marketing—are embracing it as a means of

The art of Canaletto brought to you by the master of the art of travel.

CANALETTO
The Metropolitan Museum of Art, New York
November 2, 1989 - January 21, 1990

This exhibition is made possible by Louis Vuitton.
Additional support has been provided by the National Endowment for the Arts and by an indemnity from the Federal Council on the Arts and the Humanities.

LOUIS VUITTON

Museums, like other nonprofit organizations, engage in aggressive marketing to attract customers.

growth or, in dire cases, survival. And this trend is likely to accelerate during the 1990s. Two factors fuel this trend:

- Increasing competition in the nonprofit sector.
- Nonprofit organizations' desire to improve their images and gain greater acceptance among groups that collectively determine an organization's success—groups such as donors, government agencies, news media, and of course, consumers.

## Marketing—What's in It for You?

Okay, so marketing is important globally, in our economy, and in an individual organization. But what's in it for you? Why should you study marketing? There are a number of reasons:

- The study of marketing should be interesting and perhaps exciting to you because marketing pervades so many daily activities. You buy various articles in different stores. You watch television with its commercials. You read magazine and newspaper ads. As a college student, you are part of your school's market, and you might complain about the price (tuition) of the service (education) that you are receiving. Truly, marketing occupies a large part of your daily life. If you doubt this, just imagine for a moment where you would be if there were no marketing institutions—no retail stores or no advertising to give you information, for example.
- Studying marketing will make you a better-informed consumer. You'll understand more about what underlies a seller's pricing and branding policies as well as the role of promotion and middlemen (wholesalers and retailers) in distribution.

- Lastly, marketing probably relates—directly or indirectly—to your career aspirations. Marketing majors can learn about the many career opportunities in the field. We especially suggest you read Appendix A, Careers in Marketing, following this chapter. Those planning a career in accounting, finance, or other business field can learn how marketing affects managerial decision making in their field. Finally, if you are thinking about a career in a nonbusiness field such as health care, government, music, or education, you can see how marketing is relevant to these organizations.

## SUMMARY

The foundation of marketing is exchange, in which one party provides to another party something of value in return for something else of value. In a broad sense, marketing consists of all activities designed to generate or facilitate an exchange intended to satisfy human needs.

In a more traditional sense, marketing is a total system of business activities designed to plan, price, promote, and distribute want-satisfying products to target markets to achieve organizational objectives. There are important differences between marketing and selling. In selling the emphasis is on the product, whereas in marketing the emphasis is on customers' wants.

Business firms and nonprofit organizations carry out marketing. Products marketed include intangible services, ideas, people, and places as well as tangible goods. Marketing activities are targeted at markets, consisting of direct consumers of products and also other individuals and groups that influence the success of an organization.

Marketing's evolution in the United States has gone through three stages: production orientation, sales orientation, and marketing orientation. For various reasons, some companies remain at the first or second stage, not progressing to the marketing-orientation stage. In this third stage a company's efforts are focused on identifying and satisfying customers' needs.

A business philosophy called the marketing concept was developed to aid companies with supply capabilities that exceed consumer demand. According to the marketing concept, a firm is best able to achieve its performance objectives by adopting a customer orientation and coordinating all of its marketing activities. More recently, the societal marketing concept has been proposed as a philosophy by which a company can satisfy its customers and fulfill its social responsibility.

The management process in marketing consists of planning a marketing program, implementing it, and evaluating its performance. In the planning stage, objectives must be set and strategies and tactics established to achieve these objectives. Strategic planning in marketing essentially consists of selecting target markets and designing a marketing mix consisting of product, price, distribution, and promotion.

Marketing is practiced today in all modern nations, regardless of their political philosophies. As international competition has heated up, the attention paid to marketing has increased. In the United States, between one-fourth and one-third of the civilian work force is involved with marketing, and about one-half of consumer spending covers the cost of marketing. Marketing creates place, time, possession, and image utilities.

Depending on circumstances, marketing can be vital to an organization's success. In recent years numerous service firms and nonprofit organizations have found marketing to be necessary and worthwhile. Marketing also can be useful to individual students, particularly in reference to career opportunities.

## KEY TERMS AND CONCEPTS

The numbers next to the terms refer to the pages on which the terms and concepts are defined. In addition, the glossary at the end of the book defines all key terms and concepts.

Exchange 5
Marketing 5
Production-orientation stage 7
Sales-orientation stage 7
Marketing-orientation stage 8
Marketing concept 8
Societal marketing concept 9
Management (synonymous with administration) 10
Management process 10
Objective (synonymous with goal) 11
Strategy 12

Tactic 12
Strategic planning 12
Strategic marketing planning 12
Market 12
Target market 12
Marketing mix 13
Utility 16
Place utility 16
Time utility 17
Possession utility 17
Image utility 17
Form utility 17

## QUESTIONS AND PROBLEMS

1. Explain the concept of an exchange, including the conditions that must exist for an exchange to occur.
2. In the following exchanges, what is the "something of value" that each party contributes in the exchange?
   a. Your school ⟷ You as a student.
   b. Fire department ⟷ People in your hometown.
   c. Flour miller ⟷ Bakery.
   d. United Way ⟷ Contributors.
   e. Hilton Hotel ⟷ Rotary Club meetings.
3. Name some companies that you believe are still in the production or sales stage in the evolution of marketing. Explain why you chose each of them.
4. Explain the three elements that constitute the marketing concept.
5. "The marketing concept *does not* imply that marketing executives will run the firm. The concept requires only that whoever is in top management be marketing-oriented." Give examples of how a production manager, company treasurer, or personnel manager can be marketing-oriented.
6. Explain the difference between marketing and selling.
7. In light of recent criticisms, do you think the marketing concept should be revised? Support your position.

8. Select a lodging chain (such as Hyatt or Motel 6) with which you are familiar.
   a. Develop one marketing objective that you think would be reasonable for this company.
   b. Develop two marketing strategies that would help achieve this objective.
9. For each of the following organizations, describe (1) the target market and (2) what is being marketed.
   a. San Francisco 49ers professional football team.
   b. Airline Pilots Association labor union.
   c. Professor teaching a first-year chemistry course.
   d. Police department in your city.
10. For a nonprofit organization to which you belong or with which you are familiar, describe (1) the organization's target markets and (2) its marketing mix.
11. One way of explaining the benefits of marketing in our economy is to consider how we would live if there were no marketing facilities. Describe some of the ways in which your daily activities would be affected under such circumstances.
12. Each of the companies listed in Table 1-1 obtains a significant share of its total sales from foreign markets.
    a. Why do these firms emphasize international marketing?
    b. What do you suppose are some of the reasons

why these firms have been so successful in foreign markets?

13. Give some examples of:
    a. Time utility.
    b. Place utility.
    c. Image utility.
    d. Form utility (marketing's contribution).

14. Name service firms that, in your opinion, do a good marketing job. Then name some that you think do a poor marketing job. Explain your reasoning in each case.

# CAREERS IN MARKETING

Sooner or later (hopefully sooner!), you will graduate from college. Then you'll need a job that not only pays well but also matches your interests and talents. In addition, your first postgraduation job should serve as a springboard to a successful career.

To find a suitable postgraduation job, you should launch your search at least one term, and preferably 9 months, prior to graduation. To get you thinking about your postgraduation ambitions and upcoming job search, this appendix first discusses considerations about choosing a career. Then career opportunities in marketing are explored. Finally, in a section that is relevant to all students regardless of major, guidelines on obtaining a postgraduation job are presented.

**CHOOSING A CAREER**

One of the most significant decisions you will ever make is choosing a career. This career decision will influence your future happiness, self-fulfillment, and well-being. Yet, unfortunately, career decisions often seem to be based on insufficient information, analysis, and evaluation of alternatives.

One key to a wise career decision is to get as much information about as wide a variety of career alternatives as is reasonably possible. By broadening your search you may discover some interesting fields about which you knew nothing or had gross misconceptions.

At this point let's look briefly at three key areas that you should analyze in some detail in the course of career selection.

**What Do You Want from a Career?**

Perhaps this question would be better worded if we asked, "What do you want out of life?" or "What is important to you in life?" To answer these broad questions, you first must answer several more specific ones, such as the following:

- Are you looking for a career with high financial rewards?
- How important is the social prestige of the career?
- Do you want your career to be the main thing in your life? Or do you see a career only as the means of financing leisure-time activities?
- How important are the climate and other aspects of the physical environment in which you live?
- Would you take less money and a less prestigious job in order to live in a pleasant environment?
- Would you prefer to work for a large company or a small organization?
- Would you prefer living and working in a small town or in a major urban center?

Another way to approach the key questions in this section is to identify—in writing—your goals in life. Identify both your intermediate-term goals (3 to 5 years from now) and your long-term goals (10 years or more).

Still another approach is to state your self-image in some detail. By describing yourself, you may be able to identify various careers that would (or would not) fit your self-image.

## What Do You Have to Offer?

Next you have to identify in some detail your strong and weak points. Why would anyone want to hire you? What are your qualifications? What experience—work, education, extracurricular activities—do you have that might be attractive to prospective employers?

A key point to assess is whether you are more interested in people or in things. In the field of marketing, for example, a people-oriented person might be attracted to a career in personal selling. A things-oriented person might prefer a job in advertising, marketing research, or physical distribution.

## Career Factors to Consider

You should consider several major factors when evaluating a job or career in any given field. To some extent these issues reflect the first two general topics already discussed in this section.

- Will you be happy in your work? Normally, half or more of your waking hours will be spent at work, commuting to and from work, or doing job-related work at home. So you should look for the job and career that you will enjoy during that big chunk of your waking time. Also keep in mind that many people in society do not seem to be happy with their jobs. We speak of "Blue Monday" (the wonderful weekend is finished and I have to go back to work). The saying "TGIF" (Thank God it's Friday) did not enter our vocabulary because people love their work.
- Does the career fit your self-image? Are the job and career in line with your goals, dreams, and aspirations? Will they satisfy you? Will you be proud to tell people about your job? Will your spouse (and someday your teenage children) be proud of you in that career?
- What demands or pressures are associated with the career? Some people thrive on pressure. They constantly seek new challenges in their work. Other people look for a more tranquil work experience. They do not want a job with constant demands, deadlines to meet, and heavy pressures.
- Do the financial factors meet your needs? How does the starting salary compare with those of other jobs? Consider what the job is likely to pay after you have been there 3 to 5 years. Some engineering jobs, for example, have high starting salaries, but soon hit a salary ceiling. In contrast, some marketing jobs have lower starting salaries but no upper limits.
- Are there opportunities for promotion? You should evaluate the promotion patterns in a job or in a firm. Try to find out how long it normally takes to reach a given executive level. Study the backgrounds of presidents in a number of large companies. Did they come up through engineering, the legal department, sales or marketing, accounting, or some other area?
- Are the travel considerations suitable? Some jobs involve a considerable amount of travel whether you are an entry-level worker or an executive. Other jobs are strictly in-house, with no travel at all. You need to assess which situation would meet your needs.
- Is there job or career "transportability"? Are there similar jobs in many other geographic areas? If you and your spouse both are career-oriented, what will happen to you if your spouse is transferred to another city? One nice thing about such careers as teaching, retailing, nursing, and personal selling is that generally these jobs exist in considerable numbers in many different locations.
- What qualifications are needed? Determine what qualifications are needed to enter (and later to prosper in) a given field. Then review your own

background to see whether there is a close fit between the job requirements and your qualifications.

● What is the supply and demand situation in this field? Determine generally how many job openings currently exist in a given field, as compared with the supply of qualified applicants. At the same time, study the future prospects regarding this supply and demand condition. Determine whether a present shortage or overcrowding of workers in a field is a temporary situation or is likely to exist for several years.

**WHAT ARE THE JOBS?**

In Chapter 1 we noted that about one-quarter to one-third of all civilian jobs are in the field of marketing. These jobs cover a wide range of activities. Furthermore, this variety of jobs also covers a great range of qualifications and aptitudes. For instance, jobs in personal selling call for a set of qualifications that are different from those in marketing research. A person likely to be successful in advertising may not be a good prospect in physical distribution. Consequently, the personal qualifications and aptitudes of different individuals make them candidates for different types of marketing jobs.

In this section we shall briefly describe the major jobs in marketing, grouping them by title or activity. The types of positions most often open to graduating students are summarized in Table A-1.

**TABLE A-1 Eight entry-level marketing jobs for college graduates**

| Job title | Comments |
| --- | --- |
| Sales representative | Responsible for selling the organization's goods or services to customers. Customers may be ultimate consumers, middlemen, or other organizations. |
| Sales (or marketing) support person | Assists sales manager and staff in implementing programs, such as trade shows and dealer or sales force incentive programs. Position may be broader and report to a marketing executive. |
| Customer service representative | Assists customers after the sale, often by handling complaints and requests for information and/or service. Particularly common in the business-goods sector. |
| Retail management executive trainee | Position is common in department-store chains. After training, usually moves through rotating assignment in buying and management of selling department. Ultimately, person focuses on either buying or store management. |
| Assistant store manager | Position is common in chains that have small specialty stores in shopping centers. Assists in overseeing day-to-day activities of the store, especially staffing and display. In effect, is a trainee position. |
| Assistant media buyer | Common starting position in an advertising agency. Assists buyer in purchasing advertising space and time for business firms that are the agency's clients. Another entry-level position, working for either an agency or an advertiser, is junior copywriter. |
| Research trainee | Found in various large organizations and in marketing research firms. After or during training, assists with one or more phases of the research process such as data collection, data analysis, or report preparation. |
| Assistant (or assistant to) product manager | Assists in planning and, especially, implementing marketing program for a specific brand or product line. Most commonly found in large companies that sell consumer goods or services. |

## Personal Selling

By far, sales jobs are the most numerous of all the jobs in marketing. Personal selling spans a broad array of activities, organizations, and titles. Consider the following people: a driver–sales person for Coca-Cola, a sales clerk in a department store, a sales engineer providing technical assistance in sales of hydraulic valves, a representative for Boeing selling a fleet of airplanes, and a marketing consultant selling his or her services. All these people are engaged in personal selling, but each sales job is different from the others.

Sales jobs of one sort or another are available in virtually every locality. This means you can pretty well pick the area where you would like to live, and still get involved in personal selling.

There are opportunities to earn a *very* high income in personal selling. This is especially true when the compensation plan is straight commission, or is a combination of salary plus a significant incentive element.

A sales job is the most common entry-level position in marketing. Furthermore, as illustrated in Figure A-1, a sales job is a widely used stepping-stone to a management position. Many companies recruit people for sales jobs with the intention of promoting some of these people into management positions. Personal selling and sales management jobs are also a good route to the top in a firm because it is relatively easy to measure a person's performance and productivity in selling. Sales results are highly visible.

A sales job is different from other jobs in several significant ways that will be discussed in Chapter 17. Sales people represent their company to customers and to the public in general. The public ordinarily does not judge a firm by its factory or office personnel. Also, outside sales people (those who go to the customers) operate with very little or no direct personal supervision. They must have considerable creativity, persistence, and self-motivation. Furthermore, sales jobs often involve traveling and require much time away from home and family. Personal selling jobs generally rate low in social status and prestige.

All in all, selling is hard work, but the potential rewards are immense. Certainly no other job contributes as much to the success of an organization. Remember—nothing happens until somebody sells something!

## Store Management

Retailing is second only to personal selling in terms of number of job opportunities for new college graduates. The two primary areas of opportunity in department store, specialty, and discount chains are in merchandising or buying (described in the next section) and store management.

Store managers have a great deal of responsibility and authority. A store manager's authority related to acquiring merchandise (the buying function)

**FIGURE A-1** Typical career path starting in personal selling.

Source: Noxell Corporation.

varies greatly from one firm to the next. However, once the merchandise arrives in the store, the manager has the responsibility and authority for displaying, selling, and controlling the inventory. Store managers in most companies oversee, either directly or indirectly through department heads, the following activities: personal selling, promotion, credit, personnel management, and store security.

The entry-level position for store management typically is assistant department manager, department manager, or assistant store manager, depending on the size of the store. The performance of a store or department manager is directly measurable in terms of sales or profits. Therefore, speed of advancement into higher positions is determined primarily by the quality and quantity of results produced by the manager.

## Buying and Purchasing

Most medium-size and larger organizations employ people who specialize in buying, rather than selling, goods and services. In one type of position, people select and acquire merchandise for resale. In another type of position, people purchase goods and services not for resale but for use in a manufacturing process or in operating an organization.

Every retail organization needs people to buy the merchandise that is to be resold. Frequently the route to the top in retailing is through the buying (also called merchandising) division of the business. Large retailers have many positions for buyers and assistant buyers. Each merchandise department normally has a buyer. Consequently, you often have a chance to work with particular products that interest you.

There also are centralized buying offices that buy for several different stores or chains. These resident buying offices usually are in New York City and a few other large cities.

A purchasing agent is the business-market counterpart of the retail-store buyer. Virtually all firms in the business market have purchasing departments. People in these departments buy for the production, office, and sales departments in their firms.

Retail buyers and purchasing agents need many of the same skills. They must be able to analyze markets, determine merchandise needs, and negotiate with sellers. It also helps to have some knowledge of credit, finance, and physical distribution.

## Advertising

Opportunities in advertising can be found in many different jobs in various organizations. The three primary areas of opportunity are:

- Advertisers, including manufacturers, retailers, and service firms. Many of these organizations prepare and place their own ads. In some of these firms the advertising department is a large one.
- Various media (including newspapers, radio and TV stations, and magazines) that carry ads.
- Advertising agencies that specialize in creating and producing individual ads and entire promotion campaigns.

Jobs in advertising encompass a number of aptitudes and interests—artistic, creative, managerial, research, and sales. The advertising field holds real opportunity for the artistic or creative person. Agencies and advertising departments need copywriters, artists, photographers, layout designers, printing experts, and others to create and produce ads.

Account executive is a key position in advertising agencies. People in this position are the liaisons between the agency and its clients (the advertisers). Account executives coordinate the agency's efforts with the clients' marketing programs.

Another group of advertising jobs involves buying and selling media time and space. Advertisers and agencies also often need people who can conduct buyer-behavior studies and other marketing research.

## Sales Promotion

The main function of sales promotion is to tie together the activities in personal selling and advertising. Effective sales promotion requires imagination and creativity, coupled with a sound foundation in marketing fundamentals.

One aspect of sales promotion is the design and creation of retailers' in-store displays and window displays. Another aspect deals with trade shows and other company exhibits. Sales promotion activities also include the development and management of premium giveaways, contests, product sampling, and other types of promotion.

## Marketing Research

Marketing research jobs cover a broad range of activities that will be outlined in Chapter 3. People are hired for marketing research jobs by manufacturers, retailers, services marketers, government agencies, and other organizations. There also are a large number of specialized marketing research companies. Generally, however, there are fewer jobs in marketing research than in personal selling or in retailing.

Marketing research people are problem solvers. They collect and analyze masses of information. Thus they need an aptitude for methodical, analytical work. Typically some quantitative skills are needed. It helps if you understand statistics and have good computer skills.

## Product/Brand Management

In Chapter 7 we discuss briefly the position of product manager in connection with the organizational structure for new-product planning and development. Product managers (sometimes called brand managers) are responsible for planning and directing the entire marketing program for a given product or group of products.

Early on, product managers make decisions about packaging, labeling, and other aspects of the product itself. Product managers also are responsible for the marketing research necessary to identify the market. They plan advertising, personal selling, and sales promotional programs for their products. Product managers are concerned with pricing, physical distribution, and legal issues of the product.

Being a product manager is almost like running your own business. The product manager often has much responsibility for a product's performance. But this person does not have commensurate authority to see that his or her directives and plans are put into effect.

## Physical Distribution

Many jobs exist in this field, and the prospects are even brighter as we look ahead to the year 2000. More and more firms are expected to adopt the systems approach in physical distribution to control the huge expenses involved in materials movement and warehousing.

Manufacturers, retailers, and all other goods-handling firms have jobs that involve two stages of physical distribution. First the product must be moved to the firm for processing or resale. Then the finished products must be distributed to the markets. These physical distribution tasks involve jobs in transportation management, warehousing, and inventory control. In addition, many transportation carriers and warehousing firms also provide a variety of jobs that may interest you.

**Public Relations**

The public relations department in an organization is the connecting link between that organization and its various publics. The department must deal with, or go through, the news media to reach these publics. Public relations people must be especially good in communications. In fact, these people tend to have educational backgrounds in communications or journalism, rather than in marketing.

In essence, the job of public relations is to project the desired company image to the public. More specifically, public relations people are responsible for telling the public about the company—its products, community activities, social programs, environmental improvement activities, labor policies, and views regarding controversial issues. Public relations specialists are particularly important—and very visible—when a company responds to adverse publicity. Such publicity may come from a governmental investigation or a charge of unethical practices or unsafe products, for example. Whether disseminating favorable publicity or responding to adverse publicity, the company's position must be stated in a clear, understandable, and above all, believable fashion.

**Consumer Affairs and Protection**

This broad area encompasses several activities that provide job and career opportunities. Many of these jobs are an outgrowth of the consumer movement to be discussed in Chapter 24. Many companies have a consumer affairs department to handle consumer complaints. Several federal and state agencies are set up to keep watch on business firms and to provide information and assistance to consumers. Grocery products manufacturers and gas and electric companies regularly hire college graduates to aid consumers in product use. Government and private product-testing agencies hire people to test products for safety, durability, and other features.

**Other Career Areas**

In this short appendix it is not possible to list all the careers stemming from marketing. We have, however, covered the major areas. You may get additional career ideas from the next section, which deals with organizations that provide these opportunities.

**WHERE ARE THE JOBS?**

In this section we briefly describe the types of companies and other organizations that provide jobs in marketing. This section also includes comments on jobs in international marketing and a comparison of job opportunities in large versus small organizations.

**Types of Organizations**

Literally millions of organizations provide jobs and career opportunities in marketing. The organizations can be grouped into the following categories.

**MANUFACTURING**

Most manufacturing firms provide career opportunities in all the activities discussed in the previous section. In their promotional mix, some manufacturers stress personal selling while others rely more on advertising. Even small companies offer job opportunities in most of the categories covered previously.

Large manufacturers typically have good training programs, and many of them visit college campuses as part of their recruiting programs. Starting salaries often are higher in manufacturing firms than in retailing and the other organizations described next.

### RETAILING

Retailing firms provide more marketing jobs by far than does any other organizational category, but most of these jobs are not intended for college graduates. Careers in retailing are not well understood by college students who may equate retailing with clerking in a department store or filling shelves in a supermarket. Students often perceive that retail pay is low and that retail work-hours include a lot of evenings and weekends.

Actually a career in retailing offers many attractive features for college graduates. There are opportunities for very rapid advancement for those who display real ability. Performance results, such as sales and profits, are quickly and highly visible. So if you can produce, management will generally note this fact in a hurry.

While the starting pay in many (but not all) stores is lower than in manufacturing, the compensation in higher-level retailing jobs typically is excellent. There are good retailing jobs in virtually every geographic area. Also, large retail chains (such as the May Company and K mart) generally have excellent management-training programs for newly hired college graduates.

Perhaps the main attractions in retailing are less tangible. Retailing can be an exciting field. You are involved constantly with people—customers, suppliers, and other workers. And there are challenges in merchandise buying, especially that of finding out what will sell well—what customers really want.

It is easier to start a career in retailing than in many other fields. In large stores there are jobs involving personnel management, accounting controls, and store operations (receiving, credit, and customer service departments). However, the lifeblood of retailing is the buying and selling of merchandise or services. Thus the more numerous and better-paying positions are in merchandising and store management. A typical career path is presented in Figure A-2. Note that after several years a retail manager often decides to concentrate on merchandising or store management.

**FIGURE A-2** Typical career path in a department store chain.

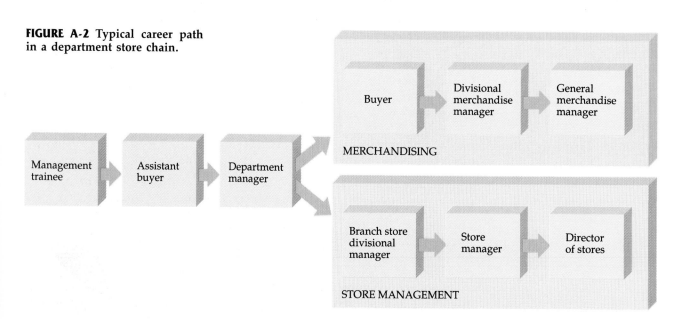

## WHOLESALING

Career opportunities in wholesaling generally are less well understood and appreciated than those in retailing or manufacturing. Wholesaling firms typically do not recruit on college campuses, and they generally have a low profile with students.

Yet the opportunities are there. Wholesalers of consumer products and industrial distributors provide many jobs in buying, personal selling, marketing research, and physical distribution. Manufacturers' agents, brokers, and the other agent middlemen discussed in Chapter 13 also offer jobs and careers. Wholesaling middlemen are increasing in numbers and in sales volume, and their future is promising.

## SERVICES MARKETING

The broad array of service industries that will be discussed in Chapter 19 provides a bonanza of job and career opportunities in marketing. Many of these fields are expected to experience rapid growth during the 1990s. The travel, hospitality, entertainment, health care, communications, and professional-services fields are prime examples. Recognizing the importance of marketing, many of these industries and organizations within them are now adding marketing-related personnel. Most of these firms really are retailers of services. Consequently, many of the statements we made earlier about retailing careers are relevant here.

## OTHER BUSINESS AREAS

Besides the general types of organizations just described, more specialized business firms hire college graduates for marketing-related positions. Entry-level opportunities can be found with communications media (such as TV stations), advertising agencies, franchise systems, energy utilities, and transportation firms (such as truck lines).

## NONPROFIT ORGANIZATIONS

As will be described in Chapter 20, nonprofit organizations are realizing that marketing is key to their success. Consequently, it is likely that jobs and careers in many nonprofit organizations will open up in large numbers during the 1990s. Consider the wide variety of nonprofit organizations—hospitals, museums, educational institutions, religious organizations, foundations, charities, and political parties, among others. Given this diversity, you can expect to find a wide range of marketing-related positions in nonprofit organizations.

## GOVERNMENT

Countless federal and state government organizations hire people for marketing positions. Here we include the major cabinet departments—agriculture, defense, human services, and the others. We also include all the regulatory agencies. Government organizations employ people in purchasing, marketing research, public relations, physical distribution, consumer affairs and protection, and even advertising and sales promotion. Sometimes students tend to overlook the many marketing career opportunities with the government.

## Careers in International Marketing

Students who like to travel and experience different cultures may want to work at least part of the time in foreign countries. They may be interested in careers in international marketing, and they may even major in international business in college. Typically, however, companies do not hire college graduates and assign them to jobs in international marketing. People are normally hired for entry-level positions in the domestic divisions of a company's operations. Then, after some years of experience with the firm, an employee may have an opportunity to move into the firm's international divisions.

## Large versus Small Companies

Should you go to work for a large company or a small firm? Or should you go into business for yourself upon graduation? For over a decade now, more and more students have been saying that they want to work for a small company. They feel there is more freedom of action, more rapid advancement, and less restraint on their life-styles in smaller firms.

Perhaps so. And certainly no one should discourage you from a career in small business. *But* we typically recommend to students (who ask for advice) that they start their careers in a big company. Then, after a few years, they can move into a smaller firm. There are three reasons for this recommendation:

- A large firm is more likely to have a good training program in your chosen field of activity. Many students have little or no practical marketing experience. The fine training programs provided by numerous large manufacturers, retailers, and major service marketers can be critical in launching a career.
- You can learn something about how a big company operates. After all, when you go into a smaller firm, large companies will be your competitors. So the more you know about them, the better able you will be to compete with them.
- After working awhile for a big company you may change your mind and decide to stay with the larger firm after all. On the other hand, let's say that you want to go to a small company after you have worked a few years at a big firm. At that point it will be relatively easy to move from a large company to a smaller one. If you start in a small firm, however, and later want to move into big business, it is not so easy to make such a move.

We have discussed various career fields and types of organizations that hire people in these fields. Now let's take a brief look at how you should go about getting a job with one of these organizations.

## HOW DO YOU GET A JOB?

This book and your entire course are designed to teach you the fundamentals involved in developing and managing a marketing program. These fundamentals are applicable regardless of whether you are marketing a good, service, idea, person, or place. They are equally applicable to (1) large and small organizations, (2) domestic and international marketing, and (3) business and nonbusiness organizations.

Now let's see whether we can apply these fundamentals to a program designed to market a person—YOU! We shall discuss a marketing approach that you can use to get a job and to start a career. Here we are talking about a *marketing* career. This same approach, however, can be used in seeking jobs and careers in any field.

## Identify and Analyze the Market

The first step in building a marketing program is to identify and analyze the market. In this case the market consists of prospective employers. Right now you don't know exactly who comprises that target market. So you must research several possible markets and then eventually narrow down your choice. In effect, we are talking about "choosing a career." Much of what we discussed in the first section of this appendix is applicable here.

You should initially get as much information as you can regarding various career opportunities in marketing. For information sources you might start with one or two professors whom you know reasonably well. Then turn to the placement office in your school, or wherever postgraduation jobs are listed. Many companies prepare recruiting brochures for students, explaining the company and its career opportunities.

Newspapers and business journals are another good information source. *The Wall Street Journal* and the business sections of large-city newspapers can be useful. Periodicals such as *Business Week, Marketing News, Advertising Age,* and trade publications in many individual industries are helpful. Sometimes, looking carefully through *Moody's Manual of Investments,* Standard and Poor's *Register,* or even a series of company annual reports can give you ideas of firms you might like to work for. You should exchange information with other students who also are in the job market.

In summary, learn all you can about various firms and industries. Then, from this information search, zero in on the group of companies that are your leading choices. You will now be ready to develop the marketing mix that will be effective in marketing yourself to your target markets.

**Product**  In this case the "product' you are planning and developing is yourself and your services. You want to make yourself as attractive as possible to your market—that is, prospective employers.

Start your product planning by listing in some detail your strong and weak points. These will lead into another list—your qualifications and achievements. This self-analysis is something we discussed in the first section of this appendix in connection with choosing a career.

When you are considering your qualifications, it may help to group them into broad categories such as these:

- Education—schools attended, degree earned, grade point average, major subjects.
- Work experience—part-time and full-time.
- Honors and awards.
- Extracurricular activities and organizations—membership, offices, committees.
- Hobbies.

Later we will discuss the presentation of your qualifications in a personal data sheet.

An important aspect of product planning is product differentiation. How can you differentiate yourself from all the other college grads? What did you do that was different, unusual, or exceptional?

Another part of product planning is packaging. When you go for an interview, be sure that the external package looks attractive. People do judge you by your appearance, just as you judge products by the way they look. This means paying attention to what you wear and how you are groomed. A good impression starts with prospective employers' first meetings with you.

**Price**  "What salary do you want?" "How much do you think we should pay you?" These are two of the questions a prospective employer might ask in a job interview. These questions may throw you if you have not done some thinking in advance regarding the price you want for your services.

As part of your marketing program, find out what the market price is for people entering your field. Talk with placement officers, career counselors, professors, and other students who are in the job market. From these sources you should get a pretty good idea of starting salaries in entry-level positions. Use this information to decide *before* the interview on a range of salaries for yourself.

## Distribution Channel

There are only a few major channels you are likely to use in marketing yourself to prospective employers. The simplest channel is your placement office, assuming there is one on your campus. Most colleges, through their placement offices, host and assist companies that send job recruiters to do on-campus interviewing.

Another channel is help-wanted ads in business journals, trade journals, and newspapers. Perhaps the most difficult, but often the most rewarding, channel is going directly to firms in which you are especially interested—knock on doors or write letters seeking a job interview. Many employers look favorably on people who display this kind of initiative in their job search.

## Promotion

Other than planning and developing an excellent product, the most important ingredient in your marketing mix is a good promotion (or communications) program. Your promotion will consist primarily of written communications (a form of advertising) and interviewing (a form of personal selling).

Frequently your first contact with a prospective employer is a cover letter in which you state briefly why you are writing to that company and what you have to offer. You enclose a personal résumé, and you request an appointment for an interview.

### COVER LETTER

In the opening paragraph of your cover letter, you should indicate why you want to work for the firm. Mention a couple of key points regarding the firm—points you learned from your research. In the second paragraph, you can present a few highlights of your own experience or personality that make you an attractive prospect. In the third paragraph, state that you are enclosing your résumé, and request an appointment for an interview, even suggesting some dates.

### RÉSUMÉ

A résumé (also called a personal data sheet) is really a brief history of yourself. You can start with biographical information such as your name, address, and phone number. Then divide the résumé into sections, including education, work experience, and activities that were listed in the product section.

At the end of your résumé, provide information about your references. One approach is to simply state, "References furnished upon request." The rationale for this approach is that interested employers will ask for names and addresses of references if or when they want to contact them. An alternative approach is to list your references by name (along with their titles, addresses, and phone numbers) at the bottom of your résumé or on a separate sheet. The thinking behind this approach is that you should make it as easy as possible for a prospective employer to check your references.

It is difficult to overstate the value of a persuasive cover letter and a distinctive résumé. They are critically important elements in your job search. They certainly are two of the most important ads you will ever write.

## INTERVIEW

Rarely is anyone hired without one or more interviews. In some cases, as when recruiters visit your campus, the interview is your initial contact with the firm. In other situations the interviews come as a result of your letter of introduction and résumé.

The interview is an experience in personal selling—in this case, you are selling yourself. People are often uncomfortable and uptight in interviews, especially their first few, so don't be surprised or disappointed if you are. One way to reduce your anxiety and increase the likelihood of impressing the interviewer is to prepare yourself to answer tough questions that may be asked during the interview: "Why should we hire you?" "What are your distinctive strengths?" "Do you have any weaknesses, and how do you plan to overcome them?" "What kind of job do you expect to have in five years?"

Your performance in an interview often determines whether or not you get the job. So be on your toes—be honest in your answers, and try to look relaxed and confident (even though you may not feel that way).

After interviews with a company have been completed, it is worthwhile to write a letter to each of the interviewers. Thank them for the opportunity to learn about their company, and state that you hope to hear from them soon regarding the job.

## EVALUATING JOB OFFERS

You are likely to receive multiple job offers *if*:

- The economy is fairly healthy, *and*
- You have at least an acceptable academic record,
- You conduct an aggressive job search,
- You develop a persuasive cover letter and professional résumé, and
- You are well prepared for job interviews.

You should evaluate the suitability of a single job offer or compare multiple job offers against a set of criteria that are important to you. These criteria should be based on your answers to the questions presented in the first section of this appendix. Recall that these questions dealt with choosing a career and determining what type of postgraduation job would best meet your needs.

We encourage you to keep in mind the questions and guidelines presented in this appendix as you take this course and progress through your academic program. It's not too early to start thinking about—and planning—your search for a postgraduation job!

# THE MARKETING ENVIRONMENT

## CHAPTER 2 GOALS

Various environmental forces influence an organization's marketing system. Some are external to the firm and thus are largely uncontrollable by the organization. Other forces are within the firm and generally controllable by management. An organization must plan, implement, and evaluate—that is, manage—its marketing system within this external and internal environment. After studying this chapter, you should be able to explain:

- How the following macroenvironmental factors can influence a company's marketing system: / Demography. / Social and cultural forces. / Economic conditions. / Political and legal forces. / Competition. / Technology.
- How the external microenvironmental factors of the market, suppliers, and marketing intermediaries can influence an organization's marketing program.
- How the nonmarketing resources within a company can influence that firm's marketing system.

Recognizing that we live in a world of accelerated change, what major developments are likely to occur between now and the year 2000? John Naisbitt, a noted and somewhat controversial futurist, in 1988 presented the following list of 10 major trends expected through the 1990s.

1. The big story will not be technology, but a renaissance in the arts, literature, and spirituality.
2. As we move more into an information-based service economy, the middle class will become larger and more affluent.
3. In mature, *developed* countries, cities will continue to decline as people leave them. Among *developing* countries, on the other hand, cities will grow to unprecedented sizes. In 1950, 6 of the 10 largest cities in the world were in Europe or the United States. By the year 2000 there will be only one—New York City. In 2000 the two largest cities in the world will be Mexico City and São Paulo, Brazil.
4. We will witness the end of the welfare state and the death of socialism.
5. English will emerge as the universal language.
6. There is increasing individualization in a growing global economy. Personal computers and cellular telephone technology, for example, move communication and information power to the level of the individual.
7. Quality of life will be the basis of competition for economic development. In an information-service-electronics age, a business can be located almost anywhere. Thus, quality of life will be a key factor in choosing industrial plant sites.
8. In our politics there will be a continuing shift to individuals and away from political parties.
9. In an information-based economy almost everything is self-generating. Therefore, there will be virtually no limits to economic growth.
10. We are approaching worldwide free trade.[1] •

[1] Adapted from a speech by John Naisbitt at the International Winter Cities Conference in Edmonton, Alberta, Canada on Feb. 18, 1988. Also see John Naisbitt, *Megatrends*, Warner Books, New York, 1982.

Domino's strategy of rapid home delivery is a successful marketing response to consumers' demand for convenience.

The trends predicted by Naisbitt may or may not occur. Part of the challenge (and opportunity) in marketing is to correctly identify developing trends and their impacts. Consider how Tom Monaghan, founder of Domino's Pizza, successfully entered the crowded pizza market by recognizing and responding to the trends toward convenience and time consciousness by providing quick home delivery.

An organization operates within an *external* environment that is continually changing and generally *cannot* be controlled by an individual organization. At the same time, a set of marketing and nonmarketing resources *within* the organization generally *can* be controlled by its executives.

External forces can be divided into two groups:

- *Macro* influences (so called because they impact all firms) include demographics, economic conditions, culture, and laws.
- *Micro* influences (so called because they affect a particular firm) consist of suppliers, marketing intermediaries, and customers. These micro elements, while external, are closely related to a specific company and are part of the company's total marketing system.

Successful marketing depends largely on a company's ability to manage its marketing program within its environmental framework. Thus management must strive to forecast the direction and intensity of changes in the external environment and to respond to these changes through effective utilization of its controllable resources.

## EXTERNAL MACROENVIRONMENT

Six interrelated macroenvironmental forces have considerable effect on any organization's marketing system (see Figure 2-1).

- Demography.
- Economic conditions.
- Competition.
- Social and cultural forces.
- Political and legal forces.
- Technology.

These forces are largely not controllable by management; however, they are not *totally* uncontrollable. A company may be able to manage its external environment to some extent. Through company and industry lobbying and contributions to a political action committee, a company may have some influence on the political-legal forces in its environment. Or new product research and development on the technological frontier can influence a firm's competitive position. In fact, *our* company's technology may be the external environmental force of technology that is affecting *other* organizations.[2]

If there is one similarity among the above environmental factors, it is that they are subject to change—and at an ever-increasing rate. We noted some changes and new environmental conditions at the beginning of this chapter. Others will be discussed in the remainder of this section.

## Demography

The statistical study of human population and its distribution is called **demography.** It is of special interest to marketing executives because people constitute markets. Demography will be discussed in greater detail in Chapter 4. At this point we shall mention just a few examples of how demographic factors influence marketing systems.

[2]For several examples of environmental management strategies that companies can use to influence the uncontrollable environment, see Carl P. Zeithaml and Valarie A. Zeithaml, "Environmental Management: Revisiting a Marketing Perspective," *Journal of Marketing*, Spring 1984, pp. 46–53.

THE MARKETING ENVIRONMENT

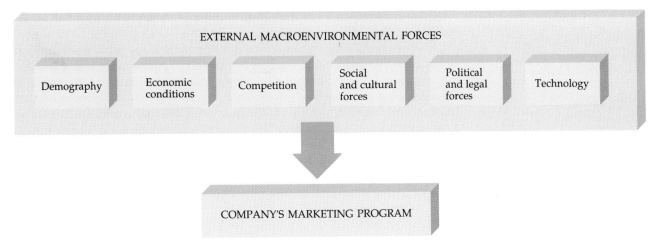

EXTERNAL MACROENVIRONMENTAL FORCES

| Demography | Economic conditions | Competition | Social and cultural forces | Political and legal forces | Technology |

COMPANY'S MARKETING PROGRAM

**FIGURE 2-1** Major forces in a company's macroenvironment.

In the mid-1980s, for the first time in our history, the number of people aged 65 and over surpassed the number of teenagers—and this gap will widen considerably in the 1990s. The marketing implications of this trend are substantial. Older people are being used to promote goods and services. Cosmetic firms, for example, feature such actresses as Joan Collins and Sophia Loren, who are over 50. This is quite a contrast to the youth-oriented promotion of a decade or more ago. Movie theaters offer discounts to people over 65, and several Colorado ski resorts have reduced prices on ski-lift tickets for skiers over 65.

Internationally the growing population of older people also is having an effect on marketing. In England, for instance, American financial services firms have found that people over 55 hold two-thirds of that country's savings. And for insurance companies with agents in France, a new market in

Our changing demographics make old folks an attractive target market.

retirement insurance is booming, because people there are worried about the stability of their government's pension system.[3]

Another significant demographic development is the rapid growth of minority markets—especially markets comprised of Hispanics, blacks, and Asians. Actually none of these three ethnic groups is a homogeneous unit. The so-called Hispanic market, for example, really consists of separate markets built around subethnic groups of Cubans, Puerto Ricans, Mexicans, and other Latin Americans. Many consumer products companies are just beginning to realize the importance—and also the great difficulty—of targeting their advertising, products, and distribution systems at Hispanic groups. These companies simply cannot ignore a total market whose population increase in the 1980s was five times the growth rate of non-Hispanics.[4]

## Economic Conditions

People alone do not make a market. They must have money to spend and be willing to spend it. Consequently, the **economic environment** is a significant force that affects the marketing activities of just about any organization. A marketing program is affected especially by such economic considerations as the current stage of the business cycle, inflation, and interest rates. One forecast for the 1990s in these three areas projects that: (1) the business cycle will be more calm than in the 1980s; (2) inflation will remain low; and (3) interest rates should drop.[5]

### STAGE OF THE BUSINESS CYCLE

Marketing executives need to know which stage of the business cycle the economy currently is in, because this cycle has such an impact on a company's marketing system. The traditional business cycle goes through four stages—prosperity, recession, depression, and recovery. However, economic strategies adopted by the federal government have averted the depression stage in the United States for over 50 years. Consequently, today we think in terms of a three-stage cycle—prosperity, recession, and recovery—then returning full cycle to prosperity.

A company usually operates its marketing system quite differently during each economic stage. Prosperity is a period of economic growth. During this stage organizations tend to expand their marketing programs as they add new products and enter new markets. A recession, on the other hand, is a period of retrenchment for consumers and businesses. People can become discouraged, scared, and angry. Naturally these feelings affect their buying behavior, which, in turn, has major implications for the marketing programs in countless firms.

Recovery finds the economy moving from recession to prosperity. The marketers' challenge is to determine how quickly prosperity will return and to what level. As unemployment declines and disposable income increases, companies expand their marketing efforts to improve sales and profits.

### INFLATION

Inflation is a rise in price levels. When prices rise at a faster rate than personal incomes, consumer buying power declines. Many countries today are

[3] See "Grappling with the Graying of Europe," *Business Week,* Mar. 13, 1989, pp. 54–56.
[4] See José de Cordoba, "More Firms Court Hispanic Consumers—But Find Them a Tough Market to Target," *The Wall Street Journal,* Feb. 18, 1988, p. 25.
[5] See Sylvia Nasar, "Preparing for a New Economy," *Fortune,* Sept. 26, 1988, p. 86.

plagued with extremely high rates of inflation. During the late 1970s and early 1980s, the United States experienced what for us was a high inflation rate of 10 to 14 percent. While inflation has declined in recent years, the nagging fear that higher rates may return continues to influence government policies, consumer psychology, and business marketing programs.

Inflation presents some real challenges in the management of a marketing program—especially in the area of pricing and cost control. Consumers are adversely affected as their buying power declines. At the same time, they may overspend today for fear that prices will be higher tomorrow.

### INTEREST RATES

Interest rates are another external economic factor influencing marketing programs. When interest rates are high, for instance, consumers tend to hold back on long-term purchases such as housing. Consumer purchases also are affected by whether they think interest rates will increase or decline. Marketers sometimes offer below-market interest rates (a form of price cut) as a promotional device to increase business. Auto manufacturers used this tactic extensively in the late 1980s.

## Competition

A company's competitive environment obviously is a major influence on its marketing system. Skillful executives constantly gather intelligence and otherwise monitor all aspects of competitors' marketing activities—their products, pricing, distribution systems, and promotional programs. A significant related force shaping the destiny of many American firms today is international competition. Foreign companies are selling their products in the United States, and U.S. firms are marketing in foreign countries. To compete in the international arena, many U.S. firms have formed alliances with foreign companies, some of which once were competitive enemies. For example, Ford and Volkswagen merged in Brazil and Argentina to create "Autolatina." The Bechtel Group (U.S.) joined with Siemens (West Germany) to service American nuclear power plants. Corning Glass Works penetrates foreign markets and gets infusions of technology through its alliances with companies in 10 different countries.[6]

### TYPES OF COMPETITION

A firm generally faces competition from three different sources:

- *Brand competition* from marketers of directly similar products. Thus United Airlines competes with Continental Airlines in several markets. Fischer skis compete internationally with Dynastar, Atomic, K-2, and Rossignol. And, yes, even the American Cancer Society competes with the American Heart Association for charitable contributions.
- *Substitute products* that satisfy the same needs. For instance, a manufacturer of vinyl record albums must compete with laser discs and tape cassettes in the home-entertainment field. Telecommunications companies want to install fiber-optic wiring in our homes and then sell us video entertainment in competition with cable TV operators.[7]
- In the third type of competition—more general in nature—*every company* is a rival for the customer's limited buying power. So the competition

[6]Louis Kraar, "Your Rivals Can Be Your Allies," *Fortune,* Mar. 27, 1989, p. 66.
[7]Joel Dreyfuss, "The Coming Battle over Your TV Set," *Fortune,* Feb. 13, 1989, p. 104.

Johnson & Johnson stresses the unique features that differentiate its baby shampoo from competing brands.

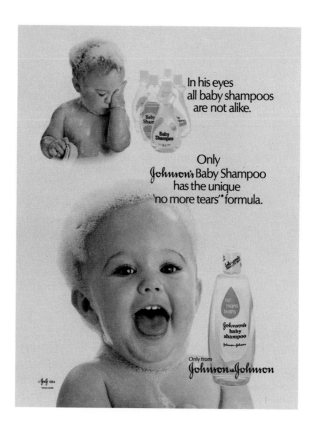

faced by a producer of tennis rackets might be a new pair of slacks, a car repair bill, or a cash contribution to a university.

## Social and Cultural Forces

The impact of the sociocultural environment on marketing systems is reflected in several sections of this book. Most of chapters 5 and 24 is devoted to the topic. To add to the complexity of the task facing marketing executives, cultural patterns—life-styles, social values, beliefs—are changing much faster than they used to. At this point we note a few changes that have significant marketing implications.

### EMPHASIS ON QUALITY OF LIFE

Our emphasis is increasingly on the *quality* of life rather than the *quantity* of goods. The theme is, "Not more—but better." We seek value, durability, and safety in the products we buy. Looking ahead, we will worry more about inflation, crime in the cities, and family stability. And we'll pay less attention to keeping up with our peers in material things like autos, homes, or where we go on vacation. Our growing concern for the physical environment and our discontent with pollution and resource waste are leading to significant changes in our life-styles. And life-style changes affect marketing. Furthermore, as our International Perspective indicates, concern for the physical environment also has begun to influence international marketing programs in Europe.

### ROLE OF WOMEN

One of the most dramatic occurrences in our society in recent years has been the changing role of women. What is especially significant is the erosion of

Toyota aimed this ad at women, thus acknowledging that women influence the purchase of a substantial percentage of autos sold in the United States.

stereotypes regarding the male-female roles in families, jobs, recreation, product use, and many other areas. Women's growing political power, economic power, and new job opportunities have considerably changed perspectives of women and those of men as well.

The evolving roles of women have many implications for marketers. Well over one-half of the women in America are working outside the home today. This has changed some traditional buying patterns in households. Many men now shop for groceries, while women buy gas and arrange for auto maintenance. Women working outside the home buy different clothing than women working at home. With both spouses working, the demand for microwave ovens and household services, for example, has increased because time-saving and convenience are major factors in buying. Half the women with children under 6 years old work outside the home, increasing the demand for day-care centers and nursery schools.

### ATTITUDES TOWARD HEALTH AND FITNESS

An increased interest in health and physical fitness in recent years seems to have cut across most demographic and economic segments of our society. Participation in fitness activities from aerobics to yoga (we could not think of an activity beginning with a Z) is on the increase. As a result sporting good stores, fitness centers, and other firms catering to this trend have multiplied. Public facilities such as bicycle paths, hiking trails, jogging paths, and playgrounds also have been improved.

Paralleling the fitness phenomenon, we see significant changes in the dietary habits of Americans. Our awareness of the relationship between diet and heart disease and cancer is being raised. Consequently, there is a growing interest in diets for weight loss, foods low in salt, additives, and cholesterol; and foods high in vitamins, minerals, and fiber content. Health foods truly have moved into supermarkets.

### IMPULSE BUYING

Recently there has been a marked increase in impulse buying—purchases made without much advance planning. A shopper may go to the grocery store with a mental note to buy meat and bread. When in the store he may also select some fresh peaches because they look appealing or are priced attractively. Another shopper, seeing cleansing tissues on the shelf, may be reminded that she is running low and so may buy two boxes. These are impulse purchases.

A key point to understand is that some impulse buying is done on a very rational basis. Self-service, open-display selling has brought about a marketing situation wherein planning may be postponed until the buyer reaches the retail outlet. Because of the trend toward impulse buying, emphasis must be placed on promotional programs designed to get people into a store. Displays must be appealing because the manufacturer's package must serve as a silent sales person.

### DESIRE FOR CONVENIENCE

As an outgrowth of the increase in discretionary purchasing power and the importance of time, there has been a substantial increase in the consumer's desire for convenience. We want products ready and easy to use, and convenient credit plans to pay for them. We want these products packaged in a

Consumers' demand for convenience shapes 7-Eleven's marketing program.

---

## AN INTERNATIONAL PERSPECTIVE: The greening of international markets in Europe

Early in the 1990s the physical environment is a major political issue in the United States. Any company, foreign or domestic, that wants to market its products in the United States must conform to our rising environmental standards. This same development is evident throughout the 12-nation European Community (EC). Environmentalists in Europe have become a most formidable and well-organized pressure group. As the chairman of Shell Oil Company in the United Kingdom said, "No business has a secure future unless it is environmentally acceptable."

Many companies marketing in Europe have adjusted their product offerings to respond to this strong macroenvironmental force. To mention some examples: French companies advertise phosphate-free detergents; Scandinavian paper manufacturers produce bleach-free products that do not pollute waterways; the entire Italian chemical industry has a reconstruction program designed to reduce toxic wastes; and a French-

produced mercury-free battery was a big market success. Sales of unleaded gasoline, recycled paper, and biodegradable disposable diapers are growing rapidly in Europe.

Some of these changes are "old news" to American environmentalists and consumers, because the environmental movement started later in Europe than in the United States. Even today pollution-control standards differ greatly from one European country to another. However, European consumers are increasingly intolerant of companies and products that pollute the air or water. And the creation of a unified European Community market starting in 1992 should reduce pollution-control differences among member countries.

Any company planning to market in the European Community must adapt its marketing programs to growing environmental concerns there.

Source: "The Greening of Europe's Industries," *U.S. News & World Report*, June 5, 1989, p. 45.

variety of sizes, quantities, and forms. We want stores located close by, and open at virtually all hours. Supermarkets and convenience stores (such as 7-Eleven) have responded to this consumer desire by remaining open 24 hours a day in some metropolitan areas.

Every major phase of a company's marketing program is affected by this desire for convenience. Product planning is influenced by the need for customer convenience in packaging, quantity, and selection. Pricing policies must be established in conformity with the demand for credit and with the costs of providing the various kinds of convenience. Distribution policies must allow for convenient locations and store hours.

## Political and Legal Forces

To an increasing extent every company's conduct is influenced by the political-legal processes in society. The political-legal influences on marketing can be grouped into five categories. In each the impact stems both from legislation and from policies established by myriad government regulatory agencies. The categories are:

- *General monetary and fiscal policies.* Marketing systems obviously are affected by the level of government spending, the money supply, and tax legislation.
- *Broad social legislation and accompanying policies set by regulatory agencies.* Civil rights laws and programs to reduce unemployment fall in this category. Also included is legislation controlling the environment—antipollution laws, for example—and regulations set by the Environmental Protection Agency.
- *Governmental relationships with individual industries.* Here we find subsidies in agriculture, shipbuilding, passenger rail transportation, and other industries. Tariffs and import quotas also affect specific industries. In the 1990s government *deregulation* continues to have a significant effect on financial institutions and on the airline, rail, and trucking industries.
- *Legislation specifically related to marketing.* Marketing executives do not have to be lawyers. But they should know something about these laws, especially the major ones—why they were passed, their main provisions, and current ground rules set by the courts and regulatory agencies for administering these laws.

The laws fall into two groups. One group is designed primarily to regulate and maintain competition; the other is intended to protect the consumer. Table 2-1 summarizes the main laws in each group. You may note that there has been no new major regulatory legislation affecting marketing since 1980. This fact reflects the political climate in Washington during the 1980s. We will cover relevant legislation in appropriate places throughout this book.

Up to this point our discussion of governmental influences on marketing has dealt essentially with the activities of the *federal* government. However, there are also strong political-legal influences at the *state and local* levels. The marketing programs in many firms are affected by zoning laws, sign laws, interest-rate regulations, state and local taxes, and laws affecting door-to-door selling.

- *The provision of information and the purchase of products.* This fifth area of government influence in marketing is quite different from the other four. Instead of telling marketing executives what they must do or cannot do—instead of legislation and regulations—the government is clearly helping

Environmental concerns have prompted curbs on hazardous practices such as the use of water-polluting phosphates in detergents.

## TABLE 2-1 Summary of selected major legislation affecting marketing

**Designed primarily to protect consumers:**

1. *Pure Food and Drug Act* (1906). Regulates labeling of food and drugs and prohibits manufacture or marketing of adulterated food or drugs. Amended in 1938 by Food, Drug, and Cosmetics Act.

2. Various *textile labeling laws* that require the manufacturer to indicate what the product is made of:
   a. Wool Products Labeling Act (1939).
   b. Fur Products Labeling Act (1951).
   c. Flammable Fabrics Act (1953).
   d. Textile Fiber Products Identification Act (1958).

3. *Automobile Information Disclosure Act* (1958). Requires manufacturers to post suggested retail prices on new passenger vehicles.

4. *Kefauver-Harris Drug Amendments* (1962). Requires that (a) drugs be labeled with their generic names, (b) new drugs be pretested, and (c) new drugs get approval of Food and Drug Administration before being marketed.

5. *National Traffic and Motor Vehicle Safety Act* (1966). Provides safety standards for tires and autos.

6. *Fair Packaging and Labeling Act* (1966). Regulates packaging and labeling.

7. *Cigarette Labeling and Advertising Acts* (1966, 1969). Require manufacturers to label cigarettes as being hazardous to health and prohibit TV advertising of cigarettes.

8. *Consumer Credit Protection Act* (1968). The "truth in lending" law that requires full disclosure of interest rates and other financing charges on loans and credit purchases.

9. *Consumer Product Safety Act* (1972). Establishes the Consumer Product Safety Commission with broad powers to regulate the marketing of products ruled unsafe by the commission.

10. *Consumer Product Warranty Act* (1975). Increases consumers' rights and sellers' responsibilities under product warranties.

11. *FTC Improvement Act* (1980). Limits the power of the Federal Trade Commission to set and enforce industry trade regulations. In effect, reverses the trend toward more FTC protection of consumers.

**Designed primarily to regulate competition:**

1. *Sherman Antitrust Act* (1890). Prohibits monopolies and combinations in restraint of trade.

2. *Federal Trade Commission (FTC) Act* (1914). Prohibits unfair competition.

3. *Clayton Antitrust Act* (1914). Regulates several activities, notably price discrimination.

4. *State Unfair Trade Practices Acts* (1930s). Prohibit "loss-leader" pricing (selling below cost). Laws still in effect in about half the states.

5. *Robinson-Patman Act* (1936). Amends the Clayton Act by strengthening the prohibition of price discrimination. Regulates price discounts and allowances.

6. *Wheeler-Lea Act* (1938). Amends the FTC Act; broadens and strengthens regulation of unfair or deceptive competition.

7. *Lanham Trademark Act* (1946). Regulates brands and trademarks.

8. *Consumer Goods Pricing Act* (1975). Repeals *federal* laws supporting *state* fair-trade laws. Does away with state laws allowing manufacturers to set retail prices.

9. Various *deregulation* laws pertaining to specific industries:
   a. Natural Gas Policy Act (1978).
   b. Airline Deregulation Act (1978).
   c. Motor Carrier Act (1980).
   d. Staggers Rail Act (1980).
   e. Depository Institutions Act (1981).

them. The federal government is the largest source of secondary marketing information in the country. And the government is the largest single buyer of goods and services in the nation.

**Technology**

Technology has a tremendous impact on our lives—our life-styles, our consumption patterns, and our economic well-being. Just think of the effect of major technological developments like the airplane, plastics, television, computers, antibiotics, and birth control pills. Except perhaps for the airplane, all these technologies reached their major markets only in your lifetime or your parents' lifetime. Think how your life in the future might be affected by cures for the common cold, development of energy sources to replace fossil fuels, low-cost methods for making ocean water drinkable, or even commercial travel to the moon.

Consider for a moment some of the dramatic technological breakthroughs that will expand our horizons in the 1990s. The role of robots undoubtedly will expand considerably. At the heart of a robot's operating mechanism is a miniature electronic computer system, which leads us into another technological breakthrough area—miniature electronic products. It's hard to grasp the fantastic possibilities in this field. Then there is the awesome potential of the superconductor—a means of transmitting electrical energy with virtually no

New technology such as fiber optics—these men are burying fiber-optic cable—can have a major impact on the marketing programs in many companies.

resistance. Further developments in fiber optics and high-definition television will open vistas in communications that we never dreamed of 10 to 15 years ago.[8]

Major technological breakthroughs carry a threefold market impact. They can:

- Start entirely new industries, as computers, robots, and lasers have done.
- Radically alter, or virtually destroy, existing industries. Television crippled the radio and movie industries; hand-held calculators did in the slide-rule industry.
- Stimulate other markets and industries not related to the new technology. New home appliances and frozen food gave homemakers additional free time to engage in other activities.

Technology is a mixed blessing in other ways also. A new technology may improve our lives in one area, while creating environmental and social problems in other areas. The automobile makes life great in some ways, but it also creates traffic jams and air pollution. Television provides built-in baby-sitters, but it also can have an adverse effect on family discussions and on children's reading habits. It is a bit ironic that technology is strongly criticized for creating problems (air pollution, for example), but at the same time is expected to solve these problems.

**Monitor the Environment**

Now that we have finished our discussion of the external environmental forces that shape an organization's marketing system, you may appreciate what a monumental task a marketing executive has in adjusting to these external influences. Obviously the more executives know about their environment, the better they can plan and carry out their company's marketing programs. One key to learning about the environment is to monitor it in a systematic, ongoing fashion. In each of the six environmental categories, marketing executives should be alert to trends, new developments, and other changes that may present marketing opportunities or problems for their particular firm.

**EXTERNAL MICROENVIRONMENT**

Three environmental forces are a part of a company's marketing system but are external to the company. These are the firm's market, producer-suppliers, and marketing intermediaries. While generally classified as noncontrollable forces, these external elements can be influenced to a greater degree than the macro forces. A marketing organization, for example, may be able to exert some pressure on its suppliers or middlemen. And, through its advertising effort, a firm should have some influence on its present and potential market. (See Figure 2-2.)

**The Market**

As both an external force and a key part of every marketing system, the market is really what marketing and this book are all about—how to reach the market and serve it profitably and in a socially responsible manner. The market is (or should be) the focal point of all marketing decisions in an organization. This tremendously important factor is the subject of Part 2 (Chapters 4 to 6), and it arises frequently throughout the text.

---

[8]See "Super Television: The High Promise—and High Risks—of High-Definition TV," *Business Week,* Jan. 30, 1989, p. 56.

**FIGURE 2-2** External microenvironment of a company's marketing program.

## WHAT IS A MARKET?

The word *market* is used in a number of ways. There is a stock *market* and an automobile *market*, a retail *market* for furniture and a wholesale *market* for furniture. One person may be going to the *market*; another may plan to *market* a product. What, then is a market? A *market* may be defined as a place where buyers and sellers meet, goods or services are offered for sale, and transfers of ownership occur. A *market* may also be defined as the demand made by a certain group of potential buyers for a good or service. For instance, there is a farm *market* for petroleum products. The terms *market* and *demand* are often used interchangeably; they may also be used jointly as *market demand*.

These definitions are not sufficiently precise to be useful to us here. For business purposes we define a **market** as people or organizations with *wants (needs) to satisfy, money to spend, and the willingness to spend it.* Thus in the market demand for any given product or service, there are three factors to consider—people or organizations with wants (needs), their purchasing power, and their buying behavior.

We shall employ the dictionary definition of *needs:* the lack of anything that is required, desired, or useful. As noted in Chapter 1, we do not limit needs to the narrow physiological requirements of food, clothing, and shelter essential for survival. In our discussion the words *needs* and *wants* are used synonymously and interchangeably.

**Suppliers**   Because you can't sell a product if you can't first make it or buy it, **producer-suppliers** of goods and services are critical to the success of any marketing organization. In our economy a buyer's market exists for most products. That

### AN ETHICAL DILEMMA?

The manufacturers of disposable diapers have been informed that the plastic portion (about 20 percent) of the product is not biodegradable and therefore will cause environmental problems. Assume you are a product manager having responsibility for disposable diapers at one of these firms. Three options have been proposed by your staff:

- Ignore the information.
- Appeal to the ecology minded by claiming that your product is "more than 80% biodegradable!"
- Inform your customers of the problem and use a less effective ingredient until a better alternative can be found.

Which options do you consider ethical?

is, there is little problem in making or buying a product; the big problem is usually how to sell it.

Marketing executives often do not concern themselves enough with the supply side of the exchange transaction. However, the importance of suppliers in a company's marketing system comes into focus sharply when shortages occur. Shortages highlight the importance of cooperative relationships with suppliers. Suppliers' prices and services are a significant influence on any company's marketing system. At the same time these prices and services can very often be influenced by careful planning on the part of the buying organization.

**Marketing Intermediaries**

**Marketing intermediaries** are independent business organizations that directly aid in the flow of goods and services between a marketing organization and its markets. These intermediaries include two types of institutions: (1) resellers—the wholesalers and retailers—or the people we call *middlemen* and (2) various *facilitating organizations* that provide such services as transportation, warehousing, and financing that are needed to complete exchanges between buyers and sellers.

These intermediaries operate between a company and its markets and between a company and its suppliers. Thus they complete what we call *channels of distribution*.

In some situations it may be more efficient for a company to operate on a "do-it-yourself" basis without using marketing intermediaries. A producer can deal *directly* with its suppliers or sell *directly* to its customers and do its own shipping, financing, and so on. But marketing intermediaries do perform a variety of services. They are specialists in their respective fields. They justify their economic existence by doing a better job at a lower cost than the marketing organization can do by itself.

**ORGANIZATION'S INTERNAL ENVIRONMENT**

An organization's marketing system is also shaped to some extent by *internal* forces that are largely controllable by management. These internal influences include a firm's production, financial, and personnel capabilities. If the Dial Corporation is considering adding a new brand of soap, for example, it must determine whether existing production facilities and expertise can be used. If the new product requires a new plant or machinery, financial capability en-

**FIGURE 2-3** Internal environment of a company's marketing program.

ters the picture. Other nonmarketing forces are the company's location, its research and development (R&D) strength as evidenced by the patents it holds, and the overall image the firm projects to the public. Plant location often determines the geographic limits of a company's market, particularly if high transportation costs or perishable products are involved. The R&D factor may determine whether a company will lead or follow in the industry's technology and marketing. (See Figure 2-3.)

Another environmental consideration here is the necessity of coordinating the marketing and nonmarketing activities in a company. Sometimes this can be difficult because of conflicts in goals and executive personalities. Production people, for example, like to see long production runs of standardized items. However, marketing executives may want a variety of models, sizes, and colors to satisfy different market segments. Financial executives typically want tighter credit and expense limits than the marketing people feel are necessary to be competitive.

To wrap up our discussion of the marketing environment, Figure 2-4 shows the environmental forces that combine to shape an organization's marketing program. Within the framework of these constraints, management should develop a marketing program to provide want-satisfaction to its markets. Permeating the planning and operation of this program is the company's marketing information system—a key marketing subsystem intended to aid management in its decision making. The next chapter is devoted to the subjects of marketing information systems and marketing research.

**FIGURE 2-4** A company's marketing environment.

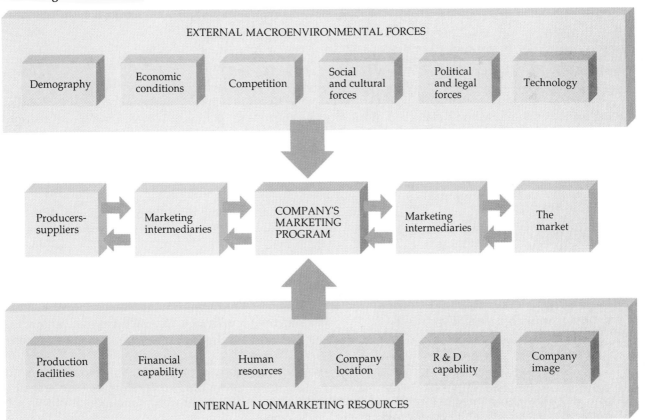

**SUMMARY**
A company operates its marketing system within a framework of ever-changing forces that constitute the system's environment. Some of the forces are broad, external variables that generally cannot be controlled by the executives in a firm. Demographic conditions are one of these macro influences. Another is economic conditions such as the business cycle, inflation, interest rates, and unemployment. Management must be aware of the various types of competition and the competitive structure within which a given firm operates. Social and cultural forces, including cultural changes, are another factor with which to contend. Political and legal forces, along with technology, round out the group of external macroenvironmental influences. Management should establish a system for monitoring these external forces.

Another set of environmental factors—producer-suppliers, marketing intermediaries, and the market itself—is also external to the firm. But these elements clearly are part of the firm's marketing system and can be controlled to some extent by the firm. At the same time a set of nonmarketing resources *within* the firm (production facilities, personnel, finances) influences its marketing system. These variables generally are controllable by management.

**KEY TERMS AND CONCEPTS**

Demography 38
Economic environment 40
   Business cycle 40
   Inflation 40
   Interest rates 41
Types of competition 41
Social and cultural forces 42

Political and legal forces 45
Technology 47
Environmental monitoring 48
Market 49
Producer-suppliers 49
Marketing intermediaries 50

## QUESTIONS AND PROBLEMS

1. It is predicted that college enrollments will decline during the next several years. What marketing measures should your school take to adjust to this forecast?
2. For each of the following companies, give some examples of how its marketing program is likely to differ during periods of prosperity as contrasted with periods of recession.
   a. Campbell soups.
   b. Schwinn bicycles.
   c. Chain of movie theaters.
   d. Salvation Army or Red Cross.
3. What would be the likely effect of high interest rates on the market for the following goods or services?
   a. Timex or Swatch watches.
   b. Building materials.
   c. Nursery school programs.
4. Explain the three types of competition faced by a company. What marketing strategies or programs would you recommend to meet each type?
5. Name three U.S.-manufactured products that

you think would be highly acceptable from a physical-environment standpoint in Western European markets. Name three products that you think would be environmentally unacceptable.
6. Give some examples of how the changing role of women has been reflected in American marketing.
7. What are some marketing implications of the increasing public interest in health and physical fitness?
8. Why was there so little marketing-related federal regulatory legislation during the 1980s?
9. Give examples of the effects of marketing legislation in your own buying, recreation, and other everyday activities. Do you believe these laws are effective? If not, what changes would you recommend?
10. Using examples other than those in this chapter, explain how a firm's marketing system can be influenced by the environmental factor of technology.

11. Specify some external macroenvironmental forces affecting the marketing programs of:
    a. Pizza Hut.
    b. Your school.
    c. A local nightclub.
    d. Clairol (hair-care products).

12. Explain how each of the following resources within a company might influence that company's marketing program.
    a. Plant location.      c. Financial resources.
    b. Company image.      d. Personnel capability.

13. Explain how or under what conditions a company might exert some control over its suppliers and intermediaries in its marketing program.

As different as they are, all these organizations had one thing in common. They needed information to assist them in decision making. Management in any organization needs information—and lots of it—about potential markets and environmental forces discussed in Chapter 2. One requirement for success in strategic marketing planning is effectively managed information. A mass of data is available both from external sources and from within a firm. The challenge is sorting through it and using it effectively, that is, managing it.

We will begin our discussion with a description of marketing information systems. We will then examine the actual performance of marketing research.

## WHAT IS A MARKETING INFORMATION SYSTEM?

With the popularization of computers as business tools in the late 1950s and early 1960s, expanded data manipulation and storage capability became important aids in marketing decision making. What quickly developed was the **marketing information system (MkIS)**—a concept that is still evolving today. An MkIS is an ongoing, organized set of procedures and methods designed to generate, analyze, disseminate, store, and retrieve information for use in making marketing decisions. The ideal MkIS has the ability to:

- Generate regular reports and ad hoc studies as needed.
- Integrate old and new data to provide information updates and identify trends.
- Analyze data using mathematical models that represent the real world.
- Allow managers to get answers to "what if" questions. (For example, "What if we increase our TV advertising in the Southwest 20 percent and add 10 percent to inventories?")

The increased use of personal computers, "user friendly" software, and the ability to link computer systems at different locations (networking) have greatly enhanced the potential of MkIS.

The value and, ultimately, success of an MkIS depends on three factors:

- The nature and quality of the data available to it.
- The accuracy and realism of the models and analytic techniques applied to the data.
- The working relationship between the operators of the MkIS and the managers who use the output.

## Need for a Marketing Information System

Today many environmental forces dictate that every firm manage its marketing information as effectively as possible. Let's consider some of these factors and their relationship to information management:

- Executives have less time for decision making. Companies are being forced to develop and market new products more quickly than ever before.
- Marketing activity is becoming increasingly complex and broader in scope. Companies are expanding their markets, and many operate in both domestic and foreign markets.
- Energy, labor, and other raw materials are becoming more costly. Firms must make more efficient use of resources and labor in order to complete.
- Customer expectations are growing. The lack of timely, adequate information about a problem with some aspect of an organization's marketing program can result in lost business.
- The quantity of information is expanding. Computer technology has made

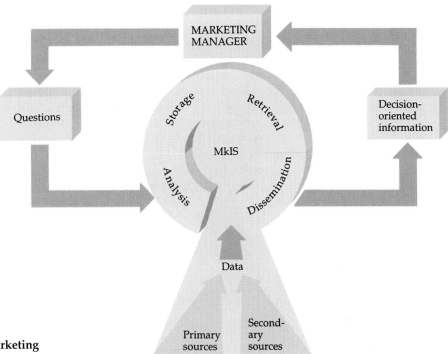

**FIGURE 3-1** The structure of a marketing information system.

so much information available that the challenge often is to figure out what to do with it.

A marketing information system can help marketers cope with each of these dynamic forces.

## Benefits of an MkIS

An organization generates and gathers much information in its day-to-day operations, and much more is available to it. But unless the company has some system to retrieve and process these data, it is unlikely that it is using its marketing information effectively.

A well-designed MkIS can provide a fast and more complete information flow for management decision making. The storage and retrieval capability of an MkIS allows a wider variety of data to be collected and used. Management can continually monitor the performance of products, markets, sales people, and other marketing units in detail.

A marketing information system is of obvious value in a large company where information is likely to get lost or distorted as it becomes widely dispersed. However, experience shows that integrated information systems can also upgrade management's performance in small and medium-sized firms.

The broad array of types and prices of computer hardware and software currently available brings MkIS capability to almost any organization. Figure 3-1 illustrates the characteristics and operation of an MkIS.

## Relationship between MkIS and Marketing Research

The relationship between marketing information systems and marketing research is perceived quite differently by different people. Some see an MkIS as a logical, computer-based extension of marketing research. Others see the two as distinctly different activities, related only to the extent that they both deal with the management of information.

When this latter approach is accepted, marketing research tends to be conducted on a project-by-project basis, with each project having a starting and ending point. Projects often tackle unrelated problems on an intermittent, almost as-needed basis. Marketing research focuses on past events and their consequences to solve current problems.

This project orientation is reflected in the definition endorsed until recently by the American Marketing Association (AMA): Marketing research is the "systematic gathering, recording, and analyzing of data relating to the marketing of goods and services."[1] By this definition marketing research is a small part of the MkIS. Its function is simply to provide and process data. But researchers have taken issue with this limited role, suggesting that it excludes involvement with problems, ideas, actions, and decisions from marketing research.[2] According to the definition, a researcher would not generate hypotheses, test theories, or participate in setting strategy.

Thus, the AMA has adopted a new definition, which is intended to reflect marketing research in the 1990s. This definition states that **marketing research**

> links the consumer, customer, and public to the marketer through information—information used to identify and define marketing opportunities and problems; generate, refine, and evaluate marketing actions; monitor marketing performance; and improve understanding of marketing as a process. Marketing research specifies the information required to address these issues; designs the methods for collecting information; manages and implements the data collection process; analyzes the results; and communicates the findings and their implications.[3]

This rather lengthy definition differs from its predecessor in two major ways. First, it emphasizes the researcher's responsibility to develop managerially useful *information* rather than simply generate data. Second, the new definition proposes greater *involvement* for researchers in the decision-making process. If it is widely accepted and implemented, the definition will resolve the debate and the MklS will become part of marketing research.

At this point we will turn to the subject of marketing research. We will discuss (1) its scope within organizations, (2) typical procedures in a marketing research study, (3) organizational structures for conducting research, and (4) the current status of the field.

### SCOPE OF MARKETING RESEARCH ACTIVITIES

The broad scope of marketing research activities and the percentage of firms engaging in each are summarized in Table 3-1. The most common activities are studies of industry and market trends and market share analyses. It is interesting to note that despite claims of a global economy, a relatively small proportion of firms are researching export and international markets.

### PROCEDURE USED IN MARKETING RESEARCH

The general procedure illustrated in Figure 3-2 is applicable to most marketing research projects. Some of the steps are not needed in every project, however. The numbers in the following section headings correspond to the steps in Figure 3-2.

### 1. Define the Objective

Researchers should have a clear idea of what they are trying to accomplish in a research project—that is, the goal of the project. Usually the objective is to solve a problem, but this is not always so. Often the purpose is to *define* the problem, or to determine whether the firm even *has* a problem. To illustrate, a manufacturer of commercial air-conditioning equipment had been enjoying a

---

[1] "Report of the Definitions Committee of the American Marketing Association," American Marketing Association, Chicago, 1961.
[2] Lawrence D. Gibson, "What Is Marketing Research?" *Marketing Research,* March 1989, pp. 2–3.
[3] "New Marketing Research Definition Approved," *Marketing News,* Jan. 2, 1987, p. 1.

**TABLE 3-1 Selected marketing research activities of 587 U.S. companies**

| Subject areas examined | % doing |
|---|---|
| 1. Business/Economic and Corporate Research | |
| a. Industry/market characteristics and trends | 83 |
| b. Market share analyses | 79 |
| 2. Pricing | |
| a. Market potential | 74 |
| b. Sales potential | 69 |
| c. Sales forecasts | 67 |
| d. Competitive pricing analyses | 63 |
| 3. Product | |
| a. Concept development and testing | 68 |
| b. Competitive products | 58 |
| c. Product testing of existing products | 47 |
| d. Test marketing | 45 |
| 4. Distribution | |
| a. Channel performance | 29 |
| b. Export and international | 19 |
| 5. Promotion | |
| a. Advertising effectiveness | 65 |
| b. Public image | 60 |
| c. Media research | 57 |
| d. Copy research | 50 |
| 6. Buying Behavior | |
| a. Product satisfaction | 68 |
| b. Purchase behavior | 61 |
| c. Purchase intentions | 60 |
| d. Segmentation | 60 |
| e. Brand awareness | 59 |

Source: Thomas C. Kinnear and Ann R. Root, *1988 Survey of Marketing Research*, American Marketing Association, Chicago, 1989, p. 43.

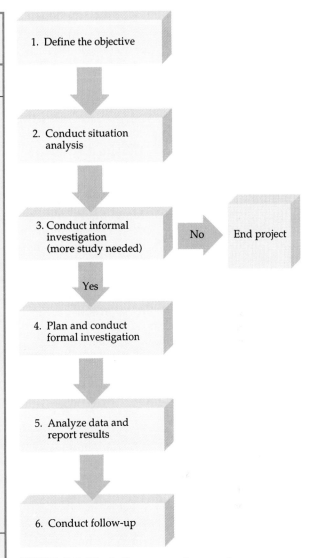

**FIGURE 3-2** Marketing research procedure.

steady increase in sales volume over a period of years. Management decided to make a sales analysis. This research project uncovered the fact that, although the company's volume had been increasing, its share of the market had declined. In this instance marketing research uncovered a problem that management did not know existed.

The following case history illustrates the first three steps in a marketing research project—namely, problem definition, situation analysis, and informal investigation. A small manufacturer of camera accessories developed a compact, 4-pound rechargeable power cell for use in professional flash photography. The general problem, as presented to an outside marketing research firm, was to determine whether the company should add this product to its line. A breakdown of the problem into parts that could be handled by research resulted in the following specific questions:

- What is the market demand for such a product?
- What additional features are desired, if any?
- What channels of distribution should be used for such a product?
- What will technology be like in the next 5 years?
- What will the competition be like in the next 5 years?

With this tentative restatement of the problem, the researchers were ready for the next procedural step—the situation analysis.

## 2. Conduct Situation Analysis

The **situation analysis** involves obtaining information about the company and its business environment by means of library research and extensive interviewing of company officials. The researchers try to get a "feel" for the situation surrounding the problem. They analyze the company, its market, its competition, and the industry in general.

In the situation analysis, researchers also try to refine the problem definition and develop hypotheses for further testing. A research **hypothesis** is a tentative supposition or a possible solution to a problem. A well-run project generates information to support or reject each hypothesis.

In the camera accessory case the situation analysis suggested the following hypotheses:

- There is adequate demand for the product.
- To reach the professional market, full-line camera stores should be emphasized in distributing the product.
- Advances in technology will not quickly make the product obsolete.
- Competition is not a serious threat to the product's success.

## 3. Conduct an Informal Investigation

Having gotten a feel for the problem, the researchers are now ready to collect some preliminary data from the marketplace. This **informal investigation** consists of gathering information from people outside the company—middlemen, competitors, advertising agencies, and consumers.

The researchers in the camera accessory case talked with many people outside the company. From telephone conversations with officials of the Photo Marketing Trade Association, the researchers developed an estimate of the potential market for the product. This estimate suggested that the market was large enough to warrant further investigation. Fifteen photographers in three cities were then asked to evaluate the product itself as well as photographic practices in general. All liked the product, but they did suggest some product modifications.

To investigate channels of distribution, the researchers talked by telephone with several photo retailers around the country. The consensus was that the retailers would not stock this new product. The researchers then visited the annual Photo Marketing Trade Show to talk with more retailers and to get a line on the competition. Again, the retailers' reaction was negative. The researchers also learned that three major competitors soon would introduce rechargeable batteries that would compete directly with the new product. Furthermore there was a rumor that the Japanese soon would be entering the market.

The informal investigation is a critical step in a research project because it will determine whether further study is necessary. Decisions on the main problem can often be made with information gathered in the informal investigation. In fact, at this point the camera accessory company decided not to market its portable power cell.

## 4. Plan and Conduct the Formal Investigation

If the project warrants continued investigation, management and the researcher must determine what additional information is needed. The next step for the researcher is to plan where and how to get the desired data and then to gather it.

### SELECT SOURCES OF INFORMATION

Primary data, secondary data, or both can be used in an investigation. **Primary data** are original data gathered specifically for the project at hand. **Secondary data** have already been gathered for some other purpose. For example, when researchers stand in a supermarket and observe whether people use shopping lists, they are collecting primary data. The Census of Population compiled by the federal government is a secondary source.

One of the biggest mistakes made in marketing research is to collect primary data before exhausting the information available in secondary sources. Ordinarily secondary information can be gathered much faster and at far less expense than primary data.

**Sources of secondary data**  Several excellent sources of secondary information are readily available to marketing researchers.[4] One such source, of course, is the multitude of records and reports *within* the firm itself. *Outside* the firm the major sources are as follows:

The Thomas Register is one of many useful secondary sources available in most public libraries.

- *Libraries.* Probably the best all-around source of secondary information is a good library. All of the publications mentioned below, as well as many other useful sources, are available there.
- *Government.* The federal government furnishes more marketing data than any other source. It has access under the law to types of data (company sales and profits, personal income, and the like) that are impossible for private companies to get. The monthly *Catalog of United States Publications* lists all U.S. government publications.

    State and local governments provide many sources of information. Tax records, license applications, and other registration systems are potentially valuable data sources.
- *Trade, professional, and business associations.* Associations frequently conduct and publish member surveys. The *Encyclopedia of Associations*, an index of all associations, provides details on how to contact them. Some associations also maintain libraries. For example, the American Marketing Association has a library with 4,000 books. Groups such as The Conference Board and the American Management Association publish reports and statistical studies on special topics.
- *Private business firms.* Private marketing research firms produce a wealth of information. Nielsen Media Research, for instance, has for years reported how many households watch various television programs during a given week. Audits & Surveys measures retail sales, retail distribution, and retailer inventory bimonthly for specific product categories. There are also firms producing information for the business-to-business markets. Market Statistics lists the number and size of firms for all Standard Industrial Classifications (SICs) for every Zip code and county in the United States.

---

[4]For an excellent reference list of major secondary sources of business information, see James Woy, ed., *Encyclopedia of Business Information Sources*, Detroit, Mich., Gale Research, Inc., 1988.

*Findex*, a directory of marketing studies, lists over 400 private research companies and over 13,000 studies, reports, and surveys that are available for sale.

- *Advertising media.* Many magazines, newspapers, and radio and television stations publish useful information. *Sales & Marketing Management* magazine annually puts out the "Survey of Buying Power." This report gives the population, retail sales, income, and effective buying power for all U.S. states, counties, metropolitan areas, and cities.
- *University research organizations.* Most large universities publish research and statistics on their local areas.

The risk with secondary data is that the user has no control over how, when, or why it was collected. As a result, the information may be inaccurate or dated. Or the definitions may not meet the user's needs. For example, a secondary source may define the "youth market" in terms of school grade but the user may need information by age. Thus researchers should check the source, motivation for the study, and key definitions before relying on secondary data.

**Sources of primary data** After exhausting all reasonable secondary sources of information, researchers may still lack sufficient data. Then they will turn to primary sources and gather the information themselves. In a company research project, for instance, a researcher may interview that firm's sales people, middlemen, or customers to obtain the pertinent market information.

### DETERMINE METHODS FOR GATHERING PRIMARY DATA

There are three widely used methods of gathering primary data: survey, observation, and experimentation. Normally all three are not used on one project. The choice of method will be influenced by the availability of time, money, personnel, and facilities.

**Survey Method** A **survey** consists of gathering data by interviewing people. The advantage of a survey is that information is firsthand. In fact, it may be the only way to determine the opinions or buying intentions of a group.

Inherent in the survey method are certain limitations. There are opportunities for error in the construction of the survey questionnaire and in the interviewing process. Moreover, surveys can be very expensive, and they are time-consuming. Other weaknesses are that potential respondents sometimes refuse to participate and the ones who do respond often cannot or will not give true answers.

Survey interviews may be done by the researcher in person, by telephone, or by mail. **Personal interviews** are more flexible than the other two types because interviewers can probe more deeply if an answer is incomplete. Ordinarily it is possible to obtain more information by personal interview than by telephone or mail. Also the interviewer, by observation, can obtain data regarding the respondents' socioeconomic status—their home, neighborhood, and apparent standard of living.

Rising costs and other problems associated with door-to-door interviewing have prompted many market researchers to survey people in central locations, typically regional shopping centers. This technique is called the **shopping mall intercept** method of interviewing. A study by Market Facts, Inc., found that mall intercepts are used by 90 percent of market researchers and

With mall intercept interviewing, the researcher knows that the respondents are actual shoppers.

that 65 percent of the largest consumer product companies spend the majority of their research budgets on studies that employ mall intercepts.[5]

Another popular tool for face-to-face data gathering is the **focus group.** In a focus group, 4 to 10 people meet with the researcher. Open-ended questions are often used to prompt participants into freely discussing the topic. The researcher can ask follow-up questions to probe deeper into their attitudes. The purpose of focus groups is to generate concepts and hypotheses that can be tested on large, representative samples of people.

In addition to their high cost and time-consuming nature, personal interviews also face the possible limitation of the researcher introducing personal bias into an interview. Sometimes, for example, respondents will give the interviewer the answer they think is desired.

In a **telephone survey** the respondent is approached by telephone, and the interview is completed at that time. Telephone surveys can usually be conducted more rapidly and at less cost than either personal or mail surveys. Since a few interviewers can make any number of calls from a few central points, this method is quite easy to administer. Computer-assisted techniques have broadened the scope of telephone interviewing. These techniques involve automatic random-number dialing, a recorded voice asking the questions, and a machine to record the respondents' answers.

A telephone survey can be timely. For instance, people may be asked whether they are watching television at the moment and, if so, the name of the program and the sponsor. One limitation of the telephone survey is that interviews must be short. Lengthy interviews cannot be conducted satisfactorily over the phone. Also about 20 percent of households have unlisted numbers, have moved since the directory was printed, or have no telephone.

Telephone surveys have been used successfully with executives at work. When preceded by a letter introducing the study and a short call to make an appointment for the actual interview, these surveys can elicit a very high cooperation rate.

**Interviewing by mail** involves mailing a questionnaire to potential respondents and having them return the completed form by mail. Since no interviewers are used, this type of survey is not hampered by interviewer bias or problems connected with the management of interviewers. Mailed questionnaires are more economical than personal interviews and are particularly useful in national surveys. If the respondents remain anonymous, they are more likely to give true answers because they are not biased by the presence of an interviewer.

A major problem with mail questionnaires is the compilation of a good mailing list, especially for a *broad-scale* survey. If the sample can be drawn from a *limited* list, such as property taxpayers in certain counties or subscribers to a certain magazine, the list presents no problem. Another significant limitation concerns the reliability of the questionnaire returns. The researchers have no control over who actually completes the questionnaire or how it is done. For example, a survey may be addressed to the male head of the household but because he is unavailable or not interested, his teenage daughter "helps out" by completing it. In addition, because there is no personal contact with the respondents, it is impossible to judge how much care and thought went into providing the answers.

---

[5] Katherine T. Smith, "Most Research Firms Use Mall Intercepts," *Marketing News*, Sept. 11, 1989, p. 16.

## AN ETHICAL DILEMMA?

A recent mailing to consumers began with the following statement: "You may never have another chance like this. If you want to see America's National Park System survive, it is *extremely* important you complete and return the enclosed National Survey to the National Parks and Conservation Association *immediately*." The survey consists of 12 questions. A typical one is, "Great Smoky Mountain and Shenandoah National Parks are being heavily, perhaps irreversibly, damaged by acid rain. Do you favor current legislation requiring federal controls on acid rain?" The final question is a request for donations to the association. If you were a marketing researcher, would you consider soliciting donations to be an ethical use of a survey? What impact might it have on the attitudes of consumers toward surveys?

Still another limitation is that there is usually a low response rate to a mail survey. It is not uncommon to receive completed replies from only 10 to 30 percent of those contacted. This is particularly important because if the respondents have characteristics that differentiate them from nonrespondents on certain dimensions of the survey, the results will be invalid. Techniques for improving mail response rates have been the subject of hundreds of experiments.[6]

**Observational method**   In the **observational method** data are collected by observing the actions of a person. There are no interviews, though an interview may be used as a follow-up to get additional information. For instance, if customers are observed buying soft drinks in cans instead of plastic bottles, they may be asked why they prefer that form of packaging.

Information may be gathered by *personal* or *mechanical* observation. In one kind of personal observation, the researcher poses as a customer. This technique is useful to get information about the caliber of sales people or to determine what brands they favor. Mechanical observation takes many forms. One we have all become familiar with is the scanners used in supermarkets to record purchases. Other, more dramatic forms are eye cameras used in laboratory settings to record a person's response to a visual stimulus, such as an ad, and brain wave monitors to test whether reactions to a commercial are primarily emotional or logical.

The observational method has several merits. It can provide highly accurate data about what consumers do in given situations. Usually consumers are unaware that they are being observed, so presumably they behave in their usual fashion. Thus the observational technique eliminates bias resulting from the interaction of the data gatherer and the persons observed. However, the technique is limited in its application. Observation tells *what* happens, but it cannot tell *why*. It cannot delve into motives, attitudes, or opinions.

[6]See, for example, Srinivasan Ratneshwar and David W. Stewart, "Nonresponse in Mail Surveys: An Integrative Review," *Applied Marketing Research*, Summer 1989, pp. 37–46; Bruce J. Walker, Wayne Kirchmann, and Jeffery S. Conant, "A Method to Improve Response to Industrial Mail Surveys," *Industrial Marketing Management*, November 1987, pp. 305–14.

Initially viewed as a way of increasing check-out efficiency, electronic scanners have become a valuable tool in capturing purchase behavior data.

To overcome the biases inherent in the survey method, sophisticated observational techniques have been developed. One such method is called **single-source data,** so named because exposure to television advertising and product purchases can be traced to individual households, providing a *single source* for both types of data. It combines a cable television monitoring system with electronic scanners in supermarkets. The result is that household demographics can be correlated to television advertising exposure and product purchases. One company, Information Resources, Inc., has a panel of 12,000 participants in four small U.S. cities to collect this type of data.

**Experimental method**   An **experiment** is a method of gathering primary data in which the researcher is able to observe the results of changing one variable in a situation while holding all others constant. Experiments are conducted in laboratory settings and in the field. In marketing research the word *laboratory* is used to describe an environment over which the researcher has complete control during the experiment.

Consider this example. A small group of consumers is assembled and presented with a brief product description and proposed package for a new breakfast cereal. After examining the package the people are asked whether they would buy the product and their responses are recorded. Next a similar

Product tests involving potential consumers can provide valuable preliminary information.

group of consumers is brought together and presented with the identical package and product information, except that a nutritional claim is printed on the package. This group is also asked if it would buy the product. Because the researcher had complete control over the test environment and the only thing changed was the nutritional claim on the package, any difference in buying intentions can be attributed to the claim.

Laboratory experiments can be used to test virtually any component of marketing strategy. However, it is important to recognize that the setting is unnatural and consumers' responses may be biased by the situation.

An experiment in the *field* is called test marketing. It is similar to a laboratory experiment but is conducted under more realistic conditions. The researcher therefore has less control. In **test marketing** the researcher duplicates real market conditions in a small geographic area to measure consumers' responses to a strategy before committing to a major marketing effort. Test marketing may be undertaken to forecast sales (discussed in Chapter 22) or to evaluate different marketing mixes.

The advantage of field experiments over laboratory experiments is their realism. However, there are several disadvantages. Test marketing is expensive ($500,000 is not uncommon), time-consuming (9 to 12 months is normal), and impossible to keep secret from competitors (who may intentionally disrupt the test by temporarily changing their marketing mixes). Another problem is the researcher's inability to control the situation. For example, RJR Nabisco test-marketed its innovative, low-nicotine Premier brand of cigarettes. However, the product—dubbed the ''smokeless'' cigarette by the media—attracted an inordinate amount of attention. As a result, it was difficult to determine what portion of sales resulted from the actual product and its marketing program rather than from publicity.[7]

Because of its inherent limitations, the use of traditional test marketing declined as faster, less expensive alternatives were developed. One of these alternatives is the **simulated test market,** in which a sample of consumers is shown ads for the product being tested as well as for other products. The subjects are then allowed to ''shop'' in a test store that resembles a small grocery store. Follow-up interviews may be conducted immediately and also after the products have been used to better understand the consumers' behavior. The entire set of data goes into a statistical model and sales for the product are forecast.

The potential benefits of simulated test marketing include:

- Lower costs than a traditional test market.
- Results in as little as 8 weeks.
- A test can be kept secret.

The drawbacks are:

- Questionable accuracy for unique, new products.
- Application limited to traditional packaged goods.
- Inability to predict the response of competitors or retailers.
- Inability to test changes in marketing variables like packaging or distribution due to the simulation's short duration.[8]

---

[7] Pat Seelig, ''All Over the Map,'' *Sales & Marketing Management,* March 1989, pp. 58–64. See also ''The Nation's Most Popular Test Markets,'' *Sales & Marketing Management,* March 1989, pp. 65–69.

[8] Howard Schlossberg, ''Simulated Vs. Traditional Test Marketing,'' *Marketing News,* Oct. 23, 1989, pp. 1–2, 11.

---

### Test marketing point-of-purchase advertising

Before risking a national introduction, the manufacturer of VideOcart decided to use a test market to measure consumer reaction. Their product is an interactive video screen attached to the handle of a shopping cart. The screen can carry manufacturers' ads, information on store specials for the day, recipes, and even games (to be played while waiting in the checkout line). It also provides research data on the shopper's buying patterns.

The initial test was done at Dominick's in a Chicago suburb. Based on information learned there, tests with different types of advertising have been undertaken in Marietta, Georgia, and Los Angeles. Are VideOcarts a success? The "judges" are still deciding. Maybe you will soon find out on a visit to your favorite supermarket.

Source: Pat Seelig, "All Over the Map," *Sales & Marketing Management*, March 1989, p. 60.

---

Simulated test marketing has not replaced traditional test markets because of these limitations. In fact, the two methods are often used together, with the simulation results used to make marketing mix modifications before beginning the traditional test market.[9]

### PREPARE FORMS FOR GATHERING DATA

When interviewing or observing subjects, data collectors use forms on which there are instructions as well as space to record the information. The importance of the survey questionnaire and the difficulty of designing it cannot be overemphasized. Extreme care and skill are needed to minimize bias, misunderstanding, and respondent irritation.

### PLAN THE SAMPLE

It is unnecessary to survey or observe every person who could shed light on a research problem. It is sufficient to collect data from a sample if its reactions are representative of the entire group. However, before data can be gathered, researchers must determine who the subjects will be; that is, they must select a sample. We all employ sampling in our everyday activities. Often we base our opinion of a person on only one or two conversations. And we taste food before taking a larger quantity. The key issue in this kind of sampling and in marketing research is whether the sample provides accurate information.

The fundamental idea underlying sampling is that a small number of items (a sample), if properly selected from a larger number of items (a universe), will have the same characteristics and in about the same proportion as the universe. The key to obtaining reliable data with this method is to use the right technique in selecting the sample.

Improper sampling is a source of error in many studies. In one survey an opinion on student government was derived by interviewing a sample of fraternity and sorority members. Because no dormitory students, off-campus residents, or commuters were included, this was a biased (nonrepresentative) sample of student opinion.

---

[9] A useful comparison of various test marketing techniques is found in Patricia Greenwald and Marshall Ottenfeld, "New Product Testing: A Review of Techniques," *Applied Marketing Research*, Summer 1989, pp. 17–24.

**AN INTERNATIONAL PERSPECTIVE: What's different about marketing research in Asia?**

When American researchers work overseas, they are often faced with an entirely different set of "rules." New data sources and methods of conducting research must be developed to fit the particular market. For example:

- Secondary data bases vary considerably across countries because censuses are conducted in different years using different definitions and category sizes.
- Providing incentives (such as small gifts or sums of money) to research respondents is fairly common in the United States, the Philippines, and Japan, but this practice is viewed negatively in China.
- In Japan research is done methodically, with careful planning and every contingency anticipated. In contrast, the Koreans have a very entrepreneurial attitude, making decisions and taking action quickly.
- Written and oral Cantonese are sufficiently different that the same questionnaire cannot be used for a self-administered survey, a personal interview, and a telephone survey in Hong Kong.

- The Japanese, who desire not to be disagreeable, have a greater tendency than Westerners to give answers they think will please the interviewer. In certain countries correlations exist between some variables. For instance, in Hong Kong square footage of living space and income are correlated. However, this relationship does not necessarily hold in other countries.
- Postage in Japan makes a mail survey expensive. Mailing something as small as a double postcard costs the equivalent of 55 cents.
- Telephone surveys are out of the question in many Asian countries since only the wealthy have phones.

Sources: Sabra E. Brock, "Marketing Research in Asia: Problems, Opportunities, and Lessons," *Marketing Research*, September 1989, pp. 44–51; and Denison Hatch, "Reaching Consumers in Asia Can Be Tricky," *Adweek's Marketing Week*, Aug. 21, 1989, p. 67.

Though numerous sampling techniques are used, only probability or random samples are appropriate for making generalizations to a universe. A **random sample** is one that is selected in such a way that every member of the universe has an equal chance of being included.

All other (nonrandom) samples are known as **convenience samples.** In reality, convenience samples are quite common in marketing research. There are two reasons for this. First, random samples are very difficult to get. Even though the researcher may *select* the subjects in a random fashion, there is no guarantee that they will all *participate.* Some will be unavailable and others will refuse to cooperate. As a result, researchers often resort to carefully designed convenience samples that reflect the characteristics of the universe as closely as possible. Second, not all research is done with the objective of generalizing to a universe. For example, to confirm the judgment of the advertising department, a researcher may be satisfied with the finding that a small group of respondents all take a similar message away from an ad.

A common question regarding sampling is, How large should a sample be? With random methods a sample must be large enough to be truly representative of the universe. Thus the size will depend on the diversity of characteristics within the universe. All basic statistics books contain general formulas for calculating sample size. In the case of nonrandom samples, since the objective is not to make generalizations, researchers can select any size sample they feel comfortable with.

### COLLECT DATA

The collection of primary data by interviewing, observation, or both is often the weakest link in the research process. Ordinarily, in all other steps, reasonably well-qualified people are working carefully to ensure the accuracy of the results. However, the fruits of these labors may be lost if the data gatherers are inadequately trained or supervised.

Motivating data gatherers is difficult because they frequently are part-time workers doing what is often a monotonous task. As a result many problems may crop up at this point. For instance, poorly trained data gatherers may be unable to establish rapport with respondents. Or the interviewers may revise the wording of questions and thus obtain invalid responses. Finally, some interviewers even attempt to fake data.

### 5. Analyze the Data and Present a Report

The value of research is determined by the results. And since data cannot speak for themselves, analysis and interpretation are key components of any project. Computers have made it possible for researchers to tabulate and process masses of data quickly and inexpensively. This tool can be abused, however. Managers have little use for reams of computer printouts. The researcher's ability to identify pivotal relationships, spot trends, and find patterns is what transforms data into useful information.

The end product of the investigation is the researcher's conclusions and recommendations. Most projects require a written report, often accompanied by an oral presentation to management.

### 6. Conduct Follow-up

Researchers should follow up their studies to determine whether their recommendations are being used. For several reasons management may choose not to use a study's findings. The original problem may have been misdefined, become less urgent, or even disappeared. Or the project may have been completed too late to be useful. Without a follow-up, the researcher has no way of knowing if the project was on target and met management's needs or if it fell short. Thus an important source of information for improving research performance in the future would be ignored.

### WHO DOES MARKETING RESEARCH?

Marketing research can be done by a firm's own personnel or by an outside organization.

### Within the Company

Most business firms have formal marketing research departments, although according to the American Marketing Association survey mentioned earlier, since 1983 the proportion with research departments has declined in all areas except financial services. Table 3-2 shows that business-to-business firms appear less committed to marketing research than consumer product firms and that in the consumer area, health services have significant research growth potential.

### Outside the Company

Independent marketing research firms tend to specialize and can be grouped into three categories:

- Firms that maintain large data bases (such as data on a particular industry) or data sources (such as a consumer panel).
- Firms that design quantitative models for predicting the effects of price changes, measuring advertising effectiveness, forecasting sales, and doing other sophisticated analyses.
- Firms that collect, process, and analyze survey data.

These organizations employ qualified specialists who often bring to a given problem the experience acquired from working on similar studies with other clients.

### TABLE 3-2 Internal organization of marketing research

| Type of firm | % with formal dept | % with one person | % with no one assigned |
|---|---|---|---|
| Manufacturers of consumer products | 77 | 18 | 5 |
| Publishing and broadcasting | 78 | 18 | 4 |
| Manufacturers of business-to-business products | 51 | 33 | 16 |
| Financial services | 82 | 14 | 4 |
| Advertising agencies | 72 | 17 | 11 |
| Health care | 42 | 42 | 16 |

Source: Thomas C. Kinnear and Ann R. Root, *1988 Survey of Marketing Research,* American Marketing Association, Chicago, 1989, p. 10.

## STATUS OF MARKETING RESEARCH

Significant advances have been made in both quantitative and qualitative research methodology, and researchers are making effective use of the behavioral sciences, mathematics, and statistics. Still, far too many companies are spending dollars on manufacturing research, but only pennies on determining market opportunities for their products.

Several factors account for the less-than-universal acceptance of marketing research. Unlike the results of a chemical experiment, the results of marketing research cannot always be measured in direct returns to the organization. It is improbable that a researcher can conduct a study and then point to a specific increase in sales as a result of that effort.

Because of the many variables involved, marketing research often cannot accurately predict future market behavior. Yet that is what is expected of it in many firms. When dealing with consumer behavior, the researcher may be hard-pressed to determine present attitudes or motives (for reasons that will be explained in Chapter 5), much less those of next year.

Possibly a more fundamental reason for the modest status of marketing research has been the failure of researchers to communicate adequately with management. Admittedly there are inept researchers and badly administered research. Sometimes the mentality of the decisive, pragmatic executive may be at odds with the cautious, scientific intellect of a market researcher. However, researchers, like many managers, are often product-oriented when they should be market-oriented. They concentrate on research techniques rather than on how to use these methods to assist management in making better decisions.

Another problem is the apparent reluctance of management to treat marketing research as a continuous process. Too often marketing research is viewed in a fragmented, one-project-at-a-time manner. It is used only when management realizes that it has a marketing problem. One way to change this attitude is for firms to implement the American Marketing Association's definition of marketing research.

Despite these difficulties, the prospects for marketing research are encouraging. As more and more top executives recognize the benefits of strategic marketing planning, there will be a growing respect for marketing research and marketing information systems. The strategic planning process requires

Researchers' predictions of consumers' reactions are sometimes too optimistic and sometimes not optimistic enough. The Mazda Miata (above) surpassed marketing expectations. In contrast, sales of the Yugo (right) were far fewer than anticipated.

the generation and careful analysis of information. Marketing researchers have the training, capabilities, and techniques necessary to perform those tasks.[10]

**SUMMARY**  For a company to operate successfully today, management must develop an orderly method for gathering and analyzing relevant information. A valuable tool for doing this is a marketing information system—ongoing procedures and methods designed to generate, analyze, disseminate, store, and retrieve information for use in making marketing decisions. The traditional view of marketing research positioned it as the data gathering and analyzing component of a marketing information system. However, a new, broader definition of marketing research includes information management.

In a marketing research study the problem to be solved is first identified. Then a researcher conducts a situation analysis and an informal investigation. If a formal investigation is needed, the researcher decides which secondary and primary sources of information to use. To gather primary data, a survey, observation, or the experimental method may be used. The project is completed when data are analyzed and the results reported. Follow-up provides information for improving research.

Marketing research has not yet achieved its potential within organizations because researchers have not effectively communicated with management and because research is used in a fragmented manner.

[10] For more on the status of marketing research see William D. Neal, "The Profession of Marketing Research: A Strategic Assessment and a Prescription for Improvement," *Marketing Research,* September 1989, pp. 13–23.

**KEY TERMS AND CONCEPTS**

Marketing information system (MkIS) 56
Marketing research 58
Situation analysis 60
Hypothesis 60
Informal investigation 60
Primary data 61
Secondary data 61
Survey 62
Personal interview 62
Shopping mall intercept 62
Focus group 63
Telephone survey 63

Mail questionnaire 63
Observational method 64
Personal observation 64
Mechanical observation 64
Single-source data 65
Experiment 65
Laboratory experiment 65
Field experiment 66
Test marketing 66
Simulated test market 66
Random sample 68
Convenience sample 68

## QUESTIONS AND PROBLEMS

1. Why does a company need a marketing information system?

2. Compare the definition of a marketing information system with the latest definition of marketing research presented in the chapter.

3. Do you think marketing researchers should be involved in setting strategy for their organizations? Why or why not?

4. A group of wealthy business executives regularly spend time each winter at a popular ski resort—Aspen, Colorado; Sun Valley, Idaho; Snow Valley, Vermont; or Squaw Valley, California. The executives were intrigued with the possibility of forming a corporation to develop and operate a large ski resort in the Colorado Rockies. This would be a totally new venture and would be on U.S. Forest Service land. It would be a complete resort with facilities appealing to middle- and upper-income markets. What types of information might they want to have before deciding whether to go ahead with the venture? What sources of information would be used?

5. A manufacturer of a liquid glass cleaner competitive with Windex and Glass Wax wants to determine the amount of the product that he can expect to sell throughout the country. To help him in this project, prepare a report that shows the following information for your home state and, if possible, your home city or county. Carefully identify the source you use for this information, and state other sources that provide this information.
   a. Number of households or families.
   b. Income or buying power per family or per household.
   c. Total retail sales in the most recent year for which you can find reliable data.
   d. Total annual sales of food stores, hardware stores, and drugstores.
   e. Total number of food stores.

6. Explain, with examples, the concepts of a situation analysis and an informal investigation in a marketing research project.

7. Evaluate surveys, observation, and experimentation as methods of gathering primary data in the following projects:
   a. A sporting goods retailer wants to determine college students' brand preferences for skis, tennis rackets, and golf clubs.
   b. A supermarket chain wants to determine shoppers' preferences for the physical layout of fixtures and traffic patterns, particularly around checkout stands.
   c. A manufacturer of conveyor belts wants to know who makes buying decisions for his product among present and prospective users.

8. Carefully evaluate the relative merits of personal, telephone, and mail surveys on the bases of flexibility, amount of information obtained, accuracy, speed, cost, and ease of administration.

9. Would it be appropriate to interview 200 students as they left their college football stadium about their feelings toward funding for athletics and then generalize the results to the student body? Why or why not?

10. If you were the research manager, what suggestions would you have for your management if they proposed that you conduct a consumer study to determine the feasibility of introducing a new laundry detergent in several Asian countries?

11. If you were designing an academic program for the marketing researcher of the future, what areas of study would you include?

## CASE 1

## SIERRA NATIONAL BANK* Applying the Marketing Concept

The top management at the Sierra National Bank was trying to figure out why the introduction of the marketing concept had been a failure in the bank. These executives were aware of excellent results from introducing the marketing concept in manufacturing firms. But some of them were beginning to wonder whether different conditions were required for successful implementation of the marketing concept in banking. Sierra's management began a self-analysis to determine where the bank went wrong and what should be done at this stage.

The Sierra National Bank was a large commercial bank with headquarters in San Francisco and branches throughout the state of California. Regional offices, each headed by a vice president, were located in San Diego, Los Angeles, Bakersfield, Sacramento, and Redding. Major policy matters were handled in the head office. At the same time, much authority on loans and other matters was decentralized—that is, delegated to the regional offices. Sierra's early expansion had come through internal growth and mergers. The bank's growth was satisfactory until the late 1940s, but it really boomed between 1950 and 1970. During that period, the number of branches tripled, and net profits, assets, and foreign currency holdings more than doubled.

Then, during the 1970s and 1980s, Sierra experienced increasing competition from several sources. Other commercial banks and savings and loan associations were becoming more sophisticated and more aggressive in their marketing. Securities brokers such as Merrill Lynch and E. F. Hutton were expanding the financial services that they offered and were advertising heavily. Even product retailers such as Sears, Kroger, and K mart were entering the financial services field.

These winds of change that were blowing through the banking business made Sierra's management realize that it had to do something if it wanted to maintain the bank's market share and growth patterns. About two years ago a few of Sierra's top executives had come in contact with some marketing professors at a business conference. The executives were impressed by what they heard about the marketing concept. They thought that by applying the marketing concept in the bank they could better adapt to their changing environment. Consequently, they decided to introduce the marketing concept on an experimental basis in a few of the branches in the San Francisco Bay Area.

Sierra's main target markets were big businesses and large accounts. Not much attention was given to attracting small depositors and investors. However, management now believed that the bank needed to change its image and outlook. The total population and personal incomes were increasing considerably in California. Sierra needed to change its attitude, approach, and distorted image if it wanted to tap into this potential market.

The responsibility for these changes would be placed in a marketing department, if the executives correctly understood the professors' explanation of the marketing concept. The only previous activity conducted by the bank in the field of marketing had been in the area of public relations and advertising. In the late 1950s, the bank had established a separate public relations and advertising department, headed by a manager who reported to a bank officer (the corporate secretary). This department supplied ink blotters and book covers for students, posters that were displayed at branches, advertising cards for use on public transportation, small information folders for branch disposal, and many similar items. The common characteristic of each of these items was a message from Sierra National—for instance, a message with descriptive pictures telling of the advantages of a savings account or a safety deposit box.

*Adapted from a case prepared by Prof. Lionel A. Mitchell, Acadia University.

This type of promotion may have been adequate in the beginning, but the bank soon found that it must do a lot more. This led to more intensive promotional activities such as the establishment of student tours, sponsorship of prizes at regional fairs, student scholarships, and display booths at industrial fairs. Because banking had become more complex and competitive, the bank was outgrowing its public relations and advertising department.

Charles Fleming, who came to Sierra National from the marketing department of a leading consumer goods manufacturing firm in 1989, was named to head the new marketing department. He carried the title of assistant general manager of marketing, and he reported directly to Louis Beam, the general manager. Beam gave Fleming complete charge of the marketing department and full rein to implement any new marketing feature.

As his first objective, the new department head planned a major reorganization designed to (1) upgrade and modernize all services, (2) handle customer services more efficiently, and (3) listen to and act upon customers' suggestions and complaints.

The public relations and advertising department was placed under the new marketing department. One of the first projects of the marketing department was to redesign the banking forms, using the new bank logo and colors. The uniforms of messengers and mail and service staff were redesigned to reflect the bank's new image. Banking hours were to be extended for customer convenience. Fleming suggested that marketing departments be established in each of the five regional offices.

After nine months the marketing department's staff numbered 29 people. Most of the proposed projects had been initiated. The public relations and advertising department was virtually absorbed by the marketing department. Research and planning were under way to establish marketing departments in the five regions.

About this time, however, problems began to arise and conflicts developed. Doubts were raised about the number and frequency of changes. Many of the changes did not transpire as well as the bank had expected. Mr. Fleming, who was inexperienced in banking matters, had plunged into his job of introducing a marketing orientation into the bank. But he received little or no cooperation or assistance from the older staff members—that is, the experienced bank personnel. Fleming relied entirely on his previous marketing knowledge and experience. But some of his ideas were considered unorthodox by the banking public as well as by many of the staff, including his subordinates and his superiors. Fleming secretly admitted that he did not care what the staff thought of the new concept—it was a good thing and it would be implemented.

In the meantime, Fleming clashed with Beam, and in the weeks that followed, Fleming was unable to patch up this relationship. This situation eventually led to Fleming's dismissal from the bank. The marketing department was dissolved as an organizational unit. A new public relations and advertising department was set up to perform the marketing activities, and Peter Hudson was installed as manager of this new department.

## QUESTIONS

1. Why did the introduction of the marketing concept fail at Sierra National?
2. Should the introduction of the marketing concept in a service industry be different from that in retailing or manufacturing?
3. If you were Peter Hudson, what approach would you adopt in your new position? Evaluate Peter Hudson's chances of success.

---

CASE 2

## HARLEY-DAVIDSON*  Applying the Marketing Concept in a Changing Market

In the 1950s motorcyclists acquired the image of "outlaws." The general opinion was that respectable people did not own motorcycles, and those who did were either gang members or rebels. This stereotype was confirmed by Marlon Brando in the movie *The Wild Ones*. The major U.S. motorcycle manufacturer at the time was Harley-Davidson (H-D), and its powerful, easily identifiable "Harley Hog" was associated with the negative image.

Honda entered the United States in the late 1950s, determined to expand the motorcycle market by asso-

*Based on "How Harley Beat Back the Japanese," *Fortune*, Sept. 25, 1989, pp. 155–63; Sarah Smith, "Personal Investing: Hogs on Wheels," *Fortune*, April 10, 1989, pp. 38–39; Tom Incantalupo, "Motorcycle Makers Emphasize Safety in Sales Pitch," *The Coloradoan*, Sept. 24, 1989, p. E6; and "Honda Hopes to Win New Riders by Emphasizing 'Fun' of Cycles," *Marketing News*, Aug. 28, 1989, p. 6.

ciating its product with good, clean fun. Their advertising slogan, "You meet the nicest people on a Honda," apparently struck a responsive chord with consumers. Sales of the smaller street bikes grew rapidly, and new competitors such as Yamaha, Kawasaki, and Suzuki entered the market. Along with sales, product variety expanded to include off-road bikes and a variety of street bikes. One type that grew in popularity as consumers traded up was the super-heavyweight motorcycle. This category was dominated by Harley-Davidson. In 1969 H-D was selling 15,000 motorcycles a year. By 1975 that figure had risen to 75,000 units, which amounted to a 75 percent share of the super-heavyweight category.

However, Harley's position was deteriorating. Its product quality had slipped badly, and its engines were outdated in comparison to Japanese models. AMF, owner of the company, put Vaughn Beals in charge to reverse the trend. One of his first moves was to ask styling vice president William G. Davidson, grandson of

The Sportster® 883 Deluxe features a two-up seat, passenger pegs, and classic laced wheels.

one of the firm's founders, to design some new models. Davidson, himself a biker who favors black leather jackets and jeans, spends considerable time with Harley enthusiasts. He had already created the highly successful Super Glider, a model that emulated the look of Harleys customized by owners. Following his advice, several other models were introduced, including the Low Rider, with low handlebars, a low seat, and special paint. These variations were essentially cosmetic changes. As Davidson said, "They [bikers] rank the Harley look right up there with motherhood and God, and they don't want us to screw around with it." Still, the changes gave the firm time to improve the basic product.

In 1981 Beals and 12 other Harley executives bought the company from AMF in a leveraged buyout. At the time, sales were still strong, but market share had declined to 30 percent of the super-heavyweight market as Japanese firms continued to add models. Beginning with manufacturing, Beals set out to revamp the company. A team concept of management was introduced and a just-it-time (JIT) production system was installed. Employees were taught techniques for monitoring and controlling quality,

and suppliers were schooled in working more closely with production. Despite product improvements, market share continued to decline, reaching an all-time low of 23 percent of the super-heavyweight market. In 1982 the firm lost $25 million as the costs of production improvements were not offset by increased sales.

H-D had to convince potential buyers that it had solved its quality problems. To do so, the company committed $3 million to a unique program called SuperRide. Television commercials invited bikers to come to any of the 600 H-D dealers for a ride on a new Harley. Over three weekends 90,000 rides were taken by consumers, half of whom owned other brands. Though the program didn't pay for itself immediately, many who took rides came back in a year or two when they were ready to buy. SuperRide proved so successful in generating sales leads that H-D has continued it.

To develop a closer relationship with its customers, H-D formed the Harley Owners Group (HOG). HOG has over 100,000 members, a bimonthly newsletter, and weekly motorcycling events spread all over the country from April to November. To support the company credo, "The sale begins after the sale," H-D management uses HOG to keep in touch with the market.

In 1988 H-D celebrated its 85th birthday with a party in Milwaukee, site of the firm's headquarters. For a donation of $10 to charity, any biker (including those who didn't ride Harleys) was invited, and 40,000 accepted. Groups rode in from as far away as Orlando and San Francisco. Each group was led by an H-D executive. Along the way the executives auctioned off Harley memorabilia for the benefit of charity. Beals even sold his pewter belt buckle and rode into Milwaukee with his pants held up by a rope. The event included musical entertainment and activities like a slow race—the last bike to cross the finish line without stopping won. The event, which raised half a million dollars for charity, brought thousands of bikers together to talk about, look at, and try H-D products. Not only did it reinforce brand loyalty, but it also contributed to a more positive image for the industry.

The strategy appears to be working. H-D finished 1989 with sales of $800 million and a 59 percent share of the super-heavyweight market.

Looking to the future, H-D and the rest of the industry are faced with some important considerations. The motorcycle buyers of the 1960s were baby boomers of college age. Today they are in their 40s, and the prime group of motorcycle buyers—males aged 18–24—is much smaller. In addition, increased competition for the outdoor recreation dollar is coming from four-wheel-drive vehicles, R-Vs, and boats.

Some people in the industry feel that the softer image developed in the 1960s may have slipped, as many recreational riders lost interest and manufacturers developed more powerful machines to appeal to hard-core enthusiasts. But a survey conducted by Honda suggests that consumers aren't negative about motorcycles—they just aren't thinking about them at all. The problem may be that the general public hasn't seen a noticeable change in motorcycles in years.

Motorcycles have also experienced price increases that might shock a consumer who has not been in the market for a while. Even the smaller cycles cost at least $2,500 and the large bikes can go for well over $10,000.

Finally, there is the issue of safety. The motorcycle fatality rate is four times that of passenger cars. Not only is more attention being given to the risks of motorcycling, but consumers in the older market segments are also likely to be more conscious of the dangers.

## QUESTIONS

1. How did changes in the marketing environment impact Harley-Davidson?
2. How did Harley-Davidson apply the marketing concept in its successful turnaround?
3. What should the company do in the 1990s to continue its success?

## CASE 3

## McDONALD'S PIZZA*  New Product Marketing Research

In early 1990 executives at Pizza Hut, Domino's, and Little Caesars—the big three in the pizza business—were analyzing their initial responses to a new pizza marketer and deciding what they should do next. McDonald's, the strongest force in the fast-food business, had decided to test-market pizza. If it chose to, McDonald's could make pizza available at thousands more outlets (over 9,000 in the United States) than the largest of the pizza chains (Pizza Hut with 6,000). The implications of such a development were hard to imagine, but one thing was certain—none of the three wanted to compete with McDonald's in the pizza business. One observer suggested that the pizza chains should respond by selling hamburgers, but the management of these organizations did not view this incursion into their market with much amusement.

McDonald's expansion beyond burgers was not something new for the chain. The average outlet has 41 items on its menu. Recent big successes included the Egg McMuffin and prepackaged salads. But there have been disappointments too, most notably McChicken and McRib sandwiches. Also tested were prepackaged carrot and celery sticks, burritos, an omelet, a three-piece fish entree with coleslaw and fries, low-fat shakes, and sherbet. However, by moving into pizza, McDonald's would be taking on formidable opponents.

What motivated the move by McDonald's? Burgers are a $30-billion-plus industry, but growth is only 6 to 8 percent a year and competition from Burger King and Wendy's has been intense. (Recall the "burger wars" of the 1980s.) In contrast, though the pizza business is smaller ($20 billion), the industry is growing at an 11 percent annual rate with 40 percent of the volume done by vulnerable "mom and pop" outlets. Additionally, there is concern that tastes are changing. In a survey of Iowa teens reported in the *Des Moines Register*, 57 percent said they eat more pizza than burgers. Thus, with increasingly saturated markets and possibly changing tastes, the future growth of the burger chains could depend on their ability to steal business from one another.

*Based on material in Ronald Henkoff, "Big Mac Attacks with Pizza," *Fortune*, Feb. 26, 1990, pp. 87–89; Brian Bremmer, "Two Big Macs, Large Fries—and a Pepperoni Pizza, Please," *Business Week*, Aug. 7, 1989, p. 33; Brian Bremmer, "McDonald's Stoops to Conquer," *Business Week*, Oct. 30, 1989, pp. 120–21; Richard Gibson, "Two Giants Make Ready for Pizza War over Which Gets What Slice of the Pie," *The Wall Street Journal*, Sept. 15, 1989, p. B1; and Stephen Phillips, "The Burger Wars Were Just a Warmup for McDonald's," *Business Week*, May 8, 1989, pp. 67–68.

McDonald's began test-marketing pizza in July 1989 in Evansville, Indiana. Shortly thereafter, the test was expanded to a total of 24 stores by adding neighboring Owensboro, Kentucky. The product is a 14-inch pizza made with frozen dough and fresh toppings. It comes in four varieties and is priced from $5.87 for a standard cheese pizza to $9.49 for the deluxe version with cheese, sausage, pepperoni, green peppers, onions, and mushrooms. Preparation time is said to be no more than 5½ minutes. Pizza is sold only after 4 p.m. to increase volume in the sluggish evening hours. The product is called McDonald's Pizza (as opposed to McPizza) to signify that it is a traditional pizza product, not a specialized item like the Big Mac.

Newspaper, radio, and TV advertising was used in the test market. The television ads emphasized the quick service at McDonald's, contrasting it with the normal waiting time at a pizza parlor. The ads carried the tag line, "The pizza you won't believa." In the radio spot, a character named Captain Pizza descended on a crowd of grumbling teenagers who told him that by the time they are 19 years old, they will have spent several months of their lives waiting for pizza orders. A representative of Little Caesars in the Evansville market said McDonald's blitzed the market with ads "just about every hour, day and night."

In the test market, Pizza Hut counterattacked with an ad campaign combining humor and nastiness. One ad likened McDonald's dough to a hockey puck and advised, "Don't be McFooled." Pointing out that Pizza Hut uses only fresh dough, the ad recommended that viewers "Get a fresh-baked pan pizza from Pizza Hut." The ad also described McDonald's aborted 1987 test of pizza with frozen dough that "received a cold reception." In the Evansville newspaper, Pizza Hut proclaimed in full-page ads that "Great-tasting pizza is nothing to be clowned around with." The ad went on to say good pizza isn't "McFrozen"; that Pizza Hut offers a choice of three crusts, not just "McOne"; and that its pizzas are available for lunch and dinner, not just after "McFour."

In contrast to Pizza Hut, Domino's and Little Caesars adopted a wait-and-see approach. Domino's strategy was to analyze the impact of the test market on its outlets in the area and determine who the McDonald's pizza customers were before responding. Little Caesars took an even more relaxed attitude, acknowledging that McDonald's would sell "some pizza," but observing that when consumers think of pizza, they don't think of McDonald's.

After 6 months and what it reported as promising results, McDonald's expanded the test. McDonald's pizza was introduced in single outlets in Hartford, Connecticut; Fresno, California; and Las Vegas, Nevada.

## QUESTIONS

1. Was test-marketing McDonald's Pizza a good idea? What alternatives did McDonald's have?
2. What do you think of the initial reactions of the pizza chains to McDonald's test?
3. When McDonald's Pizza was in test market, should the pizza chains have been doing research of their own?

# PART TWO

# TARGET MARKETS

An analysis of the people and organizations who buy,
why they buy, and how they buy

In Part 1 we stressed the importance of customer orientation in an organization's marketing efforts. We also defined strategic planning as the process of matching an organization's resources with its market opportunities. It stands to reason then that early in the strategic marketing process, an organization should determine who its potential customers are. Only then can management develop a marketing mix that will satisfy the wants of these customers. Part 2 examines the selection of an organization's intended customers—that is, its target market.

We review the concept of a target market and discuss market segmentation in Chapter 4. Chapter 5 is devoted to the buying behavior and the buying process in consumer markets. Chapter 6 covers the business organizational market.

# MARKET SEGMENTATION AND DEMOGRAPHICS

## CHAPTER 4 GOALS

This is the first of three chapters on target markets—the ultimate consumers and business users. In it we consider the selection of target markets and the strategic concept of market segmentation and discuss the demographic and buying-power bases for segmenting consumer and business markets. After studying this chapter, you should be able to explain:

- Fundamentals of target-market selection.
- The concept of market segmentation—its meaning, benefits, limitations, and conditions for use.
- The difference between ultimate consumer markets and business user markets.
- Bases for segmenting consumer markets.
- Segmentation implications in the distribution and composition of population.
- Segmentation implications in consumer income distribution and spending patterns.
- Bases for segmenting business markets.
- Target-market strategies—aggregation, concentration, and multiple segmentation.

The promotional program for Viadent toothpaste is targeted at people who want to control tartar and plaque on their teeth. What's Left, a mail-order firm near Philadelphia, offers products designed for left-handed people—scissors, can openers, bread knives, rulers (numbered from right to left), measuring cups, potato peelers, and others.

As the number of college-age people declines, many universities are aiming their educational services at older people who did not attend college in their earlier years and at executives interested in continuing education. Several hotel chains try to attract the family trade by not charging for children under 14 who occupy a room with their parents.

Canon, a Japanese firm, entered the American market with a simplified, low-cost, desktop copying machine targeted at markets that previously had been ignored by producers of large, floor-type copiers. Several manufacturers of small computers have designed laptop models especially for sales people and other business people who travel.

Campbell Soup introduced a line of food products under the Casera label for Hispanic markets. In Texas and California, Campbell markets a nacho cheese soup that is spicier than the same soup sold in other parts of the country. San Francisco TV station KTSF runs programs in Filipino, Vietnamese, and other Asian languages.

For several decades Lane Bryant stores have specialized in apparel for women who wear size 14 or larger. Now many other stores specialize in apparel for large women or at least have one full department catering to this market. On the other hand, stores such as Petite and Short Stuff stock a wide range of fashion apparel for women who wear size 5, 3, or smaller.

Target markets for The American Cancer Society's "no smoking" campaign include teenagers (urge them not to start smoking), longtime smokers (get them to quit), and legislatures (get them to further restrict advertising of tobacco products and to establish "no smoking" areas).

The common thread in all of these situations is that each organization adopted a strategy of market segmentation as part of its target market selection. Strategic planning was defined in Chapter 1 as the matching of an organization's resources with its market opportunities. In this chapter we discuss market opportunities, focusing on the selection of target markets and decisions regarding market segmentation. The segmentation discussion will include a consideration of the geographic-demographic and buying-power dimensions of target markets.

## SELECTING A TARGET MARKET

In Chapter 1 we defined a *market* as people or organizations with (1) wants (needs) to satisfy, (2) money to spend, and (3) the willingness to spend it. A **target market** is a group of customers (people or firms) at whom the seller specifically aims its marketing efforts. The careful selection and accurate definition (identification) of target markets are essential for the development of an effective marketing mix.

### Guidelines in Market Selection

Four general guidelines govern the selection of target markets. The first one is that target markets should be compatible with the organization's goals and image. A firm that is marketing high-priced personal computers should not sell through discount chain stores in an effort to reach a mass market.

A second guideline—consistent with our definition of strategic planning—is to match the market opportunity with the company's resources. Liggett & Myers followed this guideline when it entered the market for low-cost, unbranded cigarettes. Management decided not to spend the huge sums for advertising that would be necessary for a new cigarette brand to compete with established national brands. Instead the company introduced and marketed a nonadvertised, "no brand" generic cigarette through supermarkets at a lower price. Thus the company matched its limited marketing-mix resources with its intended market.

Over the long run a business must generate a profit if it is to survive. This rather obvious, third guideline translates into what is perhaps an obvious market selection guideline. That is, an organization should consciously seek markets that will generate sufficient sales volume at a low enough cost to result in a profit. Surprisingly, companies often have overlooked the profit factor in their quest for high-volume markets. The goal was sales volume alone, not *profitable* sales volume.

Finally, a company ordinarily should seek a market wherein the number of competitors and their size are minimal. An organization should not enter a market that is already saturated with competition unless it has some overriding competitive advantage that will enable it to take customers from existing firms.

### Market Opportunity Analysis

Theoretically a market opportunity exists any time and any place there is a person or an organization with an unfilled need or want. Realistically, of course, a company's market opportunity is much more restricted. Thus selecting a target market requires an appraisal of market opportunities available to the organization. A market opportunity analysis begins with a study of the environmental forces (as discussed in Chapter 2) that affect a firm's marketing program. Then the organization must analyze the three components of a market—people or organizations, their buying power, and their willingness to spend. Analysis of the "people" component involves a study of the geographic distribution and demographic composition of the population. The second component is analyzed through the distribution of consumer income and consumer expenditure patterns. Finally, to determine consumers' "willingness to spend," management must study their buying behavior. Population and buying power are discussed more fully later in this chapter. Buying behavior is covered in Chapter 5.

**Target-Market Strategy: Aggregation or Segmentation**

In defining the market or markets it will sell to, an organization has its choice of two approaches. In one, the total market is viewed as a single unit—as one mass, aggregate market. This approach leads to the strategy of *market aggregation*. In the other approach, the total market is seen as many smaller, homogeneous segments. This approach leads to the strategy of *market segmentation*, in which one or more segments are selected as top target markets. Deciding which of the two strategies to adopt is a key step in selecting target markets. We shall discuss market aggregation and segmentation in more detail later in this chapter.

**Measuring Selected Markets**

When selecting target markets a company should make quantitative estimates of the potential sales volume of the market for its good or service. This process requires estimating, first, the total industry potential for the company's product in the target market and second, its share of this total market. It is essential that management also prepare a sales forecast, usually for a 1-year period. A sales forecast is the foundation of all budgeting and short-term operational planning in all departments—marketing, production, and finance. Sales forecasting will be discussed in more detail in Chapter 22, after we build a foundation in marketing fundamentals.

**NATURE OF MARKET SEGMENTATION**

The total market for most types of products is too varied—too heterogeneous—to be considered a single, uniform entity. To speak of the market for vitamin pills or electric razors or education is to ignore the fact that the total market for each good or service consists of submarkets that differ significantly from one another. This lack of uniformity may be traced to differences in buying habits, in ways in which the good or service is used, in motives for buying, or in other factors. Market segmentation takes these differences into account.

Not all consumers want to wear the same type of clothing, use the same hair shampoo, or participate in the same recreational activities. Nor do all business firms want to buy the same kind of word processors or delivery trucks. At the same time a marketer usually cannot afford to tailor-make a

Computer firms can develop more effective marketing programs by dividing their total market into meaningful segments.

different good or service for every single customer. Consequently market segmentation is the strategy that most marketers adopt as a compromise between the extremes of one good or service for all and a different one for each customer. A major element in a company's success is its ability to select the most effective location on this segmentation spectrum between the two extremes.[1]

**What Is Market Segmentation?**

**Market segmentation** is the process of dividing the total heterogeneous market for a good or service into several segments, each of which tends to be homogeneous in all significant aspects. Management selects one or more of these market segments as the organization's target market. A separate marketing mix is developed for each segment or group of segments in this target market.

Market aggregation is the opposite of market segmentation. **Market aggregation** is the strategy whereby an organization treats its total market as a unit—that is, as one mass aggregate market whose parts are considered to be alike in all major respects. The organization then develops a single marketing mix to reach as many customers as possible in this aggregate market.

In the language of economic theory, in market aggregation the seller assumes there is a single demand curve for its product. In effect the product is assumed to have a broad market appeal. In contrast, in market segmentation the total market is viewed as a series of demand curves. Each one represents a separate market segment calling for a different product, promotional appeal, or other element in the marketing mix. (See Figure 4-1.) Thus, instead of speaking of one aggregate market for personal computers, this total market can be segmented into several submarkets. We then will have, for example, a college student market segment for personal computers. Other submarkets might consist of segments representing homemakers, professors, traveling executives, traveling sales people, or small businesses. Stated another way, in market segmentation we employ a "rifle" approach (separate programs, pinpointed targets) in marketing activities. In contrast, market aggregation is a "shotgun" approach (one program, broad target).

**FIGURE 4-1** Demand curves representing market aggregation and market segmentation.

The object of aggregation is to fit the market to the product. Segmentation is an attempt to fit the product to the market.

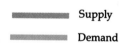

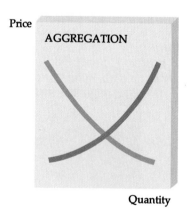

[1]For a thoughtful analysis of the meaning and use of market segmentation and an effort to distinguish segmentation from product differentiation, see Peter R. Dickson and James L. Ginter, "Market Segmentation, Product Differentiation, and Marketing Strategy," *Journal of Marketing*, April 1987, pp. 1–10.

Business users constitute a major market segment that is quite different from the consumer market.

the customer's *reason for buying*. **Ultimate consumers** buy goods or services for their own personal or household use. They are satisfying strictly nonbusiness wants, and they constitute what is called the "consumer market"—the topic of this chapter and Chapter 5.

**Business users** are business, industrial, or institutional organizations that buy goods or services to use in their own businesses or to make other products. A manufacturer that buys chemicals with which to make fertilizer is a business user of these chemicals. Farmers who buy the fertilizer to use in commercial farming are business users of the fertilizer. (If homeowners buy fertilizer to use on their yards, they are ultimate consumers because they buy it for personal, nonbusiness use.) Supermarkets, art museums, and paper manufacturers that buy the service of a certified public accountant (CPA) are business users of this service. Business users constitute the "business market"—the topic of Chapter 6.

The segmentation of all markets into two groups—consumer and business—is extremely significant from a marketing point of view because the two markets buy differently. Consequently the composition of a seller's marketing mix—products, distribution, pricing, and promotion—will depend on whether it is directed toward the consumer market or the business market.

## BASES FOR CONSUMER MARKET SEGMENTATION

Dividing the total market into consumer and business segments is a worthwhile start toward useful segmentation, but it still leaves too broad and heterogeneous a grouping for most products. We need to identify some of the bases commonly used to segment these two markets further.

As shown in Table 4-1, the consumer market may be segmented on the basis of the following characteristics:

- Geographic.
- Demographic.
- Psychographic.
- Behavior toward product (product-related bases).

Marketing executives should be especially aware of trends in each subcategory of these segments.

In using these bases to segment markets, we should bear in mind two points. First, buying behavior is rarely traceable to only one segmentation factor. Useful segmentation is developed by including variables from several bases. To illustrate, the market for a product rarely consists of all people living in Pacific Coast states or all people over 65. Instead, the segment is more likely to be described with a few of these variables. Thus a market segment for a financial service might be families living on the Pacific Coast, having young children, and earning above a certain income. As another example, one clothing manufacturer's target market might be affluent young women (income, age, sex).

The other point to observe is the interrelationships among these factors, especially among the demographic factors. For instance, age and life-cycle stage typically are related. Income depends to some degree on age, life-cycle stage, education, and occupation.

| TABLE 4-1 Segmentation bases for consumer markets | |
| --- | --- |
| **Segmentation basis** | **Typical market segments** |
| **Geographic:** | |
| Region | New England, Middle Atlantic, and other census regions. |
| City or MSA size | Under 25,000; 25,000–100,000; 100,000–500,000; 500,000–1,000,000; etc. |
| Urban-rural | Urban; suburban, exurban, rural. |
| Climate | Hot, cold, sunny, rainy-cloudy. |
| **Demographic:** | |
| Age | Under 6, 6–12, 13–19, 20–34, 35–49, 50–64, 65 and over. |
| Sex | Male, female. |
| Family life cycle | Young single, young married no children, etc. |
| Income | Under $10,000; $10,000–$25,000; $25,000–$35,000; $35,000–$50,000; over $50,000. |
| Education | Grade school only, high school graduate, college graduate. |
| Occupation | Professional, manager, clerical, craftsman, sales, student, housewife, unemployed. |
| Religion | Protestant, Catholic, Jewish, other. |
| Ethnic background | White, black, Oriental, Hispanic, Scandinavian, Italian, German, Middle Eastern, etc. |
| **Psychographic:** | |
| Social class | Upper class, upper middle, lower middle, upper lower, etc. |
| Personality | Ambitious, self-confident, aggressive, introverted, extroverted, sociable, etc. |
| Life-style | Conservative, liberal, health and fitness oriented, "swinger," adventuresome. |
| **Behavior toward product (or product-related bases):** | |
| Benefits desired | Examples vary widely depending on product: Appliance: cost, quality, life, repairs. Toothpaste: no cavities, plaque control, bright teeth, good taste, low price. |
| Usage rate | Nonuser, light user, heavy user. |

## Geographic Segmentation

Subdivisions in the geographical distribution and demographic composition of the population are widely used bases for segmenting consumer markets. The reason for this is simply that consumers' wants and product usage often are related to one or more of these subcategories. Geographic and demographic groupings also meet the conditions for effective segmentation—that is, they are measurable, accessible, and large enough. Let's consider how the geographic distribution of population may serve as a segmentation basis.

### REGIONAL POPULATION DISTRIBUTION

Many firms market their products in a limited number of geographic regions, or they may market nationally but prepare a separate marketing mix for each region. Supermarket chains such as Alpha Beta and Winn-Dixie concentrate their marketing efforts in specific geographical regions. Even supermarket giants such as Kroger and Safeway are unknown in some parts of the country. Campbell Soup Company has altered some of its soup and bean recipes to suit regional tastes, and General Foods has developed regionally oriented promotional campaigns for Maxwell House coffee.

The regional distribution of population is important to marketers because people *within* a given region generally tend to share the same values, attitudes, and style preferences. However, significant differences do exist *among* regions because of differences in climate, social customs, and other factors. Thus bright, warm colors are preferred in Florida and the Southwest, while grays and cooler colors predominate in New England and the Midwest. People in the West are less formal than Easterners, and they spend more time outdoors. Consequently, in the Western region there is a large market for patio furniture, sports clothes, and barbecue equipment.

Marketing executives should understand existing patterns and projected trends in regional population. Figure 4-2 shows the population distribution in 1990 and its projected growth from 1980 to 2000 by census regions. The biggest markets are in the East North Central, South Atlantic, and Middle Atlantic census regions. These three areas together account for a little over half of the nation's population. However, the greatest rate of population growth

Producers of outdoor furniture typically segment their markets by geographic region.

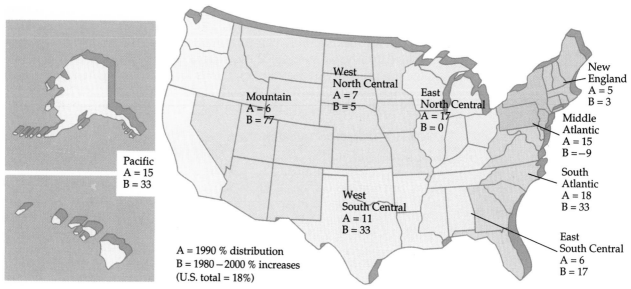

**FIGURE 4-2** Regional distribution of population, 1990, and projected growth, 1980–2000.

The East North Central, South Atlantic, and Middle Atlantic census regions account for the largest part of our total population. However, the Southern and Western regions show a more rapid growth rate. Movement of the population center of the United States is still generally south and westward.

over the past four decades has occurred in the "Sun Belt"—the Southern and Western regions. By the year 2000 the three most populous states will be California, Texas, and Florida, in that order.

## URBAN, SUBURBAN, AND RURAL DISTRIBUTION

Many organizations segment their markets on the basis of city size or urban-suburban-rural distribution. Toys "R" Us, the largest chain of toy stores in the United States, locates its stores only in metropolitan areas with populations exceeding 250,000. Within large cities the company segments further in that it usually places its warehouse-style outlets away from busy shopping centers.

The U.S. farm population has been declining for many years, and this trend is expected to continue. This decline has led some marketing people to undervalue the rural market. Both as a business market for farm equipment and supplies and as a consumer market with increased buying power and growing sophistication, however, the farm market still is big.

**Metropolitan Area Structure**  As the percentage of people living on farms has declined, so the percentage of people choosing an urban life-style has increased. In recognition of the urbanization of the American market, the federal government has established a three-part classification structure of metropolitan areas that serves as an excellent market measurement tool. Together the metropolitan areas included in this breakdown account for about 75 percent of the nation's population and retail sales. Obviously, for many products, these areas are attractive, geographically concentrated target markets. The three categories are as follows:

- The basic unit is the **Metropolitan Statistical Area (MSA),** of which there are about 325. An MSA has an urban population center of at least 50,000 and a total MSA population of at least 100,000. The boundaries of an MSA are drawn around county lines and may cross state borders. But the counties must be socially and economically integrated, and virtually all employment must be nonagricultural.

---

**Where they eat the *least*—**

If you are looking for a good market segment for bubble gum, stay out of Minneapolis. Prune juice? Forget Denver. How do you explain the fact that the following metropolitan areas have the lowest per-household consumption of certain products?

- Canned spinach: Minneapolis.
- Frozen waffles: Shreveport, La.; Jackson, Miss.
- Rice: Charleston–Huntington, W. Va.
- Bubble gum: Minneapolis.
- Frozen brussels sprouts: Shreveport; Jackson.
- Frozen corn dogs: Philadelphia.
- Frozen onion rings: Oklahoma City; Tulsa, Okla.
- Frozen Mexican dishes: Scranton, Pa.; Wilkes-Barre, Pa.
- Frozen Italian dishes: Shreveport; Jackson.
- Prune juice: Denver.
- Pasta: Nashville; Knoxville, Tenn.
- Tea bags: Green Bay, Wis.
- Bacon: Syracuse.
- Grits: Green Bay.

Source: Trish Hall, *New York Times*, as reported in *Daily Camera* (Boulder, Colo.), Jan. 20, 1988, p. 3. (Based on research by Selling Areas–Marketing Inc.)

---

- About 80 large MSAs are categorized as **Primary Metropolitan Statistical Areas (PMSA)** by virtue of (1) having a population of at least 1 million and (2) being part of a giant urban center or CMSA.
- A **Consolidated Metropolitan Statistical Area (CMSA)** is a giant urban center consisting of two or more contiguous PMSAs. The hub of each of the approximately 25 CMSAs is a very large city such as New York, Los Angeles, Chicago, or Philadelphia.[4]

**Suburban Growth**  Within our growing metropolitan areas, other changes have been taking place. The central cities are growing very slowly, and in some cases older established parts of the cities are actually losing population. The real growth is occurring in fringe areas of the central cities or in suburbs outside these cities. As middle-income families have moved to the suburbs, the economic, racial, and ethnic composition of many central cities (especially the core areas) has changed considerably. This has altered the nature of the market in these areas. Two changes in the suburban population have striking market implications. One is the changing racial mix in many suburbs, mainly as a result of the in-migration of minorities. The other is a significant increase in the numbers of single people and single-parent families living in suburbia.

Since a great percentage of suburban people live in single-family residences, there is a vastly expanded market for lawn mowers, lawn furniture, home furnishings, and home repair products. Suburbanites are more likely to want two cars than are city dwellers. They are inclined to spend more leisure

---

[4]For further explanation and clarification of this somewhat complex market measurement system, see James C. Douthit, "Whatever Happened to the SMSA System?" *Marketing News*, Jan. 4, 1988, p. 48.

time at home, so there is a bigger market for home entertainment and recreation items.

Service organizations typically must locate close to their market. Thus we have seen banks, insurance companies, and other financial services firms open branches or start new ventures in the suburbs. Some theaters, sports arenas, and other entertainment centers have closed their central-city sites and relocated in the suburbs. Health care organizations (American Cancer Society, American Heart Association), political parties, art museums, and other nonprofit groups use suburban Zip-code areas for their mailings that seek contributions.

**Demographic Segmentation** The most common basis for segmenting consumer markets is some demographic category such as age, sex, family life-cycle stage, income distribution, education, occupation, or ethnic origin.

### AGE GROUPS

We are well aware that our wants change as we go through life. In recognition of this fact, countless firms use age categories as one basis for segmenting the consumer market. Marketing executives should be aware of the changing nature of the age mix. Looking ahead to the year 2000, we anticipate both slower population growth and an aging population. In the mid-1980s, for the first time in our history, the number of Americans 65 and over exceeded the number of teenagers.

The *youth* market (roughly ages 5 to 13) carries a three-way marketing impact. First, these children can influence parental purchases. Second, billions of dollars are spent on this group by their parents. Third, these children themselves buy goods and services for their own personal use and satisfaction. Promotional programs are often geared to this market segment. Children's television shows, for instance, are sponsored by cereal, toy, and video-game manufacturers, among others, in an effort to develop brand preferences at an early age.[5]

The *teenage* market is large and free-spending, and yet it has proved difficult to reach. The mistake might be lumping all teenagers into one group; certainly the 13-to-16 age group is very different from the 17-to-20 age bracket. Yet marketers must try to understand teenage consumers because of the size of this market and because its members have a considerable amount of money to spend. And almost all of their money is purely discretionary. Although the number of teenagers has declined appreciably since the 1970s, going through the 1990s there still will be millions of teenagers with substantial incomes from part-time jobs and two income-earning parents. These youngsters constitute a big market for videocassettes, apparel, cosmetics, autos, stereos, records, and other products.

In the 1990s the early *middle-age* population segment (35 to 50) will be an especially large and lucrative market. These people are products of the post–World War II baby boom and were the social rebels of the 1960s and the 1970s. Now as they move toward middle age in the 1990s, they are reaching high earning years. Typically their personal values and life-styles are far different from those found among people of the same age in previous generations. Already manufacturers are adjusting to these changing demographics. Minnetonka, Colgate, Crest, and other toothpaste makers who had stressed

[5]See Patricia Sellers, "The ABC's of Marketing to Kids," *Fortune,* May 8, 1989, p. 114.

cavity prevention to those people 20 years ago now are producing toothpaste to fight plaque—an adult dental problem. Levi Strauss outfitted the bottom half of the baby boomers' wardrobes 20 years ago. Today this company markets nondenim clothes, office wear, and even blue jeans that are slightly bigger in the hips and seat to accommodate these older and bulging customers. Attractive women over 40 (Linda Evans, Catherine Deneuve, Joan Col-

**The middle-aging baby boomers may be the big market of the 1990s, but—**

**DON'T OVERLOOK THE YOUNG FOLKS**

About 65 percent of U.S. mothers are now working, and many are contributing a second income to their families. This means that children have increased purchasing power, shop for themselves, cook their own meals, and otherwise make their own decisions, so:

- Sony introduced a line of "my first Sony" audio equipment, including cassette recorders and a headset walkie-talkie.
- Fisher-Price Toys introduced a children's camcorder for $200.
- The Young American Bank in Denver is devoted solely to clients under the age of 23; the average age of their depositors is 9.
- Esprit Kids clothing accounts for 25 percent of Esprit Company sales.
- Teenagers are a lot more hip (than their parents) about the features of VCRs.
- In clothing, labels are becoming increasingly important to young people. "It's like, if you don't have Guess or Esprit jeans, you're . . . not cool" (a 12-year-old girl in Boulder, Colorado).*

**OR THE OLD FOLKS**

People over 50 make up about 25 percent of the population, but they control 75 percent of the nation's wealth and account for half of the nation's discretionary income. Only in recent years have consumer marketers finally begun to recognize and understand this market. It is a vibrant, viable, affluent market that wants quality, comfort, convenience, and financial security. But you better be careful when you market to these older people. Most of them think of themselves as 10 to 15 years younger than they really are. You cannot sell to a 60-year-old consumer by using a 60-year-old model.

- Some regional telephone companies publish a "Silver Pages" phone directory that includes services, discounts, ads, and products aimed at older consumers.
- Sears' Mature Outlook Club offers discounts on many goods and services to people over 55.
- Many companies are using middle-aged, gray-haired models in ads.
- Real estate developers are designing innovative retirement centers that include golf courses, medical services, mail service, aerobics centers, and appliances with large lettering on dials or that require no bending over to use.
- The travel industry—airlines, hotels, cruise ships—offers special tours, discount plans, and other special services for older travelers.
- Home-care products and leisure-time products are being designed especially for this older market.
- Universities now offer programs to attract students in this age market, thus offsetting the drop in enrollments caused by the decline in teenage population.

*The youth examples are from Julie Truck, "Companies Target the Young Set," *Daily Camera*, Feb. 16, 1988, p. 10.

lins) are featured in ads for cosmetics, watches, and other products aimed at this age market.

At the older end of the age spectrum are two market segments that should not be overlooked. One is the group of people in their fifties and early sixties. This *mature* market is large and financially well off. Its members are at the peak of their earning power and usually no longer have financial responsibility for their children. Thus this segment is a good target for marketers of high-priced, high-quality goods and services. The other group comprises *people over 65*—a segment that is growing both absolutely and as a percentage of the total population. Manufacturers and middlemen alike are beginning to recognize that people in this age group are logical prospects for small, low-cost housing units, cruises and foreign tours, health products, and cosmetics developed especially for older people.[6]

Companies engaging in international marketing also are paying attention to the older-age market segment. Volkswagen, for instance, has consciously segmented its European markets by age. The company has targeted the older (and wealthier) consumers for its German-made cars, while the company's manufacturing facility in Spain concentrates on producing less expensive cars for younger customers. The Dutch electronics giant, Philips Company, makes products such as VCRs and compact disc players with simpler instructions in large print for the elderly market.[7]

## SEX

For many years gender has been a common segmentation basis for many products such as clothing, shoes, autos, personal care products, and magazines. In recent years, however, there have been some interesting variations on traditional sex-based segmentation. In clothing, for example, several traditionally male products have been redesigned and repositioned for the female segment of the market. Jockey markets a line of Jockey Underwear for Her. Calvin Klein designs a line of men's-style boxer shorts for women. Blue jeans and T-shirts, once for men only, today are unisex items. Financial services firms traditionally identified men as their target market. Today VISA and the American Express Company urge women to get credit cards in their own names, while Merrill Lynch and other investment firms aim promotional campaigns at the female market.

Many products have traditionally been purchased by either men only or women only. However, some of these older buying patterns are changing. Not too many years ago, the wife did practically all the grocery shopping for her family, and the husband bought goods and services needed for the automobile. Today, however, men are frequent food shoppers, and women buy gas and arrange for car repair and maintenance.[8] Close to half of all new car purchases are made by women.

The number of women (married or single) working outside the home has

---

[6] For additional perspectives on the over-50 market, see Charles D. Schewe, "Effective Communication with Our Aging Population," *Business Horizons,* January–February 1989, pp. 19–25; Patricia Sorce, Philip R. Tyler, and Lynette M. Loomis, "Lifestyle of Older Americans," *Journal of Consumer Marketing,* Summer 1989, pp. 53–63; and Sandra van der Merwe, "GRAMPIES (Growing Retired Active Monied People In an Excellent State): A New Breed of Consumers Comes of Age," *Business Horizons,* November–December 1987, pp. 14–19.

[7] See "Grappling with the Graying of Europe," *Business Week,* Mar. 13, 1989, pp. 54–56.

[8] See Ronald D. Michman, "The Male Queue at the Checkout Counter," *Business Horizons,* May–June 1986, pp. 51–55.

Some products lend themselves nicely to market segmentation on the basis of sex.

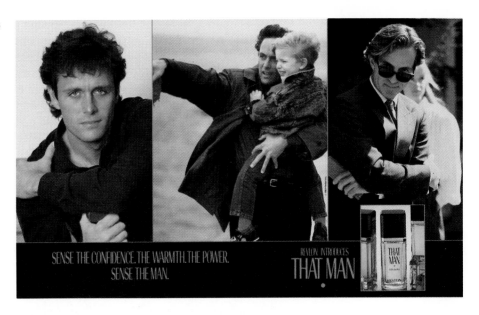

increased dramatically. Currently, well over one-half of all American women are in the labor force. About three-fourths of women in their twenties and about one-half of women with children under 6 years old are working outside the home. These facts are significant to marketers. The life-styles and buying behavior of women in the outside labor force are quite different from those of homemakers.[9]

### FAMILY LIFE CYCLE

Frequently the main factor accounting for differences in consumption patterns between two people of the same age and sex is that they are in different life-cycle stages. The concept of the family life cycle implies that there are several distinct stages in the life of an ordinary family. The traditional six-stage family cycle is shown in Figure 4-3, along with three alternative stages that reflect significant changes from traditional patterns.[10] Life-cycle position is a major determinant of buyer behavior, and thus can be a useful basis for segmenting consumer markets.

A young couple with two children (the full-nest stage) has quite different needs from those of a couple in their mid-fifties whose children no longer live at home (the empty-nest stage). A single-parent family (divorced, widowed, or never married) with dependent children faces social and economic problems quite different from those of a two-parent family. Young married couples with no children typically devote large shares of their income to clothing, autos, and recreation. When children start arriving, expenditure patterns

---

[9] To help us understand the new segmentation of the women's market, Judith Langer traces the development of the women's movement through five phases, starting with the traditional premovement phase. See "At Last, Marketers Acknowledge Women's New Role," *Marketing News*, Nov. 8, 1985, p. 45; Also see "Marketing to Women—a Special Report," *Advertising Age*, March 7, 1988, p. S1 ff.

[10] For a view of the family life cycle that reflects the growing numbers of single adults, with or without dependent children, see Patrick E. Murphy and William A. Staples, "A Modernized Family Life Cycle," *Journal of Consumer Research*, June 1979, pp. 12–22.

shift as many young families buy and furnish a home. Families with teenagers find larger portions of the budget going for food, clothing, and educational needs.

Two rapidly growing markets—reflecting our changing life-styles—are called the **singles** and the **mingles.** In 1987 the Census Bureau reported that close to 30 percent of American households consisted of just one person—a single. The number of singles households was also increasing at a much faster rate than that of family units.The impact single people of either sex have on the market is demonstrated by such goods and services as apartments for singles, social clubs for singles, and special tours, cruises, and eating places seeking the patronage of singles.

**FIGURE 4-3** The family life cycle.

1. Bachelor stage: young, single people

2. Young married couples with no children

3. Full nest I: young married couples with children

ALTERNATIVE STAGES

A. Young or middle-aged person with dependent children— the single parent

B. Divorced person without dependent children

C. Middle-aged married couples without children

4. Full nest II: middle-aged married couples still with dependent children

5. Empty nest: older married couples with no children living with them

6. Older single people, still working or retired

Singles in the 25-to-39 age bracket are especially attractive to marketers because they are such a large group. Compared with the population as a whole, this singles group is:

- More affluent.
- More mobile.
- More experimental and less conventional.
- More fashion- and appearance-conscious.
- More active in leisure pursuits.
- More sensitive to social status.

The number of mingles—unmarried couples of opposite sex living together—quadrupled between 1970 and 1987, reaching a total of 2.3 million couples. (The increase was more than eightfold for people under 25.) They still represent only a small part (2 percent) of all households. Nevertheless the social and demographic phenomenon of mingles bears watching.

### INCOME DISTRIBUTION

People alone do not make a market; they must have money to spend. Consequently income distribution is a widely used basis for segmenting consumer markets.

**Some income concepts**  There are several different concepts of income. The following "word equation" shows the relationship among some of these concepts:

PERSONAL INCOME:  Income from wages, salaries, dividends, rent, interest, businesses and professions, Social Security, and farming
  *Less:* All personal federal, state, and local taxes
  *Equals:*

DISPOSABLE PERSONAL INCOME:  The amount available for personal consumption expenditures and savings
  *Less:* (1) Essential expenditures for food, clothing, household utilities, and local transportation and (2) fixed expenditures for rent, house mortgage payments, insurance, and installment debt payments
  *Equals:*

DISCRETIONARY PURCHASING POWER:  The amount of disposable personal income available after fixed commitments (debt repayments, rent) and essential household needs are taken care of. As compared with disposable personal income, discretionary purchasing power is a better (more sensitive) indicator of consumers' ability to spend for *nonessentials.*

**Marketing significance of income distribution**  The size of a household's income is an obvious determinant of how that household spends its income. Thus, marketers should analyze the expenditure patterns of the various income classes (under $10,000; $10,000–$20,000; and so on). See Table 4-2 as an example. Some findings from Department of Labor studies of consumer expenditures are summarized as follows:

- For each product category there is a considerable *absolute* increase in dollars spent as income rises (or, more correctly, as we compare one income group with a higher income group). In other words, people in a given income bracket spend significantly more *dollars* in each product category

**TABLE 4-2  Buying patterns by income group**

| Category | Income group | | |
|---|---|---|---|
| | Lowest 20% | Middle 20% | Highest 20% |
| Average annual expenditures | $11,000 | $19,183 | $42,374 |
| | % of total | | |
| Housing and furnishings | 34 | 30 | 28 |
| Transportation | 17 | 22 | 20 |
| Food | 19 | 16 | 13 |
| Clothing | 5 | 5 | 6 |
| Health care | 7 | 5 | 3 |
| Entertainment | 4 | 5 | 6 |
| Alcohol and tobacco supplies | 3 | 3 | 2 |
| Insurance and pensions | 4 | 8 | 13 |
| Education and reading | 3 | 2 | 2 |
| Other goods and services | 4 | 4 | 7 |
| Total expenditures | 100 | 100 | 100 |

Source: Bureau of Labor Statistics, *Consumer Expenditure Survey Results from 1985,* as shown in *Sales & Marketing Management*, December 1987, p. 25.

than those in lower brackets. However, the lower-income households devote a larger *percentage* of their total expenditures to some product categories, such as food. Marketers are probably more concerned with total *dollars* available from each income group than with the *percentage* share of total expenditures.

- In each successively higher income group, the amount spent for food declines as a *percentage* of total expenditures.
- The *percentage* of expenditures devoted to the total of housing, utilities, and home operation remains reasonably constant in the middle- and high-income brackets.
- The share of expenditures for automotive goods and services tends to increase as incomes increase in low- and middle-income groups. The proportion levels off or drops a bit in higher-income brackets.
- In each successively higher income group, a greater share of total family expenditures goes for clothing.

In view of the fact that there was a general increase in incomes through the 1980s, there is likely to be significant growth in discretionary purchasing power in the 1990s. And, as discretionary income increases, so too does the demand for items that once were considered luxuries.

The middle-income market is a big market and a growing market, and it has forced many changes in marketing strategy. Many stores that once appealed to low-income groups have traded up to the huge middle-income market. These stores are upgrading the quality of the products they carry and are offering additional services.

In spite of the considerable increase in disposable income in the past 30 years, many households are still in the low-income bracket or find their higher incomes inadequate to fulfill all their wants. Furthermore, many customers are willing to forgo services in order to get lower prices. One consequence of this market feature has been the development of self-service retail outlets and discount houses.

Earlier in this chapter we noted the dramatic increase in the number of working wives. This demographic factor also has had a tremendous impact on family income levels. Today in the United States there are substantially more two-income families than families with only one provider. This increase in two-income families has significant marketing and sociological implications.

### OTHER DEMOGRAPHIC BASES FOR SEGMENTATION

The market for certain consumer products is influenced by such factors as education, occupation, religion, and ethnic origin. With an increasing number of people attaining higher levels of **education,** for example, we can expect to see (1) changes in product preferences and (2) buyers with more discriminating tastes and higher incomes. **Occupation** may be a more meaningful criterion than income in segmenting some markets. Truck drivers and auto mechanics may earn as much as young retailing executives or college professors. But the buying patterns of the first two are different from those of the second two because of attitudes, interests, and other life-style factors.

For some products it is quite useful to segment the population on the basis of **religion** or **ethnic origin.** Religious mores in Utah, for instance, affect the markets for tobacco, liquor, and coffee. There is a large market for Polish sausage in some Midwestern areas. People of Mexican descent in the Southwest have product preferences that are quite different from those of, say, Oriental consumers living on the West Coast.

In a number of cities, ethnic markets are especially large. In fact, minorities—Asians, blacks, Hispanics, and others—constitute over 50 percent of the population in 25 of the nation's largest cities. These cities include Los Angeles, San Antonio, New Orleans, Miami, Atlanta, Baltimore, Washington, D.C., Detroit, and Chicago.

One ethnic group receiving increasing attention because of its large and growing buying potential is the black American market. It contained over 30 million consumers with a combined buying power estimated at more than $200 *billion* in the late 1980s. And this figure will probably double by the year 2000, according to estimates based on Census Bureau data.

There are some distinct differences between the black American and white American markets with regard to socioeconomic characteristics (income, occupation, family structure, education, expenditure patterns, and consumption patterns). To market successfully to black consumers, a company must understand something about their buying behavior and their motivation. Furthermore, this market is not a homogeneous unit any more than any other population segment consisting of 30 million people is. The black market contains subsegments based on income, occupation, geographic location, and so on.

Another ethnic group well worth studying is made up of 20 million Spanish-speaking (Hispanic) people. This group is large and is increasing at a rapid rate. In fact, by the year 2000, Hispanics are expected to be the largest minority group in the United States, surpassing blacks in population. The Hispanic market is geographically concentrated in New York City, Miami, California, and the Southwest. This is a relatively accessible market because of its common language, geographic concentration, and relative homogeneity

To communicate, speak the language.

in terms of income. Advertisers in particular may make use of Spanish-language radio stations, television programs, movies, newspapers, and magazines. At the same time, marketers should be fully aware that this market is not a truly homogeneous unit, despite its common language. Cubans in Florida have market characteristics that differ from those of Puerto Ricans in New York. Mexican-Americans in southern Texas are not the same market as Mexican-Americans in southern California.[11]

## Psychographic Segmentation

As consumers, our buying behavior and life-styles are influenced considerably by sociological and psychological forces. Sociological influences include our culture, social class, and reference groups, whereas psychological characteristics include our learning experiences, personality, attitudes, and beliefs. (These sociological and psychological determinants of buying behavior are discussed in more depth in the next chapter.) The term *psychographics* is used today by many researchers as a collective classification for these forces. Many companies segment their consumer markets using psychographic bases such as personality characteristics, life-styles, or social class.

### PERSONALITY CHARACTERISTICS

*Theoretically,* personality characteristics should form a good basis for segmenting markets. Compulsive people buy differently from cautious consumers. Quiet introverts presumably do not make the same product choices as gregarious, outgoing people. *Realistically,* however, personality characteristics pose problems that limit their usefulness in practical market segmentation. These characteristics often are virtually impossible to measure accurately in a quantitative sense. Many studies have been made of consumer attitudes and personality traits in relation to product and brand preferences in a wide variety of product categories. But the results generally have been too limited or inconclusive to be of much practical value.

Nevertheless, many firms tailor their advertising to appeal to consumers who have certain personality traits. Even though the given market segment is immeasurable, the seller knows that it does exist and hopes to attract its members. Thus we see a brand advertised to consumers who "are on the way up," or who are "men of distinction," or who "don't want their family left helpless."

How would you describe the life-style of these two skiers?

### LIFE-STYLES

The term *life-style* is a broad concept that sometimes overlaps personality characteristics. Being cautious, skeptical, ambitious, a workaholic, a copycat—are these personality or life-style traits? Life-styles relate to your activities, interests, and opinions. They reflect how you spend your time and what your beliefs are on various social, economic, and political issues.

There is no commonly accepted terminology of life-style categories for segmenting markets. Nevertheless, people's life-styles undoubtedly affect their choice of products and their brand preferences. Marketers are well aware of this and often attempt to segment their markets on a life-style basis.

[11] For more information on the nature of the Hispanic market, see Julia Lieblich, "If You Want a Big, New Market . . . ," *Fortune*, Nov. 21, 1988, p. 181; "It's a Whole *Nuevo Mundo* Out There," *U.S. News & World Report*, May 15, 1985, p. 45; Joel Saegert, Robert J. Hoover, and Mary Tharpe Hilger, "Characteristics of Mexican-American Consumers," *Journal of Consumer Research*, June 1985, pp. 104–9; and "Marketing to Hispanics—A Special Report," *Advertising Age*, Feb. 13, 1989, p. S1 ff.

The manufacturer of Porsche automobiles, for example, has targeted "achievers" who have set for themselves extraordinarily high personal and professional goals.[12] Many retailers are successful, in part, because they regularly determine the latest consumer life-style trends and design strategies to reach these market segments.[13]

Although it is a valuable marketing tool, life-style segmentation has some of the same serious limitations ascribed to segmentation based on personality characteristics. It is very difficult to accurately measure the size of life-style segments in a quantitative manner. Another problem is that a given life-style segment simply might not be accessible at a reasonable cost through a firm's usual distribution system or promotional program.

### SOCIAL CLASS

As we will see in the next chapter, a person's social class—be it upper class, white-collar middle class, or blue-collar working class—has a considerable influence on that person's choice in many product categories. Consequently, many companies select one or two social classes as target markets and then develop a product and marketing mix to reach those segments.

## Product-Related Segmentation

Some marketers regularly attempt to segment their markets on the basis of a consumer behavioral characteristic related to the product. In this section we briefly consider two of these product-related segmentation bases—benefits desired and product usage rate.

### BENEFITS DESIRED

Conceptually it is very logical to segment a market on the basis of the different benefits customers want from the product. Certainly benefit segmentation is consistent with the idea that a company should be marketing product benefits and not simply the physical or chemical characteristics of a product. From the consumers' point of view, they really are buying product *benefits* and not the product itself. After all, a customer wants a smooth surface (the benefit), not sandpaper (the product).

For benefit segmentation to be effective, two tasks must be accomplished. First, a company must identify the various benefits that people seek in the good or service. To illustrate, in segmenting the market for its ocean cruises, the Viking Steamship Line might pinpoint such benefits as (1) the opportunity to meet people, (2) recreation, (3) education, and (4) rest and relaxation. A classic study that gave rise to the concept of benefit segmentation identified the following benefit segments for toothpaste and the benefits sought by these segments: (1) sensories—flavor and appearance; (2) sociables—brightness of teeth; (3) worriers—decay prevention; (4) independents—low price. Today "plaque control" might qualify as a fifth benefit segment.[14]

Once these separate benefits are known, the second task is to describe the

---

[12] Peter Schutz and Jack Cook, interviewed by David E. Gumpert, "Porsche on Nichemanship," *Harvard Business Review,* March–April 1986, pp. 98–106.

[13] See Max L. Densmore and Sylvia Kaufman, "How Leading Retailers Stay on Top," *Business,* April–June 1985, pp. 28–35.

[14] See Russell J. Haley, "Benefit Segmentation: A Decision Oriented Research Tool," *Journal of Marketing,* July 1968, pp. 30–35. For an update on this classic article and the concept of benefit segmentation, see Haley, "Benefit Segmentation—20 Years Later," *The Journal of Consumer Marketing,* vol. 1, no. 2, 1983, pp. 5–13.

Nikon's "red-eye" feature could appeal to both heavy-user and light-user segments of the camera market.

demographic and psychographic characteristics of the people in each segment. Then the seller is in a position to launch a product and marketing program to reach a selected target segment.

### USAGE RATE

Another product-related basis for market segmentation is the rate at which people use or consume a product. Thus we can have categories for nonusers, light users, medium users, and heavy users. Normally a company is most interested in the heavy users of its product. The 50 percent of the people who are the "heavy half" of the users of a product typically account for 80 to 90 percent of the total purchases of a given product. The remarkable feature of these usage patterns is that they seem to remain reasonably constant over time. Thus this segmentation base becomes an effective predictor of future buying behavior. Comparable studies in the 1960s and 1980s showed similar patterns in the percentage of total purchases accounted for by the heavy-user half in several product categories. Some sample products and percentages of the total market accounted for by the heavy half in 1962 and 1982 were as follows: shampoo, 81 and 79 percent; cake mixes, 85 and 83 percent; beer, 88 and 87 percent; soaps and detergents, 80 and 75 percent.[15]

Sometimes the target market is the nonuser or light user, and the objective is to woo these customers into a higher use category. Or light users may constitute an attractive niche for a seller simply because they are being ig-

[15] Victor J. Cook, Jr., and William A. Mindak, "A Search for Constants: The 'Heavy User' Revisited," *The Journal of Consumer Marketing,* vol. 1, no. 4, 1984, pp. 79–81.

nored by other firms that are targeting heavy users. Once the characteristics of these light users have been identified, management can go to them directly with an introductory low-price offer. Or a seller might increase usage rates by promoting (1) new uses for a product (baking soda as a deodorant); (2) new times for uses (off-season vacations); or (3) multiple packaging (a 12-pack of soft drinks).

## BASES FOR BUSINESS MARKET SEGMENTATION

Several of the bases used to segment the consumer market can also be used to segment the broad business market. For example, we can segment business markets on a geographical basis. Several industries are geographically concentrated, so any firm selling to these industries could nicely use this segmentation basis. Sellers also can segment on product-related bases such as usage rate or benefits desired.[16]

Let's look at three of the bases that are used solely for segmenting business markets—type of customer, size of customer, and type of buying situation.

### Type of Customer

Any firm that sells to customers in a variety of industries may want to segment its market on the basis of customer types. The federal government has developed a system for classifying the many types of industries in the United States. This system, discussed further in Chapter 6, is called the Standard Industrial Classification (SIC) code. It uses two-digit, three-digit, and four-digit codes to identify major industries plus subclasses within each industry. The SIC codes have proven to be a very useful tool for segmenting business target markets. A firm selling to manufacturers of men's clothing, for example, can start out with potential customers included in the two-digit code number 23 for apparel manufacturing. Then the three-digit code 232 identifies potential customers making men's and boys' furnishings. Finally, code number 2321 pinpoints manufacturers of dress shirts and night wear.

A firm selling janitorial supplies or small electric motors would have a broad potential market among many different industries. Management in this firm could segment its market by type of customer and then perhaps decide to sell to firms in only a limited number of these segments.

### Size of Customer

Customer size can be measured by such factors as sales volume, number of production facilities, and number of sales offices. Many industrial sellers divide their potential market into large and small accounts, using separate distribution channels to reach each segment. The large-volume accounts may be sold to directly by the company's sales force. But to reach the smaller accounts, the seller may use a manufacturers' agent or other form of middleman.

### Type of Buying Situation

It is one thing for United Airlines to buy a new model of a Boeing airplane. It is quite another buying situation for United to replenish its supply of staples or ballpoint pens. Certainly the first buying situation—called a *new buy*—is

---

[16] For examples of benefit segmentation as used in the business market, see Mark L. Bennion, Jr., "Segmentation and Positioning in a Basic Industry," *Industrial Marketing Management*, February 1987, pp. 9–18; Susan A. Lynn, "Segmenting a Business Market for a Professional Service," *Industrial Marketing Management*, February 1986, pp. 13–21; Rowland T. Moriarty and David J. Reibstein, "Benefit Segmentation in Industrial Markets," *Journal of Business Research*, December 1986, pp. 483–86; and Cornelis A. de Kluyver and David B. Whitlark, "Benefit Segmentation for Industrial Products," *Industrial Marketing Management*, November 1986, pp. 273–86.

significantly different from the second—called a *straight rebuy.* These two situations, along with an in-between one called a *modified rebuy,* are discussed in more depth in Chapter 6. These buying situations are sufficiently different that a business seller might well segment its market into these three buy-class categories. Or the seller could at least set up two segments by combining new buy and modified rebuy into one segment. Different marketing programs would be developed to reach each of these two or three segments.

## TARGET-MARKET STRATEGIES

Let's assume that a company is aware of the opportunities for segmenting its market, having analyzed different segmentation bases in relation to its product. Now management is in a position to select one or more segments as its target markets. The company can follow one of three broad strategies in this selection process. The three alternatives are market aggregation, single-segment concentration, and multiple-segment segmentation, as illustrated in Figure 4-4. Companies engaging in international marketing also need to consider the strategic use of market aggregation and segmentation, as we note in the International Perspective.

## Market Aggregation

By adopting a strategy of *market aggregation*—also known as a *mass-market* or an *undifferentiated-market* strategy—an organization treats its total market as a single unit. This unit is one mass, aggregate market whose parts are considered to be alike in all major respects. Management then develops a single marketing mix to reach as many customers as possible in this aggregate market. That is, the company develops a single product for this mass audience; it develops one pricing structure and one distribution system for its product; and it uses a single promotional program that is aimed at the entire market.

When is an organization likely to adopt the strategy of market aggregation? Generally when a large group of customers in the total market tends to have the same perception of the product's want-satisfying benefits. This strategy often is adopted by firms that are marketing a nondifferentiated, staple product such as gasoline, salt, or sugar. In the eyes of many people, cane sugar is cane sugar, regardless of the brand. All brands of table salt are pretty much alike, and one unleaded gasoline is about the same as another.

Basically market aggregation is a production-oriented strategy. It enables a company to maximize its economies of scale in production, physical distribution, and promotion. Producing and marketing one product for one market means longer production runs at lower unit costs. Inventory costs are minimized when there is no (or a very limited) variety of colors and sizes of products. Warehousing and transportation efforts are most efficient when one product is going to one market.

Market aggregation will work only as long as the seller's single marketing mix continues to satisfy enough customers to meet the company's sales and profit expectations. The strategy of market aggregation typically is accompanied by the strategy of product differentiation in a company's marketing program. **Product differentiation** is the strategy by which one firm attempts to distinguish its product from competitive brands offered to the same aggregate market. By differentiating its product, an organization hopes to create the impression that its product is better than the competitors' brands. The seller also hopes to engage in nonprice competition and thus avoid or minimize the threat of price competition.

A seller implements this strategy either (1) by changing some superficial feature of the product—the package or color, for example—or (2) by using a promotional appeal that features a differentiating benefit. Crest says that its toothpaste now fights tartar formation on teeth. Morton's claims its salt will pour even in damp, rainy weather. Ocean Spray puts its cranberry-based juices in aseptic packages that keep the product fresh without refrigeration.

**Single-Segment Concentration Strategy**

A strategy of **single-segment concentration** involves selecting as the target market one homogeneous segment from within the total market. One marketing mix is then developed to reach this single segment. A small company may want to concentrate on a single market segment, rather than to take on many competitors in a broad market. For example, a Western dude ranch got started by appealing only to guest horseback riders who also enjoyed square dancing. A large cruise-ship company, offering a round-the-world luxury cruise, targets its marketing effort at one market segment—older, affluent people who also have time to travel.

When manufacturers of foreign automobiles first entered the U.S. market,

**FIGURE 4-4** Alternative target-market strategies.

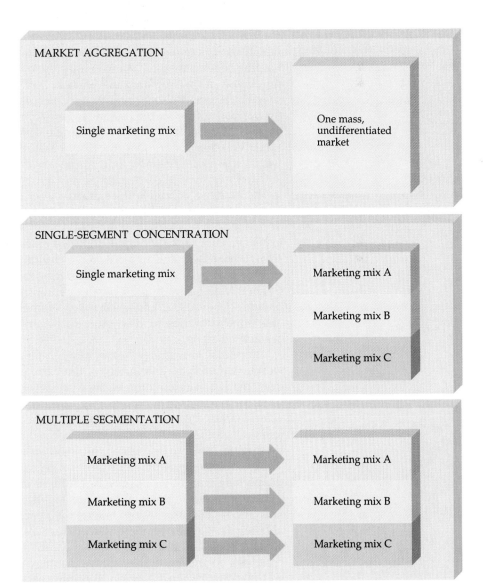

they typically targeted a single market segment. The Volkswagen Beetle was intended for the low-priced, small-car market. Honda originally sold only lower-powered motorcycles, and Mercedes-Benz targeted the high-income market. Today, of course, most of the original foreign car marketers have moved into a multisegment strategy. Only a few, such as Rolls-Royce and Ferrari, continue with a concentration strategy.

This strategy enables a company to penetrate one small market in depth and to acquire a reputation as a specialist or an expert in this limited market. A company can enter such a market with limited resources. And as long as the single segment remains a small market, large competitors are likely to leave the single-segment specialist alone. However, if the small market should show signs of becoming a large market, then the big boys may well jump in. This is exactly what happened in the market for herbal teas. Starting in 1971 Celestial Seasonings, a then-small Colorado firm, specialized in this market segment and practically owned the market for close to 10 years. But as herbal teas became more popular, this market segment began to attract major competitors such as the Lipton Tea Company.

The big risk and limitation of a single-segment strategy is that the seller has all its eggs in one basket. If that single segment declines in market potential, the seller can suffer considerably. Also, a seller with a strong name and reputation in one segment may find it very difficult to expand into another segment. Sears, Roebuck was not too successful in its move into the market for expensive furs and diamond rings. Gerber's baby food company was not successful in marketing its food in single-serving quantities to adults. Do you think Volkswagen could successfully market a high-priced car to compete with a top-of-the-line Mercedes or BMW?

**Multiple-Segment Strategy**

In the strategy of **multiple-segment target markets,** two or more different groups of potential customers are identified. Then a separate marketing mix is developed to reach each segment. A marketer of personal computers, for instance, might identify three separate market segments—college students, small businesses, and homemakers—and then design a different marketing mix to reach each segment. In segmenting the passenger automobile market, General Motors develops separate marketing programs built around its five brands—Chevrolet, Pontiac, Buick, Oldsmobile, and Cadillac. General Motors, in effect, tries to reach the total market for autos, but does so on a segmented basis.

As part of the strategy of multiple segmentation, a company frequently will develop a different variety of the basic product for each segment. However, market segmentation can also be accomplished with no change in the product, but rather with separate marketing programs, each tailored to a given market segment. A producer of cosmetics, for instance, can market the identical product to the teenage market and to the 25-to-30 age segment. But the promotional programs for the two markets will differ.

A multiple-segment strategy normally results in a greater sales volume than a single-segment approach. Multiple segmentation also is useful for a company facing a seasonal demand for its product. In England during the summer, several universities market their empty dormitory space to tourists—another market segment. A firm with excess production capacity may well seek additional market segments to absorb this capacity. Probably the biggest drawback to the multiple-segment strategy is that unit costs of production and marketing increase when multiple segments are targeted.

## AN INTERNATIONAL PERSPECTIVE: Market segmentation—a necessary strategy in Europe

In 1992 the 12-nation European Community (EC) becomes an economically united organization. Its 320 million consumers will constitute an integrated market 30 percent larger than the American market and almost double the total population of Japan. We hear about this "European Market" or the "Euro-Consumer" or the "Common Market." These terms all suggest that there is one homogeneous market that can be reached with a strategy of market aggregation. And for a handful of companies that strategy may very well work. Coca-Cola is using "Can't Beat the Feeling" as its basic promotional theme throughout the EC (and in nearly 90 other countries), making adjustments here and there for language differences. Levi Strauss can market its Levi's blue jeans throughout the EC pretty much with a standardized marketing program because of the universal appeal of the product.

In some demographic groups within the EC there is a modest degree of homogeneity. Trendy teenagers throughout the EC seem to crave the latest in Benetton sweaters. And wealthy, highly educated consumers in several European countries want Rolex watches and Dior clothes.

But for a considerable majority of Europeans, the idea of a homogeneous Euro-Consumer is a misleading myth. To market successfully in the EC in the 1990s, most companies must recognize that this market consists of many segments by virtue of cultural differences in language and social customs. Here are a few examples of this diversity:

- In France, Italy, and Spain, oil-based cooking is preferred, whereas cooks in Germany and Great Britain are butter- and margarine-oriented.
- British homemakers prefer front-loading washing machines; the French insist on top-loaders.
- It will be a long time before the French will accept the instant coffee that the British like so much.
- One study reported that 43 percent of British respondents owned a microwave oven, compared with only 3 percent of Italian households.
- A single brand name across the EC is still a dream for many sellers. Unilever sells a liquid cleaner that is called Viss in Germany, Vif in Switzerland, Jif in Britain and Holland, and Cif in France and Spain.

Yes, 12 European nations are to become an economically integrated unit in 1992. But it will be a long time, if ever, before many companies can successfully adopt a European strategy of market aggregation with a standardized product and promotional program.

Source: Barbara Toman, "Now Comes the Hard Part: Marketing," *The Wall Street Journal*, Sept. 22, 1989, p. R10; and Janette Martin, "Beyond 1992: Lifestyle Is Key," *Advertising Age*, July 11, 1988, p. 57.

---

Earlier we defined a market as people with wants to satisfy, money to spend, and the willingness to spend it. In this chapter we have analyzed the population and income factors in that definition. However, these people with money to spend must be *willing* to spend it before we can say that a market exists. In the next chapter we shall look into consumer motivation and buying behavior—the "willingness-to-buy" factor in our definition of a market.

**SUMMARY** A sound marketing program starts with the identification and analysis of target markets for whatever it is that an organization is selling. A market consists of people or organizations with needs or wants, money to spend, and the willingness to spend it. There are some general guidelines to follow when selecting target markets.

Some form of market segmentation is the strategy that most marketers adopt as a compromise between the extremes of an aggregate, undifferentiated market and a different product tailor-made for each customer. Market segmentation is the process of dividing the total heterogeneous market into several homogeneous segments. A separate marketing mix is developed for each segment that the seller selects as a target market. Market segmentation is a customer-oriented philosophy that is consistent with the marketing concept.

Market segmentation enables a company to make more efficient use of its marketing resources. Also, this strategy allows a small company to compete effectively in one or two segments. The main drawback of market segmentation is that it requires higher production and marketing costs than does a one-product, mass-market strategy. The requirements for effective segmentation are that (1) the bases for segmentation be measurable with accessible data; (2) the segments themselves be accessible to existing marketing institutions; and (3) the segments be large enough to be potentially profitable.

The total market may be divided into two broad segments—ultimate consumers and business users. The four major bases that may be used for further segmenting the consumer market are: (1) geographic—the distribution of population; (2) demographic—the composition of population such as age, sex, and income distribution; (3) psychographic—personality traits and lifestyles; and (4) product-related—product benefits desired and product usage rates. Firms selling to the business market may use several of these same bases for segmentation. In addition, the business market may be segmented on the bases of type of customer, size of customer, and type of buying situation. Normally, in either the consumer or business market, a seller will use a combination of two or more segmentation bases.

There are three alternative segmentation strategies a marketer can choose from when selecting a target market. They are market aggregation, single-segment concentration, and multiple segmentation. Market aggregation involves using one marketing mix to reach a mass, undifferentiated market. In single-segment concentration a company still uses only one marketing mix, but it is directed at only one segment of the total market. The third alternative entails selecting two or more segments and developing a separate marketing mix to reach each one.

## KEY TERMS AND CONCEPTS

## QUESTIONS AND PROBLEMS

1. Distinguish between market aggregation and market segmentation.
2. What benefits can a company expect to gain from segmenting its market?
3. Cite some regional differences in product preferences caused by factors other than climate.
4. Give several examples of goods or services whose market demand would be particularly affected by each of the following population factors:
   a. Regional distribution.
   b. Marital status.
   c. Sex.
   d. Age.
   e. Urban-rural-suburban distribution.
5. List three of the major population trends noted in this chapter (for instance, a growing segment of the population is over 65 years of age). Then carefully explain how *each* of the following types of retail stores might be affected by *each* of the trends.
   a. Supermarket.
   b. Sporting goods store.
   c. Drugstore.
   d. Restaurant.
6. In which stage of the life cycle are families likely to be the best prospects for each of the following goods or services?
   a. Braces on teeth.
   b. Suntan lotion.
   c. Second family car.
   d. Vitamin pills.
   e. Refrigerators.
   f. Life insurance.
   g. Jogging suits.
   h. 46-day Mediterranean cruise.
7. In what ways has the rise in disposable personal income since 1960 influenced the marketing programs of a typical department store? A supermarket?
8. Give examples of products whose demand is substantially influenced by changes in discretionary purchasing power.
9. Using the demographic and income segmentation bases discussed in this chapter, describe the segment likely to be the best market for:
   a. Snow skis.
   b. Good French wines.
   c. Power hand tools.
   d. Birthday cards.
   e. Outdoor barbecue grills.
10. Explain how the concept of benefit segmentation might be applied by marketing executives for a symphony orchestra or an art museum.
11. What users' benefits would you stress in advertising each of the following three products to each of these three markets?

    | Product | Market |
    | --- | --- |
    | a. Stereo tape player. | a. Schoolteachers. |
    | b. Toothpaste. | b. Retired people. |
    | c. 10-day Caribbean cruise. | c. Working women. |

12. Describe what you believe to be the demographic characteristics of heavy users of:
    a. Dog food.
    b. Ready-to-eat cereal.
    c. Videocassette recorders.
    d. Pocket calculators.
13. How would you segment the market for copying machines such as Xerox or Canon photocopiers?
14. Explain the similarities and differences between a single-segment and a multiple-segment target-market strategy.
15. U.S. manufacturers of Levi's and Wrangler blue jeans have been selling in Western European markets for several years, and now they want to enter markets in Eastern Europe, especially Poland, East Germany, and Hungary. In what ways, if any, will these producers have to adapt their market segmentation strategies for Eastern European countries?
16. How might the following organizations implement the strategy of market segmentation?
    a. Manufacturer of personal computers.
    b. American Heart Association.
    c. Universal Studios (Hollywood movies).
    d. Producer of CDs.

# CHAPTER 5
# CONSUMER BUYING BEHAVIOR

Americans spend more than $190 billion on new cars and trucks each year. In cars alone there are 572 different models available in the United States (up from 408 in 1980). Except in the smallest U.S. cities, urban "auto-dealer strips" are commonplace. In Atlanta there are 24 dealers along a 5-mile stretch of suburban Cobb Parkway.

The market's size combined with the competitive pressure of so many brands and models has led to greater market segmentation. In 1985 General Motors (GM) described the car and truck market in terms of 7 market segments. Now they identify 19 segments for cars and 11 for trucks and vans.

Malcolm McDougal, an advertising executive, says the number of choices in the car market is causing consumer stress. A GM marketing research executive agrees that the consumer is faced with more information to digest and interpret, but points out that because of the many choices available the consumer does not have to accept as many compromises in making a selection.

A recent survey found that 53 percent of new car buyers switch brands. In attempts to gain even the smallest margin of advantage, dealers and manufacturers have tried a number of tactics, including:

- An Atlanta dealer reserves a special area in the service department for cars less than a year old to speed up service for recent buyers.
- A Volvo dealership encourages shoppers to test-drive its cars to other dealers in order to compare the competing cars side by side.
- Cadillac advertises safety features despite a belief in the auto industry that safety is not a reason people buy since all cars are seen as equally safe (or dangerous).
- Pontiac offers a turbo-charged engine as an option in its Grand Prix even though it foresees a market of only 4,000 buyers.[1]

---

[1]Adapted from Paul Ingrassia and Gregory A. Patterson, "Is Buying a Car a Choice or a Chore?" *The Wall Street Journal*, Oct. 24, 1989, p. B1.

Why has marketing to consumers become more complicated? The reason is simple. Our understanding of consumer buying behavior is constantly improving, forcing marketers to refine their efforts. But there is much more to learn. And because marketing success largely depends on the ability to anticipate what buyers will do, in this chapter we examine the challenging topic of consumer buying behavior. First we develop an overview with a description of the buying-decision process. Next we consider the sources of information used by consumers—without information there are no decisions. We then describe the various social and group forces in society that influence decision making and the psychological characteristics of the individual that affect the decision process in buying. In the final section our focus shifts to the role in buying played by situational factors.

Figure 5-1 brings all of these dimensions of buying behavior together in a model that provides the structure for our discussion. The model features a six-stage **buying-decision process** influenced by four primary forces.

## DECISION MAKING AS PROBLEM SOLVING

To deal with the marketing environment and make purchases, consumers engage in a decision process. The process, which divides nicely into six stages, can be thought of as a problem-solving approach. When faced with a buying problem ("I'm bored. How do I satisfy my need for entertainment?"), the consumer goes through a series of logical stages to arrive at a decision.

As shown in the center of Figure 5-1, the stages are:

1. *Need recognition:* The consumer is moved to action by a need.
2. *Choice of an involvement level:* The consumer decides how much time and effort to invest in the remaining stages.
3. *Identification of alternatives:* The consumer collects information about products and brands.
4. *Evaluation of alternatives:* The consumer weighs the pros and cons of the alternatives identified.
5. *Decision:* The consumer decides to buy or not to buy.
6. *Postpurchase behavior:* The consumer attempts to resolve anxieties about the choice made.

Though this model is a useful starting point for examining purchase decisions, the process is not always as straightforward as it may appear. First, the potential buyer can withdraw at any stage prior to the actual purchase. If, for example, the strength of the need diminishes or no satisfactory alternatives are available, the process will come to an abrupt end. Second, it is not uncommon for some stages to be skipped. All six stages are likely to be used only in certain buying situations—for instance, when buying high-priced, infrequently purchased items. However, for many products purchasing is a routine affair in which the aroused need is satisfied by repurchasing a familiar brand and thus the third and fourth stages are bypassed. Third, the stages are not necessarily of the same length. In the purchase of a new car the need might be recognized the moment a mechanic tells you that your car's engine needs an overhaul, but the evaluation of alternatives may go on for weeks. Finally, some stages may be performed consciously in certain purchase situations and subconsciously in others. We do not calculate for every purchase the amount of time and effort we will put forth. Yet the fact that we spend more time on some purchases and less on others indicates that choice of involvement level is part of the process.

In the following discussion we assume that these stages generally charac-

Are these Olympic skiers effective reference individuals for a brand of sunglasses?

Going downhill at 40 mph is no time to dim your lights.

The trouble with all of the so-called premium sunglasses is that in their quest to eliminate harmful ultra-violet and infrared radiation, they sacrifice something else. Light. And color.

They darken your view. They distort color. So they end up robbing you of the visual cues you need to see what's waiting for you down the slopes. Like those nasty moguls hiding in the 3 o'clock light.

That's why CooperVision created Révo. A revolutionary new kind of sunglasses that actually improve your vision by letting in more light. Yet you get this extra light without any of the glare or brightness that might make your eyes uncomfortable. What will all this do for your skiing?

You don't have to be an Olympic champion to figure out that it's better to fly over the bumps in the light than to stumble over them in the dark.

For further information call (800) THE-RÉVO. In Arizona call (800) 453-1114.

RēVO

with the place of consumption (public or private) we get four situations with different reference-group influence:

- Publicly consumed luxuries—influence on the product and the brand.
- Privately consumed luxuries—influence on the product only.
- Publicly consumed necessities—influence on the brand only.
- Privately consumed necessities—no influence.

The role of reference groups as behavior determinants presents the marketer with a challenge. In a given buying situation, it must first be determined whether reference-group influence operates on the product and/or the brand. Then in situations with reference-group influence, the relevant groups must be identified. The result of this process is reflected in advertising appeals using specific reference groups, such as Nike's "Bo knows" campaign, featuring Bo Jackson and other well-known athletes.

## Family and Household Influence

A **family** is a group of two or more people related by blood, marriage, or adoption living together in a household. During their lives many people will belong to at least two families—the one into which they are born and the one they form at marriage. The birth family primarily determines core values and attitudes. The marriage family, in contrast, has a more direct influence on specific purchases. For example, family size is important in the purchase of a car.

A **household** is a broader concept than a family. It consists of a single person, a family, or any group of unrelated persons who occupy a housing unit. Thus an unmarried home owner, college students sharing an off-campus apartment, and cohabiting couples (mingles) are examples of households.

This distinction between family and household stems from relatively recent changes in the "typical" household. At one time marketers could safely assume that a household consisted of a married couple and their children.

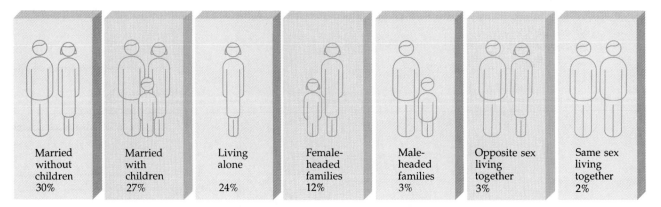

| Married without children 30% | Married with children 27% | Living alone 24% | Female-headed families 12% | Male-headed families 3% | Opposite sex living together 3% | Same sex living together 2% |

**FIGURE 5-3** "Traditional" families are a small segment of today's 91 million households.

Source: Allan Ball, "Here's Who's Living with Whom," *Adweek's Marketing Week,* Nov. 13, 1989, p. HM 11.

Not any more. Married couples with and without children account for about 55 percent of U.S. households in 1990. This, of course, means that 45 percent of households are of the nontraditional variety. Figure 5-3 shows the current mix of U.S. households. Sensitivity to household structure is important in designing marketing strategy. It affects such dimensions as product size (How large should refrigerators be?) and the design of advertising (Is it appropriate to depict a traditional family in a TV ad?).

In addition to the direct, immediate impact households have on the purchase behavior of members, it is also interesting to consider the buying behavior of the household as a unit. Who does the buying for a household? Marketers should treat this question as four separate ones because each may call for different strategies:

- Who influences the buying decision?
- Who makes the buying decision?
- Who makes the actual purchase?
- Who uses the product?

Different people may assume these various roles, or one individual may play several roles in a particular purchase. In families, for many years the female household head did most of the day-to-day buying. However, this behavior has changed as more women have entered the work force and men have assumed greater household responsibility. Night and Sunday business hours in stores in suburban shopping centers also encourage men to play a bigger role in family purchasing.

In recent years teenagers and young children have become decision makers in family buying, as well as actual shoppers. Teenagers spent $78 billion in 1987, certainly enough to warrant the attention of many manufacturers and middlemen![3] Even very young children influence buying decisions today because they watch TV advertising and ask for products when they shop with their parents. Purchasing decisions are often made jointly by husband and wife. Young married couples are much more likely to make buying decisions on a joint basis than older couples are. Apparently the longer a couple lives together, the more they feel they can trust each other's judgment.

Knowing which family member is likely to make the purchase decision will influence a firm's entire marketing mix. If children are the key decision

[3]"Teens' Spending Tops $78 Billion," *Marketing Communications,* May 12, 1988, p. 13.

makers, as is often the case with breakfast cereals, then a manufacturer will produce something that tastes good to children, design the package with youngsters in mind, and advertise on Saturday morning cartoon shows. This would be done regardless of who actually makes the purchase and who else (besides the children) in the household might eat the cereal.

## PSYCHOLOGICAL FACTORS

In discussing the psychological component of consumer behavior, we will continue to use the model presented in Figure 5-1. One or more motives within a person activate goal-oriented behavior. One such behavior is perception, that is, the collection and processing of information. Other important psychological activities are learning and attitude formation. Finally we consider the roles that personality and self-concept play in buying decisions.

## Motivation—The Starting Point

To understand why consumers behave as they do, we must first ask why a person acts at all. The answer is, "Because he or she experiences a need." All behavior starts with a recognized need. A **motive** is a need sufficiently stimulated that an individual is moved to seek satisfaction. Security and prestige are examples of needs that may become motives.

A need must be aroused or stimulated before it becomes a motive. We have many dormant needs that do not activate behavior because they are not sufficiently intense. Thus hunger that is strong enough that we search for food and fear great enough that we seek security are examples of aroused needs that become motives for behavior.

Explanations for behavior can range from simple to unexplainable. To illustrate, buying motives may be grouped on three different levels depending on consumers' awareness of them and their willingness to divulge them. At one level, buyers recognize, and are quite willing to talk about, their motives for buying certain products. At a second level, they are aware of their reasons for buying but will not admit them to others. A man may buy a luxury car because he feels it adds to his social position in the neighborhood. Or a woman may buy a leather coat to keep up with her peer group. But when questioned about their motives, they offer other reasons that they think will be more socially acceptable. The most difficult motives to uncover are those at the third level, where even the buyers themselves cannot explain the real factors motivating their buying actions.

To further complicate our understanding, a purchase is often the result of multiple motives. Moreover, various motives may conflict with one another. In buying a new dress, a young woman may want to (1) please herself, (2) please her boyfriend, (3) be considered a fashion leader by other young women in her social circle, and (4) strive for economy. To accomplish all of these objectives in one purchase is truly a difficult assignment. Also a person's buying behavior changes because of changes in income, life-style, and other factors. Finally, identical behavior by several people may result from quite different motives, and different behavior by the same person at various points in time may result from the same motive.

### CLASSIFICATION OF MOTIVES

Psychologists generally agree that motives can be grouped in two broad categories: (1) needs aroused from *physiological states* of tension (such as the need for sleep) and (2) needs aroused from *psychological states* of tension (such as the needs for affection and self-respect).

The psychologist Abraham Maslow formulated a theory of motivation

**FIGURE 5-4** Maslow's hierarchy of needs.

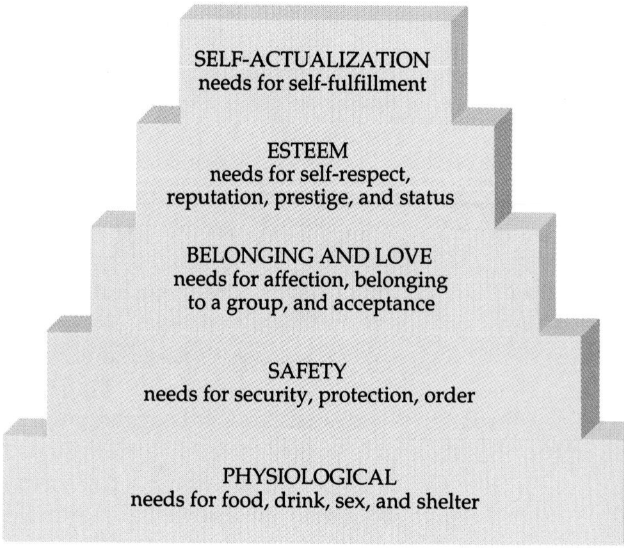

SELF-ACTUALIZATION
needs for self-fulfillment

ESTEEM
needs for self-respect,
reputation, prestige, and status

BELONGING AND LOVE
needs for affection, belonging
to a group, and acceptance

SAFETY
needs for security, protection, order

PHYSIOLOGICAL
needs for food, drink, sex, and shelter

based on needs. He identified a hierarchy of five levels of needs, arrayed in the order in which people seek to gratify them.[4] This hierarchy is shown in Figure 5-4. Maslow recognized that a normal person is most likely to be working toward need satisfaction on several levels at the same time and that rarely are all needs on a given level fully satisfied. However, the hierarchy indicates that the majority of needs on a particular level must be reasonably well satisfied before a person is motivated at the next higher level.

In their attempts to market products or communicate with particular segments, marketers often must go beyond a general classification like Maslow's to understand the specific motives underlying behavior. For example, to observe that a woman on a shopping trip may be satisfying physiological and social needs because she purchases food and talks to friends in the store may be correct, but it is not very useful. Addressing this issue, Edward Tauber described 13 specific motives reported by shoppers including recreation, self-gratification, sensory stimulation, peer group attraction, and status.[5] Using these motives, marketers are better prepared to design appealing products and stores. Much more needs to be done, however, to identify marketing-specific motives and to measure their strengths.

**Perception**   A motive is an aroused need. It, in turn, activates behavior intended to satisfy the aroused need. One form that behavior takes is collecting and processing information from the environment, a process known as **perception.** We constantly receive, organize, and assign meaning to stimuli detected by our five senses. In this way we interpret or give meaning to the world around us. Perception plays a major role in the alternative identification stage of the buying-decision process.

What we perceive—the meaning we give something sensed—depends on the object and our experiences. In an instant the mind is capable of receiving information, comparing it to a huge store of images in memory, and provid-

[4]A. H. Maslow, *Motivation and Personality*, Harper & Row, New York, 1954, pp. 80–106.
[5]Edward M. Tauber, "Why Do People Shop?" *Journal of Marketing*, October 1972, pp. 46–49.

**FIGURE 5-5** Perception is a combination of what our senses tell us and information stored in memory.

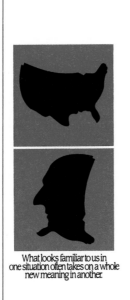

What looks familiar to us in one situation often takes on a whole new meaning in another.

We often think we understand something when a closer examination shows us there's a whole new side to it. At U S WEST Communications, we find this to be especially true in the business world.

You see, we believe every corporation is unique because of its employees, functions, goals and the very industry it's in. So when we see a problem at one business that we've seen before at another, we realize that it may require a completely different solution.

Which is exactly why we offer such a wide range of communication services. From central office switching to digital services to fiber optics, together we will design and develop a system that's right for you.

We'll also ask you questions. Get your ideas. Look at a situation from your point of view as well as ours. And do anything else we can to better understand your needs.

So give us a call at 1-800-328-4535, ext. 3005. We'll take a fresh, new look at your business. **U S WEST**
*COMMUNICATIONS* ©

ing an interpretation. For instance, the different meanings we give the same shape in Figure 5-5 depend on something as simple as the angle at which the information is presented.

Every day we come in contact with an enormous number of marketing stimuli. However, a process of selectivity limits our perceptions. As an illustration, consider that:

- We pay attention by exception. That is, of all the marketing stimuli our senses are exposed to, only those with the power to capture and hold our attention have the potential of being perceived. This phenomenon is called **selective attention.**
- We may alter information that is inconsistent with our beliefs and attitudes. Thus someone may say, "Despite the evidence, I don't believe smoking will be hazardous to my health." This is **selective distortion.**
- We retain only part of what we have selectively perceived. We may read an ad but later forget it. This is known as **selective retention.**

There are many communications implications in this selectivity process. For years advertisers in magazines have felt that the upper-left corner of a page gets more attention since we read from left to right and top to bottom. In a study for Bombay gin, researchers found that an ad got 28 percent more attention when it appeared above a magazine article rather than below it.

To gain attention, a stimulus must be sufficiently different from what the consumer expects or is used to. For example, Benetton ran ads for its Sisley clothing line upside down in *Rolling Stone* and *Sassy*. In another bid for attention, an ad for Libby's canned meats in *Redbook* had the product protruding outside the normal rectangular space into the editorial copy.[6] You have proba-

---

[6] These examples are from Ronald Alsop, "Advertisers See Big Gains in Odd Layouts," *The Wall Street Journal*, June 29, 1988, p. 25.

White space calls attention to an otherwise very familiar product.

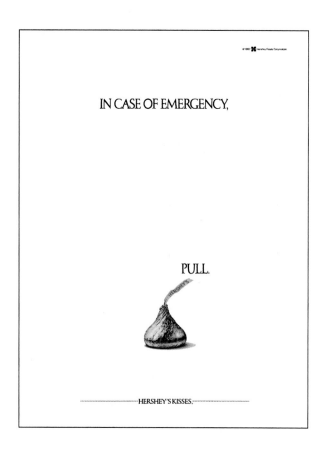

bly noticed headlines that run off the page and print ads that are mostly white space are more likely to get your attention than are traditional layouts.

As part of perception new information is compared with a person's existing store of knowledge, or frame of reference. If an inconsistency is discovered, the new information will be distorted to conform to the established beliefs. Thus if a consumer believes foreign-made cars are better built than U.S. cars, a claim of superior quality by Ford will be viewed as an exaggeration or an attempt at deception rather than as fact.

---

### Anything for attention?

Probably the most unconventional recent attempts to gain consumers' attention are what have been termed surreal ads. Honda had one of the first. Its TV ads for scooters used the rock group DEVO and flashed questions on the screen such as ''Can dogs think?'' and ''Should I buy a vowel?'' In a Reebok commercial the characters appearing on the screen included a three-legged man and a fairy godmother with a briefcase. You might ask, what do these ads accomplish? The answer is that they are intended solely as attention-getters. According to a Reebok executive, ''They are designed to stop people cold.'' One risk is that such ads may be so unusual that the devices designed to get attention may completely overshadow the products.

Source: Ronald Alsop, ''Surreal Ads Startle—But Do They Sell?'' *The Wall Street Journal,* Oct. 20, 1988, p. B1.

To reduce distortion advertisers strive for meaningful, strong messages that will be believed. A major factor influencing the believability of a message is the credibility of the source. Advertisers use recognized experts to endorse their products—Michael Jordan for Nike shoes and race car driver Richard Petty for Texaco—or someone viewed as highly trustworthy—Tip O'Neill, former Speaker of the House of Representatives, for Quality Inns—to add credibility to their messages.

Even messages received undistorted are still subject to selective retention. Consequently ads are repeated many times. The hope is that numerous exposures will etch the message into the recipient's memory. This aim partially explains why a firm like McDonald's spends over $725 million a year on advertising.

**Learning**  **Learning** may be defined as changes in behavior resulting from previous experiences. Thus it excludes behavior that is attributable to instinct such as breathing or temporary states such as hunger or fatigue. The ability to interpret and predict the consumer's learning process enhances our understanding of buying behavior since learning plays a role at every stage of the buying-decision process. No simple learning theory has emerged as universally workable and acceptable. However, the one with the most direct application to marketing strategy is the stimulus-response theory.[7]

Stimulus-response theory holds that learning occurs as a person (1) responds to some stimulus and (2) is rewarded with need satisfaction for a correct response or penalized for an incorrect one. When the same correct response is repeated in reaction to the same stimulus, a behavior pattern or learning is established.

Research has shown that attitudes and other factors also influence a consumer's response to a given stimulus. Thus a learned response does not necessarily occur every time a stimulus appears.

Four factors are fundamental to the process:

- **Drives,** or motives, are strong stimuli that require the person to respond in some way.
- **Cues** are signals from the environment that determine the pattern of response.
- **Responses** are behavioral reactions to the drive and cues.
- **Reinforcement** results when the response is rewarding.

If the response is rewarding, a connection among the drive, cues, and response will be established. Learning, then, emerges from reinforcement, and repeated reinforcement leads to a habit or brand loyalty. For example, a person motivated to shop *(drive)* who has found bargains *(reinforcement)* when going into stores *(response)* that have "sale" signs in their windows *(cues)* will respond *(learn)* by going into other stores with "sale" signs.

Once a habitual behavior pattern has been established, it replaces conscious, willful behavior. In terms of our model this means that the consumer would go directly from the recognized need to purchase, skipping the steps in between. The stronger the habit (the more it has been reinforced), the more difficult it is for a competitive product to break in. On the other hand, if the

---

[7] Other schools of thought on learning, principally the cognitive approach and gestalt learning, are discussed in books on consumer behavior. See David Loudon and Albert J. Della Bitta, *Consumer Behavior*, 3rd ed., McGraw-Hill, New York, 1988.

## AN ETHICAL DILEMMA?

Consumers have learned from experience that the size of the print used in advertising a price is usually directly related to the amount of savings. For example, in a full-page newspaper grocery ad, the items that have been reduced the most from their regular prices are shown in the largest type. If you were a retail store manager, would you consider it ethical to use large type to promote items that were reduced only a small amount or not at all?

learned response is not rewarding, the consumer's mind is open to another set of cues leading to another response. The consumer will try a substitute product or switch to another brand.

**Personality**    The study of human personality has given rise to many, sometimes widely divergent, schools of psychological thought. As a result, attempts to inventory and classify personality traits have produced a variety of different structures. In this discussion **personality** is defined broadly as an individual's pattern of traits that influence behavioral responses. We speak of people as being self-confident, aggressive, shy, domineering, dynamic, secure, introverted, flexible, or friendly and as being influenced (but not controlled) by these personality traits in their responses to situations.

It is generally agreed that personality traits do influence consumers' perceptions and buying behavior. However, there is considerable disagreement as to the nature of this relationship; that is, *how* personality influences behavior. Although we know that people's personalities often are reflected in the clothes they wear, the cars they drive (or whether they use a bike or motorcycle instead of a car), and the restaurants they eat in, we have not been successful in predicting behavior from particular personality traits. The reason is simple: many things besides personality enter into the consumer buying-decision process.

### PSYCHOANALYTIC THEORIES OF PERSONALITY

The psychoanalytic theory of personality, formulated by Sigmund Freud at the turn of the century and later modified by his followers and critics, has had a tremendous impact on the study of human behavior. Freud contended that there are three parts to the mind—the id, the ego, and the superego. The **id** houses the basic instinctive drives, many of which are antisocial. The **superego** is the conscience, accepting moral standards and directing the instinctive drives into acceptable channels. The id and the superego are sometimes in conflict. The **ego** is the conscious, rational control center that maintains a balance between the uninhibited instincts of the id and the socially oriented, constraining superego.

Freud's behavioral thesis was that we enter the world with certain instinctive biological drives that cannot be satisfied in a socially acceptable fashion. As we learn that we cannot gratify these needs in a direct manner, we develop other, more subtle means of seeking satisfaction. These other means require that the basic drives be repressed, and consequently, inner tensions and frustrations develop. Also feelings of guilt or shame about these drives cause us to suppress and even sublimate them to the point where they become subconscious. In place of drive satisfaction we substitute rationalization and socially acceptable behavior. Yet the basic urges are always there. The net result is very complex behavior. Sometimes even we ourselves do not understand why we feel or act as we do.

One significant marketing implication of psychoanalytic theory is that a person's real motive(s) for buying a product or shopping at a certain store may be hidden. Straightforward research techniques, which are adequate for compiling demographic and economic data, prove fruitless in uncovering the real reasons for subconsciously directed buying behavior. Alternative methods borrowed from psychoanalysis, such as in-depth interviews and sentence completion tests, have met with varying degrees of acceptance because they are costly and subject to interpretation problems.

Psychoanalytic theory has caused marketers to realize that they must appeal to buyers' dreams, hopes, and fears. Yet at the same time they must provide buyers with socially acceptable rationalizations for many purchases.

### THE SELF-CONCEPT

Your **self-concept,** or self-image, is the way you see yourself. At the same time it is the picture you think others have of you. Psychologists distinguish between (1) the **actual** self-concept (the way you really see yourself) and (2) the **ideal** self-concept (the way you want to be seen or would like to see

This hosiery ad relies on the ideal self-concept for its impact.

An extension

of the ego.

Ultra Silk.
In 17
couture
colors.

THE LADY PREFERS
Hanes

yourself). To some extent, the self-concept theory is a reflection of other psychological and sociological dimensions already discussed. A person's self-concept is influenced, for instance, by innate and learned physiological and psychological needs. It is conditioned also by economic factors, demographic factors, and social-group influences.

Studies of purchases show that people generally prefer brands and products that are compatible with their self-concept. There are mixed reports concerning the degree of influence of the actual and ideal self-concepts on brand and product preferences. Some psychologists contend that consumption preferences correspond to a person's *actual* self-concept. Others hold that the *ideal* self-concept is dominant in consumers' choices.

Perhaps there is no consensus here because in real life we often switch back and forth between our actual and our ideal self-concepts. A middle-aged man may buy some comfortable, but not fashionable, clothing to wear at home on a weekend where he is reflecting his actual self-concept. Then later he buys some expensive, high-fashion exercise clothing, envisioning himself (ideal self-concept) as a young, active, upwardly mobile guy. This same fellow may drive a beat-up pickup truck for his weekend errands (actual self-concept). But he'll drive his new foreign sports car to work where he wants to project a different (ideal) self-concept.[8]

**Attitudes**

A classic definition of **attitude** is: a learned predisposition to respond to an object or class of objects in a consistently favorable or unfavorable way.[9] In our model of the buying-decision process, attitudes play a major role in the evaluation of alternatives. Numerous studies have reported a relationship between consumers' attitudes and their buying behavior regarding both types of products selected and brands chosen. Surely, then, it is in a marketer's best interest to understand how attitudes are formed, the functions they perform, and how they can be changed.

All attitudes have the following characteristics in common:

- Attitudes are *learned*. The information individuals acquire through their direct experiences with a product or an idea, indirect experiences (such as reading about a product in *Consumer Reports*), and interactions with their social groups all contribute to the formation of attitudes. For example, the opinions expressed by a good friend about garage sales plus the consumer's favorable or unfavorable experience as a result of going to garage sales will contribute to an attitude toward garage sales in general.
- Attitudes have an *object*. By definition, we can hold attitudes only toward something. The object can be general (professional sports) or specific (Chicago Cubs); it can be abstract (campus life) or concrete (the computer center). In attempting to determine consumers' attitudes it is very important to carefully define the object of the attitude since a person might have a favorable attitude toward the general concept (health food) but a negative attitude toward a specific dimension (broccoli).
- Attitudes have *direction* and *intensity*. Our attitudes are either favorable or unfavorable toward the object. They cannot be neutral. In addition, they

---

[8]For an analytical review of self-concept studies, the research problems connected with these studies, and a comprehensive bibliography, see M. Joseph Sirgy, "Self-Concept in Consumer Behavior: A Critical Review," *Journal of Consumer Research*, December 1982, pp. 287–300.

[9]Gordon W. Allport, "Attitudes," in C. A. Murchinson, ed., *A Handbook of Social Psychology*, Clark University Press, Worcester, Mass., 1935, pp. 798–844.

have a strength. For example, you may mildly like this text or you may like it very much (we hope!). This factor is important for marketers since both strongly held favorable and strongly held unfavorable attitudes are difficult to change.

- Finally, attitudes are arranged in structures that tend to be *stable* and *generalizable*. Once formed, attitudes usually endure, and the longer they are held, the more resistant to change they become. People also have a tendency to generalize attitudes. For instance, if a person is treated nicely by a sales clerk in a particular store, there is a tendency to form a favorable attitude toward the entire store.

A consumer's attitudes do not always predict purchase behavior. A person may hold very favorable attitudes toward a product but not buy it because of some inhibiting factor. Typical inhibitors are not having enough money or discovering your preferred product or brand is not available when the purchase must be made. Under such circumstances purchase behavior may even contradict attitudes.

As the preceding discussion suggests, it is extremely difficult to change strongly held attitudes. Consequently when the marketer is faced with negative or unfavorable attitudes, there are two options. The first is to try to change the attitude to be compatible with the product. The second is to determine what the consumers' attitudes are and then change the product to match those attitudes. Ordinarily it is much easier to change the product than it is to change consumers' attitudes.

Nevertheless in some situations attitudes have been changed. Consider how negative attitudes have changed in favor of small cars, yellow tennis balls, off-season vacations, and coed dorms in colleges.

## SITUATIONAL INFLUENCE

Often the situations in which we find ourselves play a large part in determining how we behave. Students, for example, act differently in a classroom than they do when they are in a stadium watching a football game. The same holds true of buying behavior. You might get your hair cut because of an upcoming job interview. On spring break you might buy a souvenir that seems very strange when you get home. For a close friend's wedding gift, you might buy a fancier brand of small appliance than you would buy for yourself. These are all examples of **situational influences,** temporary forces associated with the immediate purchase environment that affect behavior. Situational influence tends to be less significant when the consumer is very loyal to a brand and when the consumer is highly involved in the purchase. However, it often plays a major role in buying decisions. The five categories of situational influences are explained next.

## When Consumers Buy— The Time Dimension

Marketers should be able to answer at least two time-related questions about consumer buying: Is it influenced by the season, week, day, or hour? What impact do past and present events have on the purchase decision?

The time dimension of buying has implications for promotion scheduling. Promotional messages must reach consumers when they are in a decision-making frame of mind. Marketers also adjust prices in an attempt to even out demand. For instance, supermarkets may offer double coupons on Wednesdays, usually a slow business day. If seasonal buying patterns exist, marketers can sometimes extend the buying season. There is obviously little opportunity to extend the buying season for Easter bunnies or Christmas ornaments.

But the season for vacations has been shifted to such an extent that winter and other "off-season" vacations are now quite popular.

The second question concerns the impact of past or future events. For example, the length of time since you last went out to dinner at a nice restaurant may influence a decision on where to go tonight. Or the significance of an upcoming event, such as a spring break trip to a resort area, could result in a greater than normal amount of clothing purchases. Marketers need to know enough about the targeted consumers to anticipate the effects of these past and future events.

### Where Consumers Buy—The Physical and Social Surroundings

Physical surroundings are the features of a situation that are apparent to the senses, such as lighting, smells, weather, and sounds. Think of the importance of atmosphere in a restaurant or the sense of excitement and action created by the sights and sounds in a gambling casino. Music can be an important element in a store's strategy. Limited, Inc., plays elegant, classical music in its Victoria's Secret intimate apparel stores. In contrast, in its high-fashion Limited Express shops, European pop tunes create an international, youthful feeling.

The social surroundings are the number, mix, and actions of other people at the purchase site. You probably would not go into a strange restaurant with an empty parking lot. And in a crowded store with other customers waiting, you will probably ask the clerk fewer questions and spend less time comparing products.

### How Consumers Buy—The Terms and Conditions of the Purchase

How consumers buy refers to the terms and conditions of sale as well as the transaction-related activities that buyers are willing to perform. Many more retailers sell on credit today than just a few years ago. Not only do consumers use credit for installment purchases (to buy things today with future income), but many now use credit for convenience. The ability to use Visa, MasterCard, or Discover to make a wide variety of purchases while not carrying cash is an attractive option to many consumers. Another recent development is the increase in purchases made by mail and phone. The growth of catalog advertising and telephone shopping services has enabled consumers to buy everything from jewelry to food without setting foot in a store. Finally the trend toward one-stop shopping has encouraged retailers to add even unrelated items to their basic mix of products. Consider, for example, the wide variety of goods found in what we call a drug store.

Marketers have also experimented with transferring functions or activities

The payment convenience of credit cards has been a major factor in the explosive growth of catalog retailing.

to consumers. For instance, consumers have shown a willingness to assemble products, sack their own groceries, and buy in case quantities—all in exchange for lower prices.

## Why Consumers Buy— The Objective of the Purchase

The intent or reason for a purchase affects the choices made. We are likely to behave very differently if we are buying a product for a gift as opposed to buying the same product for our personal use. When purchasing a wristwatch, a consumer may be most interested in one that will provide accurate time at a reasonable price. However, the appearance of a watch bought as a graduation present can be very important.

A marketer must understand the consumer's objective in buying the product in order to design an effective marketing mix. For example, the failure by most watchmakers to appeal to the functional, nongift watch market is what allowed Timex to be so successful with its reasonably priced product.

## Conditions under Which Consumers Buy—States and Moods

Sometimes consumers are in a temporary state that influences their buying decisions. When you are ill or rushed, you may be unwilling to wait in line or you do not take the time or care that a particular purchase deserves. Moods can also influence purchases. Feelings such as anger or excitement can result in purchases that otherwise would not have been made. In the exciting atmosphere of a rock concert, for example, you might pay more for a commemorative T-shirt than you would under normal circumstances. Sales people must be trained to recognize consumers' moods and adjust their presentations accordingly.

Marketers have noticed the impact of a variety of situational influences, some easy to interpret and others somewhat baffling. For instance, the sale of lip balm can be explained by a combination of temperature, humidity, and wind. And a McCann-Erickson researcher noted that people are more susceptible to food ads on the day they shop for groceries, but food commercials on TV are not advisable too soon after the dinner hour. On the other hand, how do you explain why soft drink consumption goes up with wind velocity? When a particular situational influence becomes widely accepted and strongly embedded (such as the notion that orange juice is for morning consumption), overcoming it can be difficult. The marketer may have to carry out an extensive campaign utilizing various techniques with no guarantee of success.

## SUMMARY

The focus of this chapter is ultimate consumers, as distinguished from business firms that also purchase goods and services. The discussion is built around a five-part model—the buying-decision process, information, social and group forces, psychological forces, and situational factors.

The buying-decision process is composed of six stages consumers go through in making purchases. The stages are need recognition, choice of an involvement level, identification of alternatives, evaluation of alternatives, decision, and postpurchase behavior.

Information is the fuel that drives the buying-decision process. Without it, there would be no decisions. There are two information sources—the commercial environment and the social environment. Commercial sources include advertising, personal selling, telemarketing, and personal involvement with a product. Word of mouth, observation, and experience with a product owned by someone else are social sources.

Social and group forces are composed of culture, subculture, social class, reference groups, family, and households. Culture has the broadest and most general influence, while household has the most immediate impact. Social and group forces have a direct impact on the individual purchase decisions and on the psychological makeup of an individual.

Psychological forces that impact buying decisions are motivation, perception, learning, personality, and attitudes. All behavior is motivated by some aroused need. Perception is the way we interpret the world around us and is subject to three types of selectivity: attention, distortion, and retention. Learning is a change in behavior as a result of experience. Stimulus-response learning involves drives, cues, responses, and reinforcement. Continued reinforcement leads to habitual buying and brand loyalty.

Personality is the sum of an individual's traits that influence behavioral responses. The Freudian psychoanalytic theory of personality, which includes the concepts of the id, ego, and superego, has had a significant impact on marketing. It has caused marketers to realize that the true motives for behavior are often hidden. The self-concept, or the way we see ourselves and the way we think others see us, is related to personality. Because purchasing and consumption are very expressive actions, they allow us to communicate to the world our ideal self-concepts.

Attitudes are learned predispositions to respond to an object or class of objects in a consistent fashion. Besides being learned, all attitudes are directed toward an object, have direction and intensity, and tend to be stable and generalizable. Strongly held attitudes are difficult to change.

Situational influences deal with when, where, how, and why consumers buy, and the consumer's personal condition at the time of purchase. Situational influences are often so powerful that they can override all of the other forces in the buying-decision process.

## KEY TERMS AND CONCEPTS

Buying-decision process 112
Need recognition 113
High involvement 113
Low involvement 114
Impulse buying 115
Patronage buying motives 115
Satisfaction 117
Postpurchase behavior 117
Cognitive dissonance 117
Commercial information 118
Social information 118
Culture 118
Subculture 119
Social class 120
Reference groups 122
Family 123
Household 123
Motive 125
Maslow's need hierarchy 126

Perception 126
Selective attention 127
Selective distortion 127
Selective retention 127
Learning 129
Stimulus-response theory 129
Drives 129
Cues 129
Responses 129
Reinforcement 129
Personality 130
Id 130
Ego 130
Superego 130
Self-concept 131
Actual self 131
Ideal self 131
Attitude 132
Situational influence 133

# QUESTIONS AND PROBLEMS

1. Describe a high-involvement purchase you recently made in terms of each of the stages described in the chapter. Assume you are going to purchase that same item again today. How might the stages be different this time? Why?
2. When might the purchase of a color television be low involving?
3. When a consumer's experience with a product *equals* her expectations for the product, the person is satisfied. Is there any disadvantage to an organization if the consumer's experience *greatly exceeds* expectations?
4. Describe a situation in which you experienced postpurchase cognitive dissonance and what you did to relieve it. What kinds of reinforcement could a furniture store use to reduce the cognitive dissonance of its customers?
5. Which source of information do consumers normally have the most confidence in? Why? Is it possible for an advertiser to simulate this source?
6. Describe how a subculture of which you are a member influences your purchasing behavior.
7. From a consumer behavior perspective, why is it incorrect to view the European Community or the countries of Asia as single markets?
8. It is possible that a person in the lower-middle social class could have an income as high as a person in the upper-middle class. In this case would you expect their purchases to be very similar? Why or why not?
9. Explain why reference-group influence would affect the choice of the product, the brand, or neither for the following items:
   a. Bath soap.
   b. Lawn tractor.
   c. Office furniture.
   d. Camera.
   e. Waterbed.
10. What roles would you expect a husband, a wife, and their young child to play in the purchase of the following items?
    a. Nintendo.
    b. Choice of a fast food outlet for dinner.
    c. Personal computer.
    d. Lawn mower.
    e. Auto tune-up.
    f. Lawn care service.
11. Which needs in the Maslow hierarchy might be satisfied by each of the following products?
    a. Home burglary alarm system.
    b. Pepsi-Cola.
    c. Encyclopedias.
    d. Sunscreen lotion.
    e. Donation to United Way.
    f. BMW automobile.
12. Describe a situation in which the selectivity process in perception might operate.
13. Using the concepts of stimulus-response learning theory, explain why a person might buy five new Chevrolets over a period of 25 years.
14. Does the psychoanalytic theory of personality have any practical application in the marketing of cars that have a top speed of 120 mph when the highest speed limit is 65 mph?
15. Explain how self-concept might come into play in the purchase of the following products:
    a. Eyeglasses.
    b. Condominium.
    c. Man's suit.
    d. Golf clubs.
    e. Eye shadow.
    f. College education.
16. Describe an attitude you have toward a career in marketing using the four characteristics that all attitudes have in common.
17. What situational influences might affect a family's choice of a motel in a strange town while on a vacation?

How would you like to enjoy the rich taste of premium ice cream, but at less than half the calories of present brands? Would you try a salad dressing, mayonnaise, yogurt, or margarine with the old-time taste but with a 70 to 80 percent savings in calories? Or how about eating all the tasty french-fried potatoes and potato chips you want, knowing all the time that the oil used in the frying process does not contain any calories, cholesterol, or fat? All of these products have one thing in common: they contain fat substitutes—Simplesse in the dairy products and olestra in the fried foods. By the early 1990s both of these fat alternatives, along with similar products being developed by Unilever, Frito-Lay, and others, are expected to be in great demand. In fact, Unilever started using a fat substitute (with a 50 percent savings in calories) in two brands of margarine marketed in Europe in the late 1980s.

Simplesse is brought to you by those wonderful people who gave us NutraSweet sugar substitute, not many years ago. Made completely with natural ingredients—primarily egg and milk proteins—Simplesse's only significant drawback is that it cannot be used in cooking. Thus its use is limited primarily to dairy products—still a huge potential market. Olestra is a synthetic calorie-free chemical developed by Procter & Gamble for use in deep frying and in many cooked and uncooked foods.

Once these fat substitutes receive government approval for U.S. distribution, their producers will face many questions of marketing strategy. Can NutraSweet move further into the food business by introducing or acquiring food brands in which Simplesse could be used as a fat substitute? If so, the products' labels would clearly feature the fact that the product was made with Simplesse. Should Procter & Gamble introduce a line of health foods made with olestra? Should olestra be packaged and sold to consumers as a substitute for cooking oils that are high in calories and fat?

Whatever marketing strategies the makers of Simplesse and olestra adopt, one thing is clear. The primary target markets for each of these products are business firms that will use Simplesse or olestra in making other products. Thus Simplesse and olestra are business products marketed to business users in the business market—the topics we'll be talking about in this chapter. The business market is big, rich, and widely diversified. It employs millions of workers in thousands of different jobs. Firms producing for this market are usually not criticized for extreme claims in selling or advertising. They are not accused of offering duplicate brands or of handing middlemen exorbitant profits.

## NATURE OF THE BUSINESS MARKET

The **business market** consists of all business users. In Chapter 4 we defined **business users** as organizations that buy goods and services for one of the following purposes:

- *To make other goods and services.* Campbell's buys fresh vegetables to make soup, and Henredon buys wood to make furniture.
- *To resell to other business users or to consumers.* Kroger's buys canned tuna fish to sell to consumers, and Western Pipe Supply Company sells lawn sprinkler equipment and supplies to sprinkler contractors.
- *To conduct the organization's operation.* The University of Vermont buys office supplies and electronic office equipment for use in the registrar's office, and the Denver General Hospital buys supplies to use in its surgical operating rooms.

In the business market we deal with both consumer products and business products. **Business marketing,** then, is the marketing of goods and services to business users, as contrasted to ultimate consumers.

Because the business market is largely unknown to the average consumer, we are apt to underrate its significance. Actually this market is a huge one in terms of total sales volume and the number of firms involved in it. About 50 percent of all manufactured products are sold to the business market. In addition, about 80 percent of all farm products and virtually all minerals and forest and sea products are business goods. These are sold to firms for further processing.

The magnitude and complexity of the business market are also evident from the many transactions required to produce and market a product. Consider, for example, the business marketing transactions and total sales volume involved in getting a pair of cowhide work shoes to their actual user. First the cattle are sold through one or two middlemen before reaching a meat-packer. Then the hides are sold to a tanner, who in turn sells the leather to a shoe manufacturer. The shoe manufacturer may sell finished shoes to a shoe wholesaler, who markets the products to retail stores or to factories that supply shoes to their workers. Each sale is a business marketing transaction.

In addition, the shoe manufacturer buys metal eyelets, laces, thread, steel safety toe plates, heels and soles, and shoe polish. Consider something as simple as the shoelaces. Other industrial firms must first buy the raw cotton and then spin, weave, dye, and cut it so that it becomes shoestring material. All the manufacturers involved have factories and offices with furniture, machinery, and other equipment—and these also are business goods that have to be produced and marketed. Factories also are business products, as are the heating and maintenance equipment and supplies required to run them. In short, thousands of business products and business marketing activities come into play before almost any product—consumer good or business good—reaches its final destination.

The magnitude and complexity of the business market loom even larger when we consider all the business services involved throughout our work-shoe example. Each firm engaged in any stage of the production process probably uses outside accounting and law firms. Several of the producers may use advertising agencies. And all of the companies will use services of various financial institutions.

## Scope of the Business Market

Another indication of the scope of the business market is the range of industries it includes:

- Agriculture, forestry, and fishing.
- Mining and quarrying.
- Contract construction.
- Manufacturing.
- Transportation, communication, and other public utilities.
- Wholesale trade and retail trade.
- Finance, insurance, and real estate.
- Services.
- Government—federal, state, and local.
- Nonbusiness (nonprofit) organizations.

Every retail store and wholesaling establishment is a business user. Every bus company, airline, and railroad is part of this market. So is every hotel, restaurant, bank, insurance company, hospital, theater, and school. In all, there are close to 15 million business users in the United States. While this is far short of the approximately 250 million consumers, the total sales volume in the business market far surpasses total sales to consumers. This difference is due to the very many business marketing transactions that take place before a product is sold to its ultimate user.

## Overlooked Business Market Segments

Traditionally, business markets were referred to as industrial markets, often construed to mean manufacturing firms. But as you can see from the above list, the business market is quite large and varied. In recognition of this fact, a few years back the American Marketing Association renamed its Industrial Marketing Division the Business Marketing Division.[1] Among the nonmanufacturing segments of the business market, five very large ones stand out. These segments—farmers, resellers, government agencies, service companies, and nonprofit organizations—often are underrated or overlooked because of the heavy attention devoted to manufacturing.

### THE FARM MARKET

The high level of cash income from the sale of farm products—over $160 billion in 1990—gives farmers, as a group, the purchasing power that makes them a highly attractive market. Moreover, world population forecasts and food shortages in many countries undoubtedly will keep pressure on farmers to increase their output. Companies hoping to sell to the farm market must analyze it carefully and be aware of significant trends. For example, both the proportion of farmers in the total population and the number of farms have

[1] See "AMA Restructures the Industrial Marketing Division into Business Marketing Division," *Marketing News*, Aug. 17, 1987, p. 13.

The farm market is a huge business market for a wide variety of products.

been decreasing and probably will continue to decline. Counterbalancing this has been an increase in large corporate farms. Even the surviving "family farms" are tending to expand in size. Farming is becoming more automated and mechanized. This means, of course, that capital investment in farming is increasing. **Agribusiness** (farming, food processing, and other large-scale farming-related businesses) is becoming big business in every sense of the word.

As business buyers, most farmers—especially the owners of large farms—are quite discerning and well informed. Like other business executives, farmers are looking for better ways to increase their crop yields, to cut their expenses, and to manage their cash flow. And, as farms become fewer, larger, and more sophisticated, manufacturers must change their distribution and promotion strategies to reach the farm market effectively.

In distribution, for instance, producers must recognize the key role played by farm equipment dealers and feed-seed suppliers located in farm communities. Farmers usually buy locally, where they can get repair service, parts, and supplies from people they know. Even a major capital expenditure for large equipment usually is made through a local dealer. This is unlike the buying behavior of most users, who typically buy large equipment directly from the manufacturer.

When promoting their products, manufacturers should be aware of the high degree of specialization in the farm market. Some producers of fertilizer (International Minerals and Chemical Company is one) will send a sales person directly to a large farm. There, working with the farmer, the sales rep will analyze the soil and determine exactly what fertilizer mix is best for that particular farm. From that analysis the manufacturer will prepare, as a special order, the appropriate blend of fertilizers.

On the other side of a farm-market transaction, *buying from* farmers sometimes is done on a contract basis. In fact, **contract farming,** while it has existed for a long time, seems to have increased in recent years. Under one type of contract-farming arrangement, one firm (a middleman or a manufacturer) agrees to furnish the farmer with supplies and possibly with equipment and working capital to grow a crop. The farmer, in turn, agrees to sell the entire crop to this supplier at some predetermined price. In effect, the farmer is an employee of this supplier. In another type of contract farming, the farmer furnishes the supplies and equipment. But a processor (perhaps a canner or freezer of fruits or vegetables) agrees in advance to buy that farmer's entire crop. The price may be set before the growing season, or it may be negotiated at some time during the season. Contract farming also affects the marketing of farm supplies and equipment. Often it is difficult for the seller to determine who makes a buying decision. Is it the farmer, the contract buyer, or both?

## THE RESELLER MARKET

Intermediaries in the American marketing system—approximately 500,000 wholesaling middlemen and 2 million retailers—constitute the **reseller market.** This is a large segment of the total business market. The basic activity of resellers—unlike any other business market segment—is buying products from supplier organizations and reselling these items in essentially the same form to the resellers' customers. In economic terms, resellers create time, place, and possession utilities, rather than form utility.

Resellers also buy many goods and services for use in operating their businesses—items such as office supplies and equipment, warehouses, materials-handling equipment, legal services, electrical services, and janitorial supplies. In these buying activities, resellers are essentially no different from manufacturers, financial institutions, or any other segment of the business market.

It is their role as buyers for resale that differentiates resellers and attracts special marketing attention from their suppliers. To resell an item, you must please your customer. Usually it is more difficult to determine what will please your outside customers than to find out what will satisfy somebody within your own organization. Thus, buying for resale typically is more difficult and risky than buying for use within a firm.

Buying for resale, especially in a large reseller's organization, can be a complex, sophisticated procedure. Buying for a supermarket chain, for example, is frequently done by a *buying committee.* Department stores may retain *resident buyers*—independent buying agencies—located in New York or other major market centers. Careful inventory management is essential for a profitable operation. Computerized inventory-control systems are used to minimize overstocking, obsolete merchandise, or out-of-stock conditions.

The wholesaling and retailing institutions that constitute the reseller market are discussed in more detail in Chapters 13 and 14.

## THE GOVERNMENT MARKET

The fantastically large government market includes over 80,000 federal, state, and local units buying for countless government institutions, such as schools, offices, hospitals, and military bases. Spending by the federal government alone accounts for about 20 percent of our gross national product. Spending at the state and local levels accounts for another 10 percent. The government as a buyer is so big and complex, however, that it is difficult to comprehend. Government procurement processes are different from those in the private sector of the business market.

A unique feature of government buying is the *bidding system.* Much government procurement, by law, must be done on a bid basis. That is, the government advertises for bids, stating product specifications. Then it must accept the lowest bid that meets these specifications. In other buying situations, the government may *negotiate* a purchase contract with an individual supplier. This marketing practice might be used, for instance, when the Department of Defense wants someone to develop and build a new weapons system and there are no comparable products on which to base bidding specifications.

Many companies make no real effort to sell to the government, preferring not to contend with the red tape. Yet government business can be quite profitable. Dealing with the government to any significant extent, however, usually requires specialized marketing techniques and information.

### THE SERVICES MARKET

Currently service firms greatly outnumber the producers of tangible goods—manufacturers, mining companies, construction firms, and firms engaged in farming, forestry, and fishing. The services market includes all transportation carriers and public utilities, and the many financial, insurance, and real estate firms. This market also includes organizations that produce and sell such diverse services as rental housing, recreation and entertainment, repairs, health care, personal care, and business services.

These service firms constitute a huge buying market for tangible products and other services. Hilton Hotels, for example, buy blankets and sheets from textile manufacturers. Hospitals in the United States and abroad buy supplies from Baxter Healthcare Company. The Chicago Cubs and other major league teams buy their Louisville Slugger baseball bats from Hillerich and Bradsby. And all these service firms buy legal, accounting, and consulting advice from other service marketers. Because of the size of the services market and its unique features, we later devote a separate chapter to services marketing (Chapter 19).

### THE "NONBUSINESS" BUSINESS MARKET

In recent years we have been giving some long-overdue marketing attention to the multibillion-dollar market comprised of so-called nonbusiness or nonprofit organizations. This business market segment includes such diverse institutions as churches, colleges and universities, museums, hospitals and other health institutions, political parties, labor unions, and charitable organizations. Actually each of these so-called nonbusiness organizations is a business organization. However, our society (and the institutions themselves) in the past did not perceive a museum or a hospital as being a business organization. And many people today still feel uncomfortable thinking of their church, school, or political party as being a business organization. Nevertheless, these are business organizations with real marketing problems. If you don't think so, just take a look at some of the advertising being done by universities and hospitals to attract customers.

These organizations also conduct marketing campaigns—albeit under a different name—in an effort to attract billions of dollars in contributions. In turn, they spend billions of dollars buying goods and services to run their operations. Marketing to, and by, these organizations is discussed in more detail in Chapter 20.

## CHARACTERISTICS OF BUSINESS MARKET DEMAND

Four general demand characteristics help to differentiate the business market from the consumer market: (1) demand is derived, (2) demand is inelastic, (3) demand is widely fluctuating, and (4) the market is well informed.

### Demand Is Derived

The demand for each business product is derived from the demand for the consumer products in which the business item is used. Thus the demand for

You could go to great lengths to keep ugly spills off your carpets.
Or you could simply get Du Pont Certified Stainmaster™ carpet.
Then, you can handle most common household spills with soap and water.
Even if they've sat for hours.
And that'll leave you leaping for joy. Instead of other things.

## What would you do without Stainmaster carpet?

DUPONT
CARPET FIBERS

The derived-demand feature of business markets often stimulates business producers to advertise to ultimate consumers.

steel depends partially on consumer demand for automobiles and refrigerators, but it also depends on the demand for butter, baseball gloves, and bongo drums. This is because the tools, machines, and other equipment needed to make these items are made of steel. Consequently, as the demand for baseball gloves increases, glove manufacturers may buy more steel sewing machines or filing cabinets.

There are several marketing implications in the fact that business market demand is a derived demand. The producer of a business product may run an advertising campaign promoting consumer goods or services using the firm's product. Du Pont ran an advertising campaign aimed at consumers, for instance, urging them when buying carpeting to ask specifically for products made with Du Pont's stain-resistant "Stainmaster" fiber. Similarly, the manufacturer of NutraSweet ran a consumer advertising campaign designed to build consumer loyalty for products sweetened with NutraSweet. The idea was that this consumer demand would, in turn, trigger a derived demand for NutraSweet on the part of food and soft-drink processors.

### Demand Is Inelastic

Another significant characteristic of the business market is related to the derived-demand feature: The demand for many business products is relatively inelastic. That is, the demand for a product responds very little to changes in price. If the price of buttons for men's jackets should suddenly rise or fall considerably, there would probably be no appreciable change in the demand for buttons. (If you would like to review some economics, the concept of demand elasticity is explained early in Chapter 10.)

The demand for business products is inelastic because ordinarily the cost of a single part or material is a small portion of the total cost of the finished product. The cost of the chemicals in paint is a small part of the price that a consumer pays for paint. The cost of the enamel on a refrigerator is a small part of its retail price. Even the cost of expensive capital equipment, when distributed over thousands of units of a product, becomes a very small part of the unit cost. As a result, when the price of the business product changes, there is very little shift in the demand for the related consumer products. If there is no appreciable shift in the demand for the consumer goods, then (by virtue of the derived-demand feature) there is no change in the demand for the business product.

From a marketing point of view, there are three factors that can moderate inelasticity of business demand:

- The first is the position of an entire industry as contrasted with that of an individual firm. An industry-wide cut in the price of steel belts used in tires will have little effect on the demand for automobile tires. Consequently, it will cause little change in the total demand for steel belts. The pricing policy of an individual firm, however, can substantially alter the demand for that firm's products. If one supplier significantly cuts the price of its steel belts, the drop in price may draw a great deal of business away from competitors. The advantage will be temporary, of course, because competitors will undoubtedly retaliate in some way to recapture their lost business. Nevertheless, in the short run, the demand curve faced by a single firm is much more elastic than the industry's curve.
- The second marketing factor that can affect the inelasticity of demand is time. Much of our discussion here applies to short-term situations. Over the long run, the demand for a given industrial product is more elastic. If the price of cloth for women's suits is raised, there probably will be no immediate change in the price of the finished garment. However, the increase in the cost of materials could very well be reflected in a $50 rise in suit prices for next year. This rise could then influence the demand for suits, and thus for cloth, a year or more hence.
- The third factor is the relative importance of a specific business product in the cost of the finished good. We may generalize to this extent: The greater the cost of a business product as a percentage of the total price of the finished good, the greater the elasticity of demand for this business product.

**Demand Is Widely Fluctuating**

Although the demand for business goods does not change much in response to price changes, it is far from steady. In fact, market demand for most classes of business goods fluctuates considerably more than the demand for consumer products. The demand for installations—major plant equipment, factories, and so on—is especially subject to change. Substantial fluctuations also exist in the market for accessory equipment—office furniture and machinery, delivery trucks, and similar products. These tend to accentuate the swings in the demand for business raw materials and fabricating parts. This is exemplified by downturns in the construction and auto industries, which affect suppliers of lumber, steel, and other materials and parts. One exception to this generalization is found in agricultural products intended for processing. There is a reasonably consistent demand for animals intended for meat products, for fruits and vegetables that will be canned or frozen, and for grains and dairy products.

Fluctuations in the demand for business products can influence all aspects of a marketing program. In product planning they may stimulate a firm to diversify into other products to ease production and marketing problems. Distribution strategies may be affected. Consider a firm's sales force. When demand declines, the sales force must be either trimmed back or maintained at full strength (but at a loss). Rather than try to cope with this problem, a seller may decide to make greater use of wholesalers to reach its market. In its pricing, management may attempt to stem a decline in sales by cutting prices, hoping to attract customers away from competing firms.[2]

---

[2]See William S. Bishop, John L. Graham, and Michael H. Jones, "Volatility of Derived Demand in Industrial Markets and Its Management Implications," *Journal of Marketing,* Fall 1984, pp. 95–103.

Well-informed buyers in business markets call for a high level of customer service from sellers.

## Market Is Well Informed

Unlike ultimate consumers, typical business buyers are usually well informed about what they are buying. They know the relative merits of alternative sources of supply and competitive products. The position of purchasing agent has been upgraded in many firms, and purchasing executives are using sophisticated tools to improve their performance.

These improvements in purchasing skills carry significant marketing implications for the sellers of business products. For example, producers of business goods place greater emphasis on personal selling than do firms marketing consumer products. Business sales people must be carefully selected, properly trained, and adequately compensated. They must give effective sales presentations and furnish satisfactory service both before and after each sale is made. Sales executives are devoting increased effort to the assignment of sales people to key accounts to ensure that these reps are compatible with business buyers.

## DETERMINANTS OF BUSINESS MARKET DEMAND

To analyze a *consumer* market, a marketer would study the distribution of population and income and then try to determine the consumers' buying motives and habits. Essentially the same type of analysis can be used by a firm selling to the *business* market. The factors affecting the market for business products are the number of potential business users and their purchasing power, buying motives, and buying habits. In the following discussion, we identify several basic differences between consumer markets and business markets.

## Number and Types of Business Users

### TOTAL MARKET

The business market contains relatively few buying units when compared with the consumer market. In the United States there are approximately 15 million business users, in contrast to about 250 million consumers divided among more than 85 million households. The business market seems even more limited to most companies, because they sell to only a small segment of the total market. A firm selling to U.S. manufacturers of metal cans in 1988, for example, had only 178 potential customer plants with 100 or more employees. In that same employment-size class, there were only 35 plants producing synthetic rubber and 41 plants making luggage.[3] Consequently, marketing executives must try to pinpoint their market carefully by type of industry and geographic location. A firm marketing hard-rock mining equipment is not interested in the total business market, or even in all 30,000 firms engaged in mining and quarrying.

One very useful information source developed by the federal government is the **Standard Industrial Classification (SIC) system,** which enables a company to identify relatively small segments of its business market.[4] In this system all types of businesses in the United States are divided into 10 groups. Then a range of two-digit code numbers is assigned to each group as follows:

| SIC range | Industry group |
|-----------|----------------|
| 01 to 09 | Agriculture, forestry, fishing |
| 10 to 14 | Mining |
| 15 to 19 | Contract construction |
| 20 to 39 | Manufacturing |
| 40 to 49 | Transportation and other public utilities |
| 50 to 59 | Wholesale and retail trade |
| 60 to 67 | Finance, insurance, and real estate |
| 70 to 89 | Services |
| 90 to 97 | Government—federal, state, local, and international |
| 99 | Others |

A separate two-digit number is assigned to each major industry within each of the above groups. Then three- and four-digit classification numbers are used to subdivide each major industry into smaller segments. Figure 6-1 illustrates the SIC codes for the dairy industry—a segment of the food-products group within the broad category of manufacturing.

The federal government publishes a considerable amount of marketing research information for each four-digit industry classification. These data include the number of establishments, employment, and sales volume—all by geographic area.

One limitation of SIC codes is that a multiproduct company is listed in only a single four-digit category. Also, the government's nondisclosure rules prevent revealing information that will identify a given establishment. Consequently, four-digit detail is not available for an industry in a geographic location where this information would identify a certain company.

### SIZE OF BUSINESS USERS

While the business market may be limited in the total number of buyers, it is large in purchasing power. A relatively small percentage of firms account for the greatest share of the value added to products by manufacturing. Let's look at some examples from the latest available *Census of Manufactures.* Less than 2 percent of the firms—those with 500 or more employees—accounted for almost 50 percent of the total dollar value added by manufacturing and for almost 40 percent of the total employment in manufacturing. Firms with fewer than 100 employees accounted for 90 percent of all manufacturing es-

---

[3]"1988 Survey of Industrial & Commercial Buying Power," *Sales & Marketing Management,* Apr. 25, 1988, pp. 20–21.

[4]For a description of the Standard Industrial Classification system and a complete listing of all SIC numbers and classifications, see *Standard Industrial Classification Manual,* U.S. Government Printing Office, Washington, D.C., 1972 and also 1987 Supplement. Also see "SIC: The System Explained," *Sales & Marketing Management,* Apr. 22, 1985, pp. 52–53.

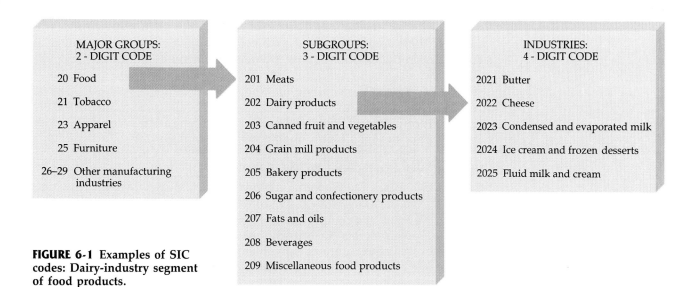

**FIGURE 6-1** Examples of SIC codes: Dairy-industry segment of food products.

tablishments, but they produced only 23 percent of the value added by manufacturing.

The marketing significance of these facts is that buying power in the business market is highly concentrated in a relatively few firms. Therefore, sellers have the opportunity to deal directly with business users. Middlemen are not as essential as in the consumer market.

Of course, these statements are broad generalizations covering the *total* business market. They do not take into account the variation in business concentration from one industry to another. In some industries—women's dresses and ready-mix concrete, for example—there is a relatively low level of concentration, as shown in Table 6-1. Nevertheless, even a so-called low-concentration industry represents far, far more concentration than anything in the consumer market.

### REGIONAL CONCENTRATION OF BUSINESS USERS

There is substantial *regional* concentration in many major industries and among business users as a whole. A firm selling products used in copper

---

**TABLE 6-1 Concentration in the business market**

| High concentration | ← In each industry → | Low concentration | |
|---|---|---|---|
| **Market share held by 4 largest companies*** | | **Market share held by 20 largest companies*** | |
| Hard-surface floor coverings | 99% | Special dies, tools, jigs | 13% |
| Chewing gum | 95% | Ready-mix concrete | 16% |
| Household refrigerators, freezers | 94% | Commercial printing | 16% |
| | | Women's dresses | 17% |
| Motor vehicles | 92% | Screw machine products | 17% |
| Light bulbs | 91% | | |

*Based on value of shipments.     Source: *Census of Manufactures*, 1982.

mining will find the bulk of its American market in Utah and Arizona. Hat manufacturers are located mostly in New England, and a large percentage of American-produced shoes come from New England, St. Louis, and the Southeast.

The eight states constituting the Middle Atlantic and East North Central census regions account for almost 50 percent of the total value added by manufacturing. Just 10 Standard Metropolitan Areas alone account for about 25 percent of the total U.S. value added by manufacturing.

### VERTICAL AND HORIZONTAL BUSINESS MARKETS

For effective marketing planning, a company should know whether the market for its products is vertical or horizontal. If a business product is usable by virtually all firms in only one or two industries, it has a **vertical** market. For example, some precision instruments are intended only for the marine market, but every boatbuilder or shipbuilder is a potential customer. If the product is usable by many industries, its market is said to be broad, or **horizontal.** Business supplies, such as lubricating oils and greases, small motors, and some paper products, may be sold to a wide variety of industries.

## AN INTERNATIONAL PERSPECTIVE: Business markets are big business internationally

Business-to-business marketing is a significant economic activity internationally, as well as in the domestic U.S. economy. Consider the following list of the largest exporting companies in the United States, ranked by export sales volume in 1988:

1. General Motors.
2. Ford Motor Company.
3. Boeing (aircraft).
4. General Electric.
5. IBM.
6. Chrysler Motors.
7. Du Pont.
8. McDonnell Douglas (aircraft).
9. Caterpillar (earth-moving equipment).
10. United Technologies (jet engines, helicopters).

Seven of the top 10 firms export products to end users in the business market. Only the three auto firms market products for which some end users are household consumers. And even in these cases, the products first are exported to the business reseller market (wholesalers and retailers) in various parts of the world.

Exporting by U.S. firms to international business markets increased during the 1980s, and this upward trend is likely to continue throughout the 1990s. In the early 1980s, for example, USX, the nation's largest steel producer, abolished its export sales unit. Then near the end of that decade, the company assembled a new overseas sales team and exported 1 million tons of steel in 1989. POM, a small manufacturer of parking meters

in Arkansas, has a larger market share overseas than at home. The firm sells to city governments in such far-flung places as Malaysia, Chile, and Holland. And recently POM introduced its first solar-powered parking meter in Shepparton, Australia. The Mead Corp. spent $550 million to expand an Alabama mill that produces coated paperboard, with the intent of exporting half of the plant's output. The Mazda auto company planned to ship to Japan in one year $100 million of North American–made auto parts.

Business-to-business international marketing is not limited to physical products. Many services firms are finding very attractive business markets in foreign countries. Law firms and management consulting firms are setting up offices in Japan, Western Europe, and Russia. In the field of financial services, Japan's huge banks are making significant inroads in the U.S. market. Some Japanese officials forecast that these banks could increase their share of the U.S. commercial bank market to 25 percent by the mid-1990s.

Truly, the scope of international trade involving business markets is huge and is continuing to grow. The range of business goods and services that can be marketed internationally seems almost limitless.

Sources: Top 10 list from Edward Prewitt, "America's 50 Biggest Exporters," *Fortune,* July 17, 1989, pp. 50–51. Other material from Ralph E. Winter, "U.S. Exporters Find the Party's Not Over," *The Wall Street Journal,* Oct. 4, 1989, p. A2; and Christopher Knowlton, "The New Export Entrepreneurs," *Fortune,* June 6, 1988, p. 98.

A company's marketing program ordinarily is influenced by whether that firm's markets are vertical or horizontal. In a vertical market, a product can be tailor-made to meet the specific needs of one industry. In a horizontal market, a product must be developed as an all-purpose item. Moreover, advertising and personal selling efforts can be directed more effectively in vertical markets.

**Buying Power of Business Users**

Another determinant of business market demand is the purchasing power of business customers. This can be measured either by the expenditures of business users or by their sales volume. Many times, however, such information is not available or is very difficult to estimate. In such cases it is more feasible to use an **activity indicator**—that is, some market factor related to income generation and expenditures. Sometimes an activity indicator is a combined indicator of purchasing power and the number of business users. Following are examples of activity indicators that might give some idea of the purchasing power of business users.

### MEASURES OF MANUFACTURING ACTIVITY

Firms selling to manufacturers might use as market indicators such factors as the number of employees, the number of plants, or the dollar value added by manufacturing. One firm selling work gloves determined the relative values of various geographic markets from the number of employees in manufacturing establishments. Another company that sold a product that controls stream pollution used two indicators: (1) the number of firms processing wood products (paper mills, plywood mills, and so forth) and (2) the manufacturing value added by these firms.

### MEASURES OF MINING ACTIVITY

The number of mines operating, the volume of their output, and the dollar value of the product as it leaves the mine all may indicate the purchasing power of mines. This information is useful to any firm marketing business products to mine operators.

The major business markets for some companies are in foreign countries.

### MEASURES OF AGRICULTURAL ACTIVITY

A company marketing fertilizer or agricultural equipment can estimate the buying power of its farm market by studying such indicators as cash farm income, acreage planted, or crop yields. The chemical producer that sells to a fertilizer manufacturer might study the same indices, because the demand for chemicals in this case derives from the demand for fertilizer.

### MEASURES OF CONSTRUCTION ACTIVITY

If an enterprise is marketing building materials, such as lumber, brick, gypsum products, or builders' hardware, its market depends on construction activity. This can be gauged by the number and value of building permits issued or by the number of construction starts by type of housing (single-family residence, apartment, or commercial).

## BUSINESS BUYING BEHAVIOR

Business buying behavior, like consumer buying behavior, is initiated when an aroused need (a motive) is recognized. This leads to goal-oriented activity designed to satisfy the need. Once again, marketing practitioners must try to determine what motivates the buyer, and then understand the organizational buying process and buying patterns.

### Buying Motives of Business Users

Business buying motives, for the most part, are presumed to be rational, and a business purchase normally is a methodical, objective undertaking. Business buyers are motivated primarily by a desire to maximize their firms' profits. More specifically, their buying goal is to achieve the optimal combination of price, quality, and service in the products they buy. On the other hand, sales people would maintain that some business buyers seem to be motivated more toward personal goals that are in conflict with their employers' goals.

Actually business buyers do have two goals—to improve their position in their firms (self-interest) and to further their company's position (in profits, in acceptance by society). Sometimes these goals are mutually consistent, but sometimes they are in conflict. Obviously the greater the degree of consistency, the better for both the organization and the individual. Probably it is more typical to find some overlap of interests, with a significant area where the buyer's goals do not coincide with those of the firm. In these cases a seller might appeal to the buyer both on a rational, "what's-good-for-the-firm" basis and on an ego-building basis. Promotional efforts attuned to the buyer's ego are particularly useful when two or more competing sellers are offering essentially the same products, prices, and services.

### Buying-Decision Process in Business

Competition and the complexity of business markets encourage companies to focus on the *total* buying process and treat buying as an ongoing relationship of mutual interest to both buyer and seller. As one example of this systems approach, we'll examine the buying-decision process in business markets. This process is a sequence of five stages similar to the ones experienced by consumers, discussed in the preceding chapter. Not every purchase involves all five steps. Routine purchases usually are low-involvement situations for the buyer, and some stages typically are skipped. But the first-time purchase of an expensive good or service is likely to be a high-involvement, total-stage buying decision.

To illustrate the process, let's assume that a company wants to buy 10 videocassette recorders (VCRs) for use in its branch-office sales training programs.

## AN ETHICAL DILEMMA?

It is not uncommon for companies to incorporate a "business gifts" category in their marketing or sales budgets. These gifts (including such articles as sweaters and attaché cases) are presented to current and prospective customers. Their value is usually based on an account's importance as measured by potential sales. Some people see business gifts as bribery. Others view them as effective promotional tools. Do you think giving business gifts is unethical? Assume you have just been appointed marketing vice president of a firm that has had a business gifts budget category for ten years. In preparing the budget for next year, should you include business gifts?

- *Problem recognition.* The sales executives are dissatisfied with the audiovisual equipment currently being used in their sales training programs. They have decided to buy VCRs so they can tape the buyer-seller role-playing exercises. The opportunity for instant replay will enable management to review and critique a trainee's performance.
- *Gathering information.* The sales executives draw up a list of product-performance specifications for the VCRs. The purchasing department then identifies the alternative brands, models, and sources of supply that generally meet these specifications.
- *Evaluation of alternatives.* The sales and purchasing people jointly evaluate both the alternative products and the alternative sources of supply. The buyer considers such factors as product quality, performance, and price, as well as a supplier's ability to meet commitments.
- *Purchase decision.* The buyer decides on a specific brand, model, and supplier. The purchasing department negotiates the final contract with the supplier.
- *Postpurchase behavior.* The buyer continues to evaluate the performance of the product and the supplier to ensure that both are "as advertised." Future dealings with this supplier will depend on this performance evaluation and on how well the supplier handles any problems that may later arise involving the product.

**Types of Buying Situations**

In Chapter 5 we observed that consumer purchases can range from routine to complex buying decisions. In like manner the buying situations in business organizations vary widely in their complexity, number of people involved, and time required. Researchers in organizational buying behavior have identified three classes of business buying situations. The three (called *buy classes*) are new-task buying, straight rebuy, and modified rebuy.[5]

- **New-task buying.** This is the most difficult and complex of the three. More people are involved in new-task buying than in the other two situations. Information needs are high and the evaluation of alternatives is

[5]Patrick J. Robinson, Charles W. Faris, and Yoram Wind, *Industrial Buying and Creative Marketing*, Allyn and Bacon, Boston, 1967. For a more current perspective, see Erin Anderson, Wujin Chu, and Barton Weitz, "Industrial Purchasing: An Empirical Exploration of the Buyclass Framework," *Journal of Marketing*, July 1987, pp. 71–86.

A product like this one typically is a new-task buying situation for a physician or hospital.

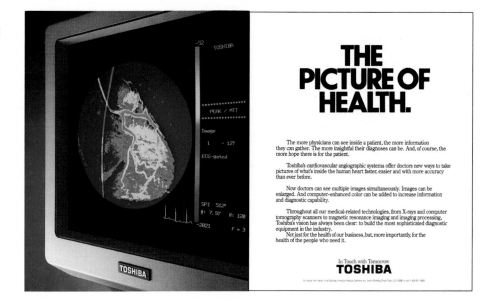

critical. Sellers have a great opportunity to display their creative selling abilities in satisfying the buyer's needs. A hospital's first-time purchase of laser surgical equipment or a company buying robots for a factory (or buying the factory itself) are new-task buying conditions.

- **Straight rebuy.** This is a routine, low-involvement purchase with minimal information needs and no great consideration of alternatives. Examples are repeat purchases of office supplies, janitorial supplies, and lubricating oils. Buying decisions are made in the purchasing department, usually from a predetermined list of acceptable suppliers. Suppliers who are not on this list may have difficulty getting in to make a sales presentation to the buyer.
- **Modified rebuy.** This buying situation is somewhere between the other two in terms of time and people involved, information needed, and alternatives considered.

**Multiple Buying Influences—The Buying Center**

One of the biggest challenges in business-to-business marketing is to determine which individuals in the organization play the various buying roles. That is, who influences the buying decision, who determines product specification, and who makes the buying decision? In the business market these activities typically involve several people. In other words, there is a **multiple buying influence,** particularly in medium-sized and large firms. Even in small companies where the owner-managers make all major decisions, knowledgeable employees are usually consulted before certain purchases are made.

Understanding the concept of a buying center is helpful in identifying the multiple buying influences and understanding the buying process in business organizations. A **buying center** may be defined as all the individuals or groups who are involved in the purchasing decision-making process. Thus a buying center includes the people who play any of the following roles:[6]

[6]Frederick E. Webster, Jr., and Yoram Wind, "A General Model for Understanding Organizational Buying Behavior," *Journal of Marketing,* April 1972, pp. 12–19. Also see Webster and Wind, *Organizational Buying Behavior,* Prentice-Hall, Englewood Cliffs, N.J., 1972, especially pp. 75–87.

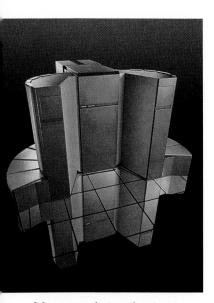

Many people in a buying center will influence the purchase of a product such as this computer.

- **Users.** The people who actually use the product—perhaps a secretary, a production-line worker, or a truck driver.
- **Influencers.** The people who set the specifications and aspects of buying decisions because of their technical expertise, their financial position, or even their political power in the organization.
- **Deciders.** The people who make the actual buying decision regarding the product and the supplier. A purchasing agent may be the decider in a straight rebuy situation. But someone in top management may make the decision regarding whether to buy an expensive computer.
- **Gatekeepers.** The people who control the flow of purchasing information within the organization as well as between the firm and potential vendors. These people may be purchasing agents, secretaries, receptionists, or technical personnel.
- **Buyers.** The people who select the suppliers, arrange the terms of sale, and process the actual purchase orders. Typically this is the purchasing department's role. But again, if the purchase is an expensive, complex new buy, the buyer's role may be filled by someone in top management.

Several people in an organization may play the same role—for instance, there may be several users of the product. Or the same person may occupy more than one role. A secretary may be a user, an influencer, and a gatekeeper in the purchase of an office machine.

The size and composition of a buying center will vary among business organizations. Within a given organization, the size and makeup of the buying center will also vary depending on the product's cost, complexity, and length of life. The buying center for a straight rebuy of office supplies will be quite different from the center handling the purchase of a building or a fleet of trucks.

It is probably obvious that the variety of people involved in any business buying situation, plus the difference among companies, present real challenges to sales people. As they try to determine "who's on first"—that is, determine who does what in a buying situation—sales reps often will call on the wrong executives. Even knowing who the decision makers are is not enough, because these people may be very difficult to reach.

Certainly the challenges presented in the business buying-decision process should suggest the importance of coordinating the selling activities of the business marketer with the buying needs of the purchasing organization.[7]

**Buying Patterns of Business Users**

Overt buying behavior in the *business* market differs significantly from *consumer* behavior in several ways. These differences obviously stem from differences in products, markets, and buyer-seller relationships.

### DIRECT PURCHASE

Direct sale from the producer to the ultimate consumer is rare, except in the case of services. In the business market, however, direct sale from the producer to the business user is quite common. This is true especially when the order is large and the buyer needs much technical assistance. From a seller's

[7]See Robert E. Spekman and Wesley J. Johnston, "Relationship Management: Managing the Selling and the Buying Interface," *Journal of Business Research*, December 1986, pp. 519–31; and Paul A. Dion and Peter M. Banting, "Industrial Supplier-Buyer Negotiations," *Industrial Marketing Management*, February 1988, pp. 43–47.

point of view, direct sale is reasonable, especially when there are relatively few potential buyers and the buyers are big and geographically concentrated.

### FREQUENCY OF PURCHASE

In the business market, firms buy certain products very infrequently. Large installations are purchased only once in many years. Smaller parts and materials to be used in the manufacture of a product may be ordered on long-term contracts, so that an actual selling opportunity exists one time a year. Even standard operating supplies, such as office supplies or cleaning products, may be bought only once a month.

Because of this buying pattern, a great burden is placed on the advertising and personal selling programs of business sellers. Their advertising must keep the company's name constantly before the market. The sales force must call on potential customers often enough to know when a customer is considering a purchase.

### SIZE OF ORDER

The average business order is considerably larger than its counterpart in the consumer market. This fact, coupled with the infrequency of purchase, spotlights the importance of each sale in the business market. Losing the sale of a pair of shoes to a consumer is not nearly so devastating as losing the sale of 10 airplanes.

### LENGTH OF NEGOTIATION PERIOD

The period of negotiation in a business sale is usually much longer than in a consumer market sale. General Electric, for example, negotiated over a 5-year period before completing the purchase of a $9.5 million Cray supercomputer.[8] Some of the reasons for extended negotiations are: (1) several executives participate in the buying decision; (2) the sale often involves a large amount of money; and (3) the business product is often made to order and considerable discussion is required to establish the specifications.

### RECIPROCITY ARRANGEMENTS

A highly controversial business buying practice is **reciprocity**—the policy of "I'll buy from you if you'll buy from me." Traditionally, reciprocity was common among firms marketing homogeneous basic business products (oil, steel, rubber, paper products, and chemicals). In these industries price competition generally did not exist, and a firm in one industry was a major supplier to a firm in another industry. Then, through the years, reciprocal selling expanded to a broad array of industries. Many companies established "trade relations" departments to make effective use of this powerful selling tool.

Today, however, most of these departments have vanished. There has been a significant decline (but not total elimination) in the practice of reciprocity on a *systematic* basis. This decline has occurred for two reasons—one legal and the other economic. Both the Federal Trade Commission and the Antitrust Division of the Department of Justice have forbidden the practice of reciprocity in any *systematic* manner, particularly in large companies. From an economic point of view, reciprocity may not make sense because the morale of both the sales force and the purchasing department may suffer. It is diffi-

---

[8]"Where Three Sales a Year Make You a Superstar," *Business Week*, Feb. 17, 1986, p. 76.

cult to justify purchasing from customers unless the buyer is getting competitive price, quality, and service from the seller.

### DEMAND FOR PRODUCT SERVICING

The user's desire for excellent service is a strong business buying motive that may determine buying patterns. Consequently, many sellers emphasize their service as much as their products. Frequently a firm's only differentiating feature is its service, because the product itself is so standardized that it can be purchased from any number of companies.

Sellers must stand ready to furnish services both before and after the sale. A manufacturer of computers may study a customer firm's accounting operations and suggest more effective systems that involve using the seller's products. The manufacturer will also arrange to retrain the present office staffs. After the machines have been installed, other services, such as repairs, may be furnished.

### DEPENDABILITY OF SUPPLY

Another business buying pattern is the user's insistence on an adequate quantity of uniform-quality products. Variations in the *quality* of materials going into finished products can cause considerable trouble for manufacturers. They may be faced with costly disruptions in their production processes if the imperfections exceed quality-control limits. Adequate *quantities* are as important as good quality. A work stoppage that is caused by an insufficient supply of material is just as costly as one that is caused by inferior quality of material. In one study of problems faced by purchasing agents for smaller manufacturers, the problem most often reported was the failure of sellers to deliver on schedule.

Adequacy of supply is a problem especially for sellers and users of raw materials such as agricultural products, metal ores, or forest products. Climatic conditions may disrupt the normal flow of goods—logging camps or mining operations may become snowbound. Agricultural products fluctuate in quality and quantity from one growing season to another. These "acts of God" create managerial problems for both buyers and sellers with respect to warehousing, standardization, and grading.

Heavy construction equipment frequently is leased, an arrangement that benefits both the user and the lessor.

### LEASING INSTEAD OF BUYING

A growing tendency among firms in the business market is **leasing** business products instead of buying them outright. In the past this practice was limited to large equipment, such as data processing machines (IBM), packaging equipment (American Can Company), and heavy construction equipment. Presently industrial firms are expanding leasing arrangements to include delivery trucks, sales-force automobiles, machine tools, and other items generally less expensive than major installations.

Leasing has several merits for the firm leasing out its equipment:

- Total net income—after charging off pertinent repair and maintenance expenses—is often higher than it would be if the unit were sold outright.
- Its market may be expanded to include users who could not afford to buy the product, especially large equipment.
- Leasing offers an effective method of getting distribution for a new product. Potential users may be more willing to rent a product than to buy it. If they are not satisfied, their expenditure is limited to a few monthly payments.

From the customer's point of view, the benefits of leasing may be summarized as follows:

- Leasing allows users to retain their investment capital for other purposes.
- There may be significant tax advantages. Rental payments are totally tax-deductible and usually are larger than corresponding depreciation charges on owned products.
- New firms can enter a business with less capital outlay than would be necessary if they had to buy the equipment outright.
- Leased products are usually serviced by lessors. This eliminates one headache associated with ownership.
- Leasing is particularly attractive to firms that need the equipment seasonally or sporadically, as in food canning or construction.

This ends our discussion of the consumer and business markets. When a company's executives know their markets, they are in a position to capture their desired share of those markets. They have the four components of the marketing mix—product, price, distribution system, and promotion—with which to attain their goals. Each of Parts 3, 4, 5, and 6 is devoted to one of these components.

## SUMMARY

The business market consists of organizations that buy goods and services to use in their firms or to resell. It is an extremely large, complex, and important market that covers a wide variety of business users that buy a broad array of business goods and services.

Business market demand may be generally characterized as being derived, inelastic, and widely fluctuating. Business buyers usually are quite well informed about what they are buying. Business market demand is analyzed by evaluating the same three basic factors as those in the consumer market: (1) the number and kinds of business users, (2) their buying power, and (3) their motivation and buying behavior. Business buying motives generally are rational, but the purchasing agent's self-interest must also be considered.

The buying-decision process in business markets may involve as many as five stages. The actual number of stages preceding a given purchase depends largely on the buying situation, whether new-task buying, straight rebuy, or modified rebuy.

The concept of a buying center reflects the multiple buying influences often involved in business purchasing decisions. In a typical buying center are people playing the roles of users, influencers, deciders, buyers, and gatekeepers. Buying patterns (habits) of business users often are quite different from patterns in the consumer market. In the business market, the negotiation period usually is longer, and purchases are made less frequently. Orders are larger, and direct purchases (no middlemen) are more common. Reciprocity arrangements and leasing (rather than product ownership) are quite common in business marketing.

## KEY TERMS AND CONCEPTS

Business market 140
Business products 140
Business marketing 140
Farm market 141
Agribusiness 142
Contract farming 142
Reseller market 143

Government market 143
Services market 144
Nonbusiness market 144
Derived demand 144
Inelastic demand 145
Standard Industrial Classification (SIC) system 148

## QUESTIONS AND PROBLEMS

1. "About 80 percent of all farm products are business goods." Give some examples of farm products that are consumer goods.

2. How does the government market differ from other business market segments?

3. If the demand for most business goods is inelastic, why is it that sellers do not raise their prices to maximize their revenues?

4. Why does the demand for business goods usually fluctuate more widely than that for consumer goods?

5. What are some marketing implications in the fact that the demand for business goods:
   a. Fluctuates widely?
   b. Is inelastic?
   c. Is derived?

6. What are the marketing implications for a seller in the fact that business customers are geographically concentrated and limited in number?

7. What differences would you expect to find between the marketing strategies of a company selling to horizontal business markets and those of a company selling to vertical business markets?

8. Select three advertisements for business goods or services and identify the buying motives appealed to in the ads.

9. An American manufacturer has been selling word processors to a large oil company in Norway. In which of the three buy classes would you place this buyer-seller relationship? Is there any aspect of the relationship that is likely to fall into the straight-rebuy category?

10. Explain how the five stages in the buying-decision process might be applied in the following buying situations:
    a. New-task buying of a conveyor belt for a soft-drink bottling plant.
    b. Straight rebuy of maintenance services for that conveyor belt.

11. What suggestions do you have to help sellers determine who influences the buying decision among business users?

12. In the buying center in a business organization, discuss briefly the role of each of the following:
    a. Influencers.
    b. Buyers.
    c. Gatekeepers.

13. Explain the ways in which the buying patterns in the business market typically differ from those in the consumer market.

14. NCR, IBM, Xerox, and other manufacturers of office machines make a substantial proportion of their sales directly to business users. At the same time, wholesalers of office equipment are thriving. Are these two market situations inconsistent? Explain.

## NIKE, INC.*  Analysis of a Changing Market

Jim Addison, the director of strategic planning at Nike, Inc., was wondering what marketing strategies his company should employ to effectively meet the competitive conditions he expected to encounter in the early 1990s. Nike no longer had the growth rate or market share that it once had enjoyed, so Addison's task was to design a marketing program to recapture the company's former market position. His experience told him that his first step should be to identify and analyze in some detail Nike's target market (the market demographics, consumer characteristics relevant to Nike products, and alternative market segmentation strategies).

Nike produces and markets a wide line of athletic shoes for track, tennis, football, basketball, soccer, and other sports. In addition, the company manufactures a line of leisure apparel such as shirts, shorts, socks, and warm-up suits. The company name was taken from Greek mythology where Nike is the goddess of victory and the speedy messenger for "top management"—Zeus and Athena. The company (originally called "Blue Ribbon Sportshoes") was started by a former member of the University of Oregon track team, Philip Knight, and his coach, Bill Bowerman.

Nike began by specializing in competitive running shoes, and the company's initial marketing program consisted of Knight persuading several top U.S. distance runners to try out the new shoe. In effect, Nike employed the testimonial approach, relying on a type of reference group influence that is used today by most athletic equipment marketers. The idea is for prominent athletes in a given sport to be seen using a certain brand of equipment. The hope of that brand's marketer is that other athletes and recreational sports participants then will purchase the brand.

In the 1970s Nike's growth was aided considerably by an important socio-cultural development: A

strong adult health and physical fitness movement began and gained momentum during the decade. Jogging and running became very popular, especially with the very large market of people in their 20s and 30s—the products of the baby boom following World War II. Running marathons (a race of 26.2 miles), formerly the domain of a few elite athletes, became the goal of thousands. Weekend races and fun runs to raise money for charity became commonplace in towns and cities across the country. Everyone seemed to be running or at least wearing running shoes, and Nike was in the right place with the right product at the right time. During those years the company's sales and market share increased dramatically.

Nike continued to build its marketing strategy around increasing the product's visibility. To this end, the company sponsored various athletic events and made payments to teams and to individual athletes for wearing Nike shoes in athletic competition. In the late 1970s, the company expanded its product line by marketing a variety of shoes for different track events. The company also added walking, casual, and leisure-time shoes appealing to people of all ages.

In the 1980s Nike's growth rate slowed and its market share declined. In fact, some knowledgeable people in the industry estimated that Nike's U.S. market share of athletic shoes dropped from a high of over 50 percent at the start of the decade to around 20 percent by the mid-1980s. A series of factors converged to cause that decline.

One factor was an increase in competition. Nike, of course, had always had strong competition. When Nike entered the athletic shoe market, Adidas, a German company, dominated the industry and another German firm, Puma, was also a strong competitor. In the United States, probably the best-known manufacturers were Converse, Rawlings, and Wilson. In the 1980s, however, the competitive situation changed. First, firms looked for ways to differentiate shoes.

---

*Adapted from a case prepared by Donald D. Bergh under the direction of Prof. James E. Nelson, University of Colorado.

**FIGURE 7-1** A product is more than just a product.

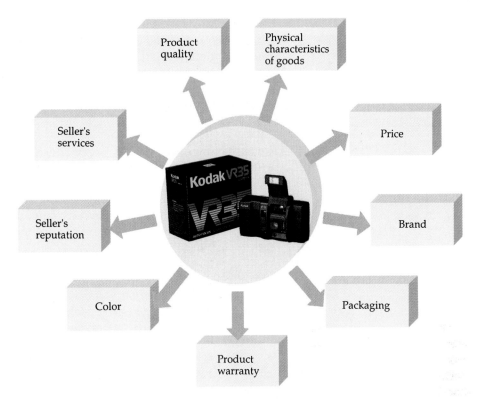

place, person, or idea. (See Figure 7-1.) In essence, then, consumers are buying more than a set of physical attributes. They are buying want-satisfaction in the form of product benefits.

## CLASSIFICATIONS OF PRODUCTS

Just as it is necessary for many firms to segment markets to improve marketing programs in many firms, so also it is helpful to separate *products* into homogeneous classifications. First we shall divide all products into two groups—consumer products and business products—in a classification that parallels our segmentation of the market. Then we shall divide each of these two categories still further.

### Consumer Products and Business Products

**Consumer products** are intended for use by household consumers for nonbusiness purposes. **Business products** are intended primarily for use in producing other products or for providing services in a business. The fundamental basis for distinguishing between the two groups is the *ultimate use* for which the product is intended in its present form.

Particular stages in a product's distribution have no effect on its classification. Cornflakes and children's shoes are classed as consumer goods, even if they are in the manufacturers' warehouses or on retailers' shelves, *if ultimately they will be used in their present form by household consumers*. Cornflakes sold to restaurants and other institutions, however, are classed as business goods.

Often it is not possible to place a product only in one class or the other. A personal computer may be considered a consumer good if it is purchased by a student or a homemaker for nonbusiness use. But if the same computer is bought by a traveling sales representative for business use, it is classed as a business good. The manufacturer of such a product recognizes that the product falls into both categories and therefore develops separate marketing programs for the two markets.

The two-way product classification is a useful framework for the strategic planning of marketing operations. Each major class of products ultimately goes to a different type of market and thus requires different marketing methods.[1]

## Classification of Consumer Goods

The marketing differences between consumer and business goods make this two-part classification of products valuable. Yet the range of consumer goods is still too broad for a single class. Consequently, consumer products are further classified as convenience goods, shopping goods, specialty goods, and unsought goods. (See Table 7-1.) This subdivision is based on consumer *buying behavior*—particularly the time and effort expended—rather than on *types of products*.

### CONVENIENCE GOODS

The significant characteristics of convenience goods are that (1) the consumer has adequate knowledge of the particular product wanted *before* going out to buy it and (2) the product is purchased with a minimum of effort. Normally the advantages resulting from shopping around to compare price and quality are not considered worth the extra time and effort required. A consumer is willing to accept any of several brands and thus will buy the one that is most accessible. For most buyers, this subclass of goods includes groceries, tobacco products, inexpensive candy, drug sundries such as toothpaste, and staple hardware items such as light bulbs and batteries.

Convenience goods typically have a low unit price, are not bulky, and are not greatly affected by fad and fashion. They usually are purchased frequently, although this is not a necessary characteristic. Items such as Christmas-tree lights or Mother's Day cards are convenience goods for most people, even though they may be bought only once a year.

A convenience good must be readily accessible when consumer demand arises, so the manufacturer must secure wide distribution. But since most retail stores sell only a small volume of the manufacturer's output, it is not economical to sell directly to all retail outlets. Instead the producer relies on wholesalers to reach part of the retail market.

Retailers usually carry several brands of a convenience item, so they are not able to promote any single brand. They are not interested in doing much advertising of these articles because many other stores carry them. Thus any advertising by one retailer may help its competitors. As a result, virtually the entire advertising burden is shifted to the manufacturer.

### SHOPPING GOODS

Shopping goods are products for which customers usually wish to compare quality, price, and style in several stores before purchasing. This search continues only as long as the customer believes that the gain from comparing products offsets the additional time and effort required. Examples of shop-

---

[1] For a different classification scheme that provides strategic guidelines for management by relating products and prices, along with an excellent bibliography on product classification, see Patrick E. Murphy and Ben M. Enis, "Classifying Products Strategically," *Journal of Marketing*, July 1986, pp. 24–42. Also see Ernest F. Cooke, "The Relationship between a Product Classification System and Marketing Strategy," *Journal of Midwest Marketing*, Spring 1987, pp. 230–40.

### TABLE 7-1 Consumer goods: characteristics and marketing considerations

| Characteristics and marketing considerations | Type of product* | | |
|---|---|---|---|
| | Convenience | Shopping | Specialty |
| **Characteristics:** | | | |
| Time and effort devoted by consumer to shopping | Very little | Considerable | Cannot generalize; consumer may go to nearby store and buy with minimum effort or may have to go to distant store and spend much time and effort |
| Time spent planning the purchase | Very little | Considerable | Considerable |
| How soon want is satisfied after it arises | Immediately | Relatively long time | Relatively long time |
| Are price and quality compared? | No | Yes | No |
| Price | Usually low | High | High |
| Frequency of purchase | Usually frequent | Infrequent | Infrequent |
| Importance | Unimportant | Often very important | Cannot generalize |
| **Marketing considerations:** | | | |
| Length of channel | Long | Short | Short to very short |
| Importance of retailer | Any single store is relatively unimportant | Important | Very important |
| Number of outlets | As many as possible | Few | Few; often only one in a market |
| Stock turnover | High | Lower | Lower |
| Gross margin | Low | High | High |
| Responsibility for advertising | Producer's | Retailer's | Joint responsibility |
| Importance of point-of-purchase display | Very important | Less important | Less important |
| Brand or store name imporant | Brand name | Store name | Both |
| Importance of packaging | Very important | Less important | Less important |

*Unsought products are not included. See text explanation.

ping goods include women's apparel, furniture, major appliances, and most automobiles.

With shopping goods, buying habits affect the distribution and promotional strategy of both manufacturers and middlemen. Manufacturers of shopping goods require fewer retail outlets because consumers are willing to look around for what they want. To increase the convenience of comparison shopping, manufacturers try to place their products in stores located near other stores carrying competing items. Similarly, department stores and other retailers who carry primarily shopping goods like to be grouped together.

Manufacturers usually work closely with retailers in the marketing of shopping goods. Since manufacturers use fewer retail outlets, they are more dependent on those they do select. Retail stores typically buy shopping goods in large quantities. Distribution direct from manufacturer to retailer is common. Store names often are more important to buyers of shopping goods than manufacturers' names.

### SPECIALTY GOODS

Specialty goods are those products for which consumers (1) have a *strong* brand preference and (2) are willing to expend special time and effort in purchasing them. The consumer is willing to forgo more accessible substitutes in order to procure the wanted brand. Examples of products usually classified as specialty goods include expensive men's suits, stereo sound equipment, health foods, photographic equipment, and, for many people, new automobiles and certain home appliances.

Since consumers *insist* on a particular brand and are willing to expend considerable effort to find it, manufacturers can afford to use fewer outlets. Ordinarily the manufacturer deals directly with these retailers. The retailers are extremely important, particularly if the manufacturer uses only one in each area. And where the franchise to handle the product is a valuable one, the retailer may become quite dependent on the producer. Manufacturers and retailers are interdependent; the success of one is closely tied to the success of the other.

Because brand is important and because only a few outlets are used, both the manufacturer and the retailer advertise the product extensively. Often the manufacturer pays some portion of the retailer's advertising costs, and the retailer's name frequently appears in the manufacturer's ads.

When buying shoes, do you consider them to be a shopping good or a specialty good?

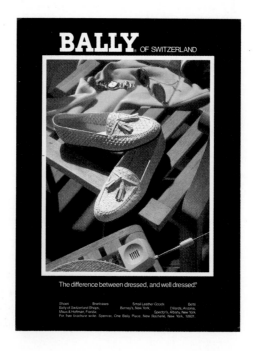

## UNSOUGHT GOODS

The very title of this category suggests a somewhat unusual type of product that does not parallel the three categories already discussed. For this reason unsought goods are not included in Table 7-1.

There are two kinds of unsought products: (1) new products that the consumer is not yet aware of, and (2) products that right now the consumer does not want. For some people products in the first group might include computers that speak or video telephones. Examples of the second type of product might include prepaid burial insurance or gravestones. The title of this product category suggests that a seller faces a monumental advertising and personal selling job when trying to market these products.[2]

**Classification of Business Goods**

As is the case with consumer goods, the general category *business goods* is too broad to use in developing a marketing program. Consequently, we separate business goods into five categories: raw materials, fabricating materials and parts, installations, accessory equipment, and operating supplies. (See Table 7-2.) This classification is based on the broad *uses* of the product.

## RAW MATERIALS

Raw materials are business goods that will become part of another physical product. They have not been processed in any way, except as necessary for economy or protection during physical handling. Raw materials include: (1) goods found in their natural state, such as minerals, land, and products of the forests and the seas; and (2) agricultural products such as wheat, cotton, fruits, vegetables, livestock, and animal products like eggs and raw milk. These two groups of raw materials are marketed quite differently.

The marketing of raw materials in their natural state is influenced by several factors. The supply of these products is limited and cannot be substantially increased. Usually only a few large producers are involved. The products must be carefully graded and, consequently, are highly standardized. Because of their great bulk, their low unit value, and the long distances between producer and business user, transportation is an important consideration. These products generally are of a commodity nature with no product differentiation within a given grade or quality level. Thus their prices are set by supply and demand, approximating the conditions of perfect competition.

These factors necessitate short channels of distribution and a minimum of physical handling. Frequently, raw materials are marketed directly from producer to business user. At most, one intermediary may be used. The limited supply forces users to assure themselves of adequate quantities. Often this is done either by (1) contracting in advance to buy a season's supply of the product or (2) owning the source of supply. Advertising and other forms of demand stimulation are rarely used. There is very little branding or other product differentiation. Competition is built around price and the assurance that a producer can deliver the product as specified.

Agricultural products used as business raw materials are supplied by many small producers located some distance from the markets. The supply is largely controllable by producers, but it cannot be increased or decreased

---

[2] For examples of how some companies handle the problem of promoting unsought products, see Lenora Skenazy, "Burial Marketer Undertakes TV Spots," *Advertising Age*, Nov. 30, 1987, p. 30; and Paul A. Engelmayer, "Cemetery Companies Aggressively Market Burial Plots as Costs Soar and Business Falls," *The Wall Street Journal*, Jan. 24, 1984, p. 35.

rapidly. The product is perishable and is not produced at a uniform rate throughout the year.

Close attention must be given to transportation and warehousing. Transportation costs are high relative to unit value, and standardization and grading are very important. Because producers are small and numerous, many middlemen and long channels of distribution are needed. Very little promotional activity is involved.

**TABLE 7-2 Classes of business goods: characteristics and marketing considerations**

| Characteristics and marketing considerations | Type of product | | | | |
|---|---|---|---|---|---|
| | Raw materials | Fabricating parts and materials | Installations | Accessory equipment | Operating supplies |
| **Example:** | Iron ore | Engine blocks | Blast furnaces | Storage racks | Paper clips |
| **Characteristics:** | | | | | |
| Unit price | Very low | Low | Very high | Medium | Low |
| Length of life | Very short | Depends on final product | Very long | Long | Short |
| Quantities purchased | Large | Large | Very small | Small | Small |
| Frequency of purchase | Frequent delivery; long-term purchase contract | Infrequent purchase, but frequent delivery | Very infrequent | Medium frequency | Frequent |
| Standardization of competitive products | Very much; grading is important | Very much | Very little; custom-made | Little | Much |
| Quantity of supply | Limited; supply can be increased slowly or not at all | Usually no problem | No problem | Usually no problem | Usually no problem |
| **Marketing considerations:** | | | | | |
| Nature of channel | Short; no middlemen | Short; middlemen only for small buyers | Short; no middlemen | Middlemen used | Middlemen used |
| Negotiation period | Hard to generalize | Medium | Long | Medium | Short |
| Price competition | Important | Important | Not important | Not main factor | Important |
| Presale/postsale service | Not important | Important | Very important | Important | Very little |
| Promotional activity | Very little | Moderate | Sales people very important | Important | Not too important |
| Brand preference | None | Generally low | High | High | Low |
| Advance buying contract | Important; long-term contracts used | Important; long-term contracts used | Not usually used | Not usually used | Not usually used |

### FABRICATING MATERIALS AND PARTS

Fabricating materials and parts are business goods that become an actual part of the finished product. They have already been processed to some extent, in contrast to raw materials. Fabricating **materials** will undergo further processing. Examples include pig iron going to steel, yarn being woven into cloth, and flour becoming part of bread. Fabricating **parts** will be assembled with no further change in form. They include such products as zippers on clothing and semiconductor chips in computers.

Fabricating materials and parts are usually purchased in large quantities. To ensure an adequate, timely supply, a buyer may place an order a year or more in advance. Because of such buying habits, most fabricating products are marketed on a direct-sale basis from producer to user.

Middlemen are used most often if the buyers are small or if small fill-in orders for rapid delivery are placed. Normally buying decisions are based on the price and the service provided by the seller. Branding is generally unimportant. However, some firms have made successful attempts to pull their products out of obscurity by identifying them with a brand. Talon zippers and the NutraSweet brand of sweetener are notable examples.

### INSTALLATIONS

Installations are manufactured business products—the long-lived, expensive, major equipment of a business user. Examples are large generators in a dam, a factory building, diesel engines for a railroad, blast furnaces for a steel mill, and jet airplanes for an airline. The differentiating characteristic of installations is that they *directly affect the scale of operation in a firm.* Adding 12 new typewriters will not affect the scale of operation at American Airlines, but adding 12 new jet airplanes certainly will. Therefore, the airplanes are classed as installations, but the typewriters usually are not.

The marketing of installations presents a real challenge to management because every single sale is important. Usually no middlemen are involved; sales are made directly from producer to business user. Typically the unit sale is large, and often the product is made to the buyer's detailed specifications. Much presale and postsale servicing is required. A high-caliber sales force is needed to market installations, and sales engineers are frequently used. Promotional emphasis is on personal selling rather than advertising, although some advertising is used.

Airplanes are considered installations for American or Northwest Airlines because they affect the company's scale of operations. But company planes for executives' transportation are accessory equipment.

### ACCESSORY EQUIPMENT

Accessory equipment is used in the production operations of a business firm, but it does not have a significant influence on the scale of operations. Accessory equipment does not become an actual part of the finished product. The life of accessory equipment is shorter than that of installations, and longer than that of operating supplies. Some examples are cash registers in a retail store, small power tools, forklift trucks, and the typewriters mentioned above.

It is difficult to generalize about the distribution policies of firms marketing accessory equipment. In some cases direct sale is used. This is true particularly when an order is for several units of the product or when the product is of relatively high unit value. A firm that manufactures forklift trucks may sell directly because the price of a single unit is large enough to make this distribution policy profitable. In the main, however, manufacturers of accessory equipment use middlemen. They do so because (1) the market is geographically dispersed, (2) there are many different types of potential users, and (3) individual orders may be relatively small.

### OPERATING SUPPLIES

Operating supplies are the "convenience goods" of the business sector. They are short-lived, low-priced items usually purchased with a minimum of effort. They aid in a firm's operations but do not become a part of the finished product. Examples are lubricating oils, pencils and stationery, registration supplies in a university, heating fuel, and washroom supplies.

Like consumer convenience products, business operating supplies must be distributed widely. The producing firm makes extensive use of wholesaling middlemen because the product is low in unit value, is bought in small quantities, and goes to many users. Price competition is heavy because competitive products are quite standardized and there is little brand insistence.

## IMPORTANCE OF PRODUCT INNOVATION

The social and economic justification for the existence of a business is its ability to satisfy its customers while making a profit. A company meets this basic responsibility to society through its products. Effective new-product planning and development are vital to a company today. Good executive judgment elsewhere cannot offset weaknesses in product planning. A company simply cannot successfully sell a bad product over the long run.

### Requirement for Growth

A watchword for management is "innovate or die." For many companies a substantial portion of sales volume and net profit this year will come from

### AN ETHICAL DILEMMA?

A magazine ad for Log Cabin syrup points out that it is the only leading brand made with pure maple syrup. The claim is true, but a careful reading of the list of contents on the package label reveals that only two percent of Log Cabin is pure maple syrup. Is it ethical to emphasize maple syrup as an ingredient when it makes up such a small proportion of the product?

products that did not exist 5 to 10 years ago. Because products, like people, go through a life cycle, new products are essential for sustaining a company's expected rate of profit. They grow (in sales), then decline, and eventually are replaced.

The concept of the product life cycle is discussed in more detail in Chapter 8, but we mention it here because it has two significant implications for product innovation. First, every company's present products will eventually become obsolete as their sales volume and market share are reduced by competitive products. Second, as a product ages, its profits generally decline. The introduction of a new product at the proper time will help maintain a company's desired profit level.

## Increased Consumer Selectivity

In recent years, consumers have become more selective in their choice of products. As consumers' disposable income has increased, and as an abundance of products has become available, consumers have fulfilled many of their wants. The large middle-income group is reasonably well fed, clothed, housed, transported, and equipped. If market satiation—in terms of quantity—does exist to some extent, it follows that consumers may be more critical in their appraisal of new products. While the consumer has become increasingly selective, the market has been deluged with products that are imitations or that offer only marginal competitive advantages. This may lead to "product indigestion." The cure is to develop *truly* new products—to *innovate* and not just *imitate*.

## Resources and Environmental Considerations

We are finally realizing that the supply of many of our natural resources is limited and irreplaceable. These two conditions clearly demonstrate the importance of careful new-product planning. Increasingly, environmental factors will influence product decisions, because we simply cannot afford to continue wasting our natural resources and polluting our environment. Both K mart and Wal-Mart, for example, have publicly stated a commitment to carry merchandise and packaging that are better for the environment in their manufacturing, use, and disposal.

## DEVELOPMENT OF NEW PRODUCTS

It has been said that nothing happens until somebody sells something. This is not entirely true. First there must be something to sell—a good, a service, or an idea—something that is in some way new. And that "something" must be developed.

## What Is a "New" Product?

Just what is a "new" product? Are the new models that auto manufacturers introduce each autumn new products? If a firm adds a wrinkle-remover cream to its assortment of women's cosmetics, is this a new product? Or must an item be totally new in concept before we can class it as a *new* product?

Here we need not seek a very limited definition. Instead, we can recognize several possible categories of new products. What is important, however, is that each separate category may require a quite different marketing program to ensure a reasonable probability of success.

Three recognizable categories of *new products* are as follows:

- Products that are *really* innovative—truly unique. Examples would be a hair restorer or a cancer cure—products for which there is a real need but for which no existing substitutes are considered satisfactory.
- Replacements for existing products that are *significantly* different from the

Some new products are significantly better than existing ones. The picture on the left shows an improved-definition TV screen. On the right is the same image photographed from an ordinary color-television screen.

existing ones. Disposable contact lenses and improved-definition television (much sharper image) are replacing some traditional models. Michael Foods Company in Minneapolis has developed a technology for removing most of the cholesterol from fresh eggs, while at the same time extending their shelf life. Compact disc players are replacing conventional stereo record players. In certain years, annual model changes in autos and new fashions in clothing are different enough to fit into this category.

- Imitative products that are new to a particular company but not new to the market. A company may simply want to capture part of an existing market with a "me-too" product. Thus Polaroid broke its long-standing policy when it introduced a line of conventional (noninstant) film to compete directly with Kodak, Fuji, and others. Several hotel chains have added all-suite hotels. Although not new to the market, these services were new to particular chains such as Marriott or Quality Inns.

In the final analysis, of course, whether a given product is new depends on how the intended market perceives it. If buyers perceive that a given item is significantly different from competitive goods in some characteristic (appearance, performance), then it is a new product.

## Selection of New-Product Strategy

The development process for new products should begin with the selection of an explicit new-product strategy. This strategy then can serve as a meaningful guideline throughout the step-by-step development process for each new product.

The purpose of an effective overall new product strategy is to identify the strategic role new products will play in achieving corporate and marketing goals.[3] For example, a new product might be designed to defend a market-share position or to maintain the company's position as a product innovator.

[3] See *New Products Management for the 1980s*, Booz, Allen & Hamilton, New York, 1982, pp. 10–11.

**AN INTERNATIONAL PERSPECTIVE: New-product development for international markets**

The people who brought you Toyotas, Nikons, VCRs, and the Walkman are preparing to branch out across the globe with new high-tech products and an array of services. Here is a sample of what can be expected from Japan in international marketing during the 1990s:

- Matchbox-size tape recorders that do not need cassettes.
- High-definition TV sets that have the clarity of movies.
- TV sets that can also serve as home computers.
- Magnetic-levitation trains that travel 320 miles per hour.
- Robots that sew, wash windows, or smooth concrete floors better and faster than humans.
- Air conditioners that use much less power than current models.
- Telephones that translate foreign languages as you talk.
- Sports cars to compete with Ferrari and Lamborghini, but at about half the price.

- Personal computers a fraction of the size of current IBM and Apple models.
- JCB Company, Japan's credit-card giant, plans to expand internationally from its present 30,000-card level into a multimillion-card level.
- Japanese banks, already comprising 9 of the 10 largest banks in the world, will continue expanding their financial services in many foreign countries.
- Retail stores (Sogo, Takashimaya, and others) are opening branches in Hong Kong, Singapore, California, and New York.
- Investments in travel services (hotels, resorts, golf courses) to accommodate the vast Japanese tourist spending.
- In construction services, 5 of the world's top 10 revenue-producing firms are Japanese, and they are expanding their activity in Europe and the United States.

Source: Gene Bylinsky, "Where Japan Will Strike Next," *Fortune*, Sept. 25, 1985, p. 42.

Or the product's role might be to meet a specific return-on-investment goal or to establish a position in a new market.

A new product's intended role also will influence the *type* of product to be developed. To illustrate:

| Company goal | | Product strategy |
|---|---|---|
| To defend a market-share position. | ⟶ | Introduce an addition to an existing product line, or revise an existing product. |
| To further the company's position as an innovator. | ⟶ | Introduce a *really* new product—not just an extension of an existing one. |

Only in recent years have many companies consciously identified new-product strategies as a separate activity in the development process. Since then, however, there has been a dramatic increase in the efficiency of the development process. A survey by the Booz, Allen & Hamilton management consulting firm reported that in 1968 there were 58 new-product ideas considered for every successful new product introduced. In 1981 only seven new-product ideas were required to generate one successful new product—truly a dramatic reduction in the mortality rate for new-product ideas.[4]

[4]*New Products Management for the 1980s,* p. 14. For a report on several new product strategies and their impact on performance results, see Robert G. Cooper, "Industrial Firms' New Product Strategies," *Journal of Business Research,* April 1985, pp. 107–21; and Robert G. Cooper, "Overall Corporate Strategies for New Product Programs," *Industrial Marketing Management,* August 1985, pp. 175–93.

**Steps in the Development Process**

With the company's new-product strategy as a guide, the development of a new product can proceed through a series of six steps, as shown in Figure 7-2. During each stage management must decide whether to move on to the next stage, abandon the product, or seek additional information.

The first two steps—idea generation and evaluation—are tied closely to the overall new-product strategy. This strategy can provide (1) a focus for generating new-product ideas and (2) a criterion for screening and evaluating these ideas.

1. *Generation of new-product ideas.* New-product development starts with an idea. It is particularly important to develop a system within an organization for stimulating new ideas and then acknowledging and reviewing them promptly. Customers can also be encouraged to design ways to generate new-product ideas.

2. *Screening and evaluation of ideas.* New-product ideas are evaluated to determine which ones warrant further study.

3. *Business analysis.* A new-product idea that survives to this stage is expanded into a concrete business proposal. Management (*a*) identifies product features, (*b*) estimates market demand, competition, and the product's profitability, (*c*) establishes a program to develop the product, and (*d*) assigns responsibility for further study of the product's feasibility.

**FIGURE 7-2** Major stages in the new-product development process.

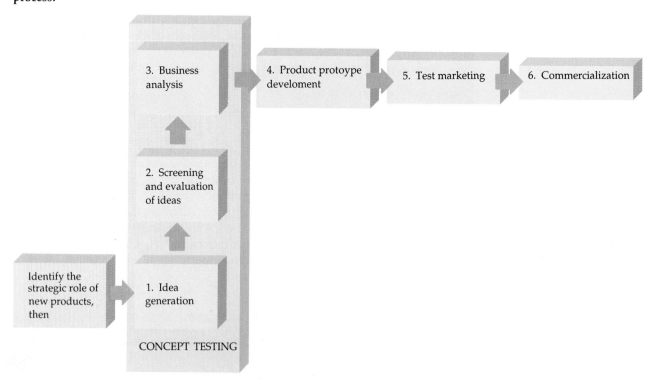

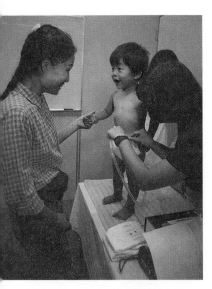

Procter & Gamble did extensive product and market testing of its Pampers disposable diapers in Japan.

These first three steps are together referred to as *concept testing*. This is pretesting of the product *idea*, as contrasted to later pretesting of the product itself and its market.[5]

4. *Product development.* The idea-on-paper is converted into a physical product. Pilot models or small quantities are manufactured to designated specifications. Laboratory tests and other technical evaluations are made to determine the production feasibility of the article.

5. *Test marketing.* Market tests, in-use tests, and other commercial experiments in limited geographic areas are conducted to ascertain the feasibility of a full-scale marketing program. In this stage, design and production variables may have to be adjusted as a result of test findings. Management must now make a final decision regarding whether or not to market the product commercially.

6. *Commercialization.* Full-scale production and marketing programs are planned, and the product is launched. Up to this point in the development process, management has virtually complete control over the product. Once the product is "born" and enters its life cycle, however, the external competitive environment becomes a major determinant of its destiny.

In this six-step evolution, the first three—the idea, or concept, stages—are the critical ones. They are the least expensive, as each stage becomes progressively more costly in dollars and scarce human resources. But more important, many products fail because either the idea or the timing is wrong—and these three stages are designed to identify such situations.[6]

## Producer's Criteria for New Products

When should a proposed new product be added to a company's existing product assortment? Here are guidelines that some producers use in answering this question:

- There should be an *adequate market demand*. This is by far the most important criterion to apply to a proposed product. Too often management begins with a question such as, "Can we use our present sales force?" or "Will the new item fit into our production system?" The basic question is, "Do enough people really want this product?"
- The product should fit from a *financial* standpoint. At least three questions should be asked: Is adequate financing available? Will the new item increase seasonal and cyclical stability in the firm? Are the profit possibilities worthwhile?
- The product must be compatible with current *environmental and social standards*. Do the production processes heavily pollute air or water (as do steel or paper mills)? Will the use of the finished product be harmful to the environment (as are automobiles)? After being used, is the product harmful to the environment (as are DDT and some detergents)? Does the product have recycling potential?

---

[5]For a further discussion of concept testing, with an excellent bibliography, see William L. Moore, "Concept Testing," *Journal of Business Research*, September 1982, pp. 279–94; and David A. Schwartz, "Concept Testing *Can* Be Improved—and Here's How to Do It," *Marketing News*, Jan. 6, 1984, p. 22.

[6]For a report on the criteria used in making go/no-go decisions at major stages in the product-development process, see Ilkka A. Ronkainen, "Criteria Changes across Product Development Stages," *Industrial Marketing Management*, August 1985, pp. 171–78.

Reebok believed that there was a strong market demand for the pump feature of its new athletic shoes.

the
pump
Pump it up.
Introducing The Pump™ by Reebok.® It's the first shoe with a built-in pump that inflates to give you a personalized fit you control with your fingertips. You pump up by squeezing the ball on the tongue, and release air with the valve on back. You've never seen or felt a shoe like this before. Check it out.
Reebok
Basketball

- The product should fit into the company's present *marketing* structure. The general marketing experience of the company is important here. Bill Blass probably would find it easy to add designer sheets and towels to his clothing line, whereas paint manufacturers would find it quite difficult to add margarine to theirs. More specific questions may also be asked regarding the marketing fit of new products: Can the existing sales force be used? Can the present channels of distribution be used?
- A new-product idea will be more favorably received by management if it fits in with existing *production* facilities, labor, and management capabilities.
- There must be no *legal* objections. Patents must be applied for, labeling and packaging must meet existing regulations, and so on.
- *Management* in the company must have the experience, time, and ability to deal with the new product.
- The product should be in keeping with the *company's image and objectives.* A firm stressing low-priced, high-turnover products normally should not add an item that suggests prestige or status.

## Middleman's Criteria for New Products

Retailers and wholesalers considering whether to take on a new product should apply the above criteria except those related to production. In addition, a middleman should consider:

- *The relationship with the producer.* The producer's reputation, the possibility of getting exclusive sales rights in a given geographic territory, and the type of promotional and financial help given by the producer.
- *In-store policies and practices.* What kind of selling effort is required for the

new product? How does the proposed product fit with store policies regarding repair service, alterations (for clothing), credit, and delivery?

**NEW-PRODUCT ADOPTION AND DIFFUSION PROCESSES**

The opportunity to market a new product successfully is increased if management understands the adoption and diffusion processes for that product. The **adoption process** is the decision-making activity of *an individual* through which the new product—the innovation—is accepted. The **diffusion** of the new product is the process by which the innovation is spread through a *social system* over time.[7]

**Stages in Adoption Process**

A prospective user goes through the following six stages during the process of deciding whether to adopt something new:

| Stage | Activity in that stage |
|---|---|
| Awareness.<br>↓ | Individual is exposed to the innovation; becomes a prospect. |
| Interest.<br>↓ | Prospect is interested enough to seek information. |
| Evaluation.<br>↓ | Prospect mentally measures relative merits. |
| Trial.<br>↓ | Prospect adopts the innovation on a limited basis. A consumer buys a small sample; if for some reason (cost or size) an innovation cannot be sampled, the chances of its being adopted will decrease. |
| Adoption.<br>↓ | Prospect decides whether to use the innovation on a full-scale basis. |
| Postadoption confirmation. | The innovation is adopted; then the user continues to seek assurance that the right decision was made |

**Adopter Categories**

Some people will adopt an innovation quickly after it has been introduced. Others will delay before accepting a new product, and still others may never adopt it. Researchers have identified five categories of individuals, based on the point in time when they adopt a given innovation. Nonadopters are excluded from this categorization. Characteristics of early and late adopters are summarized in Table 7-3.

**INNOVATORS**

Innovators, a *venturesome* group, constitute about 3 percent of the market and are the first to adopt an innovation. In relation to later adopters, the innovators are likely to be younger, have a higher social status, and be in a better financial position. Innovators also tend to have broader, more cosmopolitan social relationships. They are likely to rely more on impersonal sources of information, rather than on sales people or other word-of-mouth sources.

**EARLY ADOPTERS**

Early adopters—about 13 percent of the market—tend to be part of a local social system. Whereas innovators have broad social involvements *outside* a local community, early adopters are more likely to function *within* a local

---

[7]For foundations of diffusion theory, a review of landmark studies on diffusion of innovation, and extensive bibliographic references, see Everett M. Rogers, *Diffusion of Innovations,* 3rd ed., The Free Press, New York, 1983.

**TABLE 7-3 Characteristics of early and late adopters of new products**

|  | Early adopters | Late adopters |
|---|---|---|
| **Key characteristics:** | | |
| Venturesome | Innovators (3% of total adopters) | |
| Respected | Early adopters (13%) | |
| Deliberate | Early majority (34%) | |
| Skeptical | | Late majority (34% of total adopters) |
| Tradition-bound | | Laggards (16%) |
| **Other characteristics:** | | |
| Age | Younger | Older |
| Education | Well educated | Less educated |
| Income | Higher | Lower |
| Social relationships: within or outside community | Innovators: outside Others: within | Totally local |
| Social status | Higher | Lower |
| Information sources | Wide variety; many media | Limited media exposure; limited reliance on outside media; reliance on local peer groups |

community. Thus the early-adopter category includes more opinion leaders than any other adopter group. Early adopters are greatly *respected* in their social system. A change agent is a person who is seeking to speed up the diffusion of a given innovation. A change agent often will try to work through the early adopters because they are not too far ahead of others in their peer group. As information sources, sales people are probably used more by early adopters than by any other category.

### EARLY MAJORITY

The more *deliberate* group, the early majority, represents about 34 percent of the market. This group often accepts an innovation just before the "average" adopter in a social system. This group is a bit above average in social and economic measures. Its members rely quite a bit on advertisements, sales people, and contact with early adopters.

### LATE MAJORITY

Representing about another 34 percent of the market, the late majority is a *skeptical* group. Usually its members adopt an innovation in response to an economic necessity or to social pressure from their peers. They rely on their peers—late or early majority—as sources of information. Advertising and personal selling are less effective with this group than is word-of-mouth.

### LAGGARDS

This *tradition-bound* group—16 percent of the market—includes those who are last to adopt an innovation. Laggards are suspicious of innovations and innovators. By the time laggards adopt something new, it may already have been discarded by the innovator group in favor of a newer idea. Laggards are older and usually are at the low end of the social and economic scales.

At this point we might recall that we are discussing only *adopters* (early or late) of an innovation. For most innovations there still are many people who are *not* included in our percentages. These are the people who *never* adopt the innovation—the nonadopters.

**Innovation Characteristics Affecting Adoption Rate**

The following five characteristics of an innovation, as perceived by individuals, seem to influence the adoption rate:[8]

- *Relative advantage.* The degree to which an innovation is superior to preceding ideas. Relative advantage may be reflected in lower cost, higher profitability, or some other measure.
- *Compatibility.* The degree to which an innovation is consistent with the cultural values and experiences of the adopters.
- *Complexity.* The more complex an innovation is, the less quickly it will be adopted.
- *Trialability.* The degree to which the new idea may be sampled on some limited basis. For instance, a central home air-conditioning system is likely to have a slower adoption rate than a new seed or fertilizer, which may be tried on a small plot of ground.
- *Observability.* The more an innovation can be seen to work, the more likely it is to be adopted. A weed killer that works on existing weeds will be accepted sooner than a preemergent weed killer. The reason is that the latter—even though it may be a superior product—produces no dead weeds to show to prospective buyers.

## ORGANIZING FOR PRODUCT INNOVATION

For new-product programs to be successful, *they must be supported by a strong and continuing commitment from top management over the long term.* Furthermore, this commitment must be maintained even in the face of the failures that are sure to occur in some individual new-product efforts. To effectively implement this commitment to innovation, new-product programs must be soundly organized.

## Types of Organization

There is no "one best" organizational structure for new-product planning and development. Many companies use more than one structure to manage these activities. Some widely used organizational structures for planning and developing new products are:

- *Product-planning committee.* Members usually include the company president and executives from major departments—marketing, production, finance, engineering, and research.
- *New-product department.* Generally these units are small, consisting of four or five or even fewer people, and the department head reports to the president.
- *Venture team.* A venture team is a small, multidisciplinary group, organizationally segregated from the rest of the firm. It is composed of representatives of engineering, production, finance, and marketing research. The team operates in an entrepreneurial environment, in effect being a separate small business. Typically the group reports directly to top management.[9]

On completion of the development process, responsibility for marketing a

---

[8] Rogers, op. cit.
[9] See Frank G. Bingham and Charles J. Quigley, Jr., "Venture Team Application to New Product Development," *Journal of Business and Industrial Marketing,* Winter–Spring 1989, pp. 49–59.

new product usually is shifted to another organizational unit. This unit may be an existing department or a new department established just for this new product. In some cases the team that developed the product may continue as the management nucleus of a newly established division in the company.

Which of these particular organizational structures is chosen is not the critical point here—each has its strengths and weaknesses. The key point is to make sure that some person or group has the specific organizational responsibilities for new-product development—and is backed by top management. Product innovation is too important an activity to handle in an unorganized, nonchalant fashion, figuring that somehow the job will get done.

However, integrating new products into departments that are already marketing established, mature products does carry at least two risks. First, the executives involved with ongoing products may have a short-term outlook as they deal with day-to-day problems of existing products. Consequently, they tend to put the new products on the back burner, so to speak. Second, managers of successful existing products often are reluctant to assume the risks inherent in marketing new products.

---

### Some novel approaches to product innovation—

For years the 3M Company (Scotch Tape, Post-it note pads) has been a case study in successful new-product development. To continue as a smooth-running "innovation machine," the company relies on a few simple rules, such as:

- Keep divisions small. Division managers must know each staffer's first name.
- Tolerate failure. Encouraging experimentation and risk-taking increases chances for a new-product hit.
- Motivate the winners. Salaries and promotions are tied to a product's progress. The successful innovator has a chance to run his or her own product division someday.
- Stay close to the customer. 3M people routinely visit customers and invite them to help brainstorm product ideas.
- Don't kill a product. A 3M employee can devote 15 percent of his or her time to prove a project is workable. And $50,000 "Genesis" grants are awarded to those who need seed money.

Other companies ranked among the "innovation elite" have their own approaches to product innovation:

- Rubbermaid. Thirty percent of sales must come from products developed during the past 5 years.
- Hewlett-Packard. Researchers are urged to spend 10 percent of their time on their own pet projects, with 24-hour access to labs and equipment.
- Dow Corning. Forms research partnership with customers.
- Merck. Gives researchers time and resources to pursue high-risk, high-payoff products—such as Mevacor, an anticholesterol drug that is a potential gold mine, yet experts believed the research leading to its development would be fruitless.
- General Electric. Develops products jointly with customers.
- Johnson & Johnson. The freedom to fail is a built-in corporate cultural prerogative.

Source: "Masters of Innovation," *Business Week*, Apr. 10, 1989, p. 62.

## PRODUCT MANAGER

In many companies, a product manager—sometimes called a brand manager or a merchandise manager—is responsible for planning related to *new* products as well as to *established* ones. A large company may have many product managers who report to higher marketing executives.

In many large firms—Procter & Gamble, Pillsbury, and General Foods, to name a few—the product manager's job is quite broad. This executive is charged with *planning the complete marketing program* for a brand or group of products. Responsibilities may include developing new products along with improving established products. Setting marketing goals, preparing budgets, and developing plans for advertising and field selling activities are some of the product manager's tasks. At the other extreme, some companies limit product managers' activities essentially to the areas of selling and sales promotion.

Probably the biggest problem in the product-manager system is that a company will saddle these executives with great responsibility, yet it may *not* give them the corresponding authority. They must develop the field selling plan, but they have no line authority over the sales force. Product managers do not select advertising agencies, yet they are responsible for developing advertising plans. They have a profit responsibility for their brands, yet they are often denied any control over product costs, prices, or advertising budgets. Their effectiveness depends largely on their ability to influence other executives to cooperate with their plans.

Interestingly enough, there are some indications that the product-manager system may change considerably in the 1990s. The product-manager system was widely adopted and thrived during the period of economic growth and market expansion in the 1950s to 1970s. In the 1980s, however, many industries experienced slow economic growth in maturing markets, coupled with a trend toward strategic planning that stressed centralized managerial control. Because of these environmental forces, one study concludes that the product-manager system is being modified in many companies and eventually will be abolished in some firms.[10]

**SUMMARY**

If the first commandment in marketing is "Know thy customer," then the second is "Know thy product." A firm can best serve its customers by producing and marketing truly want-satisfying goods or services. In light of a scarcity of resources and a growing concern for our environment, socially responsible product innovation becomes even more crucial. The new products marketed by a firm are a prime determinant of that company's growth rate, profits, and total marketing program.

To manage their product assortments effectively, marketers should understand the full meaning of the term *product* and the different concepts of what a *new product* is. Products can be classified into two broad categories—consumer products and business products. Then each of these two major groups should be further subdivided, because a different marketing program is required for each subgroup.

Six steps in the development process for new products are built on the initial, clear statement of the intended new-product strategy. The early stages

---

[10]See Victor P. Buell, "Firms to Modify, Abolish Product Manager Jobs Due to Sluggish Economy, Centralized Planning," *Marketing News*, Mar. 18, 1983, p. 8. Also see Al Urbanski, "Repackaging the Brand Manager," *Sales & Marketing Management*, April 1987, pp. 42–45.

in this process are especially important. If a firm can make an early (and proper) decision to drop a product, a lot of money and labor can be saved. In its decision regarding whether to accept or reject a new product, there are several criteria for a manufacturer or middleman to consider. The product should fit in with marketing, production, and financial resources. But the key issue is that there *must* be an adequate market demand for the product. Management should understand the adoption and diffusion processes for a new product. Adopters of a new product can be divided into five categories, depending on how quickly they adopt a given innovation. In addition, there usually is a group of nonadopters.

Organizational relationships are typically reported as a major problem in new-product planning and development. Top management must be deeply committed to product innovation and must support this activity in a creative fashion. Most firms that report reasonable success in product innovation seem to use one of these four organizational structures for new-product development: product-planning committee, new-product department, venture team, or product-manager system.

| KEY TERMS AND CONCEPTS | | |
|---|---|---|
| Product 168 | Relation of sales volume and profit over life of a product 177 | |
| Consumer products 169 | New product 177 | |
|    Convenience goods 170 | New-product strategy 178 | |
|    Shopping goods 170 | New-product development process 180 | |
|    Specialty goods 172 | | |
|    Unsought goods 173 | Concept testing 181 | |
| Business products 169 | Test marketing 181 | |
|    Raw materials 173 | Adoption process 183 | |
|    Fabricating materials and parts 175 | Diffusion 183 | |
|    Installations 175 | New-product adopter categories 183 | |
|    Accessory equipment 176 | Product manager 187 | |
|    Operating supplies 176 | | |

## QUESTIONS AND PROBLEMS

1. In what respects are the products different in each of the following cases?
   a. A Whirlpool dishwasher sold at an appliance store and a similar dishwasher sold by Sears under its Kenmore brand name. Assume Whirlpool makes both dishwashers.
   b. A Sunbeam Mixmaster sold by a leading department store and the same model sold by a discount house.
2. a. Explain the various interpretations of the term *new product*.
   b. Give some examples, other than those cited in this chapter, of products in each of the three new-product categories.
3. "As brand preferences are established with regard to women's clothing, these items, which traditionally have been considered shopping goods, will move into the specialty-goods category. At

the same time, women's clothing is moving into supermarkets and variety stores, thus indicating that some articles are convenience goods." Explain the reasoning in these statements. Do you agree that women's clothing is shifting away from the shopping-goods classification? Explain.

4. In what way is the responsibility for advertising a convenience good divided between the producer and the retailers? A shopping good? A specialty good?
5. Compare the elements of a producer's marketing mix for a convenience good with those of the mix for a specialty good.
6. In which of the five subclassifications of business products should each of the following be included? Which products may belong in more than one category?
   a. Trucks.

b. Medical X-ray equipment.
c. Typing paper.
d. Copper wires.
e. Printing presses.
f. Nuts and bolts.
g. Paper clips.
h. Land.

7. What factors account for the growing importance of product planning?

8. In developing new products, how can a firm make sure that it is being socially responsible in regard to scarce resources and our environment?

9. What are some of the questions that management is likely to want answered during the business analysis stage of new-product development?

10. Assume that the following organizations are considering the following additions to their product lines. In each case, should the proposed product be added?
    a. McDonald's—salad bar.
    b. Safeway—automobile tires.
    c. Exxon—personal computers.
    d. Banks—life insurance.
    e. General Motors—outboard motors for boats.

11. Several new products from Japan were described in the International Perspective. In your opinion, which ones will enjoy the greatest market success in the United States? Explain your choices.

12. In the "trial" stage of deciding whether to adopt an innovation, the likelihood of adoption is reduced if the product cannot be sampled because of its cost or size. What are some products that might have these drawbacks? How might these problems be overcome?

13. Describe the people likely to be found in (a) the innovator category of adopters and (b) the late-majority category.

14. What are some of the problems typically connected with the product-manager organizational structure?

# CHAPTER 8
# PRODUCT-MIX STRATEGIES

# CHAPTER 8 GOALS

At any given time, a firm may be marketing some new products and some older ones, while others are being planned and developed. This chapter focuses on managing the entire range of products. After studying this chapter, you should be able to explain:

- The difference between product mix and product line.
- The major product-mix strategies
  a. Positioning.
  b. Expansion.
  c. Trading up and trading down.
  d. Alterations.
  e. Contraction.
- The management of a product throughout its life cycle.
- Planned obsolescence
  a. Style and fashion.
  b. The fashion-adoption process.

Toyota and Nissan have positioned their new luxury cars, the Lexus and the Infiniti, to compete directly against Cadillac, Lincoln, Mercedes, and BMW. Maxwell House introduced Private Collection gourmet coffees, and Marriott moved into the medium-priced motel market with Courtyard Hotels. The Gap clothing chain tested a store for high-income shoppers, and several pet-food producers traded up into superpremium pet foods. Eastman Kodak began to market disposable cameras, and Polaroid added conventional (noninstant) film to its product assortment. Campbell Soup added Great Starts Budget Breakfasts (frozen) suitable for microwave ovens. Johnson & Johnson, makers of Band-Aids and Tylenol, moved into the field of disposable contact lenses.

Gillette has altered its pivot-head razor in what appears to be another breakthrough in shaving comfort and closeness. Several firms are planning to substitute olestra or Simplesse for fat in their food products. General Mills, the producer of Wheaties and Betty Crocker products, discontinued marketing toys, games, and Izod (alligator label) clothing. The makers of Retin-A rejuvenated the product by marketing it as an effective wrinkle-remover, and the various producers of aspirin have found new life for their product as a medicine against heart attacks. Cajun cuisine became very popular in the late 1980s, so many restaurants and food producers moved to capitalize on this current fashion. Benetton, called the McDonald's of fashion, has learned to adapt its fashion merchandise to local tastes in different markets around the world. •

One common thread permeates this wide array of product changes. All illustrate strategies related to the company's mix of products. The management of that assortment is the topic of this chapter.

## PRODUCT MIX AND PRODUCT LINE

The **product mix** is the full list of all products offered for sale by a company. The structure of the product mix has dimensions of both breadth and depth. Its breadth is measured by the number of product lines carried; its depth, by the variety of sizes, colors, and models offered within each product line. A product-mix structure is illustrated in Figure 8-1.

A broad group of products, intended for essentially similar uses and possessing reasonably similar physical characteristics, constitutes a **product line.** Wearing apparel is one example of a product line. But in a different context, say, in a small specialty shop, men's furnishings (shirts, ties, and underwear) and men's ready-to-wear (suits, sport jackets, topcoats, and slacks) would each constitute a line. In another context, men's apparel is one line, as contrasted with women's apparel, furniture, or sporting goods.

## MAJOR PRODUCT-MIX STRATEGIES

Several major strategies used by producers and middlemen in managing their product mix are discussed next. Later in the chapter we'll look at planned obsolescence as a product strategy and fashion as an influence on the product mix.

### Positioning the Product

Management's ability to position a product appropriately in the market is a major determinant of company profit. A product's **position** is the image that the product projects in relation to competitive products as well as to other products marketed by the same company.

Marketing executives can choose from a variety of positioning strategies, some of which are as follows:[1]

- *Positioning in relation to a competitor.* For some products the best position is directly against the competition. Thus, Campbell Soup's Casera brand of Caribbean-style Hispanic foods was promoted head-to-head against Goya

**FIGURE 8-1 Product mix—breadth and depth.**
Part of the product mix in a lawn and garden store.

| | Breadth (different lines) | |
|---|---|---|
| Lawn mowers | Gardening tools | Lawn furniture |
| Power rotary | Rakes | Chairs |
| Power reel-type | Hoes | Chaise lounges |
| Hand-powered | Pruning shears | Benches |
| ——————— | Shovels | ——————— |
| Each in various sizes and prices | ——————— | Various sizes and prices in redwood or aluminum with plastic webbing |
| | Each in various sizes and prices | |

Depth (assortment within a line)

[1]Adapted from David A. Aaker and J. Gary Shansby, "Positioning Your Product," *Business Horizons,* May–June 1982, pp. 56–58.

Sears is using specialty departments to position its large stores against competition from specialty retailers.

Foods.[2] Cadillac introduced its Allante car to compete directly with the European prestige cars, and Coca-Cola and Pepsi-Cola meet each other head-on. For other products, head-to-head positioning is exactly what *not* to do, especially when a competitor has a strong market position. Canon entered the office-copier market with a desktop model—thus seeking a market niche that would avoid any head-on confrontation with Xerox.

Sears repositioned itself against its competitors when it recognized that old-line department stores no longer were so dominant on the retailing scene. Sears faced stiff competition on two fronts: specialty retailers such as The Limited and Circuit City appliance stores, and low-overhead price discounters such as Wal-Mart and K mart. To meet this competition Sears established specialty departments; for example, its "Brand Central" appliance department carries major name-brands in addition to the Sears' Kenmore brand. Sears now markets a specialty line of children's clothing called McKids, under an agreement with McDonald's. To meet the discounters' challenge, Sears made major organizational changes to speed up decision making, reduce overhead costs, and unsnarl a cumbersome bureaucracy. The company also adopted a strategy of "everyday low prices" to replace the strategy of frequent sales.[3]

- *Positioning in relation to a target market.* To reach younger, more fashion-oriented consumers (who are heavy users of paint), Sherwin-Williams repositioned its 80-year-old Dutch Boy brand of paint. This repositioning strategy involved redesigning the packaging and the color system. Also, an advertising campaign that was quite different (at least for the paint industry) emphasized fashion and the finished appearance of the painted surface. This new strategy was in contrast to the traditional strategy of stressing paint's durability, washability, and one-coat coverage.[4] As another example, consider the positioning of Miller Lite beer. Other reduced-calorie beers were introduced before Miller Lite. However, they typically had been promoted as low-calorie beers and were targeted at diet-conscious consumers who usually drank very little beer. In contrast,

[2]See Alfredo Corchado, "Campbell Soup Is Seeking to Be Numero Uno Where Goya Reigns," *The Wall Street Journal*, Mar. 28, 1988, p. 24.
[3]See "The Big Store's Big Trauma" *Business Week*, July 10, 1989, p. 50.
[4]Cyndee Miller, "Dutch Boy Repositions Itself to Reach Upscale, Fashion-Oriented Consumers," *Marketing News*, July 4, 1988, p. 1.

Miller Lite was aimed at the male blue-collar worker (a heavy-user beer-drinking market). The new promotional appeal is that Miller Lite is a beer that beer lovers can drink more of because it is less filling.

- *Positioning in relation to a product class.* Sometimes a company's positioning strategy entails associating its product with (or dissociating it from) a common class of product. Libby's, Del Monte, Campbell Soup, Kellogg's cereals, and other food processors introduced product lines with one common denominator—no salt (or very little) was added. Thus these items were positioned against food products that are packed with the conventional (larger) amounts of salt.
- *Positioning by price and quality.* Certain retail stores are known for their high-quality merchandise and high prices (Saks Fifth Avenue, Neiman-Marcus). Positioned at the other end of the price and quality scale are discount stores such as Target and K mart. In recent years both K mart and J.C. Penney have tried to *reposition* themselves on the price-quality spectrum by upgrading their apparel lines and stressing designer names. Their goal is to upgrade their fashion and quality image, while retaining their low-price image. Price and quality repositioning can be a dangerous strategy, however. A company runs the risk of blurring its image and confusing its present customers, yet the firm may not gain many new customers for the higher-price quality merchandise.

## Expansion of Product Mix

A firm may elect to expand its present product mix by increasing the number of lines and/or the depth within a line. The new lines may be related or unrelated to present products.

Dannon increased the depth of its yogurt line by adding liquid yogurt and Dannon Light (lower in calories, sweetened with NutraSweet). Eastman Kodak added a 35mm disposable camera called Fling. Several large securities brokers (Merrill Lynch was the first) have started credit-card operations, financial planning services, and other cash management services. Arthur Andersen Company and other public accounting firms have expanded into management consulting services. Universities now offer programs to appeal to prospective older students. The Roman Catholic church broadened its line of religious services by adding Saturday and Sunday evening masses.

Expanding into an unrelated line, Johnson & Johnson (Band-Aid, Tylenol) introduced a line of disposable contact lenses called Acuvue. Swatch, a Swiss watch company, added a line of clothes. Sony, a Japanese company, increased its international presence by purchasing Columbia movie studios. Banks are using their Automatic Teller Machines (ATMs) to sell rail passes in Portland, Oregon, gift certificates in Tacoma, Washington, postage stamps in Pittsburgh, and discount movie tickets in Phoenix.[5]

## Trading Up and Trading Down

As product strategies, trading up and trading down involve, essentially, an expansion of the product line and a change in product positioning. **Trading up** means adding a higher-priced, prestige product to a line to attract a higher-income market. At the same time, the seller intends that the prestige of its new product will help the sale of its existing lower-priced products. For instance, to its line of inexpensive sport watches Swatch added a Limelight model with four diamonds set in its face and priced at around $100. Maxwell

[5]Christopher J. Chipello, "Banks Start Spicing Up Their ATM Menus," *The Wall Street Journal,* Oct. 5, 1989, p. B1.

House coffee introduced its Private Collection gourmet coffees targeted at a market of younger, more active people. Manufacturers of pet foods also traded up to superpremium lines as exemplified by Kal Kan's Pedigree, Quaker Oats' King Kuts, Carnation's Grand Gourmet, and Ralston Purina's O.N.E. Holiday Inn's Crowne Plaza Hotels, a chain of high-rise upscale hotels, are targeted at more affluent business travelers. K mart traded up with designer-labeled women's clothing (Gloria Vanderbilt, Jonathan Logan), German wines, gourmet pots and pans, and other higher-priced, name-brand merchandise. The company hopes to attract higher-income shoppers without losing its traditional customer base of discount shoppers.

When a company embarks on a policy of trading up, at least two avenues are open with respect to promotional emphasis:

- The seller may continue to depend on the older, lower-priced product for the bulk of the sales volume and promote it heavily.
- The seller may gradually shift promotional emphasis to the new product and expect it to produce the major share of sales volume. In fact, the lower-priced line may be dropped altogether after a transition period.

A company is said to be **trading down** when it adds a lower-priced item to its line of prestige products. The firm expects that people who cannot afford the original product will want to buy the new one because it carries some of the status of the higher-priced product. In line with this strategy, the Marriott Corporation has been building Courtyard by Marriott hotels, which are targeted at the mid-price market now dominated by chains such as Holiday Inn and Ramada Inn, and Fairfield Inns to compete in the low-priced market. Sometimes the effect of trading down can be achieved through advertising,

Trading down can be an effective but risky product strategy.

without introducing new, lower-priced products. Thus, both the Steuben Glass and Waterford Glass companies traded down simply by advertising some of their lower-priced pieces of crystal.[6]

Trading up and trading down are perilous strategies because the new products may confuse buyers, so that the net gain is negligible. Nor is any useful purpose served if sales of the new item are generated at the expense of the older products. When *trading down* is employed, the new article may permanently hurt the firm's reputation and that of its established high-quality product.

In *trading up*, on the other hand, the seller's major problem is to change the firm's image enough so that new customers will accept the higher-priced product. At the same time, the seller does not want to lose its present customers. The real risk is that the company will lose *both* customer groups through this change in its product positioning. Former customers may become confused because the company has clouded its image; and the new target market may not believe that the company is marketing truly high-quality merchandise.

## Alteration of Existing Products

As an alternative to developing a completely new product, management should take a fresh look at the company's existing products. Often improving an established product can be more profitable and less risky than developing a completely new one. The substitution of NutraSweet for saccharin in diet soft drinks increased sales of those drinks. Many food producers expect similar sales gains when the government approves the use of Procter & Gamble's olestra and NutraSweet's Simplesse fat substitutes. Olestra will be used in baked and fried foods. Simplesse will replace fat in dairy products such as ice cream, margarine, processed cheese, and salad dressing.

For some products, *redesigning* is the key to their renaissance. Scott Paper Company produced a narrower paper towel, Scott Towel, Jr., in an effort to carve a new niche in the highly competitive paper towel market. *Packaging* is another popular type of product alteration, especially for consumer products. Sales of Aziza nail polish increased considerably when this product was repackaged in a felt-tip applicator pen. The d-Con Company also put its ant and cockroach insecticide in a felt-tip pen with which invisible, insect-killing lines could be drawn in places that were difficult to spray. Even something as mundane as bread, glue, or cheesecloth can be made more attractive by means of creative packaging and display.

## Contraction of Product Mix

Another product strategy is to thin out the product mix, either by eliminating an entire line or by simplifying the assortment within a line. The shift from fat and long lines to thin and short lines can weed out low-profit products and get higher profits from fewer products. General Mills (Wheaties, Betty Crocker, Gold Medal flour) decided to concentrate on its food business and, consequently, sold its interest in Izod (the "alligator" apparel maker) and its line of toys and Parker Brothers games. Similarly, some travel agencies have discontinued selling a full line of travel services and are concentrating on specialized tours and trips to exotic places. And numerous physicians eliminated their line of obstetrical services in order to reduce their liability risks and insurance costs.

The practice of slimming the product mix has long been recognized as an

---

[6]See Ronald Alsop, "Companies Pitch Elite Brands to Less Elite Target Audience," *The Wall Street Journal,* Nov. 6, 1986, p. 35.

important product strategy. However, during the past decade it has been used extensively to cope with economic and competitive conditions as well as to retrench from the highly expansionary strategies of earlier years.

## THE PRODUCT LIFE CYCLE

As we saw in Chapter 7, products have life cycles that can have a direct bearing on a company's survival. The life cycle of a product can be divided into four stages: introduction, growth, maturity, and decline. It is essential to note that the product life-cycle concept applies to a generic category of product (microwave ovens, for example) and not to specific brands (such as Amana). A product life cycle consists of the aggregate demand for all brands comprising a generic product category. A company's marketing success can be affected considerably by its ability to understand and manage the life cycles of its products. The product life cycle can be illustrated with the sales volume and profit curves, as shown in Figure 8-2. The *shapes* of these curves will vary from product to product. However, the basic shapes and the relationship between the two curves are usually as illustrated.

The profit curve for most new products is negative through most of the introductory stage. Also, in the latter part of the growth stage, the profit curve starts to decline while the sales volume is still ascending. This occurs because a company usually must increase its advertising and selling effort or cut its prices (or do both) to continue its sales growth during the maturity stage in the face of intensifying competition. Introducing a new product at the proper time will help maintain the company's desired level of profit.

## Characteristics of Each Stage

Management must recognize what part of the life cycle its product is in at any given time. The competitive environment and resultant marketing strategies ordinarily will differ depending on the stage.

### INTRODUCTION

During the first stage of a product's life cycle, it is launched into the market in a full-scale promotion and marketing program. It has gone through the embryonic stages of idea evaluation, pilot models, and test marketing. The entire

**FIGURE 8-2** Typical life cycle of a product—sales and profit curves.

Profit usually starts to decline while a product's sales volume is still increasing. How does the relationship between these curves influence the time at which additional new products should be introduced?

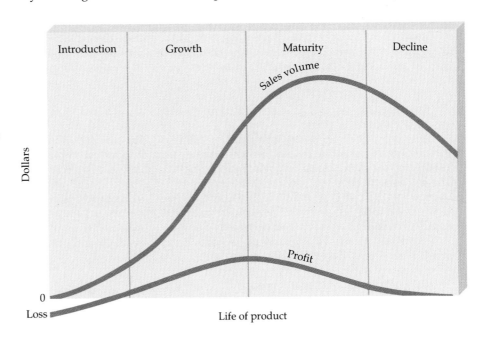

product may be new, like a machine that cleans clothes electronically without using any water. Or the basic product may be well known but have a new feature or accessory that is in the introductory stage—a gas turbine engine in an automobile, for example.

There is a high percentage of product failures in this stage. Operations in the introductory period are characterized by high costs, low sales volume, net losses, and limited distribution. In many respects the pioneering stage is the most risky and expensive one. However, for really new products, there is very little direct competition. The promotional program is designed to stimulate *primary*, rather than *secondary*, demand, by emphasizing the *type of product*, rather than the *seller's brand*.

### GROWTH

In the growth, or market-acceptance, stage, both sales and profits rise, often at a rapid rate. Competitors enter the market—in large numbers if the profit

---

**AN INTERNATIONAL PERSPECTIVE: Product strategies for international markets**

The first wave of Japanese products to hit the American shoreline—autos, TVs, VCRs, microchips—relied largely on low-cost labor and high-quality manufacturing to compete with domestically produced goods. Now a second wave is quietly building up. It consists of inexpensive consumer goods that couple product innovation with an obsessive dedication to customer service. Large Japanese companies such as Suntory, Shiseido, Kao, and Nissin want to go international with such products as soft drinks, cosmetics, laundry detergent, and soup. When they do, they will be bucking strong marketers such as Coca-Cola, Estée Lauder, Procter & Gamble, and Campbell Soup.

Suntory and Kirin have been exporting beer to the United States for about 20 years, so they know better than to position their soda head-to-head against Coca-Cola or Pepsi-Cola. Instead, seeking a noncola niche, they are gradually introducing into the United States their fresh-tasting canned coffee and tea drinks, which are highly popular in Japan.

Shiseido, a giant cosmetics firm, failed in its initial venture into the American market because the company attempted to sell the same products it sold in Japan. Those products required too many time-consuming steps, so the company withdrew temporarily from the U.S. market and designed a new line of cosmetics to appeal to American women. Shiseido's reentry into the American market was accompanied by a lavish treatment of customers. Since then the company's U.S. sales have increased at an annual rate of 25 percent.

Kao Corporation, the largest marketer of detergents, diapers, and toothpaste in Japan, introduced a super-concentrated (one spoonful per wash) laundry detergent. This new product, named Attack, soon captured 30 percent of the Japanese market, reducing Procter & Gamble's market share from over 20 percent to 8 percent. Analysts believe that eventually Kao will export Attack to the United States. Already Kao has acquired an established distribution system by virtue of buying the Andrew Jergens Company, an American manufacturer of skin lotion and soap.

Nissin, a Japanese noodlemaker, has quietly expanded its position in the dry-soup market in the United States. Nissin's Oodles of Noodles competes against Campbell with advertisements claiming that dry soup tastes better than canned soup. And Nissin's two U.S. manufacturing plants enable it to provide frequent delivery of small quantities. Thus the company claims a freshness advantage over its major dry-soup competitor, Lipton's Cup-a-Soup.

The Japanese realize that these inexpensive consumer goods markets won't be as easy to enter as were the auto and electronics markets. U.S. firms, several of which have competed for years in Japan's home markets, are not likely to be caught sleeping again. But the Japanese will continue to be formidable competitors in product innovation. Their long-run outlook enables them to accept early market setbacks and product mistakes. They simply pull back temporarily, revamp their products and marketing strategies, and try again.

Source: Brian Dumaine, "Japan's Next Push in U.S. Markets," *Fortune*, Sept. 26, 1988, p. 135.

outlook is particularly attractive. Sellers shift to a secondary-demand rather than a primary-demand promotional strategy. The number of distribution outlets increases, economies of scale are introduced, and prices may come down a bit. Typically, profits start to decline near the end of the growth stage.

### MATURITY

During the first part of this period sales continue to increase, but at a decreasing rate. While sales are leveling off, the profits of both the producer and the retailers are declining. Marginal producers are forced to drop out of the market. Price competition intensifies. The producer assumes a greater share of the total promotional effort in the fight to retain dealers and shelf space in their stores. New models are introduced as producers broaden their lines, and trade-in sales become significant.

### DECLINE AND POSSIBLE ABANDONMENT

For virtually all products, obsolescence inevitably sets in as new products start their own life cycles and replace the old ones. Cost control becomes increasingly critical as demand drops. Advertising declines, and a number of competitors withdraw from the market. Whether the product has to be abandoned or whether the surviving sellers can continue on a profitable basis often depends on management's abilities.

**Length of Product Life Cycle**

The length of the life cycle varies among products. It will range from a few weeks or short season (for a fad or clothing fashion) to many decades (for autos or telephones). In general, however, product life cycles are getting shorter. Rapid changes in technology can make a product obsolete virtually overnight. Or if competitors can quickly introduce a "me-too" version of a popular product, this product may move swiftly into the maturity stage.

Are fax machines in the introductory or growth stage of their life cycle?

Although Figure 8-2 suggests that the life-cycle stages cover nearly equal periods of time, the stages in any given product's life cycle usually last for *different* amounts of time. Also the duration of each stage will vary among products. Certain products take years to pass through the introductory stage, whereas others are accepted in a few weeks. Moreover, not all products go through all the stages. Some fail in the introductory stage, and others are not introduced until the market is in the growth or maturity stage. In most cases, however, decline and possible abandonment are inevitable for one of the following reasons:

- The need for the product disappears (as when frozen orange juice generally eliminated the market for juice squeezers).
- A better or less expensive product is developed to fill the same need (electronic microchips made possible many replacement products).
- People simply grow tired of a product (a clothing style, for instance), so it disappears from the market.

## Life Cycle Is Related to a Market

When we say a product is in its growth stage or some other stage, implicitly we are referring to a specific market. A product may be well accepted (growth or maturity stage) in a number of markets but be in the introductory stage in other markets. To illustrate, Ortho Pharmaceutical's Retin-A was introduced as a treatment for teenage acne. In the late 1980s this product was in the maturity stage in the teenage market. Having proven to be a wrinkle-remover, however, in the late 1980s Retin-A entered the introductory stage in the market of middle-aged and older people.

In terms of an international market, a product may be in its maturity stage in one country, and be in the introductory stage or perhaps even unknown in another country. Sink-installed garbage disposals, for example, are well known and widespread in the United States. Yet they are very rare in Japan and virtually unknown in many parts of Italy. Steel-belted radial auto tires were in their maturity stage in Western Europe well before they were introduced broadly in the United States. Soccer (called football in the rest of the world) is in its maturity stage as a spectator sport and recreational activity in most countries, but in the United States it is still in the introductory stage.

## Management of the Product Life Cycle

The shape of a product's sales and profit curves is not predetermined. To a surprising extent, the shape can be controlled. Successful life-cycle management strategies are (1) to predict the shape of the proposed product's cycle even before it is introduced and (2) at each stage to anticipate the marketing requirements of the following stage. The introductory period, for instance, may be shortened by broadening the distribution or by increasing the promotional effort.[7]

### STRATEGY FOR ENTRY STAGE

In the management of a product's life cycle, a crucial question concerns the timing of entry into the new market. Should we enter during the introductory stage? Or should we wait and plunge in during the early part of the growth stage, after innovating companies have proved that there is a viable market?

The strategy of entering during the introductory stage is based on the idea

---

[7]For an excellent discussion of strategies that can be employed in managing a product's life cycle, see Sak Onkvisit and John J. Shaw, "Competition and Management: Can the Product Life Cycle Help?" *Business Horizons*, July–August 1986, pp. 51–62.

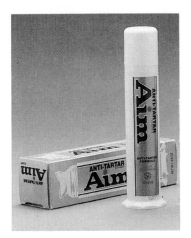

Pump-dispenser packaging worked for mustard and skin lotions, so let's try it for toothpaste.

of building a dominant market position and thus lessening the effectiveness of competition. This was the tactic pursued by Sony Walkman, Amana and Litton in microwave ovens, Perrier in bottled sparkling water, and Nike in running shoes. Marketing executives and published research generally support this strategy. The hurdles may be insurmountable when you enter with a "me-too" product and try to play catch-up.

At the same time, there are compelling reasons for delaying entry until the market is proven. Pioneering requires a large investment, and the risks are great—as demonstrated by the high failure rate among new products. Later-entry success stories usually come out of large companies with the marketing resources to overwhelm smaller innovating firms. In one such case, Royal Crown's Diet Rite Cola, an early pioneer, was later surpassed by Tab, Diet Coke, and Diet Pepsi. And after Apple proved there was a viable market, IBM successfully entered the personal computer field.

There is no clear-cut answer as to which is the better timing strategy. Perhaps the best answer is that old reliable in marketing—it all depends. Each strategy has its advantages and limitations, its successes and failures. Certainly sound executive judgment is critical, whatever decision is made.[8]

### MANAGING DURING MATURITY STAGE

A product's line may be extended during the maturity stage of its life cycle by making product modifications, designing new promotion, or devising new uses. We find one example of this in the refrigerator industry—an industry considered dull and mature even by some people in it. Admiral rejuvenated this staid product by adding features that enable the user to make ice cream, cold soup, and slush drinks. The company also built in a wine rack and microwave storage trays.

In 1988 Du Pont's Teflon celebrated its fiftieth birthday. But management continues to keep this mature product very much alive and growing by devising new uses for it. For instance, Teflon was packaged in a spray can to be used (among other purposes): on walls to protect against fingerprints; on neckties to repel food stains; and on ski clothes to keep them dry in snow.[9] Even aspirin—certainly the epitome of a mundane, mature product—found a new market among people who have survived one heart attack. Aspirin was proven to reduce considerably the chances of a second attack.

### AN ETHICAL DILEMMA?

In advertising copy prepared for local newspapers, Firestone's Traxx radial tires are described as "the tire America needs, the price America wants." However, the ad also states that Firestone dealers will no longer be selling the tire after the current inventory is gone. If you were a store manager and you knew the tire model was being discontinued, would you consider it ethical to run the ad in your community's newspaper?

---

[8]For more on this subject, see Steven P. Schnaars, "When Entering Growth Markets, Are Pioneers Better than Poachers?" *Business Horizons*, March–April 1986, pp. 27–36.

[9]Laurie Hays, "Teflon Is 50 Years Old, but Du Pont Is Still Finding New Uses for Invention," *The Wall Street Journal*, Apr. 7, 1988, p. 30.

---

### Ten ways to dream up new products and revitalize older ones

Originally, some of these ideas were intended to stimulate new-product development and others were for revitalizing older products. Whatever the case may be, they can create additional sales for a company.

- *Take something out of the product.* Removing caffeine and sugar from soft drinks and some of the sodium from various processed foods resulted in new products.
- *Add something to the product.* Extra-large chocolate chips boosted sales of Keebler's Chips Deluxe. Periodically, soap and detergent makers add something new to a basic product—bleach, softener, lemon scent, or an antistatic agent.
- *Listen to consumers' complaints.* "The smell of my antiperspirant clashes with my perfume." "Why is the fruit in my yogurt always at the bottom?" Listening to these gripes resulted in an odorless antiperspirant and a yogurt with fruit dispersed throughout.
- *Transfer success from one product category to another.* Pump dispensers proved popular with mustard, ketchup, and skin lotion, so this form of packaging was used for toothpaste.
- *Make the task easier.* Combining shampoo with hair conditioner eliminates one task. And microwaving is a lot easier than traditional methods of cooking many foods, and the results are just as tasty.
- *Dream up new uses.* Chex cereals are the key ingredient in a line of party snacks. Sales of Arm & Hammer baking soda increased considerably after the product was advertised as a refrigerator deodorant.
- *Add new distribution channels.* Woolite, a soap for woolen items, for years was sold only in department stores. When the company made this product available in supermarkets, sales tripled the first year.
- *Add a dramatic guarantee.* Spray 'n Wash sales were declining as competitive products were introduced. The company then made this guarantee: "If Spray 'n Wash doesn't remove a stain from a shirt—any shirt—we'll buy you a new shirt." This guarantee boosted sales considerably, and only a few people requested a new shirt.
- *Don't stymie creativity.* A Sony executive walking through a laboratory saw a miniature tape recorder project and a headphone project. Creative thinking combined the two projects, resulting in the Walkman.
- *Look overseas for inspiration.* Europe gave us mineral water, hair mousse, aseptic packaging, and soft-batch cookies.

Source: Adapted from Calvin L. Hodock, "Nine Surefire Ways to Cook Up New Ideas," *Sales & Marketing Management*, August 1988, p. 40; and Gerald Schoenfeld, "Treat Old Products Like New," *Marketing News*, July 31, 1989, p. 15.

---

### MANAGING DURING SALES-DECLINE STAGE

Perhaps it is in the sales-decline stage that a company finds its greatest challenges in life-cycle management. At some point in the product's life, management may have to consider whether to abandon the product. The costs of carrying profitless products go beyond the expenses that show up on financial statements. The real burdens are the insidious costs accruing from managerial time and effort that are diverted to sick products. Management often seems reluctant to discard a product, however.

When sales are declining, management has the following alternatives, some of which are reflected in the box above.

Identifying new uses for a mature product can do wonders to rejuvenate that product.

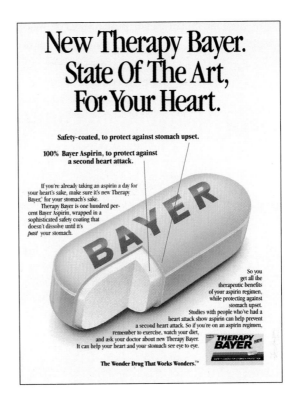

- Improve the product in a functional sense, or revitalize it in some manner.
- Make sure that the marketing and production programs are as efficient as possible.
- Streamline the product assortment by pruning out unprofitable sizes and models. Frequently this tactic will *decrease* sales and *increase* profits.
- "Run out" the product; that is, cut all costs to the bare-minimum level that will optimize profitability over the limited remaining life of the product.

In the final analysis the only reasonable alternative may be simply to abandon the product. Knowing when and how to abandon products successfully may be as important as knowing when and how to introduce new ones. Certainly management should develop a systematic procedure for phasing out weak products.[10]

**PLANNED OBSOLESCENCE AND FASHION**

The American consumer seems to be on a constant quest for the "new" but not "*too* new." The market wants newness—new products, new styles, new colors. However, people want to be moved gently out of their habitual patterns, not shocked out of them. Consequently, many manufacturers opt for a product strategy of planned obsolescence. Its objective is to make an existing product out of date and thus to increase the market for replacement products.

[10]For suggestions on how to recognize the technological limits of an existing product—in effect, knowing when to get off the curve for an existing product and to jump on the curve for the next product—see Richard Foster, "When to Make Your Move to the Latest Innovation," *Across the Board*, October 1986, pp. 44–50.

## Nature of Planned Obsolescence

The term **planned obsolescence** may be interpreted two ways:

- *Technological or functional obsolescence.* Significant technical improvements result in a more effective product. For instance, pocket calculators made slide rules technologically obsolete. This type of obsolescence is generally considered to be socially and economically desirable.
- *Style obsolescence.* This is sometimes called "psychological" or "fashion" obsolescence. Superficial characteristics of the product are altered so that the new model is easily differentiated from the previous model. The intent is to make people feel out of date if they continue to use old models.

When people criticize planned obsolescence, they usually have in mind the second interpretation—style obsolescence. In our discussion, planned obsolescence will mean *only* style obsolescence, unless otherwise stated.

## Nature of Style and Fashion

Although the words *style* and *fashion* are often used interchangeably, there is a clear distinction between the two. A **style** is a distinctive manner of construction or presentation in any art, product, or endeavor (singing, playing, behaving). Thus we have styles in automobiles (sedans, station wagons), in bathing suits (one-pieces, bikinis), in furniture (Early American, French Provincial), and in dancing (waltz, rumba).

A **fashion** is any style that is popularly accepted and purchased by successive groups of people over a reasonably long period of time. Not every style becomes a fashion. To be rated as a fashion, or to be called "fashionable," a style must become popularly accepted. A **fad** normally does not remain popular as long as a fashion, and is based on some novelty feature.

Basic styles never change, but fashion is always changing. Fashions are found in all societies, including primitive groups, the great Oriental cultures, and the societies of ancient and medieval Europe.

Fashion is rooted in sociological and psychological factors. Basically people are conformists. At the same time, they yearn to look, act, and be a *little* different from others. They are not in revolt against custom; they simply wish to be a bit different and still not be accused of bad taste or disregard for convention. Fashion discreetly furnishes them the opportunity for self-expression.

## Fashion-Adoption Process

The fashion-adoption process reflects the concepts of (1) large-group and small-group influences on consumer buying behavior and (2) the diffusion of innovation, as discussed in Chapters 5 and 7. People usually try to imitate others in the same social stratum or those on the next higher level. They do so by purchasing the fashionable product. This shows up as a wave of buying in that particular social stratum. The **fashion-adoption process,** then, is a series of buying waves that arise as the given style is popularly accepted in one group, then another and another, until it finally falls out of fashion. This wavelike movement, representing the introduction, rise, popular culmination, and decline of the market's acceptance of a style, is referred to as the **fashion cycle.**

Three theories of fashion adoption are recognized (see Figure 8-3):

- **Trickle-down,** where a given fashion cycle flows *downward* through several socioeconomic classes.
- **Trickle-across,** where the cycle moves *horizontally* and *simultaneously within* several social classes.

**FIGURE 8-3** Fashion-adoption processes.

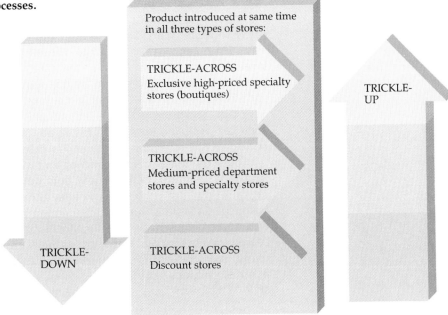

● **Trickle-up,** where the cycle is initiated in lower socioeconomic classes, then later the style becomes popular among higher-income and social groups.

Traditionally, the *trickle-down* theory has been used as the basic model to explain the fashion-adoption process. As an example, designers of women's apparel first introduce a style to the leaders—the tastemakers who usually are social leaders in the upper-income brackets. If they accept the style, it quickly appears in leading fashion stores. Soon the middle-income and then the lower-income markets want to emulate the leaders, and the style is mass-marketed. As its popularity wanes, the style appears in bargain-price stores and finally is no longer considered fashionable.

To illustrate the *trickle-across* process, let us again use the example of women's apparel. Within a few weeks at the most, at the beginning of the fall season the same style of dresses appears (1) in small, exclusive dress shops

---

**The "trickle-up" process**

Blue jeans, denim jackets, T-shirts, and pasta in the 1990s. Years earlier there were popular styles of music we call jazz and the blues. These all have one thing in common. They are styles that *trickled up* in popularity; that is, they were popular first with lower socioeconomic groups. Later, their popularity trickled up as these styles gained wide acceptance among higher-income markets. T-shirts—once the domain of beer-drinking blue-collar workers and radicals—have moved up considerably in social respectability and price. Now they are designed by Yves St. Laurent, Calvin Klein, Ralph Lauren, and others.

appealing to the upper social class, (2) in large department stores appealing to the middle social class, and (3) in discount houses and low-priced women's ready-to-wear chain stores, where the appeal is to the upper-lower social class. Price and quality mark the differences in the dresses sold on the three levels—*but the style is basically the same*. Within each class the dresses are purchased early in the season by the opinion leaders—the innovators. If the style is accepted, its sales curve rises as it becomes popular with the early adopters, and then with the late adopters. Eventually, sales decline as the style ceases to be popular. This cycle, or flow, is a horizontal movement occurring virtually simultaneously within each of several social strata.

Today the trickle-across concept best reflects the adoption process for most fashions. Granted, there is some flow downward, and obviously there is an upward flow. But present market conditions seem to foster a horizontal flow. By means of modern production, communication, and transportation methods, we can disseminate style information and products so rapidly that all social strata can be reached at about the same time. In the apparel field particularly, manufacturing and marketing programs foster the horizontal movement of fashions. Manufacturers produce a wide *variety* of essentially one style. They also produce different *qualities* of the same basic style so as to appeal to different income groups simultaneously. When an entire cycle may last only one season, sellers cannot afford to wait for style acceptance to trickle down. They must introduce it into many social levels as soon as possible.

## Marketing Considerations in Fashion

When a firm's products are subject to the fashion cycle, management must know what stage the cycle is in at all times. Managers must decide at what point to get into the cycle and when they should get out.

Accurate forecasting is of inestimable value in achieving success in fashion merchandising. This is an extremely difficult task, however, because the forecaster is often dealing with complex sociological and psychological factors. Frequently a retailer or manufacturer operates largely on intuition and inspiration, tempered by considerable experience.

Management also must know what market it is aiming for. Ordinarily a retailer cannot successfully participate in all stages of the fashion cycle at the same time. A high-grade specialty apparel store—whose stocks are displayed in limited numbers without price tags—should get in at the start of a fashion trend. A department store appealing to the middle-income market should plan to enter the cycle in time to mass-market the style as it is climbing to its peak of popularity.

## SUMMARY

To make the product-planning phase of a company's marketing program most effective, it is imperative that management select appropriate strategies for the company's product mix. One strategy is to appropriately position the product, relative to competing products or other products sold by the firm. Another strategy is simply to expand the product mix by increasing the number of lines and/or the depth within a line. Alternatively, management may elect to trade up or trade down relative to its existing products. Altering the design, packaging, or other features of existing products is still another option. The product mix also can be changed by eliminating an entire line or by simplifying the assortment within a line.

Executives need to understand the concept of a product's life cycle and the characteristics of each stage in the cycle. The task of managing a product as it moves through its life cycle presents both challenges and opportunities—perhaps most frequently in the sales-decline stage.

An especially controversial product strategy is that of planned obsolescence, built around the concepts of style, fashion, and the fashion cycle. Fashion—essentially a sociological and psychological phenomenon—follows a reasonably predictable pattern. With advances in communications and production, the fashion-adoption process has moved away from the traditional trickle-down pattern. Today the process is better described as trickle-across. There also are some noteworthy examples of fashions trickling up. Style obsolescence is based on consumer psychology.

| **KEY TERMS AND CONCEPTS** | Product mix 192 | Planned obsolescence 204 |
|---|---|---|
| | Product-mix breadth and depth 192 | Fashion (style) obsolescence 204 |
| | Product line 192 | Style 204 |
| | Product positioning 192 | Fashion 204 |
| | Expansion of product mix 194 | Fad 204 |
| | Trading up 194 | Fashion-adoption process 204 |
| | Trading down 195 | Fashion cycle 204 |
| | Product alteration 196 | Trickle-down 204 |
| | Contraction of product mix 196 | Trickle-across 204 |
| | Product life cycle 197 | Trickle-up 205 |

## QUESTIONS AND PROBLEMS

1. "It is inconsistent for management to follow concurrently the product-line strategies of *expanding* its product mix and *contracting* its product mix." Discuss.

2. "Trading up and trading down are product strategies closely related to the business cycle. Firms trade up during periods of prosperity and trade down during recessions." Do you agree? Why?

3. After reviewing the International Perspective in this chapter:
   a. What positioning strategy should Shiseido use against other brands of cosmetics in the U.S. market?
   b. What target market should Suntory and Kirin aim for initially when introducing their canned coffee and tea drinks in the United States?

4. Name some goods and services you believe are in the introductory stage of their life cycles. Identify the market that considers your examples to be new products.

5. Give examples of products that are in the stage of market decline. In each case point out whether you think the decline is permanent. What recommendations do you have for rejuvenating the demand for the product?

6. How might a company's pricing strategies differ, depending on whether its product is in the introductory stage or maturity stage of its life cycle?

7. What advertising strategies are likely to be used when a product is in the growth stage?

8. What products, other than wearing apparel and automobiles, stress fashion and style in marketing? Do styles exist among business products?

9. Select a product and trace its marketing strategies through a complete fashion cycle. Particularly note and explain the changes in the distribution, pricing, and promotion of the product in the various stages of the cycle.

10. Is the trickle-across theory applicable to the fashion-adoption process in product lines other than women's apparel? Explain, using examples.

11. Planned obsolescence is criticized as a social and economic waste because we are urged to buy things we do not like and do not need. What is your opinion? If you object to planned obsolescence, what are your recommendations for correcting the situation?

12. What effects might a recession have on:
    a. Product life cycles?
    b. Planned obsolescence?
    What marketing strategies might a firm employ to counter (or take advantage of) these effects?

Lauren (Classifications), Perry Ellis (Portfolio), Bill Blass (Blassport), and Anne Klein (Anne Klein II).

## The Battle of the Brands

Middlemen's brands have proved to be eminently successful in competing with producers' brands. However, neither group has demonstrated a convincing competitive superiority over the other in the marketplace. Consequently, the "battle of the brands" shows every indication of continuing and becoming more intense.

In the late 1970s, several supermarket chains introduced products sold under their generic names. The products were simply labeled as pork and beans, peanut butter, cottage cheese, paper towels, and so on. These unbranded products generally sell for 30 to 40 percent less than manufacturers' brands and 20 percent less than retailers' brands. Although they are the nutritional equivalent of branded products, the generics (graded "standard" in industry terms) may not have the color, size, and appearance of the branded items (graded "fancy"). Most chains sell these products completely unbranded—referring to them as "generic products" in the store's advertising. In effect, "generic" becomes an unofficial brand name in that it is the identifying name used by stores and consumers.

Generic products now account for a large enough share of total sales in their respective product lines to be a major factor in the battle of the brands. In the late 1980s, the generics' market share leveled off, and even declined, in some product lines. Apparently the low inflation rate had dulled consumers' price sensitivity, and also producers fought back with extensive use of coupons for their brands. Nevertheless, in the early 1990s, generics still are a strong force.

Several factors account for the success of middlemen's brands and generic products. The thin profit margins on producers' brands have encouraged retailers to establish their own labels. The improved quality of retailers' brands has boosted their sales. Consumers have become more sophisticated in their buying and their brand loyalty has declined, so they do consider alternative brands. It is generally known that retailers' brands usually are produced by large, well-known manufacturers. Generic products, with their low-price, no-frills approach, appeal to price-conscious consumers.

Manufacturers do have some effective responses to combat generics and retailers' brands. Producers can, for example, devote top priority to product innovation and packaging, an area in which retailers are not as strong. Manu-

Now *this* is a battle of the brands.

facturers' research and development capacity also enables them to enter the market in the early stages of a product's life cycle, whereas retailer brands typically enter after a product is well established.[3]

## Trademark Licensing

An effective branding strategy that has grown by leaps and bounds in recent years is trademark (or brand) licensing. During the 10-year period of 1977 to 1986, sales of licensed products in the United States soared from $5 billion to over $54 billion.[4] The owner of a trademark grants permission (a license) to other firms to use the owner's brand name, logotype (distinctive lettering and coloring), and/or character on the licensee's products. The licensee pays a royalty of about 5 percent on the wholesale price of the product that carries the licensed trademark. However, this figure can vary depending on the perceived strength of the licensor's brand.

As examples of trademark licensing, the Walt Disney Company granted Sears the right to use Disney characters on Sears' products. So you might see a Snow White sweatshirt or Pinocchio shaving lotion. Sears also markets a line of McKid's children's clothing under an agreement with McDonald's. Pepsi-Cola and Burger King have also licensed their names for use on wearing apparel. In fact, it was the highly successful licensing of the Coca-Cola name for use on apparel made by Murjani in the mid-1980s that sparked the growth of brand licensing in clothing.[5]

Using licensing, several companies have successfully extended their brand into related fields. Thus we see Old Spice safety razors and shaving mugs, Winnebago camping equipment, Louisville Slugger batting gloves, Astroturf sports shoes for playing on Astroturf fields, and After Six bridal gowns licensed by the country's largest marketer of men's formal wear.

Strategy decisions must be made by both parties—the licensor and the licensee. Pierre Cardin (a licensor) must ask, "Should we allow other firms to use our designer label?" A manufacturer of eyeglasses (a licensee) must ask, "Do we want to put out a line of high-fashion eyeglasses under the Pierre Cardin name?"

Owners of well-known brands are interested in licensing their trademarks for various reasons. First, it can be very profitable since there is little expense involved on the part of the licensor. Second, there is a promotional benefit, because the licensor's name gets circulation far beyond the original trademarked article. Third, licensing can help protect the trademark. If Coca-Cola licenses its brand for use in an array of product categories, it can block any other company from using that brand legally in those product categories.

For the company receiving the license—the licensee—the strategy is a quick way to gain market recognition and to penetrate a new market. Today the financial cost of establishing a new brand name is high. And there is no guarantee of success. It is a lot easier for an unknown firm to gain consumer acceptance of its product if that item carries a well-known brand.

[3] For a review of manufacturer and retailer strategies in the past regarding generic products, and suggestions for future strategies now that generics have reached maturity in many product categories, see Brian F. Harris and Roger A. Strang, "Marketing Strategies in the Age of Generics," *Journal of Marketing*, Fall 1985, pp. 70–81.

[4] "The Licensing Letter" as cited in Lori Kessler, "Extensions Leave Brand in New Areas," *Advertising Age*, June 1, 1987, p. S1.

[5] See Cyndee Miller, "Sears Gets Merchandising Rights to Disney Characters," *Marketing News*, Dec. 18, 1987, p. 1; and Joe Agnew, "Brand Licensers Become Increasingly Clothes-Minded," *Marketing News*, July 31, 1987, p. 1.

## Strategic Branding of Services

Earlier in this chapter we discussed the competitive edge that a well-selected brand can give to a product. These advantages are equally applicable to tangible goods and intangible services. Furthermore, the marketers of services have to make many of the same strategic branding decisions as do the marketers of tangible products. Perhaps the first of these decisions is to select a good brand name for the service.[6] In services marketing, more so than in the marketing of tangible goods, the company name typically serves as the brand name.

The characteristics of an effective service brand are much the same as for tangible goods. Thus, a service brand should be:

One strategy in international marketing is to use the same brand all over the world.

- Relevant to the service or its benefits. Ticketron, for example, conveys the nature of the service and the electronic speed by which it is delivered. VISA suggests an international activity and thus is relevant for a global financial service. Humana is a good name for a health-care organization, and Holiday Inn implies positive benefits for travelers.
- Distinctive. This characteristic is difficult to communicate. Names such as Allied or United should be avoided because, standing alone, they tell us nothing about the service or its benefits. The company needs to add words such as Allied *Van Lines*, United *Airlines*, or United *Parcel Service*. (We wonder how many First National Banks there are in the U.S.)

    Some service marketers differentiate by using a symbol or a color. AT&T's lined globe, Prudential's Rock of Gibraltar, and the Girl Scouts' three-leaf clover are distinctive symbols. For color, we see Avis red, Hertz black and gold, and UPS brown delivery vans. The use of a person's name (Marriott, McDonald) or a coined word (NYNEX, Primerica) also offers distinctiveness. But it tells us little or nothing about the service being offered.
- Easy to pronounce and remember. Simple, short names (such as Pan Am or Delta) usually meet this criterion. But not always. NYNEX and Aetna, for instance, pose pronunciation problems for some people. Sometimes unusual spelling aids the memory factor—the reverse R in Toys "R" Us, for example.
- Adaptable to additional services that may be offered. Companies can change their mix of services and their geographical locations over time, so ideally a service brand should be flexible enough to adapt to these expansions. Names like Alaska Airlines and America West pose more geographical limits than does Allstate.

Another branding decision is whether or not to use family branding. Insurance companies and financial services firms often use the same brand name for the variety of services offered. On the other hand, when the parent company of United Airlines also owned Hertz rental cars and Westin Hotels, separate brand names were retained for each line of services.

Whether or not to engage in trademark licensing is a strategic branding decision faced by many services firms. Companies, entertainers, and most professional sports teams license their brand (name) for use on countless products.

---

[6] For a good discussion of this topic, see Leonard L. Berry, Edwin F. Lefkowith, and Terry Clark, "In Services, What's in a Name?" *Harvard Business Review,* September–October 1988, pp. 28–30. Some of the examples in this section are drawn from this source.

## PACKAGING

**Packaging** may be defined as all the activities of designing and producing the container or wrapper for a product. There are three reasons for packaging:

- Packaging serves several *safety and utilitarian purposes.* It protects a product on its route from the producer to the final customer, and in some cases even while it is being used by the customer. Effective packaging can help prevent ill-intentioned persons from tampering with products. Some protection is provided by "child-proof" closures on containers of medicines and other products that are potentially harmful to children. Also, compared with bulk items, packaged goods generally are more convenient, cleaner, and less susceptible to losses from evaporation, spilling, and spoilage.
- Packaging may be a *part of a company's marketing program.* Packaging helps identify a product and thus may prevent substitution of competitive products. At the point of purchase, the package can serve as a silent sales person. Furthermore, the advertising copy on the package will last as long as the product is used in its packaged form. A package may be the only significant way in which a firm can differentiate its product. In the case of convenience goods or business operating supplies, for example, most buyers feel that one well-known brand is about as good as another.

    Some feature of the package may add sales appeal—a no-drip spout, a reusable jar, or a self-applicator (a bottle of shoe polish or glue with an applicator top, for example). By packaging their toothpaste in a pump dispenser—a product long used in Europe—Colgate and Close-Up brands increased their sales considerably. Crest and Aim later adopted the same type of packaging.
- A firm can package its product in a way that *increases profit and sales volume.* A package that is easy to handle or minimizes damage losses will cut marketing costs, thus boosting profit. On the sales side, packaged goods typically are more attractive and therefore better than items sold in bulk. Many companies have increased the sales volume of an article simply by redesigning its package. A little later we'll speak more about the strategy of changing packages.

### Importance of Packaging in Marketing

Historically, packaging was a production-oriented activity in most companies, performed mainly to obtain the benefits of protection and convenience. Today, however, the marketing significance of packaging is fully recognized, and packaging is truly a major competitive force in the struggle for markets. The widespread use of self-service selling and automatic vending means that the package must do the selling job at the point of purchase. Shelf space is often at a premium, and it is no simple task for manufacturers even to get their products displayed in a retail outlet. Most retailers are inclined to cater to producers that have used effective packaging.

In addition, the increased use of branding and the public's rising standards in health and sanitation have contributed to a greater awareness of packaging. Safety in packaging has become a prominent marketing and social issue in recent years. Extensive consumer use of microwave ovens has had a significant impact on packaging. Many food products are now packaged so that they may go straight from the shelf or freezer into a microwave oven. In this vein, Campbell Soup announced that in the early 1990s it will completely discontinue the use of cans for soup packaging in favor of microwaveable containers.

A package that can be reclosed after opening can keep a product clean and fresh and can also serve as a promotional appeal.

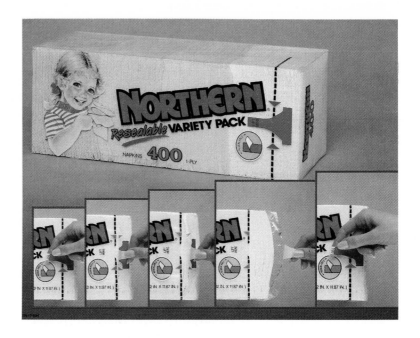

New developments in packaging, occurring rapidly and in a seemingly endless flow, require management's constant attention. We see new packaging materials replacing traditional ones, new shapes, new closures, and other new features (measured portions, metered flow). These all increase convenience for consumers and selling points for marketers. One new development in packaging that will be particularly interesting to watch in the coming years is the aseptic container—a "paper bottle" made of laminations of paper, aluminum foil, and plastic. Its airtight feature keeps perishables fresh for 5 months without refrigeration, and it costs about one-half as much as cans and 30 percent as much as bottles. Already being used to package many drink products, its future prospects are exceptionally bright.[7]

Packaging is attracting special managerial attention as American firms prepare for the unified European Community starting in 1992. Packages that work in the United States may not be successful in Europe. In general, European consumers are used to a more sophisticated package design than are Americans. Colors are more subtle, illustrations are used more commonly than photography, and consumers are more conscious of typography.[8]

## Packaging Strategies

When managing the packaging component of a product, executives must make the following decisions regarding various packaging policies.

### CHANGING THE PACKAGE

There may be several reasons for considering a package change. A firm may want to correct a poor feature in an existing container or take advantage of a new material. To increase sales volume, many companies find that it costs much less to redesign a package than to conduct an expensive advertising

[7] For recommendations on managing the product-packaging phase of a company's marketing mix, see Richard T. Hise and James U. McNeal, "Effective Packaging Management," *Business Horizons*, January–February 1988, pp. 47–51.

[8] Janice Ashby, "European Unification in 1992 Challenges U.S. Expert Packaging," *Marketing News*, Oct. 10, 1988, p. 12.

**AN ETHICAL DILEMMA?**

A coffee producer has developed a new roasting method that enables consumers to brew the same number of cups from 13 oz. of coffee as were formerly produced with 16 oz. As a result, the firm can charge the same price for 20 percent less coffee. If you were the brand manager for this coffee, would you consider it ethical to continue using the 16-oz. can for less coffee to avoid having a smaller container than the competition? Would your answer be different if the instructions on the can explained that a smaller amount of coffee produces the same flavor?

campaign. Coca-Cola increased its sales of Cherry Coke in Salt Lake City by placing a ski scene on the can and dropping the cherry-red motif. The Kroger supermarket chain boosted sales of its store brand ice cream by 20 percent in one year simply by changing the printing and photo on the package. Sales of Wheatena hot cereal went up 25 percent in test markets when the box was redesigned.[9]

### PACKAGING THE PRODUCT LINE

A company must decide whether to develop a family resemblance in the packaging of its several products. **Family packaging** uses identical packages for all products or packages with some common feature. Campbell Soup, for instance, uses virtually identical packaging on its condensed soup products. Management's philosophy concerning family packaging generally parallels its feelings about family branding. When new products are added to a line, promotional values associated with old products extend to the new ones. On the other hand, family packaging makes sense only when the products are related in use and are of similar quality.

### REUSE PACKAGING

Another strategy to be considered is reuse packaging. Should the company design and promote a package that can serve other purposes after the original contents have been consumed? Glasses containing cheese can later be used to serve fruit juice, for instance. Reuse packaging also should stimulate repeat purchases as the consumer attempts to acquire a matching set of containers.

### MULTIPLE PACKAGING

For many years there has been a trend toward multiple packaging—the practice of placing several units in one container. Dehydrated soups, motor oil, beer, golf balls, building hardware, candy bars, towels, and countless other products are packaged in multiple units. Test after test has proved that multiple packaging increases total sales of a product.[10]

[9] Alecia Swasy, "Sales Lost Their Vim? Try Repackaging," *The Wall Street Journal*, Oct. 11, 1989, p. B1.

[10] For a further discussion of package design strategies that can boost sales and profit, see Sue Bassin, "Innovative Packaging Strategies," *Journal of Business Strategy*, January–February 1988, pp. 38–42.

## Criticisms of Packaging

Packaging is in the socioeconomic forefront today because of its relationship to environmental pollution issues. Perhaps the biggest challenge facing packagers is how to dispose of used containers, which are a major contributor to the solid-waste disposal problem. Consumers' desire for convenience in the form of throw-away containers conflicts with their desire for a clean environment.[11]

Other socioeconomic criticisms of packaging are:

- Packaging depletes our natural resources. This criticism is being offset to some extent as packagers increasingly use recycled and biodegradable materials. Another offsetting point is that effective packaging reduces spoilage (another form of resource waste).
- Packaging is excessively expensive. Cosmetic packaging is often cited as an example here. But even in seemingly simple packaging—beer, for example—half the production cost goes for the container. On the other hand, effective packaging reduces transportation costs and losses from product spoilage.
- Health hazards occur from some forms of plastic packaging and some aerosol cans. Government regulations have banned the use of several of these suspect packaging materials.
- Packaging is deceptive. Government regulation plus improvements in business practices regarding packaging have reduced the intensity of this criticism, although it still is heard on occasion.

Marketing executives face real challenges in satisfying these complaints while at the same time retaining the marketing-effectiveness, consumer-convenience, and product-protection features of packaging.

## LABELING

Labeling is another product feature that requires managerial attention. A **label** is the part of a product that carries information about the product or the seller. A label may be part of a package, or it may be a tag attached directly to the product. Obviously there is a close relationship among labeling, packaging, and branding.

## Types of Labels

Labels are classified as brand, grade, or descriptive. A **brand label** is simply the brand alone applied to the product or package. Thus, some oranges are brand-labeled (stamped) Sunkist or Blue Goose, and some clothes carry the brand label Sanforized. A **grade label** identifies the quality with a letter, number, or word. Canned peaches are grade-labeled A, B, and C, and corn and wheat are grade-labeled 1 and 2. **Descriptive labels** give objective information about the use, construction, care, performance, or other features of the product. On a descriptive label for a can of corn, there will be statements concerning the type of corn (golden sweet), style (creamed or in niblet kernels), can size, number of servings, other ingredients, and nutritional contents.

### RELATIVE MERITS

Brand labeling creates very little stir among critics. While it is an acceptable form of labeling, its severe limitation is that it does not supply sufficient

---

[11] See Elliott D. Lee, "Opposition to Plastic Packaging Is Intensifying As the Nation's Solid-Waste Problem Grows Acute," *The Wall Street Journal,* Nov. 25, 1987, p. 38.

information to a buyer. The real fight centers on grade versus descriptive labeling and on whether grade labeling should be mandatory.

The proponents of grade labeling argue that it is simple, definite, and easy to use. They also point out that if grade labels were used, prices would be more closely related to quality, although grade labeling would not stifle competition.

Those who object to grade labeling argue that a very low score on one grading characteristic can be offset by very high scores on other factors. Companies selling products that score high *within* a given grade would be hurt by grade labeling. These companies could not justify a higher price than that charged for a product that scored very low in the same grade. And some people feel that grades are an inaccurate guide for consumer buying. It is not possible to grade the differences in flavor and taste, or in style and fashion, yet these are the factors that often influence consumer purchases.

## Statutory Labeling Requirements

Several of the public's criticisms of marketing have centered on charges of false or deceptive packaging and labeling. These criticisms have led to a considerable amount of federal legislation. The Federal Trade Commission Act of 1914 and its Wheeler-Lea Amendment (1938) state that unfair competition is illegal. False or deceptive labels or packages are specific instances of unfair competition.

In spite of this legislation, consumer discontent with packaging and labeling continues to mount. Consumers have charged, for example, that there are a confusing number of sizes and shapes of packages for a given product. Critics also have claimed that some packages are only partially filled and that some package shapes are deceptive. Also when contents are measured in odd amounts (such as 6½ ounces), it is very difficult to make unit-price comparisons.

Congress responded with the Fair Packaging and Labeling Act (1966). This law provides for (1) *mandatory* labeling requirements, (2) an opportunity for business to *voluntarily* adopt packaging standards that will limit the proliferation of weights and measures, and (3) administrative agencies (the Food and Drug Administration and the Federal Trade Commission) with the *discretionary* power to set packaging regulations where deemed necessary.

In the past, labeling of clothing, furs, and piece goods (fabrics to make clothes and home furnishings) was often confusing and misleading to consumers. To correct this problem, Congress passed three labeling laws: the Wool Products Labeling Act (1940), the Fur Products Labeling Act (1951), and the Textile Fiber Products Identification Act (1958). Each of these laws requires sellers to provide consumers with relevant and accurate information on product labels to aid in making purchase decisions.

The Food and Drug Administration established a set of labeling standards for processed foods to ensure full disclosure of their nutritional content. Labels must clearly state the amount of protein, fat, carbohydrates, and calories contained in the contents of the package. Vitamin and mineral content must be expressed as a percentage of the recommended daily allowance.

A 1962 law pertaining to production and marketing of prescription and nonprescription drugs requires that labels and advertising must prominently state the *generic* name of the drug, in addition to the *brand* name. A 1977 law requires that the main ingredients in cosmetics must be disclosed on the label.

The Food and Drug Act of 1906 and its 1938 amendment, the Food, Drug,

The label on this coat must state the generic name of the fur and its country of origin.

and Cosmetic Act, provide explicit regulations for labeling drugs, foods, cosmetics, and therapeutic devices.

## OTHER IMAGE-BUILDING FEATURES

A well-rounded program for product planning and development will include a company policy on several additional product attributes: product design, color, quality, warranty, and servicing.

### Product Design and Color

One way to satisfy customers and gain a competitive advantage is through skillful **product design.** In fact, a distinctive design may be the only feature that significantly differentiates a product. Many firms feel that there is considerable glamour and general promotional appeal in product design and the designer's name. In the field of business products, *engineering* design has long been recognized as extremely important. Today there is a realization of the marketing value of *appearance* design as well. Office machines and office furniture are examples of business products that reflect recent conscious attention to product design, often with good sales results. The marketing significance of design has been recognized for years in the field of consumer products, from big items like automobiles and refrigerators to small products like fountain pens and apparel.

Good design can improve the marketability of a product by making it easier to operate, upgrading its quality, improving its appearance, and/or reducing manufacturing costs. Recognizing the strategic importance of design, many companies have elevated the design function in the corporate hierarchy. In a number of firms the director of design (sometimes called the director of human factors) participates in strategic planning and reports directly to top management.[12]

**Color** often is the determining factor in a customer's acceptance or rejection of a product, whether that product is a dress, a table, or an automobile. Color by itself, however, is no selling advantage because many competing firms offer color. The marketing advantages comes in knowing the right color and in knowing when to change colors. If a garment manufacturer or a retail

[12]See "Smart Design: Quality Is the New Style," *Business Week,* Apr. 11, 1988, p. 102; and "How Do We Confuse Thee? Let Us Count the Ways," *Forbes,* March 1988 p. 156.

store's fashion coordinator guesses wrong on what will be the fashionable color in women's clothing, disaster may ensue.

## Product Quality

The quality of a product is extremely significant, but it is probably the most difficult of all the image-building features to define. Users frequently disagree on what constitutes quality in a product, whether it be a cut of meat or a work of art or music. Personal tastes are deeply involved. One guideline in managing product quality is that the quality level should be compatible with the intended use of a product; the level need not be any higher. In fact, *good* and *poor* sometimes are misleading terms for quality. *Correct* and *incorrect* or *right* and *wrong* may be more appropriate. If a person is making a peach cobbler, grade B or C peaches are the correct quality. They are not necessarily the best quality, but they are right for the intended use. It is not necessary to pay grade-A prices for large, well-formed peaches when these features are destroyed in making the cobbler. Another key to the successful management of quality is to maintain *consistency* of product output at the desired quality level.

In recent years, American manufacturers have been increasingly concerned about the quality of their products. And well they should be! For many years, consumers have complained about the poor quality of some products—both materials and workmanship. Foreign products—Japanese cars, for example—have made serious inroads into the American market because these products are perceived as being of better quality than their American counterparts.

Quality of output also is a primary consideration in the production and marketing of services. The quality of its service can determine whether a firm

One key to marketing success in the 1900s is to provide product quality consistently at a level expected by customers.

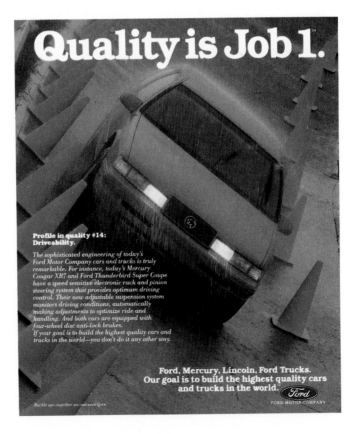

will be successful. Yet it is virtually impossible for a firm to standardize performance quality among its units of service output. We frequently experience differences in performance quality from the same organization in appliance repairs, haircuts, medical exams, football games, or marketing courses. Consequently, it is essential that management do all it can to ensure consistency of quality at or above the level expected by the firm's present and potential customers.[13]

To aid in determining and maintaining the desired level of quality in its goods and services, a company should establish a quality-improvement program. This should be an ongoing group effort of the design, production, marketing, and customer-service departments. Such a program is in sharp contrast to a simple inspection of finished goods or parts on a production line—what some firms call quality control. A total quality-management program should also include provisions for communicating to the market its commitment to quality. A firm may then justifiably claim in its advertising that its product quality has improved. The problem is getting consumers to believe this fact.[14]

## Warranty and Product Liability

The general purpose of a warranty is to give buyers some assurance that they will be compensated in case the product does not perform up to reasonable expectation. In years past, courts seemed generally to recognize only **express warranties**—those stated in written or spoken words. Usually these were quite limited in their coverage and seemed mainly to protect the seller from buyers' claims.

But times have changed! Consumer complaints have led to a governmental campaign to protect the consumer in many areas, one of which is product warranty. Today courts and government agencies are broadening the scope of warranty coverage by recognizing the concept of **implied warranty.** This means that a warranty was *intended* by the seller, although not actually stated. Producers are being held responsible, even when the sales contract is between the retailer and the consumer. They are held liable for product-caused injury, whether or not they are to blame for negligence in manufacturing. It all adds up to "Let the seller beware."

In recent years, producers have responded to legislation and consumer complaints by broadening and simplifying their warranties. Many sellers are using their warranties as promotional devices to stimulate purchases by reducing consumers' risks. The effective handling of consumers' complaints related to warranties can be a significant factor in strengthening a company's marketing program. General Electric's warranty on large appliances (return them within 90 days if you are not satisfied) and Chrysler's 7 years or 70,000 miles warranty on its cars are just two examples of the strategic use of warranties in a company's marketing program.

[13] For more on service quality, see Leonard L. Berry, A. Parasuraman, and Valarie A. Zeithaml, "The Service-Quality Puzzle," *Business Horizons*, September–October 1988, pp. 35–43. Service quality also is discussed further in Chapter 19.

[14] For more on quality-improvement programs, see David W. Cravens, Charles W. Holland, Charles W. Lamb, Jr., and William C. Moncrief III, "Marketing's Role in Product and Service Quality," *Industrial Marketing Management*, November 1988, pp. 285–304; Valarie A. Zeithaml, Leonard L. Berry, and A. Parasuraman, "Communication and Control Processes in the Delivery of Service Quality," *Journal of Marketing*, April 1988, pp. 35–48; and Stephen B. Castleberry and Anna V. A. Resurrecion, "Communicating Quality to Consumers," *Journal of Consumer Marketing*, Summer 1989, pp. 21–28.

Another very compelling reason for management to pay special attention to its warranties and product quality is the threat of a costly **product-liability** claim. This is a legal action claiming that an illness, accident, or death resulted from the named product because it was harmful, faulty, or inadequately labeled. Product-liability claims are a major and growing problem, creating bitter disputes between business groups and consumer advocates. Tens of thousands of suits are filed every year claiming alleged defects in a wide variety of products. This product list includes autos, stepladders, asbestos products, tampons, toys, pharmaceuticals, birth-control devices, chain saws, tires, and others. And juries seem inclined to award large settlements to the plaintiffs.

The Consumer Product Safety Act (1972) is typical of the changed attitude regarding product liability and injurious products. The act created the Consumer Product Safety Commission (CPSC) that has authority to establish mandatory safety standards for many consumer products. (The CPSC has no authority over autos, food, drugs, tobacco products, and other products that are covered by separate laws or other agencies.) It can publish information regarding injurious products—naming brands and producers. It can ban the distribution of these products without a court hearing. And top management of offending companies may face criminal—not just civil—charges.

Congress has been wrestling with this highly controversial issue of product-liability legislation. It has proven to be difficult to write a law that is considered fair by groups on either side of the issue. Yet everybody recognizes the need for legislation to bring some uniformity to the existing chaos created by the great variations in state laws, court decisions, and financial settlements. And product-liability problems are likely to increase for companies marketing in Western Europe. Recent European laws for the first time provide redress for consumers against bodily injury or property damage from products—even when there is no negligence on the part of the seller.[15]

**Product Servicing**   A problem related to product liability is that of providing adequate postsale services such as maintenance and repairs. Product servicing becomes essential as products become more complex and consumers grow increasingly dissatisfied and vocal. To cope with these problems, management can consider several courses of action. For instance, a producer can establish several geographically dispersed factory service centers, staff them with well-trained company employees, and strive to make servicing a separate profit-generating activity. Or the producer can shift the main burden to middlemen, compensate them for their efforts, and possibly even train their service people.

Today the provision of adequate product servicing should be high on the list of topics calling for managerial action. A perennial major consumer complaint is that manufacturers and retailers do *not* provide adequate repair service for the products they sell. Often the situation is simply that the consumers wish to be *heard*. That is, they simply want someone to listen to them regarding their complaints. In response to this situation, a number of producers have established toll-free telephone lines to their customer service departments.

---

[15] For a good review of the product-liability problem, see Ronald J. Adams and John M. Browning, ''Product Liability in Industrial Markets,'' *Industrial Marketing Management*, November 1986, pp. 265–71; and Fred W. Morgan, ''Marketing and Product Liability: A Review and Update,'' *Journal of Marketing*, Summer 1982, pp. 69–78.

**SUMMARY** Managing the various features of a product—its brand, package, labeling, design, color, quality, warranty, and servicing—is an integral part of effective product planning. A brand is a means of identifying and differentiating the products of an organization. Branding aids sellers in managing their promotional and pricing activities. Brand ownership carries the dual responsibilities of promoting the brand and maintaining a consistent level of quality. Selecting a good brand name—and there are relatively few really good ones—is a difficult task. A good name should suggest a product's benefits, be easy to pronounce and remember, lend itself to product-line additions, and be eligible for legal registration and protection.

Manufacturers must decide whether to brand their products and whether to sell under a middleman's brand. Middlemen must decide whether to carry producers' brands alone or whether to establish their own brands as well. Both groups of sellers must set policies regarding branding of groups of products and branding for market saturation. Customer acceptance of generic products has heated up the "battle of the brands." Another branding strategy is trademark licensing, which is being employed to an increasing extent by owners of well-known brands. The owner allows the use of (licenses) its name or trademarked character to another firm that is looking for a quick, relatively low-cost way of penetrating a market.

Packaging is becoming increasingly important as sellers recognize the problems, as well as the marketing opportunities, involved in packaging. Labeling is a related activity. Marketers should understand the merits and problems of grade labeling and of descriptive labeling. Many consumer criticisms of marketing center on packaging and labeling, and there are several federal laws regulating these activities.

Companies are now recognizing the marketing value of product design, color, and quality. Projecting the appropriate quality image and then delivering the level of quality desired by customers is essential to marketing success. In addition, warranties and servicing require considerable management attention these days because of consumer complaints and governmental regulations in these areas. The prevalence of product-liability claims is a major problem that is getting worse and needs remedial action by the U.S. Congress.

**KEY TERMS AND CONCEPTS**

Brand 210
Brand name 210
Brand mark 210
Trademark 210
Brand names becoming generic names 213
Branding of parts and materials 215
Producer's brand (national brand) 214
Middleman's brand (private brand) 215
Family brands 216
Branding for market saturation 217
Battle of the brands 218

Generic products 218
Trademark licensing 219
Packaging 221
Family packaging 223
Grade label 224
Descriptive label 224
Major labeling laws 225
Product design 226
Product color 226
Product quality 227
Product warranty 228
    Express warranty 228
    Implied warranty 228
Product liability 229
Consumer Product Safety Act 229

## QUESTIONS AND PROBLEMS

1. List three brand names that you think are good ones and three that you consider poor. Explain the reasoning behind your choices.

2. Evaluate each of the following brand names in light of the characteristics of a good brand, indicating the strong and weak points of each name.
   a. Catviar (cat food).
   b. Kodak (cameras).
   c. Metropolitan (insurance).
   d. Hush Puppies (shoes).
   e. Federal Express (delivery service).
   f. Whirlpool (appliances).

3. Suggest some brands that are on the verge of becoming generic. What course of action should a company take to protect the separate identity of its brand?

4. Under what conditions would you recommend that a producer brand a product that will be used as a part or material in the production of another product?

5. In which of the following cases should the company adopt the strategy of family branding?
   a. A manufacturer of men's underwear introduces similar products for women.
   b. A manufacturer of hair-care products introduces a line of portable electric hair dryers.
   c. A chain of luxury hotels adds one chain of medium-priced, all-suite hotels and another chain of lower-priced, no-frills hotels.

6. A manufacturer of a well-known brand of ski boots acquires a division of a company that markets a well-known brand of snow skis. What brand strategy should the new organization adopt? Should all products (skis and boots) now carry the boot brand? Should they carry the ski brand? Is there still some other alternative that you feel would be better?

7. Why do some firms sell an identical product under more than one of their own brands?

8. Assume that a large department store chain proposed to the manufacturers of Maytag washing machines that Maytag supply the department store with machines carrying the store's brand. What factors should Maytag's management consider in making a decision? If the product were General Foods' Jell-O, to what extent would the situation be different?

9. An American manufacturer plans to introduce its line of camping equipment (stoves, lanterns, ice chests) in several Western European countries. Should management select the same brand for all countries or have a different brand in each country? What factors should influence the decision?

10. Give examples of products that are excellently packaged. Mention some that are very poorly packaged. Support your choices.

11. What changes would you recommend in the packaging of these products?
    a. Coke Classic.
    b. Hairspray.
    c. Potato chips.
    d. Toothpaste.

12. If grade labeling is adopted, what factors should be used as bases for grading the following products?
    a. Lipstick.
    b. Woolen sweaters.
    c. Diet-food products.

13. Give examples of products for which the careful use of color has increased sales. Can you cite examples to show that poor use of color may hurt a company's marketing program?

14. Explain the relationship between a warranty on small electric appliances and the manufacturer's distribution system for these products.

15. How would the warranty policies set by a manufacturer of toasters differ from those adopted by an automobile manufacturer?

## THE GILLETTE SENSOR RAZOR*  Positioning a New Product

When you hear "Gillette," one thing comes to mind—*razors*. That's to be expected since the safety razor was invented by King C. Gillette in 1903 and the company that bears his name is one of the foremost manufacturers of razors in the country.

The Gillette Co. had a 64 percent share of the U.S. market for razors in the late 1980s and intends to maintain its position of dominance in the 1990s. As a first step toward achieving that objective, Gillette introduced the new Sensor razor in January 1990. Its primary goal: Win back men who now use disposable razors (made by Bic, Schick, Wilkinson, and Gillette itself). A second goal: Attract current users of top-of-the-line razors, especially those made by Gillette's competitors.

A major challenge Gillette faced in introducing Sensor was how to position the product in relation to key factors such as its target market, main competitors, other razors, and price and quality. These positioning decisions are likely to determine the success or failure of the new product, which in turn will have a significant impact on the entire company.

In a way, Gillette created its own problem. In the mid-1970s Gillette introduced Good News, the first disposable razor. Rather than serving only a small segment of the market, Good News and its imitators have attracted large numbers of customers. What Gillette didn't count on was that the disposable's customers included many people who previously used Gillette's more profitable Atra and Trac II razors.

Disposables currently account for 40 to 50 percent of razor blade sales in the United States. Shavers who use disposable razors are not seeking the best shave; rather, they want value and convenience. Value may be a particularly important factor because men think they spend more money on shaving than they actually do. According to Gillette research, men estimate they spend about $50 annually on razors and blades, but the actual figure is less than $20.

Along with the popularity of disposables, Gillette faces two other problems: (1) competitors such as Bic, Wilkinson, and Schick are strong and aggressive; (2) the number of young adults (new shavers) in the United States is declining. Gillette's response to these challenges is the new Sensor razor. According to Peter Hoffman, Gillette's marketing VP, "We've found that the three most important attributes of a razor are closeness, comfort, and safety." Hoffman believes the Sensor combines all three features and, as a result, its introduction "will lead to a decline in sales of disposables."

What's new about Sensor? The biggest differences between Sensor and other cartridge razors are: Sensor's twin blades are mounted on tiny springs that allow each blade to move separately; it pivots in a concave (rather than convex) arc in order to remain in close contact with the face; and its skin guard is also spring-mounted to keep the blades on the face. The critical question is whether shavers will perceive these differences as important benefits.

Besides being an innovative product, Sensor differs from other Gillette cartridge razors in price. The

*Based on Dan Koeppel, "Gillette's Rivals Predict a Razor War," *Adweek's Marketing Week,* Oct. 16, 1989, p. 3; Martha T. Moore, "Gillette Arms Itself with Sensor Razor," *USA Today,* Oct. 4, 1989, p. B6; Lawrence Ingrassia, "A Recovering Gillette Hopes for Vindication in a High-Tech Razor," *The Wall Street Journal,* Sept. 29, 1989, pp. A1, A6.

razor and three cartridges initially carried a suggested retail price of $3.75; a pack of five replacement cartridges cost about the same amount. At these prices the Sensor was about 25 percent more expensive than Gillette's Atra Plus razor and cartridges and about twice as costly as a package of disposables.

## QUESTIONS

1. a. How new a product is Sensor? Is it truly innovative—a significantly different replacement—or simply imitative?

   b. Given your answer to (a), what special marketing challenges does Gillette face?

2. Do you think consumers will view Sensor's new product features as beneficial enough to abandon their present razor? Why or why not?

3. Gillette's executives intend that the primary buyers of the Sensor razor will be people who presently use either the top-of-the-line razors of competitors (Schick, Wilkinson) or disposable razors, rather than other Gillette products. With this goal in mind, how should Gillette position Sensor with respect to (a) competitors, (b) target market, (c) product class, and (d) price and quality?

---

## CASE 8

## AMERICAN EXPRESS COMPANY* Trading Down for Market Expansion

In preparation for the 1990s, the American Express Company (AmEx) wanted to broaden the base of retailers that would accept AmEx credit cards. One strategy was to get fast-food chains and discount retailers to honor the cards. The fast-food target market included McDonald's, Burger King, Wendy's, Domino's Pizza, Kentucky Fried Chicken, and Arby's. Credit-card sales in 1990 accounted for only about 1 percent of the $55 billion total sales in the fast-food industry. The target market of discount retailers included Wal-Mart, K mart, and Target stores.

The American Express Company is a large, global, financial-services organization. Credit cards are marketed through an AmEx subsidiary, the Trade Related Services Company. Currently AmEx offers four types of credit cards with annual user fees as follows: Green Card—$55; Gold Card—$75; Platinum Card—$300. The fourth type, Optima Card at $15 per year, is an installment-credit card available only in conjunction with one of the other three.

AmEx's major credit-card competitors are VISA and MasterCard, and AmEx is the smallest in terms of numbers of cards issued and retailers honoring the cards. In 1989 worldwide market-penetration figures for all three of the firms were approximately as follows:

|  | Number of cards issued | Number of retailers accepting the card |
|---|---|---|
| American Express | 30 million | 2.5 million |
| VISA | 185 million | 6.5 million |
| MasterCard | 137 million | not available |

All three of these firms test-marketed the idea of expanding into the fast-food field in 1989, and all reported very good results. VISA said that its credit-card purchases were 75 percent higher than the average sale at fast-food outlets. AmEx reported that the average charge sale was $15 compared with the average cash transaction of $5 in a Nashville, Tennessee, chain of family restaurants.

Two trends drove the credit-card firms into fast foods: the saturation in traditional markets and the fact that only about 12 percent of total consumer expenditures were made by credit card. To broaden their markets the firms were looking into other "small-unit transaction" markets such as movie theaters, parking lots, convenience stores, and long-distance telephoning.

People who evaluated AmEx's move into the fast-food and discount-retailer fields did not question the size of these potential markets. Entry into them would attract new card members, boost the company's credit-card sales volume, and expand the retailer base where the AmEx card could be used. The key question was whether these advantages would be more than offset by damage to the company's image and to its standing in its traditional markets.

*Based on Judith Graham, "AmEx Card on the Road Downscale," *Advertising Age*, Apr. 3, 1989, p. 1; Barbara Marsh, "American Express Chases After the Fast-Food Market," *The Wall Street Journal*, Apr. 5, 1989, p. B1; and "Can AmEx Win the Masses—and Keep Its Class?" *Business Week*, Oct. 9, 1989, p. 134.

The American Express Company has always aimed at upscale markets—upper-middle income and above—especially in its credit-card promotion. Ads showed classy people dining in luxurious settings at exciting, exotic locations. One long-running advertising theme featured cardholders who were celebrities in sports, entertainment, and other fields. Another series of ads pictured stores and restaurants that accepted AmEx cards exclusively. Later promotions focused on health care and family dining. But through all these campaigns the company consistently projected an upscale image to an upscale market.

Now this question arises: Can American Express reinforce its upscale image and yet broaden its base to include less prestigious outlets? Can the company stay upscale and trade down at the same time? At a Wendy's in Chicago, a bond salesman, who incidentally carried an AmEx card, described the conflict this way: "They've got us all convinced of the image of the debonair guy, with a woman on his arm, being in only the finest hotels and restaurants. Now they want to get into McDonald's and Wendy's. It just doesn't compute."

AmEx officials claimed that the card's status would not be hurt. They don't consider fast-food outlets as being downscale. The new plan would simply give cardholders more places to use the card. One AmEx survey of its cardholders showed that 76 percent of the respondents had visited a fast-food restaurant within the previous 3 months. The percentage was even higher among cardholders under 35 years old and for those with children.

**QUESTION**

Should American Express continue to expand its credit-card service to include fast-food chains and discount retailers?

## CASE 9

## MURATA BUSINESS SYSTEMS* Managing a Product throughout Its Life Cycle

In the hot market for facsimile (fax) machines in the United States, Murata Business Systems jumped from tenth place in 1986 to second place as the 1990s began. With strong demand for facsimile machines expected to continue indefinitely, Murata's executives face the challenge of choosing marketing strategies that keep pace with changes in the market.

A fax machine allows a user to transmit a document over telephone lines. A facsimile version of the document arrives at its destination within seconds of transmission. Technically, a fax is a scanning device that converts a document's optical image into equivalent electrical signals, which are then converted into audio tones for transmission over telephone lines. At the receiving end, another fax reverses the conversion process and prints out the document.

Fax technology was actually invented more than 150 years ago by a Scottish clockmaker, but the first commercially successful fax was introduced by Xerox only in 1970. Early fax producers in the United States were discouraged by consumer response. Then, in the late 1970s, Japanese-produced faxes began to appear in more and more offices throughout Japan. Shortly thereafter successful Japanese brands such as Ricoh and Panasonic entered the U.S. market.

A brief chronology of the fax industry in the United States during the 1980s follows:

- 1983—Seven fax producers (the entire industry) sell 50,000 units.
- 1984—Sharp introduced no-frills fax with a $2,000 price, thereby creating the "low end" of the market.
- 1987—Sales spurt, totaling 475,000 units.
- 1988—Distribution emphasis shifts from manufacturers' sales forces to equipment dealers and retail stores. Rapid growth occurs in low end of market, with sales of about 700,000 units.
- 1989—At least 25 manufacturers with 60 brands sell about 1.4 million units worth $2 billion. De-

*Based on Brian Bagot, "Brand Report: Fax Facts," *Marketing and Media Decisions*, December 1989, pp. 129–30ff.; Frederick H. Katayama, "Who's Fueling the Fax Frenzy?" *Fortune*, Oct. 23, 1989, pp. 151–52ff.; and Sherli Evans, "Fax in '88: More Models, More Features," *Industry Week*, May 16, 1988, pp. BC3–BC4ff.

mand is particularly strong among small and medium-size businesses. Industry's leaders—Sharp and Murata—focus on low end of market.

Fax machines are increasingly being used to speed up business affairs and also for personal convenience. They can transmit important documents in seconds rather than the next day. Office workers even fax documents to each other to avoid walking from one building to another or from one floor to the next. Business firms accept orders via fax machines. And restaurants are installing faxes to take reservations and orders.

Established in 1982, Murata Business Systems is the U.S. subsidiary of Murata Machinery of Kyoto, Japan. The U.S. operation started with only a president (Robert Franz), one employee, and a single fax model. Franz's early strategies for Murata included heavy advertising (approaching $10 million annually in the late 1980s) and undercutting its competitors' prices. In 1989 Murata introduced a new low-end product—the M1200 with an $899 price tag, which was about $600 below competitors' prices. More than 100,000 units of the M1200 were sold in the first year—making it the industry's best seller.

Murata aims its advertising at 25- to 55-year-old males. The ads are concentrated in three media: television, newspapers, and radio. Murata relies on two main distribution channels: office equipment dealers and consumer electronics outlets.

As the 1990s began, fax industry forecasts pointed to strong growth, stiff competition, and product refinements and innovations. Among the forecasts:

- Sales will total more than 3 million units in 1993.
- About 70 percent of sales will be at the low end, with vigorous competition among companies selling to cost-conscious customers interested in a no-frills fax.
- The variety of business customers will increase as creative uses of faxes expand. Heavy fax usage for international communication across many time zones is anticipated.
- The home fax market shows promise.

- New product features such as color capability and greater transmission speed will be added.
- Some fax producers concentrate on features appealing to high-end corporate customers.
- Prices on no-frills machines will drop further, perhaps as low as $300.
- Only 10 of 25 existing manufacturers will survive to 1995.

Entering the 1990s, Murata certainly wanted at least to maintain its second-place standing (as well as acceptable levels of financial performance). Doing so will be all the more difficult because of strong competition from well-known brands, including Sharp, Canon, Ricoh, and Pitney Bowes, and emerging competition from South Korea.

Murata is implementing or considering various strategies to adapt to a changing market situation. Not surprisingly, it intends to remain aggressive at the market's low end, with even higher levels of advertising.

Murata also plans, however, to put more emphasis on fax machines with more features and price tags up to $5,000. These higher-end machines print and transmit simultaneously, transmit the same document to hundreds of destinations sequentially, and have better security devices to maintain the confidentiality of incoming documents. They also have memories that hold incoming documents for later printing.

Murata recognizes that selling higher-end machines to corporate customers will not be easy because these firms have longstanding business relationships with other suppliers. To gain better access to this target market, Murata will add computer dealers to its distribution channels.

## QUESTIONS

1. As the 1990s began, in which stage of the product life cycle was the fax machine in the United States?
2. Should Murata concentrate on the low end or the high end of the fax market or both?
3. Considering the product's life-cycle stage and your target-market recommendation, what marketing-mix strategies would be effective for Murata in the early 1990s?

# PART FOUR

# THE PRICE

The development and use of a pricing structure as part of
the firm's marketing mix

We are in the process of developing a marketing mix to reach our target markets and achieve our marketing goals. With product planning completed, we now turn our attention to pricing. In strategic planning for—and development of—the pricing structure, we face two broad tasks. First, we must determine the base price for a product that is consistent with our pricing objectives. This is covered in Chapter 10. Second, we must decide on strategies (such as discounts) to employ in modifying and applying the base price. These strategies are discussed in Chapter 11.

# PRICE DETERMINATION

In 1988 a French company, Société Bic, introduced a line of perfumes in France, Italy, and Belgium. The company then planned to expand its distribution system by exporting to the United States. This is the same company that produces and markets Bic disposable cigarette lighters, Bic disposable razors, and Bic ballpoint pens, all at very low prices.

Even though Bic enjoyed huge market shares in most of its products—65 percent in lighters and 50 percent in pens—management realized that the company faced some major environmental threats. With cigarette lighters, Bic faced an inevitable long-run decline as people quit smoking. Bic lost the market share in disposable razors after Gillette introduced its MicroTrac razor as a low-priced alternative to Bic. In pens, Japanese imports and Gillette (Paper Mate, Flair, Write Brothers) were growing competitive threats.

Consequently Bic's search for hot, new growth products led the company to French perfumes. Bic estimated that retail sales of perfume in the United States were about $3 billion a year, and growth prospects were favorable. Perfume is considered a high-priced luxury good. Prices at the time for ¼-ounce bottles of some competitive brands were:

| | |
|---|---|
| Obsession: $60 | Opium: $67.50 |
| Chanel No. 5: $60 | Giorgio: $55 |
| Joy: $90 | |

Bic, however, initially priced its imported French perfume at $5 for a ¼-ounce spray bottle. The perfume was sold through Bic's traditional distribution channels, which included drugstores and supermarkets.

Do you think this product was properly priced at $5? Or will people reject Bic perfume because its price is too low? "It can't be real perfume at only $5." "I'd be embarrassed if my friends knew I was wearing $5 perfume." Such reactions can result in what economists call an inverse demand curve (a concept discussed later in this chapter), which means the lower your price is, the less you sell.

What would be a good brand name for this perfume? How about Eau de Bic? Actually the company exported four scents to the United States—two for women and two for men—and named them Nuit, Jour, Bic for Men, and Bic Sport for Men.[1]

[1] Adapted from "Will $4 Perfume Do the Trick for Bic?" *Business Week*, June 20, 1988, p. 89; and Andrea Rothman, "France's Bic Bets U.S. Consumers Will Go for Perfume on the Cheap," *The Wall Street Journal*, Jan. 12, 1989, p. B6.

"How much will people in America pay for our perfume?" Société Bic had to answer that question in the course of planning to introduce its perfumes to the U.S. market. In effect, this question is asked any time an organization introduces a new product or considers changing the price on an existing one. This question also reminds us that *prices are always on trial.* A price is simply an offer or an experiment to test the pulse of the market. If customers accept the offer, then the price is fine. If they reject it, the price usually will be changed quickly, or the product may even be withdrawn from the market. In this chapter we shall discuss some major methods used to determine a price. Before being concerned with actual price determination, however, executives should understand the meaning and importance of price. They must also decide on their pricing objectives.

## MEANING OF PRICE

Undoubtedly many difficulties associated with pricing occur because we do not know the meaning of the word *price,* even though the concept is quite easy to define in familiar terms. In economic theory, price, value, and utility are related concepts. **Utility** is the attribute of an item that gives rise to want satisfaction. **Value** is the quantitative measure of the worth of a product in an exchange for other products. We may say the value of a certain hat is three baseball bats or 15 gallons of gasoline. Because our economy is not geared to a slow, ponderous barter system, we use money as a common denominator of value. And we use the term *price* to describe the monetary value of an item. **Price** is value expressed in terms of dollars and cents, or any other monetary medium of exchange.

Practical problems arise in connection with a definition of price, however, when we try to state simply the price of a product—say, an office desk. Suppose the price quoted to Helen for an office desk was $525, but Bill paid only $275. At first glance it looks as if Bill got a better deal. Yet, when we get all the facts, we may change our opinion. Helen's desk was delivered to her office, she had a year to pay for it, and it was beautifully finished. Bill bought a partially assembled desk with no finish on it. (He was a do-it-yourself fan.) He had to assemble the drawers and legs and then painstakingly stain, varnish, and hand-rub the entire desk. He arranged for the delivery himself, and he paid cash in full at the time of purchase. Now let us ask who paid the higher price in each case. The answer is not as easy as it first seemed.

Defining the price of a product can be tricky because of the difficulty of determining exactly what the sale price will buy.

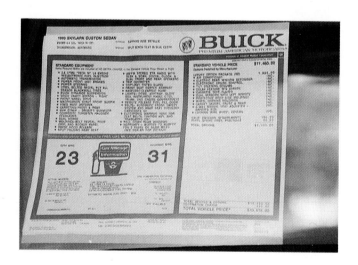

> **Price is what you pay for what you get**
>
> "That which we call a rose by any other name would smell as sweet."
> —*Romeo and Juliet*, Act II, Scene 2
>
> - Tuition—Education
> - Interest—Use of money
> - Rent—Use of living quarters or a piece of equipment for a period of time
> - Fare—Taxi or bus ride
> - Fee—Services of a physician or lawyer
> - Retainer—Lawyer's services over a period of time
> - Toll—Long-distance phone call or travel on some highways
> - Salary—Services of an executive or other white-collar worker
> - Wage—Services of a blue-collar worker
> - Commission—Sales person's services
> - Dues—Membership in a union or a club
>
> And in socially undesirable situations, some people pay a price called blackmail, ransom, or bribery.
>
> Source: Suggested, in part, by John T. Mentzer and David J. Schwartz, *Marketing Today*, 4th ed., Harcourt Brace Jovanovich, San Diego, 1985, p. 599.

This example illustrates how difficult it is to define price in an everyday business situation. The definition hinges on the problem of determining exactly what is being sold. In pricing, we must consider more than the tangible good alone. A seller usually is pricing a combination of a tangible good and several services and want-satisfying benefits. Sometimes it is difficult even to define the price of the tangible good alone. On one model of automobile, a stated price may include radio, power steering, and power brakes. For another model of the same make of car, these three items may be priced separately.

In summary, price is the value placed on goods and services. Price is the amount of money and/or goods needed to acquire some combination of another good and its accompanying services.

## IMPORTANCE OF PRICE

### In the Economy

Pricing is considered by many to be the key activity within the free enterprise system. A product's price influences wages, rent, interest, and profits. That is, the price of a product influences the price paid for the factors of production—labor, land, capital, and entrepreneurship. Price thus is a basic regulator of the economic system because it influences the allocation of these factors of production. High wages attract labor, high interest rates attract capital, and so on. As an allocator of scarce resources, price determines what will be produced (supply) and who will get the goods and services that are produced (demand).

Criticism of the American system of reasonably free enterprise and public demand for further restraints on the system are often triggered by negative reactions to price or pricing policies.

### In the Individual Firm

A product's price is a major determinant of the market demand for the item. Price affects a firm's competitive position and its market share. As a result, price has a considerable bearing on a company's revenue and net profit. It is only through price that money comes into an organization.

What do you think is the price and quality level of this watch?

At the same time, several factors usually limit the importance of pricing in a company's marketing program. Differentiated product features or a favorite brand may be more important to consumers than price. In fact, as noted in Chapter 9, one object of branding is to *decrease* the effect of price on the demand for a product. To put the role of pricing in a company's marketing program in its proper perspective, then, let us say that price is important, but not all-important, in explaining marketing success.

### Relationship to Product Quality

Consumers rely heavily on price as an indicator of a product's quality, especially when they must make purchase decisions with incomplete information. Some consumers' perceptions of product quality vary directly with price. Thus, the higher the price, the better the quality is perceived to be. Consumers make this judgment particularly when no other clues as to product quality are available. Consumers' quality perceptions can, of course, also be influenced by such things as store reputation and advertising.[2]

## PRICING OBJECTIVES

Every marketing task—including pricing—should be directed toward a goal. Management should decide on its pricing *objective* before determining the price itself. Yet, as logical as this may sound, very few firms consciously establish, or explicitly state, a pricing objective. We shall discuss the following pricing objectives:

- Profit-oriented:
  - To achieve a target return.
  - To maximize profit.
- Sales-oriented:
  - To increase sales volume.
  - To maintain or increase market share.

[2]For an in-depth discussion of this topic, along with excellent bibliographies, see David J. Curry and Peter C. Riesz, "Prices and Price/Quality Relationships: A Longitudinal Analysis," *Journal of Marketing,* January 1988, pp. 36–51; and Valarie A. Zeithaml, "Consumer Perceptions of Price, Quality, and Value: A Means-End Model and Synthesis of Evidence," *Journal of Marketing,* July 1988, pp. 2–22.

- Status quo–oriented:
  - To stabilize prices.
  - To meet competition.

The pricing objective management selects should be entirely compatible with the goals set for the company and its marketing program. To illustrate, let's assume that the company's goal is to increase return on investment from its present level of 15 percent to 20 percent at the end of a 3-year period. It follows that the pricing goal during this period must be to achieve some stated percentage return on investment. It would not be logical, in this case, to adopt the pricing goal of maintaining the company's market share or of stabilizing prices.

**Profit-Oriented Goals**  A company may select one of two profit-oriented goals for its pricing policy. Profit goals may be set for the short run or for a longer period of time.

### ACHIEVE A TARGET RETURN

A firm may price its products to achieve a certain percentage return on its *sales* or on its *investment*. Such goals are used by middlemen and producers. Many retailers and wholesalers use a target return on *net sales* as a pricing objective for short-run periods such as a year or a fashion season. They set a percentage markup on sales that is large enough to cover anticipated operating costs plus a desired profit for the period. Safeway or Kroger, for example, may price to earn a net profit of 1 percent on a store's total sales. A chain of men's clothing stores in Colorado has a net profit target of 6 percent of sales, and prices its products accordingly. (Markup and other operating ratios are discussed fully in Appendix B, which immediately follows this chapter.)

Achieving a target return on *investment* is often selected as a pricing goal by manufacturers that are leaders in their industry, such as Du Pont, Alcoa, or Exxon. These firms may price so that they earn a net profit that is 15 or 20 percent of the firm's investment—the company's assets minus its liabilities. Target-return pricing is typically used by industry leaders because they can set their pricing goals more independently of competition than can smaller firms in the industry.

### MAXIMIZE PROFITS

The pricing objective of making as much money as possible is probably followed by a larger number of companies than any other goal. The trouble with this goal is that the term *profit maximization* has an ugly connotation. It is sometimes connected in the public mind with profiteering, high prices, and monopoly.

In economic theory or business practice, however, there is nothing wrong with profit maximization. Theoretically, if profits become unduly high because supply is short in relation to demand, new capital will be attracted into the field. This will increase supply and eventually reduce profits to normal levels. In the marketplace it is difficult to find many situations where profiteering has existed over an extended period of time. Substitute products are available, purchases are postponable, and competition can increase to keep prices at a reasonable level. Where prices may be unduly high and entry into the field severely limited, public outrage soon balances the scales. If market conditions and public opinion do not do the job directly, government restraints will soon bring moderation.

A profit maximization goal is likely to be far more beneficial to a company and to the public if practiced over the *long run*. To do this, however, firms sometimes have to accept short-run losses. A company entering a new geographic market or introducing a new product frequently does best by initially setting low prices to build a large clientele.

The goal should be to maximize profits on *total output* rather than on each single product. In fact, a company may maximize total profit by setting low, relatively unprofitable prices on some products in order to stimulate sales of others. Through its sponsored broadcasts and telecasts of athletic events, the Gillette Company frequently promotes razors at very low prices. The firm hopes that once customers acquire Gillette razors, they will become loyal customers for Gillette blades, which generate healthy profits for the company.

## Sales-Oriented Goals

In some companies, management's pricing attention is focused on sales volume. The pricing goal may be to increase sales volume or to maintain or increase the firm's market share.

### INCREASE SALES VOLUME

This pricing goal is usually stated as a percentage increase in sales volume over some period of time, say, 1 year or 3 years. Management may decide to increase sales volume by discounting or by some other aggressive pricing strategy, perhaps even incurring a loss in the short run. Thus, clothing stores run end-of-season sales, and auto dealers offer rebates and below-market financing rates on new cars to stimulate sales. Many vacation resorts reduce their prices during off-seasons to increase sales volume.

### MAINTAIN OR INCREASE MARKET SHARE

In some companies, both large ones and small ones, the major pricing objective is to maintain or increase the firm's market share. In the late 1980s, for instance, the Japanese yen rose considerably in relation to the U.S. dollar. Consequently, Japanese products—autos, for example—became more expensive in U.S. dollars and Japanese companies faced the prospect of losing market share. To maintain their market shares, Toyota, Nissan, and Honda accepted smaller profit margins and reduced their costs so that they could lower their selling prices.

Occasionally a price war is started when one firm cuts its price in an effort to increase its market share. A gas station may lower the price of its gasoline below market level, or an airline may cut fares on certain routes. Other gas stations and airlines in those markets usually are forced to cut their prices just to maintain their market shares.

## Status Quo Goals

Two closely related goals—**stabilizing prices** and **meeting competition**—are the least aggressive of all pricing goals, because they are designed to maintain the pricing status quo. The primary intention of a firm that adopts these goals is to avoid any form of price competition—to "live and let live."

Price stabilization often is the goal in industries where the product is highly standardized (steel, gasoline, copper, bulk chemicals) and one large firm historically has acted as a leader in setting prices. Smaller firms in these industries simply adopt a follow-the-leader policy (meeting competition) when setting their own prices. A major reason for seeking price stability is to avoid price wars.

Even in industries where there are no price leaders, countless firms consciously price their products to meet the competitive market price. This pricing policy gives management an easy means of avoiding difficult pricing decisions.

Just because firms adopt status quo pricing goals that circumvent price competition does not mean that they are unaggressive in marketing. Quite the contrary! Typically these companies compete aggressively using the other major elements in the marketing mix—product, distribution, and especially promotion. This approach is called nonprice competition.

## FACTORS INFLUENCING PRICE DETERMINATION

Knowing its objective, a company then can move to the heart of price management—the actual determination of the base price of a product. By **base price** (or **list price**), we mean the price of one unit of the product at its point of production or resale. This is the price before provision is made for discounts, freight charges, or any other modification, such as those discussed in the next chapter.

The same general procedure is followed in pricing both new and established products. However, pricing an established product usually involves less difficulty, because the exact price or a narrow range of prices may be dictated by the market. In pricing new products, though, the decisions are difficult, but very important. Pricing objectives certainly guide price setting in the price determination process. Other key factors that influence price determination are discussed next.

### Estimated Demand for the Product

In pricing, a company must estimate the total demand for the product. Obviously this is easier to do for an established product than for a new one. Two steps in demand estimation are (1) to determine whether there is a price that the market expects and (2) to estimate the sales volume at different prices.

#### THE "EXPECTED" PRICE

The "expected" price of a product is the price at which customers consciously or unconsciously value it—what they think the product is worth. Expected price usually is expressed as a *range* of prices, rather than as a specific

Retailers often are very good at estimating the price that consumers will pay for a product.

## Elasticity of demand
Review of a basic economic concept

Elasticity of demand refers to the effect that unit-price changes have on the number of units sold and total revenue. (Total revenue—total dollar sales volume—equals the unit price times the number of units sold.) We say that the demand is **elastic** when (1) reducing the unit price causes an increase in total revenue or (2) raising the unit price causes a decrease in total revenue. In the first case, the cut in unit price results in a boost in quantity sold and more than offsets the price cut—hence the increase in total revenue.

These situations are illustrated in Figure 10-A. We start with a situation where, at $5 a unit, we sell 100 units and the total revenue (TR) equals $500. When we lower the price to $4 a unit, the quantity sold increases to 150 and total revenue also goes up—to $600. When the unit price is boosted to $6, however, the quantity sold drops off so much (to 70 units) that total revenue also declines (to $420).

Demand is **inelastic** when (1) a price cut causes total revenue to decline or (2) a price raise results in an increase in total revenue. In each of these situations, the changes in unit price more than offset the relatively small changes in quantities sold. That is, when the price is cut, the increase in quantity sold is not enough to off-set the price cut, so total revenue goes down. When the unit price is raised, it more than offsets the decline in quantity sold, so total revenue goes up.

In Figure 10-B, again we start with a unit price of $5, we sell 100 units, and total revenue is $500. When we lower the unit price to $4, the quantity sold increases to 115. But this is not enough to offset the price cut, so total revenue declines to $460. When we raise the unit price to $6, the quantity sold falls off to 90. But the price increase more than offsets the drop in quantity sold, so total revenue goes up to $540.

As a generalization, the demand for necessities (salt, sugar, cigarettes, gasoline, telephone service, gas and electric service) tends to be inelastic. If the price of gasoline goes up or down, say, 10 or 15 cents a gallon, the total number of gallons sold does not change very much. On the other hand, the demand for products purchased with discretionary income (luxury items, large appliances, furniture, autos) typically is much more elastic. Moreover, the demand for individual *brands* is much more elastic than is the demand for the broader *product* category. Thus the demand for Continental Airlines or Hertz rental cars is far more elastic (price-sensitive) than is the demand for air travel or rental cars in general.

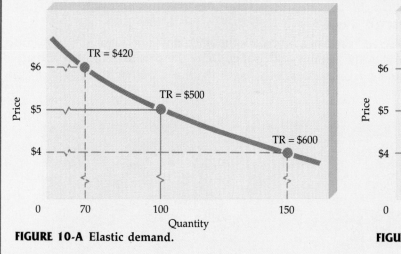

**FIGURE 10-A** Elastic demand.

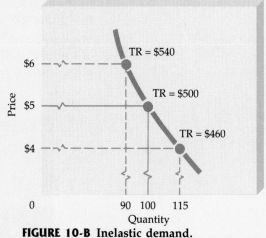

**FIGURE 10-B** Inelastic demand.

amount. Thus the expected price might be "between $250 and $300" or "not over $20." Consumers can be surprisingly shrewd in evaluating a product and its expected price.

A producer must also consider the middleman's reaction to price. Middlemen are more likely to give an article favorable treatment in their stores if they

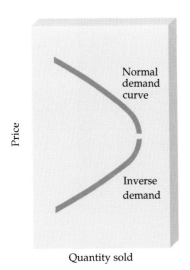

**FIGURE 10-1** Inverse demand.

approve of its price. Retail or wholesale buyers can frequently make an accurate estimate of the selling price that the market will spend for a particular item.

It is possible to set a price too low. If the price is much lower than what the market expects, sales may be lost. For example, it would probably be a mistake for a well-known cosmetics producer to put a 49-cent price tag on its lipstick or to price its imported perfume at $2.29 an ounce. Either customers will be suspicious of the quality of the products or their self-concepts will not let them buy such low-priced products. Many sellers have raised the price of a product and experienced a considerable increase in sales. This situation is called **inverse demand**—the higher the price, the greater the unit sales. Inverse demand usually exists only within a given price range and only at low price levels. Once a price rises to some particular point, inverse demand ends and the usual-shaped demand curve takes over. Demand then declines as prices rise. (See Figure 10-1.)

How do sellers determine expected prices? They may submit articles to experienced retailers or wholesalers for appraisal. A manufacturer of business products might get price estimates by showing models or blueprints to engineers working for prospective customers. Another alternative is to test-market the product in a few limited areas. By trying different prices under controlled test-market conditions, the seller can determine a reasonable range of prices.

### ESTIMATES OF SALES AT VARIOUS PRICES

It is extremely helpful to estimate what the sales volume will be at several different prices. By doing this, the seller is, in effect, determining the demand curve for the product and thus determining its demand elasticity. Estimates of sales at different prices also are useful in determining break-even points—a topic that we discuss later in this chapter.

There are several methods sellers can use to estimate potential sales at various prices. To illustrate, a company can conduct a survey of buyer intentions to determine consumer buying interest at different prices. Or management can conduct test-market experiments, offering the product at a different price in each market and measuring consumer purchases at these different prices. A seller may be able to design a computerized model that would simulate field selling conditions and sales responses at various prices. Firms can get sales estimates by surveying their wholesalers and retailers. For some

**AN ETHICAL DILEMMA?**

A store receives a special shipment of costume-jewelry earrings and prices them with its normal markup. After two weeks, despite some interest on the part of consumers, the earrings are not selling, even though they are a good value. Assume you are the store manager and a young executive suggests to you that the reason the earrings are not selling is that consumers judge quality by price. He proposes increasing the price from $2.99 (which produces a profit margin of 100 percent) to $7.99. How would you respond?

The alternative methods of transportation available to shippers will influence the price that Santa Fe charges for hauling freight.

# With a name like Santa Fe, you expect us to be super.

In the past, you've looked to Santa Fe for quality and service. In the future, you'll recognize the same quality and service in our new red and silver Super Fleet™ trains.

Super Fleet from Santa Fe is the industry's elite—in service, performance and competitive spirit. You'll find it in the increased availability of our intermodal equipment. And in our commitment to developing services such as our warehouse program (QDC), our high speed, short-haul network (QSN), and our coast-to-coast double stack service (QSS).

At Santa Fe, being super has always meant being first with innovations too. Our articulated flat car pioneered a smooth, damage-free ride for our customers. Now, it's standard equipment for the industry.

Finally, being super means being productive for our customers. We realize that service is the most important thing we have to sell. So you can expect responsiveness from an organization that has been reorganized to meet your needs more effectively.

Superiority. It isn't just a claim with us. It's a commitment we're willing to put behind our name.

To find out how Super Fleet can work for you, call 1-800-234-9852.

**Super Fleet**
Setting the track record in transportation.

The Atchison, Topeka and Santa Fe Railway Company, 80 E. Jackson Boulevard, Chicago, Illinois 60604-2491

business products, sales estimates can be generated by using the sales-force composite method of forecasting, a topic to be discussed in Chapter 22.[3]

## Competitive Reactions

Present and potential competition greatly influences base price. Even a new product is distinctive only until the inevitable competition arrives. The threat of *potential* competition is greatest when the field is easy to enter and profit prospects are encouraging. Competition can come from these sources:

- *Directly similar products:* Nike running shoes versus Adidas or Reebok shoes.
- *Available substitutes:* Air freight versus truck or rail freight.
- *Unrelated products seeking the same consumer dollar:* Videocassette recorder (VCR) versus a bicycle or a weekend excursion.

## Other Parts of the Marketing Mix

The base price of a product is influenced considerably by the other major ingredients in the marketing mix.

### THE PRODUCT

We have already observed that the price of a product is affected substantially by whether it is a new item or an older, established one. The importance of the product in its end use must also be considered. For instance, there is little

---

[3]For a report on how marketing managers determine customers' sensitivity to price (and determine demand elasticity) in the business-to-business market, see Michael H. Morris and Mary L. Joyce, "How Marketers Evaluate Price Sensitivity," *Industrial Marketing Management*, May 1988, pp. 169–76.

price competition among manufacturers of packaging materials or producers of industrial gases, so their price structure is stable. These business products are only an incidental part of the final article, so customers will buy the least expensive product consistent with the required quality. The price of a product is also influenced by (1) whether the product may be leased as well as purchased outright, (2) whether or not the product may be returned to the seller, and (3) whether a trade-in is involved.

### CHANNELS OF DISTRIBUTION

The channels and types of middlemen selected will influence a producer's pricing. A firm selling both through wholesalers and directly to retailers often sets a different factory price for each of these two classes of customers. The price to wholesalers is lower because they perform services that the producer otherwise would have to perform itself—activities such as providing storage, granting credit to retailers, and selling to small retailers.

### PROMOTIONAL METHODS

The promotional methods used and the extent to which the product is promoted by the producer or middlemen are still other factors to consider in pricing. If major promotional responsibility is placed on retailers, they ordinarily will be charged a lower price for a product than if the producer advertises it heavily. Even when a producer promotes heavily, it may want its retailers to use local advertising to tie in with national advertising. Such a decision must be reflected in the producer's price to these retailers.

## COST-PLUS PRICING

We now are at the point in our price determination discussion where we can talk about setting a *specific* selling price. Most approaches used by companies to establish base prices are variations of one of the following methods:

- Prices are based on total cost plus a desired profit. (Break-even analysis is a variation of this method.)
- Prices are based on marginal analysis—a consideration of both market demand and supply.
- Prices are based only on competitive market conditions.

**Cost-plus pricing** means setting the price of one unit of a product equal to the unit's total cost plus the desired profit on the unit. Suppose a contractor

Should the builder use the cost-plus method when pricing these condominium units?

**TABLE 10-1 Example of cost-plus pricing**
Actual results often differ from the original plans because various types of costs react differently to changes in output.

| Costs, selling prices, profit | Number of houses built and sold | |
| --- | --- | --- |
| | Planned = 10 | Actual = 8 |
| Labor and materials costs ($75,000 per house) | $750,000 | $600,000 |
| Overhead (fixed) costs | 150,000 | 150,000 |
| Total costs | $900,000 | $750,000 |
| Total sales at $99,000 per house | 990,000 | 792,000 |
| Profit: Total | $90,000 | $42,000 |
| Per house | $9,000 | $5,250 |
| As % of cost | 10% | 5.6% |

figures that the labor and materials required to build and sell 10 houses will cost $750,000, and that other expenses (office rent, depreciation on equipment, wages of management, and so on) will equal $150,000. On this total cost of $900,000, the contractor desires a profit of 10 percent of cost. The cost plus the profit amount is $990,000, so each of the 10 houses is priced at $99,000.

While this is an easily applied pricing method, it has one serious limitation. It does not account for the fact that there are different types of costs, and that these costs are affected differently by changes in level of output. In our housing example, suppose the contractor built and sold only eight houses at the cost-plus price of $99,000 each. As shown in Table 10-1, total sales would then be $792,000. Labor and materials chargeable to the eight houses would total $600,000 ($75,000 per house). Since the contractor would still incur the full $150,000 in overhead expenses, however, the total cost would be $750,000. This would leave a profit of only $42,000, or $5,250 per house instead of the anticipated $9,000. On a percentage basis, the profit would be only 5.6 percent of total cost rather than the desired 10 percent.

**Cost Concepts**

The total unit cost of a product is made up of several types of costs that react differently to changes in the quantity produced. Thus the total unit cost of a product changes as output expands or contracts. A more sophisticated approach to cost-plus pricing takes such changes into consideration.

The cost concepts in the nearby box are fundamental to our discussion. These nine cost concepts and their interrelationships may be studied in Table 10-2 and Figure 10-2, which is based on the table. The interrelationship among the various *average unit* costs is displayed graphically in the figure and may be explained briefly as follows:

- The **average fixed cost curve** declines as output increases because the total of the fixed costs is spread over an increasing number of units.
- The **average variable cost curve** usually is U-shaped. It starts high because average variable costs for the first few units of output are high. Variable costs per unit then decline as the company realizes efficiencies in production. Eventually the average variable cost curve reaches its lowest point,

reflecting optimum output as far as variable costs (not total costs) are concerned. In Figure 10-2 this point is at three units of output. Beyond that point the average variable cost rises, reflecting the increase in unit variable costs caused by overcrowded facilities and other inefficiencies. If the variable costs per unit were constant, then the average variable cost curve would be a horizontal line at the level of the constant unit variable cost.

- The **average total cost curve** is the sum of the first two curves—average fixed cost and average variable cost. It starts high, reflecting the fact that total *fixed* costs are spread over so few units of output. As output increases, the average total cost curve declines, because the unit fixed cost and unit variable cost are decreasing. Eventually the point of lowest total cost per unit is reached (four units of output in the figure). Beyond that optimum point, diminishing returns set in and the average total cost curve rises.
- The **marginal cost curve** has a more pronounced U-shape than the other curves in Figure 10-2. The marginal cost curve slopes downward until the second unit of output, at which point the marginal costs start to increase.

Now note the relationship between the marginal cost curve and the average total cost curve. The average total cost curve slopes downward *as long as the marginal cost is less than the average total cost*. Even though the marginal cost increases after the second unit, the average total cost curve continues to slope downward until the fourth unit. This is so because marginal cost—even when it is going up—is still less than average total cost.

The marginal cost and average total cost curves intersect at the lowest point of the average total cost curve. Beyond that point (the fourth unit in the

---

### Different kinds of costs

- A **fixed cost** is an element, such as rent, executive salaries, or property tax, that remains constant regardless of how many items are produced. Such a cost continues even if production stops completely. It is called a fixed cost because it is difficult to change in the short run (but not in the long run).
- **Total fixed cost** is the sum of all fixed costs.
- **Average fixed cost** is the total fixed cost divided by the number of units produced.
- A **variable cost** is an element, such as labor or material cost, that is directly related to production. Variable costs can be controlled in the short run simply by changing the level of production. When production stops, for example, all variable production costs become zero.
- **Total variable cost** is the sum of all variable costs. The more units produced, the higher this cost is.
- **Average variable cost** is the total variable cost divided by the number of units produced. Average variable cost is usually high for the first few units produced. It decreases as production increases due to such things as quantity discounts on materials and more efficient use of labor. Beyond some optimum output, it increases, because of such factors as crowding of production facilities and overtime pay.
- **Total cost** is the sum of total fixed cost and total variable cost for a specific quantity produced.
- **Average total cost** is the total cost divided by the number of units produced.
- **Marginal cost** is the cost of producing and selling one more unit. Usually the marginal cost of the last unit is the same as the variable cost of that unit.

## TABLE 10-2 Costs for an individual firm

Total fixed costs do not change in the short run, despite increases in quantity produced. Variable costs are the costs of inputs—materials, labor, power. Total variable costs increase as production quantity rises. Total cost is the sum of all fixed and variable costs. The other measures in the table are simply methods of looking at costs per unit; they always involve dividing a cost by the number of units produced.

| (1) Quantity produced | (2) Total fixed costs | (3) Total variable costs | (4) Total costs (2) + (3) | (5) Marginal cost per unit | (6) Average fixed cost (2) ÷ (1) | (7) Average variable cost (3) ÷ (1) | (8) Average total cost per unit (4) ÷ (1) |
|---|---|---|---|---|---|---|---|
| 0 | $256 | $ 0 | $256 | | Infinity | $ 0 | Infinity |
| | | | | $ 84 | | | |
| 1 | 256 | 84 | 340 | | $256.00 | 84 | $340.00 |
| | | | | 28 | | | |
| 2 | 256 | 112 | 368 | | 128.00 | 56 | 184.00 |
| | | | | 32 | | | |
| 3 | 256 | 144 | 400 | | 85.33 | 48 | 133.33 |
| | | | | 80 | | | |
| 4 | 256 | 224 | 480 | | 64.00 | 56 | 120.00 |
| | | | | 176 | | | |
| 5 | 256 | 400 | 656 | | 51.20 | 80 | 131.20 |

**FIGURE 10-2 Unit cost curves for an individual firm.**

This figure is based on data in Table 10-2. Here we see how *unit* costs change as quantity increases. Using cost-plus pricing, two units of output would be priced at $184 each, whereas four units would sell for $120 each.

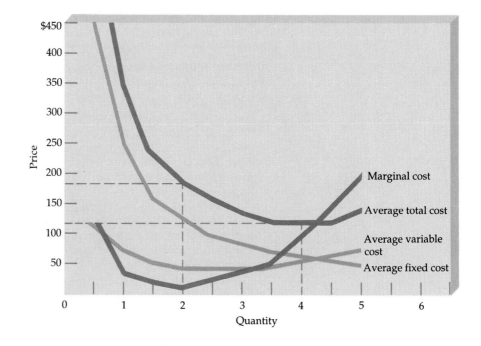

example), the cost of producing and selling the next unit is higher than the average cost of all units. Therefore, from then on the average total cost rises. This occurs because the average variable cost is increasing faster than the average fixed cost is decreasing. Table 10-2 shows that producing the fifth unit reduces the average fixed cost by $12.80 (from $64 to $51.20), but causes the average variable cost to increase by $24.

**Refinements in Cost-Plus Pricing**

Once a company understands that not all costs react in the same way to changes in output, refinements in cost-plus pricing are possible. Let's assume that the desired profit is included either in the fixed cost or the variable cost schedule. That is, profit is included as a cost in Table 10-2 and Figure 10-2. Then once the quantity to be produced has been determined, management can refer to the table or graph to find the appropriate price. If a firm decides to produce three units in our example, the selling price will be $133.33 per unit. A production run of four units would be priced at $120 per unit.

This pricing method assumes that all the intended output will be produced and sold. If fewer units are produced, each would have to sell for a higher price in order to cover all costs and show a profit. But, obviously, if business is slack and output must be cut, it is not wise to raise the unit price. Thus the difficulty in this pricing approach is that market demand is ignored.

**Prices Based on Marginal Costs Only**

Another approach to cost-plus pricing is to set a price that will cover only marginal costs, not total costs. Refer again to the cost schedules shown in Table 10-2 and Figure 10-1, and assume that a firm is operating at an output level of three units. Under marginal cost pricing, this firm can accept an order for one more unit at $80, instead of the total unit cost of $120. The company is then trying to cover only its variable costs. If the firm can sell for any price over $80—say, $85 or $90—the excess contributes to the payment of fixed costs.

Not all orders can be priced to cover only variable costs. Marginal cost pricing may be feasible, however, if management wants to keep its labor force employed during a slack season. Marginal cost pricing may also be used when one product is expected to attract business for another. A department store may price meals in its café at a level that covers only the marginal costs. The reasoning is that this café will bring shoppers to the store, where they will buy other, more profitable products.

**Cost-Plus Pricing by Middlemen**

Cost-plus pricing is widely used by retailing and wholesaling middlemen. At least it seems this way at first glance. A retailer, for example, pays a given amount to buy products and have them delivered to the store. Then the retailer adds an amount (a markup) to the acquisition cost. This markup is estimated to be sufficient to cover the store's expenses and still provide a reasonable profit. Thus a clothing store may buy a garment for $30 including freight, and price the item at $50. The price of $50 reflects a markup of 40 percent based on the selling price, or 66⅔ percent based on the merchandise cost.

Different types of retailers will require different percentage markups because of the nature of the products handled and the services offered. A self-service supermarket has lower costs and thus a lower average markup than a full-service delicatessen. Figure 10-3 shows an example of markup pricing by middlemen. The topic of markups is discussed in more detail in Appendix B.

To what extent is cost-plus pricing truly used by middlemen? At least three significant indications suggest that what seems to be cost-plus pricing is really market-influenced pricing:

1. Most retail prices set by applying average percentage markups are really only price offers. If the merchandise does not sell at the original price, that price will be lowered until it reaches a level at which the merchandise will sell.

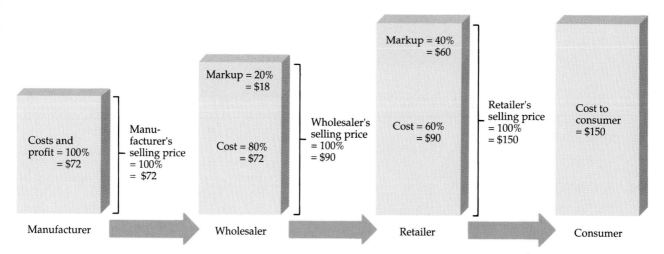

**FIGURE 10-3** Examples of markup pricing by retailers and wholesalers.

2. Many retailers do not use the same markup on all the products they carry. A supermarket will have a markup of 6 to 8 percent on sugar and soap products, 15 to 18 percent on canned fruit and vegetables, and 25 to 30 percent on fresh meats and produce. These different markups for different products definitely reflect competitive considerations and other aspects of market demand.

3. The middleman usually does not actually set a base price but only adds a percentage to the price that has already been set by the producer. The producer's price is set to allow each middleman to add the customary markup and still sell at a competitive retail price. The key price is set by the producer, with an eye on the market.

## Evaluation of Cost-Plus Pricing

We have emphasized that a firm must be market-oriented and must cater to consumers' wants. Why, then, are we now considering cost-plus pricing? Cost-plus pricing is mentioned so widely in business that it must be understood. Adherents of cost-plus pricing point to its simplicity and its ease of determination. They say that costs are a known quantity, whereas attempts to estimate demand for pricing purposes are mainly guesswork.

This opinion is questionable on two counts. First, it is doubtful that accurate cost data are available. We know a fair amount about cost-volume relationships in production costs, but what we know is still insufficient. Furthermore, information regarding marketing costs is woefully inadequate. Second, it is indeed difficult to estimate demand—that is, to construct a demand schedule that shows sales volume at various prices. Nevertheless, sales forecasting and other research tools can do a surprisingly good job in this area.

Critics of cost-plus pricing do not say that costs should be disregarded in pricing. Costs should be a determinant, they maintain, but not the only one. Costs are a floor under a firm's prices. If goods are priced under this floor for a long time, the firm will be forced out of business. But when used by itself, cost-plus pricing is a weak and unrealistic method, because it ignores competition and market demand.

## BREAK-EVEN ANALYSIS

One way to use market demand in price determination, and still consider costs, is to conduct a break-even analysis and determine break-even points. A **break-even point** is that quantity of output at which total revenue equals total costs, *assuming a certain selling price.* There is a different break-even point for each different selling price. Sales of quantities above the break-even output result in a profit on each additional unit. The further the sales are above the break-even point, the higher the total and unit profits. Sales below the break-even point result in a loss to the seller.

## Determining the Break-Even Point

The method of determining a break-even point is illustrated in Table 10-3 and Figure 10-4. In our hypothetical situation, the company's fixed costs are $250 and its variable costs are constant at $30 a unit. Recall that in our earlier example (Table 10-2 and Figure 10-2) we assumed that unit variable costs were *not* constant; they fluctuated. Now to simplify our break-even analysis, we are assuming that unit variable costs *are* constant.

Therefore, the total cost of producing one unit is $280. For five units the total cost is $400 ($30 multiplied by 5, plus $250). In Figure 10-4 the selling price is $80 a unit. Consequently, every time a unit is sold, $50 is contributed

**TABLE 10-3 Computation of break-even point**

At each of several prices we wish to find out how many units must be sold to cover all costs. At a unit price of $100, the sale of each unit contributes $70 to cover overhead expenses. We must sell about 3.6 units to cover the $250 fixed cost. See Figures 10-4 and 10-5 for a visual portrayal of the data in this table.

| (1) Unit price | (2) Unit variable costs | (3) Contribution to overhead (1) − (2) | (4) Overhead (total fixed costs) | (5) Break-even point (4) ÷ (3) |
|---|---|---|---|---|
| $ 60 | $30 | $ 30 | $250 | 8.3 units |
| 80 | 30 | 50 | 250 | 5.0 units |
| 100 | 30 | 70 | 250 | 3.6 units |
| 150 | 30 | 120 | 250 | 2.1 units |

**FIGURE 10-4 Break-even chart with selling price of $80 per unit.**

Here the break-even point is reached when the company sells five units. Fixed costs, regardless of quantity produced and sold, are $250. The variable cost per unit is $30. If this company sells five units, total cost is $400 (variable cost of 5 × $30, or $150, plus fixed cost of $250). At a selling price of $80, the sale of five units will yield $400 revenue, and costs and revenue will equal each other. At the same price, the sale of each unit above five yields a profit.

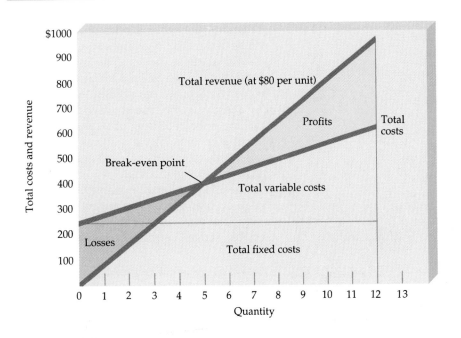

to overhead (fixed costs). The variable costs are $30 per unit, and these costs are incurred in producing each unit. But any revenue over $30 can be used to help cover fixed costs. At a selling price of $80, the company will break even if five units are sold because a $50 contribution from each of five units will just cover the total fixed costs of $250.

Stated another way, variable costs for five units are $150 and fixed costs are $250, for a total cost of $400. This is equal to the revenue from five units sold at $80 each. So, for an $80 selling price, the break-even volume is five units.

The break-even point may be found with this formula:

$$\text{Break-even point in units} = \frac{\text{Total fixed costs}}{\text{Unit contribution to overhead}}$$

$$= \frac{\text{Total fixed costs}}{\text{Selling price} - \text{Average variable cost}}$$

The basic assumptions underlying these calculations are as follows:

- Total fixed costs are constant. In reality they may change, although they usually don't in the short run. It is reasonably easy, however, to develop a break-even chart in which fixed costs, and consequently total costs, are stepped up at several intervals.
- Variable costs remain constant per unit of output. In the earlier discussion of cost structure, however, we noted that average variable costs usually fluctuate.
- Figure 10-4 shows a break-even point only where the unit price is $80. It is highly desirable to calculate break-even points for several different selling prices.

## Evaluation of Break-Even Analysis

Many of the underlying assumptions in break-even analysis—such as that costs are nonfluctuating—are unrealistic in real-world business operations. Consequently, break-even analysis has limited value in companies where demand and/or average unit costs fluctuate frequently.

Another major drawback of break-even analysis is that it ignores market demand at the various prices. Table 10-3, for example, shows what revenue will be at the different prices *if* (and it is a big if) the given number of units can be sold at these prices. The completed break-even charts show only the amount that must be sold at the stated price to break even. The charts do not tell us whether we *can* actually sell this amount. The amount the market will buy at a given price could well be below the break-even point. For instance, at a selling price of $80 per unit, the break-even point is five units. But competition and/or a volatile market may prevent the company from selling those five units. If the company can sell only three or four units, the firm will not break even. It will show a loss.

These limitations, however, should not lead management to dismiss break-even analysis as a pricing tool. Even in its simplest form, break-even analysis is very helpful because in the short run many firms experience reasonably stable cost and demand structures.[4]

---

[4] For a more sophisticated approach to break-even analysis—one that includes semifixed costs—and is of more practical value in situations typically faced by marketing executives, see Thomas L. Powers, "Breakeven Analysis with Semifixed Costs," *Industrial Marketing Management*, February 1987, pp. 35–41.

## AN INTERNATIONAL PERSPECTIVE: Pricing for export marketing

How should a company price a product for export? This question cannot be answered easily because it is difficult to generalize about export pricing. Not only are there significant differences among companies' philosophies, cultures, and products, but also pricing is affected by different constraints in the various foreign markets.

For example, intensive negotiations normally occur when selling in the Middle East. When Regal Ware, a producer of kitchen cookware, sells in these markets, the company sets a higher list price to allow room for bargaining. On the other hand, a manufacturer of grain storage and handling equipment (D. W. Witter) refuses to engage in price bargaining in the Middle East. This company is convinced that once you make price concessions, the bargaining process will continue indefinitely through future transactions.

The three major methods of export price determination are rigid cost-plus pricing, flexible cost-plus pricing, and marginal cost pricing. Seventy percent of American firms in one survey used some form of cost-plus pricing when engaging in export marketing. For these firms, pricing was a static, rather than dynamic, element in their marketing mix. In fact, over half the firms practicing cost-plus pricing reported that they adhered *rigidly* to this method of price determination. Autotrol, a Wisconsin manufacturer of water treatment and control equipment, has used rigid cost-plus pricing successfully for

the past 15 years. This company's major markets include Western Europe, Japan, Australia, and New Zealand.

In recent years competitive pressures have induced many firms to employ a more flexible cost-plus pricing method. Typically these firms offer some form of discounts or other price concessions to ensure making a sale. The Baughman Company, a producer of grain storage silos, has identical export and domestic prices, before exporting costs are added. However, the company will make price concessions when an important export sale is at stake.

The third export pricing method—marginal costs—was used by about 30 percent of the firms covered in the survey. The price is set at a level that covers only variable production costs plus exporting expenses. This price does not cover fixed costs for manufacturing and research and development, nor does it cover domestic marketing expenses. Firms using this pricing method have unused production capacity and assume that the exported products could not be sold at full cost.

Perhaps the bottom-line answer to our original question is "It all depends." Export price setting is complex, and no single method suits a company at all times.

Source: S. Tamer Cavusgil, "Unraveling the Mystique of Export Pricing," *Business Horizons*, May–June 1988, pp. 54–63.

## PRICES BASED ON MARGINAL ANALYSIS

Another method of price setting is based on marginal analysis—a consideration of both demand and costs to determine the best price for profit maximization. This policy of price determination is thus best suited for companies whose pricing goal is to maximize profit. However, firms with other pricing goals might use this method in special situations or perhaps to compare prices determined by different means.

### Determining the Price

To use marginal analysis, the price setter must understand the concepts of average and marginal revenue, in addition to average and marginal cost. **Marginal revenue** is the income derived from the sale of the last unit. **Average revenue** is the unit price at a given level of unit sales. It is calculated by dividing total revenue by the number of units sold. Referring to the hypothetical demand schedule in Table 10-4, we see that the company can sell one unit at $80. To sell two units it must reduce its price to $75 for each unit. Thus the company receives an additional $70 (marginal revenue) by selling two units instead of one. The fifth unit brings a marginal revenue of $53. After the sixth unit, however, total revenue declines each time the unit price is lowered to sell an additional unit. Hence there is a negative marginal revenue.

The price-setting process that considers both supply and demand is illustrated in Figure 10-5. We assume that a firm will continue to produce units as

## TABLE 10-4 Demand schedule for an individual firm

At each market price a certain quantity of the product will be demanded. Marginal revenue is simply the amount of additional money gained by selling one more unit. In this example the company no longer gains marginal revenue after it has sold the sixth unit at a price of $60.

| Units sold | Unit price (average revenue) | Total revenue | Marginal revenue |
|---|---|---|---|
| 1 | $80 | $ 80 | |
| 2 | 75 | 150 | $ 70 |
| 3 | 72 | 216 | 66 |
| 4 | 68 | 272 | 56 |
| 5 | 65 | 325 | 53 |
| 6 | 60 | 360 | 35 |
| 7 | 50 | 350 | −10 |
| 8 | 40 | 320 | −30 |

**FIGURE 10-5** Price setting and profit maximization through marginal analysis.

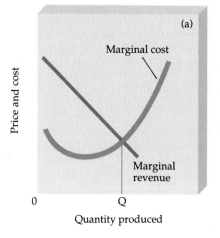

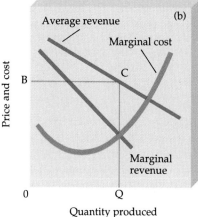

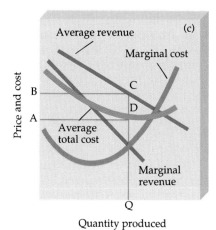

long as revenue from the last unit sold exceeds the cost of producing this last unit. That is, output continues to increase as long as marginal revenue exceeds marginal cost. At the point where they meet (quantity Q in Figure 10-5a), production theoretically should cease. Ordinarily a company will not want to sell a unit at a price less than its out-of-pocket (variable) costs of production. The optimum volume of output is the quantity level at which *marginal cost equals marginal revenue*, or quantity Q.

The unit price is determined by locating the point on the average revenue curve that represents an output of Q units. Remember that average revenue represents the unit price. The average revenue curve has been added in Figure 10-5b. The unit price at which to sell quantity Q is represented by point C. It is price B in Figure 10-5b.

The average unit total cost curve has been added in Figure 10-5c. It shows that, for output quantity Q, the average unit cost is represented by point D. This average unit cost is A. Thus, with a price of B and an average unit cost of A, the company enjoys a unit profit given by AB in the future. Total profit is represented by area ABCD (quantity Q times unit profit AB).

## Evaluation of Marginal Analysis Pricing

Marginal analysis as a basis for price setting has enjoyed only limited use. Business people claim that better data are needed for plotting the curves exactly. Marginal analysis can be used, they feel, to study past price movements, but it cannot serve as a practical basis for setting prices.

On the brighter side, management's knowledge of costs and demand is improving. Computerized data bases are bringing more complete and detailed information to management's attention all the time. Earlier we pointed out that management usually can estimate demand within broad limits, and this is helpful. And experienced management in many firms can do a surprisingly accurate job of estimating marginal and average costs and revenues.

Marginal analysis can also have practical value if management will adjust the price in light of some conditions discussed earlier in this chapter. In Figure 10-5 the price was set at point B. But, in the short run, management may price below B, or even below A, adopting an aggressive pricing strategy to increase market share or to discourage competition.

## PRICES SET IN RELATION TO MARKET ALONE

Cost-plus pricing is one extreme among pricing methods. At the other end of the scale is a method whereby a firm's prices are set in relation *only* to the market price. The seller's price may be set right at the market price to meet the competition, or it may be set either above or below the market price.

## Pricing to Meet Competition

Management may decide to price a product right at the competitive level in several situations. One such situation occurs when the market is highly competitive and the firm's product is not differentiated significantly from competing products. To some extent this method of pricing reflects market conditions that parallel those found under perfect competition. That is, product differentiation is absent, buyers and sellers are well informed, and the seller has no discernible control over the selling price. Most producers of agricultural products and small firms marketing well-known, standardized products ordinarily use this pricing method.

The sharp drop in revenue that occurs when the price is raised above the prevailing level indicates that the individual seller faces a *kinked demand* (see Figure 10-6). The prevailing price is at A. If the seller tries to go above that

**FIGURE 10-6 Kinked demand curve facing producer of product sold at prevailing price (the same type of curve faces individual oligopolist).**

The kink occurs at the point representing the prevailing price A. Above A, demand declines rapidly as price is increased. A price set below A results in very little increase in volume, so revenue is lost. Marginal revenue is negative.

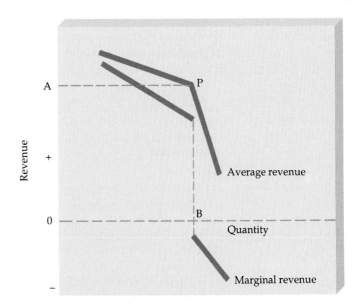

price, the demand for the product drops sharply, as indicated by the flat average revenue curve above point P. At any price above A, then, demand is highly elastic—total revenue declines. Below price A, demand is highly inelastic, as represented by the steeply sloping average revenue curve and the negative marginal revenue curve. Total revenue decreases each time the price is reduced to a level below A. The prevailing price is strong. Consequently, a reduction in price by one firm will not increase the firm's unit sales very much—certainly not enough to offset the loss in average revenue.

Up to this point in our discussion of pricing to meet competition, we have observed market situations that involve many sellers. Oddly enough, the same pricing method is often used when the market is dominated by a few firms, each marketing similar products. This type of market structure, called an **oligopoly,** exists in such industries as copper, aluminum, soft drinks, breakfast cereals, auto tires, and even among barber shops and grocery stores within a smaller community.

The demand curve facing an individual seller in an oligopoly is a kinked one, as in Figure 10-6. An oligopolist must price at market level to maximize profit. Selling *above* market price will result in a drastic reduction in total revenue, because the average revenue curve is so elastic above point P. If an oligopolist cuts its price *below* the market price, all other members of the oligopoly must respond immediately. Otherwise the price cutter will enjoy a substantial increase in business. Therefore, competitors do retaliate with comparable price cuts, and the net result is that a new market price is established at a lower level. All members of the oligopoly end up with about the same share of the market that they had before. However, unit revenue is reduced by the amount of the price cut.

Theoretically oligopolists gain no advantage by cutting prices. For their own good they should simply set prices at a competitive level and leave them there. In reality, however, price wars are common in an oligopoly because it is not possible to control all sellers of the product. In the absence of collusion, every so often some firm will cut its price. Then all others usually cut prices to maintain their respective market shares.

Pricing to meet competition is rather simple to do. A firm ascertains what the market price is, and after allowing for customary markups for middlemen, it arrives at its own selling price. To illustrate, a manufacturer of men's dress shoes knows that retailers want to sell the shoes for $70 ($69.95) a pair. The firm sells directly to retailers, who want an average markup of 40 percent of their selling price. Consequently, after allowing $28 for the retailer's markup,

---

**Flying from New York to California—the kinked demand curve in the real world**

The type of pricing situation discussed in this section is exactly what has occurred throughout the U.S. airline industry since deregulation. In an attempt to increase the number of passengers, an airline would cut its price on a heavily traveled route. However, competitors on this route usually would match that lower fare immediately. As a result, there was no significant shift in the market share held by each airline on that route. But another result was that the market price settled at the lower level, and the profits of all airlines involved generally suffered.

To accommodate local cultural traditions in Middle East markets, Regal Ware applies a pricing method different from the one used in U.S. markets.

the producer's top price is about $42. This manufacturer then has to decide whether $42 is enough to cover costs and still provide a reasonable profit. Sometimes a producer faces a real squeeze, particularly when its costs are rising but the market price is holding firm.

**Pricing below Competitive Level**

A variation of market-based pricing is to set a price at some point *below* the competitive level. This is typically done by discount retailers. These stores offer fewer services and operate on the principle of low markup and high volume. They price nationally advertised brands 10 to 30 percent below the suggested retail list price, or the price being charged by full-service retailers. Even full-service retailers may price below the competitive level by eliminating specific services. For example, some gas stations offer a discount to customers who use the self-service pumps or who pay with cash instead of a credit card.

**Pricing above Competitive Level**

Producers or retailers sometimes set their prices *above* the market level. Usually above-market pricing works only when the product is distinctive or when the seller has acquired prestige in its field. Most cities have an elite clothing or jewelry store where price tags are noticeably above the competitive level set by other stores that handle similar products. Above-market pricing often is practiced by manufacturers of prestige brands of expensive products such as autos (Ferrari, Mercedes), watches (Rolex), crystal (Waterford), and leather products (Gucci, Fendi). Above-market pricing is sometimes found even among relatively low-cost products—candies, for example, as in the case of Godiva and other brands of imported Belgian chocolates. A product with a celebrity tie-in may command an above-market price. In perfumes, Elizabeth Taylor's "Passion" was priced above market, yet it was one of the top 10 selling scents in 1989.

Most of the examples in this chapter illustrate the pricing of tangible goods. The basic pricing methods (cost-plus and marginal analysis, for instance) are equally applicable in the marketing of intangible services—a topic that is covered in more detail in Chapter 19. Pricing in nonprofit organizations, however, involves quite different considerations, and these are discussed in Chapter 20—"Marketing in Nonprofit Organizations."

**SUMMARY**     In our economy, price is a major regulator because it influences the allocation of scarce resources. In individual companies, price is one important factor in determining marketing success. However, it is difficult to define price. A rather general definition is: Price is the amount of money (plus possibly some goods or services) needed to acquire another product.

Before setting the base price on a product, management should identify its pricing goal. Major pricing objectives are to (1) earn a target return on investment or on net sales, (2) maximize profits, (3) increase sales, (4) gain or hold a target share of the market, (5) stabilize prices, and (6) meet competition's prices.

Key factors (besides the firm's pricing objective) that should influence management's decision when setting the base price are: (1) demand for the product, (2) competitive reactions, (3) other major elements in the marketing mix, (4) desired market share, and (5) the product's cost.

Three major methods used to determine the base price are cost-plus pricing, marginal analysis, and setting the price in relation only to the market.

For cost-plus pricing to be at all effective, a seller must consider several types of costs and their reactions to changes in the quantity produced. A producer usually sets a price to cover total cost. In some cases, however, the best policy may be to set a price that covers marginal cost only. The main weakness in cost-plus pricing is that it completely ignores market demand. To partially offset this weakness, a company may use break-even analysis as a tool in price setting.

In real-life situations virtually all price setting is market-inspired to some extent. Consequently, marginal analysis is a useful method for setting price. Prices are set and output level is determined at the point where marginal cost equals marginal revenue.

For many products price setting is a relatively easy job because management simply sets the price at the market level established by the competition. Two variations of market-level pricing are to price below or above the competitive level.

**KEY TERMS AND CONCEPTS**

Price 240
Pricing objectives: 242
   Target return 243
   Maximize profit 243
   Increase sales 244
   Market share 244
   Stabilize prices 244
   Meet competition 244
Base price (list price) 245
Expected price 245
Elastic demand 246
Inelastic demand 246

Inverse demand 247
Cost-plus pricing 249
Fixed cost 252
Variable cost 252
Marginal cost 252
Average cost 252
Total cost 252
Prices based on marginal costs 253
Break-even point 254
Marginal revenue 257
Price set by marginal analysis 257
Competitive market price 259

## QUESTIONS AND PROBLEMS

1. Two students paid $2.49 for identical tubes of toothpaste at a leading store. Yet one student complained about paying a much higher price than the other. What might be the basis for this complaint?

2. Explain how a firm's pricing objective may influence the promotional program for a product. Which of the six pricing goals involves the largest, most aggressive promotional campaign?

3. What marketing conditions might logically lead a

company to set "meeting competition" as a pricing objective?

4. What is the expected price for each of the following articles? How did you arrive at your estimate in each instance?

a. A new type of cola beverage that holds its carbonation long after it has been opened; packaged in 12-ounce (355-ml) and 2-liter bottles.

b. A nuclear-powered 23-inch table-model television set, guaranteed to run for years without replacement of the original power-generating component; requires no battery or electric wires.

c. An automatic garage-door opener for residential housing.

5. Name at least three products for which you think an inverse demand exists. For each product, within which price range does this inverse demand exist?

6. In Figure 10-2, what is the significance of the point where the marginal cost curve intersects the average total cost curve? Explain why the average total cost curve is declining to the left of the intersection point and rising beyond it. Explain how the marginal cost curve can be rising, while the average total cost curve is still declining.

7. In Table 10-2, what is the marginal cost of the fifth unit produced?

8. What are the merits and limitations of the cost-plus method of setting a base price?

9. In a break-even chart is the total *fixed* cost line always horizontal? Is the total *variable* cost line always straight? Explain.

10. In Table 10-3 and Figure 10-4, what would be the break-even points at prices of $50 and $90, if variable costs are $40 per unit and fixed costs remain at $250?

11. A small manufacturer sold ballpoint pens to retailers at $8.40 per dozen. The manufacturing cost was 50 cents for each pen. The expenses, including all selling and administrative costs except advertising, were $19,200. How many dozen must the manufacturer sell to cover these expenses and pay for an advertising campaign costing $6,000?

12. In Figure 10-6, why would the firm normally stop producing at quantity Q? Why is the price set at B and not at D or A?

13. Are there any stores in your community that generally price above the competitive level? How are they able to do this?

14. Evaluate the three methods of export pricing identified in the International Perspective. Under what conditions do you recommend that each be used?

# FINANCIAL ACCOUNTING IN MARKETING

Marketing involves people—customers, middlemen, and producers. Much of the business activity of these people is quantified in some manner. Consequently, knowledge of the rudiments of financial accounting is essential for decision making in many areas of marketing. Since most of you have already had a beginning course in accounting, this appendix is intended as a review. It discusses three accounting concepts that are useful in marketing: (1) the operating statement, (2) markups, and (3) analytical ratios. Another useful concept—discounts and allowances—is covered in the next chapter in connection with pricing strategies.

## THE OPERATING STATEMENT

An operating statement—often called a *profit and loss statement* or an *income statement*—is one of the two main financial statements prepared by a company. The other is the balance sheet. An **operating statement** is a summary of the firm's income and expenses—its operations—over a period of time. In contrast, a **balance sheet** shows the assets, liabilities, and net worth of a company at a given time—for example, at the close of business on December 31, 1990.

The operating statement shows whether the business earned a net profit or suffered a net loss during the period covered. It is an orderly summary of the income and expense items that resulted in this net profit or loss.

An operating statement can cover any period of time. To fulfill income tax requirements, virtually all firms prepare a statement covering operations during the calendar or fiscal year. It is also common for businesses to prepare monthly, quarterly, or semiannual operating statements.

Figure B-1 is an example of an operating statement for a wholesaler or retailer. The major difference between the operating statement of a middleman and that of a manufacturer is the cost-of-goods-sold section. A manufacturer shows the cost of goods *manufactured*, whereas the middleman's statement shows net *purchases*.

## MAJOR SECTIONS

The essence of business is very simple. A company buys or makes a product and then sells it for a higher price. Out of the sales revenue the seller hopes to cover the cost of the merchandise and the seller's own expenses and have something left over, which is called *net profit*. These relationships form the skeleton of an operating statement. *Sales minus cost of goods sold equals gross margin;* then *gross margin minus expenses equals net profit.* An example based on Figure B-1 is as follows:

|  |  |  |
|---|---|---|
|  | Sales | $80,000 |
| *less* | Cost of goods sold | −48,000 |
| *equals* | Gross margin | 32,000 |
| *less* | Expenses | −27,200 |
| *equals* | Net profit | $ 4,800 |

## FIGURE B-1 Example of operating statement for a wholesaler or retailer

**Alpha-Beta Company**
**Operating Statement for Year Ending December 31, 1990**

| | | | |
|---|---|---:|---:|
| **Gross sales** | | | $87,000 |
| *Less:* Sales returns and allowances | $ 5,500 | | |
| Cash discounts allowed | 1,500 | 7,000 | |
| **Net sales** | | | $80,000 |
| **Cost of goods sold:** | | | |
| Beginning inventory, January 1 (at cost) | | 18,000 | |
| Gross purchases | 49,300 | | |
| *Less:* Cash discounts taken on purchases | 900 | | |
| Net purchases | 48,400 | | |
| *Plus:* Freight in | 1,600 | | |
| Net purchases (at delivered cost) | | 50,000 | |
| Cost of goods available for sale | | 68,000 | |
| *Less:* Ending inventory, December 31 (at cost) | | 20,000 | |
| Cost of goods sold | | | 48,000 |
| **Gross margin** | | | 32,000 |
| **Expenses:** | | | |
| Sales-force salaries and commissions | | $11,000 | |
| Advertising | | 2,400 | |
| Office supplies | | 250 | |
| Taxes (except income tax) | | 125 | |
| Telephone and telegraph | | 250 | |
| Delivery expenses | | 175 | |
| Rent | | 800 | |
| Heat, light, and power | | 300 | |
| Depreciation | | 100 | |
| Insurance | | 150 | |
| Interest | | 150 | |
| Bad debts | | 300 | |
| Administrative salaries | | 7,500 | |
| Office salaries | | 3,500 | |
| Miscellaneous expenses | | 200 | |
| Total expenses | | | 27,200 |
| **Net profit** | | | $ 4,800 |

## SALES

The first line in an operating statement records gross sales—the total amount sold by the company. From this figure the company deducts sales returns and sales allowances. The firm also deducts discounts that are granted to employees when they purchase merchandise or services.

In virtually every firm at some time during an operating period, customers will want to return or exchange merchandise. In a *sales return,* the customer is refunded the full purchase price in cash or credit. In a *sales allowance,* the customer keeps the merchandise, but is given a reduction from the selling price because of some dissatisfaction. The income from the sale of returned merchandise is included in a company's gross sales, so returns and allowances must be deducted to get net sales.

## NET SALES

This is the most important figure in the sales section of the statement. It represents the net amount of sales revenue, out of which the company will pay for the products and all its expenses. The net sales figure is also the one upon which many operating ratios are based. It is called 100 percent (of itself), and the other items are then expressed as a percentage of net sales.

## COST OF GOODS SOLD

From net sales we must deduct the cost of the merchandise that was sold, as we work toward discovering the firm's net profit. In determining the cost of goods sold in a retail or wholesale operation, we start with the value of any merchandise on hand at the beginning of the period. To this we add the net cost of what was purchased during the period. From this total we deduct the value of whatever remains unsold at the end of the period. In Figure B-1 the firm started with an inventory worth $18,000, and it purchased goods that cost $50,000. Thus the firm had a total of $68,000 worth of goods available for sale. If all were sold, the cost of goods sold would have been $68,000. At the end of the year, however, there was still $20,000 worth of merchandise on hand. Thus, during the year the company sold goods that cost $48,000.

We just spoke of merchandise "valued at" a certain figure or "worth" a stated amount. Actually the problem of inventory valuation is complicated and sometimes controversial. The rule of thumb is to value inventories at cost or market, whichever is lower. The application of this rule in the real world may be difficult. Assume that a store buys six footballs at $2 each and the following week buys six more at $2.50 each. The company places all 12, jumbled, in a basket display for sale. Then one is sold, but there is no marking to indicate whether its cost was $2 or $2.50. Thus the inventory value of the remaining 11 balls may be $25 or $24.50. If we multiply this situation by thousands of purchases and sales, we begin to see the depth of the problem.

A figure that deserves some comment is the *net cost of delivered purchases.* A company starts with its gross purchases at billed cost. Then it must deduct any purchases that were returned or any purchase allowances received. The company should also deduct any discounts taken for payment of the bill within a specified period of time. Deducting purchase returns and allowances and purchase discounts gives the net cost of purchases. Freight charges paid by the buyer (called "freight in") are added to net purchases to determine the net cost of *delivered* purchases.

In a manufacturing concern, the cost-of-goods-sold section has a slightly different form. Instead of determining the cost of goods *purchased,* the firm determines the cost of goods *manufactured,* as in Figure B-2. Cost of goods manufactured ($50,000) is added to the beginning inventory ($18,000) to ascertain the total goods available for sale ($68,000). Then, after the ending inventory of finished goods has been deducted ($20,000), the result is the cost of goods sold ($48,000).

To find the cost of goods *manufactured,* a company starts with the value of goods partially completed (beginning inventory of goods in process— $24,000). To this beginning inventory figure is added the cost of raw materi-

---

**FIGURE B-2 Cost-of-goods-sold section of an operating statement for a manufacturer**

| | | | |
|---|---|---|---|
| Beginning inventory of finished goods (at cost) | | | $18,000 |
| Cost of goods manufactured: | | | |
|   Beginning inventory, goods in process | | $24,000 | |
|   *Plus:* Raw materials | $20,000 | | |
|     Direct labor | 15,000 | | |
|     Overhead | 13,000 | 48,000 | |
|   Total goods in process | | 72,000 | |
|   *Less:* Ending inventory, goods in process | | 22,000 | |
|   Cost of goods manufactured | | | 50,000 |
| Cost of goods available for sale | | | 68,000 |
| *Less:* Ending inventory, finished goods (at cost) | | | 20,000 |
| Cost of goods sold | | | $48,000 |

---

als, direct labor, and factory overhead expenses incurred during the period ($48,000). The resulting figure is the total goods in process during the period ($72,000). By deducting the value of goods still in process at the end of the period ($22,000), management finds the cost of goods manufactured during that span of time ($50,000).

### GROSS MARGIN

Gross margin is determined by subtracting cost of goods sold from net sales. Gross margin, sometimes called *gross profit,* is a key figure in the entire marketing program. When we say that a certain store has a "margin" of 30 percent, we are referring to the gross margin.

### EXPENSES

Operating expenses are deducted from gross margin to determine net profit. The operating expense section includes marketing, administrative, and miscellaneous expenses. It does not, of course, include the cost of goods purchased or manufactured, since these costs have already been deducted.

### NET PROFIT

Net profit is the difference between gross margin and total expenses. Obviously a negative net profit is a loss.

## MARKUPS

Many retailers and wholesalers use markup percentages to determine the selling price of an article. Normally the selling price must exceed the cost of the merchandise by an amount sufficient to cover operating expenses and still leave the desired profit. The difference between the selling price of an item and its cost is the **markup,** sometimes referred to as the "mark-on."

Typically markups are expressed in percentages rather than dollars. A markup may be expressed as a percentage of either the cost or the selling price. Therefore, we must first determine which will be the *base* for the markup. That is, when we speak of a 40 percent markup, do we mean 40 percent of the *cost* or of the *selling price?*

To determine the markup percentage when it is based on *cost*, we use the following formula:

$$\text{Markup \%} = \frac{\text{Dollar markup}}{\text{Cost}}$$

When the markup is based on *selling price,* the formula to use is:

$$\text{Markup \%} = \frac{\text{Dollar markup}}{\text{Selling price}}$$

All interested parties must know which base is being used in a given situation. Otherwise there can be considerable misunderstanding. To illustrate, suppose Mr. A runs a clothing store and claims he needs a 66⅔ percent markup to make a small net profit. Ms. B, who runs a competitive store, says she needs only a 40 percent markup and that A must be inefficient or a big profiteer. Actually both merchants are using identical markups, but they are using different bases. Each seller buys hats at $6 apiece and sets the selling price at $10. This is a markup of $4 per hat. Mr. A is expressing his markup as a percentage of cost—hence the 66⅔ percent figure ($4 ÷ $6 = .67, or 66⅔ percent). Ms. B is basing her markup on the selling price ($4 ÷ $10 = .4, or 40 percent). It would be a mistake for Mr. A to try to get by on B's 40 percent markup, as long as A uses cost as his base. If Mr. A used the 40 percent markup, but *based it on cost,* the markup would be only $2.40. And the selling price would be only $8.40. This $2.40 markup, averaged over the entire hat department, would not enable A to cover his usual expenses and make a profit.

*Unless otherwise indicated, markup percentages are always stated as a percentage of selling price.*

**Markup Based on Selling Price**

The following diagram shows the relationships among selling price, cost, and markup. It can be used to calculate these figures regardless of whether the markup is stated in percentages or dollars, and whether the percentages are based on selling price or cost.

|  |  | Dollars | Percentage |
|---|---|---|---|
|  | Selling price |  |  |
| *less* | Cost |  |  |
| *equals* | Markup |  |  |

As an example, suppose a merchant buys an article for $90 and knows the markup based on selling price must be 40 percent. What is the selling price? By filling in the known information in the diagram, we obtain:

|  |  | Dollars | Percentage |
|---|---|---|---|
|  | Selling price |  | 100 |
| *less* | Cost | 90 |  |
| *equals* | Markup |  | 40 |

The percentage representing cost must then be 60 percent. Thus the $90 cost is 60 percent of the selling price. The selling price is then $150. That is, $90 equals 60 percent of the selling price. Then $90 is divided by .6 (or 60 percent) to get the selling price of $150.

A common situation facing merchants is to have competition set a ceiling on selling prices. Or possibly the sellers must buy an item to fit into one of their price lines. Then they want to know the maximum amount they can pay for an item and still get their normal markup. Assume that the selling price of an article is set at $60 (by competition or by the $59.95 price line). The retailer's normal markup is 35 percent. What is the most the retailer should pay for this article? Again let's fill in what we know in the diagram:

|  |  | Dollars | Percentage |
|---|---|---|---|
|  | Selling price | 60 | 100 |
| *less* | Cost | | |
| *equals* | Markup | | 35 |

The dollar markup is $21 (35 percent of $60). So by simple subtraction we find that the maximum cost the merchant will want to pay is $39.

## Series of Markups

Markups are figured on the selling price at *each level of business* in a channel of distribution. A manufacturer applies a markup to determine its selling price. The manufacturer's selling price then becomes the wholesaler's cost. The wholesaler must determine its own selling price by applying its usual markup percentage based on its—the wholesaler's—selling price. The same procedure is carried on by the retailer, whose cost is the wholesaler's selling price. The following calculations illustrate this point:

Producer's cost $7
Producer's selling price $10 } **Producer's markup = $3, or 30%**

Wholesaler's cost $10
Wholesaler's selling price $12 } **Wholesaler's markup = $2, or 16⅔%**

Retailer's cost $12
Retailer's selling price $20 } **Retailer's markup = $8, or 40%**

## Markup Based on Cost

If a firm is accustomed to dealing in markups based on cost—and sometimes this is done among wholesalers—the same diagrammatic approach may be employed. The only change is that cost will equal 100 percent. The selling price will be 100 percent plus the markup based on cost. As an example, a firm bought an article for $70 and wants a 20 percent markup based on cost. The markup in dollars is $14 (20 percent of $70). The selling price is $84 ($70 plus $14):

|  |  | Dollars | Percentage |
|---|---|---|---|
|  | Selling price | 84 | 120 |
| *less* | Cost | 70 | 100 |
| *equals* | Markup | 14 | 20 |

The relationship between markups on cost and markups on selling price is important. For instance, if a product costs $6 and sells for $10, there is a $4 markup. This is a 40 percent markup based on selling price, but a 66⅔ percent markup based on cost. The following diagram may be helpful in understanding these relationships and in converting from one base to another.

*If selling price = 100%*                                                  *If cost = 100%*

$10 = 100% { 60% →                 Cost = $6.00      ←100% }
            { 40% →         Markup = $4.00      ← 66⅔% } $10 = 166⅔%

The relationships between the two bases are expressed in the following formulas:

$$\% \text{ markup on selling price} = \frac{\% \text{ markup on cost}}{100\% + \% \text{ markup on cost}}$$

$$\% \text{ markup on cost} = \frac{\% \text{ markup on selling price}}{100\% - \% \text{ markup on selling price}}$$

To illustrate the use of these formulas, let's say that a retailer has a markup of 25 percent on *cost*. This retailer wants to know what the corresponding figure is, based on selling price. In the first formula we get:

$$\frac{25\%}{100\% + 25\%} = \frac{25\%}{125\%} = .2, \text{ or } 20\%$$

A markup of 33⅓ percent based on *selling price* converts to 50 percent based on cost, according to the second formula:

$$\frac{33\tfrac{1}{3}\%}{100\% - 33\tfrac{1}{3}\%} = \frac{33\tfrac{1}{3}\%}{66\tfrac{2}{3}\%} = .5, \text{ or } 50\%$$

The markup is closely related to gross margin. Recall that gross margin is equal to net sales minus cost of goods sold. Looking below gross margin on an operating statement, we find that gross margin equals operating expenses plus net profit.

Normally the initial markup in a company, department, or product line must be set a little higher than the overall gross margin desired for the selling unit. The reason for this is that some reductions will be incurred before all the articles are sold. For one reason or another certain items will not sell at the original price. They will have to be marked down—reduced in price from the original level. Some pilferage and other shortages also may occur.

## ANALYTICAL RATIOS

From a study of the operating statement, management can develop several ratios to evaluate the results of its marketing program. In most cases net sales is used as the base (100 percent). In fact, unless specifically mentioned to the contrary, all ratios reflecting gross margin, net profit, or any operating expense are stated as a percentage of net sales.

### Gross Margin Percentage

This is the ratio of gross margin to net sales. In Figure B-1 the gross margin percentage is $32,000 ÷ $80,000, or 40 percent.

### Net Profit Percentage

This ratio is determined by dividing net profit by net sales. The ratio in Figure B-1 is $4,800 ÷ $80,000, or 6 percent. This percentage may be calculated either before or after federal income taxes are deducted, but the result should be labeled to show which it is.

### Operating Expense Percentage

When total operating expenses are divided by net sales, the result is the operating expense ratio. In Figure B-1 the ratio is $27,200 ÷ $80,000, or 34 percent. In similar fashion we may determine the expense ratio for any given cost. Thus we note in the figure that rent expense was 1 percent, advertising 3 percent, and sales-force salaries and commissions 13.75 percent.

### Rate of Stockturn

Management often measures the efficiency of its marketing operations by means of the **stockturn rate.** This figure represents the number of times the average inventory is "turned over," or sold, during the period under study. The rate is calculated on either a cost or a selling-price basis. Both the numerator and the denominator of the ratio fraction must be expressed in the same terms, either cost or selling price.

On a *cost* basis, the formula for stockturn rate is:

$$\text{Rate of stockturn} = \frac{\text{Cost of goods sold}}{\text{Average inventory at cost}}$$

The average inventory is determined by adding beginning and ending inventories and dividing the result by 2. In Figure B-1 the average inventory is ($18,000 + $20,000) ÷ 2 = $19,000. The stockturn rate then is $48,000 ÷ $19,000, or 2.5. Because inventories usually are abnormally low at the first of the year in anticipation of taking physical inventory, this average may not be representative. Consequently, some companies find their average inventory by adding the book inventories at the beginning of each month and then dividing this sum by 12.

Now let's assume inventory is recorded on a *selling-price* basis, as is done in most large retail organizations. Then the stockturn rate equals net sales divided by average inventory at selling price. Sometimes the stockturn rate is computed by dividing the number of *units* sold by the average inventory expressed in *units*.

Wholesale and retail trade associations in many types of businesses publish figures showing the average rate of stockturn for their members. A firm with a low rate of stockturn is likely to be spending too much on storage and inventory. The company runs a higher risk of obsolescence or spoilage. If the stockturn rate gets too high, the company's average inventory may be too low. Often a firm in this situation is operating on a hand-to-mouth buying system. In addition to incurring high handling and billing costs, the company is likely to be out of stock on some items.

## Markdown Percentage

Sometimes retailers are unable to sell articles at the originally stated prices, and they reduce these prices to move the goods. A **markdown** is a reduction from the original selling price. Management frequently finds it very helpful to determine the markdown percentage. Then management analyzes the size and number of markdowns and reasons for them. Retailers, particularly, make extensive use of markdown analysis.

Markdowns are expressed as a percentage of net sales and *not* as a percentage of the original selling price. To illustrate, a retailer purchases a hat for $6 and marks it up 40 percent to sell for $10. The hat does not sell at that price, so it is marked down to $8. Now the seller may advertise a price cut of 20 percent. Yet, according to our rule, this $2 markdown is 25 percent *of the $8 selling price.*

Markdown percentage is calculated by dividing total dollar markdowns by total net sales during a given period of time. Two important points should be noted here. First, the markdown percentage is determined in this fashion, whether the markdown items were sold or are still in the store. Second, the percentage is calculated with respect to total net sales, and not only in connection with sales of marked-down articles. As an example, assume that a retailer buys 10 hats at $6 each and prices them to sell at $10. Five hats are sold at $10. The other five are marked down to $8, and three are sold at the lower price. Total sales are $74 and total markdowns are $10. The retailer has a markdown ratio of $10 ÷ $74, or 13.5 percent.

Markdowns do not appear on the profit and loss statement because they occur *before* an article is sold. The first item on an operating statement is gross sales. That figure reflects the actual selling price, which may be the selling price after a markdown has been taken.

**Return on Investment**   A commonly used measure of managerial performance and the operating success of a company is its rate of return on investment. We use both the balance sheet and the operating statement as sources of information. The formula for calculating return on investment (ROI) is as follows:

$$\text{ROI} = \frac{\text{Net profit}}{\text{Sales}} \times \frac{\text{Sales}}{\text{Investment}}$$

Two questions may come to mind. What do we mean by "investment"? Why do we need two fractions? It would seem that the "sales" component in each fraction would cancel out, leaving net profit divided by investment as the meaningful ratio.

To answer the first query, consider a firm whose operating statement shows annual sales of $1,000,000 and a net profit of $50,000. At the end of the year the balance sheet reports:

| Assets | $600,000 | Liabilities | | $200,000 |
|--------|----------|-------------|----------|----------|
| | | Capital stock | $300,000 | |
| | | Retained earnings | 100,000 | 400,000 |
| | $600,000 | | | $600,000 |

Now is the investment $400,000 or $600,000? Certainly the ROI will depend on which figure we use. The answer is contingent on whether we are talking to the stockholders or to the company executives. The stockholders are more interested in the return on what they have invested—in this case, $400,000. The ROI calculation then is:

$$\text{ROI} = \frac{\text{Net profit } \$50,000}{\text{Sales } \$1,000,000} \times \frac{\text{Sales } \$1,000,000}{\text{Investment } \$400,000} = 12\tfrac{1}{2}\%$$

Management, on the other hand, is more concerned with total investment, as represented by total assets ($600,000). This is the amount that the executives must manage, regardless of whether the assets were acquired by stockholders' investment, retained earnings, or loans from outside sources. Within this context the ROI computation becomes:

$$\text{ROI} = \frac{\text{Net profit } \$50,000}{\text{Sales } \$1,000,000} \times \frac{\text{Sales } \$1,000,000}{\text{Investment } \$600,000} = 8\tfrac{1}{3}\%$$

Regarding the second question, we use two fractions because we are dealing with two separate elements—the rate of profit on sales and the rate of capital turnover. Management really should determine each rate separately and then multiply the two. The rate of profit on sales is influenced by marketing considerations—sales volume, price, product mix, advertising effort. Capital turnover is a financial consideration not directly involved with costs or profits—only sales volume and assets managed.

To illustrate, say our company's profits doubled with the same sales volume and investment because of an excellent marketing program this year. In effect, we doubled our profit rate with the same capital turnover:

$$\text{ROI} = \underbrace{\frac{\text{Net profit } \$100,000}{\text{Sales } \$1,000,000}}_{10\%} \times \underbrace{\frac{\text{Sales } \$1,000,000}{\text{Investment } \$600,000}}_{1.67} = 16\frac{2}{3}\%$$

$$10\% \times 1.67 = 16\frac{2}{3}\%$$

As expected, this 16⅔ percent is twice the ROI calculated above.

Now assume that we earned our original profit of $50,000 but that we did it with an investment reduced to $500,000. We cut the size of our average inventory, and we closed some branch offices. By increasing our capital turnover from 1.67 to 2, we raised the ROI from 8⅓ percent to 10 percent, even though sales volume and profits were unchanged:

$$\text{ROI} = \underbrace{\frac{\$50,000}{\$1,000,000}}_{5\%} \times \underbrace{\frac{\$1,000,000}{\$500,000}}_{2} = 10\%$$

$$5\% \times 2 = 10\%$$

Now let us say that we increased our sales volume—we doubled it—but did not increase our profit or investment. The cost-profit squeeze has brought us "profitless prosperity." The following interesting results occur:

$$\text{ROI} = \underbrace{\frac{\$50,000}{\$2,000,000}}_{2\frac{1}{2}\%} \times \underbrace{\frac{\$2,000,000}{\$600,000}}_{3.33} = 8\frac{1}{3}\%$$

$$2\frac{1}{2}\% \times 3.33 = 8\frac{1}{3}\%$$

The profit rate was cut in half, but this was offset by a doubling of the capital turnover rate, leaving the ROI unchanged.

## QUESTIONS AND PROBLEMS

1. Construct an operating statement from the following data and compute the gross margin percentage:

| | |
|---|---|
| Purchases at billed cost | $15,000 |
| Net sales | 30,000 |
| Sales returns and allowances | 200 |
| Cash discounts given | 300 |
| Cash discounts earned | 100 |
| Rent | 1,500 |
| Salaries | 6,000 |
| Opening inventory at cost | 10,000 |
| Advertising | 600 |
| Other expenses | 2,000 |
| Closing inventory at cost | 7,500 |

2. Prepare a retail operating statement from the following information and compute the markdown percentage:

| | |
|---|---|
| Rent | $ 9,000 |
| Closing inventory at cost | 28,000 |
| Sales returns | 6,500 |
| Gross margin as percentage of sales | 35 |
| Cash discounts allowed | 2,000 |

| | |
|---|---|
| Salaries | $ 34,000 |
| Markdowns | 4,000 |
| Other operating expenses | 15,000 |
| Opening inventory at cost | 35,000 |
| Gross sales | 232,500 |
| Advertising | 5,500 |
| Freight in | 3,500 |

3. What percentage markups on cost correspond to the following percentages of markup on selling price?
   a. 20 percent.  c. 50 percent.
   b. 37½ percent.  d. 66⅔ percent.

4. What percentage markups on selling price correspond to the following percentages of markup on cost?
   a. 20 percent.  c. 50 percent.
   b. 33⅓ percent.  d. 300 percent.

5. A hardware store bought a gross (12 dozen) of hammers, paying $302.40 for the lot. The retailer estimated operating expenses for this product to

be 35 percent of sales, and wanted a net profit of 5 percent of sales. The retailer expected no markdowns. What retail selling price should be set for each hammer?

6. Competition in a certain line of sporting goods limits the selling price on a certain item to $25. If the store owner feels a markup of 35 percent is needed to cover expenses and return a reasonable profit, what is the most the owner can pay for this item?

7. A retailer with annual net sales of $2 million maintains a markup of 66⅔ percent based on cost. Expenses average 35 percent. What are the retailer's gross margin and net profit in dollars?

8. A company has a stockturn rate of five times a year, a sales volume of $600,000, and a gross margin of 25 percent. What is the average inventory at cost?

9. A store has an average inventory of $30,000 at retail and a stockturn rate of five times a year. If the company maintains a markup of 50 percent based on cost, what are the annual sales volume and cost of goods sold?

10. From the following data, compute the gross margin percentage and the operating expense ratio:

Stockturn rate = 9
Average inventory at selling price = $45,000
Net profit = $20,000
Cost of goods sold = $350,000

11. A ski shop sold 50 pairs of skis at $90 a pair, after taking a 10 percent markdown. All the skis were originally purchased at the same price and had been marked up 60 percent on cost. What was the gross margin on the 50 pairs of skis?

12. A men's clothing store bought 200 suits at $90 each. The suits were marked up 40 percent. Eighty were sold at that price. The remaining suits were each marked down 20 percent from the original selling price, and all were sold. Compute the sales volume and markdown percentage.

13. An appliance retailer sold 60 radios at $30 each after taking markdowns equal to 20 percent of the actual selling price. Originally all the radios had been purchased at the same price and were marked up 50 percent on cost. What was the gross margin percentage earned in this situation?

14. An appliance manufacturer produced a line of small appliances advertised to sell at $30. The manufacturer planned for wholesalers to receive a 20 percent markup, and retailers a 33⅓ percent markup. Total manufacturing costs were $12 per unit. What did retailers pay for the product? What were the manufacturer's selling price and percentage markup?

15. A housewares manufacturer produces an article at a full cost of $1.80. It is sold through a manufacturers' agent directly to large retailers. The agent receives a 20 percent commission on sales, the retailers earn a margin of 30 percent, and the manufacturer plans a net profit of 10 percent on the selling price. What is the retail price of this article?

16. A building materials manufacturer sold a quantity of a product to a wholesaler for $350, and the wholesaler in turn sold to a lumberyard. The wholesaler's normal markup was 15 percent, and the retailer usually priced the item to include a 30 percent markup. What is the selling price to consumers?

17. From the following data, calculate the return on investment, based on a definition of *investment* that is useful for evaluating managerial performance:

| | |
|---|---|
| Net sales | $800,000 |
| Gross margin | $280,000 |
| Total assets | $200,000 |
| Cost of goods sold | $520,000 |
| Liabilities | $ 40,000 |
| Markup | 35% |
| Average inventory | $ 75,000 |
| Retained earnings | $ 60,000 |
| Operating expenses | $240,000 |

# CHAPTER 11

# PRICING STRATEGIES AND POLICIES

Sears, Roebuck & Company is the largest retailer in the world, based on annual sales volume. But even a "Number 1" organization can have its problems. For several decades Sears' primary target market was the upper-lower and lower-middle social classes. Sears prospered in this market, building a solid image based on its own brands of products, low price, and a "value for your money" promotional theme.

Then in the 1970s and 1980s Sears tried to reposition itself by upgrading its fashion and quality image. The company added expensive fur coats and jewelry and apparel that featured designer and celebrity names. But this upscale move was not successful. It blurred the company's image, confused old customers, failed to tap into higher-income markets, and reduced Sears' market share.

The growing power of discounters such as K mart and Wal-Mart became strong enough in the 1990s to further erode Sears' market share. Sears decided to combat the discounters' competitive threat by adopting the strategy of price competition. During most of the 1980s many large retailers were continually running sales or price specials. Prices for some goods kept going up and down like a yo-yo. In 1988, for example, Sears sold about 55 percent of its goods at "sale" prices. Finally, in 1989 Sears discontinued its frequent use of sales and price specials. Instead it adopted a price-competition strategy of "everyday low prices" and sharply reduced its prices on many items, but especially on appliances, clothing, and cosmetics.

Major players in other industries also implemented the strategy of price competition in the late 1980s and into the early 1990s. Coca-Cola and Pepsi-Cola engaged in price competition in several geographic markets. At Fry's supermarket in the Phoenix metropolitan area, for instance, Coke sold for 10 cents a can or 59 cents for a six-pack. Across town at Smitty's supermarket, a six-pack of Pepsi was on sale at 79 cents. McDonald's and Anheuser-Busch (Budweiser beer) were both longtime advocates of nonprice competition. Yet in 1989 these companies reluctantly discounted prices on certain products in selected geographic markets.

Price competition is just one of the pricing strategies we shall discuss in this chapter. In the course of managing the price element in a company's marketing mix, management first decides on its pricing goal and then sets the base price for a good or service. The next task is to design appropriate strategies and policies concerning several aspects of the price structure. What kind of discount schedule should be adopted? Will the firm occasionally absorb freight costs?

A number of pricing issues that require strategy decisions and policy making will be examined. We also shall consider legal aspects of these activities. A company's success in pricing may depend on management's ability to design creative pricing strategies that reflect a customer orientation, rather than the traditional cost-oriented pricing methodology. See Figure 11-1.

We shall use the terms *policy* and *strategy* frequently in this chapter, so let's review their meanings. A **strategy** is a broad plan of action by which an organization intends to reach its goal. A **policy** is a managerial guide to future decision making when a given situation arises. Thus a policy becomes the course of action followed routinely anytime a given strategic or tactical situation arises. To illustrate, suppose management adopts the *strategy* of offering certain quantity discounts in order to achieve the goal of a 10 percent increase in sales next year. Then, routinely, every time the company receives an order of a given size, it is company *policy* to grant the customer the prescribed quantity discount.[1]

**FIGURE 11-1** The price-determination process.

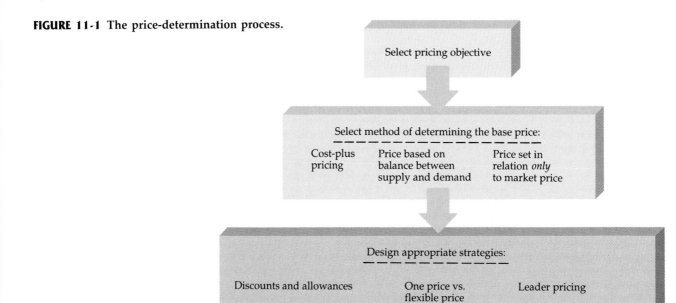

[1] For further discussion of pricing strategies and policies, see Gerard J. Tellis, "Beyond the Many Faces of Price: An Integration of Pricing Strategies," *Journal of Marketing*, October 1986, pp. 146–160.

Discounts often accompany introductory offers of goods or services.

**WITH NOTHING MORE TO BUY...EVER!**

## DISCOUNTS AND ALLOWANCES

Discounts and allowances result in a deduction from the base (or list) price. The deduction may be in the form of a reduced price or some other concession, such as free merchandise or advertising allowances.

### Quantity Discounts

**Quantity discounts** are deductions from a seller's list price that are offered to encourage customers to buy in larger amounts or to make the most of their purchases from that seller. Discounts are based on the size of the purchase, either in dollars or in units.

A **noncumulative discount** is based on the size of an *individual order* of one or more products. Thus a retailer may sell golf balls at $2 each or at three for $5. A manufacturer or wholesaler may set up a quantity discount schedule such as the following one, which was used by a manufacturer of industrial adhesives.

| Boxes purchased in single order | % discount from list price |
|:---:|:---:|
| 1–5 | 0.0 |
| 6–12 | 2.0 |
| 13–25 | 3.5 |
| Over 25 | 5.0 |

Noncumulative quantity discounts are intended to encourage large orders. Many expenses, such as billing, order filling, and salaries of sales people, are about the same whether the seller receives an order totaling $10 or $500. Consequently, selling expense as a percentage of sales decreases as orders become larger. A seller shares such savings with a purchaser of large quantities.

**Cumulative discounts** are based on the total volume purchased *over a period of time*. These discounts are advantageous to a seller because they tie customers more closely to that seller. The more total business a buyer gives a seller, the greater is the discount. Airline frequent-flyer and hotel frequent-guest programs are a form of cumulative discount. IBM offers an assortment of volume-over-time discounts, and MCI competed with AT&T in some markets by offering deep discounts to high-volume users of long-distance telephone service.[2] Cumulative discounts are common in sales of perishable products. These discounts encourage customers to buy fresh supplies frequently so that the merchandise will not become stale.

Quantity discounts can help a producer effect real economies in production as well as in selling. On the one hand, large orders (motivated by a noncumulative discount) can result in lower-cost production runs and lower transportation costs. On the other hand, frequent orders from a single cus-

[2]George S. Day and Adrian B. Ryans, "Using Price Discounts for a Competitive Advantage," *Industrial Marketing Management,* February 1988, pp. 1–14.

tomer (motivated by a cumulative discount) can enable the producer to make much more effective use of production capacity, even though individual orders are small and do not generate savings in marketing costs.

**Trade Discounts**

**Trade discounts,** sometimes called **functional discounts,** are reductions from the list price offered to buyers in payment for marketing functions that they will perform. A manufacturer may quote a retail price of $400 with trade discounts of 40 percent and 10 percent. The retailer pays the wholesaler $240 ($400 less 40 percent), and the wholesaler pays the manufacturer $216 ($240 less 10 percent). The wholesaler is given the 40 and 10 percent discounts. The wholesaler is expected to keep the 10 percent to cover costs of the wholesaling functions and pass on the 40 percent discount to retailers. Note that the 40 and 10 percent discounts do not constitute a total discount of 50 percent off list price. Each discount percentage in the "chain" is computed on the amount remaining after the preceding percentage has been deducted.

**Cash Discounts**

A **cash discount** is a deduction granted to buyers for paying their bills within a specified period of time. The discount is computed on the net amount due after first deducting trade and quantity discounts from the base price. Let's say a buyer owes $360 after other discounts have been granted and is offered terms of 2/10, n/30 on an invoice dated November 8. This means the buyer may deduct a discount of 2 percent ($7.20) if the bill is paid within 10 days after the date of the invoice (by November 18). Otherwise the entire (net) bill of $360 must be paid in 30 days (by December 8).

Every cash discount includes three elements (see Figure 11-2):

- The percentage discount itself.
- The time period during which the discount may be taken.
- The time when the bill becomes overdue.

There are many different terms of sale because almost every industry has its own traditional combination of elements.

Most buyers are extremely eager to pay bills in time to earn cash dis-

**FIGURE 11-2** Parts of a cash discount.

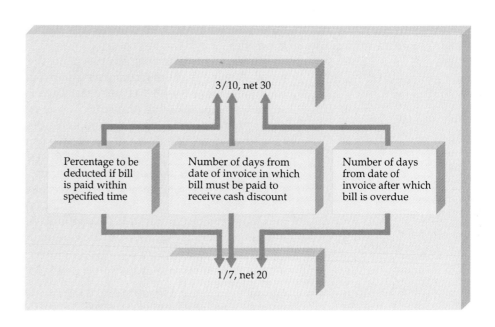

| Percentage to be deducted if bill is paid within specified time | Number of days from date of invoice in which bill must be paid to receive cash discount | Number of days from date of invoice after which bill is overdue |

3/10, net 30

1/7, net 20

counts. The discount in a 2/10, n/30 situation may not seem like very much. But this 2 percent is earned just for paying 20 days in advance of the date the entire bill is due. If buyers fail to take the cash discount in a 2/10, n/30 situation, they are, in effect, borrowing money at a 36 percent annual rate of interest. (In a 360-day year, there are 18 periods of 20 days. Paying 2 percent for one of these 20-day periods is equivalent to paying 36 percent for an entire year.)

**Other Discounts and Allowances**

A firm that produces goods such as air conditioners or toys that are purchased on a seasonal basis may consider granting a **seasonal discount.** This is a discount of, say, 5, 10, or 20 percent given to a customer who places an order during the slack season. Off-season orders enable manufacturers to make better use of their production facilities and/or avoid inventory carrying costs. Many firms that market services also offer seasonal discounts. For example, Club Med and many other vacation resorts lower prices during the off-season.

**Forward dating** is a variation of both seasonal and cash discounts. A manufacturer of fishing tackle might seek and fill orders from wholesalers and retailers during the winter months. But the bill would be dated April 1, with terms of 2/10, n/30 offered as of that date. Orders that the seller fills in December and January help to maintain production during the slack season for more efficient operation. The forward-dated bills allow the wholesale or retail buyers to pay their bills after the season has started and some sales revenue has been generated.

**Promotional allowances** are price reductions granted by a seller in payment for promotional services performed by buyers. To illustrate, a producer of builders' hardware gives a certain quantity of ''free goods'' to dealers who prominently display its line. Or a clothing manufacturer pays one-half the cost of a retailer's advertisement that features its product.

**The Robinson-Patman Act and Price Discrimination**

The discounts and allowances discussed in this section may result in different prices for different customers. Whenever price differentials exist, there is price discrimination. The terms are synonymous. In certain situations price discrimination is prohibited by the Robinson-Patman Act, which is one of the most important federal laws affecting a company's marketing program.

Any federal law regulating pricing is applicable only in cases where *interstate* trade is involved. However, many states have pricing statutes that cover sales *within* the state (intrastate trade).

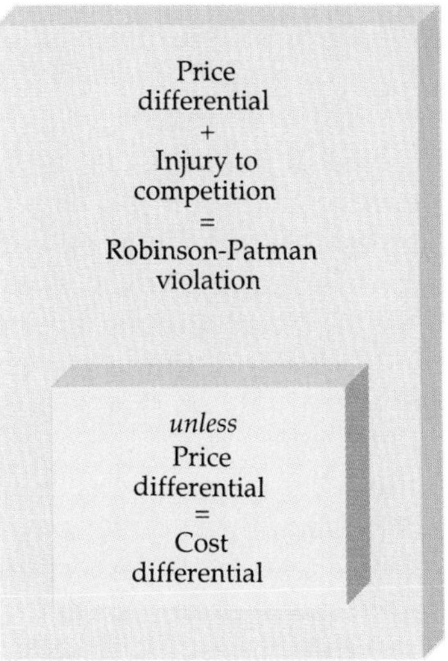

### MAIN PROVISIONS OF THE ACT

The Robinson-Patman Act, passed in 1936, was intended to curb the price-discrimination practices of large retailers only. It was written in such general terms, however, that through the years it has also become applicable to manufacturers. Not all price differentials are illegal under the act. Price differentials are unlawfully discriminatory only when their effect *may be* to substantially injure competition. In other words, a price difference is allowed if it does not substantially reduce competition. This law does *not* apply to sales to ultimate household consumers, because presumably they are not in business competition with each other.

Price
differential
+
Injury to
competition
=
Robinson-Patman
violation

*unless*
Price
differential
=
Cost
differential

**FIGURE 11-3** Robinson-Patman Act.

**Other exceptions and defenses** Price differentials are allowable in response to changing conditions that affect the marketability of goods. For example, differentials are allowed in response to seasonal obsolescence, physical deterioration of products, or going-out-of-business sales.

Price differentials may be granted if they do not exceed differences in the cost of manufacture, sale, or delivery of the product. These cost differences may result from (1) differences in the quantity sold or (2) different methods of sale or delivery of the product. Such differentials are allowable even though there is a reasonable probability of injury to competition.

**Buyer's liability**  Under the Robinson-Patman Act, the buyer is as guilty as the seller if the buyer *knowingly* induces or receives an unlawful price differential. This provision is intended to restrain large-scale buyers from demanding discriminatory prices. From a practical standpoint, however, it has been difficult to prove that the buyer *knowingly* received an unlawful price differential.

**Promotional allowances**  Various types of promotional services and facilities are lawful *only* if they are offered to all competing customers on proportionally equal terms. The real problem here is to determine what is meant by "proportionally equal terms." This concept and its practical application are examined in Chapter 16, in connection with a firm's promotional program.

### LEGALITY OF QUANTITY DISCOUNTS

Quantity discounts result in different prices to different customers. Consequently, these discriminatory prices are potentially illegal under the Robinson-Patman Act if the necessary injury to competition can be shown. To justify price differentials stemming from its quantity discount schedule, a firm must rely on the cost defense provided in the act. In a nutshell, quantity discounts are legal if the resultant price differentials do not exceed differences in the cost of manufacturing, selling, or delivering the product.

### LEGALITY OF TRADE DISCOUNTS

There is no specific statement about trade discounts in the Robinson-Patman Act nor in its predecessor, the Clayton Act. However, three court cases many years ago established that separate discounts could be given to different classes of buyers. That is, one discount could be given to wholesalers and another to retailers as long as all buyers within a given group were offered the same discount.

## GEOGRAPHIC PRICING STRATEGIES

In pricing, a seller must consider freight costs involved in shipping goods to the buyer. This consideration grows in importance as freight becomes a larger part of total variable costs. Pricing policies may be established whereby the buyer pays all the freight, the seller bears the entire costs, or the two parties share the expense. The chosen strategy can influence (1) the geographic limits of a firm's market, (2) the location of its production facilities, (3) the source of its raw materials, and (4) its competitive strength in various market areas.

### F.O.B. Point-of-Production Pricing

In one widely used geographic pricing strategy, the seller quotes the selling price at the factory or at some other point of production and the buyer pays the entire cost of transportation. This is usually referred to as **f.o.b. factory** or **f.o.b. mill** pricing. Of the four strategies discussed in this section, this is the only one in which the seller does not pay *any* of the freight costs. The seller pays only the cost of loading the shipment aboard the carrier—hence the term *f.o.b.*, or *free on board*.

Under f.o.b. factory pricing, the seller nets the same amount on each sale of similar quantities. The delivered price to the buyer varies according to the freight charge. In general, the Federal Trade Commission has considered f.o.b. factory pricing to be nondiscriminatory. However, this pricing strategy has serious economic and marketing implications. In effect, f.o.b. factory pricing establishes a geographic monopoly for a given seller, because freight rates prevent distant competitors from entering the market. The seller, in turn, is increasingly priced out of more distant markets.

## Uniform Delivered Pricing

Under the **uniform delivered pricing** strategy, the same delivered price is quoted to all buyers regardless of their locations. This is sometimes referred to as "postage stamp pricing" because of its similarity to the pricing of first-class mail service. The net revenue to the seller varies, depending on the shipping cost involved in each sale.

A uniform delivered price is typically used where transportation costs are a small part of the seller's total costs. It is also used by many retailers who feel that "free" delivery is an additional service that strengthens their market position. Buyers located near the seller's factory pay for some of the costs of shipping to more distant locations. Critics of f.o.b. factory pricing usually favor a uniform delivered price. They feel that the freight expense should not be charged to individual customers any more than other marketing or production expenses.

## Zone Delivered Pricing

**Zone delivered pricing** divides a seller's market into a limited number of broad geographic zones. Then a uniform delivered price is set within each zone. Zone delivered pricing is similar to the system used in pricing parcel post services. An Eastern firm that quotes a price and then says "Slightly higher west of the Rockies" is using a two-zone pricing system. The freight charge built into the delivered price is an average of the charges at all points within a zone area.

When adopting this pricing strategy, the seller must walk a tightrope to avoid charges of illegal price discrimination. The zone lines must be drawn so that all buyers who compete for a particular market are in the same zone. This condition is almost impossible to meet in the dense market areas of the East and the Midwest.

## Freight Absorption Pricing

A **freight absorption pricing** strategy may be adopted to offset competitive disadvantages of f.o.b. factory pricing. With an f.o.b. factory price, a firm is at a price disadvantage when it tries to sell to buyers located in markets nearer to competitors' plants. To penetrate more deeply into such markets, a seller may be willing to absorb some of the freight cost. Thus seller A will quote to the customer a delivered price equal to (1) A's factory price plus (2) the freight costs that would be charged by a competitive seller located nearest to that customer.

A seller can continue to expand the geographic limits of its market as long as its net revenue after freight absorption is larger than its marginal cost for units sold. Freight absorption is particularly useful to a firm with excess capacity whose fixed costs per unit of product are high and whose variable costs are low. In these cases, management must constantly seek ways to cover fixed costs, and freight absorption is one means.

The legality of freight absorption is reasonably clear. It is legal if it is used independently and not in collusion with other firms. Also it must be used only to meet competition. In fact, if practiced properly, freight absorption can strengthen competition by breaking down geographic monopolies.

## SKIMMING AND PENETRATION PRICING

When pricing a product, especially a new product, management should consider whether to adopt a skimming or a penetration pricing strategy.

### Market-Skimming Pricing

Market skimming involves setting a price that is high in the range of expected prices. This strategy is particularly suitable for new products because:

- In the early stages of a product's life cycle, price is less important, competition is minimal, and the product's distinctiveness creates opportunities for nonprice competition.
- The market can be effectively segmented on an income basis. Initially the product is marketed to that segment that responds to distinctiveness and is relatively insensitive to price. Later the seller can lower the price and appeal to market segments that are more sensitive to price.
- It acts as a strong hedge against a possible mistake in setting price. If the original price is too high and the market does not respond, management can easily lower it. But it is very difficult to raise a price that has proven to be too low to cover costs.
- High initial prices can keep demand within the limits of a company's productive capacity.

### Market-Penetration Pricing

In market-penetration pricing, a low initial price is set to reach the mass market immediately. This strategy can also be employed at a later stage in the product's life cycle. Penetration pricing is likely to be more satisfactory than market-skimming pricing when the following conditions exist:

Should Sharp use skimming or penetration pricing when introducing this product?

**AN INTERNATIONAL PERSPECTIVE: Is a market-skimming strategy appropriate here?**

The Burroughs Wellcome Company (BW) is a pharmaceutical manufacturer whose parent company is located in England. In 1986 the company introduced into the U.S. market a drug—azidothymidine (AZT)—that is effective in controlling advances of the AIDS virus in human beings. AZT also slows down the onset of AIDS in people who have been infected with the virus, but who do not yet show any symptoms of the disease.

In mid-1989 AZT was priced at about $8,000 for a year's supply per patient, thus making it one of the most expensive drugs ever sold. The gross margin on AZT was 70 to 80 percent—obviously high, but still in line with what other firms get for major new drugs. Later in 1989 the price was reduced to about $6,400 for a year's supply because of two factors. One was the strong protests from AIDS activists, and the other was the anticipated market growth stemming from the increasing acceptance of AZT as a treatment for AIDS.

Critics of BW's pricing strategy included not only people with AIDS, but also some medical people involved in AIDS treatment and research. These activists contended that BW was profiteering shamelessly and that the high price was both unethical and immoral.

BW, on the other hand, pointed out that the company needed to recover the high costs associated with its research, development, and production of AZT. BW also noted that it is quite usual and necessary for drug companies to use profits from successful products (1) to support R & D work for future products and (2) to recoup R & D costs from past products that failed either in the laboratory or in the market.

What pricing strategy do you think BW should employ for AZT? Would your answer be any different if AZT were a cure for cancer? For the common cold?

Source: Marilyn Chase, "Burroughs Wellcome Reaps Profits, Outrage from Its AIDS Drug," *The Wall Street Journal*, Sept. 15, 1989, p. A1; Chase, "Burroughs Wellcome Cuts Price of AZT under Pressure from AIDS Activists," *The Wall Street Journal*, Sept. 19, 1989, p. A3.

- The product has a highly elastic demand.
- Substantial reductions in unit costs can be achieved through large-scale operations.
- The product is expected to face very strong competition soon after it is introduced to the market.

The nature of potential competition will critically influence management's choice between these two pricing strategies. If competitors can enter a market quickly, and if the market potential for the product is very promising, management probably should adopt a policy of penetration pricing. Low initial pricing may do two things. First, it may discourage other firms from entering the field, because of the anticipated low profit margin. Second, low initial pricing may give the innovator such a strong hold on its market share that future competitors cannot cut into it.

**ONE-PRICE AND FLEXIBLE-PRICE STRATEGIES**

Rather early in its pricing deliberations, management should decide whether to adopt a one-price strategy or a flexible-price strategy. Under a **one-price strategy,** a seller charges the *same* price to all similar customers who buy similar quantities of a product. Under a **flexible-price** (also called a **variable-price**) **strategy,** similar customers may each pay a *different* price when buying similar quantities of a product.

In the United States a one-price strategy is more common than variable pricing. Most retailers, for example, follow a one-price policy—except in cases involving trade-ins, and then flexible pricing abounds. A one-price policy builds customer confidence in a seller, whether at the manufacturing, wholesaling, or retailing level. Also, with a one-price strategy, weak bargainers need not feel that they are at a competitive disadvantage.

This seller seems to have a one-price strategy. But at the end of the day, flexible pricing might be used to sell this produce before it spoils.

A rather extreme variation of the one-price strategy is to charge the same price for everything that a company sells. Motel 6, a chain of budget motels, chose its name because originally all rooms were priced at $6 a night for single occupancy.

With flexible pricing, often the price is set as a result of buyer-seller bargaining. In automobile retailing—with or without a trade-in—price negotiating (bargaining) is quite common, even though window-sticker prices may suggest a one-price policy. Variable pricing also may be used to meet a competitor's price. To meet Japanese competition, Ford and General Motors sold subcompact cars to West Coast dealers at a lower price than was charged to dealers elsewhere in the country. Several airlines (Continental and TWA, for instance) have used aggressive flexible pricing to enter new markets and to increase their market share on existing routes. Their new business comes from two sources—passengers now flying on other airlines and passengers who would not fly at higher prices. In the second group, especially, demand for air travel is highly elastic. The trick is to keep the market segment of price-sensitive passengers separate from the business-traveler segment, whose demand is inelastic. Airlines keep these segments apart by placing restrictions on lower-priced tickets—requiring advance purchase and a Saturday night stay in the destination city, for example.

A considerable amount of flexible pricing does exist in the United States. On balance, however, a flexible-price strategy is generally less desirable than a one-price strategy. In sales to business firms (but not to ultimate consumers), flexible pricing is likely to be in violation of the Robinson-Patman Act. Flexible pricing also may generate considerable ill will when word gets around that some buyers acquired the product at a lower price.[3]

[3]For an in-depth discussion of flexible pricing including a theoretical model and managerial implications, see Kenneth R. Evans and Richard F. Beltramini, "A Theoretical Model of Consumer Negotiated Pricing: An Orientation Perspective," *Journal of Marketing*, April 1987, pp. 58–73. For a report on managerial, legal, and ethical aspects of flexible pricing in business markets, see Michael H. Morris, "Separate Prices as a Marketing Tool," *Industrial Marketing Management*, May 1987, pp. 79–86.

## UNIT PRICING

Unit-pricing shelf labels reduce prices to a common basis.

The universal product code label from a six-pack of beer.

**Unit pricing** is a retail price-information reporting strategy that, to date, has been employed largely by supermarket chains. The method is, however, adaptable to other types of stores and products. It is a business response to consumer protests concerning the proliferation of package sizes (especially in grocery stores). Numerous package sizes made it virtually impossible to compare prices of similar products. For example: Is a can labeled "15½ avoirdupois ounces" for 39 cents a better deal than two "1-pound 1-ounce (482 grams)" cans for 89 cents?

In a unit pricing system, for each separate product and package size there is a shelf label that states (1) the price of the package and (2) this price expressed in dollars and cents per ounce, pound, pint, or other standard measure. Studies covering the early years of unit pricing showed that consumers were ignoring unit-pricing data. More recent studies show an increase in the awareness and usage of unit-pricing information. However, city residents (typically lower-income markets) still use this information significantly less than do suburban residents (typically higher-income consumers).[4]

Increasingly, supermarkets and other retail stores are using electronic scanners at checkout stands that read the universal product code on products. Many of these retailers are no longer price-marking each individual item in a store. Consequently, unit-pricing shelf signs clearly are important, if not absolutely essential, to provide consumers with price information.

## PRICE LINING

**Price lining** is used extensively by retailers of all types of apparel. A limited number of prices are selected at which a store will sell its merchandise. The Athletic Store, for instance, sells several styles of shoes at $19.88 a pair, another group at $29.88, and a third assortment at $39.88.

For the consumer, the main benefit of price lining is that it simplifies buying decisions. From the retailer's point of view, the strategy is advantageous because it helps store owners plan their purchases. A dress buyer can go into a market looking for dresses that can be retailed for $79.95 or $99.95.

Rising costs can put a real squeeze on price lines, because a company hesitates to change its price line every time costs go up. But if costs increase and prices remain stationary, profit margins are compressed and the retailer may be forced to seek products with lower costs.

## RESALE PRICE MAINTENANCE

Some manufacturers want controls over the prices at which retailers resell their products. One way in which a producer can gain a small amount of control, and perhaps provide some guidance to retailers, is with suggested list prices. These prices often are set by manufacturers at a level that will provide retailers with their normal markup. To illustrate, a manufacturer sells to a store—a hardware or sporting-goods store, for example—a certain product for which the manufacturer charges $6 a unit. For this product the suggested retail list price is $10, which would provide these retailers with their normal markup of 40 percent of selling price. This is only a *suggested* resale price. If retailers wish, they can sell below the $10 price with absolutely no objections from the manufacturer.

Other manufacturers try very hard to control the retail prices of their products. Normally such a strategy is successful only when a manufacturer sells to a few retailers that want very much to carry the product. Nevertheless, some

---

[4]See David A. Aaker and Gary T. Ford, "Unit Pricing Ten Years Later: A Replication," *Journal of Marketing*, Winter 1983, pp. 118–122.

A manufacturer's suggested price may be a starting point for a reseller's attractive discounts.

manufacturers approach the limits of antitrust laws. They may even threaten to cancel a retailer's franchise for price cutting or to stop shipping products to these retailers.

Obviously these producers are—and have been for many years—in conflict with discount retailers of various types. In the 1980s, however, a phenomenon called off-price retailing again called attention to the strategy of resale price maintenance. **Off-price retailing**—that is, selling well-known brands below the manufacturer's recommended retail price—is discussed in Chapter 14. Actually off-price retailing is not a new concept. For decades it has existed in hard goods—appliances and sporting goods, for instance. In the 1980s, however, the term became associated with soft goods—especially apparel, accessories, and footwear. The current conflict between manufacturers and retailers involving pricing strategies in the apparel industry has led to court suits and proposed legislation.

Currently a producer no longer can establish a resale price maintenance program and have it supported by law. For a period of about 45 years (1930 to 1975), a series of state and federal laws permitted manufacturers to legally set retail prices on products. The state laws—technically called resale price maintenance laws—became known as *fair-trade laws.*[5]

**LEADER PRICING AND UNFAIR-PRACTICES ACTS**

Many firms, primarily retailers, temporarily cut prices on a few items to attract customers. This pricing and promotional strategy is called **leader pricing,** and the items whose prices are cut are called **loss leaders.** These loss leaders should be well-known, heavily advertised articles that are purchased frequently. The idea is that customers will come to the store to buy the advertised leader items and also will stay to buy other regularly priced merchan-

[5] For a discussion of the current and probable future legal status of resale price maintenance, plus some steps manufacturers can take to avoid legal problems when establishing resale price maintenance programs, see Mary Jane Sheffet and Debra L. Scammon, "Resale Price Maintenance: Is It Safe to Suggest Retail Prices?" *Journal of Marketing,* Fall 1985, pp. 82–91.

### AN ETHICAL DILEMMA?

Retailers sometimes ask manufacturers to set artificially high suggested retail prices and print them on packages or on merchandise tags. The retailer then adds another tag with a lower price to give consumers the impression that the merchandise has been significantly discounted. Assume you are a manufacturer. Would you consider it ethical to put a "suggested price" on merchandise if you knew retailers did not sell the item at that price?

dise. The net result, the firm hopes, will be increased total sales volume and net profit.

Today about 22 states have laws (unfair-sales acts, unfair-practices acts) to regulate leader pricing. The states have followed two model laws: (1) A reseller is prohibited from selling an item below invoice cost (including freight) plus a stated markup. This markup is usually 2 percent at wholesale and 6 percent at retail. (2) The minimum price is set at invoice cost (including freight) plus the retailer's or wholesaler's cost of doing business.[6]

The general intent of these laws is commendable. Much predatory price cutting is eliminated. However, the laws still permit firms to use loss leaders as a pricing and promotional strategy. That is, a retailer can offer an article at a selling price that is below the store's total cost—merchandise cost plus store operating expenses. Yet this selling price still will be *above* the merchandise cost plus a 6 percent markup. Thus loss-leader legislation may be viewed as a compromise between the complete absence of pricing discretion under fair-trade laws and the possibility of predatory pricing with no regulation. Loss-leader laws do not protect high-cost retailers nor do they provide the lowest possible prices for consumers.

Another limitation of these laws is that it is difficult or even impossible to determine the cost of doing business for each individual product. Therefore, some state laws have been declared unconstitutional. Also, the purpose of a business is to make a profit on the *total* operation, and not necessarily on each sale of each product.

## ODD PRICING

We have already briefly discussed pricing strategies that might be called *psychological pricing:* price lining, prestige pricing above competitive levels, and *raising* a too-low price in order to *increase* sales. At the retail level another psychological pricing policy is commonly used. **Odd pricing** sets prices at uneven (or odd) amounts, such as 49 cents or $19.95, rather than at so-called even amounts. Autos are priced at $13,995 rather than $14,000, and houses sell for $119,500 instead of $120,000. The rationale for odd pricing is that uneven price-endings suggest lower prices.

---

[6] For a study of the effects of state unfair-sales laws on price levels and competition between small stores and large grocery warehouse operators, see Willard F. Mueller and Thomas W. Paterson, "Effectiveness of State Sales-below-Cost Laws: Evidence from the Grocery Trade," *Journal of Retailing,* Summer 1986, pp. 166–185.

Do you think this store will sell more pasta at 89 cents a pound than it would at 90 cents? Would you buy more eclairs at 89 cents than at 90 cents each?

In general, retailers believe that pricing items at odd amounts will result in larger sales. Thus a price of 49 cents or 98 cents will bring greater revenue than 50 cents or $1. However, studies have reported inconclusive results regarding the value of odd pricing. Odd pricing is often avoided in prestige stores or on higher-priced items. Expensive men's suits, for example, are priced at $750, not $749.95.

## PRICE VERSUS NONPRICE COMPETITION

In the course of developing a marketing program, management has a choice of emphasizing price competition or nonprice competition. This choice can affect other parts of the firm's marketing system.

### Price Competition

In our economy today there still is a considerable amount of price competition. A firm can effectively engage in price competition by regularly offering prices that are as low as possible. Along with this strategy, a seller usually offers a minimum of services. Discount houses and chain stores often compete in this way. A firm can also use price to compete by (1) changing its prices and (2) reacting to price changes made by a competitor.

#### PRICE CHANGES BY THE FIRM

Any one of a number of situations may prompt a firm to change prices. As costs increase, for instance, management may decide to raise the price, rather than to cut quality or to aggressively promote the product and still maintain the price. If a company's market share is declining because of strong competition, its executives may react initially by *reducing* price. In the long run, however, their best alternative may be to improve their own marketing program, rather than to rely on the price cut. *Temporary* price cuts may be used to correct an imbalance in inventory or to introduce a new product.

From the seller's standpoint, the big disadvantage in price cutting is that competitors will retaliate. This is especially true in oligopolistic markets. The net result can be a price war, and the price may even settle permanently at a lower level. Note that *oligopoly* does not necessarily imply *large* firms—it means "a few sellers." Thus a neighborhood group of small merchants—barbers, for instance—can constitute an oligopoly. In an oligopoly, large or small firms try to avoid price competition, because if one reduces prices, all must follow.

### REACTION TO COMPETITORS' PRICE CHANGES

Any firm can assume that its competitors will change prices. Consequently, every firm should have policy guidelines on how it will react. If a competitor *boosts* prices, a reasonable delay in reacting probably will not be perilous. Advance planning, however, is particularly necessary in case of a competitive price *reduction*, since time is then of the essence.

As mentioned earlier, McDonald's and Anheuser-Busch (Budweiser beer) have been very much opposed to price cutting as a means of increasing sales volume. But in 1989 both firms temporarily changed their policies. McDonald's faced increasing competition from supermarket delis, home delivery services, convenience stores, and gas stations, as well as from discount price specials offered by Wendy's, Taco Bell, and other fast-food restaurants. To meet this competition, McDonald's cut prices on its Quarter-Pounder and regular cheeseburgers in some markets. Anheuser-Busch, undercut by ongoing and deep price discounts by Miller's and Coors, decided to match competitors' prices on a market-by-market basis.[7]

Airline price wars provide a good illustration of a wrong way and a right way to respond to a competitor's price cuts. In the price wars that began soon after deregulation, when one airline cut its prices, competitors typically reacted by reducing fares generally across the board—for example, "Fly anywhere, anytime, for $99." As a result of this unsound strategy, the airlines suffered heavy financial losses. In recent years, however, the major airlines (American, United, Delta) have adopted a better strategy—that of *selective* price cutting—when low-cost carriers reduce fares. This newer strategy cuts airfares only on certain routes, places restrictions on discounted fares, and even raises prices on routes that the low-cost carriers do not fly.

## Nonprice Competition

In nonprice competition, sellers maintain stable prices. They attempt to improve their market position by emphasizing other aspects of their marketing programs. Of course, competitive prices still must be taken into consideration, and price changes will occur over time. Nevertheless, in a nonprice competitive situation, the emphasis is on something *other than* price.

By using terms familiar in economic theory, we can differentiate nonprice competition from price competition. In price competition, sellers attempt to move up or down their individual demand curves by changing prices. In nonprice competition, sellers attempt to *shift* their demand curves to the right by means of product differentiation, promotional activities, or some other technique. This is illustrated in Figure 11-4. The demand curve faced by the producer of a given model of skis is DD. At a price of $250 the producer can sell 35,000 pairs a year in the New England market. On the basis of price competition alone, sales can be increased to 55,000 if the producer is willing to reduce the price to $230. The demand curve is still DD.

However, the producer is interested in boosting sales without any decrease in selling price. Consequently, the firm embarks on a promotional program—a form of nonprice competition. Suppose enough new customers are persuaded to buy at the original $250 price so that unit sales increase to 55,000 pairs a year. In effect, the firm's entire demand curve has been shifted to position D'D'.

---

[7] See "McDonald's Stoops to Conquer," *Business Week,* Oct. 30, 1989, p. 120; and James P. Miller, "Anheuser-Busch, Slugging It Out, Plans Beer Price Cuts," *The Wall Street Journal,* Oct. 26, 1989, p. B1.

**FIGURE 11-4 Shift in demand curve for skis.**

Nonprice competition can shift the demand curve for a product. A company selling skis in the New England market used a promotional program to sell more skis at the same price, thereby shifting DD to D'D'. Volume increased from 35,000 to 55,000 units at $250 (point X to point Y). Besides advertising, what other devices might this firm use to shift its demand curve?

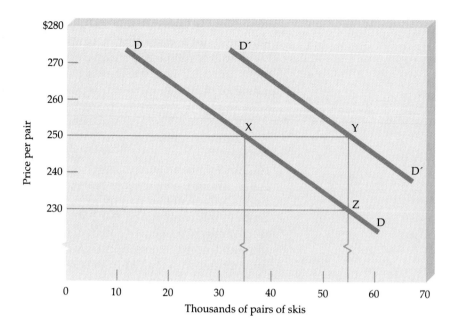

Two major methods of nonprice competition are *promotion* and *product differentiation*. In addition, some firms emphasize the *variety and quality of their services*.

Nonprice competition is being used increasingly in marketing. Companies want to be masters of their own destiny. Nonprice competition allows a seller to keep some advantage when a competitor decides to undersell. Furthermore, there is little customer loyalty when price is the only feature that distinguishes the seller. Buyers will stay only as long as that seller offers the lowest price.

**SUMMARY**

After deciding on pricing goals and setting the base (list) price, the next task in price determination is to establish specific strategies in several areas of the pricing structure. One of these areas is discounts and allowances— deductions from list price. Management has the option of offering quantity discounts, trade discounts, cash discounts, and other types of deductions. The factor of freight costs must also be considered in pricing strategy. A producer can pay all the freight (uniform delivered price) or let the buyer pay the freight bill (f.o.b. factory price). Or the two parties can share the cost in some proportion (freight absorption). Any decisions on discounts or freight allowances must be made in conformity with the Robinson-Patman Act, a federal law regulating price discrimination.

When pricing a product, especially a new product, a company should consider whether to use a market-skimming or a market-penetration pricing strategy. Management also should decide whether to charge the same price to all similar buyers (one-price strategy) or to adopt a flexible (variable) pricing strategy. Unit pricing is employed by some retailers, especially in the grocery field, to help consumers compare prices. Some firms, particularly retailers, price line. Many retailers also use leader pricing to stimulate sales. Odd pricing is a psychological pricing strategy commonly used by retailers.

Another basic decision facing management is whether to engage primarily in price or nonprice competition. Most firms prefer to use promotion, product differentiation, and other nonprice marketing activities, rather than to rely only on price as a sales stimulant.

**KEY TERMS AND CONCEPTS**

Quantity discount: 279
  Noncumulative discount 279
  Cumulative discount 279
Trade (functional) discount 280
Cash discount 280
Seasonal discount 281
Forward dating 281
Promotional allowance 281
Robinson-Patman Act provisions: 281
  Cost defense 282
  Buyer's liability 282
F.o.b. factory (mill) price 282
Uniform delivered price 283
Zone delivered price 283

Freight absorption price 283
Market-skimming pricing 284
Market-penetration pricing 284
One-price strategy 285
Flexible-price (variable-price) strategy 285
Unit pricing 287
Price lining 287
Off-price retailing 288
Resale price maintenance 288
Leader pricing 289
Odd pricing 289
Price competition 290
Nonprice competition 291

## QUESTIONS AND PROBLEMS

1. Carefully distinguish between cumulative and noncumulative quantity discounts. Which of these two types of quantity discounts has the greater economic and social justification? Why?

2. A manufacturer of appliances quotes a list price of $800 per unit for a certain model of refrigerator and grants trade discounts of 35, 20, and 5 percent. What is the manufacturer's selling price? Who might get these various discounts?

3. Company A sells to all its customers at the same published price. A sales executive finds that company B is offering to sell to one of A's customers at a lower price. Company A then cuts its price to this customer but maintains the original price for all other customers. Is this a violation of the Robinson-Patman Act?

4. Name some products that might logically be sold under a uniform delivered price system.

5. "An f.o.b. point-of-production price system is the only geographic price system that is fair to buyers." Discuss.

6. An Eastern firm wants to compete in Western markets, where it is at a significant disadvantage with respect to freight costs. What pricing alternatives can it adopt to overcome the freight differential?

7. For each of the following products, do you recommend that the seller adopt a market-skimming or a penetration pricing strategy? Support your decision in each instance.

a. High-fashion dresses styled and manufactured by Chanel or Yves St. Laurent.

b. An exterior housepaint that wears twice as long as any competitive brand.

c. A cigarette *totally* free of tar and nicotine.

d. A tablet that converts a gallon of water into a gallon of automotive fuel.

8. Under what marketing conditions is a company likely to use a variable-price strategy? Can you name firms that employ this strategy, other than when a trade-in is involved?

9. In 1990 several U.S. companies were completing their plans to enter the economically unified European Community market in 1992. Name three U.S. brands that well might adopt a skimming pricing strategy in the EC. Name three that should use a penetration pricing strategy.

10. Distinguish between leader pricing and predatory price cutting.

11. How should a manufacturer of prefinished plywood interior wall paneling react if a competitor cuts prices?

12. What factors account for the increased use of nonprice competition?

13. On the basis of the topics covered in this chapter, establish a set of price strategies for the manufacturer of a new glass cleaner that is sold through a broker to supermarkets. The manufacturer sells the cleaner at $15 for a case of a dozen 16-ounce bottles.

# CHAPTER 12

# MANAGING CHANNELS OF DISTRIBUTION

A distribution channel sometimes is a tightly coordinated system. Other times it consists of independent and competing firms. Whatever the circumstances, for a product to reach its intended market, a channel of distribution must be well managed. After studying this chapter, you should be able to explain:

- The nature and importance of middlemen.
- What a distribution channel is.
- The sequence of decisions involved in designing a channel.
- The major channels of distribution for consumer goods, business goods, and services.
- Multiple channels of distribution.
- Vertical marketing systems.
- Factors affecting the selection of a channel.
- The concept of intensity of distribution.
- The choice of individual middlemen.
- The nature of horizontal and vertical conflicts in distribution channels.
- The concept of channel control.
- Legal considerations in channels management.

Shoprite Stores required a small popcorn producer to pay $86,000 to have its product stocked in the chain's supermarkets in New York City. Pillsbury Co. was asked by a New England supermarket chain to "rent" shelf space for a fee that was greater than Pillsbury's entire budget for introducing a new brownie product across the United States.

Many supermarket chains are demanding fees for space on store shelves. These fees, called slotting allowances, suggest that the balance of power in distribution is shifting from manufacturers to retailers.

This trend is most evident in the grocery products field. In some cases, companies with new products are required to pay a slotting allowance of $100 to over $1,000 per store for each version of the product. Or payment may be in the form of free products.

Of course, not all manufacturers are paying all of these fees. And some small producers cannot afford them.

Manufacturers criticize the fees, especially slotting allowances, claiming that they stifle the introduction of new products, particularly those developed by small companies. Moreover, the fees do not seem to be related to actual costs incurred by chains in stocking or removing products from their shelves.

Retailers vigorously defend slotting allowances. Supermarkets contend they must find a way to recoup the costs of reviewing the flood of new products, stocking some of them, and removing failures. Actually slotting allowances indicate that demand for supermarket shelf space far exceeds available supply.

Are manufacturers powerless against these fees? No. They can counter them by distributing through stores that do not charge them or by building customer loyalty so supermarkets will be forced to stock popular brands. Right now, though, supermarkets and other retailers seem to have the upper hand.[1]

●

[1] Christine Donahue, "Getting Them Coming and Going," Adweek's Marketing Week, Sept. 14, 1989, pp. 20–21; "Small Companies Protest Slotting Allowances," Marketing News, Jan. 16, 1989, pp. 2, 6; and Richard Gibson, "Supermarkets Demand Food Firms' Payments Just to Get on the Shelf," The Wall Street Journal, Nov. 1, 1988, pp. 1, 14.

Even before a product is ready for market, management should determine what methods and routes will be used to get it there. This task involves establishing a strategy covering distribution channels and physical distribution of the product.

Managing a distribution channel often begins with a producer. Therefore, we will discuss channels largely from the vantage point of the producer. As you will see, however, the channel problems and opportunities of middlemen are similar to those faced by producers. Furthermore, as shown in our opening example, control of channels used by producers may actually rest with middlemen.

## MIDDLEMEN AND DISTRIBUTION CHANNELS

Product ownership has to be transferred somehow from the individual or organization making it to the consumer needing it. Goods also must be transported from the production site to the location where they are needed. (As will be discussed in Chapter 19, services ordinarily cannot be shipped but rather are produced and consumed in the same place.)

Distribution's role within a marketing mix is getting the product to its target market. Overall responsibility rests with the distribution channel, with some tasks assumed by middlemen in this channel. Thus we begin by discussing the activities and roles of middlemen and a distribution channel.

Getting a product to market entails a number of activities, most importantly arranging for its sale (and the transfer of title) from producer to final customer. Other common functions are promoting the product, storing it, and assuming some of the risk during the distribution process.

A producer can carry out these functions in exchange for an order (and, ultimately, payment) from a consumer. Or producer and consumer can divide up the activities. Typically firms called middlemen perform these activities on behalf of the producer or consumer.

A **middleman** is a business firm that renders services directly related to the purchase and/or sale of a product as it flows from producer to consumer. A middleman either owns the product or actively aids in the transfer of ownership. Often, but not always, a middleman takes physical possession of the product, whereas others do not physically handle it.

Middlemen are commonly classified on the basis of whether or not they take title to the products involved. **Merchant middlemen** actually take title to the goods they are helping to market. **Agent middlemen** never actually own the goods, but they do actively assist in the transfer of title. Real estate brokers, manufacturers' agents, and travel agents are examples of agent middlemen. The two major groups of merchant middlemen are wholesalers and retailers. Middlemen operate as vital links between producers and ultimate consumers or business users.

## How Important Are Middlemen?

Marketing's critics sometimes say that prices of products are high because there are too many middlemen who perform unnecessary, duplicate functions. While middlemen can be eliminated in attempting to reduce distribution costs, lower costs may not always be achieved. The reason for this uncertainty lies in a basic axiom of marketing: *You can eliminate middlemen, but you cannot eliminate their functions.* These functions can be shifted from one party to another in an effort to improve efficiency. However, someone has to perform the various activities—if not a middleman, then the producer or final customer.

In certain situations middlemen may be able to carry out distribution activ-

**FIGURE 12-1** Typical activities of a middleman.

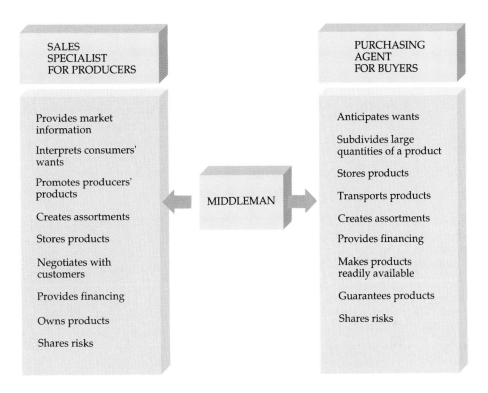

ities better or more cheaply than either producers or consumers. In fact, middlemen can be downright indispensable in many situations. It is usually not practical for a producer to deal directly with ultimate consumers. Think for a moment how inconvenient life would be if there were no retail middlemen—no supermarkets, gas stations, or ticket sales outlets, for instance.

As illustrated in Figure 12-1, middlemen serve as purchasing agents for their customers and as sales specialists for their suppliers. They provide financial services for both suppliers and customers. Middlemen's storage services, ability to divide large shipments into smaller ones for resale, and market knowledge benefit suppliers and customers alike.

## What Is a Distribution Channel?

A **distribution channel** consists of the set of people and firms involved in the flow of title to a product as it moves from producer to ultimate consumer or business user. A channel of distribution always includes both the producer and the final customer for the product in its present form as well as any middlemen (such as retailers and wholesalers).

The channel for a product extends only to the last person or organization buying it without making any significant change in its form. When its form is altered and another product emerges, a new channel is started. When lumber is milled and then made into furniture, two separate channels are involved. The channel for the *lumber* might be lumber mill → broker → furniture manufacturer. The channel for the *finished furniture* might be furniture manufacturer → retail furniture store → consumer.

Besides producer, middlemen, and final customer, other institutions aid the distribution process. Among these intermediaries are banks, insurance companies, storage firms, and transportation companies. However, because they do not take title to the products and are not actively involved in purchase or sales activities, these intermediaries are not formally included in the distribution channel.

This chapter focuses on the flow of ownership or title for a product, while Chapter 15 examines the physical flow of goods. These flows are distinct; consequently, different institutions may carry them out. For example, a contractor might order a load of roofing shingles from a local building-materials distributor. The product might be shipped directly from the shingles manufacturer to the contractor to minimize freight and handling costs. But the channel for title (and ownership) would be manufacturer → distributor → contractor.

Sofas, like many goods, are distributed through a channel consisting of the manufacturer, retailer, and final consumer.

## DESIGNING DISTRIBUTION CHANNELS

Firms that appear to be similar often have dissimilar channels of distribution. For instance, the three largest sellers of auto insurance use different channels. State Farm sells through its own sales force working out of branch offices in local communities. Allstate sales people typically sell from offices located in Sears stores. Aetna uses independent insurance brokers to reach consumers.

Why do seemingly similar firms wind up with such different channels? One reason is that there are numerous types of channels and middlemen from which to choose. Also a variety of factors related to the market, product, middlemen, and company itself influence which channel is actually used by a firm.

Essentially a company wants a distribution channel that not only meets customers' needs but also provides an edge on competition. This requires an organized approach to designing a channel. As shown in Figure 12-2, we suggest a sequence of four decisions:

1. *Delineating the role of distribution.* A channel strategy should be designed within the context of an entire marketing mix. First the firm's marketing objectives are reviewed. Next the roles assigned to product, price, and promotion are delineated. Each element may have a distinct role, or two elements may share an assignment. For example, a manufacturer of pressure gauges may use both distribution and promotion to convince prospective customers that it is committed to servicing the product following the sale.

   A company must decide whether distribution will be used defensively or offensively. If defensive, a firm will strive for distribution that is as good as, but not necessarily better than, other firms' distribution. With an offensive strategy, a firm uses distribution to gain an advantage over competitors. Recently Honda decided to seek an advantage for its Acura line of luxury cars by establishing separate Acura dealerships rather than relying on existing Honda dealerships.

2. *Selecting the type of channel.* Once distribution's role in the overall marketing program has been agreed on, the most suitable type of channel for the company's product must be determined. At this point in the sequence, a firm needs to decide whether middlemen will be used in its channel and, if so, which types of middlemen.

   To illustrate the wide array of institutions available as well as the difficulty of channel selection, consider a manufacturer of compact disc players. If the use of middlemen is deemed appropriate, the company must choose among many different types of middlemen. At the retail level the range of institutions includes specialty audio-video outlets, department stores, discount houses, and mail-order firms. Which single type or combination of types would permit the manufacturer to achieve its distribution objectives? Another choice must be made if the firm has decided to also use wholesaling middlemen. In a subsequent section this decision as

**FIGURE 12-2** Sequence of decisions to design a distribution channel.

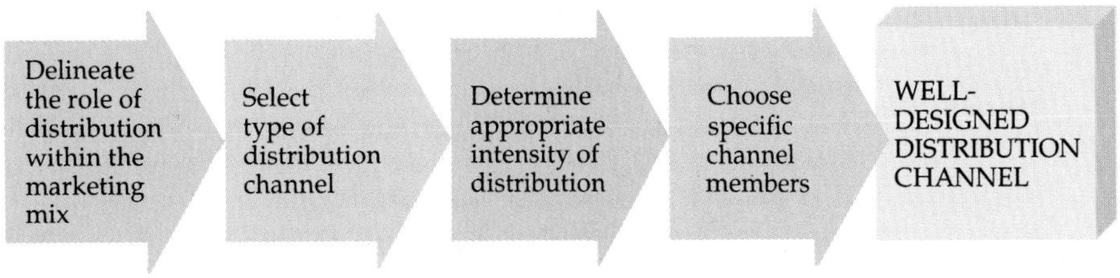

Delineate the role of distribution within the marketing mix → Select type of distribution channel → Determine appropriate intensity of distribution → Choose specific channel members → WELL-DESIGNED DISTRIBUTION CHANNEL

well as the major types of channels for goods and services will be discussed in detail.

3. *Determining intensity of distribution.* The next decision relates to **intensity of distribution,** or the number of middlemen used at the wholesale and retail levels in a particular territory. The target market's buying behavior and the product's nature have a direct bearing on this decision, as we will see later.

4. *Choosing specific channel members.* The last decision is the selection of specific firms, or ''brands'' of middlemen, to distribute the product. For each type of institution, there are usually numerous specific companies from which to choose.

Recalling our compact disc player example, assume that the manufacturer prefers two types of middlemen: department stores and specialty outlets. If the CD players will be sold in Chicago, the producer must decide which department stores—Marshall Field and/or Carson Pirie Scott—will be asked to distribute its product line. Also one or more audio-video chains—from a group including United Audio Centers, MusiCraft, and Hi Fi Hutch—must be selected. Similar decisions must be made for each territory in the firm's market.

When selecting specific firms to be part of a channel, a producer should assess factors related to the market, product, and company as well as middlemen. Another key factor is the degree of intensity necessary to serve its target market well. Two additional factors are whether the middleman sells to the market that the manufacturer wants to reach and whether its product mix, pricing structure, promotion, and customer service are all compatible with the producer's needs.[2]

## SELECTING THE TYPE OF CHANNEL

Firms may rely on existing channels or they may use new channels to better serve existing customers, reach new customers, and/or gain an edge on competitors. For instance, to attract new customers, Xerox now distributes some of its products through Sears stores. A small company named New Pig decided not to use conventional middlemen such as supermarkets and hardware stores to sell a new dust cloth that has special dirt-attracting properties. Instead, to reach a primarily female target market, it is distributing its product through beauty salons![3]

Most distribution channels include middlemen, but some do not. A channel consisting only of producer and final customer, with no middlemen providing assistance, is called **direct distribution.** In contrast, a channel of producer, final customer, and at least one level of middleman represents **indirect distribution.** One level of middleman—retailers but no wholesaling middlemen, for example—or multiple levels may participate in an indirect channel. (Sometimes a channel for consumer goods in which wholesalers are bypassed but retailers are used is termed *direct*, rather than indirect, distribution.) With indirect distribution a producer must determine the type(s) of middlemen that will best serve its needs. A wide range of options exists at both the wholesale and retail levels, and these will be described in the next two chapters.

[2] For further ideas on how to build a good producer-middleman relationship, see James A. Narus and James C. Anderson, ''Distributor Contributions to Partnership with Manufacturers,'' *Business Horizons,* September–October 1987, pp. 34–42.

[3] These examples are taken from ''Unconventional Channels,'' *Sales & Marketing Management,* October 1988, p. 38.

Selection of one type of middleman, such as a discount house, may affect whether another type, such as a specialty retailer, will participate in the channel. Or including one type may influence how much support another type will put behind the manufacturer's product. Their decisions are based on various factors that will soon be discussed.

At this point in the decision sequence, we should look at the major channels traditionally used by producers and at two special channels. Then we can consider the factors that most influence a company's choice of channels.

## Major Channels of Distribution

Diverse distribution channels exist today. However, only a handful of channels are used most often. Common channels for consumer goods, business goods, and services are described next and summarized in Figure 12-3.

### DISTRIBUTION OF CONSUMER GOODS

Five channels are widely used in marketing tangible products intended for ultimate consumers:

- *Producer → consumer.* The shortest, simplest distribution channel for consumer goods involves no middlemen. The producer may sell from door to door or by mail. For instance, Southwestern Company uses college students to market its books on a house-to-house basis.
- *Producer → retailer → consumer.* Many large retailers buy directly from manufacturers and agricultural producers.
- *Producer → wholesaler → retailer → consumer.* If there is a "traditional" channel for consumer goods, this is it. Small retailers and manufacturers by the thousands find this channel the only economically feasible choice.
- *Producer → agent → retailer → consumer.* Instead of using wholesalers, many producers prefer to use agent middlemen to reach the retail market, especially *large-scale* retailers. For example, a manufacturer of a glass cleaner selected a food broker to reach the grocery store market, including large chains.
- *Producer → agent → wholesaler → retailer → consumer.* To reach *small* retailers, producers often use agent middlemen, who in turn call on wholesalers that sell to small stores.

### DISTRIBUTION OF BUSINESS GOODS

Once again, a variety of channels are available to reach organizations that will incorporate the products into their manufacturing process or use them in their operations.[4] In the following discussion the term *industrial distributor* is synonymous with merchant wholesaler. The four most common channels for business goods are:

- *Producer → user.* This direct channel accounts for a greater *dollar* volume of business products than any other distribution structure. Manufacturers of large installations, such as airplanes, generators, and heating plants, usually sell directly to users.
- *Producer → industrial distributor → user.* Producers of operating supplies and small accessory equipment frequently use industrial distributors to

---

[4]An excellent discussion of distribution channels for business goods and services is found in Michael D. Hutt and Thomas W. Speh, *Business Marketing Management*, 3rd ed., The Dryden Press, Chicago, 1989, pp. 379–411.

**FIGURE 12-3** Major marketing channels available to producers.

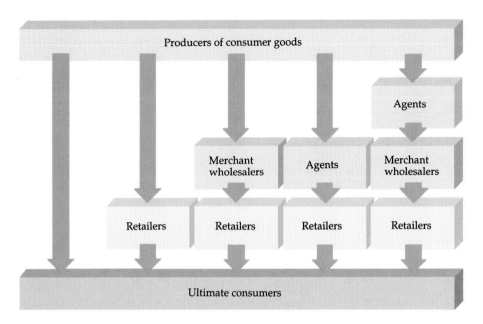

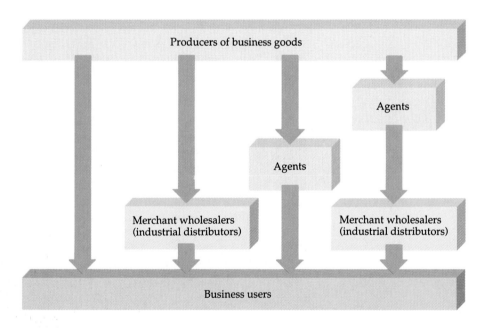

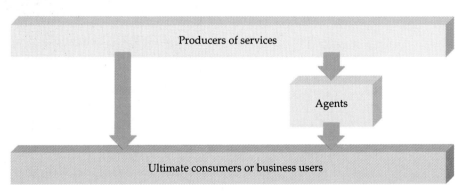

reach their markets. Manufacturers of building materials and air-conditioning equipment are two examples of firms that make heavy use of the industrial distributor.

- *Producer → agent → user.* Firms without their own sales departments find this a desirable channel. Also a company that wants to introduce a new product or enter a new market may prefer to use agents rather than its own sales force.
- *Producer → agent → industrial distributor → user.* This channel is similar to the preceding one. It is used when, for some reason, it is not feasible to sell through agents directly to the business user. The unit sale may be too small for direct selling. Or decentralized inventory may be needed to supply users rapidly, in which case the storage services of an industrial distributor are required.

### DISTRIBUTION OF SERVICES

The intangible nature of services creates special distribution requirements. There are only two common channels for services:[5]

- *Producer → consumer.* Because a service is intangible, the production process and/or sales activity often requires personal contact between producer and consumer. Thus a direct channel is used. Direct distribution is typical for many professional services, such as health care and legal advice, and personal services, such as haircutting and weight-loss counseling. However, other services, including travel, insurance, and entertainment, may also rely on direct distribution.
- *Producer → agent → consumer.* While direct distribution often is necessary for a service to be performed, producer-consumer contact may not be required for key distribution activities. Agents frequently assist a services producer with transfer of ownership (the sales task) or related tasks. Many services, notably travel, lodging, advertising media, entertainment, and insurance, use agents.

Whom does a travel agent primarily serve—airlines, lodging chains, and cruise lines, *or* final consumers?

---

[5]For an excellent discussion of this topic, see Donald H. Light, "A Guide for New Distribution Channel Strategies for Service Firms," *The Journal of Business Strategy,* Summer 1986, pp. 56–64.

## Multiple Channels of Distribution

Many, perhaps most, producers are not content to use only a single distribution channel. Instead, for reasons such as achieving broad market coverage or avoiding total dependence on a single arrangement, they employ multiple channels. (Similarly, to ensure they have products when needed, many companies establish multiple *supply* channels.)

Use of multiple channels, sometimes called **dual distribution,** occurs in several distinct situations. A manufacturer is likely to use multiple channels to reach *different types of markets* when selling:

- The same product (for example, sporting goods or typewriters) to both consumer and business markets.[6]
- Unrelated products (margarine and paint; rubber products and plastics).

Multiple channels are also used to reach *different segments within a single market* when:

- Size of the buyers varies greatly. To illustrate, an airline may sell directly to travel departments in large corporations but use travel agents to reach small businesses and ultimate consumers.
- Density differs across parts of the market. For example, a manufacturer of industrial machinery may use its own sales force to sell directly to users in concentrated markets, but may employ agents in sparsely populated markets.

A significant trend is the use of competing channel systems to sell the *same brand to a single market.* Sherwin-Williams paints and Goodyear tires are distributed through the manufacturers' own retail stores as well as through conventional channels of independent retailers and possibly wholesalers. Producers may open their own stores, thereby creating dual distribution, when they are not satisfied with the market coverage provided by existing retail outlets. Or they may establish their own stores primarily as testing grounds for new products and marketing techniques.

Although multiple distribution channels provide various benefits to the producer, they can aggravate middlemen. Disputes between producers and middlemen may occur. To mention an example, owners of franchised Häagen-Dazs stores rebelled when faced with multiple channels. They claimed their marketing efforts were undermined (and sales and profits reduced) when the producer decided to sell this premium ice cream in supermarkets as well as franchised stores.

## Vertical Marketing Systems

Historically, distribution channels stressed the independence of individual channel members. That is, various middlemen were employed to achieve a producer's distribution objectives; however, the producer typically was not concerned with middlemen's needs. In turn, wholesalers and retailers were more interested in maintaining their freedom than in coordinating their activities with a producer. These shortcomings of conventional distribution channels provided an opportunity for a new type of channel.

During the past three decades, the vertical marketing system has become a major force—perhaps *the* dominant force—in distribution. A **vertical marketing system** (VMS) is a tightly coordinated distribution channel designed to achieve operating efficiencies and marketing effectiveness.

---

[6]For extensive discussion of this strategy, see John A. Quelch, "Why Not Exploit Dual Marketing?" *Business Horizons,* January–February 1987, pp. 52–60.

Vertical marketing systems exemplify the concept of function shifting discussed earlier. No marketing function is sacred to a particular level or firm in the channel. Instead, each function is performed at the most advantageous position in the channel.

The high degree of coordination or control that characterizes a VMS is achieved through one of three means: ownership of successive levels of a channel, contracts between channel members, or the market power of one or more members. As shown in Table 12-1, there are three distinct forms of vertical marketing systems.

In a **corporate VMS,** a firm at one level of a channel owns the firms at the next level or owns the entire channel. Remember that Sherwin-Williams and Goodyear own retail outlets. Also, a growing number of apparel makers are opening their own retail stores to feature their brands of clothing.

Middlemen may also engage in this type of vertical integration. For example, many grocery chains own food-processing facilities, such as dairies, which supply their stores. And Sears has ownership interests in manufacturing facilities that supply its stores with many goods, including tools and clothing.

In a **contractual VMS,** independent firms—producers, wholesalers, and retailers—operate under contracts specifying how they will try to improve distribution efficiency and effectiveness. Three contractual systems have developed: wholesaler-sponsored voluntary chains, retailer-owned cooperatives, and franchise systems. All three will be discussed in Chapter 14.

An **administered VMS** coordinates distribution activities through the market and/or economic power of one channel member or the shared power of two channel members. This is illustrated by Corning in ovenware, Rolex in watches, and Kraft in food products. Typically a producer's brand and market position are strong enough to gain the voluntary cooperation of retailers in matters such as inventory levels, advertising, and store display.

In the distant past, competition in distribution usually involved two differ-

## TABLE 12-1 Types of vertical marketing systems

| Type of system | Control maintained by | Examples |
| --- | --- | --- |
| Corporate | Ownership | Singer (sewing machines), Goodyear (tires), Tandy Corp. (electronics) |
| Contractual: | | |
| Wholesaler-sponsored voluntary chain | Contract | Western Auto stores, Ben Franklin stores, IGA stores |
| Retailer-owned cooperative | Stock ownership by retailers | True Value hardware stores |
| Franchise systems | Contract: | |
| | Manufacturer-sponsored retailers | Ford, Chrysler, and other auto dealers |
| | Manufacturer-sponsored wholesalers | Coca-Cola and other soft-drink bottlers |
| | Marketers of services | Wendy's, Midas Muffler, Holiday Inn, National car rentals |
| Administered | Economic power | Hartman luggage, General Electric, Kraft dairy products |

In this administered VMS, Ralph Lauren and May Department Stores work toward shared goals.

ent conventional channels. More recently, competition pitted a conventional channel against some form of VMS. Presently and in the future, the most common competitive battles will be between different forms of vertical marketing systems. For example, a corporate system (such as the stores owned by Goodyear) competes with a contractual system (such as Firestone's franchised dealers). Considering the potential benefits of vertical marketing systems with respect to both operating efficiencies and marketing effectiveness, they should continue to grow in number and importance.

## Factors Affecting Choice of Channels

If a firm is customer-oriented, its channels should be determined by consumer buying patterns. Thus the nature of the market should be the key influence in management's choice of channels. Other major considerations are the product, the middlemen, and the company itself.

### MARKET CONSIDERATIONS

A logical starting point is to consider the needs, structure, and buying behavior of target markets:

- *Type of market.* Because the buying behavior of ultimate consumers ordinarily is different than that of business users, separate distribution arrangements normally must be made to reach the different markets. Retailers, by definition, serve ultimate consumers so they are not in channels for business goods.
- *Number of potential customers.* A manufacturer with relatively few potential customers (firms or industries) may use its own sales force to sell directly to consumers or business users. For a large number of customers, the manufacturer would likely use middlemen.

- *Geographic concentration of the market.* Direct sale to the textile or the garment manufacturing industry is feasible because most of the buyers are concentrated in a few geographic areas. Even in the case of a national market, some segments have a higher density rate than others. Sellers may establish sales branches in densely populated markets and use middlemen in less concentrated markets.
- *Order size.* A food products manufacturer would sell directly to large grocery chains because the large order size and total volume of business make this channel economically desirable. The same manufacturer, however, would use wholesalers to reach small grocery stores whose orders are usually too small to justify direct sale.[7]

### PRODUCT CONSIDERATIONS

While there are numerous product-related factors to consider, we will highlight three:

- *Unit value.* The price attached to each unit of a product affects the amount of funds available for distribution. For example, a company can afford to use its own employee to sell a nuclear-reactor part that costs, say, more than $10,000. But it would not make sense for a company sales person to call on a household or a business firm to sell a $2 ballpoint pen. Consequently, products with low unit values usually are distributed through long channels (that is, through one or more levels of middlemen). There are exceptions, however. For instance, if order size is large because the customer buys many products at the same time from the company, then a direct (or short) channel may be economically feasible.
- *Perishability.* Some goods, including many agricultural products, physically deteriorate fairly quickly. Other goods, such as clothing, perish in a fashion sense. As will be discussed further in Chapter 19, services are perishable due to their intangible nature. Perishable products require direct or very short channels.
- *Technical nature of a product.* A business product that is highly technical is often distributed directly to business users. The producer's sales force must provide considerable presale and postsale service; wholesalers normally cannot do this. *Consumer* products of a technical nature provide a real distribution challenge for manufacturers. Ordinarily, manufacturers cannot sell the goods directly to the consumer. As much as possible, producers try to sell directly to retailers, but even then product servicing often poses problems.

### MIDDLEMEN CONSIDERATIONS

Here we begin to see that a company may not be able to arrange exactly the channels it desires:

- *Services provided by middlemen.* Each producer should select middlemen that will provide those marketing services that the producer either is unable to provide or cannot economically perform.
- *Availability of desired middlemen.* The middlemen preferred by a producer

[7]For more on the idea that market considerations should determine a producer's channel structure, see Louis W. Stern and Frederick D. Sturdivant, "Customer-Driven Distribution Systems," *Harvard Business Review*, July–August 1987, pp. 34–41.

may not be available. They may be carrying competitive products and may not want to add another line.

- *Attitude of middlemen toward producers' policies.* Sometimes manufacturers' choices of channels are limited because their marketing policies are not acceptable to certain types of middlemen. Some retailers or wholesalers, for example, are interested in carrying a line only if they receive assurance that no competing firms will carry the line in the same territory.

## COMPANY CONSIDERATIONS

Before choosing a distribution channel for a product, a company should consider relevant factors in its own situation:

- *Desire for channel control.* Some producers establish short channels simply because they want to control the distribution of their products, even though the cost of the more direct channel may be higher than that of an indirect channel. By controlling the channel, producers can achieve more aggressive promotion and can better control both the freshness of merchandise stocks and the retail prices of their products.
- *Services provided by seller.* Some producers base channel decisions in part on their ability to carry out the distribution functions demanded by middlemen. For instance, often a retail chain will not stock a given product unless it is presold through heavy producer advertising.
- *Ability of management.* Channel decisions are affected by the marketing experience and ability of the firm's management. Many companies lacking marketing know-how prefer to turn the distribution job over to middlemen.
- *Financial resources.* A business with adequate finances can establish its own sales force, grant credit, or warehouse its own products. A financially weak firm would have to use middlemen who could provide these services.

In some cases virtually all factors point to a particular length and/or type of channel. In most situations, however, careful assessment results in mixed signals. Several factors may point to the desirability of direct channels, but others to the use of wholesalers and/or retailers. Or the company may find a desired length or type of channel is unavailable. If a company with an unproven product having low profit potential cannot place its product with middlemen, it may have no other option but to try to distribute the product directly to its target market.

**DETERMINING INTENSITY OF DISTRIBUTION**

At this stage in the design sequence, a firm knows what role within the marketing mix has been assigned to distribution, whether direct or indirect distribution is the better choice, and which types of middlemen will be used (assuming indirect distribution is appropriate). Next the company must decide on the intensity of distribution, that is, how many middlemen will be used at the wholesale and retail levels in a particular territory.

The degrees of intensity span an entire continuum. For ease of discussion and decision making, the continuum typically is broken into three categories, ranging from *intensive* to *selective* to *exclusive*. This continuum is presented in Figure 12-4.

Distribution intensity ordinarily is thought to be a single decision. For instance, after considering all factors, a firm may opt for intensive distribution. However, if the desired channel has more than one level of middlemen

**FIGURE 12-4** The intensity-of-distribution continuum.

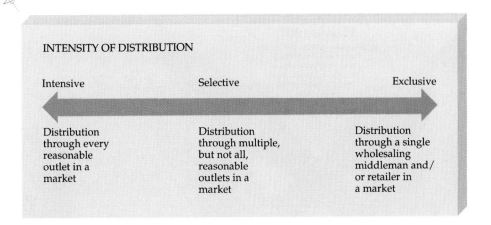

(wholesaler and retailer, for example), then the appropriate intensity must be selected for each level.

Different degrees of intensity may be appropriate at successive levels of distribution. A manufacturer can often achieve intensive retail coverage with selective, rather than intensive, wholesale distribution. Or selective intensity at the retail level may be gained through one wholesaler—that is, exclusive intensity at the wholesale level. Of course, the wholesaling firm(s) will determine which retail outlets actually receive the product. Despite this lack of control, a producer should plan the levels of intensity needed at both the wholesale and retail levels. Making only one decision is simplistic and can create serious problems.

## Intensive Distribution

Under a strategy of **intensive distribution,** a producer sells its product through every available outlet in a market where a consumer might reasonably look for it. High intensity is often used by manufacturers of convenience goods. Ultimate consumers demand immediate satisfaction with this class of product and will not defer purchases to find a particular brand. Retailers often control whether this strategy can be implemented. For example, a new manufacturer of toothpaste or a small producer of potato chips may want distribution in all supermarkets, but these retailers may limit their assortments to four fast-selling brands.

Retailers typically will not pay to advertise a product that is sold by competitors. Therefore, intensive distribution places most of the advertising and promotion burden on the producer.

## Selective Distribution

In **selective distribution,** a producer sells its product through multiple, but not all possible, wholesalers and/or retailers in a market where a consumer might reasonably look for it. Selective distribution is appropriate for consumer shopping goods, such as various types of clothing and appliances, and for business accessory equipment, such as office equipment and handheld tools.

A company may decide to adopt a selective distribution strategy after some experience with intensive distribution. The decision to change usually hinges on the high cost of intensive distribution or the unsatisfactory performance of middlemen. Certain customers perennially order in small, unprofitable amounts. Others may be poor credit risks. Eliminating such marginal middlemen may reduce the number of outlets, but it can actually increase a company's sales volume. Many companies have found this to be the case

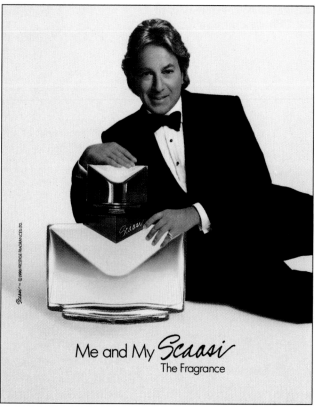

Several department store chains make up the Swatch selective distribution channel. In contrast, Scaasi Fragrances believes that exclusive distribution by a single retail chain serves its needs more effectively.

simply because they were able to do a more thorough selling job with a smaller number of accounts.

## Exclusive Distribution

Under an **exclusive distribution** strategy, the supplier agrees to sell its product only to a single wholesaling middleman and/or retailer in a given market. An exclusive distributorship with a wholesaler or an exclusive dealership with a retailer sometimes prohibits the middleman from handling a directly competing product line.

Exclusive dealerships are frequently used in the marketing of consumer specialty products such as expensive suits. Producers also often adopt an exclusive distribution strategy when it is essential that the retailer carry a large inventory. This form of distribution is also desirable when the dealer or distributor must furnish installation and repair service. Manufacturers of farm machinery and large construction equipment use exclusive distributorships for this reason.

Exclusive distribution helps a manufacturer control the last level of middleman before the final customer. A middleman with exclusive rights is usually willing to promote the product aggressively. This is because interested customers will have to purchase the product at its outlet since no other outlets in the area carry the same brand. However, a producer suffers if its exclusive middlemen in various markets do not serve customers well. Essentially a manufacturer has "all its eggs in one basket."

A significant advantage of being an exclusive dealer or distributor is the opportunity to reap all the benefits of the producer's marketing activities in a particular area. However, an exclusive middleman may become too dependent on the manufacturer. If the manufacturer fails, the middleman also fails (for that product). Another risk is that once sales volume has been built up in a market, the producer may add other dealers.

## CONFLICT AND CONTROL IN CHANNELS

Distribution occasionally is characterized by shared goals and cooperative actions. But conflict and struggles for control are more typical. Firms in one channel often compete vigorously with firms in other channels. Even within the same channel, firms argue about operating practices and try to gain control over actions of other members.

Effective management of distribution channels requires an understanding of both conflict and control, including techniques to (1) decrease conflict, or at least its negative effects, and (2) increase a firm's control within a channel. **Channel conflict** exists when one channel member perceives another channel member to be acting in a way that prevents the first member from achieving its distribution objectives. There are two types of conflict—horizontal and vertical.

**AN INTERNATIONAL PERSPECTIVE: Can U.S. companies penetrate the Japanese distribution system?**

With so many possible combinations of types of institutions, distribution intensity, and specific firms, American producers face serious challenges in arranging effective distribution channels in their own country. But the challenge is much greater, sometimes insurmountable, in Japan!

Distribution in Japan has been characterized by numerous small, family-operated retail stores, an even larger number of wholesalers, and many government regulations protecting traditional distribution channels. Ownership of goods may pass through several wholesalers before reaching retailers.

The 1.6 million "papa-mama" stores, as the Japanese call them, account for 56 percent of retail sales (compared to only 3 percent in the United States). And government regulations deter change. One law, for example, stipulates that a chain desiring to open a new store must gain the approval of *all* papa-mama stores within a third of a mile of the proposed store site. If approval is obtained, another law limits the size of the new store to less than 6,000 square feet.

Changing consumer needs and government attitudes are beginning to modify the complex and, according to many observers, inefficient Japanese distribution system. More Japanese women are employed, and they desire the convenience of one-stop shopping provided by large stores and shopping centers. Also the govern-

ment considers big stores as good for economic growth, so some restrictions are being eased.

Sensing a giant opportunity, many U.S. companies are trying to distribute their products in Japan. More success is being achieved by going around—rather than through—traditional channels. For example, importers avoid wholesalers, if possible, and deal directly with retailers. Washington State wine and Pepperidge Farm cookies made it onto store shelves in this way. American-style convenience stores (led by 7-Eleven) now compete with the traditional papa-mama stores.

What's on the horizon for Japanese distribution? Apparently, traditional wholesalers and retailers will lose ground to new distribution approaches. Discount houses, large shopping centers, home-shopping channels on TV, and catalog retailing are finding favor with Japanese consumers who want to save money and/or time. New NIE (newly *i*ndustrialized *e*conomy) stores are selling products from South Korea, Hong Kong, and elsewhere at lower prices than comparable Japanese goods sell for. Change is in the air!

Source: Adapted from Carla Rapoport, "Ready, Set, Sell—Japan Is Buying," *Fortune*, Sept. 11, 1989, pp. 159–60ff; C. William Verity, "Piercing the Ultimate Trade Barrier," *Fortune*, Dec. 19, 1988, p. 183; and Damon Darlin, "'Papa-Mama' Stores in Japan Wield Power to Hold Back Imports," *The Wall Street Journal*, Nov. 14, 1988, pp. A1, A7.

Plastic wrap plus children's toys equals scrambled merchandising.

## Horizontal Conflicts

**Horizontal conflict** occurs among firms on the same level of distribution. Such conflict may occur between:

- *Middlemen of the same type:* Maryvale True Value Hardware versus Fred's Friendly Hardware, for example.
- *Different types of middlemen on the same level:* Maryvale True Value Hardware versus Dunn Edwards Paint versus K mart.

The main source of horizontal conflict is **scrambled merchandising,** where middlemen diversify by adding product lines not traditionally carried by their type of business. Supermarkets, for instance, expanded beyond groceries by adding health and beauty aids, small appliances, records, snack bars, and various services. Retailers that sold these product lines first have become irritated both at supermarkets for diversifying and at producers for using multiple distribution channels.

Scrambled merchandising and the resulting horizontal competition may stem from the market, middleman, or producer. Many consumers (the *market*) prefer convenient, one-stop shopping, so stores broaden their assortments to satisfy this desire. *Middlemen* constantly strive for higher gross margins and more customer traffic by adding new lines. *Producers* seek to expand market coverage and reduce unit production costs by adding new types of outlets. These diversification efforts intensify the degree of horizontal conflict.

## Vertical Conflicts

Perhaps the most severe conflicts in distribution involve firms at different levels of the same channel. These **vertical conflicts** typically occur between producer and wholesaler or producer and retailer.

### PRODUCER VERSUS WHOLESALER

Tensions occasionally arise between producers and wholesalers. A producer and wholesaler may disagree about aspects of their business relationship. For instance, Deere & Co. has argued with distributors about whether they should sell farm equipment made by other companies or should restrict their efforts to the Deere brand.

Why do conflicts arise? Basically manufacturers and wholesalers have differing points of view. On the one hand, manufacturers think that wholesalers neither promote products aggressively nor provide sufficient storage services. And wholesalers' services cost too much. On the other hand, wholesalers believe producers either expect too much or do not understand the wholesaler's primary obligation to customers.

Channel conflict typically stems from a manufacturer's attempts to bypass wholesalers and deal directly with retailers or consumers. Direct sale occurs because (1) producers are dissatisfied with wholesalers' services or (2) market conditions call for direct sale. Ordinarily battles about direct sale are fought in *consumer* goods channels. Such conflicts rarely arise in channels for business goods because there is a tradition of direct sale to ultimate customers in business markets.

To bypass wholesalers, a producer has two alternatives:

- *Sell directly to consumers.* Producers may employ house-to-house or mail-order selling. They also may establish their own distribution centers in different areas or even their own retail stores in major markets.
- *Sell directly to retailers.* Under certain market and product conditions, selling directly to retailers is feasible and advisable. An ideal retail market for this option consists of retailers that buy large quantities of a limited line of products.

Direct distribution—a short channel—is advantageous when the product (1) is subject to physical or fashion perishability, (2) carries a high unit price, (3) is custom-made, or (4) requires installation and technical service. Direct distribution, however, places a financial and managerial burden on the producer. Not only must the manufacturer operate its own sales force and handle physical distribution of its products, but a direct-selling manufacturer also faces competition from its former wholesalers, which no doubt now sell competitive products.

Wholesalers too can improve their competitive position. Their options include:

- *Improve internal management.* Many wholesalers have modernized their operations and upgraded the caliber of their management. Functional, single-store warehouses have been built outside congested downtown areas, and mechanized materials-handling equipment has been installed. Computers have improved order processing, inventory control, and billing.
- *Provide management assistance to retailers.* Wholesalers have realized that improving retailers' operations benefits all parties. Wholesalers help meet certain retailers' needs, such as store layout, merchandise selection, promotion, and inventory control.
- *Form voluntary chains.* In a voluntary chain (discussed in Chapter 14), a wholesaler enters into a contract with a group of retailers, agreeing to furnish them with management services and volume buying power. In turn, retailers promise to buy all, or almost all, of their merchandise from the wholesaler.
- *Develop private brands.* Some large wholesalers have successfully established their own brands. A voluntary chain of retailers provides a built-in market for the wholesaler's brand.

Some manufacturers, such as Ralph Lauren, risk conflict by distributing their products through their own outlets as well as other retail chains.

### PRODUCER VERSUS RETAILER

Another struggle for channel control takes place between manufacturers and retailers. Conflict can arise over terms or conditions of the relationship between the two parties. Or producers may compete with retailers by selling from house to house or through producer-owned stores. A number of apparel makers—including Polo, Gucci, and Liz Claiborne—have opened retail outlets. In doing so they have aggravated department stores and specialty retailers that also carry their brands.[8]

As discussed throughout this chapter, producers and retailers both have methods to gain more control. Manufacturers can:

- *Build strong consumer brand loyalty.* To accomplish this, creative and aggressive promotion is needed.
- *Establish one or more forms of vertical marketing system.*
- *Refuse to sell to uncooperative retailers.* However, this tactic has to be defensible from a legal standpoint.

Effective marketing weapons are also available to retailers. They can:

- *Develop store loyalty among consumers.* This is done by advertising effectively and/or establishing a store's own brands.
- *Improve computerized information systems.*
- *Plan more sophisticated marketing programs.*[9]

**Who Controls Channels?** Every firm would like to determine the behavior of other companies in the same distribution channel. The ability to influence the behavior of other channel members is termed **channel control.** Traditionally, manufacturers have

---

[8] For details about this trend and the resulting conflicts, see Teri Agins, "Clothing Makers Don Retailers' Garb," *The Wall Street Journal,* July 13, 1989, p. B1.

[9] For further discussion of strategies that either create or offset conflict between manufacturers and retailers, see Allan J. McGrath and Kenneth G. Hardy, "Avoiding the Pitfalls in Managing Distribution Channels," *Business Horizons,* September–October 1987, pp. 29–33.

## AN ETHICAL DILEMMA?

In exchange for shelf space in their stores, some supermarket chains require manufacturers to pay slotting allowances (as discussed at the beginning of the chapter). Part or all of the revenues a chain receives from slotting allowances might be passed on to consumers in the form of lower prices. Or the chain could retain these revenues to cover added labor costs associated with shelving new products and/or to boost profits. Assume you are a supermarket-chain vice president responsible for establishing policies regarding relationships with suppliers. Do you consider it ethical for your chain to demand slotting allowances from manufacturers? Would your view depend on whether the revenues were passed on to consumers via lower prices?

been viewed as controlling channels—that is, making the decisions regarding types and number of outlets, participation of individual middlemen, and business practices to be followed by a channel. But this is a one-sided, outdated point of view.

Middlemen often have considerable freedom to establish their own channels. Certainly the names Macy's, Safeway, and Sears mean more to consumers than the names of most brands sold in these stores. As discussed in the opening vignette, large retailers are challenging producers for channel control, just as many manufacturers seized control from wholesalers years ago. Even small retailers may be quite influential in local markets because their prestige may be greater than that of their suppliers.

The position supporting channel leadership by manufacturers is that they create the new products and need greater sales volume to benefit from economies of scale. The argument favoring leadership by retailers is that they are closest to final customers and, as a result, are best able to know customers' wants and to design and oversee channels to satisfy them. Various factors have contributed to retailers' growing ability to control channels. To mention one, widespread introduction by retailers of electronic scanning devices has given them access to more accurate information about sales trends of individual products than producers have.[10]

**A Channel Viewed As a System**

Many producers and middlemen understand that each channel member is part of a *system* designed to provide want-satisfaction to the ultimate consumer. Consequently, coordination is needed throughout a distribution channel.

Sometimes, however, members see a channel as a fragmented collection of independent, competing firms. One possible reason for channel problems is that most producers do not have a person in the organization who is formally in charge of channels. While most firms have an *advertising* manager and a *sales* manager, few have a *channels* manager. Perhaps it is time for manufactur-

[10]Customer market power in relation to channel control is covered in Gul Butaney and Lawrence H. Wortzel, "Distributor Power Versus Manufacturer Power: The Customer Role," *Journal of Marketing*, January 1988, pp. 52–63. For more on the struggle for channel control, see Brent H. Felgner, "Retailers Grab Power, Control Marketplace," *Marketing News*, Jan. 16, 1989, pp. 1, 2.

ers to create this position. The channels manager would be directly responsible for planning, coordinating, and evaluating the firm's distribution channels.[11]

Channel members frequently do realize that benefits of cooperation and voluntary control often outweigh any reasons for conflict. Producers and middlemen alike must consider the channel as an extension of their own internal organizations.

## LEGAL CONSIDERATIONS IN MANAGING CHANNELS

Attempts to control distribution are subject to legal constraints. In this section we will discuss legal aspects of four control methods that are sometimes employed by suppliers (usually manufacturers). Each method is limited by the Clayton Antitrust Act, Sherman Antitrust Act, or Federal Trade Commission Act. None of the four methods is illegal by itself. Distribution control becomes unlawful when it (1) substantially lessens competition, (2) creates a monopoly, or (3) restrains trade.

### Exclusive Dealing

When a manufacturer prohibits its dealers from carrying products of its competitors, it is engaged in **exclusive dealing.** This arrangement is very likely to be illegal in either of two situations:

- When the manufacturer's sales volume is a substantial portion of total volume in a given market. Competitors are thus excluded from a major part of the market.
- When the contract is between a large manufacturer and a much smaller middleman, the supplier's power is considered inherently coercive, and thus in restraint of trade.

However, some court decisions have also held that exclusive dealing is permissible under some circumstances:

- When equivalent products are available in a market or when the manufacturer's competitors have access to equivalent dealers. In these cases exclusive dealing may be legal if competition is not lessened to any large degree.
- When a manufacturer is entering a market or when its total market share is so small as to be negligible. An exclusive-dealing agreement may actually strengthen the producer's competitive position.

### Tying Contracts

When a manufacturer sells a product to a middleman only under the condition that this middleman also buys another (possibly unwanted) product from the producer, the two parties have entered into a **tying contract.** In a variation of this arrangement, the middleman agrees *not* to buy the *other* product from any other supplier.

A manufacturer pushes for a tying agreement in several situations. If there are shortages of a desired product, a supplier may want to unload products that are less in demand. Or when a producer grants a franchise (as in fast foods), it may see the owners as captive buyers of all necessary equipment and supplies. Also, a supplier relying on exclusive dealers or distributors (in appliances, for example) may want them to carry a full line of its products.

In general, tying contracts are considered in violation of antitrust laws.

---

[11]Donald W. Jackson, Jr., and Bruce J. Walker, "The Channels Manager: Marketing's Newest Aide?" *California Management Review,* Winter 1980, pp. 52–58.

There are exceptions, however. Tying contracts may be acceptable:

- When a new company is trying to enter a market.
- When an exclusive dealer or distributor is required to carry the manufacturer's full line of products but is not prohibited from carrying competing products.

**Refusal to Deal**     To select—and perhaps control—its channels, a producer may refuse to sell to certain middlemen. This practice is called **refusal to deal.** A 1919 court case established that manufacturers can select the middlemen to whom they will sell, so long as there is no intent to create a monopoly.

However, a decision to cancel a wholesaler or retailer is subject to scrutiny. Generally it is illegal to drop a middleman for carrying competitors' products or for resisting a tying contract.

**Exclusive Territories**     Under an **exclusive-territory policy,** a producer requires each middleman to sell *only* to customers located within the middleman's assigned territory. In several court cases, exclusive (or closed) sales territories were ruled unlawful because they lessened competition and restrained trade. The courts sought to encourage competition among middlemen handling the *same* brand.

Exclusive territories may be permitted in a number of instances:

- When a company is small or is a newcomer in the market.
- When a producer establishes a corporate vertical marketing system and retains ownership of the product until it reaches the final buyer.
- When a producer uses independent middlemen to distribute the product under consignment, in which a middleman does not pay the supplier until after the merchandise is sold.

**SUMMARY**     The role of distribution is getting a product to its target market. A distribution channel carries out this assignment with middlemen performing some tasks. A middleman is a business firm that renders services directly related to the purchase and/or sale of a product as it flows from producer to consumer. Middlemen can be eliminated from a channel, but someone still has to carry out their essential functions.

A distribution channel is the set of people and firms involved in the flow of title to a product as it moves from producer to ultimate consumer or business user. A channel includes producer, final customer, and any middlemen that participate in the process.

Designing a channel of distribution for a product occurs through a sequence of four decisions: (1) delineating the role of distribution within the marketing mix; (2) selecting the proper type of distribution channel; (3) determining the appropriate intensity of distribution; and (4) choosing specific channel members. A variety of channels are used to distribute consumer goods, business goods, and services. Firms often employ multiple channels to achieve broad market coverage, although this strategy can alienate some middlemen. Because of deficiencies in conventional channels, vertical marketing systems have become a major force in distribution. There are three forms of vertical marketing systems: corporate, contractual, and administered.

Numerous factors need to be considered prior to selecting a distribution channel for a product. The primary consideration is the nature of the target market; other considerations relate to the product, the middlemen, and the company itself.

Distribution intensity refers to the number of middlemen used at the wholesale and retail levels in a particular territory. It ranges from intensive to selective to exclusive.

Firms distributing goods and services sometimes clash. There are two types of conflict: horizontal (between firms at the same level of distribution) and vertical (between firms at different levels of the same channel). Scrambled merchandising is a prime cause of horizontal conflict. Vertical conflict typically pits producer against wholesaler or retailer. Manufacturers' attempts to bypass middlemen are a prime cause of vertical conflict.

Channel members frequently strive for some control over one another. Depending on the circumstances, either producers or middlemen can achieve the dominant position in a channel. All parties may be served best by viewing channels as a system requiring coordination of distribution activities. Moreover, attempts to control distribution may be subject to legal constraints.

## KEY TERMS AND CONCEPTS

Middleman 304
Merchant middleman 304
Agent middleman 304
Shifting of functions 304
Distribution channel 305
Intensity of distribution 308
Direct distribution 308
Indirect distribution 308
Multiple-channel distribution 312
Dual distribution 312
Vertical marketing system 312
Corporate vertical marketing
  system 313
Contractual vertical marketing
  system 313

Administered vertical marketing
  system 313
Intensive distribution 317
Selective distribution 317
Exclusive distribution 318
Channel conflict 319
Horizontal conflict 320
Scrambled merchandising 320
Vertical conflict 320
Channel control 322
Channels manager 323
Exclusive dealing 324
Tying contract 324
Refusal to deal 325
Exclusive territory 325

## QUESTIONS AND PROBLEMS

1. "You can eliminate middlemen, but you cannot eliminate their functions." Discuss this statement.
2. Which of the following institutions are middlemen? Explain.
   a. Avon sales person.
   b. Electrical wholesaler.
   c. Real estate broker.
   d. Railroad.
   e. Auctioneer.
   f. Advertising agency.
   g. Grocery store.
   h. Stockbroker.
   i. Bank.
   j. Radio station.
3. Which of the channels illustrated in Figure 12-3 is most apt to be used for each of the following products? Defend your choice in each case.
   a. Fire insurance.
   b. Single-family residences.
   c. Farm hay balers.
   d. Washing machines.
   e. Hair spray.
   f. An ocean cruise.
4. "The great majority of business sales are made directly from producer to business user." Explain the reason for this first in terms of the nature of the market, and then in terms of the product.
5. Explain, using examples, the differences among the three major types of vertical systems—corporate, administered, contractual. Which is the best kind?

6. A small manufacturer of fishing lures is faced with the problem of selecting its channel of distribution. What reasonable alternatives does it have? Consider particularly the nature of its product and the nature of its market.

7. Is a policy of intensive distribution consistent with consumer buying habits for convenience goods? For shopping goods? Is intensive distribution normally used in the marketing of any type of business goods?

8. From a producer's viewpoint, what are the competitive advantages of exclusive distribution?

9. What are the drawbacks to exclusive distribution from a retailer's point of view? To what extent are these alleviated if the retailer controls the channel for the particular brand?

10. A manufacturer of a well-known brand of men's clothing has been selling directly to one dealer in a Southern city for many years. For some time the market has been large enough to support two retailers very profitably. Yet the present dealer objects strongly when the manufacturer suggests adding another outlet. What alternatives does the manufacturer have in this situation? What course of action would you recommend?

11. "Manufacturers should always strive to select the lowest-cost channel of distribution." Do you agree? Should they always try to use the middlemen with the lowest operating costs? Why or why not?

12. What are reasons for producers' dissatisfaction with the wholesalers' performance? Do you agree with the producers' complaints?

13. Why are full-service wholesalers relatively unimportant in the marketing of women's high-fashion wearing apparel, furniture, and large electrical equipment?

14. What advice regarding distribution channels would you give to a small American company that makes stylish women's clothing and desires to distribute the product line in Japan?

CHAPTER 13

# WHOLESALING: MARKETS AND INSTITUTIONS

The owner of a small pharmacy stands in a store aisle, checks inventory levels for different products, and uses a handheld electronic device to assemble orders. In the pharmacy area of a chain drugstore, a customer and a pharmacist obtain information about a new drug from a personal computer. Although both situations occur in retail stores, they indicate how wholesaling middlemen are trying to enhance their positions in distribution channels.

Both the order-entry device, part of a system called Economost, and the drug data base, called a Pharmacy Information Center, were developed by the McKesson Corp., a wholesaler with more than $7 billion in annual sales. Why? McKesson believes such services not only help drugstores and small pharmacies but also improve its own competitive standing.

Orders prepared with the Economost handheld device are transmitted to McKesson by telephone. McKesson fills them quickly—sometimes the same day. The new inventory is boxed according to the store's floor arrangement to make restocking easier and cheaper. In addition, McKesson supplies each pharmacy with a monthly report showing sales, profit, and turnover levels for various items and departments in the store.

Pharmacies and drugstores alike benefit from Economost in a number of ways: lower-cost ordering and restocking; fewer dollars tied up in inventory; improved sales due to fewer stockouts; and time savings from dealing with fewer suppliers. Of course, McKesson also benefits with lower-cost order processing; improved information on what is selling at the retail level; and increased loyalty from pharmacies and drugstores. In short, with Economost, both McKesson Corp. and its customers can gain a stronger competitive position and better financial performance.[1]

---

[1]Based on Eric K. Clemons and Michael Row, "A Strategic Information System: McKesson Drug Company's Economost," *Planning Review,* September–October 1988, pp. 14–19; and William P. Patterson, "Dispensing Drugs—and Data," *Industry Week,* June 6, 1988, p. 74.

At various times, consumers, business people, and government officials have proclaimed, "The middleman makes all the profit in distribution." Critics have even suggested a solution: "Let's eliminate the middleman." Such comments are most often focused on the wholesaling part of the distribution process.

As we shall see, most middlemen (especially wholesaling middlemen) typically earn a small profit. Indeed, many are fighting for survival against modified distribution patterns resulting from changing consumer needs and desires. Also, as discussed in the preceding chapter, eliminating middlemen from a distribution channel does not guarantee lower prices or better service. In fact, just the opposite may occur. Furthermore, as the profile of McKesson Corp. shows, some wholesaling middlemen perform vital services for producers and consumers in a highly efficient manner. This chapter will provide you with greater insight into both wholesale markets and wholesaling institutions as they relate to the broader marketing system.

## NATURE AND IMPORTANCE OF WHOLESALING

Wholesaling and retailing stand between production and purchases for consumption. Whereas retailing involves sales to ultimate consumers for their personal use, wholesaling has a different role in the marketing system.

### What Are Wholesaling and Wholesaling Middlemen?

**Wholesaling,** or wholesale trade, consists of the sale, and all activities directly related to the sale, of goods and services to parties for resale, use in producing other goods or services, or operating an organization. Broadly viewed, sales made by one producer to another are wholesale transactions, and the selling producer is engaged in wholesaling. Likewise, a retail variety store is carrying out wholesaling when it sells calculators and office supplies to a business firm.

Thus wholesaling includes sales by any firm to any customer except an ultimate consumer who is buying for personal, nonbusiness use. From this perspective all sales are either wholesale or retail sales, distinguished only by the purchaser's intended use of the good or service that is bought.

In this chapter we will concentrate on firms engaged *primarily* in wholesaling. This type of company is called a **wholesaling middleman.** We will not be concerned with retailers that make only occasional wholesale sales. And we will not focus on the sales of manufacturers and farmers because they are primarily engaged in production rather than wholesaling.

### Economic Justification for Wholesaling

Most manufacturing companies in the U.S. are small and specialized. They don't have the capital needed to maintain a sales force large enough to contact the many small retailers that are their customers. Even for manufacturers with sufficient capital, output frequently is too small to justify the necessary sales force. On the other hand, most retailers buy in small quantities and have only a limited knowledge of the market and sources of supply. Thus there is often a gap between the retailer (buyer) and the producer (seller). A wholesaling middleman can fill this gap by pooling the orders of many retailers and so furnish a market for the small producer. At the same time, the wholesaling middleman is performing a buying service for small retailers.

From a broad point of view, wholesaling brings to the total distribution system the economies of skill, scale, and transactions. Wholesaling *skills* are efficiently concentrated in a relatively few hands. This saves the duplication of effort that would occur if many producers had to perform wholesaling functions themselves. Economies of *scale* result from the specialization of

**FIGURE 13-1** The economy of transactions in wholesaling.

Four producers each sell directly to six retailers, resulting in 24 transactions:

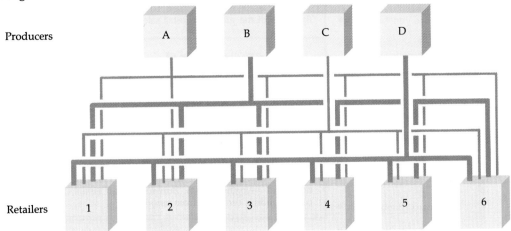

Four producers use the same wholesaling middleman, reducing the number of transactions to 10:

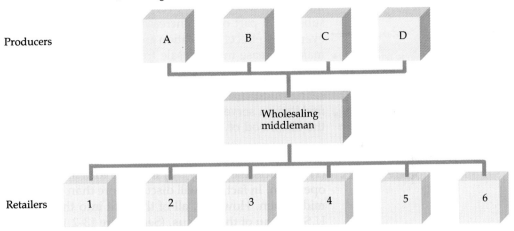

wholesaling middlemen performing functions that might otherwise require several small departments run by producing firms. Wholesalers typically can perform wholesaling functions at a lower operating-expense percentage than can most manufacturers. *Transaction* economies come into play when wholesaling or retailing middlemen are introduced between producers and their customers. To illustrate: four manufacturers want to sell to six retailers. As shown in Figure 13-1, *without* a middleman, there are 24 transactions; *with* one wholesaling middleman, the number is cut to 10. Four transactions occur when all the producers sell to the middleman, and another six occur when the middleman sells to all the retailers.

**Size of Wholesale Market**

At last count there were about 470,000 wholesaling establishments in the United States. As Table 13-1 shows, the number of establishments has greatly increased over the past 20 years. This trend dispels the notion that wholesaling middlemen are disappearing from distribution channels.

To remain competitive and profitable, many wholesalers use networked computer systems to control inventories.

acquire, be acquired, or somehow isolate themselves from this trend—perhaps by serving small market niches.

To illustrate the impact of a new institution, consider service merchandisers, which supply retail stores (particularly grocery stores) with nonfood items ranging from health and beauty aids to automotive supplies. To develop a strong seller-buyer relationship, service merchandisers ordinarily provide retail outlets with computerized order-entry systems to assist the stores in placing orders with their firms. This new type of company threatens the viability of traditional rack jobbers.

## Marketing Strategies

Like all other business firms, wholesaling middlemen must develop effective marketing strategies in the following related areas:

- *Target markets.* Wholesaling firms must decide whether to pursue diversified or niche markets. To make this decision, middlemen should classify markets by size, types of customers, and services needed by customers.

### AN ETHICAL DILEMMA?

Under gray marketing, products wind up being distributed outside a manufacturer's authorized distribution channels. For example, an exporter may establish a relationship with a European manufacturer to distribute its line of stereo equipment in South America (but not in the United States). However, without the manufacturer's knowledge, the exporter diverts a large order of equipment for sale in the United States. Assume you are the stereo-equipment buyer for a chain of discount houses. The exporter contacts you about purchasing some stereos at prices that are substantially below the normal wholesale price. Would it be ethical for you to buy these stereos for resale in your stores? Would your view depend on whether you knew for sure that the stereos were indeed "gray market" goods?

Wholesalers review manufacturers' ads before deciding what product lines and brands to carry.

- *Product.* Several strategic decisions relate to this element of the marketing mix. A wholesaling middleman must determine the breadth and depth of assortment of the firm's product mix. A middleman then has to decide whether it will actually carry stocks. A wholesaling firm may want a broad assortment and extensive inventories to satisfy customers' desires to deal with few suppliers and receive goods soon after an order is placed. However, a middleman may want to control its investment in inventory. Another key decision is what services will be performed for suppliers and customers.
- *Price.* Middlemen's prices should take into account many factors, most notably services performed. Prices are reflected in the size of markups and commissions.
- *Distribution.* The first distribution decision pertains to where the specific wholesaling middleman fits into various distribution channels. In turn, specific suppliers must be chosen. Many wholesaling middlemen face strategic decisions regarding the extent to which the firm will be involved in physical distribution of the product and where they will locate, considering such factors as access to markets, transportation requirements, and costs.
- *Promotion.* This element of the marketing mix concerns the best means of communicating with target markets. Wholesaling middlemen, like other firms, need to create an effective blend of advertising, personal selling,

sales promotion, and publicity. For most middlemen, personal-selling activities are of paramount importance.

Successful wholesaling middlemen have a true customer orientation. They identify and then satisfy the needs of their retail customers. Furthermore, they consider their suppliers as customers in that producers must perform or delegate various distribution functions, and wholesaling middlemen have to determine how they can satisfy these needs.

**SUMMARY**

Wholesaling is the sale, and all activities directly related to the sale, of goods and services to parties for resale, use in producing other goods or services, or operating an organization. In contrast, retailing involves sales to ultimate consumers. Thus all transactions are either wholesale or retail sales, depending on the purchaser's purpose in buying.

Firms primarily engaged in wholesaling are called wholesaling middlemen. Such firms provide participants in the distribution process with economies of skill, scale, and transactions. About 470,000 wholesaling firms account for more than $2.5 trillion in annual sales in the United States.

There are three major categories of wholesaling middlemen: merchant wholesalers, agent wholesaling middlemen, and manufacturers' sales facilities. The first two are independent firms whereas the third is owned by a manufacturer. Merchant wholesalers take title to products being distributed; agent wholesaling middlemen do not. Total wholesale trade is divided up as follows: merchant wholesalers, 59 percent; agent wholesaling middlemen, 10 percent; and manufacturers' sales facilities, 31 percent.

Wholesaling middlemen's operating expenses average about 11 percent of wholesale sales compared to retailers' operating expenses of about 27 percent of retail sales. Net profits in wholesaling average about 2 percent of sales.

Merchant wholesalers, whose share of wholesale trade has increased in recent years, include full-service wholesalers, rack jobbers, truck jobbers, and drop shippers. Of the three major categories of wholesaling middlemen, merchant wholesalers offer the widest range of services and consequently incur the highest operating expenses.

Agent wholesaling middlemen have lost ground to merchant wholesalers over the past several decades. The principal types of agents are manufacturers' agents, brokers, and commission merchants. Agent middlemen usually are paid on a commission basis. Because they perform more limited services, their operating expenses tend to be lower than for merchant wholesalers.

In the future, wholesaling middlemen will face challenges to their roles in distribution. To succeed, wholesaling middlemen will have to address significant trends in distribution and develop effective marketing strategies.

**KEY TERMS AND CONCEPTS**

Wholesaling 330
Wholesaling middleman 330
Merchant wholesaler 332
Agent wholesaling middleman 333
Manufacturer's sales facility 333
Manufacturer's sales branch 334
Manufacturer's sales office 334
Full-service wholesaler 337
Rack jobber 339

Limited-function wholesaler 339
Truck jobber 339
Drop shipper 340
Manufacturers' agents 342
Broker 343
Commission merchant 344
Auction company 344
Selling agent 344

# QUESTIONS AND PROBLEMS

1. A large furniture warehouse is located in a major Midwestern city. The following conditions characterize this firm:
   a. All merchandise is purchased directly from manufacturers.
   b. The warehouse is located in the low-rent wholesaling district.
   c. Merchandise remains in original crates; customers use catalogs and swatch books to see what the articles look like and what fabrics are used.
   d. About 90 percent of the customers are ultimate consumers, and they account for 85 percent of sales volume.
   e. The firm does quite a bit of advertising, stressing that consumers are buying at wholesale prices.
   f. Crates are not price-marked. Sales people bargain with customers.
   g. Some 10 percent of sales volume comes from sales to furniture stores.
   Is this furniture warehouse a wholesaling middleman? Explain.

2. Which of the following are wholesaling transactions?
   a. Color Tile sells wallpaper to an apartment building contractor and also to the contractor's wife for her home.
   b. General Electric sells small motors to Whirlpool for its washing machines.
   c. A shrimp farmer sells shrimp to a local restaurant.
   d. A family has a friend who is a home decorating consultant. The family orders carpet through the consultant at 50 percent off retail. The carpet is delivered directly to the home.

3. As shown in Figure 13-3, agent wholesaling middlemen and manufacturers' sales facilities have lost part of their share of wholesale trade to merchant wholesalers since the late 1960s. How do you explain this shift?

4. How would you explain the substantial variation in operating expenses among the major types of wholesalers shown in Figure 13-4?

5. Wholesaling middlemen typically have lower operating expenses than do retailers. How do you account for this difference?

6. What activities could full-service wholesalers discontinue in an effort to reduce operating costs?

7. What service does a full-service wholesaler provide for a manufacturer?

8. What types of retailers, other than supermarkets, offer reasonable fields for entry by rack jobbers? Explain.

9. Why would a manufacturing firm prefer to use manufacturers' agents instead of its own company sales force?

10. Why is it that manufacturers' agents often can penetrate a market faster and at a lower cost than a manufacturer's sales force?

11. What is the economic justification for the existence of brokers, especially in light of the few functions they perform?

12. Which type of wholesaling middleman, if any, is most likely to be used by each of the following firms? Explain your choice in each instance.
    a. A small manufacturer of a liquid glass cleaner to be sold through supermarkets.
    b. A small manufacturer of knives used for hunting, fishing, and camping.
    c. A small canner in Vermont packing a high-quality, unbranded fruit product.
    d. A small-tools manufacturing firm that has its own sales force selling to the business market and that wishes to add backyard barbecue equipment to its product mix.
    e. A North Carolina textile mill producing unbranded towels, sheets, pillowcases, and blankets.

13. Compared to a wholesaling middleman that distributes products only in the United States, what special challenges do you think an import or export agent faces in arranging for distribution of a product in a foreign country?

14. Looking into the future, which types of wholesaling middlemen do you think will increase in importance and which ones will decline? Explain.

# CHAPTER 14

# RETAILING: MARKETS AND INSTITUTIONS

Is there a Wal-Mart in your area? Have you ever shopped at one?

There's only about a 50 percent chance that your answers are "yes." In all likelihood some of you have never seen a Wal-Mart. Others not only shop at Wal-Mart but also know that this discount chain was the "superstar" of retailing during the 1980s.

How can this retailer be unknown to some consumers but a frequent shopping experience for many others? The explanation lies in Wal-Mart's meteoric growth and successful marketing strategies.

In 1962 Sam Walton opened the first Wal-Mart discount house in rural Arkansas. After a rocky start Wal-Mart grew to about 20 stores by the late 1960s. Since then its growth has been phenomenal—an average rate of 40 percent per year! (In the late 1980s Wal-Mart's growth "slowed" to 30 percent per year.)

By the end of the 1980s, the chain's 1,400 stores registered annual sales and pretax profits exceeding $25 *billion* and $1 *billion*, respectively. And Wal-Mart's performance is achieved with stores in only one of every two states. Particularly strong in the Southeast and South Central states, the chain has not yet penetrated New England or much of the West.

Wal-Mart's strategy emphasizes segmentation, value, people, and "little things." This retailer originally concentrated on value-conscious consumers in rural towns without discount houses; it is still stronger in small communities than in large cities. Its broad assortment of merchandise is of reasonable quality and carries very low prices.

Wal-Mart's top management believes its more than 200,000 employees, called associates, are integral to the chain's continuing success. Various programs motivate employees; for example, associates receive financial rewards if a store exceeds its profit goal. They are urged to do little things to make customers comfortable, such as making eye contact. At the entrance to each store, a "people greeter" welcomes shoppers to Wal-Mart.

Sam Walton, now in his 70s, has slowed his personal pace. But it's obvious that the chain he founded about 30 years ago is still going strong.[1]

---

[1]Based on Francine Schwadel, "Little Touches Spur Wal-Mart's Rise," *The Wall Street Journal*, Sept. 22, 1989, p. B1; and John Huey, "Wal-Mart: Will It Take Over the World?" *Fortune*, Jan. 30, 1989, pp. 52–56ff.

We all have a great deal of experience with retailing—as consumers. And many students acquire work experience in retailing. This chapter builds on that experience and provides insights about retail markets, different types of retailers, and key strategies and trends in retailing.

## NATURE AND IMPORTANCE OF RETAILING

For every superstar like Wal-Mart, thousands of tiny retailers serve consumers only in very limited areas. Despite their differences, all of these firms do have two common features: They link producers and ultimate consumers, and they perform valuable services for both parties. In all likelihood these firms are retailers, but all of their activities may not qualify as retailing. How can that be? Explanations follow.

### What Are Retailing and Retailers?

If a supermarket sells some floor wax to a gift-shop operator to polish the shop's floor, is this a retail sale? When a gas station advertises tires for sale at the "wholesale price," is this retailing? Can a wholesaler or manufacturer engage in retailing? When a service such as hair styling or auto repair is sold to an ultimate consumer, is this retailing? Obviously we need to define some terms, particularly *retailing* and *retailer*, to avoid misunderstandings later.

**Retailing** (or **retail trade**) consists of the sale, and all activities directly related to the sale, of goods and services to ultimate consumers for personal, nonbusiness use. While most retailing occurs through retail stores, it may be done by any institution. A manufacturer selling brushes or cosmetics door to door is engaged in retailing, as is a farmer selling vegetables at a roadside stand.

Any firm—manufacturer, wholesaler, or retailer—that sells something to ultimate consumers for their own nonbusiness use is making a retail sale. This is true regardless of *how* the product is sold (in person or by telephone, mail, or vending machine) or *where* it is sold (in a store or at the consumer's home). However, a firm engaged *primarily* in retailing is called a **retailer.** In this chapter, we will concentrate on retailers rather than on other types of businesses that make only occasional retail sales.

Most people associate the term *retailer* with the sale of *goods* rather than *services*. In fact, the U.S. Census of Retail Trade concentrates on goods, whereas a separate Census of Service Industries covers the wholesaling and retailing of services. While this chapter focuses primarily on retailers of *goods*, much of what is said—particularly regarding marketing strategies—applies equally well to retailers of *services*.

### Economic Justification for Retailing

As discussed in Chapter 12, all middlemen basically serve as purchasing agents for their customers and as sales specialists for their suppliers. To carry out these roles, retailers perform many activities, including anticipating customers' wants, developing assortments of products, acquiring market information, and financing.

It is relatively easy to become a retailer. No large investment in production equipment is required, merchandise can often be purchased on credit, and store space can be leased with no "down payment." This ease of entry results in fierce competition and better values for consumers.

To get into retailing is easy but to be forced out is just as easy. To survive in retailing, a company must do a satisfactory job in its primary role—catering to consumers—as well as in its secondary role—serving producers and wholesalers. This dual responsibility is both the justification for retailing and the key to success in retailing.

**FIGURE 14-1 Total retail trade in the United States.**
Sales volume has increased steadily over the past 20 years. In contrast, note that the number of retail stores rose substantially in 1977–87 after a period of relative stability in 1967–77.

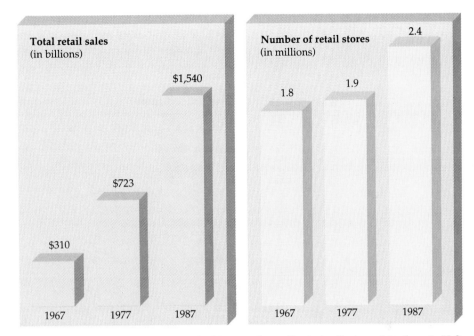

Sources: *1987 Census of Retail Trade*, Nonemployer Statistics Series—Northeast, U.S. Bureau of the Census, Washington, D.C., 1990, p. 1-3. *1977 Census of Retail Trade*, Vol. 1, Subject Statistics, 1978, p. 1-8; and *1967 Census of Business*, Vol. 1, Retail Trade—Subject Reports, 1971, p. 1-4.

## Size of Retail Market

There are just over 2.4 million retail stores in the United States, as shown in Figure 14-1. The jump in number of stores between 1977 and 1987 coincided with a growing population and rising consumer incomes.

Retail sales in 1987 (the last census year) totaled just over $1.5 *trillion*. The increase in total sales volume has been tremendous—fivefold from the late 1960s to the late 1980s. Even adjusting for the steady rise in prices, we find that total retail sales and per capita retail sales have gone up considerably. Slower sales growth is on the horizon, however.[2]

## Operating Expenses and Profits

It is estimated that average total operating expenses for retailers are about 27 percent of retail sales.[3] As discussed in Chapter 13, wholesaling expenses run about 11 percent of *wholesale* sales or 8 percent of *retail* sales. Thus, roughly speaking, retailing costs are about two and a half times the costs of wholesaling when both are stated as a percentage of the middleman in question.

Higher retailing costs are generally related to the expense of dealing directly with the ultimate consumer. Compared to wholesale customers, ultimate consumers typically demand more services. Also, compared to wholesalers, retailers have smaller sales and lower rates of merchandise turnover, and buy smaller quantities of merchandise. Furthermore, retail sales people often cannot be used efficiently because customers do not come into stores at a steady rate.

Retailers' costs and profits vary depending on their type of operations and

---

[2]"How Much Deeper Can the Consumer Dig?" *Business Week*, Jan. 13, 1986, p. 99.
[3]*1982 Census of Retail Trade*, Industry Series—Measures, U.S. Bureau of the Census, Washington, D.C., 1985, pp. 2–4.

**TABLE 14-1 Gross margins and net profits as a percentage of sales for selected types of retailers**

| Type of business | Gross margin (%) | Net profit after income taxes (%) |
|---|---|---|
| Automobile and truck dealers | 13 | 1.5 |
| Liquor stores | 19 | n.a.* |
| Grocery stores | 23 | 1.7 |
| Building materials, hardware, and farm equipment: | 28 | |
|     Building materials | | 1.9 |
|     Hardware | | 4.1 |
| Gasoline service stations | 17 | 2.1 |
| Drugstores | 27 | n.a. |
| Furniture and home-furnishings stores: | 36 | |
|     Furniture | | 3.1 |
|     Household appliances | | 3.4 |
| General merchandise stores (e.g., department stores) | 37 | 0.8 |
| Apparel and accessory stores: | 41 | |
|     Women's ready-to-wear | | 5.6 |
|     Men's & boys' clothing | | 5.0 |
|     Shoes | | 5.2 |
|     Jewelry | | 9.5 |

*Not available.
Source: Gross margins from *Cost of Doing Business: Corporations*, Dun & Bradstreet, New York, 1990; net profit figures from "The Ratios," *Dun's Business Month*, February 1983, pp. 112, 115.

major product line. Looking at Table 14-1, note how wide-ranging the gross margins are. The figures for department stores and apparel and accessory stores are more than two and a half times that for auto and truck dealers. The net profit figures in the table demonstrate that healthy gross margins do not necessarily translate into the highest levels of net profits. The small size of the net profit figures in Table 14-1—averaging about 3 percent of sales—may surprise people who believe that retailers make large profits.

**Store Size** Most retail establishments are very small. In the last available census year, about 16 percent of stores operating the full year had annual sales of less than $100,000. However, as shown in Figure 14-2, only 1 percent of all retail sales can be attributed to these stores.

At the same time there is a high degree of concentration in retailing. A small number of establishments account for a substantial share of retail trade. Only 21 percent of all stores had an annual sales volume over $1 million, but they accounted for about 77 percent of total retail sales.

**FIGURE 14-2** Distribution of stores and total retail sales by size of store.

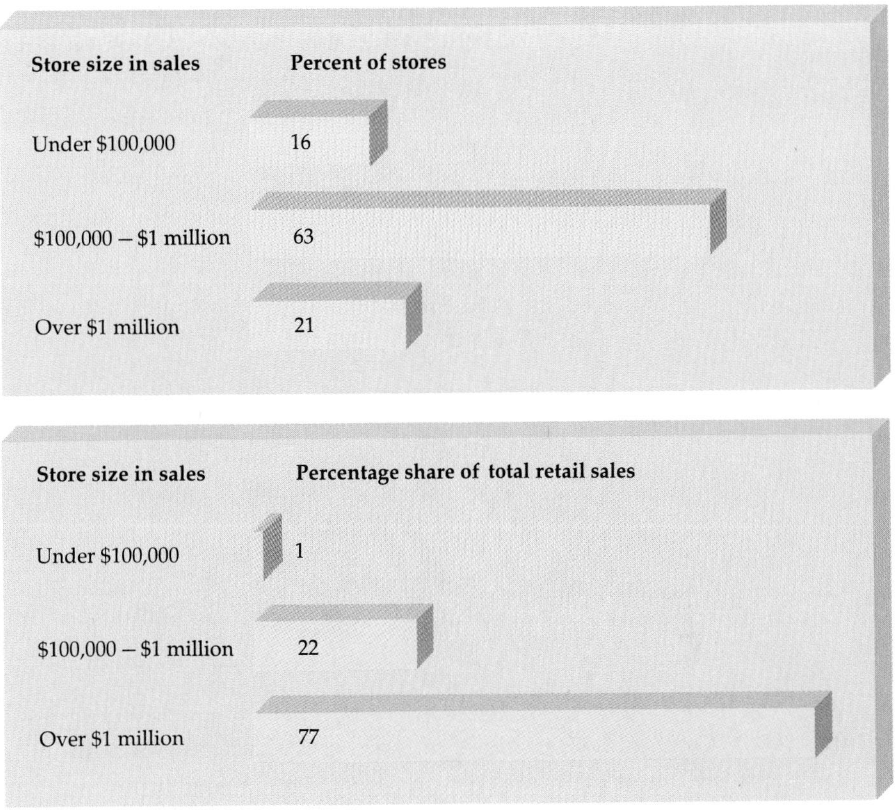

| Store size in sales | Percent of stores |
|---|---|
| Under $100,000 | 16 |
| $100,000 – $1 million | 63 |
| Over $1 million | 21 |

| Store size in sales | Percentage share of total retail sales |
|---|---|
| Under $100,000 | 1 |
| $100,000 – $1 million | 22 |
| Over $1 million | 77 |

Source: *1987 Census of Retail Trade,* Subject Series—Establishment and Firm Size, U.S. Bureau of the Census, Washington, D.C., 1990, p. 1-3.

Figure 14-2 does not tell the full story of large-scale retailing because it represents a tabulation of individual *store* sales and not *company* sales volume. A single company may own many establishments, as in the case of chain stores. When retail sales are analyzed by companies, the high degree of concentration becomes even more evident. For example, as shown in Table 14-2, the combined sales of the 10 largest retailers make up more than 14 percent of total retail trade.

Stores of different sizes present different management challenges and opportunities. Buying, promotion, personnel relations, and expense control are influenced significantly by whether a store's sales volume is large or small.

Size, or the lack thereof, brings with it certain advantages, several of which are evaluated in Table 14-3. This assessment suggests that relatively large stores have a competitive advantage over small stores. Small retailers do face many difficulties. The ones that cannot meet the challenges fail. If that's the case, how do so many small retailers succeed? The answer is twofold:

- Some small retailers have formed or joined contractual vertical marketing systems. These entities—called retailer cooperatives, voluntary chains, or franchise systems—give individual members certain advantages of large stores, such as specialized management, buying power, and a well-known store name.
- Many consumers seek benefits that small stores can often provide better

## TABLE 14-2 Worldwide sales of 10 largest U.S. retailers

| Retailer | 1989 sales (in billions) | 1989 net profit as % of sales | % change in sales, 1984–1989 |
|---|---|---|---|
| 1. Sears, Roebuck | $ 53.9 | 2.8 | + 39 |
| 2. K mart | 29.6 | 1.1 | + 40 |
| 3. Wal-Mart | 25.9 | 4.2 | +298 |
| 4. American Stores | 22.0 | 0.5 | + 82 |
| 5. Kroger | 19.1 | (0.4)* | + 20 |
| 6. J.C. Penney | 16.4 | 4.9 | + 21 |
| 7. Safeway Stores | 14.3 | 0.0 | − 27 |
| 8. Dayton Hudson | 13.6 | 3.0 | + 70 |
| 9. May Dept. Stores | 12.0 | 4.1 | +150 |
| 10. A & P | 10.1 | 1.3 | + 94 |
| Total sales volume | $216.9 | | |
| Average net profit | | 2.2 | |

*Kroger reported a loss in 1989.
Source: "The 50 Largest Retailing Companies," *Fortune*, June 4, 1990, pp. 324–25, and June 10, 1985, pp. 190–91.

## TABLE 14-3 Competitive positions of large and small retail stores

| Selected bases for evaluation | Who has the advantage? |
|---|---|
| Division of labor and specialization of management | Large-scale retailers—their biggest advantage |
| Flexibility of operations—merchandise selection, services offered, store design, reflection of owner's personality | Small retailers—their biggest advantage |
| Buying power | Large retailers buy in bigger quantities and thus get lower costs |
| Access to desirable merchandise | Large retailers promise suppliers access to large numbers of customers whereas a single small retailer may be viewed as insignificant |
| Development and promotion of retailer's own brand | Large retailers |
| Efficient use of advertising, especially in citywide media | Large retailers' markets match better with media circulation |
| Ability to provide top-quality personal service | Small retailers if owners pay personal attention to customers and also to selecting and supervising sales staff |
| Opportunity to experiment with new products and selling methods | Large retailers can better afford the risks |
| Financial strength | Large retailers have resources to gain some of the advantages noted above (such as private brands and experimentation) |
| Public image | Small retailers enjoy public support and sympathy. However, this same public often votes with its wallet by shopping at big stores |

than large stores can. For instance, some people seek high levels of shopping convenience. Small outlets located near residential areas offer such convenience. Other consumers desire high levels of personal service. A small store's highly motivated owner-manager and well-supervised sales staff may surpass a large store on this important shopping dimension.

Many small stores take advantage of their comparative strengths and compete successfully against other retailers of varying sizes and types.

**Classification of Retailers**

To understand how retailers serve both suppliers and customers, we will classify retailers on two bases:

1. Form of ownership.
2. Marketing strategies.

Each of these categories will be discussed in turn. Any retail store can be classified according to both bases, as illustrated by the following comparison of Sears and a neighborhood paint store.

| | Classification bases | |
| Sample stores | 1. Form of ownership | 2. Marketing strategies |
| --- | --- | --- |
| Sears | Corporate chain | Department store with broad, relatively deep assortments, everyday low prices, and levels of personal service that vary across departments |
| Neighborhood paint store | Independent | Limited-line store that has narrow, relatively deep assortments, avoids price competition, and provides extensive personal service |

Although both are retailers, Sears and the Johnson Paint Company differ in important ways.

## RETAILERS CLASSIFIED BY FORM OF OWNERSHIP

The major forms of ownership in retailing are corporate chain, independent, and vertical marketing system (VMS). Within the VMS category are several types of organizations: wholesaler-sponsored voluntary chains, retailer-owned cooperatives, and franchise systems.

### Corporate Chains

A **corporate chain,** sometimes called a *chain-store system*, is an organization of two or more centrally owned and managed stores that generally handle the same lines of products. Three factors differentiate a chain from an independent store and contractual vertical marketing system:

- Technically, two or more units constitute a chain. Many small merchants that have opened several units in shopping centers and newly populated areas do not think of themselves as chains, however. Consequently, it might be more meaningful to consider a larger number of units as a reasonable minimum when categorizing a retailer as a chain. (The Bureau of the Census considers 11 units to be the minimum size for a chain.)
- Central ownership distinguishes corporate chains from contractual vertical marketing systems.
- Due to centralized management, individual units in a chain typically have little autonomy. Strategic decisions are made at headquarters, and there is considerable standardization of operating policies for all the units in a chain.

Corporate chains continue to increase their share of total retail trade, as shown in Table 14-4. The predominance of chains varies considerably, however, depending on the kind of business. Chains dominate in the department store business but are not very significant among auto and home supply stores. In the grocery field there are several giant firms, yet chains account for less than 60 percent of sales made by grocery stores. Essentially chains are large-scale retailing institutions. As such, they possess the comparative strengths and weaknesses previously outlined in Table 14-3.

---

**TABLE 14-4 Corporate chains' share of total retail trade by type of business**

| Type of business | % of retail sales made by chains with 11 or more stores | |
|---|---|---|
| | 1987 | 1978 |
| Department stores | 97 | 95 |
| Variety stores | 80 | 78 |
| Drugstores | 59 | 49 |
| Grocery stores | 57 | 54 |
| Apparel and accessory stores | 37 | 54 |
| Auto and home supply stores | 27 | 24 |
| Total retail sales | 38 | 35 |

Source: *Statistical Abstract of the United States: 1989*, 109th ed., U.S. Bureau of the Census, Washington, D.C., 1989, p. 755; *Statistical Abstract of the United States: 1984*, 104th ed., 1984, p. 800.

A high degree of standardization is the hallmark of a chain of retail stores. Although a major factor in the success of chains, standardization is really a mixed blessing. Standardization means inflexibility. Often a chain cannot adjust rapidly to local market conditions. To overcome this weakness, chains give local store managers some autonomy.

## Independent Stores

An **independent retailer** is a company with a single retail store that is not affiliated with any type of contractual vertical marketing system. Most retailers are independents, and most independents are quite small. Of course, an independent department store or supermarket can have $10 million or more in annual sales, so it may have more economic power than small chains consisting of only a few stores. Still, independents usually have the characteristics of small retailers that were presented in Table 14-3.

Independents typically are viewed as having higher prices than chain stores. However, due to differences in merchandise and services, it is difficult to directly compare the prices of chains and independents. For instance, chains often have their own private brands that are not sold by independents. Also the two types of retailers frequently provide customers with different levels—and perhaps quality—of services. Many customers are willing to pay extra for services that are valuable to them, such as credit, delivery, alterations, installation, a liberal return policy, and friendly, knowledgeable personal service.

## Contractual Vertical Marketing Systems

In a contractual vertical marketing system, independently owned firms join together under a contract specifying how they will operate. The three types of contractual VMS are briefly described next.

### RETAILER COOPERATIVES AND VOLUNTARY CHAINS

Cooperatives and voluntary chains have the same basic purposes:

- To enable independent retailers to compete effectively with corporate chains.
- To provide members with management assistance in store layout, employee and management training programs, promotion, accounting, and inventory control systems.

The main difference between these two types of systems is who organizes them. A voluntary chain is sponsored by a wholesaler that enters into a contract with interested retailers. In contrast, a retailer cooperative is formed by a group of small retailers that agree to establish and operate a wholesale warehouse.

Historically these two forms of contractual VMS have been organized for defensive reasons—to maintain a competitive position against large, strong chains. Voluntary chains are most prevalent in the grocery field (IGA, Super Valu). They are also found in hardware (Ace), auto supplies (Western Auto), and variety stores (Ben Franklin). Retailer cooperatives are declining, but still have strong representatives in groceries (Certified Grocers) and hardware (True Value).

### FRANCHISE SYSTEMS

**Franchising** involves a continuing relationship in which a franchisor (the parent company) provides the right to use a trademark and management assistance in return for financial considerations from a franchisee (the owner of the

Many franchises have become very well known. Others are working toward that goal.

individual business unit). The combination of franchisor and franchisees is called a **franchise system.** This type of contractual VMS is growing rapidly.

There are two kinds of franchising:

- *Product and trade name.* Historically the dominant kind, product and trade name franchising is most prevalent in the automobile (Ford, Honda) and petroleum (Chevron, Texaco) industries. It is a distribution agreement wherein a franchisor authorizes a franchisee-dealer to sell a product line, using the parent company's trade name for promotional purposes. The franchisee agrees to buy from the franchisor-supplier and also to abide by specified policies. The focus in product and trade name franchising is on *what is sold.*

- *Business format.* Much of franchising's growth and publicity over the past two decades has been associated with business-format franchising (including names such as Kentucky Fried Chicken, Midas, and H & R Block). This kind of franchising covers an entire format for operating a business. A firm with a successful retail business sells the right to operate the same business in different geographic areas. Quite simply, the franchisee expects to receive from the parent company a proven business format; in return, the franchisor receives from the individual business owner payments and also conformance to policies and standards. The focus here is on *how the business is run.*

In business-format franchising the franchisor may be a manufacturer that provides franchisees with merchandise. More often, though, this is not the case. For example, Little Professor Book Centers, Inc., does not sell books to its franchised stores; rather the stores buy their inventory from wholesalers. What the franchisor provides to franchisees is management assistance, especially marketing expertise.

For a successful retail business that wants to expand, franchising provides critical advantages:

- Rapid expansion is facilitated because franchisees provide capital when they purchase franchises.
- Because they have an investment at risk, franchisees typically are highly motivated to work hard and adhere to the parent company's proven format.

**Numerous products reach consumer markets through business-format franchises**

| Product category | Sample franchises |
|---|---|
| Fast food and other prepared food | McDonald's, Domino's, Subway, Arby's |
| Automotive repairs | Midas, Car-X, Jiffy Lube, Lee Myles |
| Clothing | T-Shirts Plus, Just Pants, Fashions under $10 |
| Hair care | Fantastic Sam's, Supercuts, Cost Cutters |
| Groceries and other food products | 7-Eleven, Hickory Farms, Rocky Mountain Chocolate Factory |
| Education programs | Sylvan Learning Center, Arthur Murray School of Dance, Huntington Learning Centers |
| Home decorating products | Wallpapers to Go, Decorating Den, Stained Glass Overlay |

For an independent store facing stiff competition from chains and for a prospective new retail store, franchising offers advantages:

- Franchisees can use the parent company's well-known trade name, which should help attract customers.
- Various forms of management assistance are provided to franchisees prior to as well as after opening the store, including site-selection and store-layout guidance, technical and management training, promotional programs, and inventory control systems.

Continued growth in franchising is expected. Entrepreneurs will use it as an offensive tool—for rapid expansion—and many small retailers will use it defensively—to achieve a viable competitive position in battles against corporate chains.

**RETAILERS CLASSIFIED BY MARKETING STRATEGIES**

Whatever its form of ownership, a retailer must develop target-market and marketing-mix strategies. In retailing, the marketing mix typically emphasizes product assortment, price, location, promotion, and customer services. This last element consists of services designed to aid in the sale of a product. They include credit, delivery, gift wrapping, product installation, merchandise returns, store hours, parking, and—very importantly—personal service. (When this last form of customer service is aimed *directly* at creating a sale, then it is personal selling—a type of promotion.)

In this section we will describe the major types of retail stores, paying particular attention to three elements of their marketing mixes:

- Breadth and depth of product assortment.
- Price level.
- Amount of customer services.

Table 14-5 classifies retail stores on the basis of these three elements.

Some types of retail stores, such as off-price retailers, are new and growing rapidly. Others, notably variety stores, are diminishing in importance. And still others, particularly department stores, are under competitive pressure to modify some strategies. We will see that certain retailers are similar to others because new or modified institutions have filled the "strategic gaps" that once separated different types of retail institutions.

## Department Stores

Montgomery Ward is betting its future on a collection of "stores within a store."

A mainstay of retailing in the United States is the **department store,** a large-scale retailing institution that has a very broad and deep product assortment, tries not to compete on the basis of price, and provides a wide array of customer services. Familiar department store names include Filene's, Hecht's, May D&F, Dayton Hudson, Rich's, Marshall Field, Macy's, Sears, J.C. Penney, and Montgomery Ward.

Traditional department stores offer a greater variety of merchandise and services than does any other type of retail store. They feature both "soft goods"—such as apparel, sheets, towels, and bedding—and "hard goods"—including furniture, appliances, and consumer electronics. Department stores also attract—and satisfy—consumers by offering many customer services. The combination of distinctive, appealing merchandise and numerous customer services is designed to allow the stores to maintain the manufacturers' suggested retail prices. That is, department stores strive to charge "full" or "nondiscounted" prices.

Department stores face mounting problems, however. Largely due to their prime locations and customer services, their operating expenses are considerably higher than those of most other kinds of retail business. Many manufacturers' brands that used to be available exclusively through department stores are now widely distributed and often carry discounted prices in other outlets. And the quality of personal service, especially knowledgeable sales help, has deteriorated in some department stores.

Intense horizontal competition is also hurting department stores. Other types of retailers are aiming at consumers who have long supported department stores. Specialty stores, off-price retailers, and even some discount houses have been particularly aggressive in trying to lure shoppers away from department stores. To varying degrees retail chains such as K mart, Wal-Mart, Circuit City, and Highland Superstores compete against department stores.

Consequently, many department stores have modified their target markets or elements of their marketing mixes. The May Department Stores Company has targeted middle-income consumers, rejecting high-priced European designer lines and instead concentrating on fashionable apparel with moderate prices. Penney's dropped three lines of hard goods—home electronics, sporting goods, and photographic equipment. Penney's, Ward's, and Sears are all converting their very large stores into a collection of limited-line "superstores." Ward's, for instance, has created Auto Express, Electric Avenue, and Home Ideas areas within its stores.

Some department stores are also trying to be more price-competitive. Most notably, in 1989 Sears abandoned its practice of promoting temporarily reduced prices and adopted a strategy of "everyday low prices." With this policy, prices will always be lower than or as low as competitors'.

## Discount Houses

**Discount retailing** uses price as a major selling point by combining comparatively low prices and reduced costs of doing business. Several institutions, including off-price retailers and warehouse clubs, rely on discount retailing as their main marketing strategy.

Not surprisingly, the prime example of discount retailing is the **discount**

## TABLE 14-5 Retail stores classified by key marketing strategies

| Type of store | Breadth and depth of assortment | Price level | Amount of customer services |
|---|---|---|---|
| Department store | Very broad, deep | Avoids price competition | Wide array |
| Discount house | Broad, shallow | Emphasizes low prices | Relatively few |
| Catalog showroom | Broad, shallow | Emphasizes low prices | Few |
| Limited-line store | Narrow, deep | Traditional types avoid price competition; newer kinds emphasize low prices | Vary by type |
| Specialty store | Very narrow, deep | Avoids price competition | At least standard and extensive in some |
| Off-price retailer | Narrow, deep | Emphasizes low prices | Few |
| Category killer store | Narrow, very deep | Emphasizes low prices | Few to moderate |
| Supermarket | Broad, deep | Some emphasize low prices; others avoid price disadvantages | Few |
| Convenience store | Narrow, shallow | High prices | Few |
| Warehouse club | Very broad, very shallow | Emphasizes very low prices | Few (open only to members) |
| Hypermarket | Very broad, deep | Emphasizes low prices | Some |

**house,** a large-scale retailing institution that has a broad, shallow product assortment, emphasizes low prices, and offers relatively few customer services. A discount house normally carries a broad assortment of soft goods (particularly apparel) and well-known brands of hard goods (including appliances and home furnishings). It also advertises extensively. Target, K mart, and Wal-Mart are leading discount-house chains.

The success of discount houses can be attributed to two factors: First, other types of retailers normally had large markups on appliances and other merchandise, thereby providing discount houses with the opportunity to set smaller margins and charge lower prices. Second, consumers were receptive to a low-price, limited-service format. Discount houses have had a major impact on retailing, prompting many retailers to lower their prices.

Some discount chains are now trading up. For example, K mart—home of the "blue light special"—is trying to evolve from a no-frills discounter to a retailer of value-priced, top-quality merchandise, much of which carries well-known brand names. Such upgrading brings discount houses into competition with department stores and off-price retailers. This change in strategy may result in higher profit margins, but it also entails higher expenses due to nicer facilities and added customer services.

**Catalog Showrooms**  By placing a complete catalog and a number of sample items in a showroom and the remaining inventory in an attached warehouse, a **catalog showroom** sets itself apart from other types of stores. It offers a broad but shallow assortment of merchandise, low prices, and few customer services. Catalog showrooms stress selected product lines, such as photographic equipment, consumer electronics, jewelry, small appliances, luggage, and gift items.

Shoppers examine the samples and catalogs available in the showroom. Or they may have already received an abridged catalog in the mail or inserted in their newspapers. To purchase an item, the consumer fills out an order form and gives it to a clerk at the central counter. An employee takes the form and goes to the warehouse to obtain the desired merchandise.

Among the better-known chains of catalog showrooms are Best Products and Service Merchandise. In the latter part of the 1980s showrooms faced tough competition. Their price advantage disappeared as large discounters and new "category killer" stores (discussed shortly) also stressed low prices. Consequently, as the 1990s began, catalog showrooms were trying to figure out whether to seek a price advantage or to trade up and encourage shoppers to spend more time in their stores.

**Limited-Line Stores**     Much of the "action" in retailing in recent years has been in **limited-line stores.** This type of institution has a narrow but deep product assortment and customer services that vary from store to store. Traditionally, limited-line stores strived for full or nondiscounted prices. Currently, however, new types of limited-line retailers have gained a foothold by emphasizing low prices.

Breadth of assortment varies somewhat across limited-line stores. A store may choose to concentrate on:

- Several related product lines (shoes, sportswear, and accessories),
- A single product line (shoes), or
- Part of one product line (athletic footwear).

We identify limited-line stores by the name of the primary product line—furniture store, hardware store, clothing store, for example. Some retailers such as grocery stores and drugstores that used to be limited-line stores now carry much broader assortments because of scrambled merchandising.

This chain's name describes what type of retailer it is!

## SPECIALTY STORES

A very narrow and deep product assortment, often concentrating on a specialized product line (baked goods) or even part of a specialized product line (cinnamon rolls), is offered to consumers by a **specialty store.** Examples of specialty stores are bake shops, furriers, athletic footwear stores, meat markets, and dress shops. (Specialty *stores* should not be confused with specialty *goods.* In a sense, specialty stores are misnamed because they may carry any category of consumer goods, not just specialty goods.)

Most specialty stores strive to maintain manufacturers' suggested prices and provide at least standard customer services. Some specialty stores, however, emphasize extensive customer services, particularly knowledgeable and friendly sales help. The success of specialty stores depends on their ability to attract and then serve well customers whose two primary concerns are deep assortments and extensive, top-quality services.

## OFF-PRICE RETAILERS

While many discount houses attempted to trade up during the 1980s, **off-price retailers** positioned themselves below discount houses with lower prices on selected product lines. This institution concentrates on apparel and shoes, has a narrow, deep product assortment, emphasizes low prices, and offers few customer services. Store names such as Marshall's, Ross Dress for Less, T.J. Maxx, Syms, Payless Shoesource, and Athletic Shoe Factory are now well known to consumers in many areas.

Off-price retailers often buy manufacturers' excess output, inventory remaining at the end of a fashion season, or irregular merchandise at lower-than-normal wholesale costs. In turn, their retail prices are much lower than those for regular, in-season merchandise sold in other stores. Customers are attracted by the low prices and fairly current fashions.

Interestingly, many off-price retailers are owned by major retailing chains.[4] For example, T.J. Maxx is owned by Zayre, and Filene's Basement by Federated Department Stores. As the 1980s ended, prestigious chains such as Neiman-Marcus and Woodward & Lothrop also opened off-price stores for two reasons. First, major chains believe it is undesirable to keep marked-down merchandise on sales floors for extended periods. Second, they believe it can be more profitable to sell such merchandise through their own retail outlets than by using outside companies.

**Factory outlets** are a special type of off-price retailer. They are owned by manufacturers and usually sell a single manufacturer's clearance items, regular merchandise, and perhaps even otherwise unavailable items. Many well-known and popular brands, such as Esprit, Calvin Klein, Corning, L.L. Bean, Paul Revere, Royal Doulton, and Dansk, can be found in factory outlets. A growing trend is the grouping of numerous factory outlets in an outlet center.

## CATEGORY KILLER STORES

Another phenomenon of the 1980s, a **category killer store** has a narrow but very deep assortment, emphasizes low prices, and has few to moderate customer services. It is so named because it is designed to destroy all competition in a specific product category.[5] Highly successful category killers include Ikea

---

[4]Teri Agins, "Upscale Retailers Head to Enemy Turf," *The Wall Street Journal,* Aug. 25, 1989, p. B1.
[5]Sometimes category killers are referred to as superstores. Using this term can create confusion, however, because it is also applied to large supermarkets.

If you want to compare brands and models, a category killer store, like Circuit City, fills the bill.

in home furnishings, Circuit City in consumer electronics, Home Depot in building supplies, and Toys "Я" Us. Other product areas with category killers are office supplies, sporting goods, housewares, and records.

This retail institution concentrates on a single product line or several closely related lines. The distinguishing feature of a category killer is the combination of many different sizes, models, styles, and colors of the products *and* low prices. For example, Ikea stocks more than 15,000 items and Sportmart 100,000 items, including 70 models of sleeping bags and 12,000 kinds of athletic and outdoor shoes.[6]

Sustained growth is forecast for category killers. However, most kinds of merchandise as well as many geographic areas will not generate the large sales levels that permit low prices through high-volume buying power. Furthermore, existing category killers are not without problems. In particular, they face a major challenge in maintaining inventories that are large enough to satisfy customer demand but not so large as to result in excess inventories requiring significant markdowns.

## Supermarkets

As was the case with *discount*, the word *supermarket* can be used to describe a method of retailing *and* a type of institution. As a method, **supermarket retailing** features several related product lines, a high degree of self-service, largely centralized checkout, and competitive prices. The supermarket approach to retailing is used to sell various kinds of merchandise, including building materials, office products, and—of course—groceries.

The term *supermarket* usually refers to an institution in the grocery retailing field. In this context a **supermarket** is a retailing institution that has a moderately broad, moderately deep product assortment spanning groceries and some nonfood lines and offers relatively few customer services. Most supermarkets emphasize price. Some use price *offensively* by featuring low prices in order to attract customers. Other supermarkets use price more *defensively* by relying on leader pricing to avoid a price disadvantage. Since supermarkets

[6]Steve Weiner, "With Big Selection and Low Prices, 'Category Killer' Stores Are a Hit," *The Wall Street Journal,* June 17, 1986, p. 33.

## AN ETHICAL DILEMMA?

Manufacturers of grocery products heavily advertise their sales promotions (such as contests and rebates) in the mass media so that many consumers will learn about them. However, because supermarkets receive numerous sales promotion materials (such as contest entry blanks and rebate forms) from manufacturers, they do not display all of them. As a result, when consumers go to a supermarket expecting to find a promotion, it may not be available. If you were a supermarket manager, would you consider it ethical to discard sales promotion materials provided free of charge to your store by a manufacturer? Would your judgment be different if you knew that your store benefited from the additional store traffic generated by the manufacturer's ads?

typically have very thin gross margins, they need high levels of inventory turnover to achieve satisfactory returns on invested capital.

Supermarkets originated in the early 1930s. They were established by *independents* to compete with grocery chains. Supermarkets were an immediate success, and the innovation was soon adopted by chain stores. In recent decades supermarkets have added various nonfood lines to provide customers with one-stop shopping convenience and to improve overall gross margins.

Today stores using the supermarket *method* of retailing are dominant in grocery retailing. However, different names are used to distinguish these institutions by size and assortment:

- *A superstore* is a larger version of the supermarket. It offers more grocery and nonfood items than a conventional supermarket does. Many supermarket chains are emphasizing superstores in their new construction.
- *Combination stores* are usually even larger than superstores. They, too, offer more groceries and nonfoods than a supermarket but also most product lines found in a large drugstore. Some combination stores are joint ventures between supermarkets and drug chains such as Kroger and Sav-On.

For many years the supermarket has been under attack from numerous competitors. For example, a grocery shopper can choose among not only many brands of supermarkets (Publix, Safeway, Albertson's, and Vons) but also various types of institutions (warehouse stores, gourmet shops, meat and fish markets, and convenience stores). Supermarkets have reacted to competitive pressures primarily in either of two ways: Some cut costs and stressed low prices by offering more private brands and generic products and few customer services. Others expanded their store size and assortments by adding more nonfood lines (especially products found in drugstores), groceries attuned to a particular market area (foods that appeal to a specific ethnic group, for example), and various service departments (including video rentals, restaurants, delicatessens, financial institutions, and pharmacies).[7]

---

[7] See "There Are Two Kinds of Supermarkets: The Quick and the Dead," *Business Week,* Aug. 11, 1986, p. 62.

## AN INTERNATIONAL PERSPECTIVE: What's as big as six football fields, with sales of $11,000 an hour?

This monstrous retail store, highly successful in Europe, is called a *hypermarket*. Introduced unsuccessfully into the United States in the early 1970s, it was reintroduced in the mid-1980s. Ordinarily they are a joint venture between a U.S. retailer and a European hypermarket operator. American entrants include Super Valu (with Bigg's hypermarket), K mart and Bruno's (partners in American Fare), and Wal-Mart (Hypermart USA).

The hypermarket still has not achieved great success in the United States. But the inaugural stores are generating tremendous curiosity among consumer *and* retail executives. A **hypermarket** is an exceedingly large-scale retailing institution that has a very broad, moderately deep product assortment, emphasizes low prices, and offers some customer services. It is targeted at middle- and upper-income consumers. A hypermarket is split about 40/60 between groceries and nonfood products (the split of revenues is the opposite). It features well-known brands, especially in apparel lines.

Hypermarkets dwarf other retail stores, as shown in the accompanying table. In fact, a new Carrefour hypermarket in Philadelphia consumes 330,000 square feet, enough space for six football fields! Annual sales for each new hypermarket in the United States are about $100 million—or more than $11,000 an hour.

Will hypermarkets achieve success in the United States this time around? Some observers think they have strong appeal as the ultimate in one-stop shopping. But others wonder whether consumers want to spend that much time, walk that far, and buy everything from *A* to *Z* (apparel to zucchini) in the same store.

Many institutions eagerly await the verdict. One firm already has drawn a conclusion: Disappointed with the low profits of its hypermarkets, Wal-Mart announced in mid-1990 that it would open no more hypermarkets. You can be sure that other hypermarket operators with tremendous investments at stake are also monitoring performance very closely. So are many other retailers, wholesalers, and manufacturers that will be affected (many for the worse) if hypermarkets successfully draw sales away from conventional retail stores.

Sources: Based on Bill Saporito, "Retailers Fly into Hyperspace," *Fortune*, Oct. 24, 1988, pp. 148ff.; Todd Mason et al., "The Return of the Amazing Colossal Store," *Business Week*, Aug. 22, 1988, pp. 59–61; and Kevin Kelly and Amy Durkin, "Wal-mart Gets Lost in the Vegetable Aisle," *Business Week*, May 28, 1990, p. 48.

### Hypermarkets compared with other retail stores

| Type of store | Size (sq. feet) | Number of items stocked | Gross margin (%) | Labor cost (% of sales) | Weekly sales |
|---|---|---|---|---|---|
| Hypermarket | 200,000 | 50,000 | 15 | 5.0 | $1,750,000 |
| Wholesale club | 100,000 | 4,500 | 11 | 4.5 | $1,000,000 |
| Discount store | 65,000 | 80,000 | 28 | 10.0 | $ 150,000 |
| Supermarket | 39,000 | 30,000 | 24 | 12.5 | $ 250,000 |

Source: *Fortune*, Oct. 24, 1988, p. 152.

Hypermarkets, such as Carrefour, provide extensive assortments—and abundant exercise—for shoppers!

**Convenience Stores**     To satisfy increasing consumer demand for convenience, particularly in suburban areas, the **convenience store** emerged several decades ago. This retailing institution concentrates on convenience groceries and nonfoods, has higher prices than most other grocery stores, and offers few customer services. Gasoline, fast foods, and selected services (such as car washes and automated teller machines) can also be found in many convenience stores.

The name *convenience store* reflects its main appeal and explains how the somewhat higher prices are justified. Convenience stores are typically located near residential areas and are open extended hours; in fact, some never close. Examples of convenience-store chains are 7-Eleven (originally open from 7 A.M. to 11 P.M. but now open 24 hours in most locations), Circle K, and Convenient Food Mart.[8]

Convenience stores compete to some extent with both supermarkets and fast-food restaurants. Furthermore, in the 1980s, petroleum companies modified many service stations by phasing out auto repairs and adding a convenience groceries section. For example, Arco has AM/PM Mini Marts and Shell Oil and Texaco have Food Marts.

**Warehouse Clubs**     Another institution that mushroomed during the 1980s is the **warehouse club,** sometimes called a **wholesale club.** A combined retailing and wholesaling institution, it has very broad but very shallow product assortments, extremely low prices, and few customer services, and is open only to members. This format originated in Europe many years ago but was first applied successfully in the United States in the mid-1970s by the Price Club. Other warehouse clubs are Sam's (owned by Wal-Mart), BJ's, and Costco.

Warehouse clubs' target markets are small businesses (some purchasing merchandise for resale) and select groups of employees (government workers and school personnel, for example) as well as members of credit unions. Prices paid by ultimate consumers are usually about 5 percent higher than those paid by business members.

A warehouse club carries about the same breadth of assortment as a large discount house but in much less depth. For each item, the club stocks only one or two brands and a limited number of sizes and models. It is housed in a warehouse-type building with tall metal racks that display merchandise at ground level and store it at higher levels. Customers pay cash (credit cards are not accepted) and handle their own merchandise—even bulky, heavy items.

Further growth of warehouse clubs is expected during the 1990s. As with other retailing institutions, modifications and refinements can be anticipated as competition intensifies. Some warehouse clubs, for instance, are already experimenting with more service departments (such as an optical department and a pharmacy).[9]

**NONSTORE RETAILING**     A large majority—perhaps 85 percent—of retail transactions are made in stores. However, a growing volume of sales is taking place away from stores. Retailing activities resulting in transactions that occur away from a retail store are termed **nonstore retailing.**

It is ''guesstimated'' that total sales by nonstore retailing now account for

---

[8] For a good profile and assessment of the field, see Claudia H. Deutsch, ''Rethinking the Convenience Store,'' *The New York Times*, Oct. 8, 1989, pp. 1, 15 in section 3.

[9] For more on warehouse clubs, see Jack G. Kaikati, ''The Boom in Warehouse Clubs,'' *Business Horizons*, March–April 1987, pp. 68–73.

10–15 percent of total retail trade. Thus the sales volume through nonstore retailing is probably more than $200 billion annually.

We will consider four types of nonstore retailing: direct selling, telemarketing, automatic vending, and direct marketing. (These names may be confusing so don't worry about the names. Focus instead on the distinctive features and competitive standings of the four types.) Each type may be used by producers and/or retailers.

## Direct Selling

The trade association in this field defines **direct selling,** in the context of retailing, as personal contact between a sales person and a consumer away from a retail store. This type of retailing has also been called *in-home selling* but, as we shall see, the changing roles of women have made this term less accurate.

Annual volume of direct selling was about $10 billion as the 1990s began. According to a recent survey, 57 percent of consumers bought a product from a company using direct selling in the past 12 months; by way of comparison, 69 percent made a catalog purchase during the same period.[10]

There are many well-known direct selling companies, including Avon, Mary Kay, Tupperware, Electrolux (vacuums), Amway, Shaklee, West Bend (cookware), and World Book. Diverse products are sold through direct selling, most of which requires extensive demonstration (cosmetics, sewing machines). Direct selling—as well as other forms of nonstore retailing—is also employed in other countries. For example, Nissan used 2,500 white-collar workers to sell autos door to door in Japan. Amway has entered the Japanese market with its distinctive method of direct selling.

The two major kinds of direct selling are door-to-door and party plan. Sometimes door-to-door selling simply involves "cold canvassing" without any advance selection of prospects. More often there is an initial contact in a store, by telephone, or by a mailed-in coupon.

With the party-plan approach, a host or hostess invites some friends to a party. These guests understand that a sales person—say, for a cosmetics or a housewares company—will make a sales presentation. The sales rep has a larger prospective market and more favorable selling conditions than if these people were approached individually door to door. And the guests get to shop in a friendly, social atmosphere.

With so many women now working outside the home, direct selling firms have had to find new ways of making contact with prospective customers. For instance, Avon reps call on NCR employees and the West Virginia state police in their offices. Tupperware gives sales parties at lunchtime in offices. Obviously, however, some employers take a dim view of such selling in the workplace.[11]

There are other drawbacks to direct selling. It is the most expensive form of retailing, with sales commissions as high as 40 to 50 percent of the retail price. Also good sales people are extremely hard to recruit and retain. Some sales people have been too persistent or even fraudulent. As a result, a num-

---

[10] The sales figure is from *1988 Direct Selling Industry Survey,* Direct Selling Association, Washington, D.C., 1989, p. 2. The purchase incidences are from Robert A. Peterson, Gerald Albaum, and Nancy M. Ridgway, "Consumers Who Buy from Direct Sales Companies," *Journal of Retailing,* Summer 1989, p. 275.

[11] Kate Ballen, "Get Ready for Shopping at Work," *Fortune,* Feb. 15, 1988, p. 95.

Some direct-selling companies, including Amway, have found success in Japan.

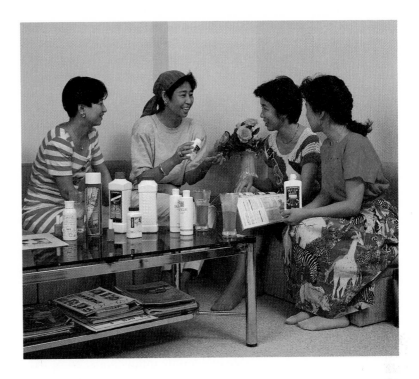

ber of states have "cooling off" laws that permit consumers to nullify a door-to-door or party-plan sale for up to several days after the transaction.

Direct selling does give consumers the opportunity to buy at home or another convenient nonstore location. For the seller, direct selling provides the most aggressive form of retail promotion as well as the chance to demonstrate a product in the shopper's (rather than the seller's) environment.

**Telemarketing**  Sometimes called *telephone selling*, **telemarketing** refers to a sales person initiating contact with a shopper and also closing a sale over the telephone. As with door-to-door selling, telemarketing may mean cold canvassing from the phone directory. Or it may rely on prospects who have requested information from the company or whose demographics match those of the firm's target market.

Several years ago annual sales by telemarketing, including sales to both consumer and business markets, were estimated to be at least $75 billion.[12] Many products that can be bought without being seen are sold over the telephone. Examples are pest-control services, magazine subscriptions, credit-card memberships, and athletic club memberships.

Telemarketing's reputation has been damaged by the unethical sales practices of some firms. These firms tell consumers that they are conducting marketing research and "are not selling anything." Such unethical procedures hurt other telemarketing companies as well as legitimate research firms that conduct telephone surveys.

Despite this problem, telemarketing sales have been increasing for several reasons. Certain consumers appreciate the convenience of making a purchase by phone. Also, the introduction of outgoing WATS lines about 20 years ago made telemarketing to consumers in distant locations more cost effective.

[12] Joel Dreyfuss, "Reach Out and Sell Something," *Fortune*, Nov. 26, 1984, pp. 127–28.

Finally, computer systems today can automatically dial a telephone number or, going a step further, play a taped message and then record information that the consumer gives to complete the sale. Such systems reduce the normally high labor costs associated with telemarketing.

**Automatic Vending**

The sale of products through a machine with no personal contact between buyer and seller is called **automatic vending** (or *automated merchandising*). Most products sold by automatic vending are convenience-oriented or are purchased on impulse. They are usually well-known, presold brands with a high rate of turnover. For many years the bulk of automatic vending sales has come from the "4 C's": cold drinks, coffee, candy, and cigarettes. It is estimated that vending rings up more than $20 billion in annual sales, representing between 1 and 2 percent of all retail trade.[13]

Vending machines can expand a firm's market by reaching customers where and when it is not feasible for stores to do so. Thus they are found virtually everywhere, particularly in schools, workplaces, and public facilities. Automatic vending has to overcome major challenges, however. Operating costs are high because of the need to continually replenish inventories. The machines also require occasional maintenance and repairs.

The outlook for automatic vending is uncertain. Some observers predict the difficulties just cited will deter further growth. Others are more optimistic due to vending innovations. Some machines are now equipped to sell "vending debit cards" that can be used to make vending purchases. When one of these cards is inserted into a vending machine, the amount of the purchase is deducted from the card's credit balance. Also there is a continuing flow of new products for vending machines, including pizzas, heatable diet dinners, and gourmet coffees.

**Direct Marketing**

There is no consensus on the exact nature of direct marketing; in a sense, it comprises all types of nonstore retailing other than the three already discussed. We define **direct marketing** as the use of nonpersonal media to contact consumers who, in turn, purchase products without visiting a retail store. (Be sure to distinguish among the terms direct *marketing*, direct *selling*, and direct *distribution*.)

To contact consumers, direct marketers use one or more of the following media: radio, TV, newspapers, magazines, catalogs, and mailings (direct mail). Consumers typically place orders by telephone or mail. Direct marketing is big business: Currently it accounts for about $200 billion—and perhaps more—in annual retail *and* wholesale sales![14]

Given its broad definition there are many forms of direct marketing. The major types are as follows:

- *Direct mail.* Companies mail consumers letters, brochures, and even product samples, and ask that orders be placed by mail or telephone.

---

[13] This statistic and the paragraph on vending innovations are from "Vending Machines of the 1990s to Offer Cappucino and Hot Pizzas," *Marketing News*, Dec. 18, 1989, p. 5.

[14] "Direct Marketing Sales Far Outpace Estimates," *Marketing News*, Nov. 23, 1984, pp. 1, 8. Although we considered it separately, telemarketing is sometimes included under the umbrella of direct marketing. Another term often associated with direct marketing, *mail order*, actually refers to the way an order is placed and/or delivered, whereas the three types we describe focus on the way contact is made with consumers.

- *Catalog retailing.* Companies mail catalogs to consumers or make them available at retail stores.
- *Televised shopping.* You are probably familiar with TV channels and shows such as the Home Shopping Network that sell consumer electronics, jewelry, and other products at relatively low prices. During the 1980s televised shopping grew dramatically, but faltered in the last years of the decade.

Some companies started out in nonstore retailing and later established massive chains of retail stores—Sears and Wards are prime examples. Other firms concentrated exclusively on direct marketing for many years—Spiegel typifies this group. An ever-larger number of the latter type of firm, among them L.L. Bean and The Sharper Image, are opening stores to expand their marketing efforts. Direct marketers can be classified as either general-merchandise firms, which offer a wide variety of product lines, or specialty firms, which carry only one or two lines such as books or fresh fruit.

Like other types of nonstore retailing, direct marketing provides consumers with shopping convenience. Direct marketers often benefit from relatively low operating expenses because they do not have the overhead of retail stores. There are drawbacks to direct marketing, however. Consumers must place orders without seeing or trying on the actual merchandise (although they may see a picture of it). To offset this limitation, direct marketers must offer liberal return policies. Furthermore, catalogs and, to some extent, direct-mail pieces are costly and must be prepared long before they are issued. Price changes and new products can be announced only through supplementary catalogs or brochures.

## RETAILING MANAGEMENT

Fundamental to managing a retailing firm is the planning of sound strategies. Central to strategic planning are the selection of target markets and development of a marketing mix. Also, during the turbulent 1990s, a factor called retail positioning will probably be critical. Let's briefly discuss these topics.

### Target Markets and Marketing Mix

As department stores are now discovering, retailers can no longer be "all things to all people." Therefore, many retail firms of various sizes are looking for unsatisfied niches that can be served profitably. However, some types of retailers—notably department stores and hypermarkets—still have fairly broad, rather than highly focused, target markets.

We have paid much attention to product assortments, price strategies, and promotional methods in preceding sections. Physical facilities, the fourth element of a retailer's marketing mix, also deserve some mention.

#### PHYSICAL FACILITIES

Firms that operate retail stores, rather than relying solely on nonstore retailing, must consider three aspects of physical facilities:

- *Location.* It is frequently stated that there are three keys to success in retailing: location, location, and location! Although overstated, this axiom does suggest the importance that retailers attach to location. Thus the store's physical site should be the first decision made about facilities. Considerations such as surrounding population, traffic, and cost determine where a store should be located.
- *Design.* This factor refers to exterior and interior appearance.

Historical shopping districts, such as the former site of the Ghirardelli chocolate factory in San Francisco, often are popular with residents and tourists alike.

- *Layout.* The amount of space allocated to various product lines, specific locations of products, and a floor plan of display tables and racks comprise the store's layout.

As might be expected, retail locations tend to follow the population. Consequently, the bulk of retail sales occur in urban areas. And suburban shopping areas have become more and more popular while many downtown areas have declined.

Planned shopping centers have become the predominant type of retail location in many suburban areas. A **shopping center** consists of a planned grouping of retail stores that lease space in a multiunit structure typically owned by a single organization. Shopping centers can be classified by size and market served:

- *Convenience center.* Usually consists of 5 to 10 outlets such as a dry cleaner, branch bank, convenience grocery store, and video rental store.
- *Neighborhood center.* Has 10 to 25 tenants including a large supermarket and perhaps a drugstore.
- *Community center.* Includes 25 to 50 stores and features a discount house or junior department store. It may also include a supermarket. Given its composition of stores, a community center draws shoppers from a larger area than does a neighborhood center.
- *Regional center.* Anchored by one or more department stores and complemented by as many as 200 smaller retail outlets; typically an enclosed climate-controlled mall.

Many regional shopping centers are giant. They have become the hub of shopping and social activities in many communities; in fact they are "the meeting place" for high school students. During the 1980s construction of new regional centers slowed considerably as the market became saturated.[15]

---

[15] Roger Lowenstein, "Regional-Mall Developers Try New Tactics as Market Shrinks," *The Wall Street Journal,* Sept. 2, 1987, p. 25.

It is expected that relatively few shopping malls will be built in the 1990s, but many existing ones will be renovated and modernized.

The growth of suburban shopping, especially in regional malls, led to decreased retail sales in many urban downtown areas. In recent years, therefore, some cities have worked to revitalize their downtown shopping districts. Often historical buildings or neighborhoods are converted to shopping areas (for example, Ghirardelli Square and The Cannery in San Francisco). Enclosed shopping malls featuring distinctive designs (for example, Water Tower Place in Chicago) have also been built in a number of downtown areas.

**Positioning**

Retailers are increasingly thinking about positioning as they develop marketing plans. **Positioning** is a retailer's strategies and actions designed to favorably distinguish itself from competitors in the minds (and hearts) of targeted groups of consumers. Positioning centers on the three variables we have stressed in this chapter: product assortment, price, and customer services.

Let's briefly examine several positioning strategies.[16] When only price and service levels are considered, two strategies that have potential value are *high price–high service* and *low price–low service*. The former is difficult to implement because it requires skilled, motivated employees (especially sales people); the latter necessitates careful management of operating expenses because gross margins are small.

When all three variables—product assortment, price, and customer services—are considered, two new options emerge. One is *product differentiation*, in which a retailer offers different brands or styles than those sold in competing stores. A second is *service and personality augmentation*, where a retailer offers similar products but sets itself apart by providing special services and also creating a distinctive personality or atmosphere for its stores.

A retailer's positioning strategy may include one or a combination of these options. Retail executives need to exhibit creativity and skill in selecting positioning strategies and then in implementing them.

**TRENDS IN RETAILING**

In the 1990s retailers face challenges perhaps unequaled since the Depression of the 1930s. Dozens of noteworthy trends present threats or, alternatively, provide opportunities for retailers. We will illustrate how dynamic retailing is by focusing on eight diverse, but highly significant trends:[17]

- *Changing demographics and industry structure.* The U.S. population is growing older, with proportional decreases in the 16-to-34 age group and increases in the 45-and-over age group. Real growth in retail sales is expected to be substantially less than in the 1970s and 1980s. Thus there may be too many shopping centers and retail stores in the 1990s.
- *Expanding computer technology.* Advancing technology dramatically affects both consumer behavior and retail management. In particular, sophisticated computer systems that capture sales and inventory data influence the items retailers stock as well as what and when they reorder. Newer

---

[16] Positioning based on price and service is discussed in George H. Lucas, Jr., and Larry G. Gresham, "How to Position for Retail Success," *Business*, April–June 1988, pp. 3–13. Positioning that combines all three variables is presented in Lawrence H. Wortzel, "Retailing Strategies for Today's Mature Marketplace," *The Journal of Business Strategy*, Spring 1987, pp. 45–56.

[17] Some of these trends as well as others are described in Richard V. Sarkissian, "Retail Trends in the 1990s," *Journal of Accountancy*, December 1989, pp. 44–46ff.

systems permit retailers to automatically place orders and reorders with suppliers that are linked to them via computer.

- *Emphasis on convenience and service.* Consumers are increasingly busy, generally older, and have more money to spend. Such consumers desire products and methods of purchase that provide maximum convenience and service. Convenience is exemplified by nearby locations, extended hours, short waiting times, and other factors that make shopping easier. Service includes some convenience factors and also friendly, knowledgeable sales help, easy credit, liberal return policies, and postsale service. The Nordstrom chain is frequently praised for having recognized—and profitably satisfied—consumers' desire for top-quality service.
- *Scrambled merchandising.* Although not new, scrambled merchandising remains a major trend. In the constant search for higher-margin items, one type of store adds products that traditionally were handled by other retail stores. This move intensifies retail competition and forces adjustments in distribution channels.
- *Increasing polarity in retail trade.* At one end are large stores with a tremendously wide variety of products; at the other extreme are small limited-line stores. As retailers carefully identify and segment their markets, specialized stores are increasing in importance.
- *Experimentation.* Largely because of competitive pressures, many retailers are experimenting with new or modified formats and also with nontraditional locations. For example, department stores are scaling back product assortments by eliminating "commodity" lines (such as fabrics and mattresses) and stressing fashion and quality. Discount houses are either trading up to become so-called promotional department stores or are digging in for price battles. Some retailers are expanding their markets through new types of locations, such as so-called "power centers" or high-rise shopping centers in downtown areas. Rather than a major anchor (such as a department store), a power center has several well-known, popular limited-line stores (such as Circuit City, Home Depot, and Toys "Я" Us).
- *Emphasis on productivity.* Extremely small profits are forcing retailers to squeeze more revenues out of their resources (floor space, people, and inventories). Hence, virtually all products are being sold, at least to some extent, on a self-service basis. To boost motivation a number of large retailers (including Macy's and Bloomingdale's) have put sales people completely on commissions rather than salaries plus commissions. Computer systems, as discussed above, can also help achieve greater productivity.
- *Continuing growth of nonstore retailing.* Retail stores will continue to be dominant. But more and more retailers are complementing their stores with one or more types of nonstore retailing. Many consumers prefer the novelty or convenience of nonstore retailing.

As consumers change, so do forms of retailing. Retail executives would like to anticipate changes in retailing before they occur. To some extent this is possible, as many of the evolutionary changes in retailing have followed a cyclical pattern called the **wheel of retailing.**[18] This theory states that a new

[18]The wheel of retailing was first described in M. P. McNair, "Significant Trends and Developments in the Postwar Period," in A. B. Smith (ed.), *Competitive Distribution in a Free, High-Level Economy and Its Implications for the University,* The University of Pittsburgh Press, Pittsburgh, 1958, pp. 17–18.

type of retailer often enters the market as a low-cost, low-price store. Other retailers as well as financial firms do not take the new type seriously. However, consumers respond favorably to the low prices and shop at the new institution. Over time this store takes business away from other retailers that initially ignored it and retained their old strategies.

Eventually, according to the wheel of retailing, the successful new institution trades up in order to attract a broader market, achieve higher margins, and/or gain more status. Trading up entails improving the quality of products sold and adding customer services. Sooner or later, high costs and, ultimately, high prices (at least as perceived by its target markets) make the institution vulnerable to new retail types as the wheel revolves. The next innovator enters as a low-cost, low-price form of retailing, and the evolutionary process continues.

There are many examples of the wheel of retailing. To mention a few, chain stores grew at the expense of independents during the 1920s, particularly in the grocery field. In the 1950s discount houses placed tremendous pressure on department stores, which had become staid, stagnant institutions. The 1980s saw the expansion of warehouse clubs and off-price retailers, which have forced many institutions—supermarkets, specialty stores, and department stores—to modify their marketing strategies.

What will be the retailing innovations of the 1990s? Perhaps electronic retailing, some other form of nonstore retailing, or a new type of low-cost, low-price store. The wheel of retailing can help retailers identify changes in retail institutions. Retail firms must identify and respond to significant trends that affect retailing, including institutional changes, by developing customer want–satisfying marketing strategies.

**SUMMARY**  Retailing is the sale of goods and services to ultimate consumers for personal, nonbusiness use. Any institution (such as a manufacturer) may engage in retailing, but a firm engaged primarily in retailing is called a retailer.

Retailers serve as purchasing agents for consumers and as sales specialists for wholesaling middlemen and producers. They perform many specific activities such as anticipating customers' wants, developing product assortments, and financing.

The 2.4 million retail stores in the United States collectively generate about $1.5 billion in annual sales. Retailers' operating expenses run about 27 percent of the retail selling price; profits are usually a very small percentage of sales.

Most retail firms are very small. However, small retailers can survive—and even prosper—if they remain flexible and pay careful attention to personally serving customers' needs.

Retailers can be classified in two ways: (1) by form of ownership, including corporate chain, independent store, and various kinds of contractual vertical marketing systems such as franchising; and (2) by key marketing strategies. Retailer types are distinguished according to product assortment, price levels, and customer service levels: department store, discount house, catalog showroom, limited-line store (including specialty store, off-price retailer, and category killer store), supermarket, convenience store, warehouse club, and hypermarket. Mature institutions such as department stores, discount houses, and supermarkets face strong challenges from new competitors, particularly different kinds of limited-line stores.

Although the large majority of retail sales are made in stores, 15 percent or more occur away from stores. And this proportion is growing steadily. Four major forms of nonstore retailing are direct selling, telemarketing, automatic vending, and direct marketing. Each type has advantages as well as drawbacks.

Retailers need to carefully select target markets and plan marketing mixes. Besides product, price, promotion, and customer services, executives also must make strategic decisions regarding physical facilities. Specific decisions concern location, design, and layout of the store. Downtown shopping areas have suffered while suburban shopping centers have grown in number and importance. Retailers also should consider positioning—how to favorably distinguish their stores from competitors' stores in the minds of consumers.

Various trends present opportunities or pose threats for retailers. Institutional changes in retailing can frequently be explained by a theory called the wheel of retailing. To succeed, retailers need to identify significant trends and ensure that they develop marketing strategies to satisfy consumers.

## KEY TERMS AND CONCEPTS

Retailing (synonymous with retail trade) 352
Retailer 352
Corporate chain 358
Independent retailer 359
Contractual vertical marketing system 359
Retailer cooperative 359
Voluntary chain 359
Franchising 359
Franchise system 360
Department store 362
Discount retailing 362
Discount house 362
Catalog showroom 363
Limited-line store 364
Specialty store 365

Off-price retailer 365
Factory outlet 365
Category killer store 365
Supermarket retailing 366
Supermarket 366
Convenience store 368
Warehouse club (synonymous with wholesale club) 368
Nonstore retailing 368
Hypermarket 369
Direct selling 370
Telemarketing 371
Automatic vending 372
Direct marketing 372
Shopping center 374
Positioning 375
Wheel of retailing 376

## QUESTIONS AND PROBLEMS

1. Explain the terms *retailing*, *retail sale*, and *retailer* in light of the following situations:
   a. Avon cosmetics sales person selling door to door.
   b. Farmer selling produce door to door.
   c. Farmer selling produce at a roadside stand.
   d. Sporting goods store selling uniforms to a professional baseball team.
2. How do you explain the wide differences in operating expenses among the various types of retailers shown in Table 14-1?
3. What recommendations do you have for reducing retailing costs?
4. Reconcile the following statements, using facts and statistics where appropriate:
   a. "Retailing is typically small-scale business."

   b. "There is a high degree of concentration in retailing today; the giants control the field."
5. Of the criteria given in this chapter for evaluating the competitive positions of large-scale and small-scale retailers, which ones show small stores to be in a stronger position than large-scale retailers? Do your findings conflict with the fact that most retail firms are quite small?
6. The ease of entry into retailing undoubtedly contributes to the high failure rate among retailers, which—in the view of some—creates economic waste. Should entry into retailing be restricted? If so, how could this be done?
7. What course of action might small retailers take to improve their competitive position?
8. In what ways does a corporate chain (Safeway,

A&P, or Sears) differ from a voluntary chain such as Super Valu?

9. What can department stores do to strengthen their competitive positions?

10. "The supermarket, with its operating expense ratio of 20 percent, is the most efficient institution in retailing today." Do you agree with this statement? In what ways might supermarkets further reduce their expenses?

11. "Door-to-door selling is the most efficient form of retailing because it eliminates wholesalers and retail stores." Discuss.

12. What is the relationship between the growth and successful development of regional shopping centers in suburban areas and the material you studied in Chapter 4 and 5 regarding consumers?

13. Which of the retailing trends discussed in the last section of the chapter do you think represents the greatest opportunity for retailers? The greatest threat?

14. Do you agree with the axiom that there are three keys to success in retailing—location, location, and location? How do you reconcile this axiom with the fact that there is so much price competition in retailing at the present time?

15. Of the types of retail stores discussed in the chapter, which one(s) do you think have been or would be most successful in foreign countries? Which one(s) have been or would be unsuccessful in other countries? Explain your answers.

# CHAPTER 15

# MANAGEMENT OF PHYSICAL DISTRIBUTION

## CHAPTER 15 GOALS

In the preceding chapters we discussed the nature and importance of distribution channels. Now we consider the physical movement of products through channels of distribution. After studying this chapter, you should be able to explain:

- What physical distribution is.
- The total-system concept of physical distribution.
- The total-cost concept of physical distribution.
- The use of physical distribution to strengthen a marketing program and reduce marketing costs.
- The five major subsystems within a physical distribution system:
  - Inventory location and warehousing.
  - Materials handling.
  - Inventory control, including the JIT concept.
  - Order processing.
  - Transportation.

The Japanese call it "Kanban." We call it "Just-in-Time" (JIT) production and inventory control. This system, to which much of Japan's manufacturing success is credited, reduces inventory at each stage in the process of producing a product and distributing it to the final user. JIT essentially is a demand-pull system in which each unit in the production-distribution process buys only the amount that the next succeeding unit wants. A firm buys in small quantities "just in time" for use in production and then produces appropriate quantities "just in time" for sales.

JIT is a philosophy that cuts across all phases of the manufacturing and marketing activities in an organization. It is a strategy marked by an environment of cooperation and coordination between buyers and sellers. Short-term relationships are replaced by long-term commitments. Fewer suppliers take the place of large numbers of materials sources.

In the United States, the JIT philosophy was first adopted in the auto industry. But the concept has been picked up by leading firms in other industries—Xerox, IBM, Apple, Black & Decker, and General Electric, to name just a few. And for some firms the results have been dramatically positive. Xerox eliminated 4,700 suppliers in 1 year, and Black & Decker cut more than 50 percent of its suppliers in 2 years.

As yet, however, all is not sweetness and light throughout American industry with respect to JIT. The slow adoption and implementation of the concept in the United States, in contrast to Japan, are traceable largely to cultural differences between the two countries. Unlike the producer-supplier relationships in Japan, the American relationships historically have been adversarial, with producers and suppliers negotiating strongly to gain an advantage over one another. Also, many producers feel more secure with a large inventory of parts and supplies. Suppliers, on the other hand, fear being cut off if producers adopt single or very limited sources of supply.

On balance, though, the JIT strategy is the only way to go. That's why some companies translate Kanban as "Survival."[1]

[1] Earnest C. Raia, "Journey to World Class (JIT in USA)," *Purchasing*, Sept. 24, 1987, p. 48; Richard C. Walleigh, "What's Your Excuse for Not Using JIT?" *Harvard Business Review*, March–April 1986, p. 38; Dexter Hutchins, "Having a Hard Time with Just-In-Time," *Fortune*, June 9, 1986, pp. 64–66.

Campbell Soup, Motorola, Intel, Xerox, Harley-Davidson, and many other companies are doing more than just reducing inventory costs with JIT. These firms are developing more effective physical distribution systems to improve their competitive positions and implement their marketing strategies. After a company has established its channels of distribution, management must arrange for the physical distribution of its products through these channels. **Physical distribution** consists of all the activities concerned with moving the right amount of the right products to the right place at the right time. The term **logistics** also is used in connection with the movement of materials. Although some people distinguish between the terms physical distribution and logistics, we treat them as synonymous.

## IMPORTANCE OF PHYSICAL DISTRIBUTION MANAGEMENT

Bernard J. LaLonde, an international authority on physical distribution, pretty well summed up the traditional attitude of top executives toward physical distribution as follows: "American management's philosophy typically has been: 'If you're smart enough to make it and aggressive enough to sell it—then any dummy can get it there.'"

Through the years, management has made substantial progress toward reducing production costs. Cost reductions have also been effected in many areas of marketing. Physical distribution is the new (and perhaps last) major frontier of cost cutting.

In recent years, American business management has been paying increasing attention to physical distribution activities because the costs are quite substantial. And the dollars saved in physical distribution have considerable impact on profit. In a supermarket operation, for instance, the net profit on sales may be 1 percent. Thus every $1 saved in physical distribution costs has the same effect on profit as an *increase of $100* in sales volume. For certain products—furniture and building materials, for example—the largest group of operating expenses comprises those relating to physical distribution. For other products, as much as one-half the wholesale cost is incurred in transportation and warehousing. The high cost of energy and high interest rates (which especially affect inventory costs) are additional forces that spotlight the need for efficient physical distribution systems.

## TOTAL-SYSTEM CONCEPT OF PHYSICAL DISTRIBUTION

Physical distribution in marketing is essentially a problem in logistics. An army cannot afford to have a battalion in position with guns but no ammunition, or with trucks but no gasoline. By the same token, a business is in a weak position when it has orders but no merchandise to ship, or a warehouse full of goods in Atlanta but insistent customers in New Orleans. These examples point up the importance of *location* in marketing, especially as regards merchandise. The appropriate assortment of products must be in the right place at the right time to maximize the opportunity for profitable sales.

*Physical distribution,* then, is the physical flow of products. **Physical distribution management** is the development and operation of efficient flow systems for products. In its full scope, physical distribution for manufacturers includes: the flow of *raw materials* from their source of supply to the production line and the movement of *finished goods* from the end of the production line to the ultimate user. Middlemen manage the flow of goods *onto* their shelves as well as *from* their shelves to customers' homes or stores.

The task of physical distribution may be divided into five parts:

- Inventory location and warehousing.
- Materials handling.

**FIGURE 15-1** Physical distribution and its subsystems.

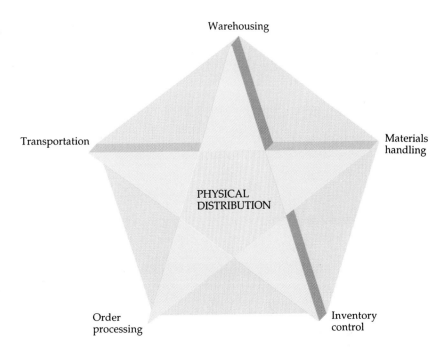

- Inventory control.
- Order processing.
- Transportation.

A decision regarding any one of these parts affects all the others. The location of a warehouse influences the selection of transportation methods and carriers; the choice of a carrier influences the optimum size of shipments. These interrelationships are illustrated in Figure 15-1.

From time to time in this book, marketing has been described as a *total system* of business action and not a fragmented series of operations. Nowhere is this clearer than in physical distribution. But it has not always been this way. Traditionally, physical distribution activities have been fragmented, and in many firms this is still the case. Managerial responsibility has been delegated to various units that often have conflicting, sometimes diametrically opposite goals. The production department, for instance, sets the production schedule. This group is interested in long production runs to minimize unit manufacturing costs, even though the result may be abnormally high inventory costs. The traffic department looks at freight rates rather than at the total cost of physical distribution. Thus carriers with low rates are often selected, even though this may mean undue time spent in transit and larger inventories to fill the long pipelines. The finance department wants a minimum of funds to be tied up in inventories. At the same time, the sales department wants to have a wide assortment of products available at locations near customers. Under such conditions it is impossible to optimize the flow of products. However, the systems approach to physical distribution can cut through these problems and result in effective coordination of these activities.

**Physical Distribution and Customer Service**

Physical distribution's major contribution to a company's marketing effort lies in its close relationship to customer service. Some years ago a landmark research study reported that top management considered customer service to

The Conrail® connection begins at the paper mill. . . .

After rolled paper is loaded onto boxcars. . .

Conrail® trains move the boxcars to the distribution center you choose . . .

where operators carefully unload your shipment for cross-dock, or . . .

for secure, clean, dry storage until an order is needed. . . .

Inventory and billing are handled by customer service representatives, who also . . .

make arrangements for local delivery when a supply is needed, and . . .

the Paper Connection℠ ends at the buyer's door.

Conrail understands that physical distribution activities are more effective when they are treated as part of a total system.

be a key element in a firm's marketing mix. The executives stated that their customers regard physical distribution activities as the major part of customer service.[2] Today many organizations, looking for ways to improve their customer service, recognize that the key ingredient is dependability. Dependability of service means *consistently* getting the right quantities of the right product to the right place at the right time.

## CUSTOMER SERVICE STANDARDS

To ensure reliable customer service, management should set standards of service performance for physical distribution activities. These standards should be measurable quantitatively. Some examples of customer service standards follow:

- Express delivery company: Deliver a package overnight to anywhere in the United States.
- Electronics manufacturer: Make delivery within 7 days after receiving an order.
- Airline: Departures and arrivals within 15 minutes of schedule on at least 85 percent of flights.
- Sporting goods wholesaler: Fill 98 percent of orders accurately.
- Industrial distributor: Maintain inventory levels that enable fulfillment of at least 85 percent of orders received.

**The Total-Cost Concept**

As part of the systems approach, executives should apply a **total-cost concept** to the management of physical distribution. A firm can choose from alternative methods of shipping, storing, and handling its products. Administrators should seek the *total set* of alternatives that optimizes the cost-profit relationship for the *entire* physical distribution system, rather than consider separate costs of individual activities.

Physical distribution activities are so interrelated that the cost of one activity often is determined by another activity. For example, if a firm increases the number of its warehouses, its total inventory costs also increase, but total transportation costs will go down. This relationship is illustrated in Figure 15-2. Increasing the number of warehouses raises the total amount of inventory carried, and thus the total inventory cost, but because inventory is located closer to customers, transportation costs are reduced.

Too often, management attempts to minimize the cost of only one aspect of physical distribution—transportation, for example. It might be upset by the high cost of air freight. But efforts to reduce that transportation expense may result in an increase in warehousing expenses that more than offsets the saving in freight costs.

The airlines particularly have been conscious of the total-cost concept, because unit freight rates are appreciably higher for air transportation than for land or sea shipment. Yet a major pharmaceutical company found that the higher costs of air freight were more than offset by savings from (1) lower inventory costs, (2) less insurance and interest expense, (3) lower crating costs, and (4) fewer lost sales due to out-of-stock conditions. The company eliminated all except one warehouse, cut inventories by 50 percent, boosted the rate of stock turnover, and found it could supply markets that had previously been inadequately served.

[2]Bernard J. LaLonde and Paul H. Zinszer, *Customer Service: Meaning and Measurement,* executive summary, National Council of Physical Distribution Management, Chicago, 1976.

**FIGURE 15-2** Relationship between number of warehouses and other physical distribution costs.

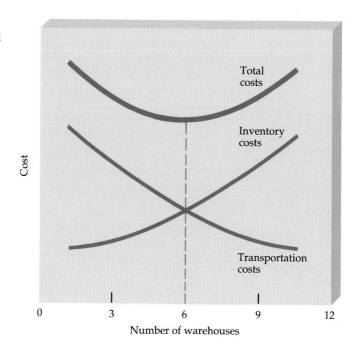

The point here is *not* that air freight is the best method of transportation. (In fact the pharmaceutical company later substantially reduced its business with airlines in some parts of the country.) Rather, the idea is that physical distribution should be viewed as a *total* process and its costs analyzed accordingly.

**Optimization and Cost Trade-Offs**

Implicit in the total-cost concept is the idea that management should strive for an optimal balance between total cost and customer services. This is what we call the concept of **optimization** in physical distribution. That is, rather than seeking *only* to minimize the total costs of physical distribution, executives should also consider customer want-satisfaction. Actually, it may be necessary to increase physical distribution costs somewhat in order to reach the desired level of customer service.

To achieve this optimal balance between physical distribution costs and customer-service levels, management must make **cost** and **customer service trade-offs.** To illustrate, let's assume that a seller wants to provide quick, frequent deliveries to customers. This seller will have to consider the trade-off between (1) an improved level of customer service and (2) the higher costs of processing and express-shipping smaller orders.

Apparel manufacturers have applied cost-service trade-offs to the locations of their production operations. A number of years ago, many companies shifted production to East Asian countries (Hong Kong, Taiwan, Korea, and others) to take advantage of very low labor costs there. Recently, however, several of these firms have moved their production operations back to the United States. It seems that improvements in customer service and cost savings related to domestic production more than offset the loss of lower-paid foreign workers. By manufacturing at home, a company can produce in smaller quantities, deliver more quickly to retail stores, and respond faster to fashion changes—all of which appeal to retailers. Also, with domestic production, a company does not pay international physical distribution costs

**FIGURE 15-3** Southland Corporation's distribution centers, dairies, food centers and other supporting operations provide 7-Eleven with better control over product supply and quality.

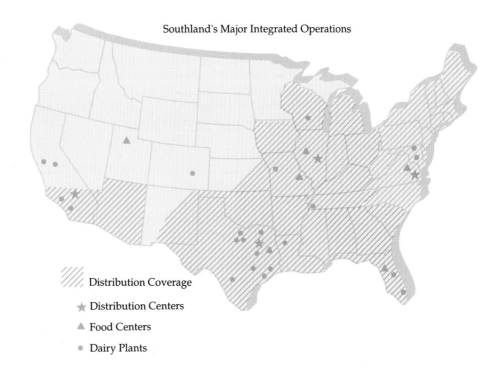

Southland's Major Integrated Operations

///// Distribution Coverage

★ Distribution Centers

▲ Food Centers

● Dairy Plants

such as overseas shipping, customs duties, import quota fees, and handling expenses of export-import middlemen.[3]

## STRATEGIC USE OF PHYSICAL DISTRIBUTION

The strategic use of business logistics may enable a company to strengthen its market position by providing more customer satisfaction and by reducing operating costs. The management of physical distribution can also affect a firm's marketing mix—particularly product planning, pricing, and distribution channels. The key here is for executives to (1) understand what their organization is trying to do and then (2) design an appropriate physical distribution system that will help, not hinder, the organization in achieving its goals.[4]

### Improve Customer Service

A well-run logistics system can improve the distribution service a firm provides its customers—whether they are middlemen or ultimate users. (See, for example, Figure 15-3.) And the level of customer service directly affects demand. This is true especially in the marketing of nondifferentiated products (chemicals, building materials) where effective customer service may be a company's only significant competitive advantage.

### Reduce Distribution Costs

Many avenues to cost reductions may be opened by effective physical distribution management. Simplifications, such as the elimination of unneeded warehouses, may lead to lower costs. Inventories—and their attendant carrying costs and capital investment—may be reduced by consolidating stocks at fewer locations.

[3]"Why Made-in-America Is Back in Style," *Business Week*, Nov. 7, 1988, p. 116.

[4]For a report on how a well-designed physical distribution system can implement a company's strategic marketing plan, see Roy D. Shapiro, "Get Leverage from Logistics," *Harvard Business Review*, May–June 1984, pp. 119–26.

## Create Time and Place Utilities

The economic value of storage (as a key part of warehousing) is the fact that it creates **time utility.** A product may be properly located with respect to its market, but the timing may be such that there is no present demand for it. Management adds precious value to this item simply by holding and properly preserving it in storage until demand rises. Time utility is created and value is added when bananas are picked green and allowed to ripen in storage, or when meat is aged in storage.

Storage is essential to correct imbalances in the timing of production and consumption. An imbalance can occur when there is *year-round consumption* but only *seasonal production,* as in the case of agricultural products. Proper use of warehousing facilities allows a producer to store the seasonal surplus so that it can be marketed long after the harvest has ended.

In other instances warehousing helps adjust *year-round production* to *seasonal consumption,* as in the case of skis. Manufacturers prefer to produce on a year-round basis to operate their plants more efficiently. Therefore, enough surplus stock must be stored during the off-season to meet peak-season demand without requiring overtime operations or additional plant capacity.

In an economic sense, the main function of the transportation subsystem in physical distribution is to add value to products through the creation of **place utility.** A fine suit hanging on a garment manufacturer's rack in New York City has less value to a retailer in Baltimore than a similar suit displayed in the retailer's store. Transporting the suit from New York to Baltimore creates place utility and thus adds value to the product.

## Stabilize Prices

Careful management of warehousing and transportation facilities can help stabilize prices for an individual firm or for an entire industry. If a market is temporarily glutted with a certain product, sellers can store the product until supply and demand conditions are more in balance. This managerial use of warehousing facilities is common in the marketing of agricultural products and other seasonally produced goods. The judicious movement of products from one market to another may enable a seller to (1) avoid a market with depressed prices or (2) take advantage of a market that has a shorter supply and higher prices.

## Influence Channel Selection and Middlemen Location

Decisions regarding inventory management have a direct bearing on a producer's selection of trade channels and the location of middlemen. Logistical considerations may become paramount, for example, when a company decides to decentralize its inventory. Now management must determine (1) how many sites to establish and (2) whether to use wholesalers, the company's own branch warehouses, or public warehouses. One producer may select merchant wholesalers that perform storage and other warehousing services. Another may prefer to use a combination of manufacturers' agents and public warehouses. These agents can solicit orders and provide aggressive selling, while the ordered products can be physically distributed through public warehouses.

One point should be kept in mind. Rarely are channels selected primarily on the basis of physical distribution considerations. Instead logistics is only one of several factors considered. Recall from Chapter 12 that the nature of the market and other factors heavily influence channel design.

## Minimize Shipping Costs

Good traffic managers ensure that their companies enjoy the fastest routes and the lowest rates for whatever methods of transportation they use. The pricing of transportation services is one of the most complicated parts of the American business scene. The rate, or tariff, schedule is the carrier's price list. To read one properly is a real art that requires considerable practice. As a simple example of some of the difficulties involved, shipping rates vary for different types of goods. Moreover, the classes of goods overlap, so that a particular product may be in two or more classes with different freight rates.

Another service that traffic managers can render their companies is the auditing (checking) of freight bills. Carriers sometimes charge a higher rate than the one that should apply. They are not intentionally trying to defraud the shipper; they are simply misinterpreting a complex rate schedule.

Proficient traffic managers can also negotiate with carriers to reclassify their products or to get special rates. A company may offer to ship larger quantities on a given carrier if lower rates are granted. Anheuser-Busch, for example, obtained reduced rates from trucking companies and railroads that netted a $3 million reduction in transportation costs over a 1-year period.

If service and control are essential for a company, traffic managers should investigate the possibility of having their own private carrier. With the present relaxed entry regulations, such a carrier could hire itself out to other companies to move their freight as well. The existence of an "in-house" carrier also serves as a powerful bargaining tool in dealing with common carriers for the portion of freight not carried by the private fleet. In-house carriers have worked well for the Southland Corporation (7-Eleven stores) and other major shippers.

**Benefit from Government Deregulation**

In the late 1970s, domestic airline, railroad, and trucking industries were largely freed from regulation. The railroad industry had been subject to federal regulations for almost a century, starting with the Interstate Commerce Commission Act in 1887. Airlines and commercial truckers have been regulated in the United States virtually from the beginning of those industries.

Because of this long history of government control, transportation firms experienced real "culture shock" after deregulation. The number of competing firms increased dramatically, especially in the airline and trucking industries. Lightly traveled routes were dropped. Competition intensified considerably on the more profitable routes. Price competition also increased considerably—sometimes to the point that carriers were pricing below cost. Many firms suffered financial losses and some were forced out of business.

But, at the same time, deregulation has provided many strategic marketing opportunities for well-managed firms both within and outside the deregulated industries. Carriers now have the flexibility to set their rates and levels of service to develop new markets. Most important, carriers can use their rates (that is, their prices) as a marketing tool. Shippers have benefited by being able to shop around for rates and service levels that best meet their needs.[5]

**MAJOR TASKS IN PHYSICAL DISTRIBUTION MANAGEMENT**

An effective physical distribution system is built around five interactive and interdependent subsystems. Consequently, each of them must be carefully coordinated with the others. The five subsystems are: inventory location and warehousing, materials handling, inventory control, order processing, and transportation.

[5] See Lewis M. Schneider, "New Era in Transportation Strategy," *Harvard Business Review*, March–April 1985, pp. 118–26; Thomas S. Robertson and Scott Ward, "Management Lessons from Airline Deregulation," *Harvard Business Review*, January–February 1983, pp. 40–44.

## Inventory Location and Warehousing

The name of the game in physical distribution is inventory management. Executive judgment must be exercised regarding the size, location, handling, and transporting of inventories. Decision making in these four areas is interrelated. The number and locations of inventory sites, for example, influence inventory size and transportation methods. These interrelationships are often quite complex.

### STORAGE VERSUS WAREHOUSING

We should distinguish carefully between these two activities in physical distribution. **Storage** is holding and preserving of products from the time of their production until their sale. **Warehousing** embraces storage plus a range of functions, such as assembling, dividing (bulk-breaking), and preparing products for reshipping. Warehousing is therefore a broader concept than storage. Storage is more passive by nature, while warehousing is more active.

### INVENTORY: CENTRALIZED OR DISPERSED?

Basic to inventory location is the company's intended strategy regarding inventory deployment. Is inventory to be heavily concentrated or dispersed throughout the market? Each strategy has its merits and limitations. A centralized inventory can be smaller in total size, can be better controlled, and is more responsive to unusual requests. Moreover, warehousing and materials handling should be more efficient. On the other hand, centralizing stocks often creates higher total transportation charges and slower delivery to some segments of the market. Dispersing inventory presents the other side of the coin on each of these points.

### THE DISTRIBUTION-CENTER CONCEPT

An effective inventory-location strategy may be a compromise—the establishment of one or more **distribution centers.** Such centers are planned around markets rather than transportation facilities. The idea is to develop under one

A modern distribution center improves considerably the efficiency of physical distribution.

roof an efficient, fully integrated system for the flow of products—taking orders, filling them, and delivering them to customers. The distribution center is a concept in warehousing that has been adopted by many well-known firms. The Limited, for example, uses its distribution center in Columbus, Ohio, as the hub of its physical distribution system, which enables the company to put apparel in its stores 60 days after placing an order with suppliers. For most competitors, the time between order placement and merchandise in store is 6 months or more. The Limited places orders by satellite with its Asian suppliers. The finished goods are taken to Hong Kong where a chartered Boeing 747 makes four flights a week to the distribution centers. There the goods are sorted, priced, and prepared for shipment by truck or airplane to the Limited's 3,200 stores, including the Limited Express and Victoria's Secret stores.[6] Another company, Nabisco Brands, opened a highly automated distribution center in Chicago, which enabled it to cut its distribution work force by more than half while at the same time increasing productivity.[7]

The use of distribution centers has lowered distribution costs by reducing the number of warehouses, cutting excessive inventories, and eliminating out-of-stock conditions. Storage and delivery time have been cut to a minimum. This puts into practice the adage that companies are in business to *sell* goods, not to *store* them.

### OWNERSHIP AND TYPES OF WAREHOUSES

A firm (producer, wholesaler, or retailer) has the option of operating its own private warehouse or using the services of a public warehouse. A **private warehouse** is more likely to be an advantage if (1) a company moves a large volume of products through a warehouse and (2) there is very little, if any, seasonal fluctuation in this flow. **Public warehouses** offer storage and handling facilities to individuals or companies. Public warehousing costs are a variable expense. Customers pay only for the space they use, and only when they use it. Major types of public warehousing facilities include:

- *General merchandise warehouses.* These store practically any product that needs protection from the weather but has no special temperature, humidity, or handling requirements.
- *Special commodity warehouses.* These are used for agricultural products such as grains, wool, cotton, or tobacco.
- *Cold storage warehouses.* For products that require refrigeration—primarily food items.

Two additional services typically provided by public warehouses are:

- *Substitute for company warehouses or wholesalers.* Public warehouses can provide office and product display space, and accept and fill orders for sellers. Producers can ship in carload quantities to a public warehouse, just as they ship to their own branches or wholesalers. Sellers thus have flexibility in inventory location. If they wish to change locations, they simply change public warehouses.
- *Financial services.* Warehouse receipts covering products stored in public warehouses may be used as collateral for bank loans. **Field (custodian)**

[6]Jeremy Main, "The Winning Organization," *Fortune*, Sept. 26, 1988, p. 50.
[7]James Aaron Cooke, "Here's a High-Tech Warehouse That Works," *Traffic Management*, April 1985, p. 76.

**warehousing** is a special service, which operates as follows: Assume that some products are stored in the owner's private warehouse. The owner wants to get a bank loan on the merchandise without the expense of moving it to a public warehouse. So the owner leases to a public warehouse company a section of the private warehouse that contains the merchandise in question. (A field warehouse need not be a portion of a regular private warehouse. It can be an office cabinet, locked desk drawer, office safe, open yard, or other storage facility.) The warehouse company then issues a receipt for the goods, and this receipt serves as collateral for a bank loan. The leased area, in effect, becomes a public warehouse, and the goods cannot be removed until the receipt is redeemed.[8]

## Materials Handling

Selection of the proper equipment to physically handle products is an important aspect of physical distribution management. Proper equipment can minimize losses from breakage, spoilage, and theft. Efficient equipment can reduce handling *costs* as well as *time* required for handling.

In this discussion of materials-handling equipment, we include the warehouse building itself. Historically, warehouses have been multistory buildings located in congested parts of town. Their operation has been characterized by the use of elevators, chutes, and other highly expensive *vertical* methods of moving products. Modern warehouses are huge one-story structures located in outlying areas where land is less expensive and loading platforms are easily accessible to motor trucks and railroad spurs. Forklift trucks, conveyor belts, motor scooters, and other mechanized equipment are used to move merchandise. In some warehouses the order fillers are even equipped with roller skates!

**Containerization** is a cargo-handling system that has gained considerable acceptance in physical distribution. Shipments of products are enclosed in large containers, usually made of metal or wood. The containers are then transported unopened from the time they leave the shipper until they reach their destination. Thus, containerization minimizes physical handling, thereby reducing damage, lessening the risk of theft, and allowing for more efficient transportation.

## Inventory Control

Essential to any physical distribution system is maintaining control over the size and composition of inventories. Inventory represents a sizable investment for most companies. The goal of inventory control is to minimize both the investment and fluctuations in inventories, while at the same time filling customers' orders promptly and accurately.

Perhaps the greatest boon to inventory control in recent years has been improvements in computer technology. These have enabled management to shorten the order delivery time and substantially reduce the size of inventories. Dillard's, a department store chain in the Midwest and Southwest, believes that the most valuable feature of its computer system is its ability to shorten the order placement–store delivery time span. Through its Quick Response inventory-control system, goods reach the selling floor 12 days after

[8] For a strategic planning model of competitive forces in the public warehousing industry and some competitive strategy options open to these firms in the early 1990s, see Michael A. McGinnis, Roger W. Carlson, and Lisa Forry, "Competitive Pressures and Emerging Strategies in Public Warehousing: Implications for Providers and Users," *Transportation Journal*, Summer 1987, pp. 43–53.

Some examples of efficient materials handling equipment.

they have been reordered electronically, instead of 30 days, the usual reorder time for similar retailers.[9]

Inventory size is determined by balancing market needs and costs. Market demands on inventory can be anticipated through sales forecasts. The more accurate the forecasts, the greater the probability of optimizing inventory size. Inventory costs include (1) acquisition costs—the costs of making or buying the products to put into inventory—and (2) carrying or holding costs—warehousing expenses, interest on investment, losses due to spoilage and pilferage, inventory taxes, and so on.

Inventory size is also influenced considerably by the desired level of customer satisfaction. What percentage of orders does the company expect to fill promptly from inventory on hand? Out-of-stock conditions result in lost sales, loss of goodwill, and sometimes even loss of customers. Yet to be able to fill 100 percent of orders promptly may require an excessively large and costly inventory. Authorities estimate that about 80 percent *more* inventory is required to fill 95 percent of the orders than to fill only 80 percent.

Management also must establish the optimal quantity for reorder when it is time to replenish inventory stocks. The **economic order quantity (EOQ)** is the volume at which the inventory-carrying costs plus the order-processing cost are at a minimum. Typically, as order size increases (1) inventory-carrying cost goes up (because the average inventory is larger) and (2) order-processing cost declines (because there are fewer orders).

In Figure 15-4, point EOQ represents the lowest-cost order quantity. Actually, the optimal order quantity often is somewhat different—usually larger—than the EOQ. Keeping in mind the need for optimization and cost trade-offs, management should balance the desire for minimum inventory costs with the desired level of customer service. This trade-off may well call for an order quantity that is larger than the EOQ—quantity $X$ in the figure, for example—in order to provide the desired level of customer service.

[9]Susan Caminiti, "A Quiet Superstar Arises in Retailing," *Fortune*, Oct. 23, 1989, p. 167.

**FIGURE 15-4** Economic order quantity.

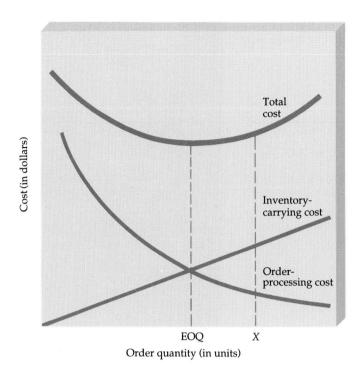

## JUST-IN-TIME (JIT) INVENTORY CONTROL

A new way of managing inventory control, purchasing, and production scheduling is the **"just-in-time"** (JIT) concept, which we described at the beginning of this chapter. JIT is attracting increasing attention from *top* management—not just marketing or physical distribution management—in many American companies. The essence of JIT is that you buy in small quantities just in time for use in production and then produce in quantities just in time for sale.

When effectively implemented, the just-in-time concept has many potential benefits. By purchasing in small quantities and maintaining low inventory levels of parts and finished goods, a company can effect dramatic cost savings. Production and delivery schedules can be shortened and made more flexible and reliable. The Japanese have found that quality levels improve with JIT purchasing. When order quantities are small and deliveries frequent, a company can spot and then correct a quality problem more quickly.

A closely coordinated, highly cooperative working relationship between producers and suppliers is absolutely essential for effective implementation of the JIT concept. As we noted in the chapter introduction, however, there still are some problems between American producers and suppliers, but the enormous benefits that JIT can provide for both groups should motivate them to make it work.[10]

[10] For further discussion of the JIT concept, see Charles R. O'Neal, "JIT Procurement and Relationship Marketing," *Industrial Marketing Management*, February 1989, pp. 55–63; Gary L. Frazier, Robert E. Spekman, and Charles R. O'Neal, "Just-in-Time Exchange Relationships in Industrial Markets," *Journal of Marketing*, October 1988, pp. 52–67; William D. Presutti, Jr., "Just-in-Time Manufacturing and Marketing—Strategic Relationship for Competitive Advantage," *Journal of Business and Industrial Marketing*, Summer 1988, pp. 27–35. Also see sources cited in the chapter introduction.

**Order Processing**

Still another part of the physical distribution system is a set of procedures for handling and filling orders. This should include provisions for billing, granting credit, preparing invoices, and collecting past-due accounts. Consumer ill will can result if a company makes mistakes or is slow in following orders. As information demands become more complex, companies are increasingly turning to computers to implement their order-processing activities.

**Transportation**

A major function of the physical distribution system in many companies is shipping products to customers. Management must decide on both the form of transportation and the particular carriers. In this discussion we will focus on *intercity* shipments.

The five major forms of transportation are railroads, trucks, water vessels, pipelines, and airplanes. The relative importance of each, along with trends in use, is shown in Table 15-1. Note that the figures reflect *intercity* freight traffic only. Ocean coastal traffic between U.S. ports is not included. Virtually all farm-to-farm and *intracity* freight movements are made by motor truck. Consequently, figures for water and truck carriers really understate the importance of these methods of transportation by a considerable margin. Nevertheless, Table 15-1 is illuminating. It shows that railroads are still by far the major intercity freight carrier. Although their relative position has declined steadily since 1950, the actual number of ton-miles of freight carried by railroads has increased considerably since that time. The use of trucks has expanded phenomenally over the past 40 years.

In Table 15-2 the major transportation methods are compared on the bases of criteria likely to be used by physical distribution management in the transportation selection process.

### SPECIAL SERVICES OFFERED BY RAILROADS

Despite the trend shown in Table 15-1, railroads are still the lowest-cost, most efficient method of transportation for many products and in many marketing situations. To meet increased competition from other carriers, especially trucks, railroads have instituted several special services and freight rates.

---

**TABLE 15-1 Distribution of intercity freight traffic in the United States by carrier**

| | % of total | |
|---|---|---|
| | 1988 | 1950 |
| Railroads | 37 | 56 |
| Trucks | 25 | 16 |
| Pipelines | 22 | 12 |
| Great Lakes | 3 | 11 |
| Rivers and canals | 13 | 5 |
| Air carriers | * | * |
| Total | 100% | 100% |

*Less than 1 percent of total.
Source: *Railroad Facts*, Association of American Railroads, Washington, D.C., 1989, p. 32.

**TABLE 15-2 Comparison of transportation methods**

| Selection criteria | Transportation method | | | | |
|---|---|---|---|---|---|
| | Rail | Water | Highway | Pipeline | Air |
| Speed (door-to-door time) | Medium | Slowest | Fast | Slow | **Fastest** |
| Cost of transportation | Medium | **Lowest** | High | Low | Highest |
| Reliability in meeting delivery schedules | Medium | Poor | Good | **Excellent** | Good |
| Flexibility (variety of products carried) | **Widest variety** | Widest | Medium | Very limited, very inflexible | Somewhat limited |
| Number of geographic locations served | Very many | Limited | **Unlimited, very flexible** | Very limited | Many |
| Products most suitable | Long hauls of carload quantities of bulky products, when freight costs are high in relation to product's value | Bulky, low-value, non-perishable | Short hauls of high-value goods | Oil, natural gas, slurried products | High value, perishable, where speed of delivery is all-important |

**Carload versus less-than-carload freight rates** Railroads offer substantial savings to firms that ship in carload (c.l.) quantities rather than less-than-carload (l.c.l.) amounts. For many items, the c.l. freight rate is as much as 50 percent less than the l.c.l. rate. This is a tremendous incentive to shippers of large quantities of products—especially minerals, agricultural products, and similar goods for which freight expenses are a significant percentage of total value.

**Combined shipments** Long ago the railroads realized that they were vulnerable to competition from other types of carriers when it came to handling l.c.l. shipments. Thus the railroads have introduced several measures designed to reduce the cost of l.c.l. shipments and to speed them up. These measures provide for combining into a carload quantity the freight from one or more companies that are shipping products to customers located in one area. The pooled freight can go at c.l. rates and can be delivered much more rapidly than if its component parts were sent separately in l.c.l. units.

**In-transit privileges** Two in-transit privileges offered by railroads are (1) diversion in transit and (2) the opportunity to process some products en route. **Diversion in transit** allows a seller to start a shipment moving in one direction and to change destination while the car is en route, just as long as the new destination involves no backtracking. The charges are computed on the basis of the *through rate* or long-haul rate from the point of origin to the ultimate destination, plus a small charge for diversion. This is a valuable service to shippers of perishable products that are subject to price variations from one city to another on any given day. A Washington cooperative can ship Red

## AN INTERNATIONAL PERSPECTIVE: Competition in global air express package delivery

The challenge is to deliver disk drives from San Jose to Seville or dresses from Hong Kong to Manhattan, door to door in 48 hours and at a lower price than the competition. This is the sort of problem facing United Parcel Service (UPS), Federal Express (Fed Ex), and Worldwide Express (DHL) as they compete in the international air express delivery segment of physical distribution. By 1990, international package delivery by air had entered the growth stage of its life cycle.

In the 1980s, competition heated up in the overnight air delivery business within the United States as Fed Ex challenged UPS, the world's largest package delivery firm. Both of these companies broadened their market in the late 1980s by expanding into the global delivery business, where they encountered competition from established firms such as DHL. Factors that prompted Fed Ex and UPS to enter global markets were:

- Domestic overnight delivery business of these two firms was being undercut by lower-priced competitors and facsimile (fax) machines.
- Manufacturers and retailers around the world increasingly were using global suppliers. Many also were adopting a just-in-time inventory philosophy that required a dependable, frequent, and speedy resupply delivery system.
- The increase in international shipments of tangible goods was accompanied by a deluge of documents—paperwork that was far too bulky and complex for fax machines to handle.

But going global in the package delivery business was not without problems.

- Start-up costs and fierce competition meant losses in the early years. UPS and Fed Ex both invested in fleets of airplanes—a heavy start-up cost. UPS did not expect any overseas net profits before 1993.
- Trade barriers added to operating expenses. Customs regulations required a considerable amount of time-consuming paperwork. Japan, for example, requires that all inbound envelopes be opened and inspected for pornographic information or products.

In spite of high costs and competition it is unlikely that any of the major express delivery firms will discontinue their international operations, because the global package delivery business is growing rapidly. The industry's annual sales were about $7 billion in 1990 and are expected to increase 20 to 30 percent each year throughout the 1990s.

Source: Clemens P. Work, "The Flying-Package Trade Takes Off," *U.S. News & World Report*, Oct. 2, 1989, p. 47.

Delicious apples from Yakima, Washington, to Indianapolis. Before the shipment reaches Indianapolis, the shipper may hear that market prices are better in Memphis. Consequently, at the appropriate "diversion point" (probably Chicago in this case), the cars will be rerouted to Memphis. The freight charges are based on the through rate from Yakima to Memphis.

Under the privilege of **processing in transit,** a shipment is unloaded and

Railroads compete with other transportation methods by providing piggyback service —and ships compete by providing fishyback service.

processed in some manner while en route. Then it is reloaded and shipped on to its final destination. Wheat may be shipped from Spokane to Minneapolis, where it is made into flour, which is then shipped to Detroit. But the through rate from Spokane to Detroit applies.

**Piggyback and fishyback services** **Piggyback service** involves carrying truck trailers on railroad flatcars. Products can be loaded on trucks at the seller's shipping dock. The truck *trailer* is later transported by train to the destination city where it is trucked to the buyer's receiving station. This combination service provides (1) more flexibility than railroads alone can offer, (2) lower freight costs than trucks alone, and (3) less handling of goods.

**Fishyback service** transports loaded trailers on barges or ships. The trailers may be carried piggyback fashion by railroad to the dock, where they are transferred to the ship. Then, at the other end of the water trip, the trailers are loaded back onto trains for completion of the haul. In an alternative use of the fishyback service, railroads are not used at all. Merchandise is trucked directly to ports, where the trailer vans are loaded on barges. At the end of the water journey the vans are trucked to the receiving station.

### FREIGHT FORWARDERS

The **freight forwarder** is a specialized marketing institution serving firms that ship in l.c.l. quantities. The typical freight forwarder does not have its own transportation equipment, but it does provide a valuable service in physical distribution.

Spurred by the opportunities provided by deregulation in the transportation field, some very large freight forwarders have established their own airlines and truck fleets. These firms—Emery and Federal Express, for example—now essentially are integrated as cargo airlines and trucking companies, but they still provide the traditional freight-forwarding services.

The main function of freight forwarders is to consolidate l.c.l. shipments, or less-than-truckload shipments, from several shippers into carload and truckload quantities. The freight forwarder's operating margin is generally the spread between c.l. and l.c.l. rates. That is, the shipper pays l.c.l. rates,

## AN ETHICAL DILEMMA?

Because their service is largely undifferentiated, trucking companies seek ways to cut expenses so that their prices will be competitive. Assume you manage a trucking business and your maintenance policies have always been more stringent than needed to meet the safety regulations of the states in which your trucks travel. An employee has proposed a cutback in maintenance to reduce expenses (for example, checking hydraulic brakes less frequently or replacing tires less often). Such inspections and maintenance would be done often enough to meet minimum government safety regulations, but not as frequently as your company has thought necessary to ensure the "roadworthiness" of your trucks. Is this cutback ethical?

and the freight forwarder transports the products at c.l. rates. The freight forwarder also picks up the merchandise at the shipper's place of business and arranges for delivery at the buyer's door. The l.c.l. shipper benefits from the speed and minimum handling associated with c.l. shipments, but pays l.c.l. rates. Also freight forwarders provide the small shipper with traffic management services, such as selecting the best transportation methods and routes.

**THE FUTURE IN PHYSICAL DISTRIBUTION**

Physical distribution management faces tremendous challenges and opportunities in the years ahead. These pressures stem both from within the companies and from external environmental forces.

Within most firms there is a need to coordinate physical distribution activities more effectively so that they function as a system. Essentially, this is a problem in organization. If you ask, "Who is in charge of physical distribution?" all too often the answer is "No one." Instead, managerial responsibility is fragmented among units that may have conflicting goals. There is currently a trend toward the establishment of an individual department responsible for all physical distribution activities. However, in many large firms this physical distribution department is separated from the marketing department. This structure causes problems when a company is trying to formulate marketing strategies.[11]

It is imperative that *top management* view logistics as one of its prime responsibilities. Physical distribution costs are the largest operating cost in many firms. For countless companies effective customer service (which involves physical distribution activities primarily) can mean the difference between a strong and a weak marketing position. If these internal conditions are not sufficient incentive to ensure effective management, then certainly macroenvironmental forces should be.

Federal deregulation of the air, rail, and trucking industries will continue

---

[11] For a report that examines why marketing and physical distribution have been separated and reasons they should be put back together to form a viable basis for business strategies in the 1990s, see Roy Dale Vorhees and John I. Coppett, "Marketing—Logistics Opportunities for the 1990s," *Journal of Business Strategy*, Fall 1986, pp. 33–38. For a report on the evolution of physical distribution organization and the structures most used by today's sophisticated firms, see Donald J. Bowersox and Patricia J. Daugherty, "Emerging Patterns of Logistics Organizations," *Journal of Business Logistics*, vol. 8, no. 1 (1987), pp. 48–60.

to be a major environmental factor affecting physical distribution in the 1990s. In addition, urban population congestion, high energy costs, and the rising concern for our environment all greatly affect physical distribution management. The entire transportation system in the United States is undergoing substantial changes. Mass urban transportation is getting increasing political attention. Air pollution controls, a national highway speed limit, and high fuel costs are altering many traditional patterns in physical distribution. Truly, the 1990s hold formidable challenges for physical distribution executives. But, at the same time, this decade also has opened unlimited opportunities for strategic marketing management.

## SUMMARY

Physical distribution is the flow of products from supply sources to the firm, and from the company to its customers. Executives who manage physical distribution are responsible for developing and operating efficient flow systems. Their goal is to move the right amount of the right products to the right place at the right time. Physical distribution costs are a substantial part of total operating costs in many firms. Moreover, physical distribution is probably the only remaining source of major cost reductions in many companies.

Physical distribution should be treated as a total system of business action. In the past (and even now in many firms), physical distribution activities have been fragmented operationally and organizationally. Applying the systems concept also means applying the total-cost approach—that is, reducing the cost of the entire system, rather than the costs of individual elements in the system. Thus management might decide to pay the high cost of air freight, if it could be more than offset by savings in warehousing and inventory-carrying costs. However, management should strive *not* for the lowest total cost of physical distribution, but for the best balance between level of customer service and total cost. Sometimes a company can improve its market position by providing a higher level of customer service, even though increased physical distribution costs result.

The actual operation of a physical distribution system requires management's attention and decision making in five areas: (1) inventory location and warehousing, (2) materials handling, (3) inventory control, (4) order processing, and (5) transportation. Again, these areas should not be approached as individual activities, but as subsystems within the whole physical distribution system.

## KEY TERMS AND CONCEPTS

Physical distribution 382
Logistics 382
Systems concept of physical distribution 383
Customer service 383
Total-cost concept 385
Optimization 386
Cost-service trade-offs 386
Time utility 388
Place utility 388
Storage 390
Warehousing 390
Centralized inventory 390
Inventory dispersal 390
Distribution center 390

Public warehousing 391
Field warehousing 391
Containerization 392
Inventory-control systems 392
Economic order quantity (EOQ) 393
"Just-in-time" concept 394
Order processing 395
Transportation methods 395
Carload versus less-than-carload freight rates 396
Railroad combined shipment services 396
Railroad in-transit services 396
Freight forwarder 398

## QUESTIONS AND PROBLEMS

1. In certain companies, activities such as processing and shipping orders, maintaining an inventory-control system, and locating inventory stocks throughout the market are treated as separate, fragmented tasks. What administrative and operational problems are likely to occur in this type of arrangement?

2. "The goals of a modern physical distribution system in a firm should be to operate at the lowest possible *total* costs." Do you agree?

3. Name some products for which the cost of physical distribution constitutes at least one-half the total price of the goods at the wholesale level. Can you suggest ways of decreasing the physical distribution cost of these products?

4. Explain how marketing managers can use transportation and warehousing facilities to stabilize prices of their products.

5. "A manufacturer follows an inventory-location strategy of concentration rather than dispersion. This company's inventory size will be smaller, but its transportation and warehousing expenses will be larger than if its inventory were dispersed." Do you agree? Explain.

6. "The use of public warehouse facilities makes it possible for manufacturers to bypass wholesalers in their channels of distribution." Explain.

7. How are transportation decisions related to packaging policies?

8. What major problems might a manufacturing firm encounter if it decides to implement the "just-in-time" concept? What suggestions do you have for overcoming each of these problems?

9. Why are l.c.l. shipments so much slower and more costly than c.l. shipments?

10. Assume that a producer must ship in l.c.l. quantities. However, the competitive price structures for this company's products are such that it cannot afford to pay the high l.c.l. freight rates. What transportation alternatives does this firm have?

11. As traffic manager of a large distribution center for a retail drugstore chain, determine the best transportation method and route for the shipment of each of the following items to your center. The distribution center is located in the city nearest to your campus. In each case your company will pay all freight charges, and, unless specifically noted, time is not important. The distribution center has a rail siding and a loading/unloading dock for trucks.
    a. Disposable diapers from Wisconsin. Total shipment weight is 112,000 pounds.
    b. A replacement memory card for your computer, which is now inoperative. Weight of shipment is 3 pounds, and you need this card in a hurry.
    c. Blank payroll checks for your company. (There is a sufficient number of checks on hand for the next two weekly paydays.) Shipment weight is 100 pounds.
    d. Ice cream from St. Louis. Total shipment weight is 42,000 pounds.
    e. Shampoo in 12-ounce bottles from Georgia. Total shipment weight is 45,000 pounds.

12. Under what conditions is a company likely to select air freight as the main method of transporting its finished products?

13. A manufacturer of precision lenses used in medical and hospital equipment wants to ship a 5-pound box of these lenses from your college town to a laboratory in Stockholm, Sweden. The lab wants delivery in 5 days or less. The manufacturer wants to use a package delivery service but is undecided as to which shipper to choose. For this situation you are asked to report on the types of services provided and prices charged by Federal Express, United Parcel Service, and one other package delivery firm.

An ad does not have to be complicated to be informative.

A direct brand comparison is one of the strongest forms of persuasive advertising.

## Purposes of Promotion

Promotion—informing, persuading, and reminding—is essential for several reasons. Distribution channels are often long, and so a product may pass through many hands between a producer and consumers. Therefore, a producer must *inform* middlemen as well as the ultimate consumer or business users about the product. Wholesalers, in turn, must promote the product to retailers, and retailers must communicate with consumers. As the number of potential customers grows and the geographic dimensions of a market expand, the problems of market communication increase. The most useful product will be a failure if no one knows it is available! Thus, a major purpose of promotion is to disseminate information—to let potential customers know.

Another function of promotion is *persuasion*. The intense competition among different industries, as well as among different firms in the same industry, puts tremendous pressure on the promotional programs of sellers. In our economy of abundance, even a product designed to satisfy a basic physiological need requires strong persuasive promotion since consumers have many brands to choose from. For a want-satisfying or luxury product, for which demand depends on a seller's ability to convince consumers that the product's benefits exceed those of other luxuries, persuasion is even more important.

Consumers also must be *reminded* about a product's availability and satisfaction potential. Sellers bombard the marketplace with thousands of messages every day in the hope of attracting new consumers and establishing

Notice the gentle message in this reminder ad. No immediate action is sought by Levi Strauss.

markets for new products. Given the intense competition for consumers' attention, even an established firm must constantly remind people about its products in order to retain a place in their minds. Much promotion, therefore, is intended simply to offset competitors' marketing activity by keeping the firm's products in front of the market.

**Promotion and Strategic Marketing Planning**

In line with the strategic approach to marketing planning, a company should treat personal selling, advertising, and other promotional activities as a coordinated effort within the total marketing program. These activities are fragmented in many firms, with potentially damaging consequences. For example, advertising managers and sales force managers may come into conflict over resources.

To be effective, promotional activities also must be coordinated with product planning, pricing, and distribution. Promotion is influenced, for instance, by the uniqueness of a product and whether a price is above or below the competition. A manufacturer or middleman must also consider its promotional interdependency with other firms in the distribution channel. For example, when developing a retail store display, a manufacturer must take into account the space constraints of the store, the availability of store personnel to assemble the display, and the presence of adequate inventory at the retail level.

Promotion should also strongly reflect a firm's strategic marketing plan.

Retail displays must get consumers' attention without disrupting the store's operation.

Suppose a company faces production limitations imposed by material shortages. This firm's marketing goal is simply to hold on to its present customers and market share. Its strategic marketing planning and promotional program will be geared toward attaining that objective. The promotional activities will be quite different from those of a company with bright prospects for market expansion brought about by new technology.

### AN INTERNATIONAL PERSPECTIVE: Will sports open the door to worldwide promotions?

Selling sports around the world is not a new idea. International tennis and golf events have generated large audiences for years. More recently Major League Baseball and the National Football League have sponsored games and TV broadcasts abroad, and they have only begun to tap their potential. The National Basketball Association (NBA) has been the most successful American sports "export," with television contracts in over 70 countries.

The most recent U.S. entrant into the international sports market is auto racing. CART (Championship Auto Racing Teams, Inc.) is negotiating with foreign cities to hold races that would carry international TV rights. This sports flow is not just one way. The World Cup of soccer, the most closely watched of all sporting events, will be held in 12 sites across the United States in 1994.

What has international sports to do with promotion? Sports events need sponsors. For example, the 1994 World Cup has signed Adidas, Procter & Gamble, and Anheuser-Busch. Television coverage provides worldwide advertising possibilities for multinational firms. In addition, sports offers opportunities for sales promotion contests that will reach large audiences, signs and displays at events, and promotional appearances by star athletes. In short, sports are ideal vehicles for many types of promotion and now they provide worldwide potential.

In the past, European governments tightly controlled major international sports events, using them to build tourism and boost nationalism. However, the privatization of much of European television and an increasing number of satellite and cable channels have created a demand for much more sports broadcasting and new promotional outlets. For instance, MasterCard International reaches consumers in Russia as a sponsor of the National Basketball Association.

What lies ahead? By the year 2000, multinational corporations will be using sports to promote worldwide, and global sports ad revenue will reach $50 billion.

Source: Bruce W. Fraser, "American Teams Play for Dollars—and McDonald's—in Rome," *Adweek's Marketing Week,* Sept. 18, 1989, p. 77.

## THE COMMUNICATION PROCESS

As noted earlier, promotion is an exercise in communication. **Communication** is the verbal and/or nonverbal transmission of information between a sender and a receiver. A conversation, an ad, and even a shrug are examples of communication.

Fundamentally, the communication process requires only four elements—a *message,* a *source* of the message, a *communication channel,* and a *receiver.* In practice, however, important additional components come into play. The information that the sending source wants to share must first be *encoded* into a transmittable form. In marketing this means changing an idea into words, pictures, or both. Once the message has been transmitted through some communication channel, the symbols must be given meaning, or *decoded,* by the receiver. If the message has been transmitted successfully, there is some change in the receiver's knowledge, beliefs, or feelings. As a result of this change the receiver *responds* in some way. The final element in the process, *feedback,* tells the sender whether the message was received and how it was perceived by the recipient. Through feedback the sender learns how to improve communication. All stages of the process can be affected by *noise*—that is, any external factor that interferes with successful communication.

Figure 16-3 illustrates these elements of a general communication process, using as examples typical promotion activities. The information source may be a marketing executive with a sales idea or proposition to communicate. After being encoded into a transmittable message, such as an ad, a display, or a sales presentation, the idea is carried by a sales force or by advertising media (the communication channel) to the receivers—perhaps different target markets. These receivers decode the message in light of their frames of reference, experiences, and memories of similar messages. The message

**FIGURE 16-3** The communication process in promotional programs.

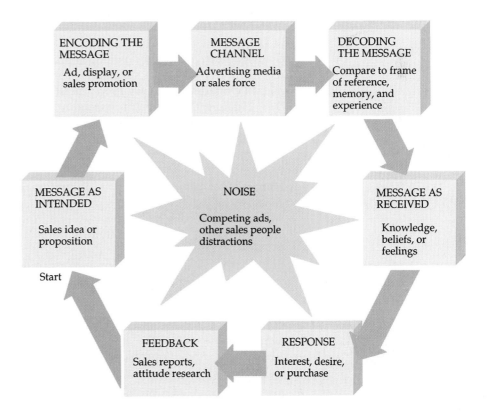

---

**Doublespeak—the art of noncommunication**

Doublespeak is language that seems to communicate information but really does not because the communicator is attempting to make things look different than they are. Examples of doublespeak from a variety of sources, including advertising, corporate annual reports, research studies, medical files, and military manuals, are:

| What Was Said | What Was Meant |
| --- | --- |
| Genuine imitation leather | Plastic |
| Faux diamonds | Pieces of glass |
| Negative deficit | Profit |
| Price enhancement | Price increase |
| Period of accelerated negative growth | Recession |
| Assigned for derecruitment | Fired |
| Energetic disassembly | Nuclear power plant explosion |
| Therapeutic misadventure resulting in a terminal episode | Death by medical malpractice |
| Career associate scanning professionals | Grocery check-out clerks |
| Social expression products | Greeting cards |
| Frame-supported tension structure | Marine Corps tent |
| Tactical redeployment | Retreat |
| Controlled flight into terrain | Plane crash |
| Television with nonmulticolor capability | Black-and-white TV |

Sources: William D. Lutz, "Corporate Doublespeak: Making Bad News Look Good," *Business and Society Review*, Winter 1983, pp. 19–22; Michael Satchell, "Could You, er, Say that Again?" *U.S. News and World Report*, April 20, 1987, p. 71; Bruce Hilton, "Doublespeak Again Comes to the Rescue," *Chicago Tribune*, Dec. 10, 1989, pp. 5–14.

---

changes the recipients' knowledge, beliefs, or feelings in some way and the recipients respond. In a successful marketing communication, the response might be interest in the product, a desire for it, or possibly the purchase of it. By evaluating the receivers' words or actions, often through marketing research, the sender gets feedback on the effectiveness of the communication. At various stages in the process the message is subject to interference or noise from competitors' messages, errors in transmission, or other distractions.

## DETERMINING THE PROMOTIONAL MIX

Management has to design the **promotional mix**—the combination of personal selling, advertising, sales promotion, publicity, and public relations that will make the most effective promotional program for a firm. This is a difficult task requiring a number of strategic decisions.

### Factors Influencing the Promotional Mix

Four factors should be taken into account when determining the promotional mix. They are (1) the nature of the market, (2) the nature of the product, and (3) the stage of the product's life cycle, and (4) the amount of money available for promotion.

#### NATURE OF THE MARKET

As is true in most areas of marketing, decisions on the promotional mix will be greatly influenced by the nature of the market. At least three variables affect the choice of a promotional method for a particular market:

- *Geographic scope of the market.* Personal selling may be adequate in a small local market, but as the market broadens geographically, greater emphasis must be placed on advertising. The exception would be a firm that sells nationally, but finds its customers concentrated in relatively few areas. For example, the market for certain plastics is heavily concentrated in Ohio and Michigan because these plastics are used by component suppliers to the auto industry. In this case emphasis on personal selling may be feasible.
- *Type of customer.* Promotional strategy depends in part on what level of the distribution channel the organization hopes to influence. Final consumers and middlemen alike may buy a product, but they require different promotion. To illustrate, a promotional program aimed at retailers will probably include more personal selling than a program designed to attract final consumers. In many situations middlemen may strongly affect a manufacturer's promotional strategy. Large retail chains may refuse to stock a product unless the manufacturer agrees to do a certain amount of advertising.

  Another consideration is the variety of final customers for a product. A market with only one type of customer will call for a different promotional mix than a market with many customer groups. A firm selling large power saws used exclusively by lumber manufacturers may have to rely only on personal selling. In contrast, a company selling portable hand saws to consumers and to construction firms will probably include a liberal portion of advertising in its mix. Personal selling would be prohibitively expensive in reaching the firm's many customers.
- *Concentration of the market.* The total number of prospective buyers is another consideration. The fewer potential buyers there are, the more effective personal selling is, compared with advertising.

### NATURE OF THE PRODUCT

Several product attributes influence promotional strategy. The most important are:

- *Unit value.* A product with low unit value is usually relatively uncomplicated, involves little risks for the buyer, and must appeal to a mass market to survive. Advertising would be the appropriate promotional tool. In contrast, high-unit-value products often are complex and expensive. These features suggest the need for personal selling.
- *Degree of customization.* If a product must be fitted to the individual custom-

### AN ETHICAL DILEMMA?

In one *Archie* comic book, Kyosho remote-control toys are the focus of an entire story. Kyosho paid the publisher a licensing fee to feature its products. The objective is to present Kyosho toys to potential consumers in a noncommercial setting. There is no indication in the publication that this exposure has been paid for. If you produced comic books, would you consider this kind of licensing agreement ethical?

er's needs, personal selling is necessary. However, the benefits of standardized products can be effectively communicated in advertising.

- *Presale and postsale service.* Products that must be demonstrated, for which there are trade-ins, or that require frequent servicing to keep them in good working order lend themselves to personal selling.

Beyond these conditions, certain products are simply more "advertisable" than others. Many years ago, advertising authority Neil Borden identified five product criteria that suggest when advertising might be most effective. If all these criteria are met, there is an excellent opportunity to advertise. When a product meets some, but not all, of these conditions, advertising may be less effective. The five criteria are as follows:

- The primary demand trend for the product should be favorable. In spite of public opinion to the contrary, advertising cannot successfully sell a product that people do not want. Nor can advertising reverse declining primary demand.
- There should be considerable opportunity to differentiate the product. Then it is easier to advertise because the company has something to say. For this reason automobiles or cosmetics are easier to advertise than salt or sugar. Products that are not easy to differentiate by *brand* may still be advertised by a trade association, such as the Beef Industry Council or the Pineapple Growers Association.
- The product should have hidden qualities. This condition affords the seller grounds for educating the market through advertising. For instance, a reclining chair or a television set is simpler to advertise than greeting cards.
- Powerful emotional buying motives should exist for the product. Buying action can be stimulated by appeal to these motives. It is easier to build an effective advertising campaign for Weight Watchers than for clotheslines or hammers.
- The company must have sufficient funds to support an advertising program adequately.

A summary of how the major financial, market, and product factors affect the decision to emphasize advertising or personal selling is shown in Figure 16-4.

**FIGURE 16-4 Financial, market, and product factors that affect the promotional mix.**

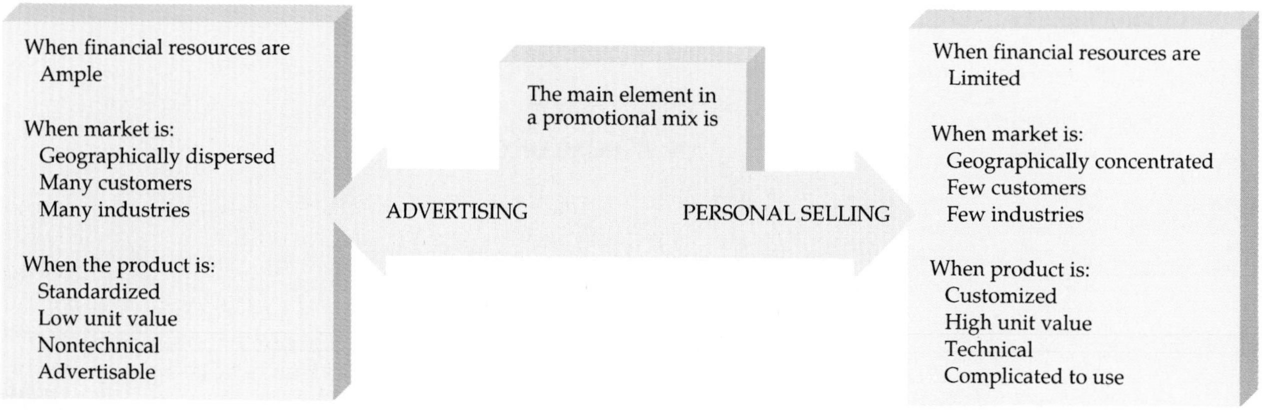

| When financial resources are Ample | The main element in a promotional mix is | When financial resources are Limited |
|---|---|---|
| When market is: Geographically dispersed Many customers Many industries | ADVERTISING ⟷ PERSONAL SELLING | When market is: Geographically concentrated Few customers Few industries |
| When the product is: Standardized Low unit value Nontechnical Advertisable | | When product is: Customized High unit value Technical Complicated to use |

| Market situation | Promotional strategy |
|---|---|
| **TABLE 16-1 Promotional strategies for different product life-cycle stages** | |
| **Introductory stage** | |
| Customers do not realize that they want the product, nor do they understand how it will benefit them. | Inform and educate potential customers. Tell them that the product exists, how it might be used, and what want-satisfying benefits it provides.<br><br>In this stage, a seller must stimulate *primary demand*—the demand for a type of product—as contrasted with *selective demand*—the demand for a particular brand. For example, producers had to sell consumers on the value of compact discs in general before it was feasible to promote a particular brand.<br><br>Normally, heavy emphasis must be placed on personal selling. Trade shows are also used extensively in the promotional mix. Rather than calling on customers individually, the company can promote its new product at a trade show where prospective customers come to the seller's exhibit. Manufacturers also rely heavily on personal selling to attract middlemen to handle a new product. |
| **Growth stage** | |
| Customers are aware of product benefits. The product is selling well and middlemen want to handle it. | Stimulate selective (brand) demand. Increase emphasis on advertising. Middlemen share more of the total promotional burden. |
| **Maturity stage** | |
| Competition intensifies and sales level off. | Advertising is used as a tool to persuade rather than only to provide information. Intense competition forces sellers to devote larger sums to advertising and thus contributes to the declining profits experienced in this stage. |
| **Sales-decline stage** | |
| Sales and profits are declining. New and better products are coming into the market. | All promotional efforts should be cut back substantially, except when attempting to revitalize the product. |

## STAGE OF THE PRODUCT LIFE CYCLE

Promotion strategies are influenced by the life-cycle stage a product is in at a given time. When a new product is introduced prospects must be informed about its existence and its benefits. Also, middlemen must be convinced to carry it. Thus both advertising (to consumers) and personal selling (to middlemen) are critical in a product's introductory stage. At this time, a product also may be something of a novelty, and excellent opportunities exist for publicity. Later in a successful product's life, as competition intensifies, more emphasis is placed on persuasive advertising. Table 16-1 shows how promotional strategies change as a product moves through its life cycle.

### FUNDS AVAILABLE

Regardless of what may be the most desirable promotional mix, the amount of money available for promotion is the ultimate determinant of the mix. A business with ample funds can make more effective use of advertising than an enterprise with limited financial resources. Small or financially weak companies are likely to rely on personal selling, dealer displays, or joint manufacturer-retailer advertising. Lack of money may even force a company to use a less efficient promotional method. For example, advertising can carry a promotional message to far more people and at a lower cost *per person* than can a sales force. Yet the firm may have to rely on personal selling because it lacks the funds to take advantage of advertising's efficiency.

## The Choice of a Push or Pull Strategy

As we have seen, in designing the promotional mix producers aim their efforts at both middlemen and end users. Promotion aimed at middlemen is called a **push strategy** and promotion directed at end users is called a **pull strategy.** Figure 16-5 contrasts these two strategies.

Using a push strategy means a producer directs promotion primarily at the middlemen that are the next link forward in the producer's distribution channel. The product is "pushed" through the channel. Take the case of a lawn fertilizer producer that sells some of its products in bags through wholesalers and retailers to household consumers. This producer will promote heavily to wholesalers, which then also use a push strategy to retailers. In turn, the retailers promote to consumers. A push strategy usually involves a lot of personal selling and sales promotion, including contests for sales people and displays at trade shows. This promotional strategy is appropriate for many

**FIGURE 16-5** Push and pull promotional strategies.

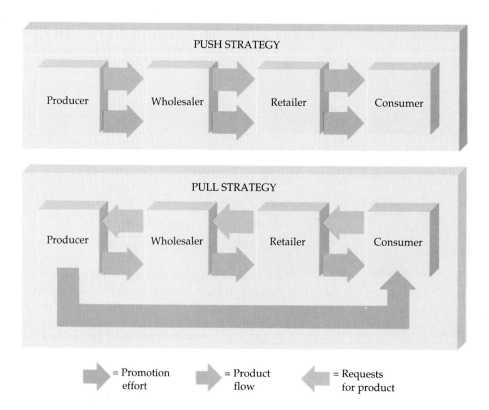

The auto industry uses a combination of push and pull strategies. Which is depicted in this photo?

manufacturers of business products, as well as for various consumer goods.

With a pull strategy, a producer aims promotion at end users—usually ultimate consumers. The intention is to motivate people to ask retailers for the product. The retailers, in turn, will request the product from wholesalers, and wholesalers will order it from the producer. In effect, promotion to consumers is designed to "pull" the product through the channel. This strategy typically calls for heavy use of advertising and possibly various forms of sales promotion such as premiums, samples, or in-store demonstrations. Manufacturers of consumer packaged goods often use a pull strategy to get products stocked on supermarket shelves.[2]

## DETERMINING THE PROMOTIONAL BUDGET

It is extremely challenging to establish promotional budgets. Management lacks reliable standards for determining (1) how much to spend altogether on advertising or personal selling and (2) how much to spend on specific activities within each area. A serious problem is that management normally cannot assess the results of promotional expenditures. A firm may decide to add 10 sales people or increase its trade show budget by $200,000 a year, but it cannot determine precisely what increase in sales or profits to expect from these moves. Nor can anyone measure with a high degree of certainty the relative values of the two expenditures.

Promotional activities generally are budgeted as current operating expenses, implying that their benefits are used up immediately. Through the years, however, several economists and executives have proposed treating advertising (and presumably other promotional efforts) as a capital investment. Their reasoning is that the benefits and returns on these investments often are not immediately evident and are spread over several years.

There are four methods of determining the budget for promotion. These are frequently discussed in connection with the advertising budget alone, but they may also be applied to the total promotional budget.

### Percentage of Sales

The promotional budget may be related in some way to company income. The expenditures may be set as a percentage of past or anticipated sales. How-

---

[2] The move from pull to push strategies is discussed in Alvin A. Achenbaum and F. Kent Mitchel, "Pulling Away from Push Marketing," *Harvard Business Review*, May–June 1987, pp. 38–40.

ever, some businesses prefer to budget a fixed amount of money per *unit* of past or expected future sales. Manufacturers of products with a high unit value and a low rate of turnover (automobiles or appliances, for example) frequently use the unit method.

This *percentage-of-sales method* is probably the most widely used of all those discussed here. It has achieved broad acceptance because it is simple to calculate. Moreover, it sets the cost in relation to sales income and thus has the effect of being a variable rather than a fixed expense.

Actually, this method is unsound and illogical if promotional expenditures are based on past sales. Management is saying that promotion is a *result* of sales when, in fact, it is a *cause* of sales. Another undesirable result of using a percentage of past sales method is that it reduces promotional expenditures when sales are declining. And this is just when promotion usually is most needed.

## Use of All Available Funds

A new company frequently plows all available funds into its promotional program. The objective here is to build sales for the first 1 to 5 years. After that period management expects to earn a profit and will budget for promotion in a different manner.

## Follow Competition

A weak method of determining the promotional budget, but one that is used occasionally, is to match the promotional expenditures of competitors. Sometimes only one competitor is followed. In other cases, if management has access to industry averages through a trade association, these become company benchmarks. There are at least two problems with this approach. First, a firm's competitors may be just as much in the dark regarding how to set a promotional budget. Second, one company's promotional goals and strategies may be quite different from those of its competitors because of differences in strategic marketing planning.

## Task or Objective

The soundest basis for establishing the promotional budget is to decide what tasks or objectives the promotional program must accomplish and then determine what they will cost. Various forms of this method are widely used today. The *task method* forces management to realistically define the goals of its promotional program.

Sometimes this approach is called the *buildup method* because of the way it operates. For example, a company may elect to enter a new geographic market. Management decides that this venture will require 10 additional sales people. Compensation and expenses of these people will cost a total of $520,000 per year. Salary for an additional sales supervisor and expenses for an extra office and administrative needs will cost $70,000. Thus in the personal selling part of the promotional mix, an extra $590,000 must be budgeted. Similar estimates can be made for the anticipated cost of advertising, sales promotion, and other promotional tools. The promotional budget is *built up* by adding up the costs of the individual promotional tasks needed to reach the goal of entering a new territory.

## THE CAMPAIGN CONCEPT

In planning the total promotional program for an organization, management should think in terms of the campaign concept. A **campaign** is a coordinated series of promotional efforts built around a single theme and designed to reach a predetermined goal. In effect a campaign is an exercise in strategic planning.

Although the term *campaign* is probably thought of most often in connection with advertising, we should apply the campaign concept first to the entire promotional program. Then the total promotional campaign can be subdivided into its advertising, personal selling, and sales promotion components. These subcampaigns can be planned in more detail, to work toward the program goal.

Many types of promotional campaigns may be conducted by a company, and some may run concurrently. Depending on available funds and objectives, a firm may have a local, regional, national, or international campaign. One campaign may be aimed at consumers, another at wholesalers and retailers. The stage of a product's life cycle may determine whether a primary or a selective demand campaign will be conducted.

A firm should first establish the goal(s) of the promotional campaign. This goal, and the buying motives of customers, will determine the selling appeals to be stressed. Assume that the goal of an airline's promotional campaign is to introduce its new jumbo jet service. The appeals might be to the customers' desire for speed, a quiet and restful trip, or fine food and courteous service. If the same airline wanted to increase its plane loadings of air freight, then the ads and personal selling might emphasize speed of delivery, reduction in losses due to spoilage and handling, or convenient schedules.

A campaign revolves around a central idea or focal point. This "theme" permeates all promotional efforts and helps to unify the campaign. A **theme** is simply the promotional appeals dressed up in a distinctive, attention-getting form. It expresses the product's benefits. Frequently the theme takes the form of a slogan. (Recall the quiz at the beginning of the chapter.) Some companies use the same theme for several campaigns; others develop a different theme for each new campaign.

This campaign included sales promotion (the coupon) along with print and TV ads. Can you recall the television ads?

For a promotional campaign to be successful, the efforts of participating groups must be carefully coordinated. This means that:

- The *advertising program* will consist of a series of related, well-timed, carefully placed ads that reinforce personal selling and sales promotional efforts.
- The *personal selling effort* will be coordinated with the advertising program. The sales force will explain and demonstrate the product benefits stressed in the ads. The sales people will also be fully informed about the advertising part of the campaign—the theme, media used, and schedule for the appearance of ads. The sales people, in turn, should carry this information to middlemen so that they take part in the campaign.
- The *sales promotional devices,* such as point-of-purchase display materials, will be coordinated with other aspects of the campaign. For each campaign new display materials must be prepared. They should reflect the ads and appeals used in the current campaign to maximize the campaign's impact at the point of sale.
- *Physical distribution management* will ensure that adequate stocks of the product are available in all outlets prior to the start of the campaign.

## REGULATION OF PROMOTIONAL ACTIVITIES

Because the primary objective of promotion is to sell something by communicating with a market, promotional activities attract attention. Consequently abuses by individual firms are easily and quickly noted by the public. This situation soon leads to (1) public demand for correction of the abuses, (2) pressure for assurances that they will not be repeated, and (3) restraints on promotional activities. Regulations have been established by the federal government and most state governments in response to public demand. In addition many individual business firms have established voluntary guidelines for their promotional activities. The advertising industry itself, through the American Association of Advertising Agencies and the National Advertising Review Board, does a considerable amount of self-regulation.

### Federal Regulation

Federal regulation of promotional activities is authorized by two major pieces of legislation: the Federal Trade Commission Act and the Robinson-Patman Act. Both laws are administered by the Federal Trade Commission (FTC).

The measure that has the broadest influence on promotional messages in interstate commerce is the Federal Trade Commission Act. The act prohibits unfair methods of competition. And, according to FTC and federal court decisions, clearly one area of unfair competition is false, misleading, or deceptive advertising.

Loopholes in the Federal Trade Commission Act led to the enactment of

Do you think this legally required message influences behavior?

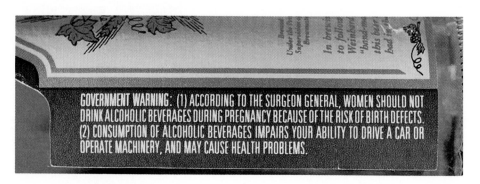

GOVERNMENT WARNING: (1) ACCORDING TO THE SURGEON GENERAL, WOMEN SHOULD NOT DRINK ALCOHOLIC BEVERAGES DURING PREGNANCY BECAUSE OF THE RISK OF BIRTH DEFECTS. (2) CONSUMPTION OF ALCOHOLIC BEVERAGES IMPAIRS YOUR ABILITY TO DRIVE A CAR OR OPERATE MACHINERY, AND MAY CAUSE HEALTH PROBLEMS.

the Wheeler-Lea Amendment in 1938. The amendment considerably strengthened the original act by specifying that an unfair competitive act violates the law if it injures the *public,* regardless of the effect this practice may have on a *competitor.* Under the original Federal Trade Commission Act, false or misleading advertising had to injure a competitor before a violation could be charged.

In the 1980s the FTC was less aggressive than in the 1970s in policing the advertising business. Nevertheless the FTC has plenty of "clout"— particularly in cases of possibly false or deceptive advertising. For example, the commission may require a company to submit test results or other research to substantiate product claims made in advertising. Furthermore, this supporting information may later be made public even if it may embarrass the company. By issuing a *cease-and-desist order,* the FTC may also compel a firm to remove from circulation advertising deemed deceptive. Although these orders may be appealed to the FTC and fought in federal court, they have been effective enforcement tools.

Another enforcement device available to the FTC is the authority to order *corrective advertising.* Cease-and-desist orders force a firm to stop running a deceptive ad, but they do not rectify the incorrect impressions already made by the ad. Corrective advertising, paid for by the offending firm and presented according to a schedule approved by the FTC, is intended to correct misinformation resulting from the allegedly false ads. Among the products for which corrective ads have been run are Hawaiian Punch, Profile Bread, STP, Listerine, and Ocean Spray cranberry juice. Because corrective ads proved to be only marginally successful in eliminating false impressions, their use has been curtailed.[3]

The Robinson-Patman Act, which outlaws price discrimination, has two sections relating to promotional allowances. (See Chapter 11 for a discussion of the provisions of the Robinson-Patman Act.) These sections state that a seller must offer promotional services and facilities, or payments for them, on a proportionally equal basis to all competing customers. Thus, if a manufacturer wants to furnish demonstrators, cooperative advertising programs, or any other type of promotional assistance, it must make them available proportionally to all firms competing in the resale of the product. *Proportionally equal basis* has sometimes been hard to define. Generally the courts have accepted the "amount purchased" as a basis for allocation. Say store A buys $150,000 worth of merchandise per year from a manufacturer and store B purchases $50,000 worth. Then store A may be offered promotional allowances valued at three times those offered to store B.

**State and Local Regulation**

At the state and local levels two types of legislation regulate promotional activities. The first of these is patterned after the model statute developed by *Printers' Ink* magazine in 1911 to establish "truth in advertising" in *intrastate* commerce. Today almost all states have a *Printers' Ink* statute or one quite similar to it. Several states have established a separate state agency to handle consumer protection.

A general type of local legislation that affects personal selling is the so-called "Green River" ordinance (so-named because Green River, Wyoming,

---

[3] For a comprehensive analysis of corrective advertising, including the historical background, the key legal concepts involved, and the pertinent managerial issues, see William L. Wilkie, Dennis L. McNeill, and Michael B. Mazis, "Marketing's 'Scarlet Letter': The Theory and Practice of Corrective Advertising," *Journal of Marketing,* Spring 1984, pp. 11–31.

was one of the first towns to enact such a law). Green River ordinances restrict sales people who represent firms located outside the affected city and who sell door to door or call on business establishments. Supposedly passed to protect local citizens from fraudulent operators, the measures also serve to insulate local businesses from outside competition.

## Regulation by Private Organizations

Numerous private organizations exert considerable control over the promotional practices of business. Many magazines, newspapers, and radio and television stations refuse to accept advertisements they feel are false, misleading, or in bad taste. For example, in 1990 the makers of Folger's coffee complained to the television networks that comparative claims made in Maxwell House coffee ads were unfair. According to Folger's, the comparison involved taste tests of a current blend of Maxwell House against an old, discontinued blend of Folger's. In another instance, Ford registered a complaint with the networks about Chevrolet pickup truck ads containing claims about truck sales in Ford County, Illinois. In cases such as these, the networks review the charges and the ads, and refuse to broadcast ads they feel are inappropriate. Some trade associations have established codes of ethics that include standards for sales force behavior and advertising activity. And Better Business Bureaus located in major cities all over the country are working to control false or misleading promotion.

## SUMMARY

Promotion is the fourth component of a company's total marketing mix. Its purpose is to inform, persuade, and remind. It is a basic ingredient of non-price competition and an essential element of modern marketing. The three primary methods of promotion are personal selling, advertising, and sales promotion. Other forms include publicity and public relations.

Promotional activity is essentially an exercise in communication. Fundamentally the communication process consists of a source sending a message through a channel to a receiver. The success of communication depends on the encoding and decoding of the message and the noise that may interfere with transmission. Feedback is a measure of how effective a communication has been.

Promotion must be integrated into a firm's strategic planning because all elements of the marketing mix—product, price, distribution, and promotion—must be coordinated in order to be effective. When deciding on the appropriate promotional mix (the combination of advertising, personal selling, and other promotional tools), management should consider four factors: (1) nature of the market, (2) nature of the product, (3) stage of the product's life cycle, and (4) money available. A push strategy involves concentrating promotional effort on the next link forward in the distribution channel. The alternative is a pull strategy, in which promotion is focused on the final buyer.

It is difficult to set a dollar figure for the total promotional budget. The most commonly used method is to set the budget as a percentage of sales, but a better approach is to establish the promotional goals and then figure out how much it will cost to achieve them. The promotional efforts of the firm should be coordinated in a campaign built around a single theme and designed to reach a predetermined goal.

In response to criticism, the federal government passed legislation regulating promotion. The main federal laws are the Federal Trade Commission Act, its Wheeler-Lea Amendment, and the Robinson-Patman Act. The FTC administers this legislation. Promotional practices also are regulated by state and local legislation, by private organizations, and by the industry itself.

**KEY TERMS AND CONCEPTS**

Promotion 410
Promotional mix 410
Personal selling 410
Advertising 410
Sales promotion 410
Publicity 410
Public relations 410
Promotion and demand elasticity 411
Communication process 415
Encoding 415
Decoding 415
Feedback 415

Noise 415
Primary demand 419
Selective demand 419
Push strategy 420
Pull strategy 420
Promotional budgeting methods 421
Campaign 422
Campaign theme 423
Federal Trade Commission Act 424
Wheeler-Lea Amendment 425
Cease-and-desist orders 425
Corrective advertising 425
Robinson-Patman Act 425

## QUESTIONS AND PROBLEMS

1. For each of the following promotional objectives, find one example of a print ad:
   a. Primarily designed to inform.
   b. Primarily designed to persuade.
   c. Primarily designed to remind.
2. Describe and explain a communication process in the following situations:
   a. A college student trying to convince her father to buy her a used car.
   b. A sales person trying to sell a car to a college student.
3. Explain how the nature of the market affects the promotional mix for the following products:
   a. Contact lenses.    d. Take-out fried chicken.
   b. Golf balls.    e. Compact discs.
   c. Plywood.    f. Mainframe computers.
4. Describe how classifying consumer goods as convenience, shopping, or specialty goods helps determine the best promotional mix.
5. Using the criteria for advertisability, evaluate each of the following products. Assume sufficient funds are available.
   a. Automobile tires.
   b. Revlon cosmetics.
   c. Light bulbs.
   d. 10-minute automobile oil changes.
   e. College education.
   f. Luggage.
6. Explain why personal selling is or is not likely to be the main ingredient in the promotional mix for each of the following products:
   a. Checking accounts.
   b. Home swimming pools.

   c. Liquid laundry detergent.
   d. Large order of McDonald's french fries.
7. Explain why retailer promotional efforts should or should not be stressed in the promotional mix for the following:
   a. Levi's 501 Jeans.
   b. Sunkist oranges.
   c. Women's cosmetics.
   d. Bank credit card.
8. Why is the percentage-of-sales method so widely used to determine promotional budgets when, in fact, most authorities recognize the task or objective method as more desirable?
9. Identify the central idea—the theme—in three current promotional campaigns.
10. Assume you are marketing a liquid that removes creosote (and the danger of fire) from chimneys used for wood-burning stoves. Briefly describe the roles you would assign to advertising, personal selling, sales promotion, and publicity in your promotional campaign.
11. Explain the term *proportionally equal basis* in connection with manufacturers' granting promotional allowances. Consider especially the situations where retailers vary in size.
12. Do you think we need additional legislation to regulate advertising? To regulate personal selling? If so, explain what you would recommend.
13. Sports are increasingly being seen as a vehicle for international promotion by multinational corporations. What issues related to the *other* marketing mix elements must be resolved before the full potential of this opportunity can be realized?

# CHAPTER 17

# MANAGEMENT OF PERSONAL SELLING

Today's top young sales people are a diverse group, but they do have some things in common. They are trained professionals who see sales experience as an important part of a total business career. Let's meet some sales people, aged 25 to 30, and find out what else they think about selling:

- Catherine Hogan is an account manager for Bell Atlantic Network Services, Inc. When she graduated from Fisk University, technical sales was not in her career plans. Now she is involved in cooperative selling, teaming up with Bell account executives to bring long distance voice or data service to customers. Hogan, a black woman, has succeeded in an environment dominated by white, middle-aged males. She says, "Minorities shouldn't overlook sales. You can adapt to your environment and make decisions that let you comfortably maintain your sense of self."
- Mark DeAngelis, an industrial distribution graduate of Clarkson University, is a sales engineer with General Electric. He feels that the way to learn a business is to be in front of the customer. "He'll [the customer] tell you exactly what he likes or doesn't like about your product." He also finds sales a good way to learn about his own company. In the course of a sales project, DeAngelis talks to marketing, manufacturing, and engineering personnel at any of five GE plants. Viewing selling in

a professional manner, he says, "This is not a back-slapping sort of business. Actually, selling is more of a service than it is 'selling.'"
- Kathy Serfilippi has an A.S. degree and is a sales representative for corporate sales at American Airlines. It is her job to build relationships with travel agents and corporate travel managers. She says, "When you come down to it, I guess I'm a people person." But liking people isn't enough. Persistence is the name of the game in her business. Serfilippi says you have to ask for the business and not be afraid to go back and ask again if you're turned down. To keep up her selling skills, she attends at least 10 training seminars a year.
- Jacques Murphy majored in marketing at the University of Colorado and is now a group vice president responsible for five divisions at The Gallup Organization, Inc. In addition to being a manager, Murphy sells marketing research services to banks, savings and loans, and credit unions. He recognizes that selling is more than just making a transaction. "When we win a contract at Gallup, that's when the selling really starts. We're constantly reinforcing the buying decision by keeping ahead on deadlines and showing how the research is useful to the buyer."[1]

[1] Martin Everett, "Selling's New Breed: Smart and Feisty," *Sales & Marketing Management*, October 1989, pp. 52–64.

Selling is essential to the well-being of our economic system, and it probably offers more job opportunities than any other single vocation. Over 13 million people in the United States are employed in sales, 6 million of them in retail organizations. In contrast, only about 500,000 people work in advertising. Personal selling is not easy, nor is it something everyone is capable of doing. Yet, as the comments above indicate, it can be an exciting and challenging occupation.

## THE NATURE OF PERSONAL SELLING

The goal of all marketing efforts is to achieve the organization's performance objectives by offering want-satisfaction to the market over the long run. **Personal selling,** the personal communication of information to persuade a prospective customer to buy a good, service, or idea, is the major promotional tool used to reach this goal. How well an organization manages its sales force often has a direct bearing on the success of its entire marketing program.

The efforts of sales people go far beyond simply making transactions. They also include:

- Explaining product benefits.
- Demonstrating the proper operation of products.
- Answering questions and responding to objections.
- Organizing and implementing point-of-purchase promotions.
- Arranging the terms of a sale.
- Following up the sale to ensure that the buyer is satisfied.
- Collecting market and competitive information to improve marketing strategy.

### Advantages and Disadvantages of Personal Selling

Compared to the impersonal promotional tools—advertising, sales promotion, publicity, and public relations—personal selling has the advantage of greater *flexibility*. Sales people can tailor sales presentations to fit the needs and behaviors of individual customers. Also, sales people can see the prospect's immediate reaction to a sales approach and make adjustments on the spot. For example, if a prospective customer appears skeptical about a particular point or shows a special interest in one product feature, the sales person can alter the presentation accordingly.

A second merit of personal selling is that it usually can be *focused* on prospective customers, thus minimizing wasted effort. By contrast, in most forms of advertising, much of the cost is devoted to sending the message to people who are not real prospects.

In most instances a third benefit of personal selling is that it *results in the actual sale*. Other forms of promotion have as their objective moving the prospect closer to the sale. Advertisements, for example, can attract attention, provide information, and even stimulate desire, but seldom do they actually cause the prospective customer to complete the transaction.

The major limitation of personal selling is its *high cost*. Using a sales force does minimize wasted effort because sales people can concentrate on legitimate prospects. However, the costs of operating a sales force are high. The average cost of a sales call in business-to-business selling, including salary, benefits, commissions, travel expenses, and sales promotion materials, is $240.[2] Excluded from this calculation are costs such as training, support staff, and supervision.

[2] "What Is the Average Cost of a Personal Sales Call?" Carr Report No. 541.1F, Cahners Publishing Co., July 1989.

Telemarketing provides inexpensive access to customers, but its success depends on the skill, training, and supervision of the callers.

One alternative to the high cost of face-to-face personal selling is **telemarketing.** Instead of the traditional sales call, a growing number of firms are using telephones or computers to talk with customers. Particularly appropriate for straight rebuy situations as well as accounts for which orders are too small to justify a personal visit, telemarketing has expanded to include providing product operating instructions and technical advice. Major U.S. auto manufacturers have progressed to the point where their computers order directly from the computers of suppliers without human intervention.

Another disadvantage of personal selling is that companies often are unable to *attract the caliber of people needed* to do the job well. At the retail level, in particular, many firms have eliminated sales forces and shifted to self-service for this reason.

**Nature of the Sales Job**

It is difficult to generalize about sales jobs because there are so many varieties. However, one trend is the broadening of the sales person's responsibilities. With greater acceptance of the marketing concept by manufacturing firms, for instance, a new type of sales position—the **territory manager**—has been created. A territory is treated as an individual profit center with the territory manager in charge. Rather than just pushing what the factory produces, this new breed of sales person works closely with customers to understand and interpret their wants. The territory manager then either fills these wants with existing products or communicates them to the producer so that adjustments can be made or new products developed. Today's territory manager engages in a total selling job—identifying customer needs, qualifying prospects, developing sales promotions, servicing customers, managing expenses, and collecting market intelligence. The job includes selling to new customers, obtaining reorders from repeat customers, selling new products, helping customers find new uses for existing products, and teaching customers to use products properly.

Due to increased responsibility, the territory manager experiences problems of **role ambiguity** and **role conflict.** Ambiguity is caused by the many different tasks modern sales people are called on to perform. Among other things they persuade prospective customers, negotiate with manufacturing, service accounts, set up displays, expedite orders, coordinate deliveries, gather information, collect past-due accounts, and help solve customers' problems. Frequently sales people must make quick decisions in the field, without all pertinent information and far removed from the advice of superiors at headquarters. The result is ambiguity about how much responsibility to assume and uncertainty about the risks of undesirable outcomes.

Role conflict occurs because several groups often place conflicting demands on the sales person. The marketing concept emphasizes satisfying the customer. But, on occasion, the best interests of the customer are inconsistent with the short-term interests of the sales person's company. As a result, sales people experience conflicts regarding whose position—the firm's or the customer's—they should support. Also, within the company, different departments (credit and production, for example) may view customers' requests from a very different perspective than does the sales person. Another potential source of conflict involves the sales person's family. The demands of sales jobs often include overnight travel, entertaining customers, and doing paperwork at home or in the evening. If the sales person feels that family obligations are at odds with the expectations of the firm, role conflict ensues. Given the nature of the sales job, it is unlikely that such conflicts can ever be completely eliminated. However, many organizations are becoming aware of the emotional stress stemming from these conflicts and try to prepare sales people for them. Some companies even conduct training for spouses so they will better understand the demands of the sales job.

## Distinctive Features of Sales Jobs

Sales jobs have a number of features that distinguish them from most other business positions:

- Sales people represent their organizations to the outside world. Consequently, attitudes about a company and its products often are based on the impressions left by sales people. The public seldom judges a firm by the appearance of its office or the behavior of its production employees.
- Sales people typically operate with little or no direct supervision. Therefore, to be successful, sales people must be creative and persistent, and show great initiative—all of which requires a high degree of motivation.
- Sales people are authorized to spend company funds. To do their jobs, sales people spend money for transportation, food, housing, entertainment, and other expenses. Spending too little can be as counterproductive as spending too much. The secret is to spend profitably.
- Sales people frequently must travel a considerable amount. Many companies have successfully reduced the number of nights sales people must be away from home by redesigning sales territories, better routing their trips, and relying more on telemarketing. However, the fact remains that most sales jobs do require travel.
- Sales people often have profit responsibility. Today's sales people may do much of the strategic planning for their individual territories. In cooperation with sales managers, they decide what target markets they will pursue, how they will deal with each market segment as well as with each individual customer, and which products they will emphasize.

## Wide Variety of Sales Jobs

No two selling jobs are alike. Even when grouped on some basis, the types of jobs and the skills needed to fill them cover a wide spectrum. Consider, for example, the job of a sales person for a Pepsi-Cola bottler who calls routinely on a group of retail stores. That job is totally different from the role of an IBM computer sales person, an Avon representative selling cosmetics door to door, or a Prudential agent selling health and disability insurance to business firms.

A way to understand the broad array of sales jobs is to think of selling as ranging from *order filling* to *order getting* positions. The following are examples of positions along such a continuum:

- Positions in which the job is primarily to deliver a product—for example, a **driver–sales person** for soft drinks, dairy products, bakery items, or fuel oil. Many of these jobs involve merchandising tasks such as arranging displays and setting up point-of-purchase material. Selling responsibilities are secondary to seeing that orders are filled correctly and on time.
- Positions in which the sales person is primarily an **inside order taker**—for example, a retail clerk behind a counter at Sears or a telephone representative at a catalog retailer such as Lands' End or L.L. Bean. Most customers have already decided to buy and the sales person's job is to serve them efficiently. Some selling may be done through suggestions, but ordinarily the sales person cannot do much more.
- Positions in which sales people are mainly **outside order takers,** going to customers in the field—for example, Procter & Gamble sales reps who call on retail stores or radio advertising sales people who sell time on their stations to local businesses. The majority of sales are of established products to repeat customers, though these sales people do introduce new products to customers and make presentations to prospects.
- Positions in which the sales people are not expected to solicit orders. Rather, their job is to influence decision makers by building goodwill, performing promotional activities, and providing service to customers. These are called **missionary sales people** in food products companies and **detail sales people** in pharmaceutical firms.
- Positions in which the major emphasis is on the sales person's ability to explain the product to a prospect as well as possibly adapt it to the customer's particular needs. A **sales engineer** is an example of this type of technically trained individual who usually sells some kind of sophisticated equipment.
- Positions that require **creative selling** of either goods or services. Often customers are not aware of their need for the product, or they may not realize how the product can satisfy their wants better than the product they are using. Creative selling often means designing a system to fit the needs of the particular customer and may require the expertise of several people who make up a sales team. Examples are construction by AT&T of a communications system for a hospital and development of a vertical lift system for a new office complex by Otis Elevator.

An organization may employ several different types of sales people. For instance, IBM has sales people who fit into all categories except driver–sales person.

**THE PERSONAL SELLING PROCESS**

The personal selling process is a logical sequence of four steps that a sales person takes in dealing with a prospective customer. The process applies equally well to any face-to-face attempt at persuasion. So whether the objective is to sell a product to a consumer, gain a retailer's participation in a sales

**FIGURE 17-1** The personal selling process.

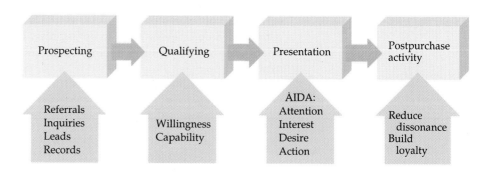

promotion program, or convince someone of the correctness of a cause, these four steps, diagrammed in Figure 17-1, should be followed.

### Prospecting for Potential Buyers

The first task of the seller is to identify prospects. If the organization has a well-designed marketing strategy, the segment(s) with the greatest potential have been identified. The sales person must take this general description (based on such descriptors as demographics, attitudes, and past purchasing behavior) and then identify specific individuals or firms that may be prospects. For example, prospects may be found in trade-association and industry directories; among people who have mailed in inquiry cards or called an 800 number featured in an advertisement; and among existing customers, suppliers, and social or professional contacts. Frequently a little thought will suggest logical prospects. For instance, sellers of home or office furnishings and telephone equipment find prospects in regularly published lists of building permits issued. Insurance, real estate, and diaper service sellers find leads in engagement, marriage, and birth announcements in newspapers.

### Qualifying the Prospect

A sales person must determine whether the prospect is qualified to buy. Qualifications include both a reasonable *willingness* to buy and the *capability* to buy. To qualify the prospect, the sales person must gather information from a wide variety of sources. To determine willingness to buy, information about a business prospect's customers, competitors, and suppliers is important. If the prospect has a special relationship with an existing supplier, for instance, there may be little possibility of getting the business, so the sales person's time would be better spent elsewhere. Also, the sales person must objectively compare the prospect's needs with the product's features. Sometimes, in their enthusiasm, sales people are unrealistic about how well a product fits a customer's situation.

The capability of a prospect to buy includes an evaluation of both short-term and long-term profit potential. The sales person, often with the aid of others in the organization, must determine whether the prospect has sufficient immediate demand for the offering to justify the selling and order-processing costs and is a reasonable credit risk. An assessment also must be made of long-term potential in deciding how much time and effort to devote to cultivating the prospect. Is the prospect's business likely to grow? Is the prospect a candidate for other products in the line?

### Presenting the Sales Message

Before preparing a presentation, sales people need to learn all they can about the individual or company to which they hope to sell. Past purchasing behavior, product preferences, and special needs are all very pertinent details. If the prospect is an organization, the sales person should discover how purchase decisions are made and who in the organization makes them. (Recall the discussion in Chapter 6 on purchase decision roles.) Knowing who is the information gatekeeper, who is likely to influence the choice of suppliers, and who ultimately will make the purchase decision allows the sales person to target the right people.

With this background information a sales person can design a presentation that will attract the prospect's *attention*. The sales person will then try to hold the prospect's *interest* while building a *desire* for the product. When the time is right, the sales person will attempt to stimulate *action* by closing the sale. This approach, called **AIDA** (an acronym formed by the first letters of *attention*, *interest*, *desire*, and *action*), is commonly used by many organizations. Each step is described next.

### ATTRACT ATTENTION

The initial objective is to generate curiosity. In some cases, for example when the prospect is already aware of the need and is seeking a solution, simply mentioning the sales person's company or product will be enough. However, more creativity is often required. If the sales person was referred to the prospect by a third party, the best approach might be to begin by mentioning this common acquaintance. An alternative is to begin with a startling statement that emphasizes the product's benefits. For instance, it would be difficult to ignore the question, "Would you give me 5 minutes to explain how I can cut your selling costs in half while doubling your sales volume?" Another method of gaining attention, particularly when the product has an unusual or novel aspect, is simply to place it in the prospect's hand. Obviously there is no limit to the variety of presentation openers. The key is remembering that attention is very valuable and can be granted only by the prospect. Therefore, the sales person must be sensitive to both the prospect's personality and circumstances in opening a presentation.

### HOLD INTEREST AND AROUSE DESIRE

After attracting the prospect's attention, the sales person can hold this interest and stimulate a desire for the product by means of the presentation itself. There is no standard pattern to follow. A number of presentation methods, each suitable for particular situations, are described in texts on selling.

Many companies insist that their sales people memorize the presentation to ensure that all key points are covered in a particular order. The problem with these "canned" presentations is that they do not permit the sales person to adapt to the customer's needs or desires. Whatever sales presentation approach is followed, the sales person must always concentrate on showing how the product will benefit the prospect.

### MEET OBJECTIONS AND CLOSE THE SALE

**Closing** means obtaining agreement to buy. It is the action step. Clearly this is the objective of the personal selling effort. On the average, it takes four personal sales calls to close a business-to-business sale. At a cost of $240 per call, the average cost of a sale is $960.[3] Thus, sellers are interested in closing sales as quickly as possible.

[3] "How Many Personal Sales Calls Does It Take to Close a Sale?" Carr Report No. 542.5A, Cahners Publishing Co., July 1989.

As part of the presentation, the sales person may periodically venture a **trial close** to measure the prospect's willingness to commit. By posing some "either-or" questions, to which both answers will result in a sale, the sales person can move the presentation toward closure. That is, the sales person might ask, "Would you prefer the red or the blue model?" or "Would you like to charge this or pay cash?"

The sales person must uncover and resolve any objections before a sale is possible. Of course, the toughest objections to answer are those that are unspoken. The trial close is useful because it frequently brings out such objections. Then the sales person has the opportunity to point out additional product features and reemphasize previously stated benefits.

As the prospect gets closer to a decision, the sales person can often finalize the sale with the **assumptive close.** In this technique the sales person assumes the prospect is going to buy and begins asking questions that will settle the details of the purchase. For example, questions like "When would you want this delivered?" and "Would one truckload be enough to get started?" indicate that the process has progressed beyond the decision to buy.

### Servicing Customers after the Sale

An effective selling job does not end when the order is written up. The final stage of the selling process is a series of postpurchase services that can build customer goodwill and lay the groundwork for future business. The alert sales person will follow up sales to ensure that no problems occur in delivery, financing, installation, routine maintenance, employee training, billing, and other areas important to customer satisfaction.

All of these activities reduce the customer's postpurchase anxiety—or **cognitive dissonance.** You may recall from Chapter 5 that dissonance leads buyers to seek reassurance that a correct choice was made and to avoid information that would suggest some other alternative would have been better. In this final stage of the selling process, the sales person can minimize the customer's dissonance by (1) summarizing the product's benefits even after the purchase, (2) repeating why the product is better than alternatives not chosen, and (3) emphasizing how satisfied the customer will be with the product.

### STRATEGIC SALES-FORCE MANAGEMENT

The management tasks of planning, implementing, and evaluating must be applied to the sales force. Sales executives begin by setting sales goals and planning sales-force activities. This involves forecasting sales, preparing sales budgets, establishing sales territories, and setting sales quotas.

When a plan is established, a sales force must be organized to carry it out. This means selecting, training, and supervising the people who will do the actual selling. The final element—performance evaluation—includes assessing the performance of individual sales people and providing compensation.

Effective sales-force management starts with a qualified sales manager. Finding the right person for this job is not easy. In many organizations the common practice when a sales management position becomes available is to reward the most productive sales person with a promotion. The assumption is that as a manager, an effective sales person will be able to impart the necessary wisdom to make others equally successful. However, as the following statements suggest, the qualities that lead to effective sales management are often diametrically opposed to the attributes of a successful sales person.[4]

---

[4] Adapted from Jack Falvey, "The Making of a Manager," *Sales & Marketing Management*, March 1989, pp. 42–47, 83.

What similarities and differences between the jobs of sales people and sales managers does this sales meeting suggest?

- A sales person must be self-driven in order to achieve results. A sales manager must be careful not to drive people to achieve results.
- A sales person must be impatient. A sales manager must let situations develop and ripen.
- A sales person requires constant recognition for results. A sales manager must learn to give recognition and accept a secondary role.
- A sales person must "make the numbers" in the short run. A sales manager must take a longer-term view of business growth and personnel development.
- A sales person must be self-reliant. A sales manager must rely almost completely on others.
- A sales person is a doer. A sales manager is an organizer.
- A sales person builds account loyalty. A sales manager builds company loyalty.
- A sales person must be tenacious, confident that with enough time and effort any prospect can be sold. A sales manager must learn to cut losses quickly and move resources to more productive opportunities.
- A sales person has considerable freedom as long as results are forthcoming. A sales manager must conform to policies and procedures and play by the rules.

Success in sales management typically requires a blend of sales experience, knowledge of the selling process, and management skill. It might be wise to identify individuals with management potential and groom them with sales training rather than selecting sales people for management positions in the hope they will develop the necessary management ability.

**OPERATING A SALES FORCE**

We will focus here on the areas of sales-force operation that take up the bulk of sales executives' time. These tasks, outlined in Figure 17-2, are recruitment and selection, training, supervision, performance evaluation, and compensa-

**FIGURE 17-2** Operating a sales force.

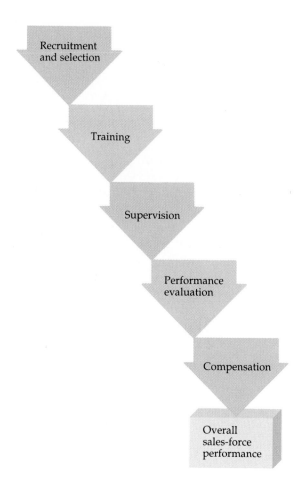

tion. Sales forecasting is discussed in Chapter 22. The topics of sales budgeting, territory design, and quotas are too specialized for treatment in this text.

**Recruiting and Selecting the Sales Force**

Staffing is the most important activity in the management process in any organization. This is true whether the organization is a business, an athletic team, or a college faculty. Consequently, the key to success in managing a sales force is selecting the right people. No matter what the caliber of sales management, if a sales force is distinctly inferior to that of a competitor, the competitor will win.

The three steps in sales force recruitment and selection are:

1. Determine the number and type of people wanted by preparing a written job description.
2. Recruit an adequate number of applicants.
3. Select the most qualified persons from among the applicants.

The turnover rate in sales personnel averages about 20 percent across all industries, with a high in auto and truck sales of 87 percent and a low in paper and allied products of 5.6 percent.[5] That means that on the average, one in

[5]"1989 Survey of Selling Costs," *Sales & Marketing Management,* Feb. 20, 1989, p. 22.

---

**The challenge of the 1990s—automating the sales force**

Sales executives today are faced with a decision that has the potential of changing how the sales job is performed—whether or not to automate sales forces. With automation, sales people are provided with desktop or laptop computers. Firms that have automated their sales forces report the following benefits:

- *Increased information accessibility.* Northwestern Mutual insurance agents can directly access the company's mainframe computer to compare coverage options or get immediate answers about the effect of changing a customer's policy.
- *Customized customer information.* With personal computers Georgia Pacific reps track customer buying habits, sales performance, and inventories more efficiently.
- *Reduced paperwork.* Sales people at Owens-Corning Fiberglas are able to electronically input and access data. Before automation each sales person received 20 pounds of reports a month.
- *Improved internal communications.* Details of new sales promotions at Black & Decker are put on the computer and are available to sales people as soon as they log on to their portable machines.
- *Strengthened sales presentations.* A Du Pont sales person, challenged by a new competitive product, can tap into a data base to see how fellow sales people in other territories have countered it.
- *Increased selling time.* IBM has found that laptops save sales people 4.4 hours per week by allowing them to avoid such tasks as traveling to a branch office to get answers to customers' questions.

What are the drawbacks of automation? Among those noted are:

- *Cost.* The necessary hardware, software, training, and support cost about $7,500 per sales person. Then there are additional costs for upgrading each year.
- *Difficulty in measuring contribution.* Though costs can be measured in dollars and cents, benefits such as time saved and improvements in information quantity and quality are harder to translate to the bottom line.
- *Sales-force resistance.* Some sales people don't want to change their behavior.

Sources: Adapted from Thayer C. Taylor, "How the Best Sales Forces Use PCs and Laptops," *Sales & Marketing Management,* April 1988, pp. 64–74; Joe Ferreira and Michael E. Treacy, "How to Justify Computers for Your Sales Force," *Sales & Marketing Management,* December 1988, pp. 46–48. The growing popularity of sales-force automation is reflected in the December issues of *Sales & Marketing Management,* which include an annual directory of PC software. The 1989 list is 30 pages long.

---

five sales people leave their jobs every year. Weaknesses in recruitment and selection are major contributors to this high rate.

## WHAT MAKES A GOOD SALES PERSON?

An organization must begin the recruitment process by determining what qualifications are needed to fill the job. Many sales managers have developed general guidelines through experience for identifying potentially successful sales people. Among the common attributes sought in prospects are a high energy level, self-confidence, competitiveness, and personal sensitivity.

Researchers have also attempted to identify generalizable traits of successful sales people. However, their efforts have not met with much success. In a review of 400 studies of relationships between personal characteristics and sales performance, six sets of variables were investigated:

## AN ETHICAL DILEMMA?

Sales contests require that sales people produce a certain volume of sales during a specified period. In order to win contests and qualify for the incentives, some sales people will build up customers' inventories beyond what is necessary. The result is that sales are shifted from a future period into the contest period and the customers have higher inventory costs than are necessary (though they will use the products eventually). Assume you are a sales manager and you suspect one of your sales people is shifting sales to earn incentives. Is this behavior ethical? What would you do about it?

- Demographic and physical attributes.
- Background and experience.
- Current marital and financial status and lifestyle.
- Intellectual aptitude and cognitive ability.
- Personality traits.
- Interpersonal, presentation, and management skills.[6]

Though intuitively it would seem that these factors are related to sales performance, none proved to be consistently related across industries and sales jobs. The apparent explanation is found in the wide variety that exists among sales jobs. The positions simply differ so much that the factors leading to success in one may be much less important in another.

The conclusion that can be drawn regarding sales person selection is that each organization must examine its own situation and determine what the particular sales job entails. This calls for a detailed job analysis and a written job description that includes specific job duties and appropriate qualifications.

The mixture of native and western cultures in many countries makes selecting sales people a challenge.

### RECRUITING APPLICANTS

A planned system for recruiting a sufficient number of applicants is the next step in selection. A good recruiting system:

- Operates continuously, not only when there are vacancies on the sales force.
- Is systematic in reaching and exploiting all appropriate sources of applicants.
- Provides a flow of qualified applicants in numbers greater than the company's needs.

To identify recruits, large organizations often use placement services on college campuses or professional employment agencies. Smaller firms needing fewer new sales people may place classified advertisements in trade publi-

[6] Neil M. Ford, Orville C. Walker, Jr., Gilbert A. Churchill, Jr., and Steven W. Hartley, "Selecting Successful Salespeople: A Meta-Analysis of Biographical and Psychological Selection Criteria," in Michael J. Houston, *Review of Marketing*, American Marketing Association, Chicago, 1987, pp. 90–131.

cations and daily newspapers and solicit recommendations of existing employees as well as referrals from customers, suppliers, or other business contacts.

## MATCHING APPLICANTS WITH HIRING SPECIFICATIONS

Sales managers use a variety of techniques to determine which applicants possess the desired qualifications, including application forms, interviews, references, credit reports, psychological tests, aptitude tests, and physical examinations. Virtually all companies ask candidates to fill out application forms. In addition to providing basic screening information, the application indicates areas that should be explored in an interview.

No sales person should be hired without at least one personal interview. And it is usually desirable to have several interviews conducted by different people in different physical settings. Pooling the opinions of a number of people increases the likelihood of discovering any undesirable characteristics and reduces the effects of one interviewer's possible bias. An interview helps an employer to determine (1) the applicant's degree of interest in the job, (2) the match between the requirements of the job and the applicant's skills, and (3) the applicant's motivation to work hard. Interviews can be **unstructured** or **patterned.** For relatively inexperienced interviewers, the patterned interview is usually preferable because the questions are planned in advance to make sure that all important issues are covered.

Testing for intelligence, attributes, or personality is somewhat controversial. Some companies avoid testing for fear that they will be accused of discrimination. However, employment tests are legitimate selection tools as long

To recruit applicants, Century 21 uses a coordinated program of mass media advertising and personal presentations.

**AN INTERNATIONAL PERSPECTIVE: Recruiting sales people overseas—the challenge for multinationals**

U.S. corporations engaged in global marketing often encounter shortages of qualified sales personnel abroad. To complicate matters, cultural, educational, ethnic, and religious differences make the use of standardized hiring criteria risky. As the following cross-national comparisons suggest, multinational companies need to be sensitive to these differences when selecting sales people for foreign markets:

- In the United States 45 percent of 18- to 21-year-olds go to college, and many study career-oriented professional subjects. In Europe there is a greater emphasis on the liberal arts and sciences, and higher education is restricted to a smaller percentage of the population. The number of educated people in developing countries is still quite small.
- Even with its various ethnic subcultures, the United States is relatively homogeneous compared to Canada, which is 25 percent French-speaking. Other countries—such as Zaire with 250 dialects and India with over 300 dialects—seem to have more ethnic differences than similarities.
- Religious friction in the United States is mild compared to other countries. Protestantism, the dominant U.S. religion, exerts little daily influence on the lives of its followers. Religions such as Hinduism, Buddhism, and Islam have a much greater influence on their adherents' behavior. Conflicts between Sunni and Shiite groups in the Middle East, Muslims and Hindus in India, and Muslims and Buddhists in Malaysia testify to the strong role that religion plays in many people's lives.
- Social class, which for the most part is based on economic considerations in the United States, has very different bases in other countries. Heredity, ethnic background, and age help determine social class in various cultures.

An examination of how these differences affect selection of sales personnel by U.S. multinationals in overseas locations showed that:

- Selection criteria, though generally the same as those used in the United States, are weighted differently overseas.
- Social class, religion, and ethnic background influence as many as a quarter of the selection decisions sales departments make abroad.
- Social class, religious, and ethnic criteria are applied in both developed and developing countries.

Source: John S. Hill and Meg Birdseye, "Salesperson Selection in Multinational Corporations: An Empirical Study," *Journal of Personal Selling & Sales Management*, Summer 1989, pp. 39–47.

as they can be validated. A **valid test** is one that accurately predicts job performance.

**Sales Force Training**

Sales training is a major expense for many organizations. According to figures developed by Dartnell Corporation, initial training costs range from $11,600 per sales person at consumer products firms to $22,200 for an industrial-products sales person, and the training period lasts from five to eight months.[7] These figures may seem high, but keep in mind that, in addition to the direct costs of training (training personnel, supplies, facilities), a firm pays the trainee a salary during this period.

Newly hired sales people know very little about the details of the job, their fellow workers, and their status in the firm. Thus the first training task is indoctrination and guidance to assimilate the person into the organization.

Designing a training program involves answering the following questions:

- What are the goals of the program? In very general terms, the aim of the program is to increase productivity and stimulate the sales force. In addition, executives must determine what specific ends they want to reach.

[7]"1989 Survey of Selling Costs," *Sales & Marketing Management*, Feb. 20, 1989, p. 23.

For instance, the goal may be to increase sales of high-profit items or to improve prospecting methods for generating new accounts.

- Who should do the training? The training program may be conducted by line sales executives, by a company training department, by outside training specialists, or by some combination of the three.
- What should be the content of the program? A well-rounded sales training program should cover three general topics: product knowledge, company policies, and selling techniques.
- When and where should training be done? Some companies believe in training new people before they go into the field. Others let new people prove that they have the desire and ability to sell first and then bring them back into the office for intensive training. Firms may employ either centralized or decentralized training programs. A centralized program, usually at the home office, may take the form of a periodic meeting attended by all sales people. A decentralized program may be held in branch offices or during on-the-job training. Decentralized programs typically cost less than centralized programs; however, the quality of instruction is often inferior.
- What instructional methods should be used? The lecture method may be employed to inform trainees about company history and practices. Demonstrations may be used to impart product knowledge or selling techniques. Role playing is an excellent device for training a person in proper selling techniques. On-the-job training may be used in almost any phase of the program.

After becoming familiar with the new work environment, sales people—both new and experienced—need regular training to enhance and refine their selling skills, to learn about new products, and to improve their time and territory management practices. The frequency and duration of refresher training depends on the company and the situation. However, most organizations recognize that learning and improving are a continuous, career-long process.

Training is often a combination of motivation and instruction.

## Supervising the Sales Force

Supervision of a sales force is difficult but essential. It is difficult because sales people often work independently where they cannot be continually observed. And yet supervision serves both as a means of continuing training and as a device to ensure that company policies are being carried out. Another value of supervision is that it creates a two-way communications channel between management and the sales force.

An issue that management must resolve is how close supervision should be. If it is too close, it will create role conflict for the sales person. One of the attractions of selling is the freedom it affords sales people to develop creative solutions to customers' problems. However, close supervision will stifle that sense of independence. Sales people will have difficulty seeing themselves as problem solvers if supervisors are constantly checking up on them. Conversely, too little supervision will contribute to role ambiguity. Sales people who are not closely supervised lack an understanding of the expectations of their supervisors and companies. They may not know, for example, how much time should be spent servicing existing accounts and how much developing new business. If they do something wrong, it may not be brought to their attention until after it has become a serious problem. As a result, they may become tentative and avoid risks.

The most effective supervisory method is personal observation in the field. Typically, at least half of a sales manager's time is spent traveling with sales people. Other supervisory tools are reports, correspondence, and sales meetings.

## Evaluating Performance

Managing a sales force includes evaluating the efforts of the sales people. Sales executives must know what the sales force is doing to be in a position to reward them or to make constructive proposals for improvement. By establishing performance standards and studying sales people's activities, management can develop new training programs for upgrading the sales force's efforts. And, of course, performance evaluation should be the basis for salary decisions and other rewards.

Performance evaluation can also help sales people identify opportunities for improving their efforts. Employees with poor sales records know they are doing something wrong. However, they may not know what the problem is if they lack objective standards by which to measure their performance.

Both quantitative and qualitative factors should serve as bases for performance evaluation. **Quantitative bases** generally have the advantage of being specific and objective. **Qualitative factors,** although often reflecting broader dimensions of behavior, are limited by the subjective judgment of the evaluators. For management the challenges are selecting measures and setting standards against which the performance measures can be compared.

Sales performance should be evaluated in terms of both **inputs** (or effort) and **outputs** (or results). Together, inputs such as call rate and customer service activity and outputs such as sales volume and gross margin provide a measure of a person's selling effectiveness.

Some *output* measures that are also *quantitative* evaluation criteria are:

- Sales volume by product, customer group, and territory.
- Sales volume as a percent of quota or territory potential.
- Gross margin by product line, customer group, and territory.
- Orders—number and average dollar amount.
- Closing rate—number of orders divided by number of calls.

- Accounts—percent of existing accounts sold and number of new accounts opened.

Useful *quantitative input* measures include:

- Call rate—number of calls per day or week.
- Direct selling expenses—total dollars or as a percent of sales.
- Nonselling activities—promotion displays set up, training sessions held with distributors or dealers.

The importance of output factors in a performance evaluation is readily recognized. Sometimes, however, the value of input factors is underestimated. Actually an analysis of input measures helps to pinpoint trouble spots. If a person's output performance is unsatisfactory, very often the cause lies in the handling of the various input factors over which the sales person has control.

One key to a successful evaluation program is appraisal of the sales person's performance on as many different bases as possible. Otherwise management may be misled. A high daily call rate may look good, but it tells us nothing about how many orders per call are being written up. A high closing rate (orders divided by calls) may be camouflaging a low average order size or a high sales volume on low-profit items.

Performance evaluation would be much easier if it could be based only on quantitative criteria. It would minimize the subjectivity and personal bias of the evaluators. However, many *qualitative* factors must be considered because they influence a sales person's performance and help in the interpretation of quantitative data. Some of these factors are:

- Knowledge of products, company policies, and competitors.
- Time management and preparation for sales calls.
- Customer relations.
- Personal appearance.
- Personality and attitude—cooperation, creativity, resourcefulness.

## Compensating Sales People

To compensate their sales forces, companies offer both financial and nonfinancial rewards. *Nonfinancial rewards* include opportunities for advancement, recognition of efforts, and a feeling of belonging. *Financial rewards* may take the form of *direct* monetary payment or *indirect* monetary payment (paid vacations, pensions, and insurance plans).

Establishing a compensation system entails decisions concerning the *level* of compensation as well as the *method* of compensation. The level refers to the total dollar income that a sales person earns over a period of time. Level is influenced by the type of person required and the competitive rate of pay for similar positions. The method is the system or plan by which the sales person will reach the intended level.

There are three widely used methods of compensating a sales force: straight salary, straight commission, and a combination plan. Today well over half the firms in the country use some kind of combination plan.

The **straight-salary plan** offers maximum security and stability of earnings for a sales person. Management can expect sales people to perform any reasonable work assignment because they receive the same pay regardless of the task performed. Under a straight salary, sales reps can consider the customers' best interests and are less likely to use high-pressure selling tactics.

A drawback of straight-salary compensation is that it does not offer ade-

---

### Sales incomes—the sky's the limit

How much do people in sales and marketing positions earn? The answer to that question is, it depends. Salaries vary by industry, by company size, and, of course, by the amount of responsibility. Recently topping the list was Robert Bardagy, Executive Vice President/President of Sales of Comdisco, Inc., a computer leasing company, who made $1,400,000. It should be noted that top management pay usually includes incentives. Mr. Bardagy is no exception. Only $200,000 of his earnings is base salary; the remainder comes from bonuses and commissions.

And other sales executives? A national survey by Sibson & Co. shows that earnings vary considerably by company size:

| Company revenues | Top sales executives' average total compensation |
|---|---|
| $100 million | $108,000 |
| $500 million | $144,000 |
| $1 billion | $164,000 |
| $5 billion | $220,000 |

But what about the young person just starting out as a sales trainee or the first-level sales manager? A survey by *Sales & Marketing Management* magazine shows that initial pay differs somewhat by industry, as shown by these 1988 figures:

| Industry | Sales trainees' average compensation | Sales supervisors' average compensation |
|---|---|---|
| Consumer goods | $23,250 | $62,621 |
| Services | $22,655 | $62,156 |
| Industrial goods | $25,812 | $60,212 |

Sources: William Keenan, Jr., "Back on the Fast Track Again," *Sales & Marketing Management*, November 1989, pp. 30–48; "1989 Survey of Selling Costs," *Sales & Marketing Management*, Feb. 20, 1989, p. 15.

---

quate incentive. Thus management has the added burden of motivating and directing sales people. The pay plan itself does not provide any appreciable direction or control. Also, under this plan compensation is a fixed cost unrelated to sales revenue. Straight-salary plans typically are used:

- For new sales people or missionary sales people.
- When opening new territories.
- When sales involve a technical product and a lengthy period of negotiation.

A **straight commission** has just the opposite merits and limitations. It provides tremendous incentive for sales people, and commission costs can be related directly to sales or gross margin. Sales representatives have more freedom in their work, and their level of income is determined largely by their own efforts. On the other hand, it is difficult to control sales people and get them to perform tasks for which no commission is paid. There is always the danger that they will oversell customers or otherwise incur customer ill will. Straight-commission plans may work well if:

**TABLE 17-1 America's best sales forces as rated by sales managers in nine industries**

| Rating Criteria | |
|---|---|
| • Recruiting top sales people<br>• Ability to keep top sales people<br>• Quality of training<br>• Opening new accounts | • Holding accounts<br>• Product/technical knowledge<br>• Reputation among customers |

| Company | Industry |
|---|---|
| Du Pont | Chemicals |
| IBM | Computers and office equipment |
| Anheuser-Busch | Food and beverage |
| Scott Paper | Forest products |
| Northwestern Mutual | Life insurance |
| Caterpillar | Industrial and farm equipment |
| Ball | Metal products |
| Merck | Pharmaceuticals |
| Xerox | Scientific and photographic equipment |

Source: "America's Best Sales Forces," *Sales & Marketing Management*, June 1989, pp. 31–48.

- Great incentive is needed to get the sales.
- Very little nonselling missionary work is required.
- The company is financially weak and must relate its compensation expenses directly to sales or gross margin.
- The company is unable to supervise its sales force.

The ideal **combination salary plan** has the best features of both the straight-salary and straight-commission plans, with as few of their drawbacks as possible. To come close to this ideal, the combination plan must be tailored to the particular firm, product, market, and type of selling.

Which organizations are the best at performing all of these sales management tasks? That is a difficult question. However, the results of a survey of sales managers, shown in Table 17-1, suggest that some companies have particularly noteworthy sales forces.

**SUMMARY** Personal selling is the main promotional method used in American business—whether measured by number of people employed, by total expenditures, or by expenses as a percentage of sales. Sales differs from other jobs because sales people represent the organization to the outside world, operate without close supervision, are authorized to spend company funds, and frequently travel. The great variety of sales jobs can be viewed as a continuum from order filling to order getting. Examples along the continuum range from driver–sales person through jobs like inside order taker, outside order taker, missionary seller, sales engineer, and creative seller.

There are four steps in the sale of a product. The first is prospecting, or identifying potential customers. In the second step, prospects are qualified to determine their willingness and capability to buy. Next the qualified prospects are presented with the sales message. Messages are often designed using a framework called AIDA, which stands for creating Attention, generating Interest, stimulating Desire, and requesting Action. The final step consists of postpurchase activities intended to reduce anxieties and increase the likelihood of repeat purchases.

Sales force management involves planning, supervising, and evaluating a sales force within guidelines set by strategic marketing planning. Major sales force operations include recruitment and selection, training, supervision, performance evaluation, and compensation. Recruiting begins with a written job description to identify necessary qualifications. In the selection process, the most common tools are the job application and the interview. Sales training is an ongoing process that should conform to guidelines delineating goals, methods, content, instructors, and timing. Performance evaluation requires quantitative and qualitative measures of both inputs (effort) and outputs (results). Compensation consists of financial and nonfinancial rewards. The most common forms of financial rewards are straight salary, straight commission, and a combination of the two.

## KEY TERMS AND CONCEPTS

Personal selling 430
Advantages of personal selling 430
Disadvantages of personal selling 430
Telemarketing 431
Territory manager 431
Role ambiguity 431
Role conflict 431
Driver–sales person 433
Inside order taker 433
Outside order taker 433
Missionary sales person 433
Detail sales person 433
Sales engineer 433
Creative selling 433
Prospecting 434
Qualifying 434
AIDA 435

Meeting objections 435
Closing a sale 435
Trial close 436
Assumptive close 436
Postpurchase service 436
Patterned interview 441
Unstructured interview 441
Valid test 442
Quantitative performance bases 444
Qualitative performance bases 444
Input performance measures 444
Output performance measures 444
Nonfinancial rewards 445
Financial rewards 445
Straight-salary compensation 445
Straight-commission compensation 446
Combination salary plan 447

## QUESTIONS AND PROBLEMS

1. The cost of a full-page, four-color advertisement in one issue of *Sports Illustrated* magazine is much more than the cost of employing two sales people for a full year. A sales-force executive is urging her company to eliminate a few of these ads and, instead, to hire a few more sales people. This executive believes that one good sales person working for an entire year can sell more than one ad in one issue of *Sports Illustrated*. How would you respond?

2. "The often conflicting demands of a sales manager, an employer, customers, and family can create heavy emotional stress for a sales person." Explain.

3. Refer to the classification of sales jobs from driver–sales person to creative seller and answer the following questions:
    a. In which types of jobs are sales people most likely to be free from close supervision?
    b. Which types are likely to be the highest paid?
    c. Which are likely to involve the most overnight traveling?
    d. For which types of jobs is the highest degree of motivation necessary?

4. What are some sources you might use to acquire a list of prospects for the following products?
   a. Bank accounts for new area residents.
   b. Dental X-ray equipment.
   c. Laptop computers.
   d. Contributors to the United Way.
   e. Baby furniture and clothes.
5. If you were preparing a sales presentation for the following products, what information about a prospect would you seek as part of your preparation?
   a. Two-bedroom condominium.
   b. New automobile.
   c. Carpeting for a home redecorating project.
6. How should a sales person respond when a prospect says the price of a product is too high?
7. "A good selection program is desirable, but not essential. Improper selection of sales people can be offset by a good training program, by good compensation, and by proper supervision." Discuss this statement.
8. What source should be used for recruiting sales applicants in each of the following firms? Explain your choice in each case.

   a. A Marriott hotel that wants companies to use the hotel for conventions.
   b. Amway, Avon, or Mary Kay Cosmetics, for sales directly to consumers.
   c. IBM, for sales of mainframe (large) computers.
9. "It is best to hire experienced sales people because they don't require training." Discuss this statement.
10. How can a sales manager evaluate the performance of sales people in getting new business?
11. What factors should be considered in determining the level of sales-force compensation?
12. Compare the merits of straight-salary and straight-commission plans of sales compensation. What are two types of sales jobs in which each plan might be desirable?
13. How might a firm determine whether a sales person is using high-pressure selling tactics that might injure customer relations?
14. For a U.S. multinational corporation hiring a sales force in a developing country, what applicant characteristics should be added to its selection criteria?

# CHAPTER 18

# MANAGEMENT OF ADVERTISING, SALES PROMOTION, PUBLIC RELATIONS, AND PUBLICITY

The power of advertising is reflected in the recognition achieved by several fictional characters used in ads. These human images, familiar to virtually all consumers, have personalized the products and brands that they symbolize. But did you know:

- Mr. Clean, the bald, muscular character used by Procter & Gamble on the product of the same name, has been around for 20 years? Or that the model for the Gerber baby is now over 60 years old?
- The maître d' for a Chicago restaurant, Frank Brown, posed for the portrait of the original Uncle Ben?
- Buster Brown was originally a cartoon-strip character that also appeared on brands of horseshoes, cigars, and bourbon?

- Quaker Oats' Aunt Jemima character first appeared on a package of pancake mix and now is over 100 years old?
- Betty Crocker has been updated six times since her original portrait appeared in 1936, going from a housedress in the first version to a business suit today?
- Morton Salt has retained the slogan "when it rains it pours" through its 75-year history, but has updated the girl on the package with contemporary hair and clothing styles?
- Sherwin-Williams's Dutch Boy has gone through nine updates, but today's version is the original 1907 image?[1]

[1]Lucy A. McCauley, "The Face of Advertising," *Harvard Business Review*, November–December 1989, pp. 155–59.

Mass communication is needed to reach mass markets at reasonable costs. Advertising, sales promotion, public relations, and publicity are the tools for this job. It is too costly and time-consuming to use only sales people in large, geographically diverse markets. However, whereas personal selling can be tailored to the individual prospect, mass communicators try to reach many people with a common message. And as the chapter-opening examples illustrate, finding images that consumers can relate to is very valuable.

## NATURE OF ADVERTISING

**Advertising** consists of all activities involved in presenting to a group a non-personal, sponsor-identified message about a product or organization. This message, called an **advertisement,** can be verbal and/or visual, and is disseminated through one or more media. Two factors differentiate advertising from publicity. The public knows who is doing the advertising because the sponsor is openly identified. And payment is made by the sponsor to the medium that carries the message.

### Types of Advertising

An organization's advertising objectives determine, to a great extent, what type of advertising should be used. Consequently, it is essential to understand the different classifications of advertising.

#### PRODUCT AND INSTITUTIONAL ADVERTISING

All advertising may be classified as product or institutional. In **product advertising,** advertisers inform or stimulate the market about their products. Product advertising is subdivided into direct-action and indirect-action advertising:

- **Direct-action advertising** seeks a quick response. For instance, a print ad with a coupon or an 800 number may urge the reader to send or call immediately for a free sample.
- **Indirect-action advertising** is designed to stimulate demand over a longer period of time. It is intended to inform or remind consumers that the product exists and to point out its benefits. Most network television advertising is of this type.

**Institutional advertising** presents information about the advertiser's business or tries to create a good attitude—build goodwill—toward the organization. This type of advertising is not intended to sell a specific product. Two forms of institutional advertising are:

- **Customer service advertising,** which presents information about the advertiser's operations. Advertisements describing the variety of automobile repairs and services available at Firestone stores are an example.
- **Public service advertising,** which is designed to improve the quality of life and show that the advertiser is a responsible member of the community. Such ads may urge the public to avoid drugs or to support a local antipollution campaign.

#### PRIMARY AND SELECTIVE DEMAND ADVERTISING

**Primary demand advertising** is designed to stimulate demand for a generic category of a product such as Colombian coffee, Florida citrus fruit, or garments made from cotton. This is in contrast to **selective demand advertising,** intended to stimulate demand for individual brands such as Folgers Coffee, Sunkist oranges, and Liz Claiborne sportswear.

Primary demand advertising is used in either of two situations. The first is

Is public service advertising of this type intended to have an immediate or a cumulative effect?

**Work with the forest as if your future depends on it.**

The paper industry was facing a no-win situation. Paper demand was growing dramatically, but overharvesting the forest would jeopardize the future.

At BASF, we looked at the problem in a new way. We found a practical, long-term solution that our paper customers could apply immediately. The key was in the paper making process. We developed a way to extract more paper pulp from each tree. Each one becomes, in effect, a super tree. Fewer trees are needed. Demand is met. The future isn't jeopardized.

In one industry after another, from paper manufacturing to magnetic recording media, our broad-based technologies help us create new worlds by seeing in new ways.

**The Spirit of Innovation**

**BASF**

when the product is in the introductory stage of its life cycle. This is called **pioneering advertising.** A firm may run an ad about its new product, explaining the product's benefits, but not emphasizing the brand name. The objective of pioneering primary demand advertising is to inform, not to persuade, the target market. The buying decision process model explains why such ads are limited to information. Recall from our discussion in Chapter 5 that a consumer must first be made *aware* of a product before becoming *interested* in or *desiring* it. Combine this with the fact that only so much information can be communicated in a single ad, and it becomes clear that only one objective can be accomplished at a time. In recent years pioneering demand ads have been run for cellular phones and video camcorders.

The second use of primary demand advertising occurs throughout the product life cycle. It is usually done by trade associations trying to stimulate demand for their industry's product. Thus the Beef Industry Council's ads urge us to consume beef products. The council doesn't care what brand of beef products we buy, just that we use more of them. Similarly, the National Dairy Association encourages us to consume more milk and dairy products.

Selective demand advertising essentially is competitive advertising—it pits one brand against another. This type of advertising typically is employed when a product has gone beyond the introductory life-cycle stage. The product is reasonably well known and in competition for market share with several brands. The objective of selective demand advertising is to increase the demand for a brand. To accomplish this goal, it emphasizes the particular benefits—the **differential advantages**—of the brand being advertised.

**Comparative advertising** is an important kind of selective demand adver-

## AN ETHICAL DILEMMA?

Sanka wants to communicate how good its product tastes. To do so, it produces a television ad that depicts a taste test at a crowded commuter train station in New Jersey. In the ad, the responses of the people tasting the beverage are outstanding, with comments like "This is great!" and "No way, this isn't Sanka." However, the test is staged, using actors and a script. If you were a television network executive, would you consider this an ethical advertising appeal?

tising that is used for a wide variety of products. In comparative advertising the advertiser either directly—by naming a rival brand—or indirectly—through inference—points out differences between the brands. Recently Kellogg's compared its Nut & Honey cereal to General Mills' Honey Nut Cheerios; Wilkinson compared its Ultra Glide blades to Gillette's Atra Plus; and AT&T and MCI both have used comparative ads in their competition for the long-distance telephone market.

Comparative advertising has been encouraged by the Federal Trade Commission as a means of stimulating competition and disseminating useful information to consumers. However, the passage of the Trademark Law Revision Act in 1988 makes it easier to sue competitors for attacks made in ads. Now misrepresentation of a firm's own or another company's products is illegal. This act closes a loophole in previous legislation, which prohibited only false claims about one's *own* goods.[2]

### COOPERATIVE ADVERTISING

**Cooperative advertising** promotes products of two or more firms that share the cost of the advertising. There are two types—vertical and horizontal. **Vertical cooperative advertising** involves firms on different levels of distribution. For example, a manufacturer and a retailer share the cost of the retailer's advertising of that manufacturer's product. Frequently the manufacturer prepares the actual ad, leaving space for the retailer's name and location. Then the manufacturer and retailer share the media cost of placing the ad. Most retail ads in newspapers are cooperative ads. Cooperative ads are also common on radio but appear less frequently on TV.

Another type of vertical cooperative advertising uses an **advertising allowance,** or cash discount offered by a manufacturer to a retailer, to encourage the retailer to advertise or prominently display a product. The difference between cooperative advertising and allowances is the amount of control exerted by the manufacturer over how the money is actually spent.

These arrangements benefit retailers by providing them with extra funds for promotion. Manufacturers benefit from advertising at the local level. In addition, ad dollars go farther because rates for local media are typically lower for ads placed by local firms than for ads placed by national advertisers.

**Horizontal cooperative advertising** is undertaken by firms on the same

[2] For a description of the Trademark Law Revision Act and its implications for advertising, see Bruce Buchanan and Doron Goldman, "Us vs. Them: The Minefield of Comparative Ads," *Harvard Business Review,* May–June 1989, pp. 38–50.

---

### Joint promotions are growing and producing some strange alliances

What do the following firms have in common?

- Dunkin' Donuts and Schick razors.
- Wolverine Hush Puppies and First Children's Bank.
- American Express and Buick.
- Sundance Juice Sparkler and Agree Shampoo.
- Campbell's Soup and Kellogg's Corn Flakes.

The answer is, they have all recently participated in joint promotions. More and more firms are discovering that they can extend their promotion dollars, benefit from the reputations of other noncompeting, successful brands, and open up new markets with joint promotional programs. A case in point is Burpee Seed Co. joining forces with McDonald's to provide garden tools and seeds with the purchase of a child's Happy Meal. Burpee received exposure in McDonald's ads and McDonald's got a premium that kids could enjoy and parents would find acceptable. The program was so successful that the two firms are considering offering it internationally.

Sources: Alecia Swasy, "Joint Promotions Creating Odd Couples," *The Wall Street Journal*, Jan. 2, 1990, pp. B1, B4; Debora Toth, "Burpee Plants Its Name in Kids' Minds," *Adweek's Marketing Week*, Sept. 11, 1989, p. 17.

---

level of distribution—such as a group of retailers—that share the costs of advertising. For example, all stores in a suburban shopping center may run a joint newspaper ad. The principal benefit is that by pooling their funds, the firms can achieve much greater exposure than if they advertised individually.

## Cost of Advertising

Advertising in one form or another is used by most marketers. The significance of advertising is indicated by the amount of money spent on it. In 1988, total advertising expenditures were about $118 billion, more than twice the amount spent in 1980. Table 18-1 shows the relative importance of each of the major advertising media. For years newspapers have been the most widely used medium, based on total advertising dollars spent. Newspapers' and radio's shares have declined, however, as expenditures for television advertising have increased.

### ADVERTISING AS A PERCENTAGE OF SALES

When gauging the importance of advertising, we should measure expenditures against a benchmark rather than simply look at the total. Frequently, advertising expenses are expressed as a percentage of a company's sales. Table 18-2 shows the 10 companies with the largest *dollar* expenditures for advertising. It is interesting to note that some of the largest advertisers (GM, Sears) actually devote a very small percentage of sales to advertising.

### ADVERTISING COST VERSUS PERSONAL SELLING COST

While we do not have accurate totals for the costs of personal selling, we do know they far surpass advertising expenditures. In manufacturing, only a few industries, such as drugs, toiletries, cleaning products, tobacco, and beverages, spend more on advertising than on personal selling. Advertising runs 1 to 3 percent of net sales in many firms, whereas the expenses of recruiting and operating a sales force are typically 8 to 15 percent of sales.

## TABLE 18-1 Advertising expenditures in the United States, by medium

Advertising expenditures reached over $118 billion in 1988, an increase of over 100 percent since 1980. Newspapers maintained their first-place position, but television is a close second and direct mail is growing rapidly.

| Medium | Dollars spent, 1988 (in billions) | 1988 % | 1980 % | 1970 % | 1960 % |
|---|---|---|---|---|---|
| Newspapers | $ 31 | 26 | 28 | 29 | 31 |
| Television | 26 | 22 | 21 | 18 | 13 |
| Direct mail | 21 | 18 | 14 | 14 | 15 |
| Radio | 8 | 7 | 7 | 7 | 6 |
| Yellow pages | 8 | 7 | — | — | — |
| Magazines | 6 | 5 | 6 | 7 | 8 |
| Business papers | 3 | 2 | 3 | 4 | 5 |
| Outdoor | 1 | 1 | 1 | 1 | 2 |
| Miscellaneous* | 14 | 12 | 20 | 20 | 20 |
| Total percentage | | 100 | 100 | 100 | 100 |
| Total dollars (in billions) | $118 | | $55 | $20 | $12 |

*Before 1988 this category included yellow pages. Also includes transportation advertising, weekly newspapers, regional farm publications, and point-of-purchase advertising.
Sources: 1988 figures from *Advertising Age*, May 15, 1989, p. 24; 1980 figures from *Advertising Age*, March 22, 1982, p. 66. Others adapted from *Advertising Age*, Nov. 17, 1975, p. 40.

## TABLE 18-2 Top 10 national advertisers in 1988, based on total expenditures in the United States

Notice how advertising as a percentage of sales varies.

| Company | Advertising expenditures | |
|---|---|---|
| | Dollars (in millions) | As % of U.S. sales |
| 1. Philip Morris | 2,058 | 9.9 |
| 2. Procter & Gamble | 1,507 | 12.8 |
| 3. General Motors | 1,294 | 1.4 |
| 4. Sears, Roebuck | 1,045 | 2.1* |
| 5. RJR Nabisco | 815 | 4.8* |
| 6. Grand Metropolitan PLC | 774 | 24.1 |
| 7. Eastman Kodak | 736 | 7.3 |
| 8. McDonald's | 728 | 6.4 |
| 9. Pepsico | 712 | 6.8 |
| 10. Kellogg | 682 | 24.7 |

*Based on worldwide sales.
Source: "100 Leading National Advertisers," *Advertising Age*, Sept. 27, 1989, pp. 59–68.

At the wholesale level, advertising costs are very low. Personal selling expenses, however, may run 10 to 15 times as high. Even among retailers in total—and this includes those with self-service operations—the cost of personal selling is substantially higher than that of advertising.

## OBJECTIVES OF ADVERTISING

The fundamental purpose of advertising is to sell something—a good, service, idea, person, or place. This broad goal is reached by setting specific objectives that can be incorporated into individual advertising campaigns. Recall again our discussion of the buying decision process. Buyers go through a series of stages from unawareness to purchase in the process of making a decision. Thus the immediate objective of an ad may be to move target customers to the next stage in the hierarchy, say from awareness to interest. Note also that advertising seldom is the only promotional tool used by a firm. Rather, it is typically one part of a strategy that may also include personal selling, sales promotion, and other tools. Therefore, the objective of advertising may be to "open doors" for the sales force.

Specific advertising objectives will be determined by the firm's overall marketing strategy. Typical objectives are:

- *Support personal selling.* Advertising may be used to acquaint prospects with the seller's company and products, easing the way for the sales force.
- *Reach people inaccessible to the sales force.* Sales people may be unable to reach top executives or may be uncertain who in the company makes the buying decisions. A well-placed ad may attract the attention of these executives.
- *Improve dealer relations.* Wholesalers and retailers like to see a manufacturer support its products.
- *Enter a new geographic market or attract a new market segment.*
- *Introduce a new product.*

**AN INTERNATIONAL PERSPECTIVE: Who spends the most on advertising outside the United States?**

Unilever, the British-Dutch conglomerate, was the top advertiser outside the United States in 1988, spending $1.2 billion in 24 countries. In second place was Procter & Gamble, with expenditures of $932 million in 18 countries. Rounding out the top 10 were:

3. Nestlé (Swiss)
4. Renault (French)
5. Matsushita (Japanese)
6. Fiat (Italian)
7. Mars (U.S.)
8. Kao (Japanese)
9. Nissan (Japanese)
10. Toyota (Japanese).

Of the top 50 spenders, 20 are Japanese firms, while 11 are U.S.-based. The rest are Western European firms with the exception of one Australian company. Product categories represented in the top 50 include 12 food companies, 11 automotive firms, 6 soap makers, and 6 electronics manufacturers.

The magnitude of these expenditures combined with a slowdown in U.S. advertising is encouraging American ad agencies to expand their international operations. Such well-known firms as BBDO Worldwide, Ogilvy & Mather, DDB Needham, and J. Walter Thompson have all recently increased their commitments of people and operations in Europe. Predictions are that major U.S.-based agencies will soon generate the majority of their new business overseas and that half of their revenues will come from advertising placed outside the United States.

Sources: Gary Levin, "Shops Shape Up for Foreign Growth," *Advertising Age*, March 6, 1989, p. 4; Julie Skur Hill, "Unilever Triumphs as Top Ad Spender," *Advertising Age*, Dec. 4, 1989, p. S-1.

- *Expand the use of a product.* Advertising may be used to lengthen the season for a product (as has been done by Lipton for iced tea); increase the frequency of replacement (as was done by Fram for oil filters); or increase the variety of product uses (as was done for baking soda by Arm & Hammer).
- *Expand industry sales.*
- *Counteract substitution.*
- *Build goodwill for the company.*

## DEVELOPING AN ADVERTISING CAMPAIGN

Once a company decides to advertise (based on the factors discussed in Chapter 16), management develops an advertising campaign; An **advertising campaign** has the same characteristics as a total promotional campaign—that is, coordination, a central theme, and a specific goal.

### Initial Planning

An advertising campaign must be planned within the framework of the overall strategic marketing program and promotional campaign. When the advertising campaign is designed, presumably management has already made decisions in several areas. Promotional goals have been established and the role of advertising in the promotional campaign has been determined. Also, the central campaign theme that will stress the product's benefits in light of the market's buying motives and habits has been chosen. The total promotion budget has been set and allocated among specific promotional methods. With these tasks completed, management can move on to the selection of advertising media and the creation and production of individual ads.

### Media Selection

Three levels of decision making enter into advertising media selection. First, the type of medium must be selected. Of the major media, will newspaper, television, radio, or magazines be used? What about the less prominent media of direct mail, billboards, specialty items, and yellow pages? Second, a particular category of the desired medium must be chosen. Television has network and cable; magazines include general-interest (*Newsweek, People*) and special-interest categories (*Popular Mechanics, Cosmopolitan*); and there are national as well as local newspapers. Finally, a specific vehicle must be chosen. An advertiser that decides first on radio and then on local stations must determine which stations to use in each city.

Factors to consider in making media decisions are:

#### OBJECTIVES OF THE AD

Media choice is influenced by the purpose of a particular ad and by the goals of an entire campaign. For example, if the campaign goal is to generate appointments for sales people, the company may rely on direct mail. If an advertiser wants to induce quick action, newspaper or radio may be the way to go.

#### AUDIENCE COVERAGE

The audience reached by the medium should fit the *geographic* distribution patterns of the product. Furthermore, the selected media should reach the desired *types of prospects* with a minimum of wasted coverage. Many media—even national and other large-market media—can be targeted at small, specialized market segments. For example, *Time* magazine publishes regional editions with different ads in the East, Midwest, and West. Large metropolitan newspapers publish suburban editions as well as regional editions within the city.

### REQUIREMENTS OF THE MESSAGE

The medium should fit the message. For example, food products, floor coverings, and apparel are best presented visually. If the advertiser can use a very brief message (the rule of thumb is six words or less), as is possible with reminder advertising, billboards may be a good choice.

### TIME AND LOCATION OF THE BUYING DECISION

The medium should reach prospects near the times they make their buying decisions and the places where they make them. Research by the Radio Advertising Bureau shows that radio scores the highest in immediacy of exposure. Over 50 percent of adults were last exposed to radio within 1 hour of making their largest purchase of the day. Many grocery store ads are placed in newspapers on Wednesday in anticipation of Thursday-through-Saturday shopping.

### MEDIA COST

The cost of advertising media should be considered in relation to the amount of funds available and the reach or circulation of the media. For example, the expense of network television exceeds the available funds of many advertisers. To determine the relationship between the cost of the medium and the size of the audience, there is a standard measure provided to prospective advertisers by all media—*cost per thousand (CPM)* persons reached. Of course, it is essential to estimate what proportion of all persons reached are truly prospects for the advertiser's product.

## Media Characteristics

When selecting media, management must consider their advertising characteristics. We have carefully chosen the term *characteristics* instead of advantages and disadvantages because a medium that works well for one product is not necessarily the best choice for another product. To illustrate, a characteristic of radio is that it makes its impressions through sound. For many products this feature is an advantage. For products that benefit from color photography, however, this characteristic of radio is a drawback.

### NEWSPAPERS

As an advertising medium, newspapers are flexible and timely. Ads can vary in size from small classifieds to multiple pages. Pages can be added or dropped, so newspapers are not limited, as are TV and radio, by constraints of time. Newspapers can be used to reach an entire city or a few urban areas. Ads can be inserted or canceled on very short notice. Newspapers also provide very intense coverage of a local market because most people read them. Cost per person reached is relatively low. On the other hand, the life of newspapers is very short—they often are discarded soon after being read.

### TELEVISION

Television's most important characteristic is obvious—the combination of motion and sound. Products can be demonstrated as well as described. TV provides wide geographic coverage and flexibility in when the message can be presented. However, television is a relatively expensive medium. One prime-time network 30-second spot can cost $100,000 or more. (Thirty seconds during the 1990 Super Bowl broadcast cost $700,000!) The broadcast nature of television means TV ads lack permanence. Therefore, they must be seen and comprehended immediately. For the same reason, TV does not lend itself to complicated messages.

Cable is also changing television as an advertising medium. Nearly 50 percent of American homes have cable, with an average of 20 broadcast stations per household. This results in more specialized broadcasting and fragmented markets, making it difficult to reach a mass market. VCRs and remote control devices have also created new problems for television advertisers. "Zapping" (changing channels when a commercial appears) and "zipping" (fast-forwarding through commercials when watching shows previously recorded) reduce audience sizes. As a result, advertisers have been forced to consider shorter, more entertaining commercials.

### DIRECT MAIL

Direct mail is the most personal and selective of all media. Highly specialized direct-mail lists can be purchased (among the thousands available are lists of air traffic controllers, wig dealers, college professors, pregnant women, and disc jockeys), but they can be expensive. Because direct mail reaches only the people the advertiser wishes to contact, there is almost no waste circulation. Printing and postage fees make the cost of direct mail per person reached quite high compared with other media.

Direct mail is pure advertising. It is not accompanied by editorial matter (unless the advertiser provides it). Therefore, a direct-mail ad must attract its own readers. This is critical when you consider that the average American home receives more than 10 direct-mail pieces a week and that the recipient of a direct-mail ad decides in 4 seconds whether to discard or open it.

### RADIO

Over the past decade radio has enjoyed a rebirth as an advertising and cultural medium. When interest in television soared after World War II, radio audiences (especially for national network radio) declined so dramatically that some people predicted radio's demise. However, since 1980 over 1,200 new radio stations (75 percent of them FM) have gone on the air. Radio is a low-CPM medium because of its broad reach. Nearly 80 percent of Americans listen to a radio daily. With programming ranging from all-talk to rock and roll to country and western music, certain target markets can be pinpointed quite effectively. Radio makes only an audio impression, relying entirely on the listener's ability to retain information after only hearing it. Also, audience attention is often at a low level, because radio is often used as background for working, studying (Is your radio on while you're reading this?), or some other activity.

### MAGAZINES

Magazines are an excellent medium when high-quality printing and color are desired in an ad. Magazines can reach a national market at a relatively low cost per reader. Through special-interest or regional editions of general-interest magazines, an advertiser can reach a selected audience with a minimum of waste circulation. Magazines are usually read in a leisurely fashion, in contrast to the haste in which other print media are read. This feature is especially valuable to the advertiser with a lengthy or complicated message. Magazines have a relatively long life, anywhere from a week to a month, and a high pass-along readership.

Here radio uses characteristics of another medium (detail and visual images) to communicate with prospects.

With less flexible production schedules than newspapers, magazines require ads to be submitted several weeks before publication. In addition, because they are published weekly or monthly, it is more difficult to use topical messages. Magazines are often read at times or in places—on planes or in doctors' offices, for instance—far removed from where a buying impulse can be acted on.

### OUTDOOR ADVERTISING

Outdoor advertising has a low cost per exposure. Because of the mobile nature of our society, outdoor ads reach a large percentage of the population. But because it is typically seen by people "on the go," billboard advertising is appropriate only for brief messages. It is excellent for reminder advertising, and it carries the impact of large size and color. Motion and three-dimensional figures can be incorporated in a billboard's design for increased attention-getting ability. Billboards provide flexibility in geographic coverage and intensity of market coverage within an area. However, unless the advertised product is a widely used good or service, considerable waste circulation will occur. Although the cost of reaching an individual person is low, the total cost of a national billboard campaign can be quite high. Finally, the landscape-defacing aspect of outdoor advertising has aroused considerable public criticism.

Three-dimensional billboards (this one using fire hoses for shoelaces) are effective attention-getters for simple messages.

## Creating Advertisements

Remember that the ultimate purpose of advertising is to sell something and that the ad itself is a sales message. The ad may be a fast-paced sales talk, as in a direct-action TV ad by a car dealership. Or it may be a very long-range, low-key message, as are many institutional ads. Whatever the method, the goal is to sell something sooner or later. Consequently advertising involves the same *AIDA* steps used in personal selling (as discussed in Chapter 17). The ad must first attract *attention* and then hold *interest* long enough to stimulate a *desire* for the product. Finally, the ad must move the prospect to some kind of *action*.

Attention can be achieved in many ways. (Recall our discussion of perception in Chapter 5.) The most common approach is to present the material in an unexpected manner. Thus a print ad might be mostly white space or a TV ad might show the product in an unusual setting. Sometimes, however, the attention-getting component may overwhelm the message. An informal poll of ad executives on the best and worst ads of the 1980s identified several of this type, including the campaigns for Reebok (U.B.U.), Infiniti's Zen-inspired ads, and Wang's computer jargon series.[3]

Maintaining interest once the audience recognizes that the communication is an ad is a challenge for advertisers. Except for people very involved with the product, most of us will quickly transfer our attention elsewhere. Therefore, advertisers must make the ad interesting through the use of humor, an attractive spokesperson, or some other device to hold the audience.

Desire for a product is stimulated by effectively presenting the product's benefits. This is the heart of the ad. Through words, pictures, and/or sounds, the advertiser must make the consumer imagine experiencing the product's benefits. The desired consumer action may be retention of new knowledge about the product or company, a change in attitude, a request for additional information, or the actual purchase of the product.

Creating an advertisement involves writing the copy, selecting the illustration (for visual media), preparing the visual or verbal layout, and reproducing the ad for the selected media. The **copy** in an ad is all the written or spoken

---

[3]Joanne Lipman, "Ads of the '80s: The Loved and the Losers," *The Wall Street Journal,* Dec. 28, 1989, pp. B1, B4.

material in it. Copy in a print ad includes the headline, coupons, advertiser's identification, and the main body of the message. In a broadcast ad the copy is the script.

For visual ads, the **illustration** is a powerful feature. The main points to consider about illustrations are (1) whether they are totally appropriate to the product advertised and (2) despite the adage "a picture is worth a thousand words," whether they are the best use of the space. The **layout** is the physical arrangement of all the elements in an advertisement. In print ads it is the appearance of the page. For television, layout is the set as well as the positioning of actors and props. The layout of a radio ad is the sequence in which information is presented. A good layout can hold interest as well as attract attention. It should lead the audience through the entire ad in an orderly fashion.

The cost of creating an ad can vary from almost nothing for a local radio spot written by the staff at a radio station to as much as $400,000 for a network television commercial. In recent years production costs for network TV ads have escalated dramatically. As a result, fewer ads are being made and they are kept on the air longer. Chanel, for example, used the same two TV ads for eight years.

## EVALUATING THE ADVERTISING EFFORT

In managing its advertising program, a company should carefully evaluate the effectiveness of previous and future ads. Shrinking profit margins and increasing competition—both foreign and domestic—force management to appraise all expenditures. Top executives want proof that advertising is justified. They want to know whether dollars spent on advertising are producing as many sales as could be reaped from the same dollars spent on other activities.

### Difficulty of Evaluation

It is very hard to measure the sales effectiveness of advertising. By the very nature of the marketing mix, all elements—including advertising—are so intertwined that measurement of any one by itself is nearly impossible. Factors that contribute to the difficulty of measuring the sales impact of advertising are:

- *Ads have different objectives.* Though all advertising is ultimately intended to increase sales, individual ads may not be aimed at producing immediate results. For example, some ads simply announce new store hours or service policies. Other ads build goodwill or contribute to a company's image.
- *Ads can have an effect over time.* Even an ad designed to have an immediate sales impact may produce results days, weeks, or months after it appears. A consumer may be influenced by an ad but not be able to act on it immediately. Or an ad may plant in the consumer's mind a seed that doesn't blossom into a sale for several weeks. It is impossible to determine, with the exception of mail-order advertising, when a particular ad or campaign produced results.
- *Measurement problems.* In most instances consumers can't say when or if a specific ad influenced their behavior, let alone caused them to buy. Human motivation is too complicated to be explained by a single factor.

In spite of these problems, advertisers do attempt to measure advertising effectiveness because they must do so—and some knowledge is better than none at all. Effectiveness may be tested before an ad is presented, while it is being presented, or after it has completed its run.

## Methods Used to Measure Effectiveness

Methods of measuring ad effectiveness can be categorized as direct and indirect. **Direct tests** measure or predict the sales volume stemming from the advertisement or campaign being tested. Tabulating the number of redemptions of a reduced-price coupon incorporated in an ad will indicate its effectiveness. Coupons frequently are coded so they can also be traced to the publications from which they came. Another type of direct test measures the number of inquiries that are received from an ad that offers additional information to prospects who call or write in.

Most other types of measures are **indirect tests** of effectiveness, or measures of something other than actual sales. *Recall tests* are based on the premise that an advertisement can have an effect only if it is remembered. Three common recall tests are:

- Recognition—showing people an ad and asking if they have seen it before.
- Aided recall—asking people if they can recall seeing any ads for a particular brand.
- Unaided recall—asking people if they can remember seeing any ads within a product category.

A well-known indirect measure is the Starch Readership Test, which measures exposure to print ads. The Starch researcher pages through magazines with people who have previously read them and notes whether the subjects remember noticing the ads, how much of the copy they read, and whether they associated the ads with the sponsors.

This ad combines sales promotion with advertising. By coding coupons and tabulating the number of coupons redeemed, manufacturers can gauge the effectiveness of a particular campaign.

Ads may also be tested before they are presented to the general public. Advertisements in nearly finished form (to save production costs) are presented to panels of consumers for their reactions. This is often done in theater settings for television ads, with the test ad shown along with other ads, in the context of a regular TV program. After viewing the program and the ads, the consumers are quizzed about the ad being tested.

Refinements are constantly being made in advertising testing. Developments in areas such as laboratory test markets and computer simulations hold promise for the future. However, the complexity of decision making combined with the multitude of influences on the buyer will continue to make measuring the effectiveness of advertising a difficult task.

## ORGANIZING FOR ADVERTISING

Now let's consider what kind of organization is needed to perform and manage advertising activities. Management has three alternatives: (1) develop an internal advertising department, (2) use an outside advertising agency, or (3) use both an internal department and an advertising agency. Regardless of which alternative is selected, generally the same specialized skills are necessary to do the advertising job. Creative people are needed to prepare the copy, generate illustrative material, and design the layouts. Media experts are required to select the appropriate media, buy the time or space, and arrange for the scheduled appearance of the ads. And managerial skills are essential to plan and administer the entire advertising program.

### Internal Departments

All of these advertising tasks, some of them, or just overall direction can be performed by an internal department. When advertising is a substantial part of the marketing mix, a company usually has its own advertising department. If the company is to implement the marketing concept, the head of this department should report to the head of marketing. Large retailers, for example, have their own advertising departments and may not use advertising agencies at all.

### Advertising Agencies

Many companies, especially manufacturers, use advertising agencies to carry out some or all of their advertising activities. An **advertising agency** is an independent company that renders specialized services in advertising in particular and in marketing in general.

Advertising agencies plan and execute entire advertising campaigns. They employ more advertising specialists than their clients do because they spread the cost over many accounts. A company can benefit from an agency's experience with other products and clients. Many advertising agencies offer a wide range of services including research, public relations, and new product development assistance. In fact, many of these firms are becoming *marketing* agencies, offering services heretofore performed by other outside specialists or by the advertisers themselves.

### Using Both a Department and an Agency

Many firms have their own advertising department and also use an advertising agency. The internal advertising department acts as a liaison between the agency and the company, giving the company greater control over this major expenditure. It approves the agency's plans and ads, is responsible for preparing and administering the advertising budget, and coordinates advertising with personal selling. The department may also handle direct mail, dealer displays, and other promotional activities if they are not handled by the agency.

Sales promotion comes in many forms. This three-story piñata was a big hit with children at a Hispanic festival.

## NATURE AND IMPORTANCE OF SALES PROMOTION

Sales promotion is one of the most loosely used terms in the marketing vocabulary. We define **sales promotion** as those promotional activities (other than advertising, personal selling, public relations, and publicity) that are intended to stimulate customer demand and improve the marketing performance of sellers. Sales promotion includes coupons, premiums, in-store displays, trade shows, samples, in-store demonstrations, and contests. Sales promotion activities may be conducted by producers or middlemen. The target for producers' sales promotion may be middlemen or end users—households, business users—or the producer's own sales force. Middlemen direct sales promotion at their sales people or prospects further down the channel of distribution.

Sales promotion is distinct from advertising and personal selling, but all three activities often are interrelated. In fact, a major function of sales promotion is to serve as a bridge between advertising and personal selling—to supplement and coordinate efforts in these two areas. For example, an in-store display (sales promotion) furnished by the manufacturer to stores selling Michelin tires may feature a slogan and illustrations from Michelin's current advertising campaign. This effective display makes retailers more receptive to talking with Michelin sales people. Or prospecting leads may be generated from people who visited the Canon copy-machines exhibit at an office equipment trade show.

Recently sales promotion has been the fastest-growing method of promotion, with dollars being shifted from advertising. Total annual expenditures for sales promotion are estimated to parallel or even exceed those for advertising. Sales promotion is also being integrated into the total marketing strategy in many firms. It is being introduced at the inception of a promotion campaign, not tacked on as an afterthought.

The numbers attached to some sales promotion activities are mind-boggling. More than *220 billion* coupons were distributed in 1988, and more than *7 billion* were redeemed by consumers.[4] Experts estimate that close to *400*

[4]Julie Liesse Erickson, "FSI Boom to Go Bust?" *Advertising Age*, May 1, 1989, pp. 1, 82.

*billion* will be distributed by 1995. Millions of people attend trade shows each year, and billions of dollars are spent on point-of-purchase displays in retail stores. The number of contests and the dollar value of their prizes more than doubled from the mid-1980s to 1990.

Several factors in the marketing environment contribute to the surging popularity of sales promotion:

- *Short-run orientation.* Sales promotions such as couponing and trade allowances produce quicker, more measurable sales results. However, critics of this strategy argue that these immediate benefits come at the expense of building a strong brand image in consumers' minds and condition buyers to expect incentives. Thus they feel an overemphasis on sales promotion will undermine a product's future.
- *Competitive pressure.* If competitors are offering buyers price reductions, contests, or other incentives, a firm may feel forced to retaliate with its own sales promotions.
- *State of the economy.* Rising prices have made consumers more price-conscious. Thus, sales promotions become more attractive to them.
- *Low quality of retail selling.* Many retailers have switched to self-service or use sales clerks who are inadequately trained. For these outlets sales promotion devices such as product displays and information booklets often are the only effective promotional tools available at the point of purchase.

## STRATEGIC MANAGEMENT OF SALES PROMOTION

Sales promotion should be included in a company's strategic marketing planning, along with advertising and personal selling. This means setting sales promotion goals, selecting appropriate strategies, and establishing a separate sales promotion budget. Management should also evaluate the performance of sales promotion activities.

One problem management faces is that many sales promotion tools are short-run, tactical actions. Coupons, premiums, and contests, for example, are designed to produce immediate (but short-lived) responses. As a result, they are frequently used as stopgap measures to shore up unexpected sales declines rather than as integrated parts of a marketing program.

## Determining Objectives and Strategies

Early in the strategic planning for sales promotion, management should (1) set goals for the current sales promotion program, (2) identify target markets, and (3) select appropriate strategies.

We identified three broad objectives of sales promotion when defining the term:

- Stimulating end-user demand (either business user or household).
- Improving the marketing performance of middlemen and sales people.
- Supplementing and coordinating advertising and personal selling.

More specific objectives of sales promotion are much like those for advertising and personal selling. Examples are:

- *To gain a trial for a new or improved product.* Procter & Gamble or Lever Brothers might send a free sample through the mail.
- *To disrupt existing buying habits.* A coupon offering a large discount might cause a consumer to switch brands of a product that is viewed as generic, such as orange juice or motor oil.
- *To attract new customers.* Financial institutions have offered small appliances and other premiums to encourage consumers to open accounts.

Does this store display for Weebok baby shoes represent a push or pull strategy?

- *To encourage greater use by existing customers.* United and most other airlines have "frequent flyer" programs to encourage travelers to use their airlines more often.
- *To combat a competitor's promotional activity.* One supermarket chain runs a lottery or game to attract shoppers and a competitor retaliates by offering triple-value coupons.
- *To increase impulse buying.* End-of-aisle and island displays in supermarkets can increase sales of a product by as much as 50 percent.
- *To get greater retailer cooperation.* A sporting-goods manufacturer gets additional shelf space by setting up excellent point-of-purchase displays, training retailers' sales people, and providing tote bags to be given away with purchases.

The choice of sales promotion tools derives directly from the objectives of the total marketing program. Consider the following situations and the different strategies available:

- A firm's objective is to increase sales, which calls for entering new geographic markets using a *pull strategy.* To encourage product trial and lure consumers away from familiar brands, possible sales promotion tactics are coupons, cash rebates, free samples, and premiums.
- A firm's objective is to protect market share in the face of intense competition. This goal suggests a *push strategy* to improve retailer performance and goodwill. Training retailers' sales forces, supplying effective point-of-purchase displays, and granting advertising allowances would be appropriate sales promotion options.

### Determining Sales Promotion Budgets

The sales promotion budget should be established when the budget for the total promotional mix is determined. Combining sales promotion with advertising or public relations for budgetary purposes or lumping it together with an appropriation labeled "advertising" is likely to prevent the development of a separate sales promotion strategy. Sales promotion may then be overlooked or poorly integrated with the other components of promotion. Setting a separate budget for sales promotion forces a company to recognize and manage this important activity.

Consistent with developing an integrated strategy, the amount budgeted for sales promotion should be determined by the task method. This forces management to consider specific objectives and the sales promotion techniques that will be used to accomplish them.

### Selecting the Appropriate Tools

A key step in sales promotion management is deciding which tools will help the organization reach its promotional goals. As shown in Table 18-3, these tools may be divided into three categories, based on the target audience: end users, middlemen, or the producer's own sales force. The same tool may be used to reach more than one audience category. For example, each year there are more than 100 auto shows in U.S. cities. These displays of new automobile models, sports cars, racing cars, and exotic custom vehicles attract huge crowds of consumers—1 million in New York and 500,000 in Los Angeles—as well as news reporters. Thus they provide excellent publicity opportunities.

Factors that influence the choice of promotional tools include:

- *The organization's promotional objectives.* Does it want to use a pull or a push strategy?

---

**TABLE 18-3 Major sales promotion tools, grouped by target audience**

| End users (consumer or business) | Middlemen and their sales forces | Producers' own sales force |
| --- | --- | --- |
| Coupons | Trade shows and exhibitions | Sales contests |
| Cash rebates | Point-of-purchase displays | Sales training manuals |
| Premiums (gifts) | Free goods | Sales meetings |
| Free samples | Advertising allowances | Packets with promotional materials |
| Contests and sweepstakes | Contests for sales people | Demonstration model of product |
| Point-of-purchase displays | Training middlemen's sales force | |
| Product demonstrations | Product demonstrations | |
| Trade shows and exhibitions | Advertising specialties | |
| Advertising specialties | | |

- *Target market for the promotion.* Is promotion aimed at ultimate consumers, middlemen, or the firm's own sales force?
- *Nature of the product.* Does it lend itself to sampling or demonstration?
- *Cost of the tool.* Sampling a large market is very expensive.
- *Current economic conditions.* Coupons, premiums, and rebates are good options during periods of recession or inflation.

### SALES PROMOTION DIRECTED AT FINAL CONSUMERS

Many of the tools in Table 18-3 probably are quite familiar to you, but a brief discussion of some of them will give you a better sense of their significance. In a 20-year time span, the number of coupons distributed by marketers has increased by over 1,200 percent (Do you remember the enormous number of coupons we said were distributed in 1988?) with no end in sight.

"Advertising specialties" is a miscellaneous category of small, usually inexpensive items imprinted with a company's name or logo that are given or sold by producers or middlemen to customers and prospects. Examples are pens, calendars, key rings, paperweights, coffee cups, hats, and jackets.

### SALES PROMOTION DIRECTED AT MIDDLEMEN

Some of the tools just discussed may also be directed at middlemen and their sales forces. In addition, trade associations in industries as diverse as shoes, travel, and furniture sponsor trade shows that are open only to wholesalers and retailers. Many producers also spend considerable time and money to train the sales forces of their wholesalers and retailers.

### SALES PROMOTION DIRECTED AT A PRODUCER'S OWN SALES FORCE

Again, there is overlap between the tools directed at middlemen and those designed for the producer's own sales force. Sales contests are probably the most significant of these tools, with about 30 percent of firms offering one kind or another.[5] The most common incentive is cash, used in over half of all contests. Other incentives include merchandise, plaques, jewelery, and travel. Visual sales aids (flipcharts, slides) are prepared for sales people and brochures are developed to reinforce sales presentations.

[5]"1989 Survey of Selling Costs," *Sales & Marketing Management*, Feb. 20, 1989, p. 26.

**EVALUATING SALES PROMOTION**

As with other components of the promotional mix, management should try to evaluate the productivity or effectiveness of sales promotion. For many sales promotion tools, this task is much easier and the results more accurate than is the case with advertising. For example, responses to a premium offer or a coupon with a specified closing date can be counted and compared to a similar period when there were no sales promotions underway. Elements that contribute to this ease of measurement are:

- Sales promotions have definite starting and ending points. Coupons must be redeemed by a certain date. Contest entries must be submitted before a particular deadline. Sales contests for the sales force count only the sales made during a specified period. This is quite different from advertising, where there can be significant residual effects and the results of one campaign may overlap another.
- Most sales promotions are designed to impact sales directly. It is more difficult to measure a change in attitude or an increase in information about a product or brand than it is to count sales.

However, there are some pitfalls in measuring sales promotion effects. First, not all sales promotions meet the conditions just mentioned. For instance, training given to a distributor's sales force may be valuable, but may not produce immediate results. Second, sales promotion results may be inflated by sales cannibalized from the future. That is, a sales promotion may get buyers to act now when they would have bought the product in the future anyway. An indication of cannibalization is a lower level of sales *after* the promotion ends compared to *before* the sales promotion began. Third, any attempt at measurement must take into consideration external conditions such as the behavior of competitors and the state of the economy. A firm's market share may not increase following an expensive sales promotion, for example, but the promotion may have offset the potentially damaging impact of a competitor's promotional activity.

## PUBLIC RELATIONS AND PUBLICITY

Public relations and publicity are the last two methods of promotion that we shall discuss in connection with an organization's total promotional program. In most organizations these promotional tools typically are relegated to stepchild status behind personal selling, advertising, and sales promotion. There are several reasons for management's lack of attention to these areas:

- *Organizational structure.* In most companies public relations and publicity are not the responsibility of the marketing department. If there is an organized effort, it is usually handled by a small public relations department that reports directly to top management.
- *Inadequate definitions.* The terms public relations and publicity are loosely used by businesses and the public. There are no generally accepted definitions of the two terms, nor is there a clear-cut distinction between them.
- *Unrecognized benefits.* Only recently have many organizations come to appreciate the tremendous value of good public relations and publicity. As the cost of promotion has gone up, firms are realizing that positive exposure through the media or as a result of community involvement can produce a high return on the investment of time and effort.
- *Adverse publicity.* In a society that is increasingly sensitive about the environment and where news media are quick to report mistakes, organiza-

tions tend to focus on the negative dimension of publicity. As a result, managers are so concerned with avoiding bad publicity that they overlook the potential of publicity for improving the firm's image.

## Nature and Scope of Public Relations

**Public relations** is a broad, overall communications effort to influence various groups' attitudes toward the organization. Public relations activities typically are designed to build or maintain a favorable image for an organization and a favorable relationship with its various publics—customers, prospects, stockholders, employees, labor unions, the local community, and the government. Note that this description is quite similar to our definition of institutional advertising. However, unlike advertising, public relations need not use the media to communicate its message.

Good public relations can be achieved by supporting charitable projects (by supplying volunteer labor or other resources), participating in community service events, sponsoring athletic teams, funding the arts, producing an employee or customer newsletter, and disseminating information through exhibits, displays, and tours. Major firms like Exxon and Johnson & Johnson sponsor shows on public television (PBS) as part of their public relations effort.

Following the major league baseball lockout, public relations became an important issue for at least one team.

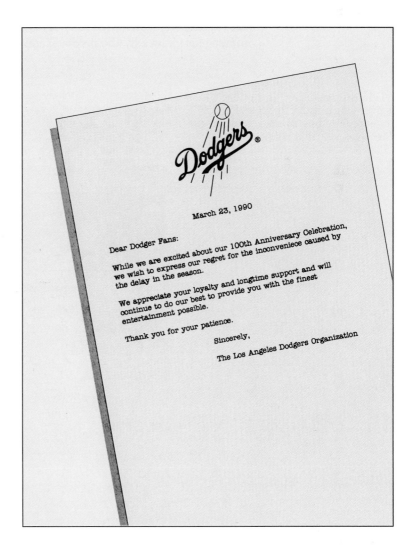

## PUBLICITY AS A FORM OF PUBLIC RELATIONS

**Publicity** is any promotional communication about an organization or its products that is presented by the media but is *not* paid for by the organization. Publicity usually takes the form of a news story appearing in a mass medium or an endorsement provided by an individual informally or in a speech or interview.

There are three channels for gaining publicity. One is to prepare a story (called a news release) and circulate it to the media. The intention is for the selected newspapers, television stations, or other media to report the information as news. The second channel is personal communication with a group. A press conference will draw media representatives if they feel the subject or speaker has news value. Company tours and speeches to civic or professional groups are other forms of individual-to-group communications. The third channel is one-on-one personal communication, often called lobbying. Companies lobby legislators or other powerful people in an attempt to influence their opinions, and subsequently their decisions. In addition, firms will give products to highly visible people in hopes that the people will be seen using them.

Publicity can help to accomplish any communication objective. It can be used to announce new products, publicize new policies, recognize employees, describe research breakthroughs, or report financial performance—if the message is viewed by the media as newsworthy or by the group or individual

Public relations or publicity? If a public relations event such as the L'eggs Mini-Marathon is reported by the news media, the sponsor receives valuable publicity.

---

**Why Elvis is more successful today than ever**

Although advertising expenditures have been modest ($100,000 in 1988), the number of visitors to Graceland—Elvis Presley's former home—continues to grow. The estate now earns about $15 million a year, twice as much as Elvis made in his best year. Most of the income comes from ticket sales to Graceland and sales of souvenirs.

The major marketing tool has been public relations. Each year Graceland sponsors an Elvis International Tribute week to commemorate his death. Other activities include hosting reunions of Elvis's high school class at the mansion, an Elvis Presley MasterCard issued by a local bank, and a quarterly newsletter sent to 900 media outlets and 3,000 subscribers.

A few marketing problems remain. Sixty percent of the visitors are female. To lure more male visitors, a million dollars was spent on the Elvis Presley Automobile Museum, located across the street from the mansion. Seasonal demand fluctuations have been another concern. In the summer 4,000 people visit every day, but during the winter the number drops to 1,000. To achieve a better balance, a Christmas program with a laser light show has been developed.

Source: Andrew Feinberg, "Elvis' Graceland, the Attraction that Sells Itself," *Adweek's Marketing Week*, July 10, 1989, p. 17.

---

recipient as interesting or useful. This is what distinguishes publicity from advertising—publicity cannot be "forced" on the audience. This is also the source of its power. The credibility level of publicity typically is much higher than advertising. If we tell you our product is great, you may well be skeptical. But if an independent, objective third party says our product is great, you are more likely to believe it.

### BENEFITS AND LIMITATIONS OF PUBLICITY

Recognizing the value of publicity, some organizations have special units to generate information. For example, Gatorade created the Sports Science Institute, Reebok operates the Aerobic Information Bureau, and Nutri-System set up the Health and Fitness Information Bureau, all designed to link their respective firms with consumer interests. However, to fulfill its potential, publicity must be treated as part of promotional strategy and coordinated with the other promotional tools. The benefits of publicity are:

- *Lower cost than advertising or personal selling.* Publicity usually costs much less than advertising and personal selling because there are no media space or time costs for conveying the message.
- *Greater credibility than advertising.* Because the source of the message is an uninvolved third party, the message is more believable than an ad.
- *Increased readership.* Many consumers are conditioned to ignore advertising or at least pay it scant attention. Publicity is presented as editorial material or news, so it gets greater readership.
- *More information.* Again, because it is presented as editorial material, publicity can contain much more detail than a standard ad. Thus more information and persuasive content can be included in the message.
- *Timeliness.* A company can put out a news release very quickly when some unexpected event occurs.

Of course, publicity also has some limitations:

- *Loss of control over the message.* An organization has no guarantee that a publicity release will appear in the media. In fact, only a small proportion of all publicity messages prepared are ever used. In addition, there is no way to control how much or what portion of a publicity release the media will print or broadcast.
- *Limited exposure.* The media will typically use publicity material only once. If the target audience misses the message when it is presented, there is no second or third chance. Thus there is no opportunity for repetition as in advertising.
- *Publicity is not free.* Even though there are no media time and space costs, there are expenses in staffing a publicity department and in preparing and disseminating messages.

**Evaluating Public Relations and Publicity**

Although few executives would argue that having a good image and staying in touch with an organization's publics are unimportant, evaluating public relations and publicity is difficult. In the past, evaluation usually involved a report of inputs or activities rather than outputs or results. Public relations departments maintained "scrapbooks" to show management what was being done. These days, to justify expenditures, more organizations are requiring departments to provide specific public relations objectives and show measurable results. Because it is impossible to relate public relations and publicity directly to sales, other measures must be used. One is behavioral research to show, for example, increased awareness of a product or brand name or changes in attitudes and beliefs about a firm.

**SUMMARY**

Advertising is the nonpersonal, mass-communications component in a company's promotional mix. The firm has the option of running product or institutional types of advertising. Product ads may call for direct or indirect action. Another useful classification of advertising is primary demand and selective demand stimulation, which include pioneering, competitive, and comparative advertising. Manufacturers and their retail dealers often employ vertical cooperative advertising, in which they share the cost of advertising the manufacturer's product at the local level. Horizontal cooperative advertising involves joint sponsorship of ads by firms at the same level of distribution.

Advertising expenditures are large, but the average cost of advertising in a firm is typically 1 to 3 percent of sales. This is considerably less than the average cost of personal selling. Most advertising dollars are spent in newspapers, with television a close second. Other important media are radio, magazines, direct mail, and outdoor displays.

Management should create an advertising campaign as part of the firm's total promotional program. The first step is to set specific goals for the particular campaign. A major task in developing a campaign is to select the advertising media—the general medium type, the particular category, and the specific vehicle. The choice should be based on the characteristics of the media and the way they fit the product and the market. The advertising message—consisting of the copy, illustration, and layout—is an integral part of an advertisement.

An especially important yet difficult task in advertising management is evaluating the effectiveness of the advertising effort—both the entire campaign and individual ads. Except for sales results tests, commonly used techniques measure only the extent to which the ad was read or recalled. To operate an advertising program, a firm may rely on its own advertising department, an advertising agency, or a combination of the two.

Sales promotion is the third major promotional tool. It is used to coordinate and supplement the advertising and personal selling programs. Sales promotion has increased considerably in importance in recent years as management has sought measurable, short-term sales results. Sales promotion should receive the same strategic attention that a company gives to advertising and personal selling. This means establishing objectives and appropriate strategies. A separate budget should be set for sales promotion. Sales promotion can be directed toward final consumers, middlemen, or a company's own employees. To implement its strategic plans, management can choose from a wide variety of sales promotion tools. Sales promotion performance also should be evaluated.

Public relations and publicity were the final promotional methods discussed. Public relations is the broad, overall promotional vehicle for improving or maintaining an organization's image and its favorable relationship with its publics. Publicity, a part of public relations, is any promotional communication regarding an organization and/or its products that is not paid for by the company benefiting from it. Typically these two activities are handled in a department separate from the marketing department in a firm. Nevertheless the management process of planning, implementing, and evaluating should be applied to their performance in the same way it is applied to advertising and personal selling.

| **KEY TERMS AND CONCEPTS** | | |
|---|---|---|
| | Advertising 452 | Horizontal cooperative advertising 454 |
| | Advertisements 452 | Advertising campaign 458 |
| | Product advertising 452 | Advertising media 458 |
| | Direct-action advertising 452 | Cost per thousand (CPM) 459 |
| | Indirect-action advertising 452 | Copy 462 |
| | Institutional advertising 452 | Illustrations 463 |
| | Customer service advertising 452 | Layout 463 |
| | Public service advertising 452 | Direct tests 464 |
| | Primary demand advertising 452 | Indirect tests 464 |
| | Selective demand advertising 452 | Advertising agency 465 |
| | Differential advantage 453 | Sales promotion 466 |
| | Pioneering advertising 453 | Sales promotion tools 468 |
| | Comparative advertising 453 | Public relations 471 |
| | Cooperative advertising 454 | Publicity 472 |
| | Vertical cooperative advertising 454 | |
| | Advertising allowance 454 | |

## QUESTIONS AND PROBLEMS

1. How do you account for the variation in advertising expenditures as a percentage of sales among the different companies in Table 18-2?

2. Several specific advertising objectives were outlined early in the chapter. Bring to class print ads that illustrate at least four of these goals. As an alternative, be prepared to describe four radio or television ads that attempt to achieve these objectives.

3. Which advertising medium would you recommend as best for each of these products?
   a. Wooden pallets.
   b. Hanes pantyhose.
   c. Tax preparation service.
   d. Mortuary.
   e. Toys for young children.
   f. Plastic clothespins.

4. Many grocery product and candy manufacturers

earmark a good portion of their advertising budgets for use in magazines. Is this a wise choice of media for these firms? Explain.

5. Why do department stores use newspapers more than local radio stations as an advertising medium?

6. Why is it worthwhile to pretest advertisements before they appear in the media? How could a test market be used to pretest an ad? (You may want to refresh your memory with a review of test marketing in Chapter 3.)

7. What procedures can a firm use to determine how many sales dollars resulted from a direct-mail ad? How would you determine whether any sales were cannibalized?

8. If a manufacturing firm finds a good ad agency, should it discontinue its own advertising department? Should it consider any changes?

9. Visit a supermarket, a hardware store, or a movie theatre and make a list of all the sales promotion tools that you observe. Which do you feel are particularly effective and why?

10. Is sales promotion effective for selling expensive consumer products such as houses, automobiles, or cruise trips? Is your answer the same for expensive business products?

11. Explain how sales promotion might be used to offset weak personal selling in retail stores.

12. Describe a recent public relations event in your community. How did it benefit the sponsor?

13. How does publicity differ from advertising?

14. Bring to class an article from a daily newspaper that appears to be the result of a firm's publicity efforts. Summarize the points made in the article that may benefit the firm. Could the same benefits be obtained through advertising?

15. Given that the United States is the largest industrial nation in the world, why do you think only 2 of the top 10 advertisers outside the United States are American firms?

## CASE 16

**PASQUINI'S PIZZERIA\*** Promotional Program for a Small Business

About 2 months ago Tony Pasquini purchased a small pizzeria, which he promptly renamed Pasquini's Pizzeria. The location had housed a pizzeria for about 2½ years with two previous owners. The first owner had operated the pizzeria successfully. Under the most recent owner, however, both in-house sales and home-delivery volume had declined considerably. In effect, Tony Pasquini had acquired an ailing business.

Tony had some experience in the pizza business. As a teenager and college student, he had worked in various capacities in a pizzeria his family owned and operated. In his current situation, Tony faced a problem that commonly confronts young entrepreneurs who have recently acquired a small business. That is, Tony was wondering what would be the most effective way to promote his products.

Pasquini's Pizzeria sold an assortment of freshly made pizzas and other products. The main product was a thick-crusted, New York–style pizza available with a choice of toppings. The restaurant also made and sold calzones (folded pizza dough stuffed with pizza toppings), submarine sandwiches, and salads. No alcoholic beverages were sold by Pasquini's Pizzeria. The restaurant provided a place to eat as well as free home delivery of all menu items within a radius of 20 blocks from the location.

Pasquini's Pizzeria was located in Denver, Colorado, on a major north-south thoroughfare about 2 miles south of the central downtown business district. The restaurant was about the same distance from Denver University, a private school with an enrollment of about 7,500.

\*Adapted from a case prepared by Anthony Pasquini, under the direction of Professor William J. Stanton.

According to Tony Pasquini, the pizza restaurant business had boomed during the past 5 years—especially in the area of home delivery. Franchises such as Domino's and Little Caesars were proliferating across the United States. Denver had followed the national trend with an increase in pizza restaurants. In Pasquini's delivery area alone, there were five pizzerias including Pizza Hut and Domino's. Three of these five competitors featured home delivery. Two of them had the ability to deliver within 30 minutes, in contrast to Pasquini's 45 minutes. However, these two competitors did not deliver all the items listed on their menus. The national chains also had the advantage of large budgets for advertising and other promotion.

During the first two months after Tony acquired the pizzeria, he concentrated on selecting and training a team of dependable workers. Now he was ready to devote his attention to the task of increasing the pizzeria's sales volume. Currently Pasquini's was taking in $3,600 a month at lunchtime and $5,500 during the evenings. "During the next 6 months," he said, "my goal is to triple our lunch business and quadruple our evening business. That should give us a sales volume of close to $400,000 per year. I realize that the increase in evening business will have to come from home-delivery sales, because at nighttime, South Broadway [his location] is dead."

Tony believed that the key to achieving these sales goals was to get people to try Pasquini's pizza. "Our pizzas taste great and their quality is top-notch. We just need to make people aware of Pasquini's Pizzeria and get them to try our pizza. Then I am sure that we will have the repeat business we need to reach our sales goal." However, to generate this customer awareness and product sampling, Tony understood

**477**

# CHAPTER 19
# MARKETING OF SERVICES

The financial services field is a whole new ball game since it underwent deregulation in the 1980s. During the years when the industry was tightly regulated by the government, competition among the institutions was minimal. Interest rates on savings accounts were standardized, for example, and financial institutions were limited with respect to the activities in which they could engage.

Today commercial banks, savings and loans, securities brokers, and other financial institutions are performing services that generally were unknown to them a few years ago. Merrill Lynch, for instance, formerly was limited to securities brokering, but now it markets a wide variety of financial services. This firm provides a cash-management program that includes check-writing privileges arranged in connection with a commercial bank. Through Merrill Lynch you can get a VISA credit card or a larger personal loan (with your home as collateral) that is much like a mortgage. As another example, some of the large New York commercial banks (Chase Manhattan, Manufacturers Hanover Trust, Citibank) have established a computer-based global information system. This network offers a worldwide cash-management program and a broad range of other information services for corporate customers. In the past, to deposit or withdraw money, you had to go to your bank in person or use the mail. Today a service and distribution innovation—automated teller machines (ATM)—can be found in convenient, freestanding locations such as shopping malls, supermarkets, and college campuses.

Financial institutions are finding that the consumer now directs decisions on what new "products" to offer and how to present them. These organizations are taking their cues from consumer packaged goods firms and are even hiring executives from these industries. However, many financial services companies have found to their disappointment that following the marketing practices of consumer packaged goods manufacturers—and even hiring executives from those industries—does not necessarily result in market success. There are too many differences between tangible goods marketing and financial services marketing. Most financial services companies are still in the learning stage with respect to effectively using marketing research, market segmentation, sales training, advertising, and other aspects of marketing.[1]

[1] Aimée L. Stern, "Now What Do We Do?" *Dun's Business Month*, January 1987, p. 54.

Financial institutions are typical of many service industries that previously had not been familiar with marketing and simply do not understand what marketing is. In the 1990s, however, it is increasingly evident that many service organizations must become more marketing-oriented if they hope to survive. This chapter will focus on significant differences between marketing services and marketing tangible goods, as well as the current growth and importance of services in our economy.

## NATURE AND IMPORTANCE OF SERVICES

In concept, goods marketing and services marketing are essentially the same. In each case the marketer must select and analyze its target markets. Then a marketing program must be built around the parts of the marketing mix—the good or service, the price structure, the distribution system, and the promotional program. In practice, there often are substantial similarities as well. However, the basic characteristics that differentiate services from goods typically lead to a quite different marketing program. The strategies and tactics used in conventional goods marketing frequently are inappropriate for services marketing.

### Definition and Scope of Services

We are talking about the marketing of services, but what do we mean by "services"? The term is difficult to define, because invariably services are marketed in conjunction with tangible goods. Services require supporting goods (you need an airplane to provide air transportation services), and goods require supporting services (to sell even a shirt or can of beans calls at least for a cashier's service). Furthermore, a company may sell a combination of goods and services. Thus, along with repair service for your car, you might buy spark plugs or an oil filter. It may be helpful to think of every product as a mix of goods and services located on a continuum ranging from pure goods to pure services, as shown in Figure 19-1.

To move closer to a useful definition, we identify two classes of services. In the first group are services that are the *main purpose or object of a transaction*. As an example, suppose you want to rent a car from Avis. Avis needs a car (tangible good) to provide the rental service. But you are buying the rental use of the car, not the car itself. The second group consists of *supplementary* services that support or facilitate the sale of a tangible good or another service. Thus, when you buy a compact disc player, you may want technical information service from a sales person and the opportunity to pay with a credit-card service.

Consequently, our definition of services in this chapter is as follows: **Services** are identifiable, intangible activities that are the main object of a transaction designed to provide want-satisfaction to customers. By this definition we

**FIGURE 19-1** A goods–services continuum.

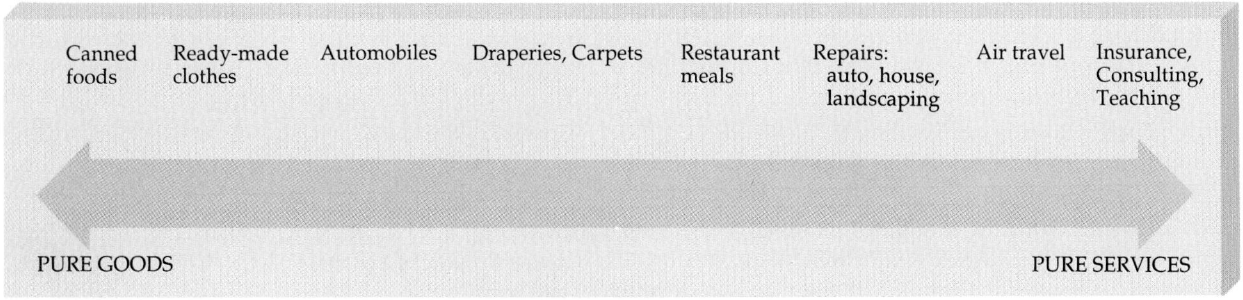

| Canned foods | Ready-made clothes | Automobiles | Draperies, Carpets | Restaurant meals | Repairs: auto, house, landscaping | Air travel | Insurance, Consulting, Teaching |

PURE GOODS

PURE SERVICES

Real estate brokerages provide a service.

exclude supplementary services that support the sale of tangible goods or other services. (In a lighter vein, a service is something that when you drop it on your foot, you don't feel anything.)

We are concerned here primarily with the services marketed by business or professional firms with profit-making motives—commercial services. This is in contrast to services of nonprofit organizations, such as churches, public schools, and the government. A useful classification of commercial services by industry is as follows:

- Housing (includes rentals of hotels, motels, apartments, houses, and farms).
- Household operations (includes utilities, house repairs, repairs of equipment in the house, landscaping, and household cleaning).
- Recreation and entertainment (includes rental and repair of equipment used to participate in recreation and entertainment activities; also admission to all entertainment, recreation, and amusement events).
- Personal care (includes laundry, dry cleaning, beauty care).
- Medical and other health care (includes all medical services, dental, nursing, hospitalization, optometry, and other health care).
- Private education.
- Business and other professional services (includes legal, accounting, management consulting, and computer services).
- Insurance, banking, and other financial services (includes personal and business insurance, credit and loan service, investment counseling, and tax services).
- Transportation (includes freight and passenger service on common carriers, automobile repairs and rentals).
- Communications (includes telephone, telegraph, computer, and specialized business communication services).

Note that no attempt was made to separate the above groups into consumer and business services, as we did with goods. In fact, most are purchased by both market groups.

## Importance of Services

The United States has moved beyond the industrial economy stage to the point where it has become the world's first service economy. Almost three-fourths of the nonfarm labor force is employed in service industries, and over two-thirds of the nation's gross national product is accounted for by services. Also, service jobs typically hold up better during a recession than do jobs in industries producing tangible goods.

During the 20-year period of 1966 to 1986, about 36 million new jobs were created in the United States—far more than in Japan and Western Europe combined. About 90 percent of these jobs were in service industries. During this same time span, some 22 million women joined the labor force—and 97 percent of these women went to work in the service sector.[2] These employment trends are expected to continue at least until the year 2000. For the period 1986–2000, the Bureau of Labor Statistics predicts that over 21 million new jobs will be created and 93 percent of them will be in service industries.[3]

Moreover, most of this explosive growth in services employment is *not* in low-paying jobs, contrary to the beliefs of many economists, business and labor leaders, and politicians. These people argue that manufacturing jobs, which have been the economic foundation of America's middle class, are vanishing. They claim that factory workers are being replaced with a host of hamburger flippers, janitors, and other low-wage earners. It is true that manufacturing jobs have declined, with many of them going to foreign countries. It is also true that there has been growth in some low-paying service jobs. Yet cooks and counter people still represent only 1 percent of the U.S. labor force today. Furthermore, for many years the fastest-growing occupational category has been "professional, technical, and related work." These jobs pay well above the average, and most are in service industries.[4]

About one-half of consumer expenditures are for the purchase of services. Projections to the year 2000 indicate that services will attract an even larger share of consumer spending. A drawback of the service economy boom is that the prices of most services have been going up at a considerably faster rate than the prices of most tangible products. You are undoubtedly aware of this if you have had your car or TV set repaired, had your shoes half-soled, or paid a medical bill in recent years.

When we say that services account for close to one-half of *consumer expenditures,* we still grossly understate the economic importance of services. These figures do not include the vast amounts spent for *business services*. By all indications, spending for business services has increased even more rapidly than spending for consumer services.

To understand the reasons for the boom in *consumer services*, we must understand what has been happening in our economy during the past 40 years. The long period of general prosperity has meant higher incomes, increased leisure time, and an overall rise in living standards. In the early stages of a period like this, people first expend their rising incomes on goods. This was particularly true after World War II, when there was a huge backlog of demand for goods. Various goods were denied to consumers in the 1930s because of the Great Depression and in the early 1940s because of the war. Then, as the years go by, the average consumer becomes sated with goods.

[2]James L. Heskett, "Thank Heaven for the Service Sector," *Business Week,* Jan. 26, 1987, p. 22.
[3]U.S. Department of Labor, Bureau of Labor Statistics, *Economic Growth and Employment Projections* program, as cited in *Sales & Marketing Management,* September 1987, p. 25.
[4]Richard I. Kirkland, Jr., "Are Service Jobs Good Jobs?" *Fortune,* June 10, 1985, p. 38.

Business services are enjoying substantial growth in the 1990s.

Consumers increasingly turn to services that heretofore they either could not afford or did not desire—services such as travel, education, personal grooming, and medical care.

The growth of *business services* may be attributed to the fact that business has become increasingly complex, specialized, and competitive. As a consequence, management has been forced to call in experts to provide services in research, taxation, advertising, labor relations, and a host of other areas.

To capitalize on the emerging service economy, many product *manufacturers* have diversified into services. Some product *retailers* have done likewise. Sears now has 40 nonmerchandise offerings, including an insurance company (Allstate), an income tax counseling firm, a car-rental agency, a securities broker (Dean Witter), and a credit-card firm (Discover). Montgomery Ward and other department stores now have in-store law and dental offices that provide services for customers.

## Characteristics of Services

The special nature of services stems from a number of distinctive characteristics. These features create special marketing challenges and opportunities. As a result, service firms often require strategic marketing programs that are substantially different from those found in the marketing of tangible goods.

### INTANGIBILITY

Because services are intangible, it is impossible for customers to sample—taste, feel, see, hear, or smell—a service before they buy it. Consequently, a company's promotional program must portray the *benefits* to be derived from

Service marketers must stress the benefits of what they offer, because of the intangibility of services.

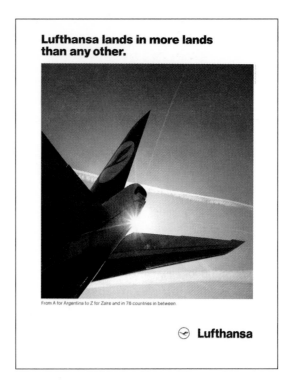

**Lufthansa lands in more lands than any other.**

From A for Argentina to Z for Zaire and in 78 countries in between.

⊛ **Lufthansa**

the service, rather than emphasizing the service itself. Four promotional strategies that may be used to suggest service benefits are as follows:[5]

- *Visualization*. For example, Carnival Cruise Lines depicts the benefits of its cruises with ads that show people dancing, dining, playing deck games, and visiting exotic places.
- *Association*. Connect the service with a tangible good, person, object, or place. The Australian airline, Qantas, uses a cuddly koala bear in its advertising to project a warm, friendly image of Australia. Prudential suggests stability and security with its Rock of Gibraltar. General Motors uses Mr. Goodwrench to build confidence in its auto repair service.
- *Physical representation*. American Express uses color—gold or platinum—for its credit-card services to symbolize wealth and prestige. Fast-food chains, telephone companies, and many other firms dress their service representatives in clean, distinctive uniforms to stress visibility, cleanliness, and dependability.
- *Documentation*. Northwest and other airlines cite facts and figures in their ads to support claims of dependability, performance, care for passengers, and safety.

**INSEPARABILITY**

Services typically cannot be separated from the creator-seller of the service. Moreover, many services are created, dispensed, and consumed simultane-

[5]Leonard L. Berry and Terry Clark, "Four Ways to Make Services More Tangible," *Business*, October–December 1986, p. 53. Also see Betsy D. Gelb, "How Marketers of Intangibles Can Raise the Odds for Consumer Satisfaction," *Journal of Services Marketing*, Summer 1987, pp. 11–17.

ously. For example, dentists create and dispense almost all their services at the same time, *and* they require the presence of the consumer for the services to be performed. Because of this inseparability feature, many people are involved concurrently in the production operations and the marketing effort in services firms. And the customers receive and consume the services at the production site—in the firm's "factory," so to speak. Consequently, customers' opinions regarding a service frequently are formed through contacts with the production–marketing personnel and impressions of the physical surroundings in the "factory." Too often, contact personnel think of themselves as producers-creators of the service rather than as marketers.

From a marketing standpoint, inseparability frequently means that direct sale is the only possible channel of distribution, and a seller's services cannot be sold in very many markets. This characteristic limits the scale of operation in a firm. One person can repair only so many autos in a day or treat only so many medical patients.

As an exception to the inseparability feature, services may be sold by a person who is representing the creator-seller. A travel agent, insurance broker, or rental agent, for instance, may represent and help promote services that will be sold by the institutions producing them.

### HETEROGENEITY

It is impossible for a service industry, or even an individual seller of services, to standardize output. Each "unit" of the service is somewhat different from

---

**This is not your common, ordinary service—**

You're invited to a fancy party, and you don't have a thing to wear. No problem—just "Rent-a-Dress."

For decades, when a man was invited to a social function that required formal evening wear, and he did not own a formal outfit, he simply *rented* a tuxedo or tails along with the appropriate accessories. Not so in the case of a woman invited to the same formal affair. She had only the alternatives of (1) buying a new dress, (2) making her own evening gown, if she was good at sewing, (3) borrowing a dress from a same-sized friend, or (4) risk wearing the same dress she had worn on a previous occasion.

But a few years ago, equal rights for women finally reached the formal-wear segment of women's apparel. In New York City there is now a shop that rents evening gowns and other party dresses. (The founder of the New York store had originally opened one in London, England, a few years earlier, and competitors have since opened similar shops in a few other large cities.) The dresses rent for $75 to $350 for a 3-day period. This service firm carries over 500 styles of dresses in a range of sizes. Some of the gowns are made by top American and European designers and would retail for thousands of dollars. Each dress is dry-cleaned after every rental, and after 10 rentals a dress is removed from inventory. It then is sold at a wholesale price—occasionally to a customer who had previously rented it and fell in love with it. This service firm appeals to budget shoppers as well as to wealthy socialites who would never wear the same dress twice. As the store's founder said, "It doesn't make sense for women to maintain an enormous wardrobe of formal dresses."

Source: "Party Time? Rent-a-Dress," *Newsweek,* Dec. 7, 1987, p. 104.

other "units" of the same service. For example, an airline does not give the same quality of service on each trip. All repair jobs a mechanic does on automobiles are not of equal quality. An added complication is the fact that it is often difficult to judge the quality of a service. (Of course, we can say the same for some goods.) It is particularly difficult to forecast quality in advance of buying a service. A person pays to see a ball game without knowing whether it will be an exciting one (well worth the price of admission) or a dull performance.

Service companies should therefore pay special attention to the product-planning stage of their marketing programs. From the beginning, management must do all it can to ensure consistency of quality and to maintain high levels of quality control. This important issue of service quality will be discussed in a later section of this chapter.

### PERISHABILITY AND FLUCTUATING DEMAND

Services are highly perishable, and they cannot be stored. Unused telephone time, empty seats in a stadium, and idle mechanics in a garage all represent business that is lost forever. Furthermore, the market for services fluctuates considerably by season, by day of the week, and by hour of the day. Many ski lifts lie idle all summer, whereas golf courses in some areas go unused in the winter. The use of city buses fluctuates greatly during the day.

There are notable exceptions to this generalization regarding the perishability and storage of services. In health and life insurance, for example, the service is purchased by a person or a company. Then it is held by the insurance company (the seller) until needed by the buyer or the beneficiary. This holding constitutes a type of storage.

The combination of perishability and fluctuating demand offers product-planning, pricing, and promotion challenges to services executives. Some organizations have developed new uses for idle plant capacity during off-seasons. Thus, during the summer, several ski resorts operate their ski lifts for hikers and sightseers who want access to higher elevations. Advertising and creative pricing are also used to stimulate demand during slack periods. Hotels offer lower prices and family packages on weekends. Telephone companies offer lower rates during nights and weekends.

## THE MARKETING CONCEPT AND SERVICES MARKETING

The growth in services has generally *not* been due to marketing developments in service industries, but rather to the maturation of our economy and our rising standard of living. Traditionally, executives in U.S. services companies have not been marketing-oriented. They have lagged behind sellers of goods in accepting the marketing concept, and have generally been slow in adopting marketing techniques. Marketing management in service firms has not been especially creative. Innovations in services marketing have usually come from goods-associated companies.

We can identify some reasons for this lack of marketing orientation. No doubt the intangibility of services creates more difficult marketing challenges for sellers of services than for sellers of goods. In many service industries—particularly professional services—the sellers think of themselves as producers or creators, and not as marketers, of the service. Proud of their abilities to repair a car, diagnose an illness, or give a good haircut, they do not consider themselves business people.

The all-encompassing reason, however, is that top management does not yet understand (1) what marketing is or (2) its importance to a company's

## AN ETHICAL DILEMMA?

In the topsy-turvey world of deregulated airlines, fares change regularly and discount fares are heavily promoted. The result is considerable variability in price (recently, comparably scheduled round-trip fares from New York to Miami ranged from $158 to $744) and confusion among consumers. In this environment, airlines prepare newspaper ads with headlines that highlight very low fares. However, there are so many restrictions—stated in fine print at the bottom of the ads—that the fares are not usable by most consumers. If you were a newspaper advertising manager, would you view this type of advertising as ethical?

success. Service executives seem to equate marketing with selling, and they fail to consider other parts of a marketing system. Most service firms also lack an executive whose sole responsibility is marketing—the counterpart of the vice president of marketing in a goods-producing company.

In defense of firms in certain service industries, however, we note that external influences have contributed to the neglect of marketing. Up until the 1980s several significant service industries were heavily regulated by federal and state governments or professional associations. Banking and all major forms of interstate transportation services, for example, were severely restricted in marketing practices such as pricing, distribution, market expansion, and product expansion. In the fields of law, accounting, and health care, various state laws and professional association regulations prevented the providers from engaging in advertising, price competition, and other marketing activities. During the past 10 to 15 years, though, consumer protests and court decisions have removed many of these restrictions—thus creating genuine competition and a growing awareness of marketing in these industries.[6]

There are, of course, exceptions to these negative generalizations. The success of such organizations as Marriott, American Express, Avis, and Federal Express is due in large part to their marketing orientation. In many services industries, the organizational concept of franchising (discussed in Chapter 14) has been applied successfully. Examples of franchising in services fields include equipment rentals, beauty salons, tax services, printing, lawn care services, and employment services. Under the umbrella philosophy of a marketing orientation, franchising organizations have used attributes such as good locations, training, and capital investment to meet services marketing challenges of intangibility, labor intensity, and quality control.[7]

The hotel industry provides an interesting example of a service industry that was not marketing-oriented in the past but has, in recent years, been

[6]For reports on professional services—an industry that traditionally has not been marketing-oriented, but is changing its ways—see Betsy D. Gelb, Samuel V. Smith, and Gabriel M. Gelb, "Service Marketing Lessons from the Professionals," *Business Horizons*, September–October 1988, pp. 29–34; Richard Cohen, "Marketing Emerges for Accounting Firms as a Formal Discipline," *Intangibles*, September 1989, pp. 9–13; Louise Myers, "Know Thy Client," *Business Marketing*, October 1988, p. 52; and Doris C. Van Doren, Louise W. Smith, and Ronald J. Biglin, "The Challenges of Professional Services Marketing," *Journal of Consumer Marketing*, Spring 1985, pp. 19–27.

[7]James C. Cross and Bruce J. Walker, "Service Marketing and Franchising: A Practical Business Marriage," *Business Horizons*, November–December 1987, pp. 50–58.

struggling to make the transition to modern times.[8] For years this industry was relatively complacent. The demand for hotel rooms usually exceeded the supply. But during the 1980s, many new hotels were built and older ones were renovated. The net result was a decline in the percentage of rooms occupied and a drop in room rates (prices).

The industry was ill-equipped to adapt to the changes in the marketing environment. A typical hotel executive had little or no expertise in marketing. Various promotional tactics were employed, but there was no real consensus on how best to market hotels and their services. Furthermore, hotels faced two problems that had little to do with the industry's general lack of marketing experience. The first was that hotels cannot be moved or easily remodeled to meet the consumer's rapidly changing wants. The other problem was lack of product differentiation among hotels. Many hotels with similar room prices look and feel alike. They all have the same facilities and offer comparable services.

To meet the challenges, many hotels started to do a little marketing. Several hotel chains employed various product-mix strategies and engaged in market segmentation. Holiday Inn, for example: (1) traded up and appealed to the luxury market by opening Crowne Plaza Hotels, (2) traded down to the economy market with a string of budget-priced Hampton Inns, and (3) reached another market segment with the all-suite Embassy Suite hotels. Other chains such as Sheraton, Marriott, and Radisson also have opened all-suite hotels to reach the market segment that wants a "home away from home." Economy chains (Super 8, Motel 6, Comfort Inn, Days Inn, and EconoLodge) are opening new units as they market aggressively to the budget-minded market segment, including economy-minded *business* travelers.

The hotel industry also is beginning to understand how to make effective use of two other powerful marketing tools—creative pricing and skillful promotion. Several chains now offer lower rates for weekend nights, and charge nothing for children accompanying their parents. Previously uninspired advertising and sales promotion are changing. Ramada Inn attracted attention with hard-hitting ads. Other chains offer premiums such as savings bonds and bonuses for "frequent stayers"—an incentive patterned after the airlines' frequent-flyer programs.

## STRATEGIC PLANNING FOR SERVICES MARKETING

Because of the characteristics of services (notably intangibility), the development of a total marketing program in a service industry is often uniquely challenging. However, as in the marketing of goods, management first should define its marketing goals and select its target markets. Then management must design and implement marketing-mix strategies to reach its markets and fulfill its marketing goals.

### Target-Market Analysis

The task of analyzing a firm's target markets is essentially the same, whether the firm is selling a good or a service. Marketers of services should understand the components of population and income—the demographic factors—as they affect the market for the services. In addition, marketers must try to

---

[8]This example is adapted, in part, from Steve Swartz, "Once-Complacent Hotel Industry Is Forced to Learn How to Market," *The Wall Street Journal,* Nov. 29, 1985, p. 11; and "Finding Lodging to Fit Your Needs," *USA TODAY,* International Edition, Feb. 24, 1987, p. 17.

determine for each market segment why customers buy the given service. That is, what are their buying *motives?* Sellers must determine buying patterns for their services—when, where, and how do customers buy, who does the buying, and who makes the buying decisions? The psychological determinants of buying behavior—attitudes, perceptions, and personality—become even more important when marketing services rather than goods, because typically we cannot touch, smell, or taste a service offering. In like manner the sociological factors of social-class structure and small-group influences are market determinants for services. The fundamentals of the adoption and diffusion of innovation are also relevant in the marketing of services.

Some of the trends noted in Chapters 4 to 6 are particularly worth watching because they carry considerable influence in the marketing of services. As an example, increases in disposable income and discretionary buying power mean a growing market for medical care, insurance, and transportation ser-

---

**Too few cavities + too many dentists = A call for marketing *or* get a free bike with your braces!**

Did you get a Christmas card from your dentist? Some people do. One dentist provides lunch for his patients, another provides chauffered limousine service for patients who don't drive, and yet another puts out a chatty newsletter containing his favorite recipes.

What's going on in the field of dental services today? Well, studies show that almost 40 percent of kids between 5 and 17 have no cavities in their teeth—a tribute to better oral hygiene and the use of fluoride toothpaste and fluoridated water. However, from 1960 to 1987 the number of dentists in the United States increased 66 percent (from about 78,000 to 130,000). The net result is that competition is increasing as the field becomes more crowded. In terms of product life cycle, dental service clearly is in the maturity stage and maybe even in the sales-decline stage.

To meet this saturated market condition, many dentists have resorted to a strategic weapon that is new and strange to most dentists—we call it marketing. Many dentists clearly have adopted a consumer orientation—a major contrast to their previous behavior. They are expanding their product lines by adding new services. They are introducing procedures that are more convenient for their customers (patients). Some are engaging in price competition. Others are using more meaningful advertising.

Some general-practice dentists now perform screening for oral cancer, treatment for complex gum diseases, and extensive cosmetic dentistry. (These are services that once were reserved for specialists in endodontics, periodontics, or orthodontics, so obviously specialists in these fields don't welcome the new competition.)

Professional dental magazines are full of articles proposing ways for dentists to spruce up their offices. Patients are being offered discounted, or even free, initial examinations. Dental appointments are easier to get, and some offices are open during evening hours and on weekends. A few dentists now even make house calls.

Sources: Paul Duke, Jr., and Albert R. Carr, "Dentists Step Up Services and Marketing as Competition Increases in Crowded Field," *The Wall Street Journal*, Nov. 20, 1987, p. 27; and "A Free Bike with Your Braces," *Newsweek*, May 5, 1986, p. 82.

vices. Shorter working hours result in increased leisure time. More leisure time plus greater income means larger markets for recreation and entertainment services.

Market segmentation strategies also can be adopted by services marketers. We find apartment rental complexes for students, for single people, and for the over-65 crowd. Some car repair shops target owners of foreign cars. Limited-service motel chains cater to the economy-minded market segment, while all-suite hotels seek to attract families and business travelers.

## Planning of Services

New services are just as important to a service company as new goods are to a goods-marketing firm. Similarly, the improvement of existing services and elimination of unwanted, unprofitable services are also key goals.

Product planning and development has its counterpart in the marketing program of a service organization. Management must select appropriate strategies based on answers to these questions:

- What services will be offered?
- What will be the breadth and depth of the service mix?
- How will the services be positioned?
- What attributes, such as branding, packaging, and service quality, will the service have?[9]

The high perishability, fluctuating demand, and inability to store services make product planning critically important to services marketers. A service organization can expand or contract its product mix, alter existing services, and trade up or down. Insurance firms that formerly specialized in fire–casualty–auto policies have added the more profitable line of life insurance policies. Some services firms have expanded their mix by working jointly with companies selling related services. For instance, automobile-rental firms have arrangements with airlines and hotels so that when customers fly to their destinations, a reserved car and hotel room are waiting. Because of the soaring costs of malpractice insurance, some physicians have contracted their service mix by discontinuing the practice of obstetrics. Holiday Inn traded up to Crowne Plaza Hotels, and Marriott traded down when it added Courtyard Hotels to its line.

In some respects product planning is easier for services than for goods. Packaging, color, and labeling are virtually nonexistent in services marketing. However, in other respects—branding and management of quality, for instance—service industries have greater challenges.

Services branding is a problem because maintaining consistent quality (a responsibility of brand ownership) is difficult. Also, a brand cannot be physically attached to a label or to the service itself. Remember, we can't see, touch, or smell the service, so the brand carries a major marketing burden. A services marketer's goal should be to create an effective brand image. To reach this goal, a key strategy is to develop a total brand theme that includes more than just a brand name. To implement this strategy, the following tactics (besides getting a good brand name) may be employed:

[9]For a model of new-service development, see Eberhard E. Scheuing and Eugene M. Johnson, "A Proposed Model for New Service Development," *The Journal of Services Marketing,* Spring 1989, pp. 25–34. Also see G. Lynn Shostack, "Service Positioning through Structural Change," *Journal of Marketing,* January 1987, pp. 34–43.

In its product planning, this cruise line positions itself as a Fun Ship.

- *Include a tangible good as part of the brand image*—like the umbrella of Travelers Insurance, Merrill Lynch's bull, or Prudential's Rock of Gibraltar.
- *Tie in a slogan with the brand*—for instance, "Fly the friendly skies of United" or "You're in good hands with Allstate."
- *Use a distinctive color scheme*—such as Avis's red or Hertz's black and gold.[10]

### MANAGEMENT OF SERVICE QUALITY

In our brief discussion of product quality in Chapter 9, we noted the elusiveness of this important product feature. Quality is difficult to define, measure, control, and communicate. Yet in services marketing, the quality of the service is critical to a firm's success. Two airlines each fly a Boeing 747 for the same fare; two auto repair shops each use Ford or Chrysler parts and charge the same price; and two banks each handle the same U.S. currency at identical interest rates. Assuming similar times and locations, quality of service is the only factor that differentiates the offerings in each of these paired situations.

However difficult it may be to define the concept of service quality, management must understand one thing: *Quality is defined by the consumer and not by the producer-seller of a service.* Your hairstylist may be delighted with the job she did on your hair. But if you think your hair looks terrible, then the service quality was poor. What counts is what consumers think about a service. Service quality that does not meet customer expectations can result in lost sales from present customers and a failure to attract new customers. Consequently, it is imperative that management strives to maintain *consistent* service quality at or above the level of consumer expectations. Yet it is sometimes virtually impossible to standardize service quality—that is, to maintain consistency in

[10]Leonard L. Berry, Edwin F. Lefkowith, and Terry Clark, "In Services, What's in a Name?" *Harvard Business Review*, September–October 1988, pp. 28–30. Also see Sak Onkvisit and John J. Shaw, "Service Marketing: Image, Branding, and Competition," *Business Horizons*, January–February 1989, pp. 13–18.

In the 1990s, consumers demand a commitment to consistently good quality.

service output. Performance quality typically varies even within the same organization. This is true in such diverse fields as opera, legal services, landscaping, baseball, hospital care, and marketing courses.[11]

As part of managing service quality, an organization should design and operate an ongoing quality-improvement program that will monitor the level and consistency of service quality. A related, but also hard, task is to evaluate service quality by measuring customer satisfaction—that is, customers' perceptions of the quality of an organization's services.[12]

## Pricing of Services

In the marketing of services, nowhere is there a greater need for managerial creativity and skill than in the area of pricing. Earlier we noted that services are extremely perishable, they usually cannot be stored, and demand for them often fluctuates considerably. All these features carry significant pricing implications. To further complicate the situation, customers may perform some services themselves (auto and household repairs, for example).

These considerations suggest that the elasticity of demand for a service should influence the price set by the seller. Interestingly enough, sellers often

[11] For a good summary of service quality, see Leonard L. Berry, A. Parasuraman, and Valarie A. Zeithaml, "The Service-Quality Puzzle," *Business Horizons*, September–October 1988, pp. 35–43.
[12] For more on the measurement of customers' perceptions of service quality, see A. Parasuraman, Valarie A. Zeithaml, and Leonard L. Berry, "SERVQUAL: A Multiple-Item Scale for Measuring Consumer Perceptions of Service Quality," *Journal of Retailing*, Spring 1988, pp. 12–40; Stephen W. Brown and Teresa A. Swartz, "A Gap Analysis of Professional Service Quality," *Journal of Marketing*, April 1989, pp. 92–98; and Kate Bertrand, "In Service, Perception Counts," *Business Marketing*, April 1989, p. 44.

Pricing strategies are especially important for service firms, because of the perishability characteristic of services.

THE

The Chan

Need f

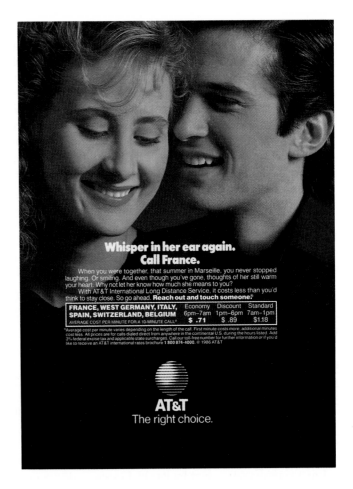

do recognize inelastic demand. They then charge higher prices. But they fail to act in opposite fashion when faced with an elastic demand—even though a lower price would increase unit sales, total revenue, utilization of facilities, and probably net profit.

Certainly, perfect competition does not apply to any great extent, if at all, in the pricing of services. Because of the heterogeneity and difficulty of standardizing quality, most services are highly differentiated. Also, it is virtually impossible to have complete market information. As an example, consider how difficult it is to get reliable, detailed information on physicians' or lawyers' prices. In any given market, such as a neighborhood, often there are geographic limits within which a buyer will seek a service. Consequently, there are not a large number of sellers. The heavy capital investment required to produce certain services (transportation, communications, medical care) often limits considerably the freedom of entry.

Nevertheless, in recent years price competition in many service areas has increased considerably, going through three identifiable phases:[13]

- In the first phase, price is barely mentioned in the organization's advertising. For example, a health maintenance organization (HMO) will run an ad explaining its services, but not dwelling much on price.

[13] This paragraph is adapted from Stephen W. Brown, ''New Patterns Are Emerging in Services Marketing Sector,'' *Marketing News*, June 7, 1985, p. 2.

# CHAPTER 20

# MARKETING IN NONPROFIT ORGANIZATIONS

Promotin

## CHAPTER 20 GOALS

In this chapter we apply many of the concepts and techniques of modern marketing to private, nonbusiness, nonprofit organizations. After studying this chapter, you should be able to explain:

- The exchange concept as applied to nonprofit organizations.
- The importance of marketing in nonprofit organizations.
- The concept of contributor markets and client markets.
- The attitudes of nonprofit organizations toward marketing.
- How market analysis and the marketing mix apply in nonprofit marketing.
- The status of marketing programs in nonprofit organizations.

To attract patients and fill empty beds, some hospitals now offer luxury suites, gourmet food, and hot tubs. Other hospitals advertise their low mortality rates in open-heart surgery. Several private and public universities have conducted advertising campaigns and other promotional activities to stem declining enrollments. Many museums, symphony orchestras, and social agencies (Girl Scouts, YMCA) use similar techniques to reverse decreasing contributions and memberships. Candidates for political office use advertising campaigns to solicit votes and survey-research techniques to determine public opinions and preferences. Many religious organizations regularly use advertising, personal selling, and other marketing techniques to add to their membership and to increase contributions. Municipal zoos are advertising, offering discounts on admission prices during off-peak times, and providing seasonal programs such as living nativity scenes at Christmastime.

Three common threads run through all these real-life situations. First, the organizations are all generally thought of as *nonbusiness* groups. Second, they are all *nonprofit* organizations—that is, profit is *not* an intended organizational goal. And third, in each situation *marketing activities* were used to solve key problems.

## NATURE AND SCOPE OF NONPROFIT MARKETING

The marketing fundamentals for nonprofit, nonbusiness organizations are the same as for the business sector. A marketing program should be strategically planned around a good or service that is effectively priced, promoted, and distributed to satisfy wants in a predetermined market. However, there are important differences in the implementation of the marketing program and in nonprofit management's understanding of and attitudes toward marketing. These differences tend to limit the marketing activities of nonprofit, nonbusiness organizations, even though these organizations need effective marketing.

Most nonprofit companies market *services*, rather than tangible goods. Consequently, many of the concepts discussed in Chapter 19 are relevant in this chapter.

---

### AN INTERNATIONAL PERSPECTIVE: Nonprofit organizations also engage in international marketing

Throughout this book, our International Perspectives have for the most part focused on profit-seeking organizations. But many private, nonprofit organizations also regularly engage in international marketing activities. The following examples illustrate the wide range of these operations.

● Very many American colleges and universities have large numbers of foreign students on campus, traceable in part to the international recruiting activities of those schools. In some engineering colleges, for instance, close to one-half of the total enrollments are foreign students. Schools with ski teams regularly recruit young people from Norway and Sweden, and numerous college hockey players come from Canada. Some college track teams have recruiting pipelines into Kenya and Nigeria, especially for distance runners. And there is a sprinkling of very tall foreign students on several college basketball teams.

In some cases, the university goes international by opening a foreign branch or merging with a foreign university, just like a multinational corporation might do. For example, Temple University and Texas A&M have branches in Japan, and Japanese universities have acquired a financial interest in Salem College in West Virginia and Westmar College in Iowa.

● Various religious organizations—Protestant, Catholic, and Mormon, for example—regularly send missionaries into foreign lands to recruit new members.

● Several cultural organizations also operate internationally. The Russian Bolshoi Ballet regularly tours in foreign countries, marketing its excellent talent to enthusiastic consumer audiences. The Egyptian National Museum sent its King Tut collection on tour to several American cities. Symphony orchestras from Vienna, Berlin, London, Philadelphia, and other cities have performed in various foreign countries.

● Charitable organizations such as the International Red Cross appeal to contributor markets in many countries. These organizations then provide services to client markets generated by natural disasters—be it earthquakes in Armenia, hurricanes in the Caribbean, hunger in Ethiopia, or local wars.

● Social causes—especially those involving the physical environment—are proving to be among the strongest nonprofit international movements in the 1990s. To illustrate, as Western Europe approaches economic unification in 1992, issues such as tobacco smoking, pollution of the Rhine and other rivers, and the destruction of forests by acid rain are attracting growing attention from many groups. Furthermore, as Eastern Europe opened up in the early 1990s, we began to learn of the extreme air and water pollution in those countries. So the international marketing of environmental causes is very likely to pick up momentum in that part of the world throughout this decade.

● Finally, in the field of health care, several nonprofit organizations have done a fine job of marketing their services across many national borders. The International Association for Medical Assistance to Travelers (IAMAT), for example, is a network of English-speaking doctors, medical centers, and hospitals in cities all over the world. IAMAT publishes a directory listing the names, addresses, and phone numbers of these institutions. IAMAT also publishes a World Immunization Chart and a World Malaria Risk Chart listing the countries where major diseases are a problem and the recommended immunization in each case.

Social-cause marketing can cross national boundaries and cultures, as this British poster illustrates.

*Sharing your mate's works means sharing with everyone he's ever shared with*

*Shooting up once can screw you up. Forever.*

## Types of Nonprofit Organizations

Nonprofit organizations number in the thousands and engage in a very wide range of activities. The following groupings will give you some idea of this broad spectrum:

- *Educational:* Private grade schools, high schools, colleges, universities.
- *Cultural:* Museums, zoos, symphony orchestras, opera and theater groups.
- *Religious:* Churches, synagogues, temples, mosques.
- *Charitable and philanthropic:* Welfare groups (Salvation Army, United Fund, Red Cross), research foundations, fund-raising groups.
- *Social cause:* Organizations dealing with family planning, civil rights, stopping smoking, preventing heart disease, environmental concerns, those for or against abortion, or for or against nuclear energy.
- *Social:* Fraternal organizations, civic clubs.
- *Health care:* Hospitals, nursing homes, health research organizations (American Cancer Society, American Heart Association), HMOs (health maintenance organizations).
- *Political:* Political parties, individual politicians.[1]

While this list generally is a classification of nonprofit organizations, note that there are some exceptions. A number of organizations within these groups—certain museums and hospitals, for example—are *profit-seeking* organizations.

## The Exchange Concept and Nonprofit Marketing

In Chapter 1, marketing was broadly defined as an exchange intended to satisfy the wants of all parties involved in the exchange. And marketing consists of all activities designed to facilitate such exchanges. A discussion of marketing in nonprofit organizations is certainly consistent with this broad, exchange-concept definition of marketing, for nonprofit organizations are also involved in exchanges.

[1] For reports on marketing programs in some of these areas, see Scott Kilman, "Facing Declining Enrollment, Instructors of Liberal Arts Jazz Up Their Courses," *The Wall Street Journal*, Dec. 26, 1985, p. 11; Larry M. Strum, "Health Care Marketers Eye Hot Topics," *Marketing News*, Feb. 27, 1989, p. 1; Thomas A. Stewart, "Turning around the Lord's Business (Churches)," *Fortune*, Sept. 25, 1989, p. 116; and Janice R. Nall and Parks B. Dimsdale, "Civic Group (Chamber of Commerce) Adopts Marketing Technique," *Marketing News*, June 21, 1985, p. 13.

As an example, the Levi Strauss Company, a business organization, sells to you, through a middleman, a pair of blue jeans in exchange for some money. In a similar vein, your local hospital, a nonprofit organization, may provide you with health care in exchange for some money. Your college, another nonprofit organization, offers an educational service to you in exchange for your money and/or your labor.

## Markets Involved in Nonprofit Marketing

A major difference between business and nonprofit marketing is that nonprofit organizations must reach more than one group with their marketing efforts. Business executives have traditionally defined their basic market as being made up of present and potential customers. They have thus directed their marketing efforts primarily toward this one group. In contrast, most nonbusiness, nonprofit organizations are involved with *two* major markets. One of these groups consists of the **contributors** (of money, labor, services, or materials) to the organization. Here the nonprofit organization's task is that of "resource attraction."

The other major target market is the organization's **clients**—the recipients of its money or services. This recipient market is much like that of the customers of a business company. However, nonprofit organizations—such as churches, Girl Scout units, nursing homes, symphony orchestras, or universities—are unlikely to refer to their client-recipients as customers. Instead these organizations use such terms as *parishioners, members, patients, audience,* or *students*.

This distinction between business and nonprofit marketing, based on the major markets involved, is significant for this reason: A nonprofit organization must develop two separate marketing programs—one looking "back" to its contributors, and the other looking "forward" to its clients. Moreover, like businesses, nonprofit organizations also have relationships with several publics in addition to their main markets. A private university, for example, must deal with government agencies, environmentalists, mass media, its faculty and staff, and the local community.

## Importance of Nonprofit Marketing

The attention that is finally being devoted to nonprofit marketing is long overdue. Thousands of these organizations handle billions of dollars and affect millions of people. Often the operation of these organizations is admittedly inefficient. Empty beds in hospitals and empty classrooms constitute a waste of resources we can ill afford. Frequently a large part of the money collected by a nonprofit organization goes to cover its administrative expenses, rather than to serve the intended markets. Then there is a dual social and economic loss—donors' gifts are wasted, and clients are not served efficiently.

Marketing's significance also becomes apparent when nonprofit organizations fail to do an effective marketing job. The result may be additional social and economic costs and waste. If the death rate from smoking rises because the American Cancer Society and other similar organizations cannot persuade people of the harm of smoking, we all lose. When antilitter organizations fail to convince people to control their solid-waste disposal, we all lose. When good museums or good symphony orchestras must cease operating because of lack of contributions or lack of attendance, again there are social and economic losses.

By developing an effective marketing program, a nonprofit organization

When business and nonprofit organizations cooperate, both can win.

can increase immeasurably its chance of (1) satisfactorily serving both its contributor and client markets and (2) improving the overall efficiency of its operations.

## NONPROFITS' ATTITUDE TOWARD MARKETING

People in most nonprofit organizations generally do not realize that they are "running a business" and should therefore employ business management techniques. It is true that making a profit is *not* the goal of these organizations. Nevertheless, they do need to identify goals, plan strategies and tactics to reach these goals, effectively execute their plans, and evaluate their performance. Yet only very recently have many nonprofit organizations started to employ accounting systems, financial controls, personnel management and labor relations, and other business management techniques.

Unfortunately, the acceptance of business management techniques often does not include planned marketing programs. Nonprofit organizations do not seem at all comfortable with marketing. To most of these groups, marketing means some form of promotion, such as advertising or personal selling. These organizations rarely understand the concept of a total marketing program.

Many nonprofit groups speak about marketing and even believe they are practicing it. But in many cases they still have a strong production orientation or, at best, a selling orientation. These organizations tend to select—on their own—the goods, services, or ideas that they *think* their customers want (or should want). Then they decide how to distribute or sell these products. Only at the end of the process do these groups analyze their markets. This really is not a marketing orientation.

People working in nonprofit organizations often have a negative attitude toward marketing. They are apt to think that having a marketing program—and using the term *marketing*—is demeaning and in bad taste. They may even feel that it is unethical to use marketing in their organizations.

Perhaps the choice of words is important. The governing body in a church, for instance, will not object to "informational notices" (don't call it "advertising") in newspapers or in the yellow pages regarding church activities. When church members go to foreign lands to bring new members into the fold, the churches don't call this activity "personal selling." It is "missionary work."

Nonprofit groups seem to face a dilemma. On the one hand, they generally are unaware of what marketing is all about or may have a negative attitude toward it. Yet, on the other hand, these organizations typically are in great need of effective marketing programs. However, as we move through the early 1990s, the marketing climate in nonprofit organizations is continually improving as the need for marketing is finally recognized.[2]

## DEVELOPING A STRATEGIC PROGRAM FOR NONPROFIT MARKETING

The basic procedure for planning and developing a marketing program is the same in any organization—profit or nonprofit. That is, first we identify and analyze the target markets, and then we develop a strategic marketing mix that will provide want-satisfaction to those markets. Throughout the process we use marketing research to help in our decision making.

### Target-Market Analysis

Nonprofit organizations need two major marketing programs—one for the contributor market and one for the client market. It is important to pinpoint each market in some detail. Market pinpointing means using market segmentation. A broad (nonsegmented) appeal to the *donor* market is likely to result in a low return. Trying to be all things to all people in the *recipient* market is likely to result in being "nothing to nobody" and going broke in the process.

The possible bases for market segmentation for nonprofit groups are generally the same as those discussed in Chapter 4. In trying to reach its *contributor* market, for example, an organization may segment its appeals by age group, geographic place of residence, record of past donations, or size of past donations. Segmentation analysis is necessary to identify the characteristics of those who donate to the organization.

Many nonprofit organizations segment their *client* markets, although they probably do not refer to this technique as market segmentation. For instance, since the Great Depression, the Democratic party has developed separate appeals to such market segments as organized labor, low-income groups, Southern Democrats, Catholics, Jews, and urban dwellers in Northeastern industrial centers. Country clubs develop different programs for golfers, tennis players, swimmers, and card players. Private colleges may segment prospective students on the basis of high school grade-point average or area of study (technical, liberal arts, professional).

A decision to employ market segmentation means that nonprofit organization must tailor all or part of its marketing program to reach each segment—be it donor or client. Thus the product offering and the promotion may have to be adapted to each major segment.

Careful market analysis requires sophisticated marketing research to identify the various markets. This poses a problem because most nonprofit organizations are not familiar with marketing research. But there are encouraging prospects in this area. Political parties and individual politicians, for example,

[2] See Kathleen Vyn, "Nonprofits Learn How-To's of Marketing," *Marketing News,* Aug. 14, 1989, p. 1; and Karen Schwartz, "Nonprofits' Bottom-Line: They Mix Lofty Goals and Gutsy Survival Strategies," *Marketing News,* Feb. 13, 1989, p. 1.

---

**If you are sending "A Message to Garcia," you'd better put it in a language that Garcia understands.**

In their attempts to avoid using such crass terms as *marketing, profit,* or *business,* some people in nonprofit fields have come up with creative terminology. Here are some examples to help you interpret business language as spoken by nonprofit people.

| Nonprofit terminology | Business translation |
|---|---|
| Revenue development (or management) | Marketing |
| Strategies for optimum occupancy | Marketing |
| Improved community awareness | Advertising and public relations |
| Needs assessment | Marketing research |
| Persuasive interpersonal communication | Salesmanship |
| Client-centered communication | Customer orientation |
| Financial stability | Net profit |
| Capital replenishment | Net profit |
| Excess of revenues over expenses | Net profit |
| Improved community utilization in health care: | Increased sales |
|     Census | Net sales |
|     Admissions personnel | Sales people |
|     Preadmission interview | Sales presentation |
| Outreach development | Broadening the customer base |

Source: Martha Rogers and Richard W. Buchman, "UnMarketSpeak: Some Services Marketers Veil Strategies with Euphemisms," *Marketing News,* Aug. 16, 1985, p. 1.

---

are frequent users of opinion polls to determine voters' preferences on candidates and issues. Segmentation research also has been used to identify the characteristics of various market segments attending art museums and presentations of the performing arts (opera, concerts, theaters).[3]

**Product Planning**  Like a profit-seeking business firm, a nonprofit organization must decide (1) what products it will offer, (2) what will be the nature of its product mix, and (3) what, if anything, it will do about product attributes such as branding and labeling. In nonprofit marketing, again, an organization needs two sets of product strategies—one for its contributor market and one for its client market.

**PRODUCT OFFERING**

In most nonprofit organizations, the "product offering" to *clients* typically is a service, an idea, a person (in politics), or a cause. In the case of foundations and charitable organizations, the product offering often is a cash grant—a form of tangible product. Other organizations may offer such tangible prod-

---

[3]See John E. Robbins and Stephanie S. Robbins, "Museum Marketing: Identification of High, Moderate, and Low Attendee Segments," *Journal of the Academy of Marketing Science,* Winter 1981, pp. 66–76; and Margery Steinberg, George Miaoulis, and David Lloyd, "Benefit Segmentation Strategies for the Performing Arts," in *1982 Educators' Conference Proceedings,* American Marketing Association, Chicago, 1982, pp. 289–93.

How would you describe the product offering of the San Francisco Ballet?

ucts as food and clothing, printed materials, or birth control devices. However, in such cases the tangible products are incidental to the main services provided by the organization.

The key to selecting a product offering is for an organization to decide (1) what "business" it is in and (2) what client markets it wants to reach. If a church views its mission only as providing religious services, its product offering will be relatively limited. On the other hand, if this church views its mission more broadly—as providing fellowship, spirituality, and personal development—it will offer more services to more markets. The church may then offer family counseling services, day-care services, religious education courses, and social activities for single people.

Planning the product offering to the *contributor* market is more difficult. An organization asks people to donate their money or time to a cause. The money or time is the price that contributors pay for the organization's "product." But what are they getting for this price? What is the product that contributors are buying with their donations? The product is an assortment of benefits for donors that includes:

- Making donors feel good.
- Supporting their favorite organizations.
- Providing them with a tax deduction.
- Contributing to their status in reference groups.
- Supporting their religious beliefs.

Management's task in product planning is to match a given benefit with the market segment that wants that benefit. Thus, the benefit of a tax deduction would be the product offering to one market segment, while another segment would be offered the benefit of furthering the organization's work. The difficulty lies in identifying the group of potential contributors (buyers) that want a particular benefit.[4]

[4] For further discussion of contributor behavior, see Bonnie S. Guy and Wesley E. Patton, "The Marketing of Altruistic Causes: Understanding Why People Help," *The Journal of Consumer Marketing*, Winter 1989, pp. 19–30.

## PRODUCT-MIX STRATEGIES

Several of the product-mix strategies discussed in Chapter 8 can be employed in nonprofit marketing. Consider, for instance, the strategy of *expanding the product line*. Symphony orchestras have broadened their lines by offering concerts appealing to children and popular-music concerts for teenagers and college-age people. Universities expanded their mix when they added adult night courses, off-campus extension programs, and concentrated between-semester courses. Hospital chains are adding their own health insurance programs, nursing homes, and home health services.

The strategy of *product differentiation* has been employed by several hospitals. These all provide basically the same health services. But to increase sales volume (number of patients), each hospital's services are differentiated by superficial features. As we noted in the chapter introduction, some hospitals offer luxury suites to attract affluent patients. Other hospitals provide gourmet food and big-screen television sets to attract the higher-income market. Still other hospitals differentiate themselves by advertising that they have the lowest mortality rates in heart surgery.[5]

The *product life-cycle* concept can be applied to nonprofit marketing. The March-of-Dimes Foundation was started many years ago to fight poliomyelitis (infantile paralysis) and to care for its victims. After the introductory stage, this organization went through its growth stage and reached maturity, partially through the support of President Franklin Roosevelt, who himself was a polio victim. Later the foundation entered the decline stage when the Salk vaccine effectively eradicated this dreaded disease. But rather than close shop (or abandon the product, in life-cycle terms), the polio foundation changed its name to the National Foundation. It also shifted its emphasis to the treatment and prevention of birth defects in children. In effect, the organization rejuvenated its services and started another life cycle by altering its product mix.

## PRODUCT ATTRIBUTES

Nonprofit groups generally do not use product strategies such as branding and labeling. The little that has been done in this area, however, suggests that a nonprofit organization can make its marketing more effective by emphasizing product attributes. For many years, colleges and universities have used nicknames (a form of brand name) primarily for their athletic teams, but also to identify their students and alumni. Most colleges and universities have school colors—another product attribute that helps increase the market's recognition and identification of the school.

Among health-research organizations, the Lung Association has registered as a trademark its double-barred Christmas-seal cross. The trademarks of the Girl Scouts, Boy Scouts, YMCA, and Salvation Army are recognized and remembered by many people.

**Price Determination**  Pricing in many nonprofit organizations is quite different from pricing in a business firm. Pricing becomes less important when profit making is not an organizational goal. Also, many nonprofit groups believe there are *no* client-market pricing considerations in their marketing because there is no charge to

---

[5] William Celis III, "Hospitals Compete for Affluent Patients by Offering Luxury Suites and Hot Tubs," *The Wall Street Journal*, Feb. 3, 1986, p. 21; and Rhonda L. Rundle, "Hospitals Cite Mortality Statistics in Ads to Attract Heart Patients," *The Wall Street Journal*, July 28, 1987, p. 25.

> ### Welcome to the wonderful world of hospital marketing! *or* Can you market hospital services the way you market soap?
>
> Apparently two hospital chains—Republic Health Corp. and Humana, Inc.—think the answer is "yes." In fact, in some circles, Republic is known as the Procter & Gamble of the hospital industry. Republic has adopted a brand-management program in an attempt to lift its services out of the generic category. Thus rather than promoting the company—Republic Hospitals—this organization promotes its *branded* services. Republic advertises in *Playboy* and *Cosmopolitan* magazines such services as "You're Becoming" plastic surgery. The company also markets "Miracle Moments" maternity care and "Gift of Sight" cataract surgery. After all, Procter & Gamble promotes its Tide, Ivory, and Head and Shoulders brands, and not the Procter & Gamble Company itself.
>
> Also, just like soap and other product companies, some hospitals are engaging in price competition. Humana's hospital in Phoenix, for example, has run the following "specials" in local newspaper ads: "Complete face lift—was $941, now $675; breast augmentation—was $504, now $315."
>
> Today some hospitals are using marketing research to determine what the customer wants. And the answers come in—no tacky linoleum, no disapproving nurses, no long hours of waiting, and so on. Hospitals are responding with re-modeled facilities, public relations programs about quality of care, and a "patient-friendly" atmosphere.
>
> Source: Ellyn E. Spragins, "A High-Powered Pitch to Cure Hospitals' Ills," *Business Week*, Sept. 2, 1985, p. 60.

the client. The organization's basic function is to help those who cannot afford to pay.

Actually, the goods or services received by clients rarely are free—that is, without a price of some kind. True, the price may not be a monetary charge. Often, however, the client pays a price—in the form of travel and waiting time and, perhaps, degrading treatment—that a money-paying client-customer would not have to pay for the same service. Poor children who have to wear donated, secondhand clothes certainly are paying a price if their classmates ridicule these clothes. Alcoholics Anonymous and some drug rehabilitation organizations that provide "free" services do exact a price. They require active participation by their clients as well as a very strongly expressed resolve by clients to help themselves.

Some nonprofit groups do face the same pricing problems discussed in Chapters 10 and 11. Museums and opera companies must decide on admission prices; fraternal organizations must set a dues schedule; and colleges must determine how much to charge for tuition. Not-for-profit organizations must (1) determine the base price for their product offering and (2) establish pricing strategies in several areas of their pricing structure.

### SETTING THE BASE PRICE

Here again we are faced with two market situations—pricing in the contributor market and pricing in the client market.

When dealing with the contributor market, nonprofit organizations really do not set the price of the donation. That price is set by contributors when they decide how much they are willing to pay for the benefits they expect to

## AN ETHICAL DILEMMA?

In recent years, colleges and universities have increased their use of marketing tools such as advertising and sales promotion. However, one area that has been largely ignored is pricing. Business firms set prices according to demand. If many buyers want a product, it can command a "premium" price. In contrast, colleges charge everyone the same tuition, usually based on credit hours. Assume you are a university vice president and a proposal has been made that tuition be adjusted according to the demand for majors. That is, to enroll in a popular major, students would have to pay more than for an unpopular major. Is such a plan ethical?

receive in return for their gifts. However, the organization may suggest a price. A charitable organization, for example, may suggest that you donate 1 day's pay or that you donate your time for 1 day a month.

Some of our discussion regarding the pricing of services (Chapter 19) is appropriate to the client market—for instance, in pricing admissions to museums, concerts, or college athletic contests. But for most nonprofit groups, the pricing methods used by business firms—cost-plus, balance of supply and demand, market alone—simply are not appropriate. Many organizations know they cannot cover their costs with prices charged to clients. The gap between anticipated revenues and costs must be made up by contributions.

As yet, there are no real guidelines—no methodology—for much nonprofit pricing. A major problem here is that most nonprofit organizations do not know the cost of the goods and services they offer in their client markets.

### PRICING STRATEGIES

Some of the pricing strategies discussed in Chapter 11 are also applicable in nonprofit marketing. Discount strategies have widespread use, for example. Some museums offer discount prices to students and senior citizens. A season ticket for many opera companies or symphony orchestras costs less per performance than tickets purchased on an individual-performance basis. This is a form of quantity discount.

Considerations regarding one price versus variable price also are strategies applicable in nonprofit marketing. Most charity hospitals charge according to the patient's ability to pay—a variable-price strategy. A one-price strategy typically is followed by private universities. That is, all students pay the same tuition (in cash or its equivalent in scholarship funds or hours of labor) for a full load of coursework.

## Distribution System

Setting up a distribution system in a nonprofit organization involves two tasks. One is to establish channels of distribution back to contributors and forward to clients. The other task, usually the more important one, is to set up a physical distribution system to reach these two markets.

### CHANNELS OF DISTRIBUTION

The channels of distribution used in nonprofit marketing ordinarily are quite simple and short. The nonprofit organization usually deals directly with its two major publics—no middlemen are involved.

Nonprofit organizations should locate as closely as possible to both contributor and client markets.

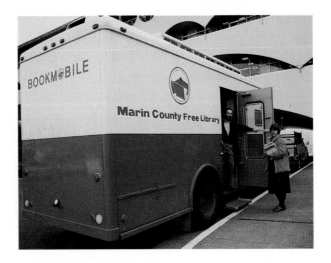

When an intermediary is used, it is an agent middleman. For instance, to generate increased contributions, a political party or a university may employ an outside fund-raising organization. To reach potential customers, opera companies or athletic terms may sell tickets through independent ticket agencies. In some cities the National Crime Prevention Council effectively uses local police personnel as middlemen. They distribute youth crime-prevention literature and programs to schools and to the general public.

Numerous nonprofit organizations have established a separate marketing program whereby they serve as a retailer of goods that are related to the organization's primary service. Thus, we see art museums selling prints of paintings, colleges selling many items through the college bookstore, local post offices selling stamps to collectors, and Planned Parenthood selling or giving away contraceptives. Over-the-counter and mail-order methods of retail selling may also be used in these situations.

### PHYSICAL DISTRIBUTION

The primary goal in physical distribution is for a nonprofit organization to locate where it can serve both contributors and clients most effectively. The organization should be as accessible as possible to its contributors so that giving is as easy and convenient as possible. Besides cash and checks, charities use payroll deductions, installment plans, and credit cards. If the donor is contributing used goods, they may collect them at the donor's residence or at some other choice location instead of forcing the donor to haul the stuff across town to a central collection point.

Location is also critical in dealing with client markets. Thus, universities set up branches around the state and offer correspondence courses. The Salvation Army locates its stores in low-income neighborhoods. Health-care organizations provide mobile units for lung X-rays, blood-pressure tests, and inoculations. Big-city museums arrange for portable exhibits to be taken to small towns.

## Promotion Program

Promotion is the part of the marketing mix that many nonprofit organizations are most familiar with and most adept at. They have regularly used advertising, personal selling, sales promotion, and publicity—often very aggressively and effectively—to communicate with both their contributors and their cli-

Nonprofit organizations, like profit-seeking firms, need to advertise to reach their markets.

**Talk about hot young management teams.**

Peter Drucker says, "The Salvation Army probably does a better job with the poor than anyone else."

"And frugally," adds *Fortune* (11/19/87). "Of each dollar it receives, 86 cents goes to the needy." In a business where 50 to 60 cents is the norm.

How do we do it? We manage.

So, kid us all you want about "saving souls." But please help us save lives.

**We're fighting for you.**

The Salvation Army of Greater New York, 132 West 14th Street, New York, NY 10011-7388. (212) 807-4200

ents. However, these organizations have not integrated their promotional mix into a total marketing program. In fact, many nonprofit groups believe that promotion and marketing are one and the same thing.

### ADVERTISING

Advertising is used extensively to reach the donor market. Many nonprofit organizations conduct annual fund-raising drives. Mass media (newspapers, magazines, television, radio) frequently are used in these efforts. Specific media also are used selectively to solicit funds. Direct mail can be especially effective in reaching segmented donor markets such as past contributors, religious or ethnic groups related to the organizations, or college alumni. Media such as alumni magazines and foreign-language newspapers can be used to pinpoint donor market segments.

Nonprofit groups also can communicate with client markets through advertising. To offset declining enrollments, colleges and universities have run ads in a variety of media. A growing number of churches are advertising aggressively in print media and on radio and TV to increase their membership and attendance. Hospitals are beginning to advertise to fill empty beds.

In some situations, a nonprofit organization can reach both its contributor and its client markets with the same ad. The American Heart Association, the American Cancer Society, or the Lung Association might advertise, asking you to contribute to its annual campaign. In the same ad, it might urge you to watch your diet, quit smoking, or get a medical checkup.

Personal selling can be very effective in fund-raising campaigns aimed at contributor markets.

### PERSONAL SELLING

Personal selling is often employed in fund-raising efforts. A door-to-door campaign may be used. At Christmastime, Salvation Army volunteers, dressed as Santa Claus, collect donations in the downtown areas of many cities. And potential large donors may be approached by sales people.

Many nonprofit organizations also use personal selling to reach their client public. These personal representatives may not be called sales people, but that is exactly what they are. For centuries, missionaries of countless religious groups have recruited new members by personal contact—personal selling. Personal selling also is employed to recruit new members for fraternal organizations such as the YMCA, Girl Scouts, and Elks. Colleges send "sales people"—admission officers, alumni, current students—to talk to high school students, their parents, and their counselors.

Using sales representatives to reach either contributors or clients poses some management problems for a nonprofit organization. In effect, the organization has to manage a sales force, including recruiting, training, compensating, supervising, and evaluating performance. Not many nonprofit organizations think in these terms, however, nor are they qualified to do this management job.

### SALES PROMOTION

Nonprofit organizations have long recognized the value of sales promotion to reach their markets. Many organizations place exhibits (including donation boxes) in local stores and shopping centers and at sporting events. Usually there is no charge for this use of the space.

## IMPLEMENTATION OF MARKETING

In this final section we discuss briefly three topics that will affect the future development of marketing in nonprofit organizations.

### Interest and Research in the Field

If nonprofit marketing is to have a future, it is important that the people in nonprofit organizations understand fully (1) what marketing is and (2) what it can do for their organization. In recent years, people in many different nonprofit fields have displayed a growing interest in marketing. Books on the topic of nonprofit marketing are now being published.[6] Several general marketing textbooks, such as this one, devote all or part of a chapter to nonprofit marketing. Doctoral dissertations, journal articles, and special sessions at professional marketing meetings are focusing on nonprofit marketing.

Just a few years ago, research in nonprofit marketing was initiated mainly by academicians and other people outside the nonprofit field being studied. Now the marketing research is being generated by people working within various nonprofit fields. This is a healthy sign for the future.

### Measuring Performance

A real managerial challenge is to establish some valid means of measuring the marketing performance of a nonprofit organization. At present this is very difficult, if not impossible, for many of these organizations. A private business can evaluate its performance by using such quantitative measures as market share or return on investment, and then compare these figures with industry-wide averages and trends. For most nonprofit organizations, however, there are no corresponding quantitative measures.

Nonprofit organizations can quantify the contributions they receive, but the result reflects only their fund-raising abilities. It does not measure the services rendered to their clients. How do you quantitatively evaluate the performance of, say, the Red Cross? Perhaps by the number of people they

---

[6]Philip Kotler and Alan R. Andreasen, *Strategic Marketing for Nonprofit Organizations*, 3rd ed., Prentice-Hall, Englewood Cliffs, N.J., 1987; and Christopher H. Lovelock and Charles B. Weinberg, *Marketing for Public and Nonprofit Managers*, John Wiley & Sons, New York, 1984.

Social-cause organizations like the American Heart Association cannot easily assess the effectiveness of their marketing efforts.

house and feed after a disaster, or by the number of people they train in first aid and lifesaving techniques?

Churches, museums, and YMCAs can count their attendance, but how can they measure the services they provide for their clients? How does the American Cancer Society or the American Heart Association assess its performance? By the decline in death rates from cancer and heart diseases? Perhaps, but such a decline may be due in part to factors other than the work of these health-research organizations. These are not easy questions to answer.

## Managing the Marketing Effort

As stressed throughout this chapter, nonprofit organizations typically are unfamiliar with marketing, even though they practice some marketing under different names. The marketing activities that they do perform (usually promotion) are not well coordinated, and the people in charge of them have other duties and titles. In a university, for example, personal selling may be managed by the director of admissions, and advertising may be done through an office of public information. Nowhere in the university will you find anyone with the title of sales manager or advertising manager.

To establish a more formal marketing structure, the organization may select a group of people to determine where the organization wants to go with its marketing effort. This group can define the organization's marketing goals and identify marketing strategies to reach these goals. Decisions can be made on the development of an internal marketing department.

As a formal marketing structure develops, the organization may create a new middle-management executive position. Such a position might carry the title of director of marketing. Typically this will be a staff position—perhaps in the organization's planning department—with little or no authority. Eventually, as a sign of marketing maturity, the nonprofit organization will establish a top-level marketing executive position. This will be a line-operating position comparable to that of vice president of marketing in a business firm.

**SUMMARY**

The marketing fundamentals apply to private, nonprofit organizations as well as to firms in the business sector. But the development and implementation of a strategic marketing program are quite different in nonprofit fields.

The nonprofit field includes thousands of organizations spanning educational, cultural, religious, charitable, social, health-care, and political activities. Because of the large amounts of money and numbers of people involved in these organizations, marketing is quite important. Yet many people in nonprofit organizations are opposed to marketing. They really do not understand what marketing is or what it can do for their organizations.

Most nonprofit organizations must deal with two major groups (markets)—the contributors to the organization and the client-recipients of the organization's money or services. Consequently, a nonprofit organization must develop two separate marketing programs—one to attract resources from contributors and one to serve its clients.

In developing its marketing programs, a nonprofit organization first must identify and analyze its markets. Market segmentation is especially helpful at this stage. Then the organization is ready to develop its strategic marketing mix. The product offering will be determined largely by deciding what business the organization is in and what client markets it wants to reach. Product-mix strategies, such as expansion of mix or product differentiation, may well be used. Pricing in many nonprofit organizations is quite different from the usual price determination in a business firm. Channels of distribution typically are quite simple in nonprofit marketing. The main distribution challenge is to physically locate the organization where it can serve both contributors and clients. In promotion, many organizations have used advertising, personal selling, and other tools extensively, aggressively, and quite effectively.

Interest and research in nonprofit marketing are growing. Both should be of help in implementing marketing programs in the future. Two important problems still to be solved are those of (1) measuring performance in a nonprofit organization and (2) developing an internal structure to manage the marketing effort.

**KEY TERMS AND CONCEPTS**

Exchange concept in nonprofit marketing 509
Contributor (donor) markets 510
Client (recipient) markets 510
Importance of nonprofit marketing 510
The antimarketing attitude in nonprofit organizations 511
Market segmentation in nonprofit organizations 512

The marketing mix in nonprofit organizations:
Product offering 513
Pricing 515
Distribution 517
Promotion 518
Measuring marketing performance in nonprofit organizations 520
Managing a marketing program in nonprofit organizations 521

## QUESTIONS AND PROBLEMS

1. Are *nonbusiness organizations* and *nonprofit organizations* synonymous terms? If not,
   a. Name some nonbusiness organizations in which profit making is a major goal.

   b. Name some business organizations that are intentionally nonprofit.
2. In this chapter it is noted that many people in nonprofit organizations have a negative attitude

toward marketing. What suggestions do you have for changing this attitude so that these people will appreciate the value of marketing for their organizations?

3. Identify the various segments of the contributor market for your school.

4. Identify the client markets for:
   a. Your school.
   b. The United Way.
   c. Your church or other place of worship.
   d. Police department in your city.

5. What are some target markets (publics), other than contributors or clients, for each of the following organizations?
   a. Girl Scouts.
   b. Community hospital.
   c. Your school.

6. What benefits do contributors derive from gifts to each of the following?
   a. The Red Cross.
   b. The Boy Scouts.
   c. A symphony orchestra.
   d. A candidate for the U.S. presidency.

7. What is the product offering of each of the following?
   a. A political candidate.
   b. A family-planning organization.
   c. An organization opposed to nuclear energy.

8. A financial consultant for a private university suggested a change in the school's pricing methods. He recommended that the school discontinue its present one-price policy, under which all full-time students pay the same tuition. Instead he recommended that the tuition vary by department within the university. Thus students majoring in high-cost fields of study, such as engineering or a laboratory science, would pay higher tuition than students in lower-cost fields, such as English or history. Should the school adopt this recommendation?

9. Explain how the concept of the marketing mix (product, price, distribution, promotion) is applicable to the marketing of the following social causes:
   a. The use of returnable bottles, instead of the throwaway type.
   b. The prevention of heart ailments.
   c. A campaign against smoking.
   d. Obeying the 55-mile-per-hour speed limit.

10. How would you measure the marketing performance of each of the following?
    a. A church.
    b. Your school.
    c. The Republican Party.
    d. A group in favor of gun control.

11. The performance of a charitable organization may be measured by the percentage of contributions distributed among its clients. Explain why you think this is or isn't an effective measure of marketing performance.

12. Assume that your college or university wants to hire a director of marketing. Prepare a job description for this position, indicating its scope, activities, location within the school's administration, and responsibilities.

13. Interview a sample of foreign students on your campus and prepare a report summarizing the differences and similarities between the colleges in their home country and your school. Include such topics as classroom atmosphere, student-professor relations, campus political activities, and campus social life.

# CHAPTER 21
# INTERNATIONAL MARKETING

A college student in Chicago, Tom Alexander, got up in the morning, brushed his teeth with Close·Up, and shaved with his Norelco razor. He then put on a new shirt and sweater (made in the U.S.A.) that a friend had bought for him as a gift at Saks Fifth Avenue. For breakfast he put fresh bananas on his cereal and drank coffee. He drove to school in his Honda Civic, stopping on the way at a Shell gas station. As he walked across campus, he noted with pleasure the growing ethnic mix on campus—especially the increasing numbers of black, Hispanic, and Asian students. At the same time, he said to himself, "I'm proud to be a 100 percent American."

Now let's examine the behavior of this "100 percent American" young man. His toothpaste is made by Lever Brothers, an English-Dutch company, and his razor is made by another Dutch firm (Philips Company). His shirt and sweater were made in the U.S.A., but were bought at a store owned by a corporation in Bahrain. His bananas and coffee were imported from South America. His car was made in Japan, and Shell Oil is a Dutch-English company. And as to the phrase "100 percent American"—the decimal (percentage) system came from the Greeks and America was named after an Italian (Amerigo Vespucci)!

Truly, today it is virtually impossible for a consumer *not* to be involved in international marketing. Marketing is becoming more global as each year goes by.

Now what do we mean by international marketing? For an organization, marketing is international if its products are marketed in two or more countries. We also hear such terms as multinational, transnational (a term used by the United Nations), and global applied to cross-border marketing. In this book we—along with most business executives—consider the word *international* in marketing to be synonymous with those other terms.

## DOMESTIC MARKETING AND INTERNATIONAL MARKETING

Marketing fundamentals are universally applicable. Whether an Ohio firm sells in Toledo, Taiwan, or Timbuktu, its marketing program should be built around a good product that is properly priced, promoted, and distributed to a market that has been carefully selected. However, strategies used to implement marketing programs in foreign countries often are quite different from domestic marketing strategies. Furthermore, for the firm that is interested in international marketing, management must make strategic decisions regarding (1) the company's degree of involvement in international marketing and (2) the organizational structure for operating in each foreign market.

## Can We Standardize International Marketing?

A continuing controversy in international marketing concerns the extent to which a company can standardize its marketing program in its various foreign markets. Two large multinational firms—Coca-Cola and Nestlé—have been immensely successful, yet they have quite opposite managerial philosophies regarding global standardization. On the one hand, Coca-Cola, following American troops around the world during World War II, established a global marketing program based on one product with one promotional message. This program was tightly managed from the company's world headquarters in Atlanta, Georgia. On the other hand, the Switzerland-based Nestlé Company historically has decentralized much of its management and marketing programs. This was done to avoid wartime disruptions in Europe and also to respond to the wants and preferences of diverse local markets.

Benetton's "United Colors of Benetton" ads reach out to young people in many cultures. This campaign is an example of a standardized approach to international marketing.

We can make a few broad generalizations regarding global standardization in marketing. The best bet for standardization is in the area of durable business goods. In such industries as aircraft, computers, and tractors, the worldwide market (at least among industrialized nations) is quite uniform. Somewhere in the middle of our standardization spectrum we can place consumer durable goods such as cameras, watches, pocket calculators, small appliances, and television sets. The most difficult goods to standardize globally are food and drink products and wearing apparel. (Here Coca-Cola is an exception.) This difficulty can be traced to national tastes and habits. Even within national markets such as the United States, we often find strong regional differences in food and clothing preferences.

Interestingly enough, the newer a product is, the more likely it will lend itself to standardized marketing across national borders. Traditional apparel such as dress shoes, business suits, and formal wear still are noticeably different from one country to another. But newer items such as T-shirts, blue jeans, athletic shoes, and sweatshirts have readily been accepted across many national borders and cultures.

We support the strategy and philosophy of market segmentation that recognizes cultural differences. It is true that satellite communications, improvements in transportation, and international travel all have contributed to greater familiarity with our neighbors around the world, but strong cultural differences remain.[1]

Different strategies are needed in foreign markets primarily because those markets exist in a different set of environments. Recall that a company operates its marketing program within the economic, political, and cultural environment of each of its markets—foreign or domestic. And none of these environments is controllable by the firm. International marketing is complicated by the fact that these environments—particularly the cultural environment—often consist of elements unfamiliar to American marketing executives. A further complication is the tendency for people to use their own cultural values as a frame of reference when in a foreign environment. Throughout this chapter, we shall point out how cultural and other environmental differences among foreign markets strongly affect an organization's international marketing program.[2]

## IMPORTANCE OF INTERNATIONAL MARKETING

Sales and profits in foreign markets are a significant part of the lifeblood of many U.S. companies. Many large American firms earn more than half their after-tax profits from overseas production and marketing operations. IBM and Boeing Aircraft regularly get about half of their annual sales revenues from foreign markets. Among the high-growth members of the American Business Conference, foreign sales grew at a 20 percent annual rate from 1981 to 1986—five times faster than their U.S. sales.[3] Moreover, there is a growing aware-

---

[1] Part of this section was adapted from J. J. Boddewyn, Robin Soehl, and Jacques Picard, "Standardization in International Marketing: Is Ted Levitt in Fact Right?" *Business Horizons*, November–December 1986, pp. 69–75; John A. Quelch and Edward J. Hoff, "Customizing Global Marketing," *Harvard Business Review*, May–June 1986, pp. 59–68; and Martin van Mesdag, "Winging It in Foreign Markets," *Harvard Business Review*, January–February 1987, pp. 71–74.

[2] For an expansion of this thesis and a more complete treatment of international marketing using the environmental approach, see Philip R. Cateora, *International Marketing*, 7th ed., Richard D. Irwin, Homewood, Ill., 1991.

[3] Richard I. Kirkland, Jr., "Entering a New Age of Boundless Competition," *Fortune*, March 14, 1988, p. 40.

ness of international marketing opportunities among U.S. companies. As domestic markets become saturated, American producers—even those with no previous international experience—look to foreign markets.

International marketing is a two-way street, however. The same expanding foreign markets that offer fine growth opportunities for American firms also have their own producers. These foreign firms are providing substantial competition both in the United States and abroad. American consumers have responded favorably, for example, to Japanese radio and TV products (Sony), motorcycles (Yamaha), cameras (Canon, Nikon), and autos (Nissan, Toyota). We buy Italian shoes, German autos, Dutch electric razors (Norelco), French wines, Austrian skis, Swiss watches, and so on.

Especially strong competition is coming from Japan and the companies in the European Community (EC), popularly known as the Common Market. The EC is a group of 12 Western European nations that have banded together in a multinational economic union. Competitive challenges are also being encountered from countries in other multinational economic organizations.

**The Changing International Scene**

As we enter the 1990s, there still are excellent marketing opportunities abroad for U.S. companies. But the scene has changed. Several factors make international marketing much tougher for American firms than it was from 1945 to 1975. Perhaps the most significant has been worldwide marketing by foreign companies of a wide variety of high-quality, relatively low-priced products. By now we are quite familiar with the flood of products from Japan. In the late 1980s, however, markets in the United States began to swell with imports

International marketing should be a two-way street, with companies in one country having equal access to markets in other countries.

*Car and Driver* 10 Best List 1986, 1987, 1988, 1989.

There are two truths about "10 Best" lists. Car magazines like making them. And car makers like appearing on them.

**One of the 10 Best. From day one.**

Saab is no different. Where we do differ is in reserving our euphoria for those times when a car magazine's passing fancy moves close to permanent endorsement.

Since we first put our Saab 9000 Turbo on the road, *Car and Driver* has put it on their list. That's four straight years as one of the world's ten best cars. Considering how good we are at making their list, perhaps we'll find our way onto yours.

**SAAB**
The most intelligent cars ever built.

**Members of the European Common Market.**

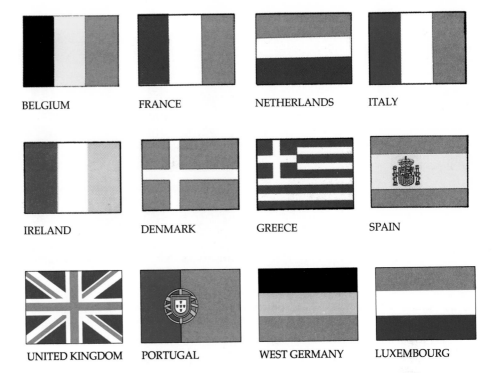

BELGIUM          FRANCE          NETHERLANDS          ITALY

IRELAND          DENMARK          GREECE          SPAIN

UNITED KINGDOM          PORTUGAL          WEST GERMANY          LUXEMBOURG

---

### Multinational economic organizations

*EC (European Community*, also known as the *Common Market): Belgium, France, West Germany, Netherlands, Luxembourg, Italy, Ireland, Great Britain, Denmark, Greece, Spain, Portugal.

*EFTA (European Free Trade Association):* Norway, Sweden, Finland, Iceland, Austria, Switzerland.

*COMECON (Council for Mutual Economic Assistance):* U.S.S.R. and other Eastern European communist nations.

*OPEC (Organization of Petroleum Exporting Countries):* Saudi Arabia, Kuwait, United Arab Emirates, Qatar, Iran, Iraq, Libya, Algeria, Nigeria, Venezuela, Indonesia.

*SERA (Latin American Economic System):* 25 nations in Central and South America.

---

from four other Asian countries—Korea, Taiwan, Hong Kong, and Singapore—sometimes referred to as Asia's "Four Tigers" or "Four Dragons." And Thailand and China are not far behind as exporters of some products to the United States. In fact, by the year 2000, Asia probably will have replaced Western Europe as the biggest trading partner of the United States.[4]

Another major change has been the shift in international investment patterns, which assumed significant proportions in the 1980s. Previously the

[4] See Liz Murphy and Richard Kern, "The Pacific Age," *Sales & Marketing Management*, April 1987, p. 64; and "Can Asia's Four Tigers Be Tamed?" *Business Week*, Feb. 15, 1988, p. 46.

A Pepsi-Cola billboard in China.

pattern was for American firms to invest abroad. At one time it was feared that U.S. firms would eventually own much of Europe's industry. Today it is the other way around. The pattern now is for foreign companies to invest in the United States. (See the box with a two-part quiz.) These firms are attracted by our political stability, economic growth potential, and limited government regulation compared to Europe. Investment alternatives for foreign companies are either to build new production facilities in the United States or to acquire existing American firms.

Perhaps the most significant development in international marketing is the forthcoming economic unification of the 12-nation European Community (EC). By the end of 1992, the EC will have removed all tariffs along with a maze of nontariff barriers within the 12 participating nations. An economically unified EC with 320 million consumers will present awesome market opportunities and challenges to companies within the EC, as well as to American, Japanese, and other foreign firms.

While the EC economic unification will eliminate internal trade barriers, non-European firms fear that external trade barriers may restrict entry of products from outside the EC. These organizations anticipate a "Fortress Europe" that will limit outside competition in EC countries. At the same time, the EC will be a major competitive force as an exporter in world markets. Consequently, many American firms moved to establish production facilities, sales branches, and other forms of business presence in the EC prior to 1992.[5]

Looking ahead to the year 2000 and thereafter, perhaps the greatest unknown factor with tremendous international marketing potential is China with its *1 billion* consumers. And, conversely, China has significant potential as an exporter of many low-priced products. Already we have seen glimpses of these possibilities. By 1990, China was a major exporter of clothing. Foreign cosmetic sales in China, unheard of a few years ago, are soaring. Kentucky Fried Chicken opened the largest store in its chain on the square across from Chairman Mao's mausoleum in Beijing. And Coca-Cola and Pepsi-Cola are aggressively competing for larger Chinese market shares.

[5]See Richard I. Kirkland, Jr., "Outsider's Guide to Europe in 1992," *Fortune*, Oct. 24, 1988, p. 121; and Shawn Tully, "Europe Gets Ready for 1992," *Fortune*, Feb. 1, 1988, p. 81.

---

**And now for a short quiz on investments in foreign countries**

*Part A.* In which of the following companies is the majority owner a foreign (non-U.S.) firm?

1. Sony (electronics).
2. Benetton (apparel).
3. Heineken (beer).
4. Volkswagen (autos).
5. Bic (pens).
6. Hyundai (autos).
7. Gucci (handbags).
8. Lipton (teas, soups).
9. Adidas (shoes).
10. Fiat (autos).

*Part B.* In which of the following firms is the majority owner a U.S. company?

1. Purolator (oil filter).
2. Shell Oil (gasoline).
3. Miles Laboratories (Alka-Seltzer).
4. Liggett Group (cigarettes—L & M, Lark, Eve; Alpo dog food).
5. Lever Bros. (soap—Lux, Wisk; toothpaste—Close·Up).
6. 20th Century–Fox (movies).
7. Carnation (dairy products).
8. Saks Fifth Avenue Stores.
9. Great Atlantic & Pacific Tea Co. (A&P supermarkets).
10. Burger King (fast food).

Answers are on the next page.

---

## STRUCTURES FOR OPERATING IN FOREIGN MARKETS

Once a company has decided to market in foreign countries, management must select an organizational structure for operating in those markets. There are several distinct methods of entering a foreign market. Each represents successively greater international involvement, leading ultimately to a truly global operation. The same firm may use more than one of these operating methods at the same time. To illustrate, it may export products to one country, establish a licensing arrangement in another, and build a manufacturing plant in a third. (See Figure 21-1.)

The simplest way of operating in foreign markets is by exporting through **import-export agent middlemen.** Very little risk or investment is involved. Also, minimal time and effort are required on the part of the exporting producer. However, the exporter has little or no control over its agent middlemen. Furthermore, these middlemen generally are not aggressive marketers, nor do they generate a large sales volume.

**FIGURE 21-1** Structures for operating in a foreign market.

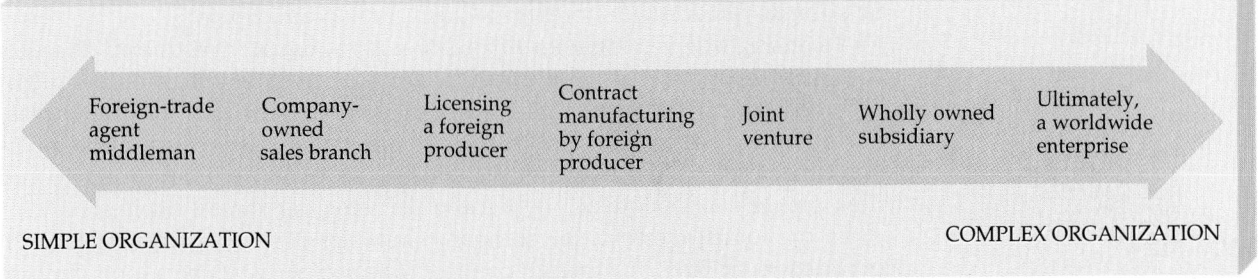

| Foreign-trade agent middleman | Company-owned sales branch | Licensing a foreign producer | Contract manufacturing by foreign producer | Joint venture | Wholly owned subsidiary | Ultimately, a worldwide enterprise |

SIMPLE ORGANIZATION                    COMPLEX ORGANIZATION

*Answers to Part A.* All 10 companies are foreign-owned. The owner's home country is as follows:

1. Japan.
2. Italy.
3. Netherlands.
4. West Germany.
5. France.
6. Korea.
7. Italy.
8. England–Netherlands.
9. West Germany.
10. Italy.

*Answers to Part B.* None of the 10 companies is American-owned. The majority owner's country in each case is as follows:

1. Australia.
2. England–Netherlands.
3. West Germany (Bayer Co.).
4. England.
5. England–Netherlands (Unilever Co.).
6. Australia.
7. Switzerland (Nestlé).
8. Bahrain (Investcorp).
9. West Germany (Tengelmann Co.).
10. England (Grand Metropolitan owns Pillsbury, which owns Burger King).

To counteract some of these deficiencies, management can move to the second stage—exporting through **company sales branches** located in foreign markets. Operating a sales branch enables a company to (1) promote its products more aggressively, (2) develop its foreign markets more effectively, and (3) control its sales effort more completely. Of course, management now has the time- and money-consuming task of managing a sales force. The difficulty here is that these sales people are either American sales people unfamiliar with the local market or foreign nationals unfamiliar with the product and the company's marketing practices.

As foreign markets expand, management may enter into licensing arrangements whereby foreign manufacturers produce the goods. **Licensing** means granting to another producer—for a fee or royalty payment—the right to use one's production process, patents, trademarks, or other assets. For example, in Japan, the Suntory brewery is licensed by Anheuser-Busch to produce Budweiser beer, while in England, Budweiser is brewed under license by the Watney brewery.

**Contract manufacturing** is related to licensing. An American marketer, such as a retail-chain organization, contracts with a foreign producer to supply products that the American firm will market in that producer's country. Sears, for instance, contracts with local manufacturers to supply many products for its department stores in Mexico, Brazil, and Spain.

Licensing offers companies flexibility with minimal investment. Through licensing or contract manufacturing, producers can enter a market that might otherwise be closed to them because of exchange restrictions, import quotas, or prohibitive tariffs. At the same time, by licensing, producers may be building future competitors. A licensee may learn all it can from the producer and then proceed independently when the licensing agreement expires.

In the fourth method, the company builds or otherwise acquires its own production facilities in a foreign country. The structure can be a joint venture or a wholly owned foreign subsidiary. A **joint venture** is a partnership arrangement in which the foreign operation is owned in part by the American company and in part by a foreign company. A Wisconsin manufacturer of children's clothing with a well-known brand name, OshKosh B'Gosh, recently began a joint venture with Poron, a French producer of children's apparel. This arrangement provides OshKosh with a network of manufacturing, sales, and distribution operations in the European market. In the early 1990s, General Mills (Wheaties, Cheerios) will enter Europe through a joint venture with Nestlé. General Mills's cereals will be produced in Nestlé plants and marketed through Nestlé's strong sales and distribution systems.[6]

When the controlling interest (more than 50 percent) is owned by foreign nationals, the American firm has no real control over any of the marketing or production activities. However, a joint venture may be the only structure (other than licensing) through which an American firm is allowed to enter a given foreign market.

**Wholly owned subsidiaries** in foreign markets are commonly used by companies that have evolved to an advanced stage of international business. With a wholly owned foreign subsidiary, a company has maximum control over its marketing program and production operations. This type of international structure, however, requires a substantial investment of money, labor, and managerial attention.

This leads us to the final evolutionary stage—one reached by very few companies as yet. It is the stage of the truly multinational corporation—the **worldwide enterprise.** Both the foreign and the domestic operations are integrated and are no longer separately identified. The regional sales office in Atlanta is basically the same as the one in Paris. Business opportunities abroad are viewed in the same way as those in the United States. That is, opportunities in the United States are no longer automatically considered to be better. A true multinational firm does *not* view itself as an American firm (Ford Motor Company), or a Swiss firm (Nestlé), or a Dutch firm (Shell Oil) that happens to have plants and markets in a foreign country. In a truly worldwide enterprise, strategic marketing planning is done on a global basis.

## A STRATEGIC PROGRAM FOR INTERNATIONAL MARKETING

Firms that have been very successful in marketing in the United States have no assurance whatsoever that their success will be duplicated in foreign markets. A key to satisfactory performance overseas lies in gauging which domestic marketing strategies and tactics should be transferred directly to foreign markets, which ones modified, and which ones not used at all. In other words, foreign markets, too, require strategic marketing planning.

### International Marketing Research

Only limited funds are invested in marketing research in foreign countries because the costs, relative to the value received, are greater abroad than at home. The reason is that environmental conditions in foreign markets often have a negative influence on some of the basic elements of marketing research.

Fundamental to marketing research is the idea that problems should be solved in a *systematic, analytical manner.* However, an orderly, rational ap-

---

[6]Timothy D. Schellhardt and E. S. Browning, "OshKosh B'Gosh Sets European Venture through Accord with Poron of France," *The Wall Street Journal*, Nov. 8, 1989, p. B6; and Richard Gibson, "General Mills Would Like to Be Champions of Breakfasts in Europe," *The Wall Street Journal*, Dec. 1, 1989, p. B6.

proach runs counter to the instincts of many people throughout the world. In many cultures, people are guided by intuition, emotional reaction, or tradition. And none of these is particularly conducive to the scientific approach. A second element in marketing research—*customer information*—depends on the willingness of people to respond accurately when researchers pose questions about attitudes or buying habits. In many societies, suspicion of strangers, distrust of government, and an individualism that holds that these things are "none of your business" compound the difficulty of gathering information.

The scarcity of *reliable statistical data* may be the single biggest problem in certain foreign markets. Figures on population, personal income, and production may be only crude estimates. Few studies have been made of such things as buying habits or media coverage. In the design of a research project, the lack of reliable data makes it very difficult to select a meaningful sample. Lack of uniformity makes intercountry comparisons very unreliable.[7]

**Analysis of Foreign Markets**

Nowhere in international marketing is the influence of the cultural and economic environments seen more clearly than in an analysis of market demand. Throughout the world, market demand is determined by population, economic ability to buy, and buying behavior. Also, human wants and needs have a universal similarity. People need food, clothing, and shelter. They seek a better quality of life in terms of lighter work loads, more leisure time, and social recognition and acceptance. But at about this point, the similarities in foreign and domestic markets end, and the differences in cultural and economic environments must be considered.

When analyzing consumers' *economic ability to buy* in a given foreign market, management may study the (1) distribution of income, (2) rate of growth of buying power, and (3) extent of available consumer financing. In emerging economies, large portions of the population have very low incomes. A much different income-distribution pattern—with resulting differences in marketing programs—is found in industrialized markets of Western Europe. In those countries there are large working-class, middle-income markets. Thus many of the products commonly in demand in Belgium or the Netherlands would find very small markets in many African or Asian countries. In Asia, Japan is an exception, of course. Rising incomes in Japan have generated huge markets for travel, sports, and other leisure-time activities. In response, some shops in London, Paris, and Rome now display window signs saying (in Japanese) "Japanese is spoken here."[8]

Here are some cultural elements that can influence a company's marketing program. The importance of specific elements in marketing varies from country to country.

- *Family.* In some countries the family is an extremely close-knit unit, whereas in others the family members act more independently. Each of these situations requires a different type of promotion, and perhaps even different types of products.

[7]See John Monaco, "Overcoming the Obstacles to International Research," *Marketing News,* Aug. 29, 1988, p. 12; and "Third World Research Is Difficult, but It's Possible," *Marketing News,* Aug. 28, 1987, p. 51. For sources of secondary data on foreign markets, see Cateora, *International Marketing,* Chapter 9.
[8]For some guidelines in determining foreign market opportunities and potential, see S. Tamer Cavusgil, "Guidelines for Export Market Research," *Business Horizons,* November–December 1985, pp. 27–33.

What cultural adjustments do you think Burger King made when entering the Finnish market?

- *Social customs and behavior.* Some cultural differences are illustrated in the boxed material on the next page.
- *Educational system.* The educational system affects the literacy rate, which in turn influences advertising, branding, and labeling. The brand may become all-important if potential customers cannot read and must recognize the article by the picture on the label.
- *Language differences.* Language differences also pose problems. Literal translations of American advertising copy or brand names may result in ridicule of, or even enmity toward, American products. Even some English words have different meanings in England and the United States.
- *Religion.* Religion is a major influence on value systems and behavioral patterns.[9]

A few examples illustrate how buying habits are influenced by cultural elements. One-stop shopping is still unknown in most parts of the world. In many foreign markets, people buy in small units, sometimes literally on a meal-to-meal basis. Also, they buy in small specialty stores. To buy food for a weekend, a *hausfrau* (housewife) in West Germany may visit the chocolate store, the dairy store, the meat market, the fish market, a dry-grocery store, the greengrocer, the bakery, the coffee market, and possibly other specialty food stores. While this may seem to be an inefficient use of her time, we must recognize that a shopping trip is more than just a chore to be done as fast as possible. It is a major part of her social life. She will visit with her friends and neighbors in these shops. Shopping in this fashion is a foreign version of the

[9]For cultural guidelines on doing business in Asia, see Frederick A. Katayama, "How to Act Once You Get There," *Fortune,* special issue, Fall 1989, p. 87; "The Delicate Art of Doing Business in Japan," *Business Week,* Oct. 2, 1989, p. 120; and John A. Reeder, "When West Meets East: Cultural Aspects of Doing Business in Asia," *Business Horizons,* January–February 1987, pp. 69–74.

---

**Marketing problems may be created by cultural differences**

---

**BODY LANGUAGE**

- Standing with your hands on your hips is a gesture of defiance in Indonesia.
- Carrying on a conversation with your hands in your pockets makes a poor impression in France, Belgium, Finland, and Sweden.
- When you shake your head from side to side, that means "yes" in Bulgaria and Sri Lanka.
- Crossing your legs to expose the sole of your shoe is really taboo in Muslim countries. In fact, to call a person a "shoe" is a deep insult.

**PHYSICAL CONTACT**

- Patting a child on the head is a grave offense in Thailand or Singapore, since the head is revered as the location of the soul.
- In an Oriental culture, touching another person is considered an invasion of privacy, while in Southern European and Arabic countries it is a sign of warmth and friendship.

**PROMPTNESS**

- Be on time when invited for dinner in Denmark or in China.
- In Latin countries, your host or business associate would be surprised if you arrived at the appointed hour.

**EATING AND COOKING**

- It is rude to leave anything on your plate when eating in Norway, Malaysia, or Singapore.
- In Egypt, it is rude *not* to leave something.
- In Italy and Spain, cooking is done with oil.
- In Germany and Great Britain, margarine and butter are used.

**OTHER SOCIAL CUSTOMS**

- In Sweden, nudity and sexual permissiveness are quite all right, but drinking is really frowned on.
- In Spain, there is a very negative attitude toward life insurance. By receiving insurance benefits, a wife feels that she is profiting from her husband's death.
- In Western European countries, many consumers still are reluctant to buy anything (other than a house) on credit. Even for an automobile, they will pay cash after having saved for some time.

---

American bridge club or neighborhood coffee break. In Japan and in Western European countries, some of the traditional shopping patterns are changing, however. Supermarkets now account for a significant and increasing percentage of retail trade in these countries.

So far in this chapter, we have stressed that significant environmental differences do exist between and within foreign countries. Yet we also see movement toward standardization of tastes, wants, and buying habits, especially in Western Europe. In some product lines there are cross-cultural similarities in demand. Pizzerias do business in Germany, lasagna is sold in Stockholm supermarkets, British fish-and-chips are wanted on the Continent, and Scotch whisky sales are large in France. To some extent travel, television, and trade are serving to homogenize European culture. But—and this should be well understood—a German is still a German, and an Italian is still an Italian. The EC will be economically unified after 1992, but a homogeneous Euro-consumer is hardly a reality.[10]

## Product Planning for International Markets

Most companies would not think of entering a domestic market without careful, extensive product planning. Yet an American firm typically enters a foreign market with essentially the same product it sells in the United States. Even when a product is changed expressly for an international market, modification is apt to be minor. A producer may convert an appliance for use with 220-volt electrical systems, or paint and package a product to protect it against a destructive tropical climate, for example.

A critical question today in product planning concerns the extent to which a company can market the same product in several different countries. While standardization obviously cannot be applied to all products, or to all international markets, certainly the situation has changed over the past 20 to 30 years. As we indicated, international communication is reducing cultural differences among some markets.

For a number of products in some markets, there is a strong common demand. One survey identified eight product categories that were highly in demand in eight major markets around the world. These products and markets are:[11]

| Products | Markets |
| --- | --- |
| Personal computers | Australia |
| Video equipment | Brazil |
| Healthful food | Britain |
| Physical fitness clothing and equipment | Canada |
| Beer and low-alcohol beverages | France |
| Convenience foods | Germany |
| Toys | Japan |
| Financial services | South Africa |

These lists still leave a lot of products and markets unaccounted for. Undoubtedly, many products have to be especially adapted for markets in a less-developed country. And by the year 2000, these countries are expected to contain 80 percent of the world's population.

In short, any marketer would be well advised to study carefully the cultural and economic environment of any market—foreign or domestic—before planning products for that particular market. In Europe, for example, a 6-cubic-foot refrigerator is the most popular size, in contrast to the larger units preferred in the United States. True, the cost difference and the prevalence of smaller kitchens in Europe are decision factors. However, the basic reasons lie in cultural behavior patterns of the consumers. As noted earlier, many European housewives shop for food daily and thus do not buy large quantities that must be stored for several days in a refrigerator. Many also do not have a car, so they walk to the store and therefore cannot carry large quantities. Frozen foods are not purchased to any great extent, so freezer storage space is not needed.

Branding and labeling are especially important in foreign marketing. As

[10] For an excellent discussion of this point with many examples, see Barbara Toman, "Now Comes the Hard Part: Marketing," *The Wall Street Journal*, Sept. 22, 1989, p. R10.
[11] Carolyn Hulse, "Popular Categories Cross Cultural Boundaries," *Advertising Age*, Dec. 24, 1984, p. 17.

---

**Adapt your product to its market—in this case, Third World markets**

---

To meet the demand in Third World markets, the Gillette Company:

- Packaged its double-edged razor blades so they can be sold one at a time.
- Packaged Silkience shampoo in half-ounce plastic bubbles, instead of the standard 7-ounce bottles.
- Packaged Right Guard deodorant in plastic squeeze bottles, instead of aerosol cans.
- Introduced plastic tubs of shaving cream that sold for half the price of the aerosol-canned cream.

As a result of these and other marketing moves from 1970 to the late 1980s, the proportion of Gillette's sales from Third World countries doubled (to 20 percent) and dollar volume increased sevenfold.

In a quite different vein, researchers at the National Autonomous University in Mexico City developed a miniature cow to help families in Third World markets. This minicow stands about 2 feet tall, and it gives one gallon of milk per day (about two-thirds the amount given by its 6-foot ancestor). Moreover, it needs only one-tenth the amount of grassland required by larger cows.

Sources: David Wessel, "Gillette Keys Sales to Third World Tastes," *The Wall Street Journal*, Jan. 23, 1986, p. 36; and Emily T. Smith, "A Miniature 'Cow' to Help Third World Families," *Business Week*, Dec. 14, 1987, p. 81.

---

suggested earlier, the brand picture may be the only part of the product that a consumer can recognize. Foreign consumers' preference for American products often overcomes their nationalistic feelings. So in many instances, a company can use the same brand overseas as in the domestic market.[12]

**Pricing in International Markets**

In earlier chapters, we recognized that determining the base price and formulating pricing strategies are complex tasks, frequently involving trial-and-error decision making. These tasks become even more complex in international marketing. An exporter faces variables such as currency conversion, a variety of bases for price quotations, and often a lack of control over middlemen's pricing.

Cost-plus pricing is probably more common in export marketing than at home. Consequently, foreign prices usually are considerably higher than domestic prices for the same product. This is because of additional physical distribution expenses, tariffs, and other export costs. At the retail level, price bargaining is quite prevalent in many foreign markets—especially in Asia, Africa, and South America.[13]

Occasionally a firm's foreign price is lower than its domestic price. The price may be lowered to meet foreign competition or to dispose of outmoded

---

[12] For an excellent discussion of positioning a product in foreign markets through branding and promotion, along with an extensive bibliography, see Teresa Domzal and Lynette Unger, "Emerging Positioning Strategies in Global Marketing," *Journal of Consumer Marketing*, Fall 1987, pp. 23–40.

[13] For a report on price bargaining by consumers in 10 developing countries, which concluded that buyer satisfaction was lower with retailers that bargain than with retailers that used a fixed-price policy, see Laurence Jacobs, Reginald Worthley, and Charles Keown, "Perceived Buyer Satisfaction and Selling Pressure versus Pricing Policy: A Comparative Study of Retailers in Ten Developing Countries," *Journal of Business Research*, March 1984, pp. 63–74.

products. Sometimes companies engage in **dumping**—that is, selling products in foreign markets at prices below the prices charged for these goods in their home market. Through the years, surplus production of certain raw materials has led to government control of world market prices. For example, individual governments have tried to stabilize the prices of coffee, nitrates, sugar, and rubber. Also, the governments of several countries have established joint agreements covering the prices of such commodities as oil, tin, potash, and cocoa.

Foreign middlemen often are not aggressive in their pricing strategies. They prefer to maintain high unit margins and low sales volume, rather than develop large sales volume by means of lower prices and smaller margins per unit sold. In fact, there is considerable price rigidity in many foreign markets. In some cases the inflexibility stems from agreements among firms that restrain independent pricing. The rigidity also sometimes results from price-control legislation that prevents retailers from cutting prices at their own discretion.

Combinations of manufacturers and middlemen are tolerated to a far greater extent in many foreign countries than in the United States. This occurs even when the avowed purpose of the combinations is to restrain trade and reduce competition. Recognizing this, Congress passed the Webb-Pomerene Act in 1918. This law allows American firms to join this type of trade combination in a foreign country without being charged with violation of American antitrust laws.

The best known of these international marketing combinations is the car-

---

### One brand—one message—eight languages

This is the package for Bircher Müsli, a popular cereal in some Western European countries. (In 1988, Kellogg's added to its U.S. product line a similar cereal, called Mueslix.) The flags and respective countries, from top to bottom, are West Germany, Great Britain, France, Spain, Italy, Netherlands, Sweden, Norway. In addition, the same package can be read in Ireland, Switzerland, Austria, Belgium, and other countries.

tel. A **cartel** is a group of companies that produce similar products and that have combined to restrain competition in manufacturing and marketing. Cartels exist to varying degrees in steel, aluminum, fertilizers, electrical products, petroleum products, rayon, dyes, and sulfur.

Prices may be quoted in U.S. dollars or in the currency of the foreign buyer. Here we encounter problems of foreign exchange and conversion of currencies. As a general rule, a firm engaged in foreign trade—whether it is exporting or importing—prefers to have the price quoted in its own national currency. Risks from fluctuations in foreign exchange then are shifted to the other party in the transaction. One way to get around currency problems, especially when dealing with Eastern European or developing nations, is through a barter arrangement in which there is an exchange of goods rather than money.

## International Distribution Systems

Understanding the environment in a foreign market helps in understanding the distribution system, because these marketing institutions result from their environment. Perceptive, and thus usually successful, retailers will capitalize on environmental change by introducing innovations that anticipate trends in the environment. Several European retailers have done a good job of innovating. Within a relatively few years, they have moved from the stage of "mom and pop" stores to a variety of retailing concepts as advanced as anything in the United States.

These innovative retailers leapfrogged several stages of institutional development. In mass retailing, the *hypermarché* in France and the *verbrauchermarkt* in Germany are huge self-service superstores operating very profitably and at much lower gross margins than similar American stores. Distribution systems in Japan, however, are another story. Producers, both foreign and Japanese, must contend with an antiquated, culture-bound, high-cost channel structure composed of "papa-mama" retail stores and a multilevel wholesaling distribution system.[14]

### MIDDLEMEN AND CHANNELS OF DISTRIBUTION

Four groups of middlemen operating in foreign trade are:

- American foreign trade middlemen.
- Foreign trade middlemen located abroad.
- Wholesalers and retailers operating within foreign markets.
- Manufacturers' sales branches and sales offices located in foreign countries.

These middlemen were introduced briefly earlier in this chapter in connection with organizational structures for international marketing. Middlemen operating *within* foreign countries are, in general, less aggressive and perform fewer marketing services than their American counterparts. The foreign marketing situation, however, usually argues against bypassing these foreign middlemen. Often the demand is too small to warrant the establishment of a sales office or branch. Also, in many foreign countries knowledge of the market may be more important than knowledge of the product, even for high-technology products. And sometimes government controls preclude the use of an American sales organization abroad. Thus, middlemen in foreign countries ordinarily are a part of the channel structure.

[14]For a brief but good description of the Japanese retailing system, see "A Land of Papa-Mama Shops," *U.S. News & World Report*, April 24, 1989, p. 47.

In Japan, foreign as well as large domestic retailers operate in an environment dominated by government-protected "papa-mama" retailers.

## PHYSICAL DISTRIBUTION

Various aspects of physical distribution in foreign marketing are quite different from anything found on the domestic scene. Generally, physical distribution expenses account for a much larger share of the final selling price in foreign markets than in domestic markets. Packing requirements, for example, are more exacting for foreign shipment. Problems caused by humidity, pilferage, breakage, and inadequate marking of shipments must be considered. Requirements regarding commercial shipping and governmental documents complicate the paperwork in foreign shipping. Marine insurance and the traffic management of international shipments are specialized fields. They involve institutions that are not ordinarily used in domestic marketing.

## BRIBERY IN INTERNATIONAL DISTRIBUTION

Bribes, kickbacks, and sometimes even extortion payments are facts of life in many international distribution systems. Bribery has existed to varying degrees in buying and selling since time immemorial. It is so rooted in many cultures that special slang words are used to designate it. In Latin America it is called the *mordida* (small bite). It is *dash* in West Africa and *baksheesh* in the Middle East. The French call it *pot de vin* (jug of wine). In Italy there is *la bustarella* (the little envelope) left on a bureaucrat's desk to cut the red tape. In Chicago we use *a little grease*.

Bribery in marketing became an international scandal in the mid-1970s. Subsequent political sensitivity in the United States resulted in several companies' establishing written ethical guidelines. In 1977 Congress passed the Foreign Corrupt Practices Act (FCPA), a far-reaching and restrictive law that limits considerably the competitive position of the United States in international trade.

What complicates this situation is the fact that bribery is not a sharply defined activity. Sometimes the lines are blurred between a bribe, a gift to show appreciation, a reasonable commission for services rendered, and a "facilitating" payment to grease the distribution channel. Realistically, in some foreign markets a seller must pay a facilitating fee or commission to an

### AN ETHICAL DILEMMA?

In most countries in the Middle East it is generally not possible for a foreign marketer to sell directly to a branch of the government or to local private firms. Invariably sales are made through local agents who have personal contacts (often family members) in the buying organizations. To make sales under these conditions, some foreign firms pay these agents commissions well beyond what is reasonable for the tasks they perform. If your firm wished to expand into international markets, would you consider it ethical to make such payments to agents?

agent in order to get in touch with prospective buyers. Without paying such fees, there is simply no effective access to those markets.[15]

**Advertising in Foreign Markets**

Rather than discuss promotion in its entirety, we limit our discussion to advertising as being illustrative of the strategic problems in international promotion. Advertising is selected because it is probably used by more firms in international marketing than a company sales force or any sales promotion technique.

A controversial issue in international advertising is the extent to which advertising can be standardized in foreign markets. In years gone by, the consensus was that a separate program (copy, appeals, and media) had to be tailored for each country, or even for regions within a country. While complete uniformity is not recommended, today there is much support for the idea of commonality in international ad campaigns. Many companies are using basically the same appeals, theme, copy, and layout in all their international advertising—particularly in Western European countries. Such standardization of advertising is spurred by the increase in international communications. Hordes of Europeans travel from one country to another while on vacation. Many radio and TV broadcasts from one country reach audiences in another country. The circulation of many European magazines and newspapers crosses national borders.

Perhaps the issue comes down to this point: The goal of advertising is essentially the same at home and abroad, namely, to communicate information and persuasive appeals effectively. It is only the media strategy and the specific messages that must be fine-tuned to each country's cultural, economic, and political environment. For some products, the appeals are sufficiently universal and the market is sufficiently homogeneous to permit the use of uniform advertising in several countries. In general, however, each country has its own national identity and characteristics that must be recognized when advertising in the given country.

#### ATTITUDE OF FOREIGN MARKETS AND GOVERNMENTS TOWARD ADVERTISING

In other parts of the world, the traditionally negative attitude toward marketing in general and toward advertising in particular is a hardship for American

[15] For more on this subject, see Jeffrey A. Fadiman, "A Traveler's Guide to Gifts and Bribes," *Harvard Business Review*, July–August 1986, pp. 122–26 ff.

firms. Some foreign consumers feel that a product is of dubious value if it has to be advertised. People in many foreign countries object especially to American hard-sell advertising.

Many countries have stringent laws regulating advertising. In those countries with government regulation of radio, television, and newspapers, the use of media as advertising vehicles is tightly controlled. For example, on government-controlled TV channels in Europe, commercials are run in 15- or 20-minute blocks of time periodically during the evening. They are not interspersed in 15-, 30-, or 60-second intervals during the programs as in the United States.

In the late 1980s, however, the winds of change (or at least slight breezes) started blowing through advertising in Western Europe. The growth of private and satellite-beamed cable TV stations is generating pressure to permit commercial advertising on state-owned TV stations. The United Kingdom now allows accountants and lawyers (but still not physicians) to advertise. Carrefour, the largest superstore *(hypermarché)* in France, began to run comparative-price ads, even though French law is unclear on the legality of this strategy.

### PREPARATION OF ADVERTISEMENTS

Most of the mistakes in writing copy and preparing individual advertisements can be traced to a lack of knowledge about the foreign market. The wrong color or a poor choice of words can completely nullify an otherwise good ad. Illustrations are of prime importance in many markets where illiteracy is common. They are, of course, effective in all markets, but they must be accurate, believable, and in accord with local cultures. The translation of advertising copy into the appropriate foreign language—especially for radio—is a major problem. The advertiser must have someone both adept and current in the idioms, dialects, and other nuances of the foreign language.

## INTERNATIONAL TRADE BALANCES

To conclude this chapter, let's move from the micro level of international marketing in the individual firm to the macro level of international trade in the total economy. To maintain equilibrium in our balance of international payments, we need to generate a substantial favorable balance of *product* trade. That is, our exports of goods and services must greatly exceed our imports. This is needed to offset the negative balances stemming from our expenditures in four areas: (1) huge imports of high-priced oil; (2) our overseas military forces; (3) foreign aid; and (4) American tourist travel abroad. Up to about 1970, the United States generally had an adequate favorable balance of product trade. But since then the balance has declined to the point where it is not sufficient to offset the outpayments from the United States. Each year throughout the 1980s, the United States ran a huge negative (unfavorable) balance of trade. This situation has had serious economic and political repercussions in the United States as well as in many foreign countries.

What caused this substantial decline in our product trade balance? In the early 1980s, a major factor was the high value of the U.S. dollar in relation to the currencies of our major trading partners. This made American exports very high priced. At the same time, foreign products were relatively inexpensive in the United States. Another factor contributing to the high prices of American products was the high labor costs in the United States relative to other countries.

However, the high value of the dollar and the high wage rates aren't the

**Sticker shock in South Korea *or* why a $10,000 imported car costs so much in Korea**

| | |
|---|---:|
| Manufacturer's delivery price | $10,000 |
| Customs duty | 4,000 |
| Defense tax | 250 |
| Consumption tax | 6,160 |
| Defense tax on consumption tax | 1,848 |
| Value-added tax | 6,048 |
| Dealer acquisition tax | 4,246 |
| Customs clearance fee and dealer markup* | 3,255 |
| Registration tax | 2,148 |
| Customer acquisition tax | 5,371 |
| Subway bonds** | 3,800 |
| Total | $47,126 |

*_Business Week_ estimate.
**Car buyers must purchase these bonds but can eventually redeem them.

In contrast, a Hyundai Excel retailed in Korea for $7,982 plus $602 in fees, taxes, and subway bonds. Since 1988, when these costs were reported, some of the import charges have been reduced. However, the spread between the manufacturer's delivery price at port of entry and the final price to the buyer still is extremely large.

Source: "Can Asia's Four Tigers Be Tamed?" _Business Week,_ Feb. 15, 1988, p. 47.

still was in the developmental stage. These cooperative ventures had not yet fulfilled the expectations of business or government.[17]

• *Relative marketing capabilities.* Foreign manufacturers (especially those in Western Europe and Asia) have improved their marketing skills over the past 25 years. These producers now compete aggressively and effectively with American firms. By being highly innovative in their product planning and more customer-oriented in their marketing, many foreign producers have been quite successful in multinational marketing.

American companies attempting to enter foreign markets may be hampered by a country's archaic, expensive internal distribution system. In Japan, for example, a lengthy, multilevel, and very expensive distribution system is built into the culture. It is likely to remain in place because it provides jobs for many people. And although this system is costly for foreign marketers and extremely difficult to bypass, it is the same one that Japanese firms have to use.[18]

• *High price of oil.* Even though the price of oil has come down from the

[17] For a discussion of American trading companies and the Export Trading Company Act, including an analysis of the types of services that export management companies currently provide for domestic producers, see Daniel C. Bello and Nicholas C. Williamson, "The American Export Trading Company: Designing a New International Marketing Institution," _Journal of Marketing,_ Fall 1985, pp. 60–69.

[18] For further discussion about marketing in Japan, see Vernon R. Alden, "Who Says You Can't Crack Japanese Markets?" _Harvard Business Review,_ January–February 1987, pp. 52–56; and William Lazer, Shoji Murata, and Hiroshi Kosaka, "Japanese Marketing: Towards a Better Understanding," _Journal of Marketing,_ Spring 1985, pp. 69–81.

heights of the 1970s, this commodity still contributes dramatically to our unfavorable balance of trade. And oil imports continue to increase both in total number of barrels and as a percentage of total oil used in the United States.

## The Changing Scene and Future Outlook

Since the late 1980s, America's balance of trade has been changing. The quality of many American manufactured products has improved considerably. Productivity improvements in the United States coupled with rising costs in foreign manufacturing and the decline in the value of the dollar have made the United States the low-cost producer in many industries. The result of these economic environmental forces has been a significant increase in America's exports of manufactured products.

One interesting aspect of this resurgence in America's export trade is that small and medium-sized firms are leading the export boom in many industries. Exports by the multinational giants *have* increased, but at the same time, their imports of parts, supplies, and other products from their foreign-based subsidiaries have also risen considerably. For example, many of Chrysler's U.S.-built cars have V-6 engines made in Japan by Mitsubishi Motor Company.[19] So the net result does not help the U.S. balance of trade as much as we might like.

On balance, then, the foreign trade situation is improving, but we still have a long way to go. U.S. imports probably will remain high because of the factors we discussed earlier. Consequently, the United States must continue to expand its exports. Success in exporting will depend on our ability to:

• Continue improving quality and productivity.
• Adapt the marketing effort to foreign cultures.
• Learn the language spoken in a foreign market.
• Take a longer-range view than currently is typical among most U.S. firms. As just one example of this point, consider that the average term for an American executive in China is 3 years. In contrast, the average term (in years) for executives from other countries is: Japan—13; Germany—8½; Australia—8; France—7; England—6.[20]

| **American manufacturing industries with the greatest foreign trade surpluses in 1988** | |
| --- | --- |
| **As Exporters** | **As Importers** |
| Aircraft | Cars and trucks |
| Chemicals | Textiles and apparel |
| Computer equipment | Steel |
| Oil-field machinery | Electronics |
| Medical equipment | Machine tools |

Source: U.S. Department of Commerce data, cited in *Business Week,* Feb. 29, 1988, pp. 64–65.

[19] See "The Long Arm of Small Business," *Business Week,* Feb. 29, 1988, p. 63; and "Help Wanted from the Multinationals," *Business Week,* Feb. 29, 1988, p. 68.
[20] Wang Beiming, "China's Business Leaders Yield on Style, Not on Ideology," *The Wall Street Journal,* Sept. 29, 1986, p. 14; and Louis R. Richman, "Lessons from German Managers," *Fortune,* April 27, 1987, p. 268.

**SUMMARY**  Many U.S. companies derive a substantial share of their total sales and profits from foreign marketing operations. These multinational marketing ventures were especially profitable between World War II and the early 1970s. Since then, however, the situation has changed. International marketing opportunities still are abundant, but it is much more difficult to capitalize on them. Competition from foreign producers, especially firms in Japan, Korea, and Western Europe, has intensified greatly.

In terms of organizational structure, the simplest way to operate in a foreign market is by exporting through foreign trade middlemen. Another method is to export through company sales branches located in foreign countries. More sophisticated structures involve licensing a foreign manufacturer, engaging in a joint venture, or forming a wholly owned subsidiary.

To develop an international marketing program, a company follows basically the same procedures it uses for domestic programs. But each step along the way involves problems and operating methods that may be different for each country, and that must take into account the foreign market environment. Marketing research is more limited overseas. Product planning, pricing, distribution, and advertising all require modification based on cultures and custom—the marketing environment.

A nation's balance of international trade is very important to that nation's economy. In recent years, the U.S. balance of trade has been adversely affected by consumers' preferences for imported products, entry barriers, and other policies of foreign governments, as well as the growing technological and marketing capabilities of other countries.

**KEY TERMS AND CONCEPTS**

Multinational economic organizations 529
Licensing 532
Contract manufacturing 532
Joint venture 533
Wholly owned subsidiary 533
International marketing research 533
Cultural differences among markets 534

Product planning for foreign markets 537
Pricing in international marketing 538
Dumping 539
Cartel 540
International distribution systems 540
Advertising in foreign markets 542
International balance of trade 543

## QUESTIONS AND PROBLEMS

1. Report on export marketing activities of companies in the state where your school is located. Consider such topics as the following. What products are exported? How many jobs are created by export marketing? What is the dollar value of exports? How does this figure compare with the value of foreign-made goods imported into the state?

2. A U.S. luggage-manufacturing company with annual sales over $120 million has decided to market its products in Western Europe. Evaluate the alternative structures this company should consider.

3. Select one product—manufactured or non-manufactured—for export, and choose the country to which you would like to export it. Then prepare an analysis of the market for this product in the selected country. Be sure to include the sources of information you used.

4. If there are foreign students on your campus, interview some of them to determine how their native buying habits differ from ours. Consider such patterns as when, where, and how people in their country buy. Who makes the family buying decisions?

5. Many countries have a low literacy rate. In what ways might a company adjust its marketing program to overcome this problem?

6. Why should special attention be devoted to labeling and branding when American products are sold in foreign markets?

7. If an American company uses foreign middlemen, it must usually stand ready to supply them with financial, technical, and promotional help. If this is the case, why is it not customary to bypass these middlemen and deal directly with the ultimate foreign buyers?

8. Why do American exporters normally prefer to have prices stated in U.S. dollars? Why should foreign importers prefer that quotations be in the currency of their country?

9. "Prices of American products are always higher in foreign countries than at home because of the additional risks, expenses of physical distribution, and extra middlemen involved." Discuss.

10. Study the advertisements in foreign newspapers and magazines available in your college or city library. Particularly note the ads for American products, and compare these with the advertisements of the same products in American newspapers and magazines. In what respect do the foreign ads differ from the domestic ads? Are there significant similarities?

11. Are U.S. manufacturers being priced out of world markets because of their high cost structures?

## CASE 19

### SANDY POINT YACHT CLUB* Promotional Program for a New Service Venture

The Sandy Point Yacht Club is being built on approximately 22 waterfront acres on a large freshwater lake in central Georgia. Richard Brinkley, the developer, is an Atlanta attorney who acquired the acreage as a result of the bankruptcy of the previous owner. Brinkley expects to profit from the yacht-club development and from the additional sales that the club will provide for nearby Brinkley Marine, his boat dealership and marine store. The yacht-club project is 4 months from completion, but advance membership sales are below expectations. Brinkley had hoped that the site's visibility and "word-of-mouth" communications would generate interest. He now is considering a more aggressive promotional approach, but time is short and funds are limited.

Sandy Point Yacht Club is a private club targeted at middle-income families. Membership initiation fees are set at $750 during the construction period and for the first year after the club's opening. If the response is good, membership fees will increase to $1,000, with possible further increases in the future. Annual maintenance fees are set at $400 per year and are also expected to increase as the club adds to its facilities. Boat-slip rental fees, ranging from $50 to $60 per month, are in line with the competition. Members who do not rent slips can park their boats and trailers in a designated area on the property at no additional charge.

Early in the planning stage Brinkley hired a marina consultant/planning specialist to develop the site plan. Thus the club's facilities are well planned, as is its site. Sandy Point Yacht Club eventually will provide a resort atmosphere with on-site conveniences.

The club is to be built in several phases over a 5-year period. The first phase of construction, which is scheduled to be completed this spring, includes the following:

- Landscaped entrance with a large sign and a card-operated entry gate.
- Paved driveway and parking areas.
- Forty-foot stationary pier and 42 covered boat slips.
- Floating ship's store with fuel dock to accommodate 30 parked boats.
- Large sandy beach and roped-off swimming area.
- Boardwalk with landscaping along back of the beach.
- Sun deck, bathhouse, and arcade building with video games and jukebox.
- Double boat-launching ramp.

Future phases of construction will provide such features as:

- An additional 258 boat slips and dry storage facilities for 400 boats.
- Showroom/sales facility for Brinkley Marine.
- Shopping area and waterfront restaurant.
- Large swimming pool and hot tub.
- Water-ski school.
- Beach club for dancing.
- Multifamily residential units on the property.

*Case prepared by Professor Thomas H. Stevenson, University of North Carolina at Charlotte. Reproduced with permission.

Nearby Macon, with its approximately 125,000 inhabitants, and the well-populated surrounding suburban area provided a population base in excess of 250,000 for use of the lake. The lake also attracts people from the eastern suburbs of Atlanta, approximately an hour's drive away. Boating, water skiing, and fishing are popular summer activities for the people of this area. Traditionally, the lake's development has consisted of second-home, summer cottages. However, the last decade brought more development on a larger scale.

Sandy Point has significant competition. Within 10 miles are two large, exclusive residential developments that offer club facilities and atmosphere. In addition, the lake already has eight marinas that provide boat-slip rental and fuel and supplies—but these offer little in terms of a resort atmosphere. Slip rentals average $50 per month. Several of these facilities have waiting lists for their slips. Many sailboats are stored not in slips, but at the marinas' docks.

Brinkley has high hopes for his venture and is very anxious about the spring opening. With opening day just 4 months away, response has been moderate. In three months, only 40 memberships have been sold. Brinkley hoped to have 200 sold by opening day. His first-year sales target is 500 memberships, the minimum needed to obtain additional financing for the second phase of the project.

Brinkley is skeptical of advertising and promotional efforts because Sandy Point is to be a private club. Nevertheless, he is aware that the two residential developments extensively advertised their open-ings. They used newspaper and radio advertisements that stressed their exclusiveness, club-type facilities, and atmosphere. Tours were conducted during the first few months after opening. Both developments targeted their promotional efforts toward home buyers. They also took advantage of publicity—each was the subject of several feature articles in local newspapers.

Brinkley also knows that the existing eight marinas use little advertising. Their major promotional efforts consists of Yellow Pages advertisements in the area telephone directories. Many of these marinas have waiting lists for their boat slips. They receive a great deal of business from the personal recommendations of their patrons. There appears to be a tendency for people to use a particular marina because it is the one that their friends use.

So far the only promotional tools Brinkley has used for Sandy Point are sales presentations to purchasers of boats at Brinkley Marine. He is beginning to wonder if these efforts are sufficient.

## QUESTIONS

1. What promotional techniques and expenditures would you recommend for the 4 months remaining before the spring opening?
2. Should there be a change in promotional strategy and budgets as additional phases of Sandy Point are completed?
3. How should the promotional program change in the years after Sandy Point is complete?

CASE 20

# VANCOUVER SYMPHONY ORCHESTRA* Expanding the Application of Marketing

On a snowy January evening—after 59 years of operation—the Vancouver (Canada) Symphony Orchestra (VSO) suspended its season. Symphony officials, facing a debt of $1.7 million and finding no way out of the dilemma, made the announcement as 84 musicians tuned up in the rehearsal hall prior to a concert. The audience was dumbfounded. Michael Adams, sitting in a choice seat, had known that the VSO was

*The case was originally prepared by Prof. Montrose S. Sommers, University of Guelph. The information was drawn from "Troubled VSO to Be Studied by City Task Force," Globe and Mail, March 5, 1988, p. C10; Audience Tells Task Force to Move Quickly on VSO," March 25, 1988, p. C11; "The Day the Music Died," MacLean's, Feb. 8, 1988, p. 50.

in trouble but the announcement shocked him as well. He also knew that within the next few days he would be involved in the aftermath of the suspension of operations. Specifically, as vice president for marketing at Pan Pacific Forest Products, he would be asked for guidance by Jesse Saunders, Pan Pacific's legal counsel and a member of both the Pan Pacific and VSO boards of directors.

Saunders had met with Adams a number of times in the last year. At each meeting it was clear to Adams that Saunders was interested in learning more about the kind of marketing ideas Michael was bringing to Pan Pacific and also what those ideas could mean to the symphony. In the three years Adams had been with Pan Pacific, he had never really thought too much about marketing beyond consumer and industrial goods. He knew that shortly he would be stretching his mind in a new direction when Jesse Saunders sought advice.

By the next morning the Vancouver media was full of the news of the suspension of the orchestra's season and by Saturday, there were news reports and commentaries across Canada. On the following Monday morning Adams began tracking what was being said so he would be prepared for his next meeting with Saunders.

There were a lot of comments and activity during the next few days. Vancouver's mayor gave a ringing endorsement of the VSO, calling it the cornerstone of the city's future. The mayor reported also that he had received many messages and phone calls telling him essentially that the public believed in music. He said many people approached him with the comment that while they hadn't been to the symphony in years, it was important to have it.

From reports in local and eastern newspapers, a number of things became obvious. First, orchestras across Canada had had their problems over the last few years; the Atlantic Symphony, the Windsor Symphony, and others had faced financial difficulties. Second, it appeared that the mounting debts frequently were the result of increasing costs and salaries for performers and musicians. Third, a popular approach to resolving the financial problems seemed to be to work harder to increase donations from public and private sources; strong local action seemed to save the troubled orchestras—at least in the short run.

Within a few days after Adams's tracking efforts had started, Vancouver's mayor had appointed a task force on the VSO's future and hearings began almost immediately. Everyone seemed to feel a sense of urgency. If immediate action was not forthcoming, members of the orchestra would have to leave Vancouver in search of other jobs, and first-class musicians would be hard to recruit. In spite of the fact that a great deal of media attention was focused on the suspension and the hearings and that public petitions

of support for the orchestra had quickly been circulated and signed by at least 10,000 people, the task force's first public forum attracted a rather small audience of about 125. Of those attending, 32 spoke about the symphony.

Adams found reports on the meeting and comments made to him by a few people who attended to be intriguing in general and especially interesting from a professional point of view. The case of the VSO seemed to run true to form. It was thought by some that the problem had started three years earlier when federal, provincial, and corporate grants reduced the orchestra's deficit from $2.5 million to $1.5 million. This gave the organization some breathing space to recover from its financial problems and try to get back to the good old days of the previous decade. At that time, the VSO performed for near-capacity audiences. However, in recent years attendance had fallen to 51 percent of capacity and a campaign to sell 25,000 season tickets for the current season had resulted in the sale of only 16,000 before the suspension was announced.

There were as many reasons advanced to explain the VSO's difficulties as there were members of the orchestra and people who attended the task force's public forum. But Adams believed the issues could be boiled down to a small number.

One problem seemed tied to the appointment of Rudolph Barshai as musical director and conductor. He arrived in Vancouver in the middle of a wage dispute between symphony management and the orchestra members, and some believed he never recovered from this introduction. Barshai's conflicts as musical director and conductor were such that many musicians were demanding that he be ousted, and the VSO Board had already decided not to renew his contract for next season. Some said Barshai was too autocratic with orchestra members. Others felt he was not in Vancouver often enough to impress either the "cultural" community or the media; he either didn't make a sincere effort or didn't have star quality or charisma and thus did not "sell" the orchestra.

A second factor was that the musical fare being presented was just not as appealing as in the past— too much classical and not enough "pops." Some commentators had noted that although Vancouver was a richer leisure and entertainment market than ever before, it also offered more choices to residents. Some symphony supporters had difficulty believing that the VSO had to compete with the Vancouver Canucks (NHL hockey team), the B.C. Lions (Canadian professional football), events at Vancouver covered stadium (B.C. Place), not to mention beaches, ski areas, theaters, clubs, and of course, Stanley Park (a 1,000-acre midtown, multipurpose recreation area).

Third, the task force was told that the problem lay in the changing nature of Vancouver's population. It was noted that 41 percent of the city's population and 53 percent of its school students listed English as a second language; these were increases over the past. One alleged result was that not only did teachers have difficulty making themselves understood, but also they were unable to instill an appreciation of music in their students. In addition, the point was made that it had been a long time since the orchestra had played at the local universities—Simon Fraser and the University of British Columbia—or given concerts in schools, parks, and other public locations.

In pondering the VSO problems, Adams was struck by how similar they seemed to the problems at Pan Pacific when he first arrived as marketing vice president. At that time, the company was being buffeted by recessionary economic conditions. The demand for traditional forest products had dropped out of sight because of the fall in new construction. The company saw itself as a producer of lumber and plywood and knew that both good times and bad were inevitable. Its response to hard times was to tighten

its belt, cut costs, and sell harder. Since Pan Pacific's supply of logs was good and secure, senior executives felt it was only a matter of time before conditions would change and sales would improve. Adams had worked hard in the last few years to persuade his department and senior management that it makes a difference if a company is production-, sales-, or marketing-oriented. It had not been easy since many in the firm believed that lumber was lumber and that builders as well as do-it-yourselfers bought raw lumber or plywood by grade, price, and delivery and that was that.

Adams was not sure about Jesse Saunders' marketing sensitivity. Saunders was an astute lawyer, but he had never worked in line management. Among the things he did as a board member was to manage Pan Pacific's donation program. Adams wanted very much to provide Saunders with sound professional advice. He needed to develop an approach to get his ideas across as well as to organize a presentation to convince Saunders that modern marketing thinking could contribute to the VSO.

## QUESTIONS

1. What kind of marketing orientation, if any, has existed at the VSO? If the issues addressed by the task force are pursued, what kind of marketing orientation would the VSO adopt?
2. Does it make sense for Adams to compare Pan Pacific with the VSO in order to convince Jesse Saunders of what could be done?
3. What should be the outline of Adams's presentation?

## CASE 21

## COOPER SUPPLY COMPANY  Distribution Channel to Reach a Foreign Market

"You know as well as I do, Ralph, that customers in Saudi Arabia, especially ARAMCO, have been our bread and butter for over 10 years. That's why I'm concerned about this new statement on procurement policy that we just received from ARAMCO. Now the Saudi government may or may not have been behind this new policy. In any case, I think we darned well better come up with the appropriate channel-of-distribution decision that will enable us to comply with this new policy. That is, if we want to continue to compete in the Saudi Arabian market." These words were spoken by Frank Broderick, the senior

sales rep in the Cooper Supply Company, in a conversation with Ralph Karras, the company's vice president of sales.

The Cooper Supply Company was a large independent distributor (wholesaler) of electrical supplies. The company had its main office and warehouse in Philadelphia, Pennsylvania, and a smaller office and warehouse in Houston, Texas. Since its founding in 1930, the firm had grown slowly but steadily until 1973, when its sales volume reached $12 million. About 25 percent of this volume was in export business, primarily to large oil companies.

Then, in the mid-1970s, the price of oil increased dramatically, thus stimulating the exploration and drilling for oil. This situation sharply increased the demand for products carried by Cooper Supply Company. Consequently, since 1973, Cooper's sales had increased considerably. By 1990, the company's annual sales volume was $50 million and net profit was $5 million. Almost one-half of this business came from export sales to companies in Saudi Arabia.

Cooper Supply carried a wide variety of electrical supplies and small electrical equipment. "We represent the finest names in the industrial electrical supply and equipment industry," Karras said. "And we got there because of our reputation for honesty and integrity in an industry that often is laced with payoffs, price fixing, and price cutting."

One particular group of products was classified as explosion-proof, hazardous-application products. This group accounted for 50 percent of Cooper's total sales and about 80 percent of its export sales volume. Intended for use in hazardous environments where toxic or inflammable particles or fumes might be in the atmosphere, these items permitted the safe transfer of electricity without the danger of igniting volatile gases or particles.

These products included switches, circuit breakers, telephones, lighting equipment, receptacles, timers, and thermostats. Cooper also carried a complete line of the same goods in the non-explosion-proof category. Other products distributed by Cooper were batteries, flashlights, light bulbs, wire, conduit, transformers, fans, and electric welders.

The large number of competitors, plus the fact that an essentially similar product could be supplied by several manufacturers, made electrical supply wholesaling an intensely competitive industry with low profit margins. However, as Ralph Karras pointed out, "Typically, export customers will pay higher prices, which makes the export business more lucrative and obviously *very* important to us. Of course, the export business is a lot more complicated and risky than is domestic selling."

Many of Cooper's customers preferred to deal with only one electrical goods supplier in order to reduce procurement costs and also to give the buyer some influence with the supplier. Cooper easily adapted to this industrial buying pattern by being able to handle a customer's total electrical supply needs. Cooper sold to firms in a variety of industries including railroads, utilities, manufacturing, engineering, construction, federal and state governments, and petroleum.

Many of Cooper's petroleum accounts were large oil companies that bought electrical merchandise in the United States for use in their foreign operations. In fact, sales to one customer alone—the Arabian-American Oil Company (ARAMCO)—accounted for 30 percent ($15 million) of Cooper's sales in 1990.

ARAMCO was jointly owned by Exxon, Texaco, and Standard Oil of California, each with a 28⅓ percent interest, and Mobil with a 15 percent interest. Because the ARAMCO account was so important to Cooper Supply, Frank Broderick was greatly concerned about ARAMCO's recently issued statement regarding its procurement policy. In effect, the statement said that, starting the first of the following year, all ARAMCO purchase orders exceeding $50,000 would be placed either through (1) a Saudi Arabian national or (2) agents or companies based in Saudi Arabia. That is, ARAMCO would no longer place orders directly with Cooper or other foreign-based suppliers.

The reason stated for the new policy was ARAMCO's dissatisfaction with the situation in which so much capital was leaving Saudi Arabia without adequately benefiting the country. In view of this line of reasoning Broderick believed that other large Cooper customers in Saudi Arabia would soon adopt a similar purchasing policy.

Despite its rapid growth since the mid-1970s, Cooper Supply still had only 10 outside sales reps and another 10 who comprised the inside sales force. The outside sales people called on customers' offices in the United States, even though many of the orders were shipped to foreign locations. The inside sales force handled all inquiries, mail orders, and telephone orders. Karras preferred to limit the size of his sales force. He wanted Cooper Supply to retain the image of being a medium-sized company that offered personalized service and quick delivery in competition with its larger competitors.

Several weeks before receiving ARAMCO's statement, Karras had received a proposal from a Saudi Arabian agent offering to represent Cooper Supply in Saudi Arabia. Karras responded to the agent's letter, saying that Cooper would study the proposal and reply within a reasonable period of time. In fact, Karras had been wondering how to respond to the Saudi's proposal when he (Karras) received the ARAMCO notice.

The proposed agency agreement was to cover a period of 3 years, and was subject to renewal in 3-year time segments. The agent would receive a commission of 2 percent of all orders shipped to Saudi Arabia. This commission was to be paid even if the agent had not been instrumental in soliciting the business or obtaining the order. In return, the agent would (1) supply local sales people in Saudi Arabia, (2) provide contacts with potential customers, and (3) use his good reputation to solicit inquiries and orders for Cooper Supply. The agent also enclosed supporting letters of recommendation from ARAMCO and Saudi government officials.

Ralph Karras was discussing the agent's proposal and the ARAMCO statement with Frank Broderick. Broderick pointed out that Cooper's annual sales to ARAMCO alone amounted to $15 million, and another $8 to $10 million came from sales to other Saudi Arabian construction projects. On the ARAMCO sales alone, the agent's 2 percent commission would amount to $300,000. "And that assumes that the agent can sell at least as much as we've been selling to ARAMCO from our United States offices," Broderick stated.

"I don't like this agent's deal at all," he continued. "We tie ourselves up in an exclusive-agency contract for 3 years. That makes us vulnerable if the guy turns out to be ineffective. Competition could kill us during that period. I think we simply ought to open our own sales office in Saudi land—either in Riyadh or in Jiddah. In that way we'd have our own people on the scene. We would avoid paying an agent's commission. We would get better market coverage and still be operating within the terms of the new ARAMCO policy."

"Frank, I'm a little leery of the financial and personnel commitment involved in establishing our own sales office over there," countered Karras. "Salaries and expenses could cost us a bundle, and with no guarantee of success. Maybe we can open an office some time in the future, but for now this agency proposal maybe is our best bet. The guy comes highly recommended, and his 2 percent fee won't put our bids above competitive level. And he will know the territory better than we do. As you well know, the hardest part of obtaining business over there is to make the initial contact—that is, to obtain inquiries from prospective accounts.

"I really don't know which way to go," concluded Karras. "Maybe there is a better alternative that we are overlooking. All I do know is that we have to do something and do it soon."

## QUESTION

What channel of distribution should the Cooper Supply Company use to reach the Saudi Arabian market?

# PART EIGHT

# MANAGING THE MARKETING EFFORT

Planning and implementing a company's marketing program,
evaluating the marketing performance of a company,
appraising the role of marketing in our society, and
considering marketing activities in the future

Up to this point, we have dealt separately with how a firm selects target markets and then develops and manages the four elements of the marketing mix. Now it is time to bring these individual areas together—to present an overview of the firm's *total* marketing program.

In Part 8 we will apply the basic management process to a company's total marketing program. Thus in Chapter 22 we discuss marketing planning and demand forecasting. Then in Chapter 23 we survey the implementation and evaluation stages of the management process as these stages relate to the marketing program in an individual firm. Finally, in Chapter 24 we appraise the current position of marketing in the American socioeconomic system and consider the future of marketing.

# MARKETING PLANNING AND FORECASTING

## CHAPTER 22 GOALS

This chapter examines the planning of a company's total marketing program with special attention to the forecasting of market demand. After studying this chapter, you should be able to explain:

- The nature, scope, and importance of planning.
- The essential difference between strategic company planning and strategic marketing planning.
- The process of strategic company planning.
- Alternative strategies by which a company can achieve its organizational mission and objectives.
- The steps involved in strategic marketing planning.
- The purpose and contents of an annual marketing plan.
- The nature and importance of demand forecasting in marketing.
- Major methods used in forecasting market demand.

Companies in the ski industry are finding out that, whereas more snow can often be made by machines, additional skiers are more difficult to come up with. As a result, the ski industry and many ski resort operators have had to rethink their marketing plans.

By the late 1980s, the number of day passes purchased annually by skiers was only 10 percent higher than a decade earlier. Why? One demographic trend is critical: The U.S. population has been aging. In particular, the group most likely to be avid skiers—18- to 34-year olds—has been shrinking compared to other age groups. While the number of skiers has gone up slightly, operating costs (especially for labor) have risen much more rapidly. The result: financial problems at many ski resorts.

Many ski areas have redefined their missions and modified strategies regarding target markets and the marketing mix. Some ski resort operators, for example, believe satisfying today's skier requires more than excellent ski facilities. So they have added restaurants, ice skating, child care, and family recreation. Some resorts are also adding convention facilities.

With the population aging, many ski areas have expanded their target markets. Some aggressively pursue foreign skiers. Aspen and Breckenridge in Colorado are targeting European and Japanese skiers, respectively. Other areas are trying to attract more families. And some are seeking to attract first-timers.

New marketing-mix strategies have been tried as well. Ski-area operators have excelled in improving their products. During the 1980s, they spent more than $1.5 billion to upgrade ski runs, add more lifts, speed up existing lifts, and expand the variety of facilities. They also are advertising more and tailoring their campaigns to reach specific groups.

In addition, price has become an offensive weapon for some resorts. Reduced prices—as low as $10 at some small areas in Colorado—are intended to attract skiers who cannot—or will not—pay the normal prices of up to $35. Some operators fear skiers will always expect low prices.

The number of ski areas declined from 1,000 to about 650 during the 1980s. Evidently, many areas are fighting not just for added profits but for survival. Those that make it are likely to have sound and creative strategic marketing plans.[1]

[1] Based on Nan O'Neal and Alan Radding, "Ski Areas Sport New Strategies," *Advertising Age*, Jan. 9, 1989, p. 38W; and William C. Symonds, "A Punishing Run for Ski Resorts," *Business Week*, Dec. 12, 1988, p. 38.

As the opening example suggests, the development of creative, yet sound, marketing plans is critical to a firm's success. Now that you have a good understanding of the fundamentals of marketing, we can discuss several aspects of planning as applied to an entire organization and its marketing activities. We shall also discuss the forecasting of market demand—an essential ingredient in marketing planning.

To begin, let's briefly review the topic of marketing management. In Chapter 1 the management process was defined as planning a marketing program, implementing the plans, and evaluating the performance results. This is illustrated in Figure 22-1, which is identical to Figure 1-3. In this chapter we focus on planning, the first step in the process.

## NATURE AND SCOPE OF PLANNING

To develop an effective marketing program, management first should prepare a strategic plan for the *total* organizational effort. This overall planning should be followed by strategic planning in the organization's various functional divisions, including marketing. But before we discuss strategic *marketing* planning, we will review the concept of planning in general as well as key aspects of strategic *company* planning.

### What Is Planning?

Quite simply, **planning** is deciding now what we are going to do later, including when and how we are going to do it. Without a plan, we cannot get anything done, because we don't know what needs doing or how to do it.

**Strategic planning** is the managerial process of matching an organization's resources with its market opportunities over the long run. Market and economic conditions during the past two decades prompted many companies to engage in more frequent and more formal strategic planning. The intent was to seize changing market opportunities and avoid imminent threats. Formal strategic planning was recognized as one of the most effective management tools for reducing risks.

### Scope of Planning Activities

Planning may cover long or short periods of time. Strategic planning is usually long-range planning that covers 3, 5, 10, or (infrequently) 25 years. It also requires the participation of top management and often involves a planning staff. Long-range planning deals with broad, company-wide issues such as expansion or contraction of production, markets, and product lines. For example, the U.S. auto industry must look ahead to the next century to specify key markets, plan new products, and update production technologies.

**FIGURE 22-1** The management process in marketing.

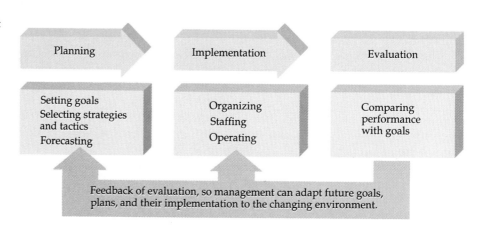

Planning → Implementation → Evaluation

Setting goals
Selecting strategies and tactics
Forecasting

Organizing
Staffing
Operating

Comparing performance with goals

Feedback of evaluation, so management can adapt future goals, plans, and their implementation to the changing environment.

In some industries, planning must extend 10—or even 25—years into the future.

Short-range planning typically covers a period of 1 year or less and is the responsibility of lower- and middle-echelon executives. It focuses on such issues as determining which target markets will receive special attention and planning next year's marketing-mix strategies. Again looking at the auto industry, Chrysler Corporation annually decides which target markets it will concentrate on and whether its basic marketing mixes need to be changed. Naturally, short-range plans have to be compatible with the organization's long-range plans.

Planning activities that determine marketing strategy in a firm may be conducted on three different levels:

- *Strategic company planning*. At this level management defines the organization's mission, sets long-range goals, and formulates broad strategies to achieve these goals. These company-wide goals and strategies then become the framework for planning in different functional areas. Company-wide planning considers an organization's requirements and capabilities in the areas of production, finance, human resources, research and development, and marketing.

- *Strategic marketing planning*. The top marketing executives set goals and strategies for the organization's marketing effort. Strategic *marketing* planning obviously should be coordinated with *company-wide* planning. It includes the selection of target markets and the development of long-range programs for the major ingredients in the marketing mix. In Parts 3 through 6 of this text, the major elements of the marketing mix were considered individually. Realistically, however, planning in all these areas must occur almost simultaneously and must be carefully coordinated, because each element in the mix interacts with every other element.

- *Annual marketing planning*. Annual plans should be prepared for all of the firm's major functions. Covering one time segment, the annual marketing plan is based on the firm's ongoing strategic marketing planning. It is a master plan laying out a year's marketing activities for a given product line, major product, brand, or market. Thus this plan serves as an operational guide to the executives in each phase of the marketing effort for the given product or market.

**FIGURE 22-2** Three levels of organizational planning.

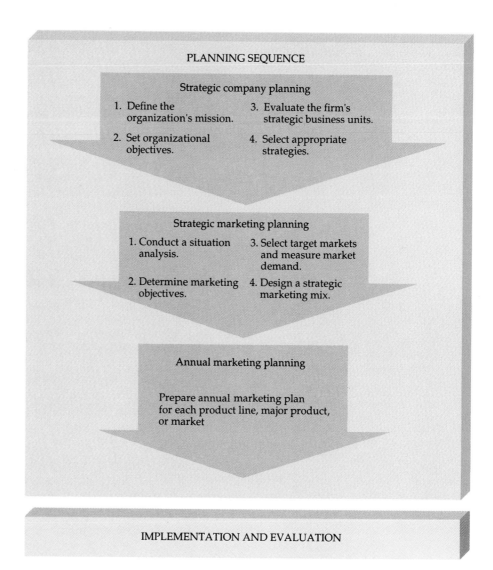

PLANNING SEQUENCE

**Strategic company planning**

1. Define the organization's mission.
2. Set organizational objectives.
3. Evaluate the firm's strategic business units.
4. Select appropriate strategies.

**Strategic marketing planning**

1. Conduct a situation analysis.
2. Determine marketing objectives.
3. Select target markets and measure market demand.
4. Design a strategic marketing mix.

**Annual marketing planning**

Prepare annual marketing plan for each product line, major product, or market

IMPLEMENTATION AND EVALUATION

## STRATEGIC COMPANY PLANNING

**Strategic company planning** consists of (1) defining the organization's mission, (2) setting organizational objectives, (3) evaluating the firm's strategic business units, and (4) selecting appropriate strategies to achieve the organization's objectives. The process is shown in the top part of Figure 22-2.

Strategic planning will be influenced considerably by *external macroenvironmental forces* such as economic conditions, technology, and competition.[2] We have discussed frequently the impact of these forces on target markets and the four elements in a company's marketing mix. Management's planning will also be affected by the organization's *internal resources*, such as its financial condition, production facilities, research and development capabilities, and strengths and weaknesses in marketing.

[2] Techniques for identifying and monitoring nontraditional competitors are discussed in William E. Rothschild, "Who Are Your Future Competitors?" *The Journal of Business Strategy*, May/June 1988, pp. 10–14.

**Define Organizational Mission**

The first step in strategic planning for the organization as a whole is to clearly define its mission. For some firms, this step requires only the review and confirmation of a previously disseminated mission statement. But for many firms this critical step has never been formally carried out.

Defining **organizational mission** means answering the question, "What business are we in?" Consider a well-known French company that found success in the United States during the 1980s (but experienced a setback in 1990 when a potential health hazard led to a total product recall). What business is Perrier in? Soft drinks? Or simply water? Neither is correct. Based on the views of consumers, Perrier executives have determined that the company is in the *natural beverages* business. This business definition, in turn, influences planning decisions.

The organization's statement of purpose, or mission, should specify the consumer groups to be served, needs that will be satisfied, and—very generally—how this goal will be accomplished. A mission statement should be neither too broad and vague nor too narrow and specific. To say that the mission is "to benefit American consumers" is too vague. To state that the purpose is "to make tennis balls" is too narrow. Neither statement outlines meaningful benefits for identified groups of consumers or provides much guidance to management. Unless the firm's basic purpose is clear to all executives, strategic planning efforts will lack direction and will likely result in considerable disagreement and confusion.

Traditionally, companies stated their missions in production-oriented terms, such as "We make furnaces" (or telephones, or tennis rackets). Today, in line with the marketing concept, organizations are urged to be customer-oriented in their statements of purpose. Executives should think in terms of the wants they are satisfying and the benefits they are providing. Thus, instead of "We make furnaces," Lennox Company's statement of mission should be "We provide home climate control." Table 22-1 contrasts production- and customer-oriented statements.

**TABLE 22-1 What business are you in?**

| Company | Production-oriented answer | Customer-oriented answer |
|---|---|---|
| AT&T | We operate a long-distance telephone company. | We provide multiple forms of reliable, efficient, and inexpensive telecommunications services. |
| Exxon | We produce oil and gasoline products. | We provide various types of safe and cost-effective energy. |
| Penn Central | We run a railroad. | We offer a transportation and materials-handling system. |
| Levi Strauss | We make blue jeans. | In wearing apparel we offer comfort, fashion, and durability. |
| Xerox | We make copy machines. | We automate offices. |
| Eastman Kodak | We make cameras and film. | We help preserve beautiful memories |
| Revlon Cosmetics (in the words of its founder) | "In the factory, we make cosmetics." | "In the drugstore, we sell hope." |

To fulfill its mission, Lennox markets various climate-control products, including heat pumps.

Benefit-oriented mission statements focus management's attention on fundamental consumer needs that must be satisfied by the business. If the company's mission is to make furnaces, it will be out of business if furnaces are replaced by heat pumps or solar heating units. But if its mission is to provide climate control, the firm is more likely to recognize emerging technology and be willing to switch to alternative energy sources.

**Determine Organizational Objectives**

The next step in strategic planning is for management to decide on a set of objectives that will guide the organization in accomplishing its mission. If mission addresses the question, "What business are we in?" then objectives answer the question, "What do we want to accomplish?" Recall from our earlier discussion that an **objective** is a desired outcome. Organizational objectives can also serve as guides for managerial planning at lower levels in a company. And they provide standards for evaluating an organization's performance.

Objectives should stimulate action because they are achieved by actions that carry out plans. To fulfill this purpose, objectives must possess a number of attributes. They should be:

- Clear and specific.
- Stated in writing.
- Ambitious, but realistic.
- Consistent with one another.
- Quantitatively measurable wherever possible.
- Tied to a particular time period.

The following objective is unsatisfactory because it is too general and not really measurable: "To improve the company's public image." A more suitable objective would be: "To receive favorable recognition awards next year from at least three consumer or environmental groups."

In effect, delineating what business it is in and stating its goals (synonymous with objectives) direct a company's total planning effort as well as more specific efforts in different functional areas. The mission statement tells something about the needs to be served, and the objectives set priorities regarding important performance areas (such as profits, market share, customer satisfaction, and repeat purchases). Together, the statements of mission and objectives should help a firm to be marketing-oriented rather than production- or sales-oriented.

## Evaluate Strategic Business Units

A small, single-product company can conduct a company-wide performance analysis. However, most large and medium-sized companies—and even some smaller firms—are multiproduct and perhaps multibusiness organizations. In such diversified firms, company-wide planning cannot serve as an effective guide for executives who oversee the organization's various divisions. Consider the Philip Morris Company, for example. The mission, objectives, and strategies in its tobacco division are—and should be—quite different from those in the Miller brewing or Kraft foods divisions.

Consequently, for more effective planning and operation, a multiproduct or multibusiness organization should be divided into major product or market divisions. These divisions are called **strategic business units** (SBUs). Each SBU may be a major division in an organization, a group of related products, or even a single major product or brand.

To be identified as an SBU, a unit should:

- Be a separately identifiable business.
- Have a distinct mission.
- Have its own competitors.
- Have its own group of executives with profit responsibility.

The trick is to set up the *optimum* number of SBUs in an organization. If there are too many, top management can get bogged down in details associated with planning, operating, and reporting. However, if there are too few SBUs, each unit covers too broad an area to be useful for managerial planning

---

**Dividing up the "pie"**

Possible SBU divisions for two giant companies and a nonprofit organization are as follows:

- *General Electric:* Electrical motors, major appliances, jet engines, lighting equipment, and commercial credit.
- *Your university or college:* Different schools (such as business, engineering, and education) *or* different delivery systems (such as on-campus curriculum and televised courses).
- *Sears:* Department stores, insurance (Allstate), real estate brokerage (Coldwell Banker), securities brokerage (Dean Witter), consumer credit (Discover card), and shopping-center development (Homart).

and control. In 1990 the right number for AT&T was 19 SBUs, ranging from long-distance service to computers. Of course, most companies have fewer SBUs than AT&T.

After SBUs have been satisfactorily delineated, the total organization may be viewed as a "portfolio" of businesses or product lines. An essential step in strategic planning is an **organizational portfolio analysis,** which identifies the present status of each SBU and determines its future role in the company. This evaluation also provides guidance to management in designing strategies and tactics for an SBU.

Management typically has limited resources to support its SBUs. Thus management needs to know how best to allocate these resources. Which SBUs should be stimulated for growth, which ones maintained in their present market position, and which ones eliminated? An organizational portfolio analysis is designed to aid management in this decision making.[3] For example, in the past several years, the Marriott Corp. has thoroughly analyzed its portfolio of businesses. As a result, this very large services firm sold some businesses (including its chain of Roy Rogers restaurants in 1990) and focused on various forms of lodging (such as Fairfield Inns, Marriott Suites, and Residence Inns).

## Select Organizational Strategies

By this point in its strategic planning, the organization has determined where it wants to go. The next step is to address the question "How are we going to get there?" Answers are found in **organizational strategies**—broad, basic plans of action by which an organization intends to achieve its goals and fulfill its mission. Strategies are selected for (1) the total organization in a small, single-product company or (2) each SBU in a large, multiproduct or multibusiness organization.

On the basis of its organizational portfolio analysis, management can select from four strategic alternatives for the company in total or for a given SBU:

- Intensify the marketing effort to strengthen and build the SBU (this might be termed an *invest* strategy).
- Help the SBU maintain its present market position *(protect)*.
- Use the SBU as a cash-flow source to help other SBUs grow or maintain position *(harvest)*.
- Get rid of the SBU *(divest)*.

Most statements of mission and objectives reflect an organization's desire to grow—to increase revenues and profits. An organization may take either of two routes in its strategy design. One route is to do what it is now doing regarding products and markets—only do it better. Or, as shown in Figure 22-3, the organization can venture into new products or markets. These two routes, when applied to markets and products, result in four product–market growth strategies:[4]

[3] Several approaches have been developed for conducting an organizational portfolio analysis. For more on these methods, see William A. Cohen, *The Practice of Marketing Management,* Macmillan Publishing Co., New York, 1988; and David W. Cravens, *Strategic Marketing,* 2nd ed., Richard D. Irwin, Homewood, Ill., 1987.

[4] First proposed by H. Igor Ansoff, "Strategies for Diversification," *Harvard Business Review,* September–October 1957, pp. 113–24. An excellent article stressing that strategy should focus on customer needs, not just on beating competition, is Kenichi Ohmae, "Getting Back to Strategy," *Harvard Business Review,* November–December 1988, pp. 149–56.

**FIGURE 22-3** Product–market growth strategies.

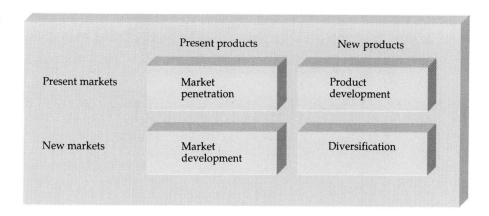

- *Market penetration.* A company tries to sell more of its present products to its present markets. Supporting tactics might include greater spending on advertising or personal selling. For example, a company tries to become a single supply source for its customers. The company's intent is that customers concentrate all their purchases with this firm in order to gain preferential treatment.
- *Market development.* A firm continues to sell its present products, but to a new market. Thus a manufacturer of power tools now selling to business users might decide to sell its small portable tools to household consumers. Ski resort operators' efforts to attract families and foreigners represent market development.
- *Product development.* This strategy calls for a company to develop new products to sell to its existing markets. A recent example is Sony's introduction of the Watchman TV following its success with the Walkman personal stereo. To remain competitive, Kodak has to develop and introduce improved color film as often as every 2 years.
- *Diversification.* A company develops new products to sell to new markets. Philip Morris, for instance, acquired various companies (such as Kraft) during the 1980s and, as a result, became the biggest spender on advertising in the United States.

Sony's Video Walkman, nicknamed "Watchman," illustrates a strategy of product development.

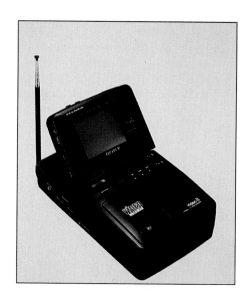

## AN ETHICAL DILEMMA?

Assume you are the brand manager for a line of sophisticated hand-held calculators used by executives and engineers. In the past year, your brand has fallen from #2 to #3 in terms of sales. You attribute the decline to an unfair comparative advertising campaign run by the new #2 firm; the ads pointed to alleged shortcomings in your calculators. Now you can regain the upper hand because one of your sales people just brought you a copy of the competitor's marketing plan for next year. The sales person found it on a chair following a seminar attended by representatives from a number of calculator makers. After studying this plan, you could adjust your plans to counter the other firm's strategies. However, even though you didn't buy or steal the plan, is it ethical to read it?

## MARKETING PLANNING

After completing the strategic planning for the total organization and for each SBU, management can plan for each major functional division, such as marketing or production. Planning for each functional area should be guided by the organization-wide or SBU mission and objectives. In marketing, strategic and annual plans need to be developed.

### Strategic Marketing Plans

**Strategic marketing planning** is a four-step process: (1) conduct a situation analysis; (2) determine marketing objectives; (3) select target markets and measure market demand; and (4) design a strategic marketing mix. These steps are shown in the middle part of Figure 22-2.

*Situation analysis* is a review of the company's existing marketing program. By analyzing where the program has been and where it is now, management can determine where the program should go in the future. Situation analysis normally includes an analysis of external environmental forces[5] and nonmarketing resources (such as R&D capabilities, financial strength, and human resources) that surround the organization's marketing program. A situation analysis also reviews in detail the company's present marketing mix.

The next step in the marketing planning process is to *determine marketing objectives*. Goals at the marketing level are closely related to company-wide goals and strategies. In fact, a *company strategy* often translates into a *marketing goal*. For example, to reach an organizational objective of a 20 percent return on investment next year, one organizational strategy might be to reduce marketing costs by 15 percent. This company strategy would become a marketing goal. In turn, converting all sales people from salaried compensation to a commission basis might be one of the marketing strategies adopted to achieve this goal.

*Selection of target markets* is a key step in marketing planning. In a new company, management should analyze markets in detail and identify potential target markets. In an existing firm, management should routinely reassess its choice of target markets to make sure they are still sound considering any changes in their characteristics and those of other markets. At this point man-

---

[5]A graphical approach for assessing a firm's strengths and weaknesses in relation to other firms in an industry is presented in Emilio Cvitkovic, "Profiling Your Competitors," *Planning Review,* May–June 1989, pp. 28–30.

# ...And The Presentation Starts In Ten Minutes.

**Thank Goodness For The Howard Johnson Road Warrior Emergency Kit.**

It could be the most important meeting of your year. And you were totally prepared...until you snagged your stockings. But, being a Road Warrior, you're staying at Howard Johnson,® where they keep a Road Warrior Emergency Kit at the front desk at all times.

It's filled with the solutions to those problems that only happen at the very worst time. So, should you run your stockings, run to the front desk and get another pair. We can also give you super-strong glue. An eyeglass repair kit. Or any toiletries you've forgotten. The Emergency Kit is one more way we help the Road Warrior get ready for the road. And one more reason Road Warriors choose Howard Johnson.

## Home Of The Road Warrior.
For Reservations, Call 1-800-654-2000.

In line with employment trends, Howard Johnson's "Road Warrior" campaign targets female as well as male business travelers.

---

### HoJo greets "road warriors"

The Howard Johnson lodging chain intends to achieve success in the 1990s with a new strategic marketing plan, part of which focuses on a specific group of consumers:

- *Objective:* Increase its share of the business-travelers market. Prime competitors include Holiday Inn and Ramada.
- *Target market:* Frequent business travelers, representing 22 percent of business travelers but accounting for 56 percent of hotel rooms booked nightly.
- *Marketing mix:* A $25 million marketing effort aimed at making Howard Johnson the "home of the road warrior." Key elements include a frequent-stay promotional program that can lead to free lodging or travel to Hawaii, TV ads saluting "road warriors," and "road-warrior emergency kits" containing personal-care necessities such as a comb.

Source: "HoJo Motels Try to Capture Road Warriors," *USA Today*, Sept. 20, 1989, p. B1.

---

agement should decide to what extent and in what manner to segment the organization's markets. As part of this step in the planning process, the firm should also forecast sales in its target markets.

Next management must *design a strategic marketing mix* that enables the company to satisfy the wants of its target markets and achieve its marketing objectives. The design, and later the implementation, of the marketing-mix elements constitutes the bulk of a company's marketing effort.

## Annual Marketing Plans

The ongoing strategic marketing planning process in an organization culminates in the preparation of a short-term marketing plan, as shown in the bottom part of Figure 22-2. This plan usually covers a year—hence the name "annual marketing plan." However, in some industries it is necessary to prepare these plans for shorter time periods because of the nature of the product or market. A separate annual plan should be prepared for each product line, major product, brand, or market.

An **annual marketing plan** is the master blueprint for a year's marketing

## AN INTERNATIONAL PERSPECTIVE: What will European markets look like after EC92?

In 1992 the 12-nation European Community (EC) takes a giant step toward becoming one market of more than 320 million people. About 285 directives legislated by the European Community will dramatically change trade regulations and business practices across Europe. This program has been dubbed EC92. (See Chapter 21 for more details.)

How does EC92 affect planning by U.S. companies that do business in Europe? What does it mean for U.S. companies with no European presence? Here are some factors that will be prominent in the European operating environment:

- *Barriers to free trade and market entry will be greatly reduced but not altogether eliminated.* Restrictions and "red tape" associated with doing business in multiple European countries are being slashed. Most companies and new products will be welcome in the EC nations. However, some observers think otherwise; they foresee "Fortress Europe." This term suggests that the marketing activities of non-European companies will be discouraged or restricted. The greatest challenges will be faced by independent U.S. firms that want to sell American-made products in European markets.
- *Some European industries will be restructured.* A wave of mergers and acquisitions is already underway. European firms are combining to gain strength. For instance, two banks united to become the largest bank in Spain. Hughes Aircraft purchased a British firm to strengthen its position in the military flight-simulator industry in Europe.
- *Competition will intensify.* Merged European organizations will be stronger competitors, as will U.S. companies that enter into cooperative agreements with European firms. Also, with fewer trade barriers, more competing products will be available in each country; in turn, this should result in price cuts—or even price wars—on some products.
- *Tastes will become more standardized but not completely uniform.* Tastes and preferences will become very similar across countries. Increasingly mobile Europeans, especially younger consumers, who are exposed to a wider variety of products are likely to develop similar buying criteria and patterns. For example, Benetton clothing and Gucci leather products are popular in many countries. However, distinctive tastes—particularly related to foods and fashions—are unlikely to disappear entirely. That is why, for instance, Nestlé has many varieties of coffee in Europe.

These factors—and others, including a firm's individual circumstances—must be taken into consideration as post-EC92 objectives and strategies are developed. No single strategic plan can be prescribed. What's appropriate for a giant U.S. firm with extensive European operations (such as Heinz and Ford) is unlikely to be suitable for a medium-sized company that does business in only one EC country. U.S. firms that engage in skillful strategic planning can seize opportunities—or at least avoid serious pitfalls—in pursuing European consumers after EC92 is a reality.

Sources: John F. Magee, "1992: Moves Americans Must Make," *Harvard Business Review*, May–June 1989, pp. 78–84; and Eric G. Friberg, "1992: Moves Europeans Are Making," *Harvard Business Review*, May–June 1989, pp. 85–89.

---

activity for the given business unit or product. The plan becomes the "how-to-do-it" document that guides executives in each phase of marketing operations. The plan includes (1) a statement of objectives, (2) identification of target markets, (3) strategies and tactics pertaining to the marketing mix, and (4) information regarding budgetary support for the marketing activity.[6]

In an annual marketing plan, more attention can be devoted to tactical details than is feasible in longer-range planning. As an example, long-range marketing planning might emphasize the role of personal selling in the promotional mix. The annual plan then might recommend increased college recruiting as a source of additional sales people.

---

[6] An excellent source of information on how various companies prepare their annual marketing plans is Howard Sutton, *The Marketing Plan*, The Conference Board, New York, 1990.

## FUNDAMENTALS OF FORECASTING MARKET DEMAND

The cornerstone of successful marketing planning is forecasting the demand for a product. In general, the process of **demand forecasting** entails estimating sales of a product during some future time period. Ordinarily, executives first estimate demand for an entire industry or market. Then they forecast sales for the company's specific products.

Demand forecasting can produce various kinds of projections. For example, a forecast can refer to an entire industry or to one firm's product line or individual brand. It can apply to an entire market or a specific segment. The estimate can be based on general factors or on a specific marketing plan. Thus when confronted with a forecast, it is important to determine exactly what it describes in order to avoid misinterpretation.

The result of demand forecasting is the preparation of a sales forecast, usually for a 1-year period. A sales forecast is the foundation of all budgeting and operational planning in all departments of a company—marketing, production, and finance.

### Definitions of Basic Terms

Before discussing forecasting methods, we need to define a number of terms.

#### MARKET FACTOR AND MARKET INDEX

A **market factor** is an item or element that (1) exists in a market, (2) may be measured quantitatively, and (3) is related to the demand for a good or service. To illustrate, the "number of cars 3 years old and older" is a market factor underlying the demand for replacement tires. That is, this element affects the number of replacement tires that can be sold.

A **market index** is simply a market factor expressed as a percentage or, in another quantitative form, relative to some base figure. For instance, a market factor that affects rentals of videocassettes is "households owning videocassette recorders." A market index for this factor would relate the number of households that own VCRs in a particular year to the corresponding figure in a base year. For example, if 1985 is established as the base year with an index of 100, then the index for 1990 might be 350, which shows tremendous growth in the number of households with VCRs. An index may also be composed of multiple market factors, such as the number of cars at least 3 years old, population, and disposable personal income.

#### MARKET POTENTIAL AND SALES POTENTIAL

**Market potential** is the total sales volume that all organizations selling a product during a stated time period in a specific market could expect to achieve under ideal conditions. **Sales potential** is the portion of market potential that a specific company could expect to achieve under ideal conditions. Note that market potential refers to an entire industry whereas sales potential applies only to one company's brand of the product. Thus we may speak of the *market* potential for refrigerators, but the *sales* potential for the Maytag or Kenmore brand of refrigerator.

In the case of either market potential or sales potential, the market may encompass the entire United States or even the world. Or it may be a smaller market segmented by income, geographic area, or some other basis. For example, we may consider the market potential for refrigerators on the Pacific Coast, or the sales potential for Maytag refrigerators in homes with incomes of $25,000 to $50,000. Market potential and sales potential are the same when a firm has a monopoly in its market, as in the case of some public utilities.

With this strong guarantee, Maytag hopes to increase the sales potential of its refrigerators.

The term *potential* refers to a maximum level of sales and assumes that (1) all marketing plans are sound and effectively implemented and (2) all prospects with the desire and ability to buy do so. Of course, since few industries or companies achieve their full potential, this is a useful guideline but cannot be the final outcome of demand forecasting. We must move from maximum (or potential) sales to likely sales; this projection is made by preparing forecasts.

### MARKET SHARE

The term **market share** is used frequently in business and is particularly relevant to the area of demand forecasting. Essentially, it refers to the proportion of total sales of a product during a stated time period in a specific market that is captured by a single firm. Market share can refer to entire industries, narrow segments, or particular geographic areas and also can apply to past, present, or future time periods. For example, a company might establish an objective of achieving a 40 percent share of first-time buyers next year. Or we could discuss the respective market shares for all of the companies in the hydraulic lift industry.

### SALES FORECAST

A **sales forecast** is an estimate of probable sales for one company's brand of the product during a stated time period in a specific market and assuming the use of a predetermined marketing plan. Like estimates of market potential and sales potential, it can be expressed in dollars or product units. However, whereas market and sales potential are estimates based on general factors and assumptions, a sales forecast is based on a specific marketing plan for the product of interest.

A sales forecast can be best prepared after market potential and sales potential have been estimated. Many firms, especially small ones, forecast sales in a simple, direct manner. An illustration is presented in Figure 22-4.

Sales forecasts typically cover a 1-year period, although many firms review annual forecasts monthly or quarterly. Annual sales forecasts tie in with annual financial planning and reporting, and are often based on estimates of future economic conditions. Forecasts for less than a year may be desirable when activity in the firm's industry is so volatile that it is not feasible to look ahead a full year. As a case in point, many firms in the fashion industry—producers and retailers alike—prepare forecasts that cover only one fashion season.

There is a close relationship between a sales forecast and the marketing plan. Marketing goals and broad strategies—the core of a marketing plan—must be established before a sales forecast is made. That is, the sales forecast depends on these predetermined goals and strategies. If the marketing goal is to liquidate an excess inventory of a product, a different sales forecast will result than if the goal is to expand the firm's market share by aggressive advertising.

Once the sales forecast has been prepared, it becomes the key controlling factor in all *operational* planning throughout the company. The sales forecast is the basis of sound budgeting. Financial planning for working-capital requirements, plant utilization, and other needs is based on anticipated sales. Scheduling of all production resources and facilities, such as setting labor needs and purchasing raw materials, also depends on the sales forecast.

**FIGURE 22-4** Business application of some of our definitions.

**MARKET SHARE WORKSHEET FOR 1991**

Dan's Diaper Deliveries
Los Angeles, CA

Market factor: _Births in City A_   Number: _120,000_

Base period: _1989_   Number: _100,000_

Market index: _120,000_ ÷ _100,000_ = _120%_

Market potential @ 6 dozen per child per month:

6 × _120,000_ = _720,000_ dz/mo

Estimated market share: _20%_

Sales potential: _2 × 720,000 =   144,000_ dz/mo

## Methods of Forecasting Demand

A company can forecast sales by using either of two basic procedures—a "top-down" or a "bottom-up" approach.

Using the top-down approach, management would:

1. Develop a forecast of general economic conditions.
2. Determine the market potential for a product.
3. Measure the share of this market the firm is currently getting or plans to capture.
4. Forecast the firm's sales of the product.

In the "bottom-up" technique, management would follow a two-step procedure:

1. Generate estimates of future demand in segments of the market or from organizational units (sales people or branches) in the company.
2. Add the individual estimates to get one total forecast.

Predictions of future market demand—either sales forecasts or estimates of market potential—may be based on techniques ranging from uninformed guesses to sophisticated statistical models. Although marketing executives may not perform the actual statistical computations, they should be familiar with each technique's merits and limitations and understand when each method is best used. In addition, they should be able to ask intelligent questions regarding the assumptions underlying the methods.

Here are some commonly used methods of predicting demand.

### MARKET-FACTOR ANALYSIS

A crucial assumption underlies **market-factor analysis:** Future demand for a product is related to the behavior of certain market factors. If this statement is true and we can determine what these factors are and can measure their relationship to sales activity, we can forecast future sales simply by studying the behavior of the market factors.

The key to successful use of the method lies in selecting appropriate market factors. It is also important to minimize the number of market factors used. The greater the number of factors, the greater the chance for erroneous estimates and the more difficult it is to determine how much each factor influences demand. The procedure used to translate market-factor behavior into an estimate of future sales is the **direct-derivation method.**

Let's illustrate the use of the direct-derivation method to estimate market potential. Suppose a manufacturer of automobile tires wants to know the market potential for replacement tires in the United States in 1992. The primary market factor is the number and ages of automobiles on the road. The first step is to estimate how many cars are likely prospects for new tires.

Assume that the seller's studies show (1) the average car is driven about 10,000 miles a year and (2) the average driver gets about 30,000 miles from a set of four tires. This means that all cars that become 3 years old or multiples of 3 years old during 1992 can be considered a part of the potential market for replacement tires during that year. The seller can obtain a reasonably accurate count of the number of cars that were sold in 1989 and therefore will be 3 years old in 1992. This information is available from state and county licensing agencies as well as private organizations. In addition, the seller can determine how many cars will become 6, 9, or 12 years old in 1992 and, as such, would be ready for another set of tires.

The number of cars in these age brackets multiplied by four (tires per car) should give the approximate market potential for replacement tires in 1992. Of course, we are dealing in averages. Not all drivers will get 30,000 miles from their tires, and not all cars will be driven 10,000 miles per year.

The direct-derivation method has much to recommend it. It is relatively simple and inexpensive to use, and requires little statistical analysis. Executives who are not statistics-oriented can follow the procedure and interpret the results. The main limitation of the direct-derivation method is that demand for the product of interest must be derived from a factor that is easily measurable.

**Correlation analysis** is a statistical refinement of the direct-derivation method that takes into account the degree of association between potential sales of the product and the market factor. Detailed explanation of this statistical technique is beyond the scope of this text. However, in general, a correlation analysis measures, on a scale of 0 to 1, the variations between two data series.

Applied correctly, correlation analysis gives a more exact estimate of market demand. In direct derivation, the correlation is implicitly assumed to be 1.0 (that is, perfect). But rarely is there perfect association between a market factor and the demand for a product. Correlation analysis therefore takes history into account in predicting the future. It also allows a researcher to incorporate more than one factor into the calculation.

There are two major limitations to correlation analysis. For one thing, not all marketing people understand correlation analysis. For another, it can be used only when *both* of the following are available: (1) a lengthy sales history of the industry or the firm and (2) a history of the market factor. To do a really good job, researchers need about 20 periods of sales records. They also must assume that approximately the same relationship has existed between sales and market factors during this entire period and that this relationship will continue in the next sales period. These can be highly unrealistic assumptions.

### SURVEY OF BUYER INTENTIONS

When a firm asks a sample of current or potential customers how much of a particular product they would buy at a given price during a specified future time period, it is conducting a **survey of buyer intentions.** Some firms maintain consumer panels on a continuing basis for use in such surveys and/or to act as sounding boards for new product ideas, prices, and other product features.

Selecting the sample of potential buyers can be a problem. For many consumer products, a very large and costly sample would be needed. Aside from the extremely high cost and large amount of time this method often entails, there is another very serious limitation. It is one thing for consumers to intend to buy a product, but quite another for them to actually buy it. Surveys of buying intentions often show an inflated measure of market potential. Such surveys are probably most accurate in forecasting demand when (1) there are relatively few buyers, (2) these buyers are willing to express their buying intentions, and (3) their past record shows that their follow-up actions are consistent with their stated intentions.

### TEST MARKETING

In **test marketing**, first discussed in Chapter 3, a firm markets its product in a limited geographic area, measures sales, and then—from this sample—

projects the company's sales over a larger area. Test marketing is frequently used to determine whether there is sufficient demand for a new product. The technique also serves as a basis for evaluating various product features and alternative marketing strategies. The outstanding benefit of test marketing is that it can tell management how many people *actually buy* the product, instead of how many say they *intend to buy*.

Test marketing is expensive in time and money. Also, great care is essential to control the experiment. A competitor, learning that a firm is test marketing, can disrupt the test. By unusual promotion or other marketing activities, a competitor can create an artificial situation that distorts the test results. To avoid such test-market "wars," some companies use simulated test markets. In effect, these firms conduct a test market in a laboratory, rather than in the field.[7]

### PAST SALES AND TREND ANALYSIS

A favorite method of forecasting is based entirely on past sales. This technique is used frequently by retailers whose main goal is to "beat last year's figures." In **past sales analysis,** a flat percentage increase is applied to the volume achieved last year or to the average volume of the past few years.

This technique is simple, inexpensive, and easy to apply. For a firm operating in a stable market, where its market share has remained constant for a period of years, past sales alone can be used to predict future volume. However, few companies operate in unchanging environments. On balance, therefore, the method is highly unreliable.

**Trend analysis** is a more complicated variation of forecasting based on past sales. One type of trend analysis is a long-run projection of sales, usually computed by a statistical technique called regression. The statistical sophistication of long-run trend analysis does not remove the inherent weakness of basing future estimates only on past sales activity. A second type of trend analysis entails a short-run projection (forecasting for only a few months ahead) using a seasonal index of sales. Short-run trend analysis may be acceptable if the firm's sales follow a reliable seasonal pattern. For example, assume that sales reach 10,000 units in the first quarter of the year and, historically, the second quarter is always about 50 percent better. Then we can reasonably forecast sales of 15,000 units in the April–June period.

### SALES-FORCE COMPOSITE

This bottom-up method may be used to forecast sales or estimate market potential. In sales forecasting, the **sales-force composite** consists of collecting from all sales people and middlemen estimates of what sales in their territories will be during the future period of interest. The sum of these separate estimates is the company's sales forecast. This method can be used advantageously if the firm has competent, well-informed sales people. It is also useful for firms selling to a market composed of relatively few, but large, customers. Thus this method would be more applicable to sales of large electrical generators than small general-use motors.

The sales-force composite method takes advantage of sales people's specialized knowledge of their own markets. Furthermore, it should make them

---

[7]For more on the practical aspects of test marketing, see Pat Seelig, "All Over the Map," *Sales & Marketing Management*, March 1989, pp. 58–64; and "Special Report on Test Marketing," *Advertising Age*, Aug. 24, 1987, pp. S1–S12.

more willing to accept their assigned sales quotas. This method has limitations, though. The sales force usually does not have the time or the experience to do the research needed for sales forecasting. Additionally, such forecasts may be inaccurate because sales people are by nature optimistic and therefore may overestimate future sales levels. Or if compensation is based on meeting a sales quota, sales people may underestimate future sales.

### EXECUTIVE JUDGMENT

This method covers a wide range of possibilities. Basically, **executive judgment** entails obtaining opinions regarding future sales volume from one or more executives. If these are informed opinions, based on valid measures such as market-factor analysis, then executive judgment is useful and desirable. Certainly all forecasting methods should be tempered with sound executive judgment. On the other hand, forecasting by executive opinion alone is risky because such opinions are in some instances simply intuition or guesswork.

The **Delphi method,** named after the location of an oracle in ancient Greece, was developed by the Rand Corporation for use in environmental forecasting. However, the Delphi technique also can be applied in sales forecasting, especially in the case of products that are truly innovative or significant technological breakthroughs. First, a group of experts individually and anonymously assesses future sales. Each expert makes a prediction without any knowledge of how others in the group have responded.

The first round of estimates is summarized, and the resulting average and range of forecasts are fed back to the experts. They are then asked to make another prediction on the same issue, now knowing how the group responded. Respondents may change their predictions or stick with their original estimates. This process of estimates and feedback is continued for several rounds. In some situations—and this would usually be the case in sales forecasting—the final round may involve face-to-face discussions among executives, at which time a sales-forecast consensus would be expected.

An advantage of the Delphi method is that it avoids the biasing influence of one individual on another (for example, a top executive on a subordinate). In addition, it permits each individual to consider the combined judgment of the group. If a person's forecast is widely divergent from the group's average, the opportunity exists to justify or modify the position as the process moves through several rounds. A potential disadvantage of the Delphi method—and of any executive judgment method—is that participants may lack the necessary information on which to base their judgments.

All methods of sales forecasting have merits and drawbacks. None is perfect. An executive must choose the technique that is likely to produce the most accurate estimates of sales given the firm's particular circumstances.

## SUMMARY

The management process consists of planning, implementation, and evaluation. Management first should prepare a strategic plan for the total organization, from which strategic plans can be developed for the marketing function.

Planning is deciding now what we are going to do later, including when and how we are going to do it. Planning provides direction to an organization. Strategic planning usually takes a long-run perspective and is often a formal process.

In strategic company planning, top management defines the organization's mission ("What business are we in?"), sets its long-range goals ("What do we want to accomplish?''), and formulates broad strategies to achieve the goals (''How are we going to get there?''). As part of this planning, the firm needs to identify and evaluate its portfolio of strategic business units.

Strategic planning at the company-wide level guides planning in different functional areas, including marketing. In strategic marketing planning, goals and strategies are established for the firm's marketing effort. Coordinated strategies related to target markets and the marketing mix must be developed. Based on strategic plans, an annual marketing plan lays out a year's marketing activities for a given product line, major product, or market. This plan includes key tactics as well as strategies.

Successful marketing planning depends on accurately forecasting the demand for a product. Management usually estimates the total sales that could be expected under ideal conditions for all firms comprising the industry and for its particular product; these figures are termed market potential and sales potential, respectively. The final result of estimating demand is a sales forecast, which indicates probable sales for the company's brand of a particular product in a future time period and with a predetermined marketing program. This forecast normally covers 1 year.

Basically, there are two approaches to demand forecasting—''top-down'' and ''bottom-up.'' Specific methods used to forecast sales are market-factor analysis, survey of buyer intentions, test marketing, past sales and trend analysis, sales-force composite, and executive judgment. Each method has weaknesses and strengths. Management's challenge is to select the technique that is appropriate in a particular situation and is most likely to provide an accurate forecast.

**KEY TERMS AND CONCEPTS**

Planning 560
Strategic planning 560
Strategic company planning 562
Organizational mission 563
Objective 564
Strategic business unit 565
Organizational portfolio
  analysis 566
Organizational strategies 566
Market penetration 567
Market development 567
Product development 567
Diversification 567
Strategic marketing planning 568
Annual marketing plan 569
Demand forecasting 571

Market factor 571
Market index 571
Market potential 571
Sales potential 571
Market share 572
Sales forecast 572
Market-factor analysis 574
Direct-derivation method 574
Correlation analysis 575
Survey of buyer intentions 575
Test marketing 575
Past sales analysis 576
Trend analysis 576
Sales-force composite 576
Executive judgment 577
Delphi method 577

## QUESTIONS AND PROBLEMS

1. Should a small manufacturer or a small retailer engage in formal strategic planning? Why or why not?

2. Using a customer-oriented approach (benefits provided or wants satisfied), answer the question ''What business are we in?'' for each of the following companies:

   a. Holiday Inn.
   b. Adidas athletic shoes.
   c. Apple computers.
   d. Universal (movie) Studios.
   e. Goodyear Tire and Rubber Co.

3. Use an example to explain the concept of a strategic business unit.

4. What criteria should a division within an organization meet in order to be classified as a strategic business unit?

5. Give two examples (other than those in this chapter) of how a company might employ each of the following strategies:
   a. Market penetration.
   b. Market development.
   c. Product development.
   d. Diversification.

6. In the situation-analysis stage of the marketing planning process, what specific external environmental factors should be analyzed by a manufacturer of equipment used for backpacking in the wilderness?

7. "The economic unification in 1992 of the European Community means absolute chaos for American firms trying to market to consumers in these countries. For a number of years, the situation will be so dynamic that U.S. executives should not waste their time on formal strategic planning related to European markets." Do you agree with this statement? Support your position.

8. What logical market factors might you use in estimating the market potential for each of the following products?
   a. Central home air conditioners.
   b. Electric milking machines.
   c. Luxury airline travel.
   d. Sterling silver flatware.
   e. Personal computer repair services.

9. Carefully distinguish between market potential and a sales forecast, using an example of a consumer or business product.

10. How would you determine (a) market potential and (b) a sales forecast for a textbook for an introductory course in marketing?

11. Explain the direct-derivation method of sales forecasting, using a product example other than automobile tires. How does this forecasting method differ from the correlation-analysis method?

12. What problems does a researcher face when using test marketing to determine sales potential?

# MARKETING IMPLEMENTATION AND PERFORMANCE EVALUATION

## CHAPTER 23 GOALS

This chapter is concerned with two parts of managing a company's total marketing program—implementation and evaluation. After studying this chapter, you should be able to explain:

- The importance of implementation in the management process.
- The relationship among strategic planning, implementation, and performance evaluation.
- Organizational structures used to implement marketing efforts.
- The importance of personnel selection.
- Delegation, coordination, motivation, and communication in the implementation process.
- The concept of a marketing audit as a complete evaluation program.
- The meaning of misdirected marketing effort.
- Sales volume analysis.
- Marketing cost analysis.

Major organizational changes are occurring in the packaged consumer goods industries as producers prepare for the future. Procter & Gamble provides a good example of this restructuring.

Sixty years ago P&G instituted the brand-management system. Under this system, each brand had its own manager who served as the brand's advocate within the company. Brands competed against each other as intensely as if they belonged to separate firms. Two problems were inherent in this system. First, there was internal competition for scarce resources. Camay and Ivory, for example, competed for advertising funds. Second, brand managers were responsibile for a brand's success, but they were not given corresponding authority in advertising, pricing, and other marketing areas.

Nevertheless, as its markets expanded over the decades, P&G prospered. However, the company also became very bureaucratic and infamous for slow, highly centralized decision making.

Then, in the 1980s, the balance of power in the packaged consumer goods fields shifted from large manufacturers to large retailers such as K mart and Wal-Mart. These trends adversely affected P&G. The company's gross margins and earnings declined, and flagship brands such as Crest and Pampers lost market share. Retailers became increasingly unhappy with P&G's autocratic, arrogant behavior.

In the late 1980s, P&G underwent a major organizational restructuring designed to push authority down into middle management levels, speed up decision making, and bring the company closer to its customers. A significant organizational change in marketing was the establishment of a category-management system. P&G's brands were grouped into 39 product categories, among them laundry detergents, bar soaps, deodorants, and diapers. A "category manager" took charge of each category, and all brand managers now report to one of these executives. The intent is to look at a product group as a whole, thus strategically fitting the individual brands together, rather than having them compete against one another.

The category manager acts as the chief executive officer of a small company, with total profit responsibility for the entire category product line and authority to make quick decisions. All areas involved in producing and marketing products within a category— advertising, sales, manufacturing, research, and engineering—report to the category manager.

Procter & Gamble's restructuring is designed to increase the speed and effectiveness of the implementation stage in the company's management process. In Chapter 1 we defined the management process in marketing as planning, implementing, and evaluating the marketing effort in an organization. Most of this book has dealt with *planning* a marketing program. We discussed the selection of target markets and the strategic design of a program to deliver want-satisfaction to those markets. This program was built around the components of a marketing mix—the product, price structure, distribution system, and promotional program.

Now we are ready to devote a chapter to the implementation and evaluation stages of the management process in marketing. Implementation is the operational stage—the stage during which an organization attempts to carry out (that is, implement or execute) its strategic plan.

At the end of an operating period (or even during the period), management needs to evaluate the organization's performance. In this way management can determine how effectively the organization is achieving the goals set in the strategic planning phase of the management process.

## IMPLEMENTATION IN MARKETING MANAGEMENT

There should be a close relationship among planning, implementation, and evaluation in the management process. Without planning, a company's operational activities—its implementation—can go off in any direction like an unguided missile. In the 1970s and into the early 1980s, there was tremendous interest in strategic planning, sparked primarily by leading management consulting firms. Then as we progressed through the 1980s, disenchantment with strategic planning set in. This cooling off occurred as many companies came to realize that strategic *planning* alone was not enough to ensure a company's success. These plans had to be *effectively implemented*. Management began to realize that planners were great at telling them *what* to do—that is, designing a strategy. But planners often fell short when it came to telling *how* to do it—that is, how to implement the strategy.[1]

> "Too often those hot-shot planners could not sell a pair of shoes to a guy who is standing barefooted on a very hot sidewalk with a $50 bill in his hand."

No matter how good an organization's strategic planning is, it is virtually useless if those plans do not lead to action—are not implemented or executed. Stated another way, good planning cannot overcome poor implementation, but effective implementation often can overcome poor planning or inappropriate strategies. At this point, therefore, we shall discuss implementation in more detail because, despite its importance, it ordinarily receives so little attention. Much has been written about strategic planning, but very little has been said about *implementing* those strategies.[2]

The implementation stage in the marketing management process includes three broad activities: (1) organizing for the marketing effort; (2) staffing this organization; and (3) directing the operational efforts of these people as they carry out the strategic plans.

[1] For some guidelines to aid in identifying implementation difficulties and suggestions for remedying them, see Thomas V. Bonoma, "Making Your Marketing Strategy Work," *Harvard Business Review,* March–April 1984, pp. 69–76.

[2] See Thomas V. Bonoma, "Enough about Strategy! Let's See Some Clever Executions," *Marketing News,* Feb. 13, 1989, p. 10.

Often a sales person in the field carries the burden of *implementing* a company's strategic planning.

## Organizing for Implementation Activities

The first major activity in implementing a company's strategic marketing plan is to organize the people who will be doing the actual implementation. We must establish an organizational relationship among marketing and the other major functional areas in a firm. And, within the marketing department, we must decide on the form of organization that will most effectively aid our implementation efforts.

### COMPANY-WIDE ORGANIZATION

In Chapter 1 we stated that one of the three foundation stones of the marketing concept is to organizationally coordinate all marketing activities. In firms that are production-oriented or sales-oriented, typically we find that marketing activities are fragmented. A sales force is quite separate from advertising; physical distribution is handled in the production department; and sales training may be under the personnel department.

In a marketing-oriented enterprise, all marketing activities are coordinated under one marketing executive, who usually is at the vice presidential level. This executive reports directly to the president and is on an equal organizational footing with top executives in finance, production, and other major functions, as shown in Figure 23-1. Under the top marketing executive, the marketing activities may be grouped into line activities and staff activities. In most firms the primary line activity is personal selling. Supporting staff activities include advertising, marketing research, sales promotion, sales analysis, and sales training.

### ORGANIZATION WITHIN THE MARKETING DEPARTMENT

Within the marketing department—especially in medium-sized or large firms—the sales force frequently is specialized in some organizational fashion. This is done in order to effectively implement the company's strategic marketing plan. One of three forms of organizational specialization of line authority typically is adopted. The sales force may be organized by (1) geo-

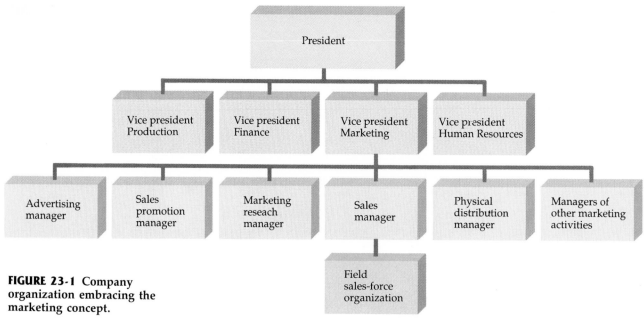

**FIGURE 23-1** Company organization embracing the marketing concept.

graphical territory, (2) product line, or (3) customer type. In very large companies, other marketing activities such as advertising or sales promotion may also be organizationally specialized in one of these three categories.

**Geographical specialization.**   Probably the most widely used method of specializing selling activities is to organize a sales force on the basis of geographical territories. Under this type of organization, each sales person is assigned a specific geographical area—called a *territory*—in which to sell. Several sales people representing contiguous territories are placed under a territorial sales executive, who reports directly to the general sales manager. These territorial executives usually are called *district* or *regional* sales managers, as shown in Figure 23-2.

A territorial organization usually ensures better implementation of sales strategies in each local market and better control over the sales force. Customers can be serviced quickly and effectively, and local sales reps can respond better to competitors' actions in a given territory.

**Product specialization.**   Another commonly used basis for organizing a sales force is some form of product specialization. As illustrated in Figure 23-3, a company may divide all of its products into two lines. Then one group of sales reps will sell only the products in line A. All sales people in group A will report to a sales manager for product A, who in turn will report to a general sales manager.

This type of organization is especially well suited for companies that are marketing:

- A variety of complex technical products—for example, electronics.
- Dissimilar or unrelated products—for example, luggage, folding chairs, and toy building blocks.
- Many thousands of items—for example, hardware.

The main advantage of this form of organization is the specialized attention each product line can get from the sales force. A potential drawback is that more than one sales rep from a company may call on the same customer. This duplication of effort not only is costly but also may irritate the customers.

A variation of product specialization is the product-manager system that we discussed back in Chapter 7. Each product manager is given the responsibility of planning and developing a marketing program for a separate group of products. The product managers report to the chief marketing executive.

**FIGURE 23-2** Sales organization specialized by geographic territories.

**FIGURE 23-3** Sales organization specialized by product.

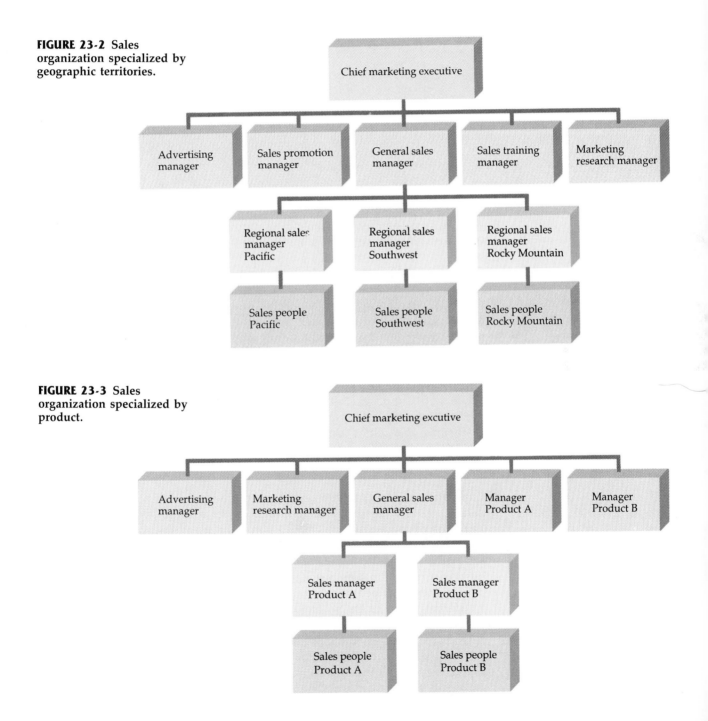

**FIGURE 23-4** Sales organization specialized by customer.

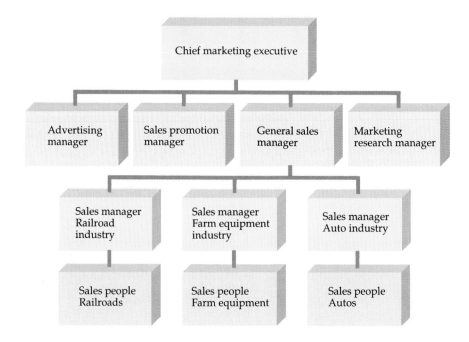

Typically product managers have no direct authority over a sales force, but act only in an advisory relationship with the sales force and line sales executives.

**Customer specialization.**   Many companies today have divided their sales departments according to type of customer. Customers may be grouped either by type of industry or by channel of distribution. Thus an oil company may divide its markets into such industry customer groups as railroads, auto manufacturers, and farm equipment producers, as shown in Figure 23-4. A firm that specializes its sales operations by channel of distribution may have one sales force selling to wholesalers and another that deals directly with large retailers.

As more companies fully implement the marketing concept, the customer-specialization type of organization is likely to increase. Certainly the basis of customer specialization is commensurate with the customer-oriented philosophy that underlies the marketing concept. That is, the organizational emphasis is on customers and markets rather than on products.

**Combination of organizational bases.**   Many medium-sized and large companies typically combine a territorial sales organization with either product or customer specialization. Thus, a hardware wholesaler operating out of a home base in Chicago may establish geographical sales districts for its sales reps. This same sales force also may be divided on a product basis. Consequently, in the one sales district that covers eastern Iowa and northwestern Illinois, there may be two or three of this company's sales reps. Each rep sells a different group of the wholesaler's products.

**Staffing the Organization**

A key step in implementing strategic planning is to staff the organization—to select the people who will be doing the actual implementation work. *Of all the specific stages in the management process, we believe selection of people is the most important.* We strongly feel this is true no matter what organization is being

## AN ETHICAL DILEMMA?

Organizations have a hard time finding qualified sales people. Even more difficult is finding *experienced* sales people who are familiar enough with an industry to begin making a contribution immediately. One way to get such sales people is to aggressively recruit them from competitors. Not only do they know the business, but they might also bring along a few customers. If you were a sales manager would you adopt this practice?

staffed. A college football coach's success depends greatly on his ability to recruit the right players. A political party's success depends on its ability to select the candidate who will attract the most votes. A sales manager's success depends in great measure on the sales people whom the manager selects. Those of you who now are single will learn that your happiness and success in life depend to a large degree on the person whom you select as a lifetime mate.

Yes, selection is critically important in *any* organization. And, tragically, most people do a horrible job of recruiting and selection. Most of us don't know how to pick appropriate people for the position being filled.

In most marketing organizations the implementation task is done largely by the sales force. So let's identify the reasons why it is important to have a good process for selecting sales people:

- Good sales people are often hard to find. There is a scarcity of prospects who have the necessary skills, experience, and interest in the work.
- Within limits, managers are no better than the people working under them. And managers are judged by the way their subordinates perform.
- A good selection job makes other managerial tasks easier. Well-chosen workers are easier to train, supervise, and motivate.
- Good selection typically reduces the turnover rate with all its attendant costs.

Regardless of the field of endeavor, the selection of people is the most important stage in the management process.

## AN INTERNATIONAL PERSPECTIVE: International sales organization

When American companies market in foreign countries, differences in cultures, business conditions, and political-legal systems present challenges unlike any found in the domestic market. Let's assume that a company wants to make a commitment to international marketing with the goal of increasing its market share in a foreign country. Either of two sales organizational structures typically is used in this situation.

One alternative is to set up a network of manufacturers' agents, distributors (wholesalers), and dealers (retailers) in each foreign country. The American firm usually grants exclusive territorial sales rights to the middlemen. A Chicago manufacturer of electronic products, for example, granted one Japanese firm the sole distributorship for all of Japan and made similar arrangements with an electronics wholesaler in Denmark.

Foreign middlemen are generally less aggressive and perform fewer services than their American counterparts. However, in many foreign countries business customs or government regulations require the use of local middlemen. In Middle Eastern countries, for instance, a local distributor's knowledge of and connections in the market often are more important than product knowledge, even for technical products. In other countries, government regulations preclude the use of an American sales force.

The other alternative is to establish a sales force in countries where the volume and profit potential warrant it and government regulations allow it. These sales forces may sell directly to the final customers or through local distributors and dealers. This organizational model has been adopted by many large American companies including Avon, Merck, NCR, Honeywell, IBM, Kimberly-Clark, and Ingersoll-Rand.

Using its own sales force enables a company to (1) promote its products more aggressively, (2) develop its foreign markets more effectively, and (3) control its sales effort more completely. Of course, management now has the time- and money-consuming task of managing a sales force. The difficulty here is that the sales people are either foreign nationals unfamiliar with the company's marketing practices or American sales people unfamiliar with the foreign culture and business customs.

**Managing the Marketing Operations**

The third activity in the implementation stage of the management process is actually directing and operating a marketing program. This activity is the guts of the entire implementation process—where strategic plans are actually carried out; where the revenue-generating activity occurs in the firm; where management directs the efforts of the people who have been selected and organized.

The guidelines for operating marketing-mix components (product, price, distribution, promotion) are probably pretty well set by virtue of the strategic marketing plan. It is up to the operating executives in the marketing department to follow these guidelines. The key to success in this stage depends on how well the executives have put into practice four concepts concerning the management of people. These four concepts are delegation, coordination, motivation, and communication.

### DELEGATION

Very often an executive's success is measured by the ability to ably delegate authority and responsibility. Executives who try to do everything themselves—who for some reason are reluctant to delegate—invariably fail to maximize the potential of their programs or their subordinates in the company.

### COORDINATION

Effective coordination will bring about a synergy in the organization whereby people working together will accomplish more than if they go off on their own in a rudderless fashion. For example, sales peoples' efforts should be

Motivation and communication in action—Black & Decker CEO discusses sales of air station compressors with employees.

coordinated with advertising activities. New-product introduction needs to be coordinated with the physical distribution of the product, and middlemen must be prepared to handle the new product.

## MOTIVATION

The success enjoyed by a leader of people in any field—athletics, education, politics, the military, business—is greatly dependent on that leader's ability to motivate people. Here we can consider economic motivation in the form of monetary payments as well as psychological motivation in the form of non-monetary rewards.

## COMMUNICATION

Finally, all implementation activities will come together in an effective manner only if the executives involved communicate effectively with their workers. In early chapters we spoke often about effectively communicating with the market. Now we are concerned with doing a good job of internal communication. It is imperative that an organization maintain open communication channels both upward and downward in the company's hierarchy. Management must communicate with sales people, and these reps must have an open channel to communicate upward to management. Often it is easier to say these things than to do them. Companies spend untold sums of money to improve the communication abilities of their executives, but the workers frequently still misunderstand management's messages. Yet this is no reason to stop trying to improve communication.

## EVALUATING MARKETING PERFORMANCE

As soon as possible after a firm's plans have been set in operation, the process of evaluation should begin. Without evaluation, management cannot tell whether a plan is working and what factors are contributing to success or failure. Evaluation logically follows planning and implementation. Planning sets forth what *should be* done, and evaluation shows what *really was* done. A circular relationship exists, as illustrated in Figure 23-5. Plans are made, they are put into action, the operational results are evaluated, and new plans are prepared on the basis of this appraisal.

Previously we discussed evaluation as it relates to individual parts of a marketing program—the product-planning process, the performance of the sales force, and the effectiveness of the advertising program, for instance. At this point let's look at the evaluation of the *total marketing effort.*

## The Marketing Audit: A Total Evaluation Program

A marketing audit is the essential element in a total evaluation program. An audit implies a review and an evaluation of some activity. Thus a **marketing audit** is a comprehensive review and evaluation of the marketing function in an organization—its philosophy, environment, goals, strategies, organizational structure, human and financial resources, and performance. A complete marketing audit is an extensive and difficult project. Therefore, it is conducted infrequently—perhaps every 2 or 3 years. However, a company should not delay a marketing audit until a major crisis arises.

The rewards of a marketing audit can be great. Management can identify problem areas in marketing. By reviewing its strategies, the firm is likely to keep abreast of its changing marketing environment. Successes can also be analyzed, so the company can capitalize on its strong points. The audit can spot lack of coordination in the marketing program, outdated strategies, or unrealistic goals. The marketing audit allows management to correctly place responsibility for good or poor performance. Furthermore, an audit should anticipate future situations. It is intended for "prognosis as well as diagnosis. . . . It is the practice of preventive as well as curative marketing medicine."[3]

## Misdirected Marketing Effort

One of the primary benefits of evaluation activities is that they can help correct misdirected or misplaced marketing effort.

### THE "80-20" PRINCIPLE

In most firms, a large proportion of the orders, customers, territories, or products accounts for only a small share of sales or profit. Conversely, a small proportion produces a large share of sales or profit. This relationship has been characterized as the **80-20 principle.** That is, 80 percent of the orders, customers, territories, or products contribute only 20 percent of sales or profit. On the other hand, 20 percent of these selling units account for 80 percent of the volume or profit. The 80-20 figure is used simply to epitomize the misplacement of marketing efforts. In reality, of course, the percentage split varies from one situation to another.

The basic reason for the 80-20 situation is that almost every marketing program includes some misdirected effort. Marketing efforts and costs are proportional to the *number* of territories, customers, or products, rather than to their actual sales volume or profit. For example, in a May Company department store, approximately the same order-filling, billing, and delivery expenses are involved whether a mink coat or a necktie is sold. Or a manufac-

**FIGURE 23-5** The circular relationship among management tasks.

---

[3] Abe Schuchman, "The Marketing Audit: Its Nature, Purpose, and Problems," in *Analyzing and Improving Marketing Performance: "Marketing Audits" in Theory and Practice,* American Management Association, New York, Management Report no. 32, 1959, p. 14. This article is the classic introduction to the marketing audit concept. For a process that proposes different uses of a marketing audit to promote strategic organizational change, see Michael P. Mokwa, "The Strategic Marketing Audit: An Adoption/Utilization Perspective," *Journal of Business Strategy,* Spring 1986, pp. 88–95.

The dangerous part of the iceberg lies beneath the surface.

turer such as Xerox may assign one sales person to each territory. Yet there may be substantial differences in the potential volume and profit from the various territories. In each case, the marketing effort (cost) is not in line with the potential return.[4]

## REASONS FOR MISDIRECTED MARKETING EFFORT

Many executives are unaware of the misdirected marketing effort in their firms. They do not know what percentage of total sales and profit comes from a given product line or customer group. Frequently, executives cannot uncover their misdirection of effort because they lack sufficiently detailed information. The analogy of an iceberg in an open sea has been used to illustrate this situation. Only a small part of an iceberg is visible above the surface of the water, and the submerged 90 percent is the dangerous part. The figures representing total sales or total costs on an operating statement are like the visible part of an iceberg. The detailed figures representing sales, costs, and other performance measures for each territory or product correspond to the important and dangerous submerged segment.

Total sales or costs as presented on an operating statement are too general to be useful in evaluation. In fact, total figures are often inconclusive and misleading. More than one company has shown satisfactory overall sales and profit figures. But when these totals were subdivided by territory or products, serious weaknesses were discovered. A manufacturer of audio equipment showed an overall annual increase of 12 percent in sales and 9 percent in net profit on one product line one year. But management wasn't satisfied with this "tip of the iceberg." When it analyzed the figures more closely, it found that the sales change within territories ranged from an increase of 19 percent to a decrease of 3 percent. In some territories profits increased as much as 14 percent, and in others they were down 20 percent.

An even more important cause of misplaced marketing effort is the fact that executives must make decisions based on inadequate knowledge of the exact nature of marketing costs. In other words, management often lacks knowledge of: (1) the disproportionate spread of marketing effort; (2) reliable

---

[4]For suggestions on how to develop and manage a program to achieve benefits from the 20 percent of marketing units that generate the 80 percent of sales volume and profit, see Richard T. Hise and Stanley H. Kratchman, "Developing and Managing a 20/80 Program," *Business Horizons*, September–October 1987, pp. 66–73.

standards for determining what should be spent on marketing; and (3) what results should be expected from these expenditures.

As an illustration, a company may spend $250,000 more on advertising this year than last year. But management ordinarily cannot state what the resultant increase in sales volume or profit should be. Nor do the executives know what would have happened if they had spent the same amount on (1) new-product development, (2) management training seminars for middlemen, or (3) some other aspect of the marketing program.

## The Evaluation Process

The evaluation process—whether it is a complete marketing audit or only an appraisal of individual components of the marketing program—is essentially a three-stage task. Management's tasks in this process are as follows:

1. Find out *what* happened. Get the facts and then compare actual results with budgeted goals to determine where they differ.
2. Find out *why* it happened. Determine what specific factors in the marketing program accounted for the results.
3. Decide *what to do* about it. Plan the next period's program so as to improve on unsatisfactory performance and capitalize on the things that were done well.

An effective way to evaluate a total marketing program is to analyze performance results. To do this, two useful tools are available—sales volume

Computers are a big help in the evaluation process.

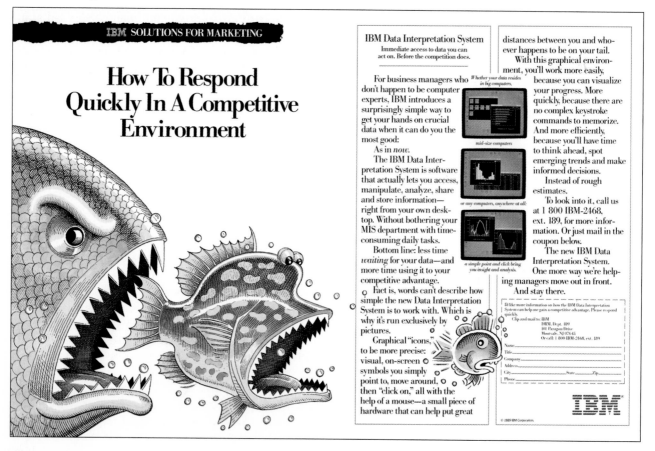

analysis and marketing cost analysis. These tools are examined in the next two sections.

Our discussion of sales volume and marketing cost analyses is built around the Great Western Company (GW)—a firm that markets office furniture. This company's 13-state Western market is divided into four sales districts, each with seven or eight sales people and a district sales manager. The company sells to office equipment wholesalers and directly to large business users. Great Western's product mix is divided into four groups—desks, chairs, filing equipment, and office accessories (wastebaskets and desk sets, for example). Some of these products are manufactured by GW and some are purchased from other firms.

## SALES VOLUME ANALYSIS

A **sales volume analysis** is a detailed study of the "net sales" section of a company's profit and loss statement (operating statement). Management should analyze its *total* sales volume, and its volume by *product lines* and *market segments* (territories and customer groups). These sales should be compared with company goals and industry sales.

### Sales Results versus Sales Goals

We start with an analysis of Great Western's total sales volume, as shown in Table 23-1. The company's annual sales doubled from $18 million to $36 million during the 10-year period ending in 1990. Furthermore, they increased each year over the preceding year, with the exception of 1987. In most of these years, the company met or surpassed its planned sales goals. Thus far the company's situation is very encouraging. When industry sales figures are introduced for comparison, however, the picture changes. But let's hold the industry-comparison analysis until the next section.

A study of total sales volume alone is usually insufficient, and maybe even misleading, because of the iceberg principle. To learn what is going on in the "submerged" parts of the market, we need to analyze sales volume by market segments—sales territories, for example.

Table 23-2 is a summary of the planned sales goals and actual sales results in Great Western's four sales districts. A key measurement figure is the *performance percentage*—actual sales divided by sales goal. A performance percentage of 100 means that the district did exactly what was expected of it. Thus, from the table we see that B and C did just a little better than was expected. District A passed its goal by a wide margin, but D was quite a disappointment.

So far in our evaluation process, we know a little about *what* happened in GW's districts. Now management has to figure out *why* it happened and *what should be done* about it. These are the difficult steps in evaluation. Great Western's executives need to determine why district D did so poorly. The fault may lie in some aspect of the marketing program, or competition may be especially strong there. They also should find out what accounts for district A's success, and whether this information can be used in the other regions.

This brief examination of two aspects of sales volume analysis shows how this evaluation tool may be used. However, for a more useful evaluation GW's executives should go much further. They should analyze their sales volume by individual territories within districts and by product lines. Then they should carry their territorial analysis further by examining volume by product line and customer group *within* each territory. For instance, even though district A did well overall, the iceberg principle may be at work *within*

**TABLE 23-1 Annual sales volume of Great Western Company, industry volume, and company's share in 13-state market**

| Year | Company volume (in millions of dollars) | Industry volume in company's market (in millions of dollars) | Company's percentage share of market |
|------|------|------|------|
| 1990 | 36.0 | 300 | 12.0 |
| 1989 | 34.7 | 275 | 12.6 |
| 1988 | 33.1 | 255 | 13.0 |
| 1987 | 30.4 | 220 | 13.8 |
| 1986 | 31.7 | 235 | 13.5 |
| 1985 | 28.0 | 200 | 14.0 |
| 1984 | 24.5 | 170 | 14.4 |
| 1983 | 22.5 | 155 | 14.5 |
| 1982 | 21.8 | 150 | 14.8 |
| 1981 | 18.0 | 120 | 15.0 |

**TABLE 23-2 District sales volume in Great Western Company, 1990**

| District | Sales goals (in millions of dollars) | Actual sales (in millions of dollars) | Performance percentage (actual ÷ goal) | Dollar variation (in millions) |
|------|------|------|------|------|
| A | 10.8 | 12.5 | 116 | +1.7 |
| B | 9.0 | 9.6 | 107 | + .6 |
| C | 7.6 | 7.7 | 101 | + .1 |
| D | 8.6 | 6.2 | 72 | −2.4 |
| Total | $36.0 | $36.0 | | |

the district. The fine *total* performance in district A may be covering up weaknesses in an individual product line or territory.

**Market-Share Analysis**     Comparing a company's sales results with its goal certainly is a useful form of performance evaluation. But it does not tell how the company is doing relative to its competitors. We need a **market-share analysis** to compare the company's sales with the industry's sales. In effect, we should analyze the company's share of the market in total, as well as by product line and market segment.

Probably the major obstacle encountered in market-share analysis is in obtaining industry sales information in total and in the desired detail. Trade associations and government agencies are excellent sources for industry sales volume statistics in many fields.

Great Western Company is a good example of the utility of market-share analysis. Recall from Table 23-1 that GW's total sales doubled over a 10-year period, with annual increases in 9 of those years. *But,* during this decade the industry's annual sales increased from $120 million to $300 million (a 150 percent increase). Thus the company's share of this market actually *declined* from 15 to 12 percent. Although GW's annual sales increased 100 percent, its market share declined 20 percent.

The next step is to determine *why* Great Western's market position declined. The number of possible causes is virtually limitless—and this is what makes management's task so difficult. A weakness in almost any aspect of GW's product line, distribution system, pricing structure, or promotional program may have contributed to the loss of market share. Or it may be that the real culprit was competition. There may be new competitors in the market that were attracted by the rapid growth rates. Or competitors' marketing programs may be more effective than Great Western's.

## MARKETING COST ANALYSIS

An analysis of sales volume is quite helpful in evaluating and controlling a company's marketing effort. A volume analysis, however, does not tell us anything about the *profitability* of this effort. Management needs to conduct a marketing cost analysis to determine the relative profitability of its territories, product lines, or other marketing units. A **marketing cost analysis** is a detailed study of the operating expense section of a company's profit and loss statement. As part of this analysis, management may establish budgetary goals, and then study the variations between budgeted costs and actual expenses.

### Types of Marketing Cost Analyses

A company's marketing costs may be analyzed:

- As they appear in the ledger accounts and on the profit and loss statement.
- After they are grouped into functional (activity) classifications.
- After these activity costs have been allocated to territories, products, or other marketing units.

#### ANALYSIS OF LEDGER EXPENSES

The simplest and least expensive marketing cost analysis is a study of the "object of expenditure" costs as they appear in the firm's profit and loss statement. These figures, in turn, come from the company's accounting ledger records. The simplified operating statement for the Great Western Company on the left side of Table 23-3 is the model we shall use in this discussion.

The procedure is to analyze each cost item (salaries and media space, for example) in some detail. We can compare this period's total with the totals for similar periods in the past, and observe the trends. We can compare actual results with budgeted expense goals. We should also compute each expense as a percentage of net sales. Then, if possible, we should compare these expense ratios with industry figures, which are often available through trade associations.

#### ANALYSIS OF FUNCTIONAL EXPENSES

Marketing costs should be allocated among the various marketing functions, such as advertising or warehousing, for more effective control. Management can then analyze the cost of each of these activities.

The procedure here is to select the appropriate groups, and then to allocate each ledger expense among those activities. As indicated in the expense distribution sheet on the right-hand side of Table 23-3, we have decided on five activity cost groups in our Great Western example. Some items, such as the cost of media space, can be apportioned directly to one activity (advertising). For other expenses, the cost can be prorated only after management has established some reasonable basis for allocation. Property taxes, for instance, may be allocated according to the proportion of total floor space occupied by each department. Thus the warehouse accounts for 46 percent of the total area (square feet) of floor space in the firm, so the warehousing and shipping function is charged with $60,000 (46 percent) of the property taxes.

A functional cost analysis gives executives more information than they can get from an analysis of ledger accounts alone. Also, an analysis of activity expenses in total provides an excellent starting point for management to analyze costs by territories, products, or other marketing units.

## ANALYSIS OF FUNCTIONAL COSTS BY MARKET SEGMENTS

The third and most beneficial type of marketing cost analysis is a study of the costs and profitability of each segment of the market. This type of analysis divides the market by territories, products, customer groups, or order sizes. Cost analysis by market segment enables management to pinpoint trouble spots much more effectively than does an analysis of either ledger-account expenses or activity costs.

By combining a sales volume analysis with a marketing cost study, a researcher can prepare a complete operating statement for each of the product or market segments. These individual statements can then be analyzed to determine the effectiveness of the marketing program as related to each of those segments.

The procedure for a cost analysis by market segments is similar to that used to analyze activity expenses. The total of each activity cost (the right-hand part of Table 23-3) is prorated on some basis to each product or market segment being studied. Let's walk through an example of a cost analysis, by

---

**TABLE 23-3 Profit and loss statement and distribution of natural expenses to activity cost groups, Great Western Company, 1990**

| Profit and loss statement ($000) | | | Expense distribution sheet ($000) | | | | |
|---|---|---|---|---|---|---|---|
| | | | **Activity (functional) cost groups** | | | | |
| | | | **Personal selling** | **Advertising** | **Warehousing and shipping** | **Order processing** | **Marketing administration** |
| Net sales | | $36,000 | | | | | |
| Cost of goods sold | | 23,400 | | | | | |
| Gross margin | | 12,600 | | | | | |
| Operating expenses: | | | | | | | |
| Salaries and commissions | $2,710 → | | $1,200 | $ 240 | $ 420 | $280 | $ 570 |
| Travel and entertainment | 1,440 → | | 1,040 | | | | 400 |
| Media space | 1,480 → | | | 1,480 | | | |
| Supplies | 440 → | | 60 | 35 | 240 | 70 | 35 |
| Property taxes | 130 → | | 16 | 5 | 60 | 30 | 19 |
| Freight out | 3,500 → | | | | 3,500 | | |
| Total expenses | | 9,700 | $2,316 | $1,760 | $4,220 | $380 | $1,024 |
| Net profit | | $2,900 | | | | | |

sales districts, for the Great Western Company, as shown in Tables 23-4 and 23-5.

First, for each of the five GW activities, we select an allocation basis for distributing the cost of that activity among the four districts. These bases are shown in the top part of Table 23-4. Then we determine the number of allocation "units" that make up each activity cost, and we find the cost per unit. This completes the allocation scheme, which tells us how to allocate costs to the four districts:

- Personal selling activity expenses pose no problem because they are direct expenses, chargeable to the district in which they are incurred.
- Advertising expenses are allocated on the basis of the number of pages of advertising run in each district. GW purchased the equivalent of 88 pages of advertising during the year, at an average cost of $20,000 per page ($1,760,000 ÷ 88).
- Warehousing and shipping expenses are allocated on the basis of the number of orders shipped. Since 10,550 orders were shipped during the year at a total activity cost of $4,220,000, the cost per order is $400.
- Order-processing expenses are allocated according to the number of invoice lines typed during the year. Since there were 126,667 lines, then the cost per line is $3.
- Marketing administration—a totally indirect expense—is divided equally among the four districts, with each district being allocated $256,000.

The final step is to calculate the amount of each activity cost to be allocated to each district. The results are shown in the bottom part of Table 23-4. We see

**TABLE 23-4 Allocation of activity costs to sales districts, Great Western Company, 1990**

| Activity | Personal selling | Advertising | Warehousing and shipping | Order processing | Marketing administration |
|---|---|---|---|---|---|
| | | **Allocation scheme** | | | |
| Allocation basis | Direct expense to each district | Number of pages of advertising | Number of orders to be shipped | Number of invoice lines | Equally among districts |
| Total activity cost | $2,316,000 | $1,760,000 | $4,220,000 | $380,000 | $1,024,000 |
| Number of allocation units | | 88 pages | 10,550 orders | 126,667 lines | 4 districts |
| Cost per allocation unit | | $20,000 | $400 | $3 | $256,000 |
| | | **Allocation of costs** | | | |
| District A < units / cost | $650,000 | 27 pages / $540,000 | 3,300 orders / $1,320,000 | 46,000 lines / $138,000 | one / $256,000 |
| District B < units / cost | $606,000 | 19 pages / $380,000 | 2,850 orders / $1,140,000 | 33,000 lines / $99,000 | one / $256,000 |
| District C < units / cost | $540,000 | 22 pages / $440,000 | 2,300 orders / $1,920,000 | 26,667 lines / $80,000 | one / $256,000 |
| District D < units / cost | $520,000 | 20 pages / $400,000 | 2,100 orders / $840,000 | 21,000 lines / $63,000 | one / $256,000 |

that $650,000 of personal selling expenses were charged directly to district A and $606,000 to district B, for example. Regarding advertising, the equivalent of 27 pages of advertising was run in district A, so that district is charged with $540,000 (27 pages × $20,000 per page). Similar calculations provide advertising activity cost allocations of $380,000 to district B; $440,000 to district C; and $400,000 to district D.

Regarding warehousing and shipping expenses, 3,300 orders were shipped to customers in district A, at a unit allocation cost of $400 per order, for a total allocated cost of $1,320,000. Warehousing and shipping charges are allocated to the other three districts as indicated in Table 23-4.

To allocate order-processing expenses, management determined that 46,000 invoice lines went to customers in district A. At $3 per line (the cost per allocation unit), district A is charged with $138,000. Each district is charged with $256,000 for marketing administration expenses.

After the activity costs have been allocated among the four districts, we can prepare a profit and loss statement for each district. These statements are shown in Table 23-5. Sales volume for each district is determined from the sales volume analysis (Table 23-2). Cost of goods sold and gross margin for each district is obtained by assuming that the company gross margin of 35 percent (12,600,000 ÷ $36,000,000) was maintained in each district.

Table 23-5 now shows, for each district, what the company profit and loss statement shows for overall company operations. For example, we note that district A's net profit was 11.8 percent of sales ($1,471,000 ÷ $12,500,000 = 11.8 percent). In sharp contrast, district D did rather poorly, earning a net profit of only 1.5 percent of net sales ($91,000 ÷ $6,200,000 = 1.5 percent).

At this point in our performance evaluation, we have completed the "what happened" stage. The next stage is to determine *why* the results are as depicted in Table 23-5. As mentioned earlier, it is extremely difficult to answer this question. In district D, for example, the sales force obtained only about two-thirds as many orders as in district A (2,100 versus 3,300). Was this because of poor selling ability, poor sales training, more severe competition in district D, or some other reason among a multitude of possibilities?

**TABLE 23-5 Profit and loss statements for sales districts ($000), Great Western Company, 1990**

|  | Total | District A | District B | District C | District D |
|---|---|---|---|---|---|
| Net sales | $36,000 | $12,500 | $9,600 | $7,700 | $6,200 |
| Cost of goods sold | 23,400 | 8,125 | 6,240 | 5,005 | 4,030 |
| Gross margin | 12,600 | 4,375 | 3,360 | 2,695 | 2,170 |
| Operating expenses: |  |  |  |  |  |
|   Personal selling | 2,316 | 650 | 606 | 540 | 520 |
|   Advertising | 1,760 | 540 | 380 | 440 | 400 |
|   Warehousing and shipping | 4,220 | 1,320 | 1,140 | 920 | 840 |
|   Order processing, billing | 380 | 138 | 99 | 80 | 63 |
|   Marketing administration | 1,024 | 256 | 256 | 256 | 256 |
| Total expenses | 9,700 | 2,904 | 2,481 | 2,236 | 2,079 |
| Net profit (in dollars) | $ 2,900 | $ 1,471 | $ 879 | $ 459 | $ 91 |
| Net profit (as percentage of sales) | 8.1% | 11.8% | 9.2% | 6.0% | 1.5% |

After a performance evaluation has determined why district results came out as they did, management can move to the third stage in its evaluation process. That final stage is, *what should management do about the situation?* This stage will be discussed briefly after we have reviewed major problem areas in marketing cost analysis.

## Problems in Cost Analysis

Marketing cost analysis can be expensive in time, money, and manpower. In particular, the task of allocating costs is often quite difficult.

### ALLOCATING COSTS

The problem of allocating costs becomes most evident when activity cost totals must be apportioned among individual territories, products, or other marketing units.

Operating costs can be divided into direct and indirect expenses. Direct, or separable, expenses are those incurred totally in connection with one market segment or one unit of the sales organization. Thus salary and travel expenses of the sales representative in district A are direct expenses for that territory. The cost of newspaper space to advertise product C is a direct cost of marketing that product. Allocating direct expenses is easy. They can be charged in their entirety to the marketing unit that incurred them.

The allocation difficulty arises in connection with indirect, or common, costs. These expenses are incurred jointly for more than one marketing unit. Therefore, they cannot be charged totally to one market segment.

Within the category of indirect expenses, some costs are *partially* indirect and some are *totally* indirect. Order filling and shipping, for example, are partially indirect costs. They would *decrease* if some territories or products were eliminated. They would *increase* if new products or territories were added. On the other hand, marketing administrative expenses are totally indirect. The cost of the chief marketing executive's staff and office would remain about the same, whether or not the number of territories or product lines was changed.

Any method selected for allocating indirect expenses has obvious weaknesses that can distort the results and mislead management. Two commonly

Warehousing costs typically are indirect costs. What basis would you use for allocating these costs to product groups?

used allocation methods are to divide these costs (1) equally among the marketing units being studied (territories, for instance) or (2) in proportion to the sales volume in each marketing unit. But each method gives a different result for the total costs for each marketing unit.

### FULL-COST VERSUS CONTRIBUTION-MARGIN APPROACH

In a marketing cost analysis, two means of allocating indirect expenses are the (1) contribution-margin (also called contribution-to-overhead) method and (2) full-cost method. A controversy exists regarding which of these two approaches is better for managerial control purposes.

In the **contribution-margin approach,** only direct expenses are allocated to each marketing unit being analyzed. These costs presumably would be eliminated if that marketing unit were eliminated. When direct expenses are deducted from the gross margin of the marketing unit, the remainder is the amount which that unit is contributing to cover total indirect expenses (or overhead).

All expenses—direct and indirect—are allocated among the marketing units under study in the **full-cost approach.** By allocating *all* costs, management can determine the net profit of each territory, product, or other marketing unit.

For any given marketing unit, these two methods can be summarized as follows:

| Contribution margin | Full cost |
|---|---|
| Sales $ | Sales $ |
| *less* | *less* |
| Cost of goods sold | Cost of goods sold |
| *equals* | *equals* |
| Gross margin | Gross margin |
| *less* | *less* |
| Direct expenses | Direct expenses |
| *equals* | *less* |
| Contribution margin (the amount available to cover overhead expenses plus a profit) | Indirect expenses |
| | *equals* |
| | Net profit |

Proponents of the *full-cost* approach contend that a marketing cost study is intended to determine the net profitability of the units being studied. They feel that the contribution-margin method does not fulfill this purpose and may be misleading. A given territory or product may be showing a contribution to overhead. Yet, after indirect costs are allocated, this product or territory may actually have a net loss. In effect, say the full-cost proponents, the contribution-margin approach is the iceberg principle in action. That is, the visible tip of the iceberg (the contribution margin) looks good, while the submerged part may be hiding a net loss.

*Contribution-margin* supporters contend that it is not possible to accurately allocate indirect costs among product or market segments. Furthermore, items such as administrative costs are not all related to any one territory or product. Therefore, the marketing units should not bear any of these costs. Advocates of the contribution-margin approach also point out that a full-cost analysis may show that a product or territory has a net loss, whereas this unit may be contributing something to overhead. Some executives might recommend that the losing product or territory be eliminated. But they are overlooking the fact that the unit's contribution to overhead would then have to be borne by other units. With the contribution-margin approach, there would be no question about keeping this unit as long as no better alternative could be discovered.

## USE OF FINDINGS FROM COMBINED VOLUME AND COST ANALYSIS

So far in our discussion of marketing performance evaluation, we have been dealing generally with the first two stages in the process. That is, we have been finding out *what happened* and *why*. To conclude this chapter, let's look at some examples of how management might use the results from a combined sales volume analysis and marketing cost analysis.

### Territorial Decisions

Once management knows the net profit (or contribution to overhead) of territories in relation to their potential, there are several possibilities for managerial action. It may decide to adjust (expand or contract) territories to bring them into line with current sales potential. Or territorial problems may stem from weaknesses in the distribution system, and changes in channels of distribution may be needed. Some firms that have been using manufacturers' agents may find it advisable to establish their own sales forces in growing markets. Intense competition may be the cause of unprofitable volume in some districts, and changes in the promotional program may be necessary.

Of course, a losing territory might be abandoned completely. An abandoned region may have been contributing something to overhead, however, even though a net loss was shown. Management must recognize that this contribution must now be carried by the remaining territories.

### Product Decisions

When the relative profitability of each product or group of products is known, unprofitable models, sizes, or colors can be eliminated. Sales people's compensation plans may be altered to encourage the sale of high-margin items. Channels of distribution may be changed. Instead of selling all its products directly to business users, for instance, a machine tools manufacturer shifted to industrial distributors for standard products of low unit value. The company thereby improved the profitability of these products.

In the final analysis, management may decide to discontinue a product. Before this is done, however, consideration must be given to the effect this will have on other items in the line. Often a low-volume or unprofitable product must be carried simply to round out the line. Customers may expect a seller to carry the item. If it is not available, the seller may lose sales of other products.

### Decisions on Customer Classes and Order Sizes

By combining a volume analysis with a cost study, executives can determine the relative profitability of each group of customers. If one group shows an unsatisfactory net profit, changes in the pricing structure for these accounts may be required. Or perhaps accounts that have been sold directly should be turned over to middlemen.

A common difficulty plaguing many firms today is the **small-order problem.** Many orders are below the break-even point. Revenue from each of these orders is actually less than allocated expenses. This problem occurs because several costs, such as billing or direct selling, are essentially the same whether the order amounts to $10 or $10,000. Management's immediate reaction may be that no order below the break-even point should be accepted. Or small-volume accounts should be dropped from the customer list. Such decisions may be harmful, however. Management should determine first *why* certain accounts are small-order problems and then adopt procedures to correct the situation. Proper handling can often turn a losing account into a satisfactory one. A small-order handling charge, which customers would willingly pay, might change the profit picture entirely.

**SUMMARY**

The management process in marketing may be defined as the planning, implementation, and evaluation of the marketing effort in an organization. Implementation is the operational stage in which an organization attempts to carry out its strategic planning. Strategic planning is virtually useless if these plans are not implemented effectively.

The implementation stage includes three broad areas of activity—organizing, staffing, and operating. In organizing, the company first should coordinate all marketing activities into one department whose top executive reports directly to the president. Then, within the marketing department, the company may utilize some form of organizational specialization based on geographical territories, products, or customer types. Selecting people is the most important step in the entire management process. To operate an organization effectively, management also needs to do a good job in delegation, coordination, motivation, and communication.

The evaluation stage in the management process involves measuring performance results against predetermined goals. Evaluation enables management to determine the effectiveness of its implementation efforts and to plan future corrective action where necessary.

A marketing audit is extremely important in a total marketing evaluation program. Most companies are victims of at least some misdirected marketing effort. That is, the 80-20 and iceberg principles are at work in most firms because marketing efforts (costs) are expended in relation to the number of marketing units, rather than to their profit potential. Fundamentally, companies do not know how much they should be spending for marketing activities, or what results they should get from these expenditures.

Two useful tools for identifying and corrrecting misdirected marketing efforts are a sales volume analysis and a marketing cost analysis. Given appropriately detailed analyses, management can study sales volume and marketing costs by product lines and market segments (sales territories, customer groups). One major problem in marketing cost analysis is that of allocating costs—especially indirect costs—to the various marketing units. But the findings from these analyses are extremely helpful in shaping decisions regarding several aspects of a company's marketing program.

**KEY TERMS AND CONCEPTS**

Brand-management system 581
Category-management system 581
Implementation (in the management process) 582
Organizational structures for implementing strategic planning 583
Importance of good selection 586
Delegating authority and responsibility 588
Coordinating marketing activities 588
Motivating people 589

Communicating inside a company 589
Marketing audit 590
Misdirected marketing effort 590
80-20 principle 590
Iceberg principle 591
Sales volume analysis 593
Market-share analysis 594
Marketing cost analysis 595
Direct costs 599
Indirect costs 599
Contribution-margin approach 600
Full-cost approach 600

## QUESTIONS AND PROBLEMS

1. Explain the relationship among planning, implementation, and evaluation in the management process.
2. "Good implementation in an organization can overcome poor planning, but good planning cannot overcome poor implementation." Explain, using examples.
3. How is the organizational placement of marketing activities likely to be different in a marketing-oriented firm as contrasted with a production-oriented firm?
4. What benefits can a company expect to gain by organizing its sales force by geographical territories?
5. Give some examples of companies that are likely to organize their sales force by product groups.
6. What organizational structures should each of the following U.S. companies use when marketing in Western Europe?
   a. Franchised chain of real estate brokerage firms such as Re/Max or Century 21.
   b. Medium-size manufacturer of women's cosmetics.
   c. Manufacturer of outboard motors.
7. What are some reasons why this book's authors believe that selecting people is such a critical aspect of the management process?
8. Why is effective delegation of authority and responsibility so important in operating a marketing program?
9. Give examples of how advertising and personal selling activities might be coordinated in a company's marketing department.
10. A sales volume analysis by territories indicates that the sales of a manufacturer of roofing materials have increased 12 percent a year for the past 3 years in the territory comprising South Carolina, Georgia, and Florida. Does this indicate conclusively that the company's sales volume performance is satisfactory in that territory?
11. A manufacturer found that one product accounted for 35 to 45 percent of the company's total sales in all but 2 of the 18 territories. In each of those two territories, this product accounted for only 15 percent of the company's volume. What factors might account for the relatively low sales of this article in the two districts?
12. Explain how the results of a territorial sales volume analysis may influence a firm's promotional program.
13. What effects may a sales volume analysis by product have on training, supervising, and compensating the sales force?
14. "Firms should discontinue selling losing products." Discuss.
15. Should a company stop selling to an unprofitable customer? Why or why not? If not, then what steps might the company take to make the account a profitable one?

# MARKETING: APPRAISAL AND PROSPECTS

## CHAPTER 24 GOALS

Throughout the book we have examined marketing within the individual firm. Now, in this final chapter, we will look more closely at marketing within our social system. After studying this chapter, you should be able to explain:

- The ideal basis for evaluating marketing performance.
- Major criticisms of marketing.
- Consumer, government, and business responses to consumer discontent.
- The significance of consumerism.
- The ethical responsibilities of marketers.
- Trends that will likely influence future marketing activity.

Marketers face a dynamic and constantly changing environment. Firms large and small encounter threats from all directions that require constant vigilance and quick responses. Consider these recent challenges:

- Avon Products, a $3 billion direct marketer of cosmetics, whose success was built on in-home sales, suffered earnings setbacks when housewives began joining the labor force in large numbers and became less accessible.
- Nintendo, a video game maker with sales over $2.5 billion and an 80 percent share of the market, came under congressional scrutiny as a result of accusations that it tried to control retail prices.
- Anheuser-Busch is engaged in a trademark dispute with the maker of a cracker called Party Animals. A-B claims the name is too close to its description of Spuds MacKenzie as the "Original Party Animal."
- Rolfs, a wallet manufacturer, has been forced to change its promotion. It once dominated the mass market, but foreign competition has forced the company to take a higher profile through more advertising, improved retail displays, and better store clerk training.
- Chrysler, having made a remarkable recovery in the early 1980s by responding to the needs of the market, ran into problems later in the decade when the market snubbed the Eagle Premier, the TC (a Chrysler/Maserati hybrid), and the Omni-Horizon.
- Kodak speeded up its new-product introduction process (80 products were introduced in 1988) largely in response to competitive pressure from Fuji and Polaroid.

As the opening examples indicate, for even the largest firms, change and challenge are probably the only certainties in marketing. Successful responses depend on understanding the proper role of marketing in business and in society.

Recall in Chapters 1 and 2 that our discussion touched on the societal dimensions of marketing as we briefly examined marketing's role in the total economy. For the most part, however, we have approached marketing from the viewpoint of the firm as we addressed the challenges facing an individual producer or middleman in managing its marketing activity. In this final chapter, we will look once again at marketing from a broader, societal perspective. We will appraise our system by identifying the major criticisms of marketing and responses to these criticisms. We conclude our discussion of marketing by looking into the crystal ball and considering some prospects for the future.

## EVALUATING THE MARKETING SYSTEM

A major goal of this chapter is to appraise American marketing. Before we can do this, however, we have to agree on what the objective of marketing should be. Recall from Chapter 1 our discussion of the marketing concept. We said the objective of an organization is to accomplish its goals through the determination and satisfaction of consumers' wants. Thus, from the point of view of the *individual organization*, if the firm's target market is satisfied and the organization's objectives are being met, then the marketing effort can be judged successful.

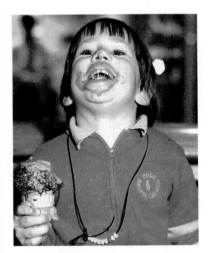

Sometimes customer satisfaction is easy to measure!

However, this standard makes no distinction between organizations whose behavior is detrimental to society and those whose activities are socially acceptable. Firms that pollute the environment or stimulate unwholesome demand would qualify as good marketers right along with firms that behave responsibly. Therefore, we must take a broader, societal view that incorporates the best interests of others as well as the desires of a particular target market and the objectives of the marketer. In other words, marketing must strike a balance among the wants of consumers, the objectives of the organization, *and* the welfare of society.

There is evidence all around us of the interrelationship of these three criteria. If a product does not *meet consumers' needs*, they will not buy it, and the product and possibly the firm that makes it will be forced from the market. In the auto industry alone, consider the recent demise of Ford's Merkur and Pontiac's Fiero, and the bankruptcy of Yugo's U.S. distributor. Likewise, if a firm behaves in a fashion viewed as *detrimental to society*, government will intervene, as it did when the grain psyllium was advertised as a cholesterol reducer. Finally, major advertising campaigns like "This is not your father's Oldsmobile" and Sears' "everyday low prices" were dropped because they failed to *achieve the organization's objectives.*

## CRITICISMS OF MARKETING

Criticisms of marketing center on actions (or inaction) that relate to the balance between organizational objectives and the wants of customers and/or the well-being of society. These issues can be categorized as follows:

- *Exploitation.* Marketers are sometimes accused of taking unfair advantage of a person or situation. Examples of exploitation are price gouging during a shortage and misleading prospects with false or incomplete information. These behaviors may meet the organization's goal of sales and profits, but they are detrimental to consumers, society, or both.
- *Inefficiency.* Some critics feel that marketing uses more resources than nec-

---

### What business practices most annoy consumers?

A survey sponsored by *The Wall Street Journal* indicated that American consumers are most annoyed by actions that are designed to benefit the seller at the expense of the consumer. That is, a balance of benefits to both parties in the exchange is absent. The seven things that bother American consumers the most, followed by the intended benefit to the seller, are:

1. Waiting in line while other windows or registers are closed.
   (Keeps the seller's costs down.)
2. Solicitation using prerecorded messages.
   (Gives the seller greater control over the message and reduces costs.)
3. Being quoted one price, then finding the real price is higher.
   (Generates interest and store traffic.)
4. Getting a sales call during dinner.
   (Reduces the number of "not at homes," lowering the seller's cost.)
5. Discovering that sale items aren't in stock.
   (Generates store traffic.)
6. Dealing with complicated health insurance forms.
   (Reduces claims and comparisons.)
7. "Urgent" mail that is only trying to sell something.
   (Increases the likelihood of the advertisement being read.)

In contrast, marketing-oriented organizations are careful to balance buyer and seller benefits.

Source: David Wessel, "Sure Ways to Annoy Consumers," *The Wall Street Journal*, Nov. 6, 1989, pp. B1, B6.

---

essary. Accusations include ineffective promotional activity, unnecessary distribution functions, and excessive numbers of brands in many product categories. Inefficiency results in higher costs to organizations, higher prices to consumers, and a waste of society's resources.

- *Stimulating unwholesome demand.* A number of marketers have been accused of encouraging consumers or businesses to purchase products that are detrimental to the individual or the organization. For example, most people believe that the marketing of pornographic material is socially unacceptable. Though it may meet the needs of some consumers and satisfy the objectives of organizations that produce and sell it, the marketing of pornography is discouraged because society views it as detrimental.
- *Illegal behavior.* Laws are passed to protect individuals, organizations, and society in general. Marketers are expected to abide by these laws, even when violating a law may benefit consumers or an organization. Price collusion, for instance, is likely to meet the needs of the organizations involved and might even result in lower prices for consumers than price competition. However, it is detrimental to competitors of the colluding firms. Therefore, since the behavior is unfair to others in society, it is unacceptable.

The major charges against marketing can be grouped according to the components of the marketing mix—product, price, distribution, and promotion. Keep in mind that these are *allegations*. Some are unsubstantiated by facts and others apply only to specific situations.[1]

## Product

INGREDIENTS: Wheat Flour, Rye Flour, Coconut Oil, Dehydrated Onions, Salt, Dextrose, Hydrogenated Vegetable Oil (soybean, cottonseed and/or palm), Yeast, Yeast Nutrients (flour, calcium sulfate, salt, ammonium chloride, calcium carbonate, potassium bromate), Sodium Diacetate (to preserve freshness), Dough Conditioner (proteolytic enzymes derived from Aspergillus Oryzae), Ferrous Sulfate (source of iron), Niacin (a B-Vitamin), Thiamine Hydrochloride (Vitamin B₁), Riboflavin (Vitamin B₂).

What do food ingredients lists tell us?

Criticisms of products generally center on how well they meet buyers' expectations. Critics charge that too many products are of poor quality or are unsafe. Examples cited include products that fail or break under normal use; prepared food that contains chemical preservatives, flavor enhancers, and coloring; commuter trains that run late; and wash-and-wear clothing that needs ironing. Also, according to some observers, products are often backed by confusing, inadequate warranties and repair service is unsatisfactory.

Other accusations include packages that appear to contain more of a product than they actually do, labels that provide insufficient or misleading information, and products advertised as "new" that appear to offer only trivial improvements. Critics also argue that style obsolescence encourages consumers to discard products before they are worn out, and that there is an unnecessary proliferation of brands in many product categories. As a result, buyers are confused and production capacity is wasted.

## Price

Everyone would like to pay less for products, but most buyers are satisfied with an equitable exchange. Complaints about prices usually stem from the perception that the seller is making an excessive profit or that the buyer has been misled about prices. We hear that prices are too high because they are controlled by the large firms in an industry. Sellers are sometimes accused of building in hidden charges or advertising false markdowns. Many critics feel that price competition has been largely replaced by nonprice competition in the form of unnecessary frills that add more to the cost than the value of a product.

## Distribution

Of the four marketing mix variables, the least understood and appreciated is distribution. This is probably because channels can take so many forms. In addition, a buyer comes in direct contact with only one level of the distribution channel, so it is difficult to appreciate the functions performed at other levels. Criticisms related to channels reflect this complexity. Channel members are accused of performing needless functions or performing them inefficiently.

## Promotion

The most common accusations against marketing focus on promotion—especially in personal selling and advertising. Most of the complaints about personal selling are aimed at the retail level and the allegedly poor quality of retail selling and service.

Criticisms of advertising may be divided into two groups—social and economic. From a social point of view, advertising is charged with overemphasizing material standards of living and underemphasizing cultural and moral values. Advertising is also accused of manipulating impressionable people, especially children. Another social criticism is that many advertising statements are false, deceptive, or in bad taste. Specifically, some say that too many of the claims made in ads are exaggerated, and fear and sexual appeals

---

[1] For an interesting perspective on the criticisms of marketing, see Steven H. Star, "Marketing and Its Discontents," *Harvard Business Review*, November–December 1989, pp. 148–54.

are overused. Critics also argue there is simply too much advertising and that ad placement is often offensive. For example, many people resent advertisements on home videos.

The economic criticism of advertising—that it unnecessarily increases the cost of products—is based on two arguments. One is that advertising, particularly persuasive as opposed to informative ads, simply shifts demand from one brand to another. Thus it only adds to the individual firms' marketing costs without increasing aggregate demand. Since the advertising must be paid for, prices go up. The other argument is that large firms can afford to differentiate their products through advertising. In this way they create barriers to market entry for new or smaller firms. The result is a high level of market concentration that leads to higher prices and higher profits. This charge was carefully refuted some years ago. A study of the effect of advertising on competition concluded that there is no relationship between advertising intensity and high concentration.[2] Nor does there seem to be any link between advertising intensity and price increases or profitability. Advertising is highly competitive, not anticompetitive. In fact, the Federal Trade Commission encourages professionals (physicians, dentists, lawyers, and optometrists, for example) to advertise in order to *increase* price competition.

## Understanding the Criticisms

To evaluate the charges against marketing, we must understand what actually is being criticized. Is the object of the complaint ultimately the U.S. economic system, an entire industry, or a particular firm? If the criticism applies to a firm, is the marketing department or some other department the cause? Our free enterprise system encourages competition, and government regulatory bodies for many years have judged competition by the number of competitors in an industry. Thus when we complain about the number of toothpaste or cereal brands on the market, we are really criticizing the system. Within a particular firm, a faulty product may result from production, not marketing problems. Clearly, though this explanation does not make the complaints less valid, it does indicate that marketing is not always to blame.

It is also instructive to consider the sources of criticism. Some critics are well-intentioned, well-informed individuals and groups. They point out legitimate weaknesses or errors that need correction, such as deceptive packaging, misleading advertising, and irresponsible pricing. A second type of detractor is simply ill-informed. For example, these people may not understand the functions associated with distribution or appreciate the costs of producing and selling a product. Although their criticisms may have some popular appeal, they cannot withstand careful scrutiny. A third group is made up of those whose views do not reflect the general sentiments of society. These people vociferously criticize behavior they find objectionable in hope of changing public opinion. Protests against the use of persuasive advertising in political campaigns come from such sources. Thus we must examine criticism carefully to separate the legitimate from the erroneous and self-serving.

Operating in a socially undesirable manner, even for a short time, is unacceptable. However, instances of this kind of behavior, though widely publicized, are few relative to the totality of marketing effort. More common, and therefore more disturbing, are the situations that are not clear-cut. These are debatable issues such as full disclosure in advertising (What is the meaning of

---

[2]Jules Backman, *Advertising and Competition*, New York University Press, New York, 1967.

How many choices is too many?

"full"?); planned obsolescence (How long should a product last?); and the subject of our next section, the cost of marketing.

## Does Marketing Cost Too Much?

Many of the censures of marketing can be generally summarized in the statement that marketing costs too much. If there is too much advertising, not enough competition, too many middlemen, or too many brands, marketing *does* cost too much. But how can we go about making those judgments? Our approach is to address the question from two points of view. The first is within the context of our total socioeconomic system, and the second is within the context of an individual firm.

### IN OUR SOCIOECONOMIC SYSTEM

It is estimated that the total cost of producing all products is about 50 percent of the final price paid by consumers. If this is the *average*, then marketing's share of the costs for some products is considerably more than 50 percent. Critics also observe that in many instances the physical product is virtually unchanged from the time it leaves the factory until the consumer buys it. Thus, though marketing costs are a substantial proportion of the final price of most products, it is unclear what value has been added by marketing efforts.

The question of whether marketing costs too much can be asked only in comparative terms. In other words, what would be the effect of spending more or less? There is insufficient accurate information with which to make that comparison. As noted in Chapter 23, we have not yet developed adequate tools to measure the return derived from a given marketing expenditure. However, in qualitative terms, saying marketing costs too much implies that one or more of the following situations must prevail:

- Firms have large amounts of money that they are willing to spend on marketing without concern for the returns produced.

- Firms benefiting from marketing expenditures (the media, advertising agencies, middlemen) are enjoying abnormally high profits.
- More services are being provided than consumers and business people demand.
- Marketing activities are being performed in a grossly inefficient manner.
- Consumption is declining, requiring more marketing effort.

The fact is that none of these situations exist. Competitive pressure ensures that the first four do not occur, and the desire for more and better products has led to continual *increases* in demand (the fifth item). What marketing expenditures produce are time, place, possession, image, and sometimes form utility (as described in Chapter 1). Thus the general criticism that marketing costs too much seems to stem from opinions more than hard evidence.

### IN AN INDIVIDUAL ORGANIZATION

Unquestionably marketing does cost too much in firms that market inefficiently or are production-oriented. Marketing costs are too high and marketing efficiency is too low in firms that:

- Do not offer a product mix desired by customers.
- Have a high rate of new product failures.
- Use improperly designed distribution channels.
- Base prices on cost rather than demand.
- Mismanage the sales force.
- Sponsor ineffective advertising and sales promotions.

In many firms, however, marketing does not cost too much. These firms have strategically planned and implemented customer-oriented marketing programs, as discussed and advocated throughout this book.

It is also important to note that examining marketing costs in isolation is misleading. A total cost approach should be adopted. In many instances a firm can reduce total costs by increasing marketing costs. To illustrate, an increase in advertising expenditures may sufficiently expand a firm's market so that unit production costs decrease due to economies of scale. If production costs go down more than marketing costs go up, *total* cost is reduced.

There is some justification for most of the criticisms of marketing. Many of these situations do occur, but not with the regularity that many critics charge. Some individuals and organizations do indeed take advantage of an economic system that places a high value on freedom. However, many of the issues are more complicated than they seem. In addition, there is in place a system of checks and balances made up of consumer activists, responsible businesses (the majority of all businesses), and government to ensure that abuses are minimized.

## RESPONSES TO MARKETING PROBLEMS

Efforts to address the problems that exist in or result from the exchange process have come from consumers, the government, and business organizations.

### Consumer Responses

One response to marketing misdeeds, both actual and alleged, has come from consumer activists. Though the term *consumerism* was popularized in the 1960s, there have been three periods of intense consumer activism in our history. The first was at the turn of the century, when the emphasis was on consumer safety, particularly the purity of food. During the Depression in the 1930s, there was another consumer movement that focused on false and misleading advertising. The most recent period of heightened consumer action occurred in the 1960s and dealt with a wide variety of issues from providing consumers with insufficient information on credit terms to grocery prices in the ghetto. This movement was characterized by President John Kennedy's "Consumer Bill of Rights"—the rights to safety, to be informed, to choose, and to be heard.

### MEANING AND SCOPE OF CONSUMERISM

The consumerism movement protests perceived injustices in exchange relationships and attempts to remedy them. Generally consumers feel that the balance of power in exchange relationships lies with the seller. Consumerism is an expression of this opinion and an effort to obtain a more equal balance of power between buyers and sellers.

Consumerism includes three broad areas of dissatisfaction and remedial effort:

- Discontent with direct buyer-seller exchange relationships between consumers and businesses. This is the original and still main focus of consumerism. Efforts to ban MSG, a flavor enhancer and preservative that can cause a severe allergic reaction in some people, would be an example.
- Discontent with nonbusiness, nonprofit organizations and governmental agencies. Consumerism extends to all exchange relationships. The performance of such diverse organizations as schools (quality of education, performance of students on standardized tests, number of class days per year), hospitals (medical care costs, smoking in rooms, malpractice), and public utilities (rate increases, eliminating service to people unable to pay their bills) has been scrutinized and subjected to organized and spirited consumer protests.
- Discontent of those indirectly affected by the behavior of others. An exchange between two parties can sometimes have a negative impact on a third party. For example, farmers buy insecticides and pesticides from chemical companies. However, these products may pollute water supplies, rivers, and the air. Thus an exchange has created a problem for a third party or group.

### CONSUMER ACTIONS

Consumer reactions to marketing problems have ranged from complaints registered with offending organizations to boycotts (refusing to buy a particular product or shop at a certain store). Consumer groups have recognized their potential power and have become more active politically than ever. They organize mass letter-writing campaigns to editors, legislators, and business executives. They support consumer-oriented political candidates, conduct petition drives, and gain media attention through sit-ins and picketing.

In recent years organizations at both the local and national levels have become consumer-oriented. Some of these organizations are multi-issue groups (Common Cause, National Consumers' League), and others are special-interest groups (American Association of Retired Persons, Mothers Against Drunk Driving). Some organizations deal primarily with buyer-seller exchange relationships (Consumers Union); others support broader causes with exchange implications (Sierra Club, Audubon Society).

Consumers sometimes react to business with more than their dollar votes.

**CONSUMERISM IN THE FUTURE**

Cultural conditions that provided impetus for the heightened level of consumerism in the 1960s are again coming into place. In our advanced stage of economic development, consumers are more sensitive to social and environmental concerns. Along with sources of dissatisfaction already described, the plight of the poor, air and water pollution, waste disposal, treatment of animals, and health and safety are other social and environmental issues that are receiving greater attention.

In addition, more people are willing and able to take an active role in consumer issues. Compared to earlier generations, young people are better educated, more articulate, and more inclined to speak out. People of all ages are generally less intimidated by large organizations and less willing to accept the status quo. Responding to this increased public sensitivity, many politicians are also demonstrating greater concern for societal issues.

Since problems remain, consumerism in the 1990s will focus on some of the same areas as in the past. It is safe to predict, for example, that fair treatment for consumers, personal well-being, and safety will be major concerns. In addition, waste management, utilization of resources, and the preservation of natural beauty are environmental issues that will likely draw increased attention.

**Government Responses**

Given society's sensitivity, it has become politically popular to support consumer concerns. Almost all states and many cities have created some kind of office for consumer affairs charged with protecting consumers' rights.

At the federal level there are many laws designed to protect consumers. One set asserts the "right to safety," including auto safety, toy safety, and the purity and integrity of virtually every product on the market. Federal legislation also supports consumers' "right to be informed." These laws deal with labeling requirements, nutritional content of food, disclosure of the interest rate on installment and credit purchases, and advertising messages.

Several federal regulatory agencies are empowered to protect consumers. Among the most significant are the Food and Drug Administration, the Federal Trade Commission, the Environmental Protection Agency, and the Consumer Product Safety Commission. The roles these agencies play are described in Chapter 2.

In state legislatures there has been considerable interest in consumer-support laws. Most states and large cities regulate door-to-door selling (as discussed in Chapter 14). Furthermore, state attorneys general have become much more active. In the past they focused on obviously fraudulent behavior such as get-rich-quick schemes and soliciting for nonexistent charities. Recently, however, many have broadened their scope and quickened their pace. For example, the attorneys general of nine states challenged the cholesterol-reducing claims in Quaker Oats' advertising of its oat bran cereal.

It is difficult to judge the effectiveness of government effort since it depends on one's perspective. From the point of view of many consumer advocates, the government is too slow and too many issues are ignored or overlooked. Alternatively, some free-market spokespersons would prefer less regulation and view government activity as interference. In evaluating consumer protection, it is important to recognize that there are trade-offs. For example, there are costs involved in providing consumers with more information, designing and manufacturing products to eliminate all hazards, and keeping the environment clean. These must be weighed against the expected benefits. Often these are difficult comparisons; some, for instance, involve costs that will be incurred now for benefits that may not be realized until some time in the future.

## Business Responses

An increasing number of businesses are making substantive responses to consumer problems. Here are a few examples:

- *Better communications with consumers.* Many firms have responded positively to the desire of consumers to be heard. No-charge 800 phone numbers have become an integral part of customer service because they are easy to use and allow consumers to speak directly to a representative of the business. In 1988 customers made 7.3 billion 800-number calls, many of which were to register complaints or to seek resolution of grievances.
- *More and better information for consumers.* Point-of-sale information is constantly improving. Manufacturers' instruction manuals on the use and care of their products are more detailed and easier to read. In many instances, package labels are more informative than in the past.
- *Product improvements.* More marketers are making a concerted effort to incorporate feedback from consumers in the designs of their products. As a result of consumer input, Pillsbury changed the consistency of its Best Sugar Cookie dough so fancy cookies could be made more easily. In response to mothers who did not like their babies awakened by the noise, General Electric added a switch on its clothes dryer so consumers could control the buzzer. And Kraft redesigned its single-serving Kool-Aid package to make it easier and less messy for kids to use.
- *More carefully prepared advertising.* Concerns about false and misleading claims as well as ads that might be offensive to some group or simply in poor taste have caused firms to review advertising content very carefully. But the system is far from perfect. Some consumers, for example, are distressed by mass media ads for personal care products and undergarments.
- *Customer service departments.* A growing number of companies have separate departments to handle consumer inquiries and complaints. General Electric, with the largest such department, spends $10 million a year on its Louisville, Kentucky, "GE Answer Center." Fidelity Bank in Philadelphia tracks all complaints and organizes them by category for a monthly report to senior management. These departments deal with complaints, but they are also used to gauge consumer tastes, as sounding boards for ideas, and to gain quick feedback on new products.[3]

Some trade associations see themselves as defenders of their respective industry or profession. In that capacity they try to moderate government antibusiness legislation through lobbying and head off criticism with arguments to justify almost any behavior. More enlightened associations have recognized the necessity for responsible corporate behavior. Though they still engage in lobbying, these groups actively respond to consumer problems by setting industry ethical standards, conducting consumer education, and promoting research among association members.

---

[3]For insights into how major corporations handle criticisms of marketing, see Patricia Sellers, "How to Handle Customers' Gripes," *Fortune,* Oct. 24, 1988, pp. 88–100.

## ETHICS AND MARKETING

Ethics are standards of conduct. To act in an ethical fashion is to conform to an accepted standard of moral behavior. Undoubtedly, virtually all people prefer to act ethically. It is easy to be ethical when no hardship is involved—when a person is winning and life is going well. The test comes when things are not going so well—when pressures build up. These pressures arise in all walks of life, and marketing is no exception.

Marketing executives face the challenge of balancing the best interests of consumers, the organization, and society into a workable guide for their daily activities. In any situation they must be able to distinguish what is ethical from what is unethical and act accordingly, regardless of the possible consequences. However, as you have seen in the "Ethical Dilemmas" presented throughout this book, there are many circumstances in which what constitutes ethical behavior is far from straightforward.

### Reasons for Ethical Behavior

Marketing executives should practice ethical behavior simply because it is morally correct. While this is simple and beautiful in concept, it is far more difficult to put into operation. Let's look at four pragmatic reasons for behaving ethically.

#### TO REVERSE DECLINING PUBLIC CONFIDENCE IN MARKETING

Marketing's image is tarnished in many people's eyes. In addition to negative attention produced by consumer issues, highly questionable practices periodically come to light. For example, we hear about misleading package labels, false claims in ads, phony list prices, and infringements on well-established trademarks. Though such practices are limited to only a small proportion of all marketing, the reputations of marketers in general are damaged.

How can this situation be reversed? Business leaders must demonstrate convincingly that they are aware of their ethical responsibility and will fulfill it. Companies must set high ethical standards and then enforce them. Moreover, it is very much in management's interest to be concerned with the well-being of consumers since they are the lifeblood of business.

#### TO AVOID INCREASES IN GOVERNMENT REGULATION

Marketing executives must act in an ethical manner to justify the privilege of operating in our relatively free economic system. Nothing worthwhile comes without a price. Our economic freedoms sometimes have a high price, just as our political freedoms do. Business apathy, resistance, or token responses to unethical behavior simply increase the probability of more government regulation. Indeed, most of the governmental limitations on marketing are the result of management's failure to live up to its ethical responsibilities at one time or other. Moreover, once some form of government control has been introduced, it is rarely removed.

#### TO RETAIN THE POWER GRANTED BY SOCIETY

The concept that social power begets social responsibility helps explain why marketing executives have a major responsibility to society. Managers wield a great deal of social power as they influence markets and speak out on economic issues. However, there is responsibility tied to that power. Thus it is logical that unethical behavior will result in an erosion of social power. If marketers do not use their power in a socially acceptable manner, that power will be lost in the long run.

## TO PROTECT THE IMAGE OF THE ORGANIZATION

Buyers of goods and services are most likely to come in contact with someone representing the marketing function, and that interaction forms their impression of the entire organization. You may base your opinion of a retail store on the behavior of a single sales clerk. As Procter & Gamble put it in an annual report: "When a Procter & Gamble sales person walks into a customer's place of business . . . that sales person not only represents Procter & Gamble, but in a very real sense, that person is Procter & Gamble."

**Setting Ethical Guidelines**

Many organizations have formal codes of ethics for their employees that identify specific acts (bribery, accepting gifts) as unethical. These guidelines lessen the chance that employees will knowingly or unknowingly get into trouble. Ethics codes strengthen a company's hand in dealing with customers or prospects that invite unethical behavior. For young or inexperienced executives, they can also be valuable guides, helping them to resist pressure to compromise personal ethics in order to move up in the firm.

However, determining what is right and what is wrong can be extremely difficult. It is not realistic for an organization to construct a two-column list of all possible practices, one headed "ethical" and the other "unethical." Rather, an executive must personally evaluate the ethical status of many actions. One simple but effective approach is to answer the following questions:

- Would I do this to a friend?
- Would I be willing to have this done to me?
- Would I be embarrassed if this action were publicized nationally?
- Is the action sound from a long-run point of view?

The last question deserves some elaboration. Marketing managers must understand that ethical behavior is not only morally right but also, over the long run, practically sound. For example, deceiving or pressuring buyers to consummate a sale can alienate customers and eliminate repeat business.[4]

**Ethics and the Consumer**

Acting ethically is not a one-way street. Consumers also have a responsibility to behave ethically in exchange situations. Business firms are increasingly experiencing unethical behavior on the part of consumers. Shoplifting, fraudulent coupon redemption, vandalism, fraudulent check cashing, and other consumer abuses have become major expense items for organizations. Although determining exactly how much consumer fraud occurs is virtually impossible, reliable estimates are disheartening:[5]

- Recent figures for shoplifting place the amount at $10 billion per year and increasing.

---

[4]Ethical issues in various areas of marketing are discussed in Shelby D. Hunt and Lawrence B. Chonko, "Ethical Problems of Advertising Agency Executives," *Journal of Advertising* 4, 1987, pp. 16–24; David J. Fritzsche, "An Examination of Marketing Ethics: Role of the Decision Maker, Consequences of the Decision, Management Position, and Sex of the Respondent," *Journal of Macromarketing,* Fall 1988, pp. 29–39; John B. Gifford and Donald G. Norris, "Ethical Attitudes of Retail Store Managers: A Longitudinal Analysis," *Journal of Retailing,* Fall 1987, pp. 298–311; and Joseph A. Bellizzi and Robert E. Hite, "Supervising Unethical Salesforce Behavior," *Journal of Marketing,* April 1989, pp. 36–47.

[5]These statistics are compiled from "Attention Shoplifters," *Forbes,* Nov. 14, 1988, p. 258; Michael Violano, "The High-Tech Future of Foiling Fraud and Forgery," *Bankers Monthly,* April 1989, pp. 34–38; and Royce D. Brown and Roger J. Snell, "Check Fraud Alert," *ABA Banking Journal,* September 1988, pp. 38–40.

A "fish eye" camera may deter shoplifting, but the problem requires a more basic solution.

- More than 500 million forged checks are written each year.
- Credit-card fraud amounts to $200 million per year, a 100 percent increase since 1982.
- The cost of check-related fraud to the retailing and banking industries is $10 billion per year.

Of course, the high incidence of unethical consumer behavior does not excuse inappropriate business practices. These examples simply illustrate how widespread unethical behavior has become. What the facts make abundantly clear is the need for a system-wide exploration of ways to reduce this problem in business, among consumers, and within all other social institutions.

### AN ETHICAL DILEMMA?

An inventor has designed a product that can reduce the effectiveness of police radar. It is referred to as the stealth "car bra" because it resembles a brassiere when it is strapped to the front of a car. Car bras were originally intended to protect a car's paint from gravel and other road debris. The stealth bra, however, is made of radar-absorbing carbon fibers that temporarily confuse police radar. This property permits the driver to get close enough to spot a speed trap with a conventional radar detector and slow down. Assume you are the vice president of an auto accessory manufacturer and the inventor would like to license your firm to make the bra. Is it ethical to produce and sell a product that is designed to circumvent law enforcement? If you owned a chain of auto accessory stores, would you stock this product?

## The Broadened Marketing Concept

At this point you may wonder about the relationship between the broadened marketing concept and the problems we have been describing. Recall the components of the broadened marketing concept:

- An emphasis on customer orientation.
- Coordination of marketing activities.
- Achieving the organization's performance objectives.
- Satisfying societal wants affected by the organization's activities.

If firms follow this approach, there shouldn't be any criticisms. Yet there are many. How can this be explained?

The major factors affecting the implementation of the broadened marketing concept revolve around the *interpretation of consumer orientation* and the *conflict in goals experienced by consumers.*

Who is the consumer, and what does it mean to be consumer-oriented? Answers to these questions have been too narrow and too short-run. It seems to be human nature to be shortsighted. We often fail to see or choose to ignore the long-run impact of our actions. For example, firms pollute the environment by making nonbiodegradable products, the effects of which won't be felt for two or three generations. However, to fully adopt the marketing concept, it is necessary to look beyond the short-run gratification of consumers or the organization. Adopting the broadened marketing concept requires that one strategic goal be defined as a consumer orientation *in the long run.* That is, we must extend the time dimension used to describe customer orientation.

We also need to expand the *breadth* of the notion of consumers. To view only the direct buyers of a company's product as the consumers is too narrow. We must expand our definition of target markets to include other groups affected by the buyer-seller exchange. Someone may buy a car and be satisfied with it. But the negative effects of pollution from the auto endanger others. In the broader context, the automobile maker has not generated customer satisfaction and thus has not successfully implemented the broadened marketing concept. We must define consumers to include not only the purchasers of a product, but also the other parts of society affected by the firm's activities. Until marketing decisions incorporate the long run and an expanded definition of consumers, criticism will continue.

The other problem area is the goal conflict experienced by many consumers. It is difficult to shift from personal to socially oriented goals. As consumers we have not abandoned our desires for possessions, but we have complicated our wants with social concerns. A simplified example illustrates the difference between our goals of the past and those of today. In the past we wanted big cars that would go fast. We paid little attention to air pollution, traffic congestion, oil reserves depletion, and water pollution. Now we still want the cars, but we also want clean air, an end to traffic jams, clean water, and independence from foreign oil resources. The former goal—a desire for autos only—was much easier to achieve because a conflict in goals was largely absent.

A related problem is the great number of publics a company must deal with and the difficulty of satisfying them all. Often the goals of the different publics are in conflict. One group may want a paper mill closed because it pollutes the air and the water. But another public wants it kept open because it provides jobs.

| TABLE 24-1 Market successes, failures, and fads of the 1980s | | |
|---|---|---|
| **Successes** | **Failures** | **Fads** |
| VCRs | Arena football | Trivial Pursuit (game) |
| Minivans | Disposable contact lenses | Cross-training shoes |
| NutraSweet | New Coke | Oat bran |
| CD players | Merkur automobile | Mountain bikes |
| Frozen yogurt | Home banking | Wine coolers |
| Fax machines | Disk cameras | Granola |
| Sunscreen lotion | Next cigarettes | Bottled water |
| Light beer | | |

## PROSPECTS FOR THE FUTURE

Predicting the future is always difficult. Consider, for example, the marketing successes, failures, and fads shown in Table 24-1. The firms that produced these products all had high hopes. But some products succeeded while many products that appeared to have considerable potential in the beginning fizzled in the marketplace.

The challenge of making accurate predictions in marketing is compounded by the fact that change is so rapid. However, none of the prospects described here should surprise you. What we have done is simply evaluate the strength of current trends and extend the strongest into the future. Most marketing successes are accomplished in the same fashion. Managers monitor what is happening in the marketplace, identify opportunities, and respond with want-satisfying products.

## Changes in Consumer Demographics

Changes in demographics—the population's age distribution, income, education, ethnic composition, and household structure—all affect marketers' activities. For example, the population is getting older and senior citizens are the fastest-growing age group. This shift creates expanded marketing opportunities in such areas as travel and tourism and health and medical care. Another demographic change is the greater ethnic diversity resulting from increases in the Hispanic and Asian populations. These groups are large enough to attract the attention of marketers, but they present interesting challenges. Some of these consumers, for example, do not speak or read English.

Another important development is the decrease in household size. More people than ever live alone. Therefore, marketers of many consumer products must consider the impact of smaller households on meal preparation, the size of appliances, and package sizes, to cite several examples. Small households also mean fewer people to perform normal maintenance functions. Therefore, time will be the currency of the 1990s.

What do these demographic changes tell us? They indicate that some markets will disappear and new ones will emerge. Marketers must remain abreast of these developments and adjust strategies accordingly. For example, the aging population has created opportunities for products modified to accommodate the physical limitations of the elderly (labels and instructions in large print, easy-to-open containers), and time pressure has spawned firms that

This ad for the California lottery is one of many aimed at ethnic groups.

will do routine errands (getting the car serviced, picking up the dry cleaning, grocery shopping).[6]

### Changes in Consumer Values

Values change slowly, but when they do, the impact on existing institutions and the opportunities for innovative marketers can be great. A good indicator of value shifts is the amount of coverage given to a particular development by the media. Three examples are discussed below.

#### ENVIRONMENT

Some forecasters see a shift away from a self-orientation to an "other-orientation." Indications are that people may be disturbed by the excesses of the 1980s, a period when self-gratification governed many choices. For example, volunteerism is on the upswing. What does this mean for marketing? In a recent Gallup poll, most Americans considered themselves environmentalists. Some cities, notably Minneapolis and St. Paul, have passed ordinances restricting the use of nonrecyclable containers. There is also evidence of heightened interest in the future quality of life. International concern over the dissipation of the atmosphere's ozone layer, acid rain, and the "greenhouse effect" shows a shift in sentiment. Of more direct interest to marketers are concerns about waste disposal and landfills, air and water pollution, and biodegradability.

Environmentally sensitive product packaging, alternatives to fossil fuel, and energy conservation are excellent marketing opportunities. Other pros-

---

[6]A number of specific implications are described in Anne B. Fisher, "What Consumers Want in the 1990s," *Fortune,* Jan. 29, 1990, pp. 108–12.

pects are not so obvious. One industry spawned by environmental interest is increased leisure travel to undeveloped areas of the world. But even this has its downside. So many tourists have visited Antarctica that its ecosystem may be in danger.

### HOME

There are several indications that consumers will focus more on the home in the years ahead. Stressful jobs and concerns about increased crime have led people to seek a place where they can relax in comfort and security. A home fulfills the desire for something stable in a dynamic world. As a result, consumers are spending more on their homes and on products that make their homes enjoyable. For instance, computerized television that will identify and record programs in preselected categories will probably be available in the 1990s. Home remodeling, lower-cost construction methods such as modular homes and prefab housing components, and fiber-optic systems to monitor lighting, security, and fire protection are predicted growth markets.

### SERVICE

The success of businesses like Nordstrom's department stores and Disney amusement parks makes it clear that consumers reward good service. It is also apparent that many firms recognize this opportunity. The effective "lonely Maytag repairman" ad campaign that has run for many years and airline ads emphasizing on-time arrival records are just two examples. Recognizing the need to offer good service is often easier than finding and training employees to provide it. A major challenge for organizations in the 1990s will be to design and implement systems that provide consumers with high-caliber service.

**The Development of Fragmented Markets**

One outcome of consumer demographic and value changes is fragmented markets. There was a time when a packaged-goods manufacturer could develop a good product, advertise it nationally to housewives using the primary media, stock retailers' shelves, and be successful. But the situation has

**AN INTERNATIONAL PERSPECTIVE: AT&T has redefined the idea of calling home**

Immigration, lower rates, and more consumers who want to maintain overseas contacts have all contributed to an increased demand for international telephone calls. To capitalize on these developments, AT&T has combined its customer data bank with advertising to expand its market.

Records on its 70 million residential customers allow AT&T to identify those who make frequent international calls and offer them special discounts on foreign holidays. Discounts have been offered on calls to France on Bastille Day, Japan on Keiro No Hi (a day honoring grandparents), Canada on Canadian Thanksgiving Day, Great Britain on Remembrance Day, and the Philippines on Philippine Independence Day. The discounts encourage consumers to call and make use of the extra capacity to foreign countries created by business closings on these holidays.

In another promotion AT&T sent 180,000 people who had placed more than one residential call to Taiwan or Hong Kong in a year a Chinese New Year greeting card. The card wished them a happy New Year and encouraged them to share the holiday by calling friends or family overseas.

Source: Calvin Sims, "Drive for Holiday Calls Abroad," *The New York Times*, Feb. 6, 1990, p. C1.

To meet the wants of the fragmented food market, Campbell Soup Company has expanded its line from condensed soups to a wide variety of niche products.

changed. Only 10 percent of women can be considered traditional housewives who stay home and raise children. Highly active consumers are less accessible through the media, and their tastes have gone in many directions. Pressed for time, many consumers are making decisions at the point of purchase. To keep up, marketers are engaging in a variety of tactics from brand extensions to new ways of conveying advertising messages.

Market fragmentation is not something new. Marketers have known about segments within markets for many years. As we discussed in Chapter 4, techniques have been developed using demographic, behavioral, and geographic data to identify market segments to enable marketers to better target their efforts.

What has changed as our society has become more complex and diversified is the number and size of market segments. Marketers can no longer expect large numbers of consumers to compromise their needs and wants and buy standardized products. Rather, they must tailor goods and services to meet the needs of these small segments. Called **niche marketing,** this strategy significantly complicates the marketer's job. One version of a product is replaced by several. Different ads must be produced and new media found to reach different consumers (see box). Retailers must choose among many product variations, not all of which can be stocked. The added variety complicates inventory management, distribution, and personal selling.[7]

Evidence of this fragmentation is everywhere. McDonald's, the king of hamburgers, not only has expanded its variety of burgers, but has also test marketed fish-and-chips, fried chicken, and pizza. From 1947 to 1984 Procter & Gamble had only one Tide. Today there are five versions including Liquid Tide and Tide with Bleach. The prices of BMW automobile models range from $25,000 to $70,000.

There are no indications that the trend to niche marketing will end. In fact, with more sophisticated electronic data collection methods being developed and the diversity of the population increasing, all indications point to even greater fragmentation in the future.[8]

## The Expansion of Information and Education

Consumers' choices and marketers' decisions are greatly influenced by the amounts and types of information they have. The quantity of information available to all segments of society continues to grow at what seem to be geometric rates. Consumers have access to dozens of television channels via cable and satellite dishes, news is available 24 hours a day, an unprecedented number of magazines and newspapers are published today, and advertising is presented in forms and places never imagined.

Businesses have amassed more detailed demographic and behavioral data about consumers, competitors, and prospects than previously imaginable (or usable!). Product sales are tracked hourly through electronic scanners. Complex systems have been designed to monitor the competition. The potential of prospects is gauged by their past purchasing tendencies, demographic characteristics, and expressed attitudes.

Of course, technology has made most of these advances possible. For example, using computer files, politicians are better able to match voters with

---

[7]For a discussion of the opportunities and risks in the particularly attractive niche market of Hispanics, see Julia Lieblich, "If You Want a Big, New Market . . . ," *Fortune,* Nov. 21, 1988, pp. 181–88.

[8]Joe Mandese, "Who Are the Targets?" *Marketing & Media Decisions,* July 1989, pp. 29–34.

---

**Consumer mobility is redefining the media**

Half the challenge in reaching fragmented markets is finding the right medium. Advertisers once preferred reaching the "masses" through traditional media—radio, television, newspapers, and magazines. In an age of fragmented markets, however, advertisers are now searching for new ways to reach busy, highly mobile consumers. Bus stop benches and mass transit are no longer considered "exotic" media. Consider also the following:

- Commercials interspersed with recorded music in grocery stores.
- Shopping carts with screens and video commercials.
- Ads on the stall doors in public restrooms.
- Magazines designed for and distributed only to doctors' waiting rooms.
- Ads on blood pressure monitors in pharmacies.
- TV monitors that show ads on gasoline pumps while people fill up their cars.

---

issues on which they are sensitive in order to more accurately target their marketing efforts. Packaged-goods firms can adjust the value of coupons individual consumers receive based on data predicting their likelihood of redeeming them. Regular users receive lower-value coupons; infrequent users and nonusers are sent coupons in larger denominations.

In sharp contrast to the growth of information technology is concern over education. Standardized tests indicate that students in many foreign countries are outperforming American students in critical subjects like science and math. A large number of young people are finishing their formal education without the basic skills needed to function in today's society. Beyond societal implications, education quality concerns marketers because it affects their ability to find capable employees and increases the difficulty of communicating with consumers.

**Global Marketing**

The cliché that we live in a "small world" is a reality for marketers. Virtually instantaneous communications have greatly increased global awareness. Economic, social, and political developments on one side of the world have an impact everywhere else. On the evening television news we are as likely to hear about developments on the Japanese stock market as we are about activity on Wall Street.

As a result, foreign firms are now major investors in the United States, and American firms in search of new mass markets have a renewed interest in opportunities overseas. Growing buying power in Asia, the elimination of trade restrictions in the European Community in 1992, and political changes in Eastern Europe have created excitement among U.S. business leaders. Major firms are quickly establishing or solidifying their positions. Procter & Gamble has a major share of the disposable diaper market in Japan; General Electric shares ownership of Tungsram, a Hungarian lighting manufacturer, giving it a strong position in Eastern Europe; and Coca-Cola and Pepsi-Cola have established strong positions in Russia. One wonders when the "cola wars" will break out in the Soviet Union!

It is also interesting to note the diversity of U.S. consumer products that have been received with open arms abroad, including dry cereal (Japan), film (Eastern Europe), ethnic foods (Northern Europe), and movies (all countries).

With the enormous potential established by the performance of the pioneering firms, many organizations are eagerly investigating global marketing. However, significant problems exist and the risks may well exceed the benefits in some cases.

Probably the biggest mistake global marketers make is a failure to recognize the diversity that exists in a target area. Some marketers, for example, envision the 320 million consumers in the European Community as a single market. They ignore the language, cultural, political, and historical differences that transcend any economic agreement. Even in a country as small as Finland, the population is a mixture of natives and immigrants from Russia, Germany, Sweden, and other Western European countries. There are two official languages and many dialects, as well as distinctive regional food preferences. These and other differences, within just one small country, suggest that global marketing faces many of the same challenges as domestic marketing.

A study of global marketing successes and failures identified five key reasons for poor performance:[9]

- Insufficient formal marketing research.
- Failure to adapt marketing to specific market differences.
- Lack of sustained marketing effort.
- Failure to decentralize decision making.
- Lack of local commitment and confidence.

Despite problems, the trend toward global marketing will accelerate. The lure of millions of consumers, combined with improved understanding of the markets and marketing practices necessary to be successful, will increase the attractiveness of such opportunities.

You have now completed your introduction to marketing (with the possible exception of a final exam!). If we have been successful, you will come away from this course with a sense of the excitement and challenges in the field. It would be great if you have been inspired to consider a career in marketing—the field can always use capable, enthusiastic people. However, whether your studies lead you to specialized marketing topics or into other areas, you now know what marketing entails and its importance to every individual and organization involved in exchanges. We hope you put the knowledge to good use!

**SUMMARY**   A firm's marketing performance should be appraised from a broad, societal perspective. When evaluating the marketing efforts of an organization, we must consider how well the firm satisfies the wants of target customers, meets the needs of the organization, and recognizes the best interests of society.

Marketing has been attacked for being exploitative, inefficient, and illegal and for stimulating unwholesome demand. Several of the criticisms are rooted in the complex question "Does marketing cost too much?" Though truly objective measures are not available, for organizations adopting the

[9]These factors are adapted from Kamran Kashani, "Beware the Pitfalls of Global Marketing," *Harvard Business Review*, September–October 1989, pp. 91–98. Other insightful articles on the realities of global marketing are Richard I. Kirland, Jr., "Who Gains from the New Europe," *Fortune*, Dec. 18, 1989, pp. 83–88; and Adam Snyder, "Reaching the New Pan-European Consumer," *Adweek's Marketing Week*, Dec. 18, 1989, pp. 20–33.

marketing concept, costs are not unreasonable. Many of the objections to marketing are valid. However, the offensive behavior is confined to a small minority of all marketers, and some of the issues are more complicated than they appear.

Responses to criticisms have come from consumers, government, and business. Consumerism—protests against perceived institutional injustices and efforts to remedy them—has had a significant impact on business behavior.

Consumer responses to marketing problems have included protests, political activism, and support of special-interest groups. Conditions providing an impetus for widespread consumerism, sensitivity to social and environmental concerns, and the willingness to become actively involved are present today. Therefore the possibility exists for a consumerism movement in the 1990s. Government at the federal, state, and local levels passes and enforces consumer protection legislation. Businesses have responded to criticism by improving communications, providing more and better information, upgrading products, producing more sensitive advertising, and enhancing customer service.

Ethical behavior by business is the best answer to the charges against marketing. Besides being morally correct, ethical behavior by organizations can restore public confidence, avoid government regulation, retain the power granted by society, and protect the image of the organization. A method of judging the ethics of a particular act is to ask four questions: Would I do this to a friend? Would I be willing to have this done to me? Would I be embarrassed if this action were publicized nationally? Is the action sound from a long-run point of view?

Consumers also have a responsibility to act ethically. The volume of credit-card misuse, check fraud, coupon misredemption, and shoplifting suggests that a system-wide exploration of ways to reduce unethical behavior is needed.

The numerous criticisms directed at marketing suggest the broadened marketing concept has not been widely adopted. If the concept is to be generally implemented, it is essential that marketers change their notion of consumer orientation. The marketing concept has been defined too narrowly and has been too short-run-oriented. In addition, consumers must resolve their conflicts between personal and societal goals.

Prospects for marketing are difficult to predict, but the strongest current trends are projected into the future. Developments likely to have major marketing implications are consumer demographic and value changes, fragmentation of markets, information expansion, and global marketing.

**KEY TERMS AND CONCEPTS**

Basis for evaluating performance 606
Nature of marketing criticisms 606
The cost of marketing 610
Consumerism 611
Scope of consumerism 612
Responses to consumer problems 613

Reasons for ethical behavior 615
Evaluating ethical merit 616
Consumer ethics 616
Broadened marketing concept 618
Fragmented markets 621
Niche marketing 622

## QUESTIONS AND PROBLEMS

1. Can all the criticisms of marketing be dismissed on the basis of critics' being poorly informed or acting in their own interest?
2. What indicates that middlemen make reasonable profits?
3. Some people believe there are too many fast-food outlets in their communities. Suggest a method for reducing the number of these outlets.
4. React to the following criticisms of advertising:
   a. It costs too much.
   b. It is in bad taste.
   c. It is false and deceptive.
   d. It creates monopolies.
5. What proposals do you have for regulating advertising to reduce the occurrence of false or misleading claims?
6. What specific recommendations do you have for reducing the cost of advertising?
7. What information do you think should be included in ads for each of the following goods or services?
   a. Snack foods.          c. Nursing homes.
   b. Jogging shoes.        d. Credit cards.
8. What are the social and economic justifications for "paternalistic" laws like seat belt regulations and warnings on cigarette and alcoholic beverage containers?
9. How would you respond to the argument that companies can absorb the cost of coupon misredemption?
10. Describe a firm whose behavior you feel reflects the adoption of the broadened marketing concept.
11. Within the overall college student market segment, describe a smaller or fragmented market that you believe exists.
12. What does global marketing have in common with domestic marketing?

## CASE 22

## VAN DER STEEN CANDY COMPANY* Designing a Strategic Marketing Plan

Joseph van der Steen had just inherited the family candy business in downtown Baltimore. Selling in limited volume to a select group of customers, his grandfather had built a loyal following among people who would pay a premium price for beautiful and authentically old-fashioned, hand-dipped chocolates. All ingredients were natural: real butter and chocolate, fresh-ground vanilla and other flavors, authentic maple sugar, and so on. All nutmeats were premium quality. Recipes and package designs were virtually unchanged since 1855, when the family had moved from Holland to Baltimore and begun selling candy.

The candy kitchens and production facilities were located in an area near the center of downtown that had been unaffected by urban renewal. The building and equipment were sturdy, spotless, and in excellent condition, according to time-honored family traditions. The small staff was expert and loyal. Current production ran from 700 pounds weekly in July to a high of 1,200 pounds weekly in December. Capacity was estimated at 2,000 pounds per week, if one or two unskilled workers were added for packing, stock control, and cleaning duties. The van der Steens also owned a larger building that backed up to the kitchen, but it had fallen into disuse.

The prices of van der Steen candy had held steady over the past couple years due to a decrease in the inflation rate. For several years prior to that, however, prices had to be raised annually to compensate for sharp jumps in the costs of sugar, chocolate, packaging materials, and other items.

Even when prices were increased, demand remained relatively stable. Sales for 1990 were $477,685 and pretax net profit was $23,358. An income statement for 1990 is shown in Exhibit 1.

The company depended entirely on walk-in traffic at their retail store, located at the candy kitchen. A survey of 87 customers in November showed van der Steen that 82 were regular repeat customers. Of the 87, 22 were businessmen buying several packages for business gifts.

The van der Steen family had never advertised, depending entirely on word-of-mouth promotion and careful maintenance of customer goodwill. Some investments had been made in new packaging, but the basic package designs were almost unchanged since the turn of the century. They featured Dutch village scenes in pastel colors and Victorian faces. The company sold different combinations of a variety of candies in 1-pound boxes.

While van der Steen had only limited experience in the family candy kitchens, he had graduated from college with a degree in marketing. After a detailed evaluation and counseling by his accountant, he decided to keep the business and build on the reputation and customer base established by earlier family members.

He allocated a promotional budget of $75,000 for the first year, based on a sales objective of $1 million

*Case prepared by Professor Ernest F. Cooke, Loyola College, Maryland, based on a case by Professor Richard J. Jeffries and Ernest F. Cooke. Used with permission.

**EXHIBIT 1 van der Steen Candy Company**

Income statement, 1990

| | |
|---|---:|
| Net sales | $477,685 |
| less Cost of goods sold* | 381,653 |
| Gross margin | 96,032 |
| less Operating expenses | 72,674 |
| Net income before taxes | $ 23,358 |

*Material, direct labor, and packaging cost for the manufacture of the candy was $342,381.

for the year. To reach that goal, the company would have to sell 2,000 pounds weekly at the current retail price of $9.95 per pound.

Van der Steen did a quick study of the competitive situation. The 1-pound Whitman's Sampler sold for $6.85 at Drugfair (a chain drugstore) and $5.19 at Giant's (a chain supermarket). A 1-pound box of Russell Stover candy sold for $5.95 at Drugfair and $6.35 at Hecht's (a department store). One pound of Godiva sold for $20.50 to $23.00 at Hecht's and at Woodward and Lothrop (a Washington, D.C., department store).

These three brands (Whitman, Russell Stover, and Godiva) were distributed nationally.

There were numerous other brands of boxed chocolates. Most were sold for under $8.00 a pound; only a few were priced at more than $15.00 a pound. Very few were sold in the $8.00 to $15.00 a pound price range. This type of candy was sold in many different sizes ranging from 2-ounce "samplers" to 5-pound boxes. The price per pound decreased as the package size increased.

Van der Steen had a number of decisions to make regarding his marketing plans for 1991. He wanted to fill in the summer sales "valley" typically experienced by the company. And he also wanted to reach his goal of doubling the company's sales volume during the coming year.

## QUESTIONS

Assume that you have been hired as a marketing consultant by Mr. van der Steen to design a strategic marketing plan for his company. As part of this plan:

1. Indicate what target markets the company should select.
2. Design in some detail a marketing mix to reach these markets.

CASE 23

## SUN ICE LIMITED* Capitalizing on Promotion of Olympic Proportions

Sun Ice Limited developed from the sewing skills of Sylvia Rempel, who made her first ski outfit for her son, only to find that his friends wanted outfits too. As news of her expertise spread, she was soon sewing ski suits for neighbors and friends in the basement of her Calgary, Canada, home. In 1978 she incorporated Sun Ice, a Calgary-based company, to design, manufacture, and market superior-quality skiwear.

By the time the 1988 Olympic Winter Games ended in Calgary, millions of people around the world had seen a lot of Sun Ice and its ski clothing, whether they realized it or not. Sun Ice had been selected as the sole licensee and official supplier of outerwear for the Olympics and had outfitted 30,000

Canadian Olympic athletes, officials, sponsors, employees, and volunteers. In addition, Sun Ice had outfitted the runners who had carried the Olympic torch across Canada in the torch relay.

Sun Ice produces an extensive line of skiwear, casual outerwear, and active sports and leisure clothing. The company's products are distributed through specialty ski stores, sporting goods stores, fashion boutiques, and department stores in Canada and, to a lesser extent, the United States. The Sun Ice collar stripes are an internationally recognized and registered trademark. Since its establishment, Sun Ice has maintained a commitment to produce outerwear that is both functional and fashionable. The company has been able to carve out a Canadian identity in a market that is extremely competitive and has been dominated by high-end European imports and low-end products from Asian countries.

The Sun Ice product line comprises almost 100

*Case prepared by Professor James G. Barnes, Memorial University, Newfoundland. The author acknowledges the support provided by Sun Ice Ltd., and particularly by Sylvia Rempel, president, and Victor Rempel, executive vice president.

styles in more than 20 fashion colors. The "Gold Label" line features Gore-Tex fabrics exclusively. Gore-Tex is produced through a patented process whereby a microthin, microporous Teflon membrane is bonded to special fabrics. The result is a fabric that is waterproof, windproof, and breathable. The latest in synthetic, high-performance insulation is used to complement the Gore-Tex fabric, to give this line the unique capacity of adjusting its thermal properties to changing weather conditions and body temperatures.

The "White Label" collection encompasses the widest selection of colors and styles to satisfy the performance and price expectations of a broader range of consumers. The fabrics used in this line are treated with Ultrex, a special coating providing protection against water and wind, while retaining breathability.

The Sun Ice Junior Collection is designed for children and looks and performs like the styles in the adult Gold Label and White Label lines. All of the styles carrying the Sun Ice label are sold through specialty ski and sporting goods stores, fashion boutiques, and selected high-image retail outlets. The company also manufactures its "Pod" line, consisting of popular styles in less costly fabrics. This line is named for Steve Podborski, a former member of Canada's National Alpine Ski Team. The Pod line was introduced in 1983 and is distributed through mid-priced high-volume department and chain stores.

The Sun Ice product assortment is rounded out by the Olympic Licensee line of insulated and noninsulated jackets, developed by the company under its agreement as official licensee for the Calgary 1988 Olympic Winter Games. By 1988 the company had begun to develop an expanded product line to complement its skiwear and outergarments. New products in 1988–89 included color- and design-coordinated gloves, headwear, turtlenecks, sweaters, fleece wear, snow boots, and other accessories.

Sun Ice uses the latest computer technology to design and produce its garments, including computerized pattern making and fabric cutting. The Sun Ice emphasis on quality has paid off. Its products have been chosen by 12 Canadian national teams in sports such as skiing, skating, bobsledding, and canoeing. In addition, Sun Ice garments were worn by five Mount Everest expeditions. In 1986 the company went public, generating funds to construct a $6 million, 68,000-square-foot manufacturing facility.

Sun Ice's sales in 1988 were $24 million, $4 million of which came from growing sales in the U.S. market. Corresponding sales figures in 1989 were $30 million and $7 million. The company's sales forecast for 1990 was $37 million. Due to a recent free-trade agreement between the two countries, the 25 percent duty charged on products shipped from Canada to the United States (and vice versa) will be reduced by 2.5 percentage points a year until it disappears after 10 years. As a result, the prices of Sun Ice's products should be increasingly competitive in the American market and growing sales are expected.

The basis of the Sun Ice marketing program since the establishment of the company has been its close involvement in the pursuits of active Canadians and support for retailers who carry Sun Ice products. Rather than place its marketing emphasis on direct-to-consumer media advertising, the company has promoted its close association with athletes and has been heavily involved in sponsorship. Sun Ice has sponsored major sporting events, including the American Ski Classic at Vail in Colorado, the Labatt's Interski, the Rothmans/Porsche Challenge car racing series, the Everest Express, the American Ski Classic, the North American Pro Ski Tour, and the Powder 8 World Championships.

Some years ago Sun Ice launched the Adult Lift Ticket Hang Tag promotion and the Junior Learn-to-Ski program. With the purchase of a Sun Ice jacket, the purchaser is given the opportunity to ski free for one day. In cooperation with retailers, Sun Ice has concentrated on developing the sport of skiing.

The largest promotional program in which Sun Ice has participated was the 1988 Winter Olympic Games in Calgary. Research conducted in connection with earlier Olympic Games showed that 83 percent of adults remember products promoted with Olympic involvement. Almost one-half of respondents to research surveys said that Olympic sponsorship raised their opinions of the sponsors' products and one-third said they were inclined to buy products that were associated with the Olympics.

The Calgary Olympics were generally considered a success. Sun Ice jackets were worn by thousands of officials and athletes and by representatives of General Motors, 3M, ABC, *Sports Illustrated*, Labatt's, IBM, and Petro-Canada, and were seen by an estimated 1.5 billion television viewers worldwide. Afterward Rempel and the senior marketing executives of Sun Ice had to decide how best to capitalize on the exposure their products had enjoyed.

## QUESTIONS

1. a. Which of the four alternative growth strategies—market penetration, market development, product development, and diversification—has Sun Ice emphasized in recent years? Was this a sound strategy?
   b. Which of the alternative strategies should Sun Ice stress in the next 3 to 5 years?
2. a. Should Sun Ice reevaluate its policy of not using media advertising to reach consumers directly?
   b. If Sun Ice wants to increase its visibility (and sales) in the United States, would a promotional program built around publicity and sponsorships be sufficient?

## CASE 24

# SEARS, ROEBUCK & CO.* In Search of Effective Strategic Marketing Plans

Looking ahead to the rest of the 1990s—and beyond to the twenty-first century—the top management of Sears, Roebuck & Co. is working feverishly to create a recipe for success in the intensely competitive retailing field. As the 1990s began, the company's chairman, Edward Brennan, and the head of its retail group, Michael Bozic, had not yet found the right mix of ingredients. Pressure on the giant chain and its executives was intense.

In the early 1970s Sears concentrated on middle-income markets and had strong store loyalty among these consumers. As a result, it was the largest retailer in the United States and its profits were strong. Among the top five general-merchandise retail chains, Sears held a commanding 44 percent market share, far ahead of the 21 percent held by second-place J. C. Penney.

During the latter part of the 1970s and throughout the 1980s, Sears' rate of growth, customer loyalty,

and market share all went down as the company found itself squeezed by three primary types of competition:

- Having lower expenses than Sears, discount-house chains such as K mart and Wal-Mart attracted many customers with lower prices.
- New specialty-store chains such as The Limited, Circuit City, and Toys "Я" Us gained footholds in the market by offering deep assortments in selected product categories.
- Other department store chains such as J. C. Penney, Montgomery Ward, Dayton Hudson, and the May Company increased their shares by sharpening their images, concentrating on fashion-oriented merchandise and some hard-goods lines.

By the end of the 1980s, Sears' market share among the top five general-merchandise chains dropped 14 points to 29 percent. K mart was positioned to overtake Sears as the largest retailer, and Wal-Mart was rapidly closing the gap as well. Profits from Sears' retail operations fell almost 8 percent per year during the late 1980s.

Although not performing at its former levels,

*Based on Kate Fitzgerald, "Sears' Plan on the Ropes," *Advertising Age*, Jan. 8, 1990, pp. 1, 42; Michael J. McDermott, "Can the Big Store Be Fixed?" *Adweek's Marketing Week*, Oct. 30, 1989, p. 2; and Brian Bremmer and Michael Oneal, "The Big Store's Big Trauma," *Business Week*, July 10, 1989, pp. 50–51.

Sears' size and strength should not be underestimated. Its total sales exceed $50 billion, with about 60 percent coming from retailing activities (catalog sales and 825 stores across the United States). Sears also owns other well-known companies—Allstate Insurance, Dean Witter financial services, and Coldwell Banker real estate. Allstate is highly profitable. In fact, it generated more than one-half of the company's total profits in 1988. Also, Sears' Discover credit card, launched in 1985, has moved steadily toward profitability. Nevertheless, it appeared that Sears' retailing activities were at the bottom and looking up.

Sears still aimed to serve and satisfy the broad middle-income market. It intended to satisfy consumers' desires for fashion in soft goods, reliability in hard goods, and quality and value in all products. In refining Sears' marketing mix, Bozic emphasized several strategies intended to make the chain more competitive against discount houses, specialty stores, and department stores. Two of the strategies—refurbished stores and friendly service—are essential to long-term success for almost any retailer.

In adopting a third strategy, Sears departed from its long-standing tradition of carrying only its own well-known private brands. Most of these brands, such as Kenmore appliances, Craftsman tools, and DieHard batteries, are recognized for high quality and good value. However, shoppers wanted national brands as well as private brands. So, in the late 1980s, Sears began to add more national brands like Sony, Levi's, RCA, OshKosh B'Gosh, and GE.

Sears plans to extend this strategy by creating in each of its stores six large "power" departments in consumer electronics (TVs, stereos), hardware, apparel, and other key lines. Its first step in this direction was to establish Brand Central departments within some stores. These departments feature both national and private brands in several product lines, including consumer electronics, appliances, computers, and telephones. Early results have been encouraging as sales at stores with Brand Central departments were up about 15 percent.

A fourth strategy, which generated much publicity and controversy, was labeled "everyday low prices." Like many traditional retailers, Sears sold some merchandise at full price and then used promotional sales featuring temporarily reduced prices to generate more shoppers and added sales volume. In the 1980s, however, some successful retailers (notably Wal-Mart and Toys "Я" Us) relied less on promotional sales and more on consistently low prices.

In early 1989, Sears closed all of its stores for 2 days, changed the price tags on most items, and reopened with "everyday low prices." Most of the prices were between the "regular" and the "sale" prices charged previously. In Brennan's words, this approach to pricing was "an idea whose time has come." Sears' ads urged consumers to think of the new approach "as a sale that never ends!" The logic of everyday low prices is that busy consumers benefit because they do not have to shop all over looking for reduced prices. Stores may attain higher sales. And they definitely should have lower expenses because there are fewer promotional sales and, as a result, less re-marking of price tags and reduced levels of advertising.

Despite great optimism and extensive advertising to tell consumers about Sears' new way of pricing, the strategy produced mixed results. Sears' sales jumped in the first months following the pricing change. For the rest of 1989, however, the news was

**631**

mostly bad. Sales leveled off and profits dropped. Critics suggest that was inevitable because Sears had relatively high operating expenses and, as a result, lower prices squeezed its profit margin. One set of statistics showed Sears with an overhead of about 32 percent of sales, compared to K mart's 23 percent and Wal-Mart's 17 percent.

Many consumers seemed to be apathetic or confused about Sears' new approach to pricing. With numerous chains touting "everyday low prices," Sears' message may not have had a lasting impact on some consumers. The retailer may have contributed to the confusion by running occasional promotional sales soon after the pricing change, even though the new approach supposedly eliminated the need for temporary price reductions. Sears apparently did not convince even its regular shoppers that its prices were lower than competitors'. According to an *Advertising Age*/Gallup Organization poll, 64 percent of Sears' customers who had an opinion thought Sears' everyday low prices were about the same as similar retailers', 14 percent judged them to be higher, and 21 percent viewed them as lower.

As the 1980s ended, Sears' financial performance was marginal at best. In 1989, Sears earned $1.5 bil-lion on sales of almost $54 billion. Sales were up 7 percent over December 1988, but profits increased only 4 percent over 1988.

Further modification of Sears' strategies is anticipated. Among the strategic options to consider are targeting different consumers, such as quality-conscious shoppers, and changing its marketing mix, perhaps deemphasizing everyday low prices and emphasizing the new variety of national brands.

## QUESTIONS

1. Evaluate the effectiveness of Sears' everyday low pricing. What did the chain do correctly with this key strategy? What did it do incorrectly?
2. Sears consists of several strategic business units (SBUs), notably Sears' retail group, Allstate, Coldwell Banker, and Dean Witter. Considering the recent performance and future prospects for its department stores, which of the following four strategies should Sears adopt for this SBU—invest, protect, harvest, or divest?
3. For Sears to gain a competitive advantage over K mart, J. C. Penney, Wal-Mart, and other significant competitors, what major target-market and marketing-mix strategies must it adopt?

# GLOSSARY

**accessory equipment**  In the business market, capital goods used in the operation of an industrial firm.

**actual self**  The way you really see yourself. To be distinguished from *ideal self*.

**ad**  See *advertisement*.

**administered vertical marketing system**  A distribution system in which channel control is maintained through the economic power of one firm in the channel.

**administration**  See *management*.

**adoption process**  The stages that an individual goes through in deciding whether or not to accept an innovation.

**advertisement**  A sponsor-identified message regarding a product or organization that can be verbal and/or visual, and is disseminated through one or more media. Same as *ad*.

**advertising**  All activities involved in presenting to a group a nonpersonal, sponsor-identified message regarding a product or organization.

**advertising agency**  An independent company rendering specialized services in advertising in particular and in marketing in general.

**advertising allowance**  A payment or cash discount offered by a manufacturer to a retailer to encourage the retailer to advertise or prominently display the manufacturer's product.

**advertising campaign**  The total advertising program for a product or brand that involves coordination, a central theme, and specific goals.

**advertising media**  The communications vehicles (such as newspapers, radio, and television) that carry advertising.

**agent middleman**  A firm that never actually owns products that are being distributed but does actively assist in the transfer of title.

**agent wholesaling middleman**  An independent firm that primarily engages in wholesaling and does not take title to the products being distributed but does actively negotiate their sale or purchase on behalf of other firms.

**agribusiness**  The business side of farming. Usually involves large, highly mechanized farming operations.

**AIDA**  A sequence of steps in various forms of promotion, notably personal selling and advertising, consisting of attracting *A*ttention, holding *I*nterest, arousing *D*esire, and generating buyer *A*ction.

**annual marketing plan**  A written document that details the planned marketing activities for the given business unit or product for the given year.

**assumptive close**  In personal selling, the stage in the selling process when the sales person can often finalize the sale by asking questions that will settle the details of the purchase.

**attitude**  A learned predisposition to respond to an object or class of objects in a consistently favorable or unfavorable way.

**auction company**  An agent wholesaling middleman that provides (1) auctioneers who do the selling and (2) physical facilities for displaying the sellers' products.

**automated merchandising**  See *automatic vending*.

**automatic vending**  A form of nonstore retailing where the products are sold through a machine with no personal contact between the buyer and seller. Same as *automated merchandising*.

**average revenue**  The unit price at a given level of unit sales. It is calculated by dividing total revenue by the number of units sold.

**average total cost**  The total cost divided by the number of units produced.

**balance of trade**  In international business, the difference between the value of a nation's imports and the value of its exports.

**base price**  The price of one unit of the product at its point of production or resale. Same as *list price*.

**battle of the brands**  Market competition between producers' brands and middlemen's brands. In recent years, generic products have entered this competitive struggle.

**brand**  A name, term, symbol, special design, or some combination of these elements that is intended to identify the products of one seller or a group of sellers.

**brand competition**  Competition among marketers of branded products that are very similar and may be substituted for each other.

**brand licensing**  See *trademark licensing*.

**brand manager**  See *product manager*.

**brand mark**  The part of a brand that appears in the

form of a symbol, picture, design, or distinctive color or type of lettering.

**brand name** The part of a brand that can be vocalized—words, letters, and/or numbers.

**breadth of product mix** The number of product lines offered for sale by a firm.

**break-even point** The level of output at which revenues equal costs, assuming a certain selling price.

**broadened marketing concept** A marketing philosophy that incorporates consumer orientation, coordination of marketing activities, achieving the organization's objectives, and satisfying societal wants affected by the organization's activities.

**broker** An independent agent wholesaling middleman that brings buyers and sellers together and provides market information to either party.

**build-up method** See *task method*.

**business marketing** The marketing of goods and services to business users.

**business product** A product that is intended for purchase and use in producing other products or in rendering services in a business.

**business user** An organization that buys goods or services to resell, use in its own business, or make other products.

**buy classes** Three typical buying situations in the business market—namely new-task buying, modified rebuy, and straight rebuy.

**buyers** The people in a buying center who select the suppliers, arrange the terms of sale, and process the actual purchase orders.

**buying center** All of the people in an organization who participate in the buying-decision process.

**buying-decision process** The series of logical stages a prospective purchaser goes through when faced with a buying problem. The stages differ for consumers and organizations.

**buying motive** The reason why a person buys a specific product or shops at a specific store.

**campaign** A coordinated series of promotional efforts built around a single theme and designed to reach a pre-determined goal.

**campaign theme** In promotion, the central idea or focal point in a promotional campaign.

**cartel** A group of companies that produce similar products and combine to restrain competition in manufacturing and marketing.

**cash discount** A deduction from list price for paying a bill within a specified period of time.

**catalog showroom** A type of retail institution that offers a complete catalog and some sample items in the showroom and the remaining inventory in an attached warehouse. It offers a broad but shallow assortment of merchandise, emphasizes low prices, and offers few customer services.

**category killer store** A type of retail institution that has a narrow but very deep assortment, emphasizes low prices, and few to moderate customer services. It is designed to "destroy" all competition in a specific product category.

**category-management system** A form of marketing organization in which an executive position called a category manager is established for each product category, and all the competing brand managers in each group report to this executive.

**cease-and-desist order** A Federal Trade Commission enforcement device requiring a firm to remove from circulation advertising deemed deceptive.

**channel conflict** A situation in which one channel member perceives another channel member to be acting in a way that prevents the first member from achieving its distribution objectives.

**channel control** The ability to influence the behavior of other channel members.

**channels manager** A person who is formally in charge of an organization's channels.

**client market** Individuals and/or organizations that are the recipients of a nonprofit organization's money and/or services. Same as *recipient market*.

**closing** In personal selling, the stage in the selling process when the sales person gets the buyer to agree to buy.

**cognitive dissonance** The anxiety created by the fact that in most purchases the alternative selected has some negative features and the alternatives not selected have some positive features.

**combination salary plan** The method of sales force compensation that combines a base salary with a commission related to some task(s).

**commercial environment** All of the marketing organizations and individuals who attempt to communicate with consumers.

**commission merchant** An independent agent wholesaling middleman, used primarily in the marketing of agricultural products, that may physically handle the seller's products in central markets and has authority regarding prices and terms of sale.

**communication process** A system of verbal and/or nonverbal transmission of information between a sender and a receiver. The four elements are message, source, communication channel, and receiver.

**comparative advertising** Selective demand advertising in which the advertiser either directly (by

**80-20 principle** A situation in which a large proportion of a company's marketing units (products, territories, customers) accounts for a small share of the company's volume or profit, and vice versa.

**elastic demand** A price-volume relationship such that a change of one unit on the price scale results in a change of more than one unit on the volume scale.

**encoding** The process of translating an idea into a message in the form of words, pictures, or both in order that it can be transmitted from a sender to a receiver.

**evaluation** The process of determining what happened, why it happened, and what to do about it.

**exchange** The voluntary act of providing a person or organization something of value in order to acquire something else of value in return.

**exclusive dealing** The practice by which a manufacturer prohibits its dealers from carrying products of competing manufacturers.

**exclusive distribution** A strategy in which a producer agrees to sell its product to only a single wholesaling middleman and/or retailer in a given market.

**exclusive territory** The practice by which a manufacturer requires each middleman to sell only to customers located within the middleman's assigned territory.

**executive judgment** A method of sales forecasting that consists of obtaining opinions regarding future sales volume from one or more executives.

**expected price** The price at which customers consciously or unconsciously value a product—what they think the product is worth.

**experimental method** A method of gathering primary data in which the researcher is able to observe the results of changing one variable in a situation while holding all others constant.

**express warranty** A statement in written or spoken words regarding restitution from seller to customer if the seller's product does not perform up to reasonable expectations.

**fabricating materials** Business goods that have received some processing and will undergo further processing as they become part of another product.

**fabricating parts** Business goods that already have been processed to some extent and will be assembled in their present form (with no further change) as part of another product.

**factory outlet** A special type of off-price retail institution that is owned by a manufacturer and usually sells only that manufacturer's clearance items, regular merchandise, and perhaps even otherwise unavailable items.

**fad** A short-lived fashion that is usually based on some novelty feature.

**family** A group of two or more people related by blood, marriage, or adoption living together in a household.

**family brands** A branding strategy in which a group of products is given a single brand.

**family life cycle** The series of life stages that a family goes through, starting with young single people and progressing through married stages with young and then older children, and ending with older married and single people.

**fashion** A style that is popularly accepted by groups of people over a reasonably long period of time.

**fashion-adoption process** The process by which a style becomes popular in a market; similar to diffusion of an innovation.

**fashion cycle** Wavelike movements representing the introduction, rise, popular acceptance, and decline in popularity of a given style.

**fashion obsolescence** See *style obsolescence*.

**Federal Trade Commission Act** A federal law, passed in 1914, prohibiting unfair competition and establishing the Federal Trade Commission.

**field experiment** An experiment in which the researcher has only limited control of the environment because the experiment is conducted in a real-world setting.

**field warehousing** A form of public warehousing that provides a financial service for a seller. Same as *custodian warehousing*.

**fishyback freight service** The service of transporting loaded truck trailers or railroad freight cars on barges or ships.

**fixed cost** A constant cost regardless of how many items are produced or sold.

**flexible-price strategy** A pricing strategy in which a company sells similar quantities of merchandise to similar buyers at different prices. Same as *variable-price strategy*.

**F.O.B. (free on board) factory price** A geographic pricing strategy whereby the buyer pays all freight charges from the F.O.B. location to the destination. Same as *F.O.B. mill price*.

**F.O.B. mill price** See *F.O.B. factory price*.

**focus group** A preliminary data-gathering method involving an interactive interview of four to ten people.

**form utility**  The utility that is created when a good is produced.

**forward dating**  A combination of a seasonal discount and a cash discount under which a buyer places an order and receives shipment during the off-season but does not have to pay the bill until after the season has started and some sales revenue has been generated.

**fragmented markets**  Small market segments that can be identified and isolated through increasingly sophisticated demographic, behavioral, and geographic data.

**franchise system**  The combination of franchisor, franchisees, and franchisor-owned business units.

**franchising**  A type of contractual vertical marketing system that involves a continuing relationship in which a franchisor (the parent company) provides the right to use a trademark plus various management assistance in opening and operating a business in return for financial considerations from a franchisee (the owner of the individual business unit).

**freight absorption**  A geographic pricing strategy whereby the seller pays for (absorbs) some of the freight charges in order to penetrate more distant markets.

**freight forwarder**  A specialized transportation agency that consolidates less-than-carload or less-than-truckload shipments into carload or truckload quantities and provides door-to-door shipping service.

**full-cost allocation**  In a marketing cost analysis, an accounting approach wherein all expenses—direct and indirect—are allocated to the marketing units being analyzed.

**full-service wholesaler**  An independent merchant middleman that normally performs a full range of wholesaling functions.

**functional discount**  See *trade discount.*

**gatekeepers**  The people in a buying center who control the flow of purchasing information within the organization and between the buying firm and potential vendors.

**generic product**  A product that is packaged in a plain label and is sold with no advertising and without a brand name. The product goes by its generic name, such as "tomatoes" or "paper towels."

**goal**  See *objective.*

**good**  A set of tangible physical attributes assembled in an identifiable form to provide want-satisfaction to customers.

**government market**  The segment of the business market that includes federal, state, and local units buying for government institutions such as schools, offices, hospitals, and military bases.

**grade label**  Identification of the quality (grade) of a product by means of a letter, number, or word.

**heterogeneity of a service**  A characteristic of a service indicating that each unit is somewhat different from other "units" of the same service.

**high involvement**  A purchase decision that involves all six stages of the buying decision process.

**horizontal business market**  A situation where a given product is usable in a wide variety of industries.

**horizontal conflict**  A form of channel conflict occurring between firms on the same level of distribution—between middlemen of the same type or between different types of middlemen.

**horizontal cooperative advertising**  Advertising that involves firms on the same level of distribution sharing the cost.

**household**  A single person, a family, or any group of unrelated persons who occupy a housing unit.

**hypermarket**  A type of exceedingly large-scale retailing institution that has a very broad and moderately deep product assortment, emphasizes low prices, and offers some customer services.

**hypothesis**  A tentative supposition or a possible solution to a problem.

**iceberg principle**  A concept related to performance evaluation stating that the summary data (tip of the iceberg) regarding an activity may hide significant variations among segments of this activity.

**id**  In Freudian psychology, the part of the mind that houses the basic instinctive drives, many of which are antisocial.

**ideal self**  The way you want to be seen or would like to see yourself. To be distinguished from *actual self.*

**illustration**  The pictorial portion of an ad.

**image utility**  The emotional or psychological value that a person attaches to a product or brand because of the reputation or social standing of that product or brand.

**implementation**  The process of organizing for the marketing effort, staffing this organization, and directing the operational efforts of these people as they carry out the strategic plans.

**implied warranty** An intended but unstated assurance regarding restitution from seller to customer if the seller's product does not perform up to reasonable expectations.

**import-export agent** An agent wholesaling middleman that arranges for distribution of goods in a foreign country.

**impulse buying** Purchases made with little or no advance planning.

**independent retailer** A company with a single retail store that is not affiliated with any type of contractual vertical marketing system.

**indirect-action advertising** Product advertising that is intended to inform or remind consumers about a product and its benefits.

**indirect costs** Expenses that are incurred jointly for more than one marketing unit and therefore cannot be totally charged to one market segment.

**indirect distribution** A channel consisting of producer, final customer, and at least one level of middleman.

**indirect tests** (in advertising) Measures of advertising effects that use something other than sales volume.

**inelastic demand** A price-volume relationship such that a change of one unit on the price scale results in a change of less than one unit on the volume scale.

**influencers** The people in a buying center who set the specifications and aspects of buying decisions because of their technical expertise, financial position, or political power in the organization.

**informal investigation** The stage in a marketing research study at which information is gathered from people outside the company—middlemen, competitors, advertising agencies, and consumers.

**innovators** The first group—a venturesome group —of people to adopt something new (good, service).

**input performance measures** In sales force performance, indications of effort expended.

**inseparability** A characteristic of a service indicating that it cannot be separated from the creator-seller of the service.

**inside order taker** A selling job in which the primary function of the sales person is to take orders in person or by phone inside a store or other type of business.

**installations** In the business market, long-lived, expensive, major industrial capital goods that directly affect the scale of operation of an industrial firm.

**institutional advertising** Advertising designed either to present information about the advertiser's business or to create a good attitude—build goodwill—toward the organization.

**intangibility** A characteristic of a service indicating that it has no physical attributes and, as a result, is impossible for customers to taste, feel, see, hear, or smell before buying.

**intensity of distribution** The number of middlemen used by a producer at the retailing and wholesaling levels of distribution.

**intensive distribution** A strategy in which a producer sells its product in every available outlet where a consumer might reasonably look for it. Same as *mass distribution.*

**inverse demand** A price-volume relationship such that the higher the price, the greater the unit sales.

**involvement level** The amount of time and effort the consumer invests in a buying decision.

**joint venture** A partnership arrangement in which a foreign operation is owned in part by an American company and in part by a foreign company.

**"just-in-time" concept** An inventory control system that involves buying parts and supplies in small quantities just in time for use in production and then producing in quantities just in time for sale.

**label** The part of a product that carries verbal information about the product or the seller.

**laboratory experiment** An experiment in which the researcher has complete control over the environment during the experiment.

**laggards** Tradition-bound people who are the last to adopt an innovation.

**late majority** The skeptical group of innovation adopters who adopt a new idea late in the game.

**layout** The physical arrangement of all of the elements of an ad.

**leader pricing** A pricing and promotional strategy in which temporary price cuts are made on well-known items with the idea that these "specials" (leaders) will attract customers to the store.

**learning** Changes in behavior resulting from previous experiences.

**leasing** A situation, found in both business and consumer markets, in which a good is rented rather than purchased outright.

**licensing** A business arrangement whereby one firm sells to another firm (for a fee or royalty) the right to use the first company's brand, patents, or manufacturing processes.

**limited-function wholesaler** A merchant wholesaler that performs only selected wholesaling functions.

**limited-line store**   A type of retailing institution that has a narrow but deep product assortment, and its customer services tend to vary from store to store.

**list price**   See *base price.*

**logistics**   See *physical distribution.*

**loss leaders**   Products whose prices are cut with the idea that they will attract customers to the store.

**low involvement**   A purchase decision in which the consumer moves directly from need recognition to purchase, skipping the stages in between.

**mail survey**   The method of gathering data by means of a questionnaire mailed to respondents and, when completed, returned by mail.

**management**   The process of planning, implementing, and evaluating the efforts of a group of people working toward a common goal. Same as *administration.*

**manufacturers' agent**   An independent agent wholesaling middleman that sells part or all of a manufacturer's product mix in an assigned geographic territory.

**manufacturer's sales branch**   A manufacturer's sales facility that carries a stock of the product being sold.

**manufacturer's sales facility**   An establishment that primarily engages in wholesaling and is owned and operated by a manufacturer but is physically separated from manufacturing plants.

**manufacturer's sales office**   A manufacturer's sales facility that does not carry a stock of the product being sold.

**marginal analysis**   A method of price setting that considers both demand and costs to determine the best price for profit maximization.

**marginal cost**   The cost of producing and selling one more unit; that is, the cost of the last unit produced or sold.

**marginal revenue**   The income derived from the sale of the last unit.

**market**   People or organizations with wants to satisfy, money to spend, and the willingness to spend it.

**market aggregation**   A strategy whereby an organization treats its total market as a unit—that is, as one mass market whose parts are considered to be alike in all major respects.

**market development**   A product-market growth strategy in which a company continues to sell its present products, but to a new market.

**market factor**   An item or element that (1) exists in a market, (2) may be measured quantitatively, and (3) is related to the demand for a good or service.

**market-factor analysis**   A sales forecasting method based on the assumption that future demand for a product is related to the behavior of certain market factors.

**market index**   A market factor expressed as a percentage, or in another quantitative form, relative to some base figure.

**market penetration**   A product-market growth strategy in which a company tries to sell more of its present products to its present markets.

**market-penetration pricing**   See *penetration pricing.*

**market potential**   The total sales volume that all organizations selling a product during a stated time period in a specific market could expect to achieve under ideal conditions.

**market segmentation**   The process of dividing the total market for a product into several parts, each of which tends to be homogeneous in all significant aspects.

**market share**   The proportion of total sales of a product during a stated time period in a specific market that is captured by a single firm. Market share can refer to entire industries, narrow segments, or particular geographic areas and also can apply to past, present, or future time periods.

**market-share analysis**   A detailed analysis of the company's share of the market in total as well as by product line and market segment.

**market-skimming pricing**   See *skimming pricing.*

**marketing**   A total system of business activities designed to plan, price, promote, and distribute want-satisfying products to target markets in order to achieve organizational objectives.

**marketing audit**   A comprehensive review and evaluation of the marketing function in an organization—its philosophy, environment, goals, strategies, organizational structure, human and financial resources, and performance.

**marketing concept**   A philosophy of doing business that emphasizes customer orientation and coordination of marketing activities in order to achieve the organization's performance objectives.

**marketing cost analysis**   A detailed study of the "operating expenses" section of a company's profit and loss statement.

**marketing information system**   An on-going organized set of procedures and methods designed to generate, analyze, disseminate, store, and retrieve information for use in making marketing decisions.

**marketing intermediary** An independent business organization that directly aids in the flow of products between a marketing organization and its markets.

**marketing mix** A combination of the four elements—product, pricing structure, distribution system, and promotional activities—that comprise a company's marketing program.

**marketing-orientation stage** The third state in the evolution of marketing management, in which a company focuses on the needs of its customers and carries out a broad range of marketing activities.

**marketing research** The process of specifying, assembling, and analyzing information used to identify and define marketing opportunities and problems; generate, refine, and evaluate marketing actions; monitor marketing performance; and improve understanding of marketing as a process.

**Maslow's needs hierarchy** A needs structure consisting of five levels and organized according to the order in which people seek need gratification.

**mass distribution** See *intensive distribution*.

**merchant middleman** A firm that actually takes title to (i.e., owns) products that are being distributed.

**merchant wholesaler** An independently owned firm that primarily engages in wholesaling and ordinarily takes title to the products being distributed. Same as *wholesaler*.

**Metropolitan Statistical Area (MSA)** An urban area in the U.S. with a center of population of at least 50,000 and a total MSA population of at least 100,000.

**middleman** A firm that renders services directly related to the purchase and/or sale of a product as it flows from producer to consumer.

**middleman's brand** A brand owned by a retailer or a wholesaler. Same as *private brand*.

**mingles** Households that consist of unmarried couples living together.

**missionary seller** A selling job in which the sales people are not expected to solicit orders but are expected to influence decision makers by building goodwill, performing promotional activities, and providing service to customers. In pharmaceuticals marketing, called detail sales person.

**modified rebuy** In the business market, a purchasing situation between a new task and a straight rebuy in terms of time required, information needed, and alternatives considered.

**motive** A need sufficiently stimulated that an individual is moved to seek satisfaction. Same as *drive*.

**multiple buying influences** A situation in which a purchasing decision is influenced by more than one person in the buyer's organization.

**multiple-segment strategy** A strategy that involves two or more groups of potential customers selected as target markets.

**national brand** See *producer's brand*.

**need recognition** The stage in the buying decision process in which the consumer is moved to action by a need.

**new product** A vague term that may refer to (1) really innovative, truly unique products; (2) replacements for existing products that are significantly different from existing ones; or (3) imitative products that are new to the given firm.

**new-product development process** Developmental stages that a new product goes through, starting with idea generation and continuing through idea screening, business analysis, limited production, test-marketing, and eventually commercialization (full-scale production and marketing).

**new-product strategy** A plan as to what role new products are to play in helping the company achieve its corporate and marketing goals.

**new-task buying** In the business market, a purchasing situation in which a company for the first time considers buying a given item.

**niche marketing** A strategy in which goods and services are tailored to meet the needs of small market segments.

**noncumulative discount** A quantity discount based on the size of an individual order of products.

**nonprice competition** A strategy in which a firm tries to compete based on some factor other than price—for example, promotion, product differentiation, or variety of services.

**nonprofit organization** An organization in which profit is not an intended organizational goal.

**nonstore retailing** Retailing activities resulting in transactions that occur away from a retail store.

**objective** A desired outcome. Same as *goal*.

**observational method** Gathering data by observing personally or mechanically the actions of a person.

**odd pricing** A form of psychological pricing that consists of setting prices at odd amounts ($4.99 rather than $5.00, for example) in the belief that these seemingly lower prices will result in larger sales volume.

**off-price retailer** A type of retail institution, often found in the areas of apparel and shoes, that has a narrow and deep product assortment, emphasizes low prices, and offers few customer services.

**off-price retailing** A strategy of selling well-known brands below the manufacturer's recommended retail price.

**one-price strategy** A strategy under which a seller charges the same price to all customers of the same type who buy the same quantity of goods.

**operating supplies** The "convenience goods" of the business market—short-lived, low-priced items purchased with a minimum of time and effort.

**organizational mission** The first step in strategic planning that defines the organization by asking the question, "What business are we in?"

**organizational portfolio analysis** A key step in strategic planning that identifies the present status of each strategic business unit and determines its future role in the company.

**organizational strategies** Broad, basic plans of action by which an organization intends to achieve its goals and fulfill its mission. These plans are for (1) the total organization in a small, single-product company or (2) each SBU in a large, multiproduct or multibusiness organization.

**output performance measures** In sales force performance, indication of results produced.

**outside order taker** A selling job in which sales people are primarily going to customers in the field.

**packaging** The activities in product planning that involve designing and producing the container or wrapper for a product.

**parcel-post pricing** See *zone-delivered price.*

**past-sales analysis** A method of sales forecasting that applies a flat percentage increase to the volume achieved last year, or to the average volume of the past few years, to predict future volume.

**patronage buying motives** The reasons why a consumer chooses to shop at a certain store.

**patterned interview** In sales force selection, an interviewing procedure in which the questions are planned in advance to ensure that all important issues are covered.

**penetration pricing** A pricing strategy in which a low initial price is set to reach the mass market immediately. Same as *market-penetration pricing.*

**percentage-of-sales method** A method of determining the promotional budget in which the amount is set as a certain percentage of past or forecasted future sales.

**perception** Collecting and processing information from the environment in order to give meaning to the world around us.

**perishability** A characteristic of a service indicating that it is highly perishable and cannot be stored.

**personal interview** A face-to-face method of gathering data in a survey.

**personal selling** The personal communication of information to persuade a prospective customer to buy a good, service, idea, or other product.

**personality** An individual's pattern of traits that influences behavioral responses.

**physical distribution** Activities involved in the flow of products as they move physically from producer to consumer or industrial user. Same as *logistics.*

**physical distribution management** The development and operation of efficient flow systems for products.

**piggyback freight service** The service of transporting loaded truck trailers on railroad flatcars.

**pioneering advertising** Primary-demand advertising in the introductory stage of the product life cycle.

**place utility** The utility created when a product is made readily accessible to potential customers.

**planned obsolescence** A product strategy designed to make an existing product out of date and thus to increase the market for replacement products. There are two forms: technological and style.

**planning** The process of deciding now what we are going to do later, including when and how we are going to do it.

**positioning** A retailer's strategies and actions related to favorably distinguishing itself from competitors in the minds (and hearts) of selected groups of consumers.

**possession utility** The utility created when a customer buys the product—that is, ownership is transferred to the buyer.

**postage-stamp pricing** See *uniform delivered price.*

**postpurchase behavior** Efforts by the consumer to reduce the anxiety often accompanying purchase decisions.

**postpurchase service** The final stage of the selling process, including delivery, financing, installation, routine maintenance, employee training, billing, and other areas important to customer satisfaction.

**price** The amount of money and/or products needed to acquire some combination of another product and its accompanying services.

**price competition** A strategy in which a firm regularly offers prices that are as low as possible, usually accompanied by a minimum of services.

**price lining** A retail pricing strategy whereby a store selects a limited number of prices and sells each item only at one of these selected prices.

**pricing objective** The goals that management tries to reach with its pricing structure and strategies.

**primary data** Original data gathered specifically for the project at hand.

**primary-demand advertising** Advertising designed to stimulate demand for a generic product.

**Primary Metropolitan Statistical Area (PMSA)** About 80 large MSAs in the U.S. that have a population of at least 1 million and are part of a giant urban center.

**private brand** See *middleman's brand*.

**private warehouse** A warehouse that is owned and operated by the firm whose products are being stored and handled at the facility.

**processing in transit** A railroad in-transit shipping privilege under which a shipper can unload its product en route, have it processed, and then reload it to the final destination while being charged only the carload rate from the original shipping point to the final destination.

**producer's brand** A brand that is owned by a manufacturer or other producer. Same as *national brand*.

**product** A set of tangible attributes, including packaging, color, price, quality, and brand, plus the services and reputation of the seller. A product may be a good, service, place, person, or idea.

**product advertising** Advertising intended to inform or stimulate the market about an organization's products.

**product development** A product-market growth strategy that calls for a company to develop new products to sell to its existing markets.

**product differentiation** The strategy in which one firm promotes the features of its product over competitors' brands offered to the same market.

**product-liability claim** A legal action alleging that an illness, accident, or death resulted from the named product because it was harmful, faulty, or inadequately labeled.

**product life cycle** The stages a product goes through from its introduction, to its growth and maturity, to its eventual decline and death (withdrawal from the market or deletion from the company's offerings).

**product line** A broad group of products, intended for essentially similar uses and possessing reasonably similar physical characteristics.

**product manager** An executive responsible for planning the marketing program for a given product or group of products. Same as *brand manager*.

**product mix** All products offered for sale by a company.

**product positioning** The decisions and activities involved in developing the intended image (in the customer's mind) for a product in relation to competitive products and to other products marketed by the same company.

**product-related segmentation** Market segmentation based on product usage rate or product benefits desired by consumers.

**production-orientation stage** The first stage in the evolution of marketing management, in which the basic assumption is that making a good product will ensure business success.

**promotion** The element in an organization's marketing mix that is used to inform, persuade, and remind the market regarding the organization and/or its products.

**promotional allowance** A price reduction granted by the seller as payment for promotional services rendered by the buyer.

**promotional mix** The combination of personal selling, advertising, sales promotion, publicity, and public relations that is intended to help an organization achieve its marketing objectives.

**prospecting** The stage in the personal selling process that involves developing a list of potential customers.

**psychographic segmentation** Market segmentation based on some aspect(s) of consumers' personality, lifestyle, or social class.

**psychographics** A concept in consumer behavior that describes consumers in terms of a combination of psychological and sociological influences.

**public relations** A broad communications effort designed to build or maintain a favorable image for an organization with its various publics.

**public-service advertising** Advertising designed to improve the quality of life and indicate that the advertiser is a responsible member of the community.

**public warehouse** An independent firm that provides storage and handling facilities.

**publicity** A news presentation for a product or organization presented in any medium that is not paid for and has the credibility of editorial material.

**"pull" promotional strategy** Promotional effort directed primarily at end users so they will ask middlemen for the product.

**"push" promotional strategy** Promotional effort directed primarily at middlemen that are the next link forward in distribution channels.

**qualifying** The stage in the personal selling process in which the sales person determines if the prospect has both the willingness and capability to buy.

**qualitative performance bases**  In sales force performance, judgmental indications of inputs and/or outputs.

**quantitative performance bases**  In sales force performance, numerical measure of inputs and/or outputs.

**quantity discount**  A reduction from list price when large quantities are purchased; offered to encourage buyers to purchase in large quantities.

**rack jobber**  A merchant wholesaler that provides its customers with the display case or rack, stocks it, and price-marks the merchandise.

**random sample**  A sample that is selected in such a way that every unit in the defined universe has an equal chance of being selected.

**raw materials**  Business goods that have not been processed in any way and that will become part of another product.

**recipient market**  See *client market.*

**reciprocity**  The situation of "I'll buy from you if you'll buy from me."

**reference group**  A group of people who influence a person's attitudes, values, and behavior.

**refusal to deal**  A situation in which a manufacturer desiring to select and perhaps control its channels may refuse to sell to some middlemen.

**reinforcement**  In learning theory, the satisfaction or dissatisfaction experienced as a result of behavior.

**resale price maintenance**  A pricing policy whereby the manufacturer sets the retail price for a product.

**reseller market**  Wholesaling and retailing middlemen that buy products for resale to other business users or to consumers. A segment of the business market.

**resident buyer**  Independent agent located in central market who buys for wholesalers and retailers located in outlying areas.

**responses**  In learning theory, the behavioral reactions to the drive and cues.

**retail trade**  See *retailing.*

**retailer**  A firm engaged primarily in retailing.

**retailer cooperative**  A type of contractual vertical marketing system that is formed by a group of small retailers who agree to establish and operate a wholesale warehouse.

**retailing**  The sale, and all activities directly related to the sale, of goods and services to ultimate consumers for personal, nonbusiness use. Same as *retail trade.*

**Robinson-Patman Act**  A federal law, passed in 1936, that amended the Clayton Antitrust Act by strengthening the prohibition of price discrimination that may injure competition.

**role ambiguity**  Confusion among sales people about how much responsibility to assume in dealing with customers.

**role conflict**  The stress created for a sales person by the often contrary demands and expectations of his or her employer, customers, and family.

**sales engineer**  A selling job, often involving technically trained individuals selling some kind of sophisticated equipment, in which the emphasis is on the sales person's ability to explain the product to the prospect and perhaps to adapt it to the customer's particular needs.

**sales-force composite**  A method of forecasting sales that consists of collecting from all sales people and middlemen an estimate of sales in their territories during the forecasting period.

**sales-force selection task**  The three steps in assembling a sales force, consisting of (1) determining the number and type of people wanted by preparing a written job description, (2) recruiting an adequate number of applicants, and (3) selecting the most qualified persons from among the applicants.

**sales forecast**  An estimate of likely sales for one company's brand of a product during a stated time period in a specific market and assuming the use of a predetermined marketing plan.

**sales-orientation stage**  The second stage in the evolution of marketing management, in which the emphasis is on selling whatever the organization produces.

**sales potential**  The portion of market potential, applying only to one company's brand of a product, that a specific company could expect to achieve under ideal conditions.

**sales promotion**  Activities, including contests for sales people and consumers, trade shows, in-store displays, samples, premiums, and coupons, that are designed to supplement advertising and coordinate personal selling.

**sales-volume analysis**  A detailed study of the "net sales" section of a company's profit and loss statement.

**satisfaction**  The consumer condition when experience with a product equals or exceeds expectations.

**scrambled merchandising**  A strategy under which a middleman diversifies its assortment by adding product lines not traditionally carried by its type of business.

**seasonal discount**  A discount for placing an order during the seller's slow season.

**secondary data**  Information already gathered by somebody else for some other purpose.

**selective attention**  The process that limits our perceptions such that, of all the marketing stimuli our senses are exposed to, only those able to capture and hold our attention have the potential of being perceived.

**selective-demand advertising**  Advertising that is intended to stimulate demand for individual brands.

**selective distortion**  The process of mentally altering information that is inconsistent with one's own beliefs or attitudes.

**selective distribution**  A strategy in which a producer sells its product through multiple, but not all, wholesalers and/or retailers in a market where a consumer might reasonably look for it.

**selective retention**  The process of retaining in memory some portion of what is perceived.

**self-concept**  A person's self-image.

**self-image**  The idea or image one has of oneself.

**selling agent**  A type of independent middleman that essentially takes the place of a manufacturer's marketing department, marketing the manufacturer's entire output and often influencing the design and/or pricing of the products.

**service**  An activity that is separately identifiable, intangible, and the main object of a transaction designed to provide want-satisfaction for customers.

**service encounter**  In services marketing, a customer's interaction with any service employee or with any tangible element, such as a service's physical surroundings.

**shopping center**  A planned grouping of retail stores in a multiunit structure, with the physical structure usually owned by a single organization.

**shopping goods**  A class of consumer products that are purchased after the buyer has spent some time and effort comparing the price, quality, color, and/or other attributes of alternative products.

**shopping-mall intercept**  A method of gathering data by conducting personal interviews in central locations, typically regional shopping centers.

**simulated test market**  A confidential variation of test marketing in which consumers are shown advertising for a product and then are allowed to "shop" in a test store in order to measure their reactions to the advertising, the product, or both.

**single-segment concentration strategy**  The selection of one homogeneous segment from within a total market to be the target market.

**single-source data**  A data-gathering method in which exposure to television advertising and product purchases can be traced to individual households.

**singles**  Households that consist of just one person.

**situation analysis**  The stage in a marketing research study that involves obtaining information about the company and its business environment by means of library research and extensive interviewing of company officials.

**situational influences**  Temporary forces, associated with the immediate purchase environment, that affect behavior.

**skimming pricing**  A pricing strategy in which the initial price is set high in the range of expected prices. Same as *market-skimming pricing*.

**social class**  A division of society based on education, occupation, and type of residential neighborhood.

**social environment**  Family, friends, and acquaintances who directly or indirectly provide information about products.

**societal marketing concept**  A revised version of the marketing concept under which a company recognizes that it should be concerned about not only the buyers of a firm's products but also other people directly affected by the firm's operations and not only with tomorrow but also with the long term.

**specialty goods**  A class of consumer products with perceived unique characteristics such that consumers are willing to expend special effort to buy them.

**specialty store**  A type of retail institution concentrating on a specialized product line, or even part of a specialized product line.

**stabilizing prices**  A pricing goal designed to achieve steady, nonvolatile prices in an industry.

**Standard Industrial Classification (S.I.C.) system**  A coding system developed by the federal government that groups firms into similar types of businesses and thus enables a company to identify and analyze small segments of its market.

**stimulus-response theory**  The theory that learning occurs as a person responds to some stimuli and is rewarded with need satisfaction for a correct response or penalized for an incorrect one.

**storage**  An activity in physical distribution that creates time utility by holding and preserving products from the time of production until their sale.

**straight commission compensation** The method of sales force compensation in which payment is directly related to the tasks performed, usually the volume of the product(s) sold.

**straight rebuy** In the business market, a routine purchase with minimal information needs.

**straight salary compensation** The method of sales force compensation in which the sales person is paid a fixed amount, regardless of tasks performed or level of performance.

**strategic business unit (SBU)** A separate division for a major product or market in a multiproduct or multibusiness organization.

**strategic company planning** The level of planning that consists of (1) defining the organization's mission, (2) setting organizational objectives, (3) evaluating the firm's strategic business units, and (4) selecting appropriate strategies so as to achieve the organization's objectives.

**strategic marketing planning** The level of planning that consists of (1) conducting a situation analysis, (2) determining marketing objectives, (3) selecting target markets and measuring the market, and (4) designing a strategic marketing mix.

**strategic planning** The managerial process of matching a firm's resources with its market opportunities over the long run.

**strategy** A broad plan of action by which an organization intends to reach its objective(s).

**style** A distinctive presentation or construction in any art, product, or activity.

**style obsolescence** A product strategy in which superficial characteristics of a product are altered so that the new model is easily differentiated from the old one in order to make people dissatisfied with the old model. Same as *fashion obsolescence*.

**subculture** Groups that exhibit characteristic behavior patterns sufficient to distinguish them from other groups within the same culture.

**substitute products** Two or more products that satisfy essentially the same need(s).

**superego** In Freudian psychology, the part of the mind that houses the conscience and directs instinctive drives into socially acceptable channels.

**supermarket** A type of retailing institution that has a moderately broad and moderately deep product assortment spanning groceries and some nonfood lines, that offers relatively few customer services, and that ordinarily emphasizes price in either an offensive or defensive way.

**supermarket retailing** A retailing method that features several related product lines, a high degree of self-service, largely centralized checkout, and competitive prices.

**survey method** Gathering data by interviewing people in person, by telephone, or by mail.

**survey of buyer intentions** A form of sales forecasting in which a firm asks a sample of current or potential customers how much of a particular product they would buy at a given price during a specified future time period.

**tactic** An operational means by which a strategy is to be implemented or activated.

**target market** A group of customers (people or organizations) at whom a seller aims its marketing effort.

**target return** A pricing goal that involves setting prices so as to achieve a certain percentage return on investment or on net sales.

**task method** A method of determining the promotional appropriation under which the organization first decides what is to be accomplished and then calculates how much it will cost to reach this goal. Same as buildup method.

**telemarketing** A form of nonstore retailing in which a sales person initiates contact with a shopper and also closes the sale over the telephone.

**telephone survey** A method of gathering data in a survey by interviewing people over the telephone.

**territory manager** A broadened concept of the sales job that includes identifying customers' needs, qualifying prospects, servicing customers, managing expenses, and collecting market intelligence.

**test marketing** A marketing research technique in which a firm markets its product in a limited geographic area, measures the sales, and then—from this sample—projects (a) the company's sales over a larger area and/or (b) consumers' response to a strategy before committing to a major marketing effort.

**time utility** The utility created when a product is available to customers when they want it.

**total cost** The sum of total fixed costs and total variable costs, or the full cost of a specific quantity produced or sold.

**total cost concept** In physical distribution, the optimization of the cost-profit relationship for the entire physical distribution system, rather than for individual activities.

**trade discount** A reduction from the list price, offered by a seller to buyers in payment for marketing activities that they will perform. Same as *functional discount*.

**trademark**   A brand that is legally protected.

**trademark licensing**   A business arrangement in which the owner of a trademark grants permission to other firms to use the owner's brand name, logotype, and/or character on the licensee's products in return for a royalty on sales of those products. Same as *brand licensing.*

**trading down**   A product-line strategy wherein a company adds a lower-priced item to its line of prestige goods in order to reach a market that cannot afford the higher-priced items.

**trading up**   A product-line strategy wherein a company adds a higher-priced, prestige product to its line in order to increase sales of the existing lower-priced products in that line and attract a higher-income market.

**trend analysis**   A method of forecasting sales over the long term by using regression analysis, or over the short term by using a seasonal index of sales.

**trial close**   The stage in the personal selling process when the sales person poses some "either-or" questions in such a way that the customer's answer is intended to close the sale.

**trickle-across cycle**   In fashion adoption, a fashion cycle that moves horizontally within several social classes at the same time.

**trickle-down cycle**   In fashion adoption, a fashion cycle that flows downward through several socio-economic classes.

**trickle-up cycle**   In fashion adoption, a fashion cycle by which a style becomes popular (fashionable) first with lower socioeconomic classes and then, later, with higher socioeconomic groups.

**truck jobber**   A limited-function merchant wholesaler that carries a selected line of perishable products and delivers them by truck to retail stores.

**tying contract**   A contract under which a manufacturer sells a product to a middleman only under the condition that this middleman also buys another (possibly unwanted) product from the manufacturer.

**ultimate consumers**   People who buy products for their personal, nonbusiness use.

**uniform delivered price**   A geographic pricing strategy whereby the same delivered price is quoted to all buyers regardless of their location. Same as *postage-stamp pricing.*

**unit pricing**   A form of price reporting where the price is stated per pound, quart, or some other standard measure in order to aid consumers in comparison shopping.

**unsought goods**   A type of consumer product that consists of new products the consumer is not yet aware of or products the consumer does not yet want.

**unstructured interview**   In sales force selection, an interviewing procedure in which the interviewer is permitted the freedom to ask questions and explore issues as they develop in the flow of the interview.

**users**   The people in a buying center who actually use a particular product.

**utility**   The attribute in an item that makes it capable of satisfying human wants.

**valid test**   In selection, an employment test that accurately predicts job performance.

**value**   The quantitative measure of the worth of a product to attract other products in exchange.

**variable cost**   A cost that varies or changes directly in relation to the number of units produced or sold.

**variable-price strategy**   See *flexible-price strategy.*

**vertical business market**   A situation where a given product is usable by virtually all the firms in only one or two industries.

**vertical conflict**   A form of channel conflict occurring between firms at different levels of the same channel, typically producer versus wholesaler or producer versus retailer.

**vertical cooperative advertising**   Advertising in which firms at different levels of the distribution channel share the cost.

**vertical marketing system (VMS)**   A tightly coordinated distribution channel designed to achieve operating efficiencies and marketing effectiveness.

**voluntary chain**   A type of contractual vertical marketing system that is sponsored by a wholesaler who enters into a contract with interested retailers.

**warehouse club**   A combined retailing and wholesaling institution that has a very broad but very shallow product assortment with very low prices and few customer services and is open only to members. Same as *wholesale club.*

**warehousing**   A broad range of physical distribution activities that include storage, assembling, bulk breaking, and preparing products for shipping.

**wheel of retailing**   The cyclical pattern of changes in retailing, whereby a new type of store enters the market as a low-cost, low-price store and over time takes business away from unchanging competitors; eventually, the successful new retailer trades up, incurring higher costs and higher prices and making the institution vulnerable to a new type of retailer.

**Wheeler-Lea Act**   A federal law, passed in 1938, that amended the Federal Trade Commission Act by strengthening the prohibition against unfair competition, especially false or misleading advertising.

**wholesale club**   See *warehouse club.*

**wholesaler**   See *merchant wholesaler.*

**wholesaling**   All activities directly related to the sale of goods and services to parties for resale, use in producing other goods and services, or operating an organization.

**wholesaling middleman**   A firm engaged primarily in wholesaling.

**wholly owned subsidiary**   A business arrangement in foreign markets in which a company owns the foreign operation in order to gain maximum control over its marketing program and production operations.

**zone-delivered price**   A geographic pricing strategy whereby the same delivered price is charged at any location within each geographic zone. Same as *parcel-post pricing.*

# NAME INDEX

State Farm, 307
Steinberg, Margery, 513n.
Stern, Aimée L., 485n.
Stern, Louis W., 315n.
Steuben Glass, 196
Stewart, David W., 64n.
Stewart, Thomas A., 509n.
STP, 425
Strang, Roger A., 219n.
Strum, Larry M., 509n.
Sturdivant, Frederick D., 315n.
Subway, 361
Sun Ice Limited, 628–630
Sun Microsystems, 15
Sunbeam, 210, 214
Sundance Juice Sparkler, 455
Sunkist, 211, 214, 224, 452
Suntory, 198, 532
Super 8, 494
Super Fleet, 248
Super Valu, 359, 368
Supercuts, 361
Surg, 212
Sutton, Howard, 570n.
Swartz, Steve, 494n.
Swartz, Teresa, 498n.
Swasy, Alecia, 85n., 223n., 455
Swatch, 194, 318
Swift Premium, 212
Sylvan Learning Center, 361
Symonds, William C., 559n.
Sysco, 210

**T**

T. J. Maxx, 365
T-Shirts Plus, 361
Tab, 201
Taco Bell, 291, 409
Takashimaya, 179
Talon zippers, 175
Tandy Corp., 313
Target, 194, 363
Tauber, Edward, 126
Taylor, Elizabeth, 261
Taylor, Thayer C., 439
TC, 605
Teflon, 201
Tellis, Gerard J., 278n.
Tengelmann, 532
Tetreault, Mary Stanfield, 502n.
Texaco, 129, 360, 369
Therapy Bayer, 203
Thomas Register, 61
3M, 15, 186
Ticketron, 220
Tide, 85, 212, 217, 516, 622
*Time*, 458
Timex, 135
Toman, Barbara, 107, 121, 537n.
Toshiba, 154
Toth, Debora, 455
Toyota, 16, 43, 179, 191, 213, 244, 457, 528
Toys "R" Us, 90, 220, 366, 376
Traxx, 201
Treacy, Michael F., 439

Truck, Julie, 93n.
True Value Hardware, 313, 320, 359
Tully, Shawn, 530n.
Tungsram, 623
Tupperware, 370
TWA, 286
20th Century-Fox, 531
Tylenol, 168
Tyler, Philip R., 94n.

**U**

Ultra Glide, 454
Ultra Silk, 131
Uncle Ben, 451
Unger, Lynette, 538n.
Unilever, 107, 139, 457, 532
Unisys, 209
United Airlines, 41, 103, 220, 291, 409
United Audio Centers, 308
United Fund, 509
United Parcel Service, 220, 397, 409
United Technologies, 150
United Way of America, 5, 55
Urbanski, Al, 187n.
US WEST Communications, 127
USX, 150

**V**

Van der Merwe, Sandra, 94n.
van der Steen Candy Company, 627–628
Van Doren, Doris C., 493n.
van Mesdag, Martin, 527n.
Vancouver Symphony Orchestra, 551–553
Variation, 217
Velveeta, 211
Verity, C. William, 319
Viadent, 81
Victoria's Secret, 116, 134, 391
Video Walkman, 567
VideOcart, 67
Vif, 107
Viking Steamship Line, 101
Violano, Michael, 616n.
VISA, 94, 134, 217, 220, 485
Viss, 107
Volkswagen, 16, 41, 94, 106, 531
Volvo, 111
Vons, 367
Vorhees, Roy Dale, 399n.
Vyn, Kathleen, 512n.

**W**

Wal-Mart, 167, 193, 277, 351, 352, 356, 362, 363, 368, 369, 581
Walgreen, 210
Walker, Bruce J., 64n., 324n., 493n.
Walker, Orville C., Jr., 440n.
Walkman, 179, 201, 202
Walleigh, Richard C., 381n.
Wallpapers to Go, 361
Walt Disney Company, 18, 213, 219, 621
Walton, Sam, 351
Wang, 462
Wang Beiming, 547n.
Ward, Scott, 389n.

Watchman, 567
Water Tower Place, 375
Waterford Glass, 196, 261
Watney, 532
Weber, Joseph, 345n.
Webster, Frederick E., Jr., 154n.
Weebok, 468
Weinberg, Charles B., 520n.
Weiner, Steve, 366n.
Weis, William L., 296n.
Weitz, Barton, 153n.
Wendy's, 291, 313
Wessel, David, 503n., 538, 607
West Bend, 370
Western Auto, 313, 359
Western Pipe Supply Company, 140
Westin Hotels, 220
Westinghouse, 216
What's Left, 81
Wheatena, 223
Wheaties, 191, 196, 533
Whitlark, David B., 103n.
Wilkie, William L., 425n.
Wilkinson, 454
Williamson, Nicholas C., 546n.
Wind, Yoram, 153n., 154n.
Winkleman Manufacturing Company, 296–298
Winn-Dixie, 89
Winnebago, 219
Winski, Joseph M., 161n.
Winston, 14
Winter, Ralph E., 150n.
Wisk, 409, 531
Wolverine Hush Puppies, 455
Woodward & Lotrop, 365
Woolite, 202
Work, Clemens P., 397
Works, The, 216
World Book, 370
Worldwide Express, 397
Worthley, Reginald, 538n.
Wortzel, Lawrence H., 323n., 375n.
Woy, James, 61n.
Wrigley, 212, 409
Write Brothers, 239

**X**

Xerox, 193, 213, 214, 381, 382, 447, 563, 591

**Y**

Yamaha, 528
YMCA, 515, 520, 521
Young American Bank, 93
Yugo, 71, 606
Yves St. Laurent, 205, 217

**Z**

Zayre, 365
Zeithaml, Carl P., 38n.
Zeithaml, Valarie A., 38n., 228n., 242n., 498n.
Zemke, Ron, 500n.
Zinszer, Paul H., 385n.

# SUBJECT INDEX